Dictionary of Literary Biography • Volume Twenty

British Poets, 1914-1945

Dictionary of Literary Biography

Dictionary of Literary Biography • Volume Twenty

British Poets, 1914-1945

Edited by
Donald E. Stanford
Louisiana State University

A Bruccoli Clark Book
Gale Research Company • Book Tower • Detroit, Michigan 48226
1983

Matthew J. Bruccoli and Richard Layman, *Editorial Directors*
C. E. Frazer Clark, Jr., *Managing Editor*

Manufactured by Edwards Brothers, Inc.
Ann Arbor, Michigan
Printed in the United States of America

Library of Congress Cataloging in Publication Data
Main entry under title:

British poets, 1914-1945.

(Dictionary of literary biography; v. 20)
"A Bruccoli Clark book."
Includes index.
1. English poetry—20th century—Bio-bibliography.
2. English poetry—20th century—History and criticism.
3. Poets, English—20th century—Biography. I. Stanford, Donald E., 1913- . II. Series.
PR610.B7 1983 821'.912'09 [B] 83-5718
ISBN 0-8103-1702-8

For Maryanna

Contents

Foreword

British poetry between 1914 and 1945 is marked by its growing Anglo-American character. This trend began before World War I with the imagist movement, but as John Masefield (who became poet laureate in 1930) predicted, once the United States entered the war in 1917, Anglo-American cultural relations became increasingly close and friendly. Masefield himself had contributed to this sense of community by touring the United States in 1916 to arouse interest among Americans in British poetry and culture and in the allied war effort, and the poet laureate Robert Bridges celebrated the Anglo-American military alliance in a sonnet addressed to Woodrow Wilson. Later, in 1924, Bridges visited America on a well-publicized tour, and British and American intellectuals became more and more interested in one anothers' countries, an interest augmented after World War II by the ease of air travel between the two countries.

In the first Anglo-American literary movement, imagism, the British poet T. E. Hulme, seconded by the British poet F. S. Flint, supplied the basic theories of imagism, but the first imagist manifesto was written and published by the American poet Ezra Pound in *Poetry* magazine in 1913, and the first poet to be called an imagist was the American H. D. (Hilda Doolittle). Of the British-born poets in this volume, Richard Aldington (who married H. D.) was recognized as an imagist. D. H. Lawrence continued to write poetry that had affinities with imagism, and T. S. Eliot, a perfect example of an Anglo-American poet, made use in *The Waste Land* of structural techniques derived from Pound's *Cantos*, which developed from Pound's earlier imagist writing. David Jones and Basil Bunting also wrote at times a kind of free verse reminiscent of imagism.

World War I produced an impressive body of verse, the chief war poets being Wilfred Owen, Siegfried Sassoon, Robert Graves, and Isaac Rosenberg. Owen wrote convincingly of the horror and the pity of war, in contrast to Rupert Brooke who wrote romantically of its glory and honor. Sassoon, Graves, and Rosenberg, also like Owen, emphasized the horror not the glory, and the four of them became quite accidentally the only well-defined "school of poetry" in the 1914-1945 period, being much more homogeneous in their approach to their subject than were the politically oriented members of the Spender, Auden, Day Lewis, MacNeice group of Oxford poets in the late 1920s and early 1930s. Of the four war poets, Sassoon and Graves survived the war and went on to develop impressive poetic careers. Graves today is noted for his complex poetry devoted to the psychic disturbances that lingered on long after the battles were over and devoted also to the mystery of the White Goddess, with its emphasis on "one story only"—the encounter between man and woman.

During the Depression of the 1930s some poets became more and more engaged with the social and political problems of their time. Auden, Spender, MacNeice, Day Lewis, and Edgell Rickword promoted left-wing causes. Spender, briefly, became a Communist, and Auden, briefly, participated in the Spanish civil war.

Auden is today considered the major poet of the 1914-1945 period although there are signs that his reputation is diminishing somewhat, partly because he was so prolific and frequently facile and clever. His career exemplifies the major trends of the Anglo-American intellectuals between the wars. He was Marxist and left wing in the early to mid-1930s, liberal and anti-Fascist in the late 1930s, and from the 1940s on more concerned with religious principles than with politics. He became an American citizen and established residence for several years in New York City.

World War II did not stimulate the remarkable body of poetry brought on by World War I. Roy Fuller and Donald Davie (to be included in *DLB, British Poets Since World War II*) are perhaps the most talented of the British poets whose poetry was affected by the war experience, but neither is known as a war poet.

Most of the poets of the 1914-1945 period are individualists, some to the point of being called eccentrics. They are difficult to classify. Elizabeth Daryush, the daughter of Robert Bridges, looked on poetry as an art dealing with universal truths unaffected by the march of current events. She wrote a number of beautiful lyrics in conventional forms and a few outstanding poems in syllabics. Ruth Pitter, Edith Sitwell, and Kathleen Raine developed their individual styles. Raine wrote private poems on personal relationships but these personal experiences are frequently seen in terms of Greek mythology and her own Platonist philosophy. David Jones, whose *In Parenthesis* (1937) established him as a modernist in the Pound-Joyce-Eliot tradition, worked on his complex, many-layered poems in seclusion and was considered an eccentric. Hugh MacDiarmid showed a lively journalistic interest in Scottish nationalism, also in communism and in other causes, although his poetry because of its language (Scots) has not been widely read. Edwin Muir, who moved from early socialist views to a preoccupation with religious principles and spiritual truths, is also difficult to classify. Dylan Thomas described his native Welsh countryside in terms of romantic pantheism and with his resonant voice delighted audiences, especially American, in his poetry readings. He was extremely popular in the 1940s and early 1950s, but most critics today consider Auden to be the only major British poet of the period (that is if he can be considered British in spite of his American citizenship and if Eliot must be considered American in spite of his British citizenship). By and large, British poetry between the wars has been heterogeneous and eclectic with—except for the World War I poets—no defined schools and no startling innovations in poetic theory, innovations which might have brought groups of poets together, as did the imagist movement of the 1910s and the "Movement" of the 1950s.

—Donald E. Stanford

Acknowledgments

This book was produced by BC Research. Karen L. Rood, senior editor for the *Dictionary of Literary Biography* series, was the in-house editor.

The production staff included Mary Betts, Patricia Coate, Angela Dixon, Lynn Felder, Joyce Fowler, Nancy L. Houghton, Laura Ingram, Sharon K. Kirkland, Cynthia D. Lybrand, Alice A. Parsons, Walter W. Ross, Joycelyn R. Smith, Debra D. Straw, Robin A. Sumner, Meredith Walker, and Lynne C. Zeigler. Joseph Caldwell is photography editor. Jean W. Ross is permissions editor. Mary Bruccoli and Charles L. Wentworth did the photographic copy work.

Valuable assistance was given by Sandra Mooney and the staff at the Louisiana State University Library and the staff at the Thomas Cooper Library of the University of South Carolina: Michael Freeman, Gary Geer, Alexander M. Gilchrist, W. Michael Havener, David Lincove, Roger Mortimer, Donna Nance, Harriet B. Oglesbee, Elizabeth Pugh, Jean Rhyne, Paula Swope, Jane Thesing, Ellen Tillett, and Beth S. Woodard.

Anthony Rota of Bertram Rota, Ltd., was especially helpful in providing illustrations for this volume.

Above all, the editor wishes to thank his wife for her indefatigable secretarial and research assistance.

Dictionary of Literary Biography • Volume Twenty

British Poets, 1914-1945

Dictionary of Literary Biography

Richard Aldington

(8 July 1892-27 July 1962)

Terry Comito
George Mason University

SELECTED BOOKS: *Images (1910-1915)* (London: Poetry Bookshop, 1915); revised and enlarged as *Images Old and New* (Boston: Four Seas, 1916); enlarged again as *Images* (London: Egoist, 1919);

The Love Poems of Myrrhine and Konallis (Cleveland: Clerk's Press, 1917); enlarged as *The Love of Myrrhine and Konallis and Other Prose Poems* (Chicago: Covici, 1926);

Images of War (London: Allen & Unwin, 1919); republished as *War and Love (1915-1918)* (Boston: Four Seas, 1921);

Images of Desire (London: Elkin Mathews, 1919);

Exile and Other Poems (London: Allen & Unwin, 1923; Boston: Four Seas, 1924);

Literary Studies and Reviews (London: Allen & Unwin, 1924);

A Fool i' the Forest (London: Allen & Unwin, 1924; New York: MacVeagh/Dial Press, 1925);

Voltaire (London: Routledge, 1925; New York: Dutton, 1925);

French Studies and Reviews (London: Allen & Unwin, 1926; New York: MacVeagh/Dial Press, 1926);

Death of a Hero (New York: Covici, Friede, 1929; London: Chatto & Windus, 1929; unexpurgated edition, 2 volumes, Paris: Babou & Kahane, 1930);

The Eaten Heart (Chapelle-Reanville, Eure, France: Hours Press, 1929; enlarged edition, London: Chatto & Windus, 1933);

Love and the Luxembourg (New York: Covici, Friede, 1930); republished as *A Dream in the Luxembourg* (London: Chatto & Windus, 1930);

Roads to Glory (London: Chatto & Windus, 1930; Garden City: Doubleday, Doran, 1930);

The Colonel's Daughter (London: Chatto & Windus, 1931; Garden City: Doubleday, Doran, 1931);

Soft Answers (London: Chatto & Windus, 1932; Garden City: Doubleday, Doran, 1932);

All Men Are Enemies (London: Chatto & Windus, 1933; Garden City: Doubleday, Doran, 1933);

Women Must Work (London: Chatto & Windus, 1934; Garden City: Doubleday, Doran, 1934);

Artifex: Sketches and Ideas (London: Chatto & Windus, 1935; Garden City: Doubleday, Doran, 1936);

Life Quest (London: Chatto & Windus, 1935; Garden City: Doubleday, Doran, 1935);

Life of a Lady: A Play, by Aldington and Derek Patmore (Garden City: Doubleday, Doran, 1936);

The Crystal World (London: Heinemann, 1937; Gar-

Richard Aldington, 1917

den City: Doubleday, Doran, 1937);

Very Heaven (London & Toronto: Heinemann, 1937; Garden City: Doubleday, Doran, 1937);

Seven Against Reeves (London & Toronto: Heinemann, 1938; Garden City: Doubleday, Doran, 1938);

Rejected Guest (New York: Viking, 1939; London & Toronto: Heinemann, 1940);

Life for Life's Sake: A Book of Reminiscences (New York: Viking, 1941; London: Cassell, 1968);

The Duke: Being an Account of the Life and Achievements of Arthur Wellesley, First Duke of Wellington (New York: Viking, 1943); republished as *Wellington: Being an Account of the Life and Achievements of Arthur Wellesley, First Duke of Wellington* (London & Toronto: Heinemann, 1946);

The Romance of Casanova (New York: Duell, Sloan & Pearce, 1946; London & Toronto: Heinemann, 1947);

Four English Portraits, 1801-1851 (London: Evans, 1948);

The Complete Poems of Richard Aldington (London: Wingate, 1948);

The Strange Life of Charles Waterton, 1782-1865 (London: Evans, 1949; New York: Duell, Sloan & Pearce, 1949);

Portrait of a Genius, But . . . : The Life of D. H. Lawrence (London: Heinemann, 1950); republished as *D. H. Lawrence: Portrait of a Genius, But . . .* (New York: Duell, Sloan & Pearce, 1950);

Pinorman: Personal Recollections of Norman Douglas, Pino Orioli, and Charles Prentice (London: Heinemann, 1954);

Lawrence of Arabia: A Biographical Enquiry (Chicago: Regnery, 1955; London: Collins, 1955);

Frauds (London: Heinemann, 1957);

Portrait of a Rebel: The Life and Work of Robert Louis Stevenson (London: Evans, 1957);

Richard Aldington: Selected Critical Writings, 1928-1960, edited by Alister Kershaw (Carbondale: Southern Illinois University Press, 1970).

It is the great irony of Richard Aldington's career that he is today chiefly remembered for his youthful involvement in a "modernist" literary movement he quickly disowned, and that much of his mature verse records his doubts about the possibility of writing poetry in the modern world. Aldington was only twenty when Ezra Pound launched him as a leading spirit of the "Imagistes," who intended to sweep away late Victorian cobwebs by devoting themselves to clear images—"hardness, as of cut stone," was Aldington's own formula—and to the flexible rhythms of vers libre. At one time or another the imagists included in their ranks, in addition to Aldington and Pound himself, such poets as H. D., F. S. Flint, John Gould Fletcher, Amy Lowell, James Joyce, D. H. Lawrence, and William Carlos Williams. Throughout the second decade of the twentieth century, "imagism" was a rallying cry, a shibboleth, and a provocation. At once an energetic publicity machine and a literary creed, it had, beyond the not inconsiderable accomplishments of its declared adherents, a far-reaching effect on the whole course of modern poetry. After an intense but relatively brief involvement in the movement, Aldington went his own rather lonely and idiosyncratic way with his poetry; and after the publication in 1929 of *Death of a Hero*, considered at the time one of the best novels to emerge from World War I, his reputation as a novelist eclipsed his poetic renown. He wrote no poetry in the last twenty-five years of his life, although he continued to produce fiction, together with a prodigious flood of literary memoirs, criticism, biographies, and translations which may today—another irony, for he considered them secondary to his more serious literary work—be his most read productions.

Richard Aldington was born in 1892 in Portsmouth, England, the son of a middle-class lawyer. His childhood provided him with the intensely idealistic devotion to literature that was to shape his whole life, together with the first seeds of disillusionment about the world in which he had to pursue his ambitions. When he was fifteen, his reading of Keats's "Endymion," he writes in his memoir, *Life for Life's Sake* (1941), was "like a combination of falling in love at first sight and finding Ali Baba's treasure cave"; and within two years he had read his way through all the major English poets and the complete Elizabethan drama. But the family's move to Dover, when Aldington was still a young boy, had introduced him into an environment—bleak treeless downs and drab provincial city streets—quite different from the world of Keatsian raptures; and his schooling confirmed him in his horror of the "narrow minded bourgeois outlook" that threatened to condemn him to the stultifying life of a "fairly prosperous provincial lawyer." "At school it was just as dull as that dull High Street," he wrote in his first book of poems. "I wanted to be alone, although I was so little,/Alone, away from the rain, the dinginess, the dullness,/ Away somewhere else—." The vision of poetry as "somewhere else," freer and at once more sensual and more intellectual than the ugliness and mediocrity he saw all around him, was a theme central to Aldington's work from the beginning of his career to the very end.

A crisis in his father's financial affairs forced Aldington to an early decision. Leaving the University of London after his first year (1911), he rejected the security of a clerk's position and plunged into the stimulating but financially precarious waters of London's literary life, working briefly as a part-time sports reporter and, as his connections grew, writing reviews and essays, working on translations, and beginning to sell his own poems. He soon fell in with three other young poets, each of whom had an important effect on his career and his life: Ezra Pound, who was energetically promoting whatever seemed new in the arts; Hilda Doolittle (H. D.), an American expatriate whom he married in 1913; and Harold Monro, already an influential editor, whose Poetry Bookshop published Aldington's first book in 1915. In the years before World War I, Aldington visited Paris, traveled through Italy, and met everyone in London who "mattered"—Yeats and his friend Sturge Moore, Ford Madox Hueffer (who later changed his name to Ford Madox Ford), D. H. Lawrence, T. E. Hulme (an essayist and theorist of imagism's earliest stage), as well as Walter de la Mare and the other more conservative young Georgian poets (whom he found provincial and old-fashioned). He paraded through the streets in "futurist" garb made of billiard cloth to hear the Italian poet Marinetti and, in general, shared enthusiastically in a "camaraderie of minds" that—for all his satirical amusement at his friends' bohemian excesses—later seemed to him as sadly unrepeatable as "the perfume of a flower which has vanished from the earth." It was from this period that emerged his lifelong dedication to the ideal of the "Good European": the life devoted not to "security and good opinion" but to "the best that had been thought and felt and known through the ages," all the pleasures of art and literature, "food and wine, France and Italy, women, old towns, beautiful country."

It was also the period of imagism. Aldington says Pound "swiped" the term from Hulme and sprang it on Aldington and H. D. one afternoon in 1911 in "some infernal bun shop full of English spinsters." By 1912, Pound had succeeded in selling three of Aldington's poems to Harriet Monroe's influential *Poetry* magazine in Chicago and followed them shortly with declarations of the principles of the new movement. "Go in fear of abstractions," he exhorted. "The natural object is always the *adequate* symbol." Although Aldington, in the preface to his *Complete Poems* (1948), disclaimed any intention of being a part of what later became regarded as the "revolution of 1912," he was for a time intensely involved in its politics, if not exactly (as he later protested) its "fuehrer." His verse appeared in Pound's 1914 anthology, *Des Imagistes*, along with contributions from Pound, H. D., F. S. Flint, Amy Lowell, William Carlos Williams, James Joyce, and others. He contributed to Amy Lowell's anthologies, *Some Imagist Poets* (1915, 1916, 1917), after Pound had split with the movement and the original group had been augmented, most notably by D. H. Lawrence; and in 1930 he put together a retrospective anthology to remind the public that the imagists, long out of the spotlight, were nevertheless alive and still writing. Furthermore, between 1914 and 1916, he was literary editor of the *Egoist*, which had become the chief organ of the movement. Imagism found in Aldington in those years its most youthfully exuberant defender. Although his editorials and articles were not as strong in theory as Pound's—the "intellectualist" cast of the movement was one of the sources of his later reservations—they were full of the high-spirited rebelliousness that characterized the decade—and Aldington himself.

His first book of poems, *Images (1910-1915)*, was published in 1915. Today it is apt to seem more innovative in form than in content. Most strikingly new to his contemporaries was the imagists' abandonment of traditional rhyme and meter in favor of free verse—which Aldington modeled, however, not on the radical experiments of the French vers libre Pound was fond of citing, but on the choruses of Greek tragedy. While the more traditional Georgian poets were celebrating the familiar beauties of the English countryside and the intimacies of domestic life, Aldington, like the other imagists, turned to more exotic sources of inspiration: Greek poetry and mythology, Japanese art and poetry, or—at the other extreme—such "unpoetic" icons of modern life as subways, movie houses, or a kitchen sink.

Most of the poems, however, evoke the pre-Raphaelite melancholy and aestheticism—"We, who have grown weary even of music"—that were rather belatedly fashionable in what Aldington later called Soho's "snob culture." The Greek poems are bittersweet celebrations of death or of the pleasures of the flesh, always shadowed by an intense, consciously pagan sense of their inevitable transience. "Choricos" in particular—it remains one of Aldington's most anthologized pieces—is pure Swinburne, with its cold lips, slim colorless poppies, and dark streams of Persephone; but Swinburne rendered marmoreal and "archaic" by being stripped of his characteristic metrical surge. Aldington's free-verse poems are typically given their rhythmic shapes by the cadences at the ends of lines, rather than by any steady impulse; and these are arranged in "Choricos" to produce an effective dancelike intricacy of dying falls. Aldington's verse is in fact probably more memorable for such rhythmic effects, mingling the cadences of biblical prose—somewhere between conversation and a formalized chant—with fleeting echos of traditional meters, rather than for any strictly visual freshness and immediacy.

Influenced by his study of Chinese ideograms, Pound had defined the image as a juxtaposition of apparently unrelated perceptions in order to evoke, through the imaginative leap required by the reader, an "intellectual and emotional complex in an instant of time." Aldington's practice is usually simpler and more traditional. Even his more "Japanese" verses (like the ones gathered together as "Images" and "Epigrams") apparently were inspired more by his fondness for Japanese prints than by any close study of such poetic forms as the haiku. In any case, they are closer to traditional uses of simile—such as, the heart is like a "flower which the wind has shaken"—than to Pound's ideographic method, the aim apparently being rather to aestheticize the emotion, by rendering it distant and static, than to complicate or intellectualize it. This intention is especially clear in the prose poems on the "Sapphic" love affair of Myrrhine and Konallis in *The Love Poems of Myrrhine and Konallis* (1917). (None were included in the *Complete Poems*, though they received high praise at the time.) He chose the subject, Aldington said, because lesbian love seemed to him so remote from "biological affection": "I wanted something sterile and passionate and lovely and melancholy." Much of Aldington's early verse is devoted to the pursuit of this sort of

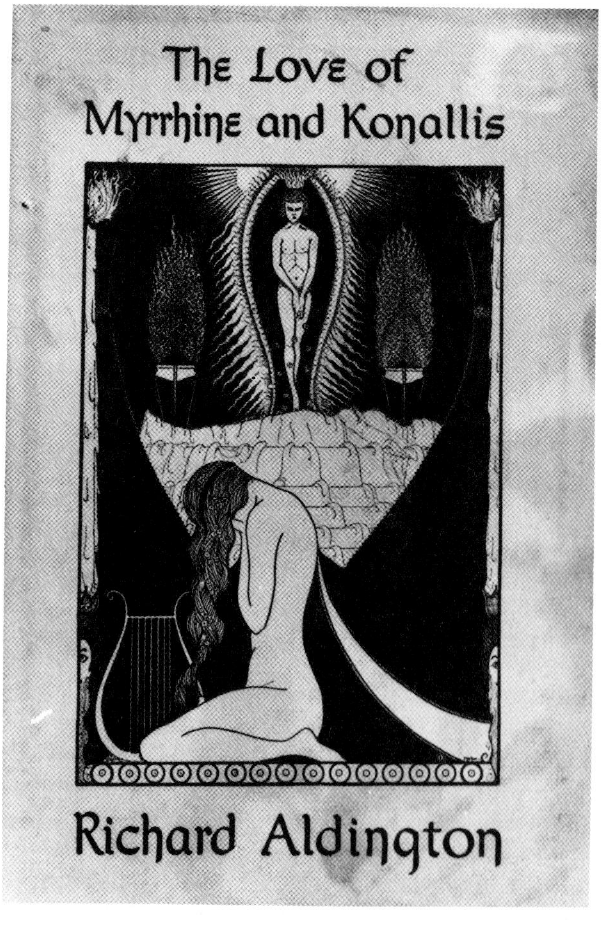

Frank Meechau dust jacket for the 1926 edition of Aldington's sequence of "Sapphic" love poems and other prose poems (Thomas Cooper Library, University of South Carolina)

beauty. Probably it is fair to say that he thought of poetry less as a means of coming to terms with his immediate experience than as an opportunity to create an alternative to it. Whatever his ostensible subject, the mood tends to be elegiac, languorous with nostalgia, as if his real theme were the distance from his own world of the beauty he evokes and the transience of his hold upon it—a lamentation for the death of the old gods.

This becomes most explicit in the poems on modern life, where the dream of classical beauty is juxtaposed, with an often shrill irony, to the vulgar debris of industrial society: Eros and Psyche "In an old dull yard near Camden Town," Helen of Sparta become a "whore in Oxford Street," the moon an "awkward Venus" rising over a kitchen sink. The poet tends to present himself, in a conventionally romantic way, as an exile struggling ineffectually in an alien world—with mawkish directness in "Childhood" ("My shrivelled wings were beaten . . . I hate that town"), more successfully in the book's last poem, where "The Captive Fawn," weary for the "old gay life of the half-god," dreams of "The lands that are free, being free of man."

In 1916, Aldington enlisted in the British army as a private, saw active combat, and emerged from the war with a captain's commission and a case of shell shock that continued to trouble him for many years. Externally at least, he slipped easily back into London's literary life, making new friends, notably T. S. Eliot (who had replaced him as editor of the *Egoist*), and securing a job as reviewer of French books for the *Times Literary Supplement*. It was not until a decade later, with the publication of his novel *Death of a Hero* (1929), that Aldington was able to give full expression of the impact, upon himself and upon the way of life to which he was dedicated, of the catastrophic war he referred to as Europe's suicide. The transparently autobiographical hero of the novel suffers less from the very considerable physical horrors of war than from the mental degradation it imposes—the utter withering away of what Aldington in his memoir calls the ability to "say 'Yes' to life with no hesitation." When Aldington's hero returns on leave to London, he finds himself alienated both from the unchanged fatuities of its intellectuals and from the affection, even the comprehension, of his wife and his mistress. Aldington, too, found himself estranged from former comrades who assumed that the old ways were still possible: they seemed to be "making vain gestures to each other across a river of death." He separated from H. D. soon after his return to London in February 1919, and by the end of the year he fled from London's "shams" to a life of almost monastic discipline in a Berkshire village.

Unlike the hero of his novel, however, Aldington did survive the war. His initial attempts to come to terms with it appeared in 1919: *Images of War* and *Images of Desire*. The poems in the first were hailed by Harold Monro as among the best to emerge from the conflict. Juxtaposing images of horror with moments of pastoral loveliness, Aldington seems to define the war as the culmination, explosive and possibly irreversible, of everything in the modern world that renders desperate the pursuit of beauty: "I have gathered sensations / Like ripe fruits in a rich orchard. . . . / All this is gone." And yet he dedicates himself, in the book's proem, to the task of extracting "out of this turmoil and passion . . . something of repose, / Some intuition of the inalterable gods." Sometimes—at considerable risk of trivializing his subject—he attempts to mythologize the horror itself, invoking death as a lover who will "stab me with a kiss like a wound/ That bleeds slowly," or hearing in an artillery bombardment "The gallop of innumerable Valkyrie." Elsewhere he abandons classical machinery and clings to simple sensations, of nature or of human warmth, rendered doubly precious by their newly perceived fragility. As he wrote in one of his uncollected prose poems: "No longer the sharp edge of Attic song, but the irrepressible pathos of the song of common men, patient under disaster." Probably the most effective verses owe less to imagism than to Walt Whitman, whose great virtue for Aldington was his honesty. A poem like "Bombardment" is simple reportage, lent dignity by the biblical cadences of Aldington's lines and by its intimations of the immutability, beyond all the "wreckage of the earth," of nature's fundamental rhythms: the battle-weary men look up "To where the white clouds moved in silent lines / Across the untroubled blue." The book ends gloomily, however, with a surrealistic vision of "The Blood of the Young Men," and with agonized doubts as to the relevance, after such an experience, of the poet's devotion to his ideal.

C. P. Snow, May Sinclair, and other admirers have included Aldington among the best love poets in the language. The full impact of *Images of Desire*, however, will be felt only if it is seen in the context of the war poems. Aldington wrote in the epilogue of *Images of War* that he had been through a hell worse than Dante's, "And yet love kept us glad." Love is a refuge from war's violence, and the lady celebrated so variously in these poems is the embodiment of whatever object of desire endures, in the senses, in nature, or in art, that might rouse the poet from his bitter apathy and persuade him once again to say yes to life. In effect, she is the goddess of poetry. Aldington inscribes classical epigrams, rewrites Catullus's most famous demand to "seize the day," turns the language of the Canticles back to its sensuous origins, perverts a medieval ballad to the Virgin into a song of earthly love and answers Dante with a defense of Paolo and Francesca, undergoes a Keatsian swoon with a lady rather than a nightingale, and writes in conventional rhyme and meter an unblushingly Swinburnian *alba*. The book is like a convocation of history's great love poets, as if Aldington were consciously seeking to regain a place for himself in the living tradition of their devotion.

Although the variety of styles in *Images of Desire* thus serves a specific expressive purpose, Aldington in both books displays an impatience with imagist tenets. The imagists seemed to him overly intellectual, absorbed in technique; he wanted to appeal directly "to people who are not enthusiasts for poetry." Aldington's admirers have often stressed his "Englishness"—a forthrightness and manly directness of expression, an impatience with theory and a refusal to regard technique as an end in itself, a kind of emotional generosity that tends toward inclusiveness rather than formal perfection. All these are virtues that perhaps find greater scope in fiction than in poetry. It is clear, in any case, that Aldington never really found congenial the imagist demand for objectivity, concision, and technical rigor. He tended always to want to speak out in his own voice, and that voice is characteristically a discursive one. He did not in fact share Pound's faith that "the natural object is always the *adequate* symbol." Images seem to have for him a purely emotional impact, evocations of Beauty or of its opposite; and when he has a serious intellectual theme to convey, he tends to do a lot of explaining, often of a prosy sort. Perhaps this inability to bring the emotional and intellectual together into a simultaneous "complex" is the most serious limitation of his verse; certainly it is a problem of which he seems to have been consciously aware.

In any case, in *Exile and Other Poems* (1923), his next book of poetry, the imagist influence is negligible. The emphasis in the first part of the book, "Exile," is almost entirely on the poet's own persona, and he speaks most of the time in blank verse or in "free" verse that slides easily into loose metrical patterns. He is exiled at once by the mediocrity of the world around him ("Deadness of English winters . . . mediocre women in dull clothes . . . embankments, coal-yards, villas, grease") and by his own war-induced vision of death ("My very mind seems gangrened"). Occasionally, in his denunciation of the baseness he finds around him, he aspires to something of the virtuous indignation of classical satire; but the tone often seems shrill, as if the moralist's anger sprang chiefly from his own inner wound. More often the mood is haunted and introspective, the tone of a man, "Faulty, imperfect, human," whose "heart is faint with the deaths of many gods." The old classical images of perfection—"Slim fauns" and the "virginal delight" of the nightingale—make their appearances only in the context of the poet's longing to escape his condition: not so much, one feels, to end his exile from the world, as to find in "indifference" a retreat from the "seething of lives, / The rage of struggle." Betrayed by reality, he writes in "Truth," his words have grown "wan and cold"; only "happy Falsehood" will once again make him a "merry fool."

The second part of the book, "Words for Music," consists of ten "Songs for Puritans" and four "Songs for Sensualists." The first are invitations to love, the second warnings about the transience of flesh. Both closely imitate the form and content of the seventeenth-century Cavalier style—the lyrics of such poets as Carew, Herrick, and Marvell. The book concludes with "Metrical Exercises," two poems in praise of country life, written in rhymed couplets in the seventeenth-century style of Jonson, Herrick, or Waller. Modern poets have often turned back to traditional poetic forms in search of better ways to express their own experiences. But Aldington's poems, although highly praised by reviewers for their craftsmanship, are quite frankly pastiches of earlier styles rather than attempts to adapt those styles to contemporary circumstances. It is difficult not to feel that the imaginative impulse behind these exercises is less a desire to say something about love or time or country life than a need to lose oneself in "happy Falsehood." It is the soothing regularity of poetic form itself that Aldington hopes will "Shut out the world that's mean and old."

In spite of the inner turmoil expressed in *Exile*, however, Aldington's years in the country were productive ones. He estimated that between 1920 and 1928 he turned out 200,000 words a year, twenty-seven books in all. In addition to his poetry, there were collections of his critical articles from the *Times* and from Eliot's *Criterion* (for which he served as editor in 1922); translations from Greek, Latin, Italian, French, Old French, and Provençal; and a biographical and critical study of Voltaire—to whose sardonic intelligence Aldington found himself increasingly attuned. He had mixed feelings about his labors. He complained that "in comparison with real writing, all this literary stuff was trivial drudgery," and at one point he was near collapse from nervous exhaustion. At the same time, he was proud of the professionalism that allowed him to make his own way without giving in to that bourgeois respectability he continued to ridicule in *Exile* ("I also might have worn starched cuffs"). All the conflicts, doubts, and dissatisfactions of the period are the substance of a long poem he produced in 1924, *A Fool i' the Forest*.

Glenn Hughes, a historian of imagism, regarded *A Fool i' the Forest* as Aldington's finest poetic achievement and noted that it was frequently associated at the time with *The Waste Land*. Despite certain external similarities, however—its "phantasmagoric" structure, its loose blank verse, the interpolation of doggerel, literary allusions, and quotations in foreign languages—Aldington's poem is not radically fragmented in the "modernist" fashion, and it is much more straightforwardly autobiographical than Eliot's. Its underlying theme is perfectly coherent, and it is the theme of most of Aldington's verse: the conflict between poetry and the world, between imagination and reason. A prefatory note by Aldington makes clear the rational structure beneath the surface dislocations of the narrative. The three main characters are "one person split in three": the unnamed protagonist is a "typical . . . man of our own time . . . shown at a moment of crisis"; Mezzetin, a commedia dell'arte fool, symbolizes "the imaginative faculties—art, youth, satire, irresponsible gaiety, liberty"; and the Conjuror represents "the intellectual faculties—age, science, righteous cant, solemnity, authority." The crisis, which the poem never manages to resolve, is precisely their splitting apart—an instance of what Eliot called the "dissociation of sensibility." The protagonist is a Byronic figure whose cynical humor is an expression of disappointed idealism. In an era when a syndicate of businessmen proposes to weatherproof the Pantheon, devotion to the imagination can only be regarded—as it had been in "Truth"—as a bitter folly. (The juxtaposition of modern banalities with fragments of traditional culture may owe something to Eliot, but it had been fundamental, in one way or another, to each of Aldington's earlier books.) Even when the Conjuror is not voicing the platitudes of bourgeois prudence ("We'll make a man of you, my son"), he dissipates the mystery of the classical heritage and thins out its dense sensuality. Yet the protagonist knows that without intelligence and maturity he is incomplete, and he protests the necessity of choosing between Mezzetin and the Conjuror: "Others have reconciled you, why not I?" The question—and it is central to Aldington's whole career—has to do not only with the poet's life, but even more crucially with his craft. In the sections that follow, the jumble of allusions, parodies, and quotations reflects the protagonist's inability to find any language of his own, anything beyond "Pallid stammering words," to unite what he knows about the world with his fleeting intuitions of the beauty he wants to create. The self-mocking irony is a mask for bitter doubt: the suspicion that nothing can any longer be said or written with conviction.

In an attempt to resolve these doubts, the poem makes two journeys, one through space and the other through time. The first part of the poem—like the first part of Aldington's life—is a pilgrimage to Greece. The Conjuror's pedantic Homeric pastiche (in the manner of Chapman's Homer) raises no classical ghosts; but under the influence of Mezzetin's nonsensical high spirits and unreflective gusto (wine, olives, "bread and sausages, / And several heads of garlic"), the rising moon does seem, for a moment at least, like "Anadyomene from the sea." "Gaiety's a kind of homage," the protagonist muses, but the Conjuror's pedantry and moralism dissipates whatever sanctity still lingers among the ruins. The core of the episode is a debate. Did the Greeks "truly reach that harmony we hear of, / Balance of thinker, athlete, artist?" And even if they did, how is their achievement relevant to a world presided over by "God the Tradesman / Playing at the pianola / 'Onward, onward, Christian soldiers?' " "How can we live like Greeks when we're not Greeks?," the protagonist later asks. "I hate *pastiches*" (a bitter reflection, coming on the heels of "Words for Music" and "Metrical Exercises"). He concludes by wondering if "Stability, perfection, harmony" really have meaning for modern man, whose virtue perhaps—he proposes this without enthusiasm—lies in his very inconsistency: for whom the contending voices are united only in their perpetual debate.

When the Greek dream vanishes, the three find themselves marching through the nightmare of history (briefly illuminated by the Renaissance) until they reach the all-too-familiar battlefields of World War I. Here the poem becomes less concerned with general ideas than with the particulars of Aldington's own life—or, rather, with his worst premonitions about the direction it was taking. In the midst of battle, the Conjuror murders Mezzetin, and the protagonist feels "something vital" leave him forever. His story will now have no conclusion, he warns the reader, but will simply subside into dullness. Delivered over to reason and "maturity," the protagonist becomes the bored observer of the Conjuror's scholarly labors in the British Museum, a prisoner in a city where a "million breathing corpses" lie "In their dark funereal cells." But when, in an outburst of rage at the Conjuror's cheery practicality, the protagonist throws him into the river, he finds himself deprived of both intellect and imagination and condemned to the life of mindless respectability, "An Empire-Builder and a taxpayer," that always haunted Aldington. The poem ends with an elegiac farewell to the deities of earth and sea, "Crushed by inscrutable Fate."

Aldington himself, however, managed to avoid this fate. Increasingly he had been feeling that "something had gone wrong with England," that he was an alien in his own land. By 1928, his earnings from his writing were sufficient to allow him to leave permanently for the Continent, where the life of the Good European still seemed possible. At the age of thirty-five, he writes in his memoir, he felt he was entering a "second youth." But in the next seven years, during which he lived a peripatetic expatriate life, mostly in France and Italy, he turned his creative energies chiefly to fiction and to the satirical, debunking side of his personality—the complement, as *The Fool i' the Forest* suggests, of his frustrated idealism. The second section of his war novel, *Death of a Hero* (1929), is an extended satirical account of the prewar literary scene, with easily recognizable lampoons of Harold Monro, Ezra Pound, and others; his second novel, *The Colonel's Daughter* (1931), is a more affectionate satire of the "fauna" of the village where he had spent his years of retirement; *Soft Answers* (1932), a collection of short stories, is a high-spirited but often bitter look at the futilities of the postwar scene, and at least one of the subjects of its caricatures, T. S. Eliot, found it "cruel and unkind."

Partly, this shift in direction must have been due to the immense popular success of *Death of a Hero*. But Aldington's choice must also have had to do with doubts about poetry in general and about his own gifts in particular—which ever since the war, he felt had been "practically dried up." Two longish poems published near the beginning of his life abroad reflect these doubts. *A Dream in the Luxembourg* (American title, *Love and the Luxembourg*), written in 1928 and published in 1930, is a narrative of the poet's attempt to recall a romantic encounter that might have been only a dream. The poem is dedicated to Brigit Patmore, the woman with whom Aldington had been traveling, and it has been said to mark the beginning of his affair with her. But even more explicitly than in *Images of Desire*, the poem's heroine, who is consistently associated with the spontaneously surging fountains of the Luxembourg, is also a symbol: the same

Beauty that inspired Catullus and the love poets of Provence, the embodiment of the allure of the old gods and of poetry itself. She mysteriously summons the poet from the dullness of his ordinary existence, initiates him into the sweetness of the "European" life ("one of those inspired ragouts / Which you can only find in France, / And some fruit"), but leaves him feeling that their nights together in "that mysterious communion of love" have been as unsubstantial as a dream. All this is recounted in loose blank verse of a quite extraordinary prosiness: Aldington's friends were distressed, and he did not have the poem published for two years. But in context, the flatness of the style has a poignant appropriateness, for the protagonist is continually aware of the inadequacy of his words to fix the shimmering outlines of his rapidly fading vision. The poem is an "incantation," the poet tells us, based on the hope that "Desire put into words may control reality." But in the end the incantation fails, the fountain jet crumbles "like dust of water," and the poet finds himself alone in "the bitterness and the drabness of the real." Poetry again seems only "a fool's dream, a fool's paradise."

The title of *The Eaten Heart* (1929) refers to a passionately violent love story set in medieval Provence, but the poem's real subject is the impossibility of telling or even comprehending such a tale in the modern world. In form, it is a rambling causerie that carries to an extreme Aldington's weakness for opinions: we hear many of his views on the difference between love and sex, the sources of modern nihilism, the sort of God in which one might believe, the errors of Dante and Petrarch, and—above all—the need for true mutuality between men and women in order to escape "the essential solitude." But after all the talk, he is forced to admit that "what we mean to say is never said." In spite of his theories, he has found no way to appropriate, for his life or for his verse, the "positive tragic intensity" of the old tale, without which, he says, one leads a merely negative existence—a "low sucking marsh / Of stagnant habit." In the end he retreats once again to an uneasy self-depreciating irony. If he is to drown in despair, his own heart eaten in a hapless pursuit of Beauty, he must do so "gracefully": "Let not your earnestness appear. . . ." Aside from some exercises in the old imagist mode for the 1930 anthology, Aldington had no more poetry published for nearly six years.

He was, in fact, to write just two more long poems, *Life Quest* (1935) and *The Crystal World* (1937). Both are attempts to articulate the positive credo of romantic love hinted at in *The Eaten Heart* and most fully developed in his third novel, *All Men Are Enemies* (1933). The novel's plot recapitulates a familiar pattern, but with intimations of a more favorable resolution than Aldington had hitherto discovered. Its hero's youthful dream of the girl he encounters on an island off Sicily (in the midst of "Immortal halcyon sea, the springtime of the world") is stripped from him by the violence of the war, and he settles into the dread half life of respectability. But by the end of the book he has once again roused himself to the pursuit of "a finer, fuller life," left his wife and his occupation, and is setting out into an uncertain future with the rediscovered sweetheart of his youth. Aldington is characteristically explicit about the "conception of life" his romance is intended to foster. The "complete human being is formed by a man and a woman," and genuine life is "the life of the here and now, the life of the senses, the life of the deep instinctive forces."

Life Quest is an attempt to get in touch with these forces by revivifying the old symbols, the "old sacred places," by which they are sustained: "The life quest falters," the poet writes, when "the ankh unlocks no door." The poem is in part a return to the jagged experimental mode of *A Fool i' the Forest*, and its early sections are full of echoes of Eliot. It is a series of loosely connected lyrical and (increasingly) rhetorical outbursts that take the protagonist, a modern Childe Harold, on a pilgrimage through "monstrous" and "half dead" cities, where the old myths are dead or impotent and new deities of modern science fail to give human life a coherent meaning. But now the pilgrim's confrontation with death—both the death of a civilization, which he sees devoured by a "mist ghost" of subhuman brutality, and the death of his own youthful dreams amid the corpses of World War I—becomes a sort of initiation. What he learns from the endless history of saviors "who never saved" is that "deep earth creativeness" is a devourer as well as a creator and that the dream of "life, more life" must learn to accommodate mortality rather than vainly seeking to evade it: "Not to live long but to live greatly." That "tainted word," the soul, can once again speak to us meaningfully only if we disentangle it from false hopes of perpetuity and understand it as the brief flowering of the moment, without knowledge of its own beginning or its end. In spite of the "brutes and priests and hucksters," the individual—"one of remnant of life-seekers"—can seek out the "still holy and unprofaned" presences of "Earth Sea and Sun." In the last section of the poem, the pilgrim, inundated by a "huge choking wave of life," utters a prophetic denunciation of the "death worship" of his fellows and a prophetic vision of the "first new men after the machines" who will perhaps replace them. The tone is closer to Whitman than to Eliot, and the substance may owe something to Aldington's intimacy with D. H. Lawrence.

The Crystal World considers how it is that a man and a woman together may draw upon the power of the "real holy ones." Its first part consists of twenty-two love lyrics, many of them reminiscent of the early *Images of Desire*, arranged so as to suggest the outlines of a story like that of *All Men Are Enemies*: ideal love possessed, lost, and regained. In the presence of the lady, "Now night and morning I say 'Yes' to life." She embodies the living power of all the old symbols (Egyptian ones here, chiefly: she is Isis restoring Osiris) by which, even in the midst of the "City of greed and bitter want," the lovers may inhabit their own world of roses, vine leaves, sun, sand, "And all the lovely things that men have made." The seventh lyric, which marks their parting, is an Eliot-like collage of the narrator's own disordered consciousness and broken fragments of a cultural tradition (echoes of Donne, Sheridan, Cole Porter) that no longer sustains him. When the lovers are reunited, it is on the understanding that they must take for granted the misery imposed upon them by a world that will always—as the title of Aldington's novel implies—be the enemy of those who seek to go their own way. Like the "little world" of Donne's lovers (to which Aldington clearly alludes) and like his own early dream of classic beauty, the lovers' "crystal world" is a refuge from the meanness of the life around them. But "It will not be given; you must make it." It is sustained not by a romantic flight from the realities of the outside world, but by a constant vigilant confrontation with its enmity.

C. P. Snow considers the love lyrics of *The Crystal World* among the best in English, and critics have generally ranked it, along with *A Fool i' the Forest* and *Life Quest*, among Aldington's more successful extended efforts. But it is not merely hindsight that suggests that the poem is at once a paean to the power of the imagination to make its own world and Aldington's own farewell to the writing of verse. In the long last section (divided into eleven parts) the lyrical mood breaks off, and we again hear the voice of Aldington the explainer, elucidating the significance of what has gone before. If Mezzetin and the Conjuror are working together again, they are not entirely at one. Furthermore, after the lover's ecstatically lyrical climax ("Beloved I go to her I love. . . .") Aldington brings us abruptly down to earth by raising all the old doubts about poetry and love—"Dead words of a dying epoch," that we use only because the "new words" have not yet been born. His purpose is not so much to call into question the reality of the lovers' experience as to reiterate his sense that we can no longer really formulate its nature. There is finally nothing to be said about the way love shapes life into "patterns of inexplicable beauty." "Inexplicable. It is inexplicable": and this conclusion leaves the love poet in a peculiar position. The lovers' crystal world is itself, of course, a kind of poetry, "the common world made vivid." But the lovers need only the "common terms of common men"—flowers, the sea, the bare word *beauty*—to remind each other of the splendor of the feelings they share. They do not require the "subtle forms of the artist / Who is always seeking exact equivalents / For the experiences of the sensibility." One has the feeling that Aldington too, for all his pride in having granted the lovers their "life-in-words," is skeptical about the possibility of "exact equivalents." He keeps nervously admitting that his language is not Shakespeare's or Proust's, and at one point he cautions the reader not to "confuse these little poems, / The attempt to express these feelings, / With the feelings themselves." In a 1933 preface to a collection of his verse, Aldington was already noting ruefully that the "old emotions and moods . . . seemed far richer than their literary expression" and wondering if his poetry is no more than "a peculiar kind of shorthand which I alone can read." Finally he seems to have settled for a kind of poetry that seeks to breathe life into the old symbols, the "common terms," by exhorting the reader to examine the springs of his own feelings—rather than attempting, perhaps Quixotically, to forge "new words" that would embody the lovers' experience on the page itself. It is possible that Aldington came to believe that the most vital task of the imagination is to build the "crystal world" in life rather than in art. If so, his early aestheticism would have come full circle. In any case, he had no more verse published after *The Crystal World*.

Aldington continued to devote himself to fiction until, at the end of the decade, the certainty of another war made it seem "absurd to denounce calamity, ignoble to satirize people fighting for their existence." Foreseeing that soon there would be "no Europe in which one might try to be good," he resolved to write a memoir in order to preserve the memory of a rapidly vanishing culture and of what he considered, in the end, his finest achievement,

Richard Aldington, Lawrence Durrell, Henry Miller, and Jacques Temple, 1959

"the evolution of an insular provincial schoolboy into an adult European." *Life for Life's Sake* was published in 1941. "I have not yet succeeded in writing either a poem or a prose book which has satisfied me entirely," he wrote in its conclusion, but added that "I can say truthfully that during approximately half a century of infesting this planet I have very seldom indeed been bored; and that is as good as any other definition of success in life."

Aldington had left Europe in 1935, visiting in the Caribbean and finally settling in the United States, where—not very happily—he waited out the war, first in Connecticut and by 1944 in Hollywood, where he lived next to Ciro's and wrote film scripts. In 1946 he returned to France, this time for good. Increasingly he turned his attention to writing biographies, the most important of which were a study of his intimate friend D. H. Lawrence, characteristically subtitled *Portrait of a Genius, But . . .* (1950); a book of indiscreet reminiscences about Norman Douglas and his circle that offended many of Douglas's friends (*Pinorman*, 1954); and a debunking account of the career of Lawrence of Arabia (*Lawrence of Arabia: A Biographical Enquiry*, 1955) that even more severely offended a large segment of England's literary establishment. Aldington's last years were embittered by the controversy over his treatment of Lawrence of Arabia, and he came to feel he was the victim of a conspiracy of silence. Nevertheless, he continued to cling with gusto to the life of the Good European; to encourage new writers (most notably, Lawrence Durrell, who referred to him affectionately as Top Grumpy, the archetypal English Exile); and in the last year of his life, 1962, he was heartened by an invitation from the Soviet Writers' Union to visit Russia, where in spite of his lifelong distaste for politics, his novels were widely read for their humanitarianism and unaffected sentiment. Two weeks after his return from Moscow, he suddenly became ill and died the same day, 27 July 1962.

At the end of his life, Aldington felt his work was unjustly neglected, and since his death there have been attempts to revive his reputation. He had a gift for evoking with considerable fluency large, uncomplicated emotions that readers have often found easy to share, and his champions frequently cite Aldington's verse in order to argue that contemporary poetry need not be obscurely intellectual. Several of his delicately crafted imagist lyrics certainly have a genuine, if somewhat dated, charm; and his longer poems remain interesting for the way they exemplify dilemmas shared by many poets of Aldington's generation. His one-time fellow imagist F. S. Flint compared Aldington to Horace and Catullus on the basis of the veracity with which he recorded his own age. But it is unlikely that his verse will ever again be read widely. His great defect—and it undermines his fiction as well as his poetry—is a tendency to prolixity and prosiness, which is in turn the symptom of a lack of any great power of invention, either in the imaginative substance of his poems or in their verbal texture. The qualities that are most winning in Aldington are all most effectively displayed in his memoir: forthrightness and gusto, a genuinely wide culture, an anecdotal vivacity that combines a sharp satirical eye with a talent for idealistic nostalgia. *Life for Life's Sake* is probably his best book and the one future generations are most likely to turn to for pleasure.

Other:

Voltaire, *Candide and Other Romances*, translated by Aldington (London: John Lane/ Bodley Head, 1927; New York: Dutton, 1927);

Fifty Romance Lyric Poems, translated by Aldington (New York: Crosby Gaige, 1928; London: Chatto & Windus, 1931);

The Decameron of Giovanni Boccaccio, translated by Aldington (New York: Covici, Friede, 1930; London: Putnam's, 1930);

The Viking Book of Poetry of the English-Speaking World, edited by Aldington (New York: Viking, 1941); republished as *Poetry of the English-Speaking World* (London & Toronto: Heinemann, 1947).

Bibliographies:

Alister Kershaw, *A Bibliography of the Works of Richard Aldington from 1915 to 1948* (Burlingame, Cal.: William Wredon, 1950);

Paul Schlueter, "A Chronological Check List of the Books by Richard Aldington," in *Richard Aldington: An Intimate Portrait*, edited by Kershaw and Frédéric-Jacques Temple (Carbondale: Southern Illinois University Press, 1965);

Norman Gates, *A Checklist of the Letters of Richard Aldington* (Carbondale: Southern Illinois University Press, 1977).

References:

Stanley K. Coffman, *Imagism: A Chapter for the History of Modern Poetry* (Norman: University of Oklahoma Press, 1951);

John T. Gage, *In the Arresting Eye: The Rhetoric of Imagism* (Baton Rouge: Louisiana State University Press, 1981);

Norman Gates, *The Poetry of Richard Aldington: A Critical Evaluation and an Anthology of Uncollected Poems* (University Park: Pennsylvania State University Press, 1974);

J. B. Harmer, *Victory in Limbo: Imagism 1908-1917* (London: Secker & Warburg, 1975);

Glenn Hughes, *Imagism and the Imagists: A Study in Modern Poetry* (Stanford: Stanford University Press, 1931);

Alister Kershaw and Frédéric-Jacques Temple, eds., *Richard Aldington: An Intimate Portrait* (Carbondale: Southern Illinois University Press, 1965);

Richard E. Smith, *Richard Aldington* (Boston: Twayne, 1977).

Papers:

The largest collection of manuscripts and letters (including those to Lawrence Durrell and to Aldington's literary executor, Alister Kershaw) is at Southern Illinois University. Other important collections of letters include those at Harvard (Amy Lowell, T. S. Eliot), Yale (Pound, H.D.), UCLA (Harold Monro), and the University of Texas (F. S. Flint, Brigit Patmore).

Kenneth Allott

(29 August 1912-23 May 1973)

Andrew Swarbrick

BOOKS: *The Rhubarb Tree*, by Allott and Stephen Tait (London: Cresset, 1937);
Poems (London: Hogarth Press, 1938);
Jules Verne (London: Cresset, 1940; New York: Macmillan, 1941);
The Ventriloquist's Doll (London: Cresset, 1943);
The Art of Graham Greene, by Allott and Miriam Ferris (London: Hamilton, 1951; New York: Russell & Russell, 1963);
A Room with a View: A Play Adapted from the Novel by E. M. Forster, by Allott and Tait (London: Arnold, 1951);
Matthew Arnold (London: Longmans, Green, 1955);
Collected Poems (London: Secker & Warburg, 1975).

Kenneth Allott

Kenneth Allott is better known as a literary critic and scholar than as a poet. His poetry has attracted comparatively little notice, except from a few isolated quarters, and has as yet established for itself only a minor place in the history of English poetry in the 1930s. Rarely has it been accorded the admiration it deserves. But Allott's poetry is too interesting and important to be viewed only as representative of a particular generation and period. While it is true that much of it does share in the characteristics and preoccupations of its time, Allott's poetic output reveals a considerable individual talent.

Kenneth Allott was born in Glamorgan but spent much of his childhood and youth in Cumberland. He was educated at various schools and at the universities of Durham (where he took first-class honors in English) and of Oxford, where he obtained a B.Litt. for his work on the poems of William Babington. He worked as a schoolmaster and journalist and between 1936 and 1939 was assistant editor of the influential journal *New Verse*, to which he was also a regular contributor. It was at this time that he began to earn his reputation as a writer. His first collection, *Poems*, was published in 1938, a year after *The Rhubarb Tree*, a novel he wrote with Stephen Tait, had appeared. In 1943 his second volume of poetry, *The Ventriloquist's Doll*, was published. He later wrote two plays: the first, *A Room with a View*, which he and Tait adapted from E. M. Forster's novel, was produced at the Cambridge Arts Theatre in February 1950; the second, *The Publican's Story*, was produced in 1953. For most of his life, however, he was a teacher, first in adult education and from 1946 as a lecturer in English literature at Liverpool University, where he was subsequently appointed Andrew Cecil Bradley Professor of Modern English Literature, a post he held until his sudden death in May 1973. As a scholar he is perhaps best known for his work on Matthew Arnold and as editor of the *Penguin Book of Contemporary Verse*; among his books of criticism are studies of Graham Greene and Jules Verne. At the time of his death, his two books of poems had long been out of print; they were republished, together with a selection of poems he had completed between about 1943 and 1957, in 1975 as his *Collected Poems*.

Poems opens with "Men Walk Upright," which in its panoramic survey of history owes something to W. H. Auden's "Spain." In 1950 Allott made high claims for Auden's poetry: "I think it true to say that no other poet writing in English today has at-

 024614

tempted as much as Auden; just as no other poet of his generation can place beside his a body of work so exciting for its peculiar insight, its range of reference and its skill in the use of language and rhythm." Like so many of his contemporaries Allott learned from Auden's techniques but adapted them to his own different purposes. In "Men Walk Upright" Allott expresses a profound despondency, an overpowering sense of irredeemable loss:

> The end of expectancy: no longer between hills
> Do we lean from saddles to see the green champaign
> Famous in legend; nor hope from the opaque deep
> To fish the perfect pearl.
>
> No longer do we believe in the masterpieces
> Growing on an exile's canvas in unfurnished rooms.
> Lost the delight in the marvellous or the antique
> Beneath the wheels of routine.

The poet acts as spokesman for his age, presenting his own intuitions as general truths, directed at an audience whose compliance he expects. Together, he and his readers suffer:

> Who can bear this? Who can face without wincing
> The noseless in the mean alley, the fellowship
> Of the loud saloon, the housewife losing a sixpence
> And hopelessly crying?

Yet it would be wrong to assume that, like others of his generation, Allott felt obliged to express in his poetry a sense of communion with his fellows. Neither was he convinced that social amelioration could be achieved by collective action. A recurring theme in his poems, including "Men Walk Upright," is that the individual remains isolated, not only unable to help others but quite incapable of helping himself and impotent before the hidden, ungovernable powers that shape his daily existence. There is no solace in the past:

> How shall we steer through the narrows, or must we founder?
> Must we sit still and regret the imaginary past,
> Weep on divans at the thought of the Elgin marbles
> Or the maypoles of England?

The individual, at the mercy of a future he cannot control, can devote himself only to making the best of the present, like "the impudent pigeon / Plaiting its nest above the ellipse of the traffic." He carves out his own existence, seeks his own fleeting and illusory comforts, "and the earth moves on / To no destination."

The tone of this first collection is undoubtedly affected by Allott's awareness of the approaching holocaust in Europe. But Allott's sense of helplessness goes beyond the temporal; having lost early his Catholic faith, he faces a blank, indifferent infinity. Skeptical about the efficacy of programmatic politics, Allott was something of a social agnostic, and this skepticism is felt in the rather severe, aloof tone of his poems. An audience is addressed, a readership envisaged, but it is as a moralist that Allott presents himself. Profoundly dismayed at his own and his fellows' situation, nevertheless he keeps his distance, watchful and reserved even as he strives for moments of release, as in these lines from "End of a Year":

> Slugged by ungainly distance you and I
> Beneath the same stars separately lie;
> But let our worlds grow singular, and let
> Those parts be mapped some do, we would forget;
> Deserts renew as gardens, so the stars
> Advise you, who for years were listeners.

This extract illustrates Allott's characteristic self-control, as well as his masterly control of verse form and syntax. The sentence unfolds over the line lengths with an unremitting logic in a manner not unreminiscent of the poetry of John Donne, not only in the imagery but in the terse, economical progression of the grammar. This adroitness sharpens Allott's keen sense of morality.

Allott's poetry could thus be described as intellectual, often difficult, and sometimes inexplicable. In particular, his adjectives are frequently far removed from the conversational and familiar idiom recommended by his masters in the 1930s. His epithets may arrest and surprise the reader, but hardly because of their accuracy, their fidelity to the phenomenon they ought to be describing. "Mild laboratories," "perfunctory west," "evangelical donkeys," "snobbish dark," "glassy hymn," "imbecile willows": the list can all too easily be extended. What they reveal is the poet's attitude toward the world around him, implicitly passing comment and evaluating whatever it is that impinges upon his senses. They reassert the poet's aloofness, his air of superiority and disenchantment, for our interest is always deflected from the things described to the voice that is describing. As these lines from "Privacy" suggest, the poet remains, in a disturbingly literal way, self-possessed:

An ample bubble blown in the solid granite,
This room has neither exits nor entrances,
Hermetically sealed against all vulgar airs
Without a stick or stitch of furniture.

Allott's intellectual quality, then, lies in the deft manipulation of the reader's responses. The things named in his poems are valuable not in themselves, as qualities of an objective reality, but only insofar as they maintain a rather one-sided dialogue between poet and reader. In this way, Allott's early poetry is very much of its time, answering to the humanist criticism of I. A. Richards, F. R. Leavis, and William Empson.

But if Allott's early poetry fails to evoke a sense of objective reality, it is remarkably successful in other ways. Roy Fuller has pointed to Allott's skill as "a great phrase-maker," and there are occasions when his lines achieve an astonishing power and resonance:

I hear the ape deafen the peninsula
Because his hands will not invent the plough.
("Historical Grimace")

The generations summer in our stead.
("End of a Year")

From this wet island of birds and chimneys.
. . . .
And I imagine sometimes at night emerging
The stunted pasty wonder of the slum,
Like a cracked bicycle frame
On which a short vocabulary is hung
("Exodus")

Allott's descriptions may sometimes fail, or they can be, as in these examples, audacious. He is often able suddenly to express an abstract concept in vividly concrete images, or to render a particular impression in a glittering phrase, as in these lines from "Morning and Evening":

The summer lightning
Flickered showing the frogs in the lily pond,
The broken panes in the greenhouse like
vowels missing. . . .

Donald Davie has recently made high claims for Allott's verbal inventiveness. He suggests, in fact, that such "inventiveness" operates at a level far below conscious deliberation, and that Allott's talent was not, indeed could not be, an acquired skill. When Allott writes in one late poem "Haunted by groan and ice-pressure of all change / When the skull-cap splits. . . ," Davie points out how, at a subliminal level, the reader will assimilate "ice-pressure" and "skull-cap" so that both "skull-pressure" and "ice-cap" are felt to be present, each making as much sense as the other. This verbal orchestration is not entirely a matter of sound, but of sound preceding and being validated by sense. Another example of this sort of interaction between sound and sense appears in "Any Point on the Circumference":

While the long figures of the years
Drum into his vexed ears
Their waxen certainties:
That trees must fall and waters freeze
And truth seduce all promises,
And men be contradicted by their fears.

"Drum" would suggest "fingers" rather than "figures"; there seems no justification for "waxen" other than its aural resemblance to "vexed"; but the "figures" are the numerals on calendars, or personified furies, and "certainties," given Allott's skepticism, may well turn out to be "waxen," drained of comfort when they are "drummed," enumerated, and sounded out. Sounds and meanings here shuttle across the poet's awareness too rapidly for a thoroughly conscious grasp to be kept on them, and it is in such cases, when Allott is not consciously striving for effect, that his writing seems most satisfying.

His second collection, *The Ventriloquist's Doll*, shows a marked falling short of such powers. Allott's wordplay is more self-conscious, his meaning more impenetrable. In his first volume there is evidence of a flirtation with surrealism and of the influence of Dylan Thomas's work in which Allott found much to praise, but the poems in this second collection suffer from phrase-making run riot, a verbal intoxication in which words are cut adrift from their referents. In the midst of war Allott, like other poets of his generation, could no longer warn and hector. His tone, once distant and aloof, now had to express a more obvious sympathy and solidarity. This urge for national communion, for egalitarianism, can be perceived in his work in the frequent recourse to catalogues. Time, in "Elegy," for example, is "like the smell of a fox's lair," "the extruded hernia / Of a middle-aged goose-stepping gauleiter," "a dream of summer and tea-roses," "a paper suit of Stock Exchange prices," "the wasp-like drone of a Lutheran hymn," "the collier's ache in the amputated limb," and "the back-payments on a bedroom suite." Everything is merged, and there are to be no distinctions. Poet and reader are granted license to mean whatever each of them wills. Yet, as he noted in his introduction to *The Penguin Book of Contemporary Verse*, Allott was well aware of the dangers in such procedures: "The neo-romantic poets lack a sense of limit provided in the 'thirties by the concern with communication. . . . [Some] have cultivated their hysteria and built themselves ivory towers. Their verse is either dark, prolix and unnecessarily involved . . . or a lisping 'silly sooth.' "

It is significant that this judgment was written in 1950, for between 1943 and his death Allott completed very few poems. This near silence has worried and perplexed critics. The poems that he did write during these years are among his very finest achievements. Gone is the superior, sometimes disdainful tone, his reserved watchfulness and morbidity. These poems are poignant, moving, and direct because the poet reveals himself, not in an extravagant or confessional manner, but as a man vulnerable before experience. Their language is unadorned, contemporary but elegant, as in "Typed with Two Fingers":

> A fault has opened here a mineral eye
> On the green innocence of grass and tree,
> Arcadia stutters,
> The houses stutter, knitting railway lines—
> What happens is a city presently

We find still the vivid descriptiveness, but now, as in "Before Breakfast," there seems a genuine and open responsiveness to the quotidian world:

> The rain sleeks its black side in rivers.
> . . . .
> Through curtains a watery knife-edge of daylight gleams.
> . . . .
> And the wild rain slake a black rage in rivers.

This vulnerability can be found in his poems concerned with personal relationships, and his lyrics, such as "Cheshire Cat," often dominated by images of parting and distance, are particularly moving and piercingly honest:

> Tonight the rain sheets down. After an hour
> It does not seem there can be any more;
> And I am moved,
> Stripped of whatever's English for *savoir-faire*,
> To tell you, where you are,
> How you are loved,
> And how your harm I mean if once believed.

In his earlier poetry Allott *would* have found "whatever's English for *savoir-faire*," and his language might have suffered; here it is disarmed and yet more probing. He now lays himself open to hurting and being hurt, whereas in his earlier style he protected himself within a rhetorical irony. The phrase-making is more muted and takes its place within the overall structure of a poem rather than overshadowing it.

Kenneth Allott's poetry deserves far more attention than passing references in literary histories and anthologies. While it lacks the philosophical scope and brilliance of Auden's, it stands up to comparison with the work of other more vaunted poets of his generation. Although his characteristic tone is one of resigned pessimism, there is a courageous and persistent endorsement of humane values and a celebration of isolated moments of joy and vision. There is a sense in which Allott's poetry yearns for the security which his rejection of the Roman Catholic faith had abandoned. His poetry refuses to be constrained within particular movements and periods; it remains throughout the work of a writer committed, as poet and scholar, to the health of his art.

Plays:

A Room with a View, by Allott and Stephen Tait, Cambridge, Cambridge Arts Theatre, February 1950;

The Publican's Story, 1953.

Other:

Poems of William Babington, edited by Allott (Liverpool: Liverpool University Press, 1948);

The Penguin Book of Contemporary Verse, edited by Allott (Harmondsworth, U.K.: Penguin, 1950; revised, 1962);

Selected Poems of Winthrop Mackworth Praed, edited by Allott (London: Routledge & Kegan Paul, 1953);

Five Uncollected Essays of Matthew Arnold, edited by Allott (Liverpool: Liverpool University Press, 1953);

Victorian Prose, 1830-1880, edited by Allott and

Miriam Allott (Harmondsworth, U.K.: Penguin, 1956);
Poems of Matthew Arnold, edited by Allott (London: Longmans, Green, 1965);
Selected Poems of Browning (London: Oxford University Press, 1967).

References:
Donald Davie, *Kenneth Allott and the Thirties* (Liverpool: Liverpool University Press, 1980);
Francis Scarfe, *Auden and After: The Liberation of Poetry 1930-1941* (London: Routledge, 1942).

W. H. Auden

Richard Johnson
Mount Holyoke College

See also the Auden entry in *DLB 10, Modern British Dramatists, 1900-1945*.

BIRTH: York, England, 21 February 1907, to Dr. George Augustus Auden and Constance Rosalie Bicknell Auden.

EDUCATION: B.A., Christ Church College, Oxford, 1928.

MARRIAGE: 15 June 1935 to Erika Mann.

AWARDS AND HONORS: King's Gold Medal for Poetry for *Look, Stranger!*, 1937; Guggenheim Fellowship, 1942; Award of Merit Medal (American Academy of Arts and Letters), 1945; Pulitzer Prize for *The Age of Anxiety*, 1948; Bollingen Prize in Poetry, 1954; National Book Award for *The Shield of Achilles*, 1956; Feltrinelli Prize (Rome), 1957; Alexander Droutzkoy Memorial Award, 1959; Guiness Poetry Award (Ireland), 1959; Honorary Student, Christ College, Oxford, 1962-1973; Austrian State Prize for European Literature, 1966; National Medal for Literature of National Book Committee, 1967; Gold Medal (National Institute of Arts and Letters), 1968; Litt.D., Swarthmore College, 1965; D.Litt., Oxford, 1971; D.Litt., London University, 1972.

DEATH: Vienna, Austria, 29 September 1973.

BOOKS: *Poems* (Oxford: Stephen Spender, 1928);
Poems (London: Faber & Faber, 1930; revised, 1933);
The Orators: An English Study (London: Faber & Faber, 1932; revised 1934, 1966; New York: Random House, 1967);
The Dance of Death (London: Faber & Faber, 1934);
Poems (New York: Random House, 1934);
The Dog Beneath the Skin, or, Where is Francis?, by Auden and Christopher Isherwood (London: Faber & Faber, 1935; New York: Random House, 1935);
The Ascent of F 6, by Auden and Isherwood (London: Faber & Faber, 1936; New York: Random House, 1937);
Look, Stranger! (London: Faber & Faber, 1936); republished as *On This Island* (New York: Random House, 1937);
Spain (London: Faber & Faber, 1937);
Letters from Iceland, by Auden and Louis MacNeice (London: Faber & Faber, 1937; New York: Random House, 1937);
Selected Poems (London: Faber & Faber, 1938);
On the Frontier, by Auden and Isherwood (London: Faber & Faber, 1938; New York: Random House, 1939);
Education Today and Tomorrow, by Auden and T. C. Worsley (London: Hogarth Press, 1939);
Journey to a War, by Auden and Isherwood (London: Faber & Faber, 1939; New York: Random House, 1939);
Another Time (New York: Random House, 1940; London: Faber & Faber, 1940);
Some Poems (London: Faber & Faber, 1940);
The Double Man (New York: Random House, 1941); republished as *New Year Letter* (London: Faber & Faber, 1941);
For the Time Being (New York: Random House, 1944; London: Faber & Faber, 1945);
The Collected Poetry (New York: Random House, 1945);

W. H. Auden, 1969 (BBC Hulton, Evening Standard *Collection)*

The Age of Anxiety (New York: Random House, 1947; London: Faber & Faber, 1948);

Collected Shorter Poems, 1930-1944 (London: Faber & Faber, 1950);

The Enchafèd Flood or, The Romantic Iconography of the Sea (New York: Random House, 1950; London: Faber & Faber, 1951);

Nones (New York: Random House, 1951; London: Faber & Faber, 1952);

The Rake's Progress: Opera in Three Acts, music by Igor Stravinsky, libretto by Auden and Chester Kallman (London & New York: Boosey & Hawkes, 1951);

The Shield of Achilles (New York: Random House, 1955; London: Faber & Faber, 1955);

The Old Man's Road (New York: Voyages Press, 1956);

The Magic Flute: An Opera in Two Acts, music by

Mozart, English libretto by Auden and Kallman (New York: Random House, 1956; London: Faber & Faber, 1957);

Making, Knowing and Judging (Oxford: Clarendon Press, 1956);

W. H. Auden: A Selection by the Author (Hammersmith: Penguin, 1958); republished as *Selected Poetry of W. H. Auden* (New York: Modern Library, 1959);

Homage to Clio (New York: Random House, 1960; London: Faber & Faber, 1960);

Elegy for Young Lovers: Opera in Three Acts, music by Hans Werner Henze, libretto by Auden and Kallman (Mainz, London & Paris: Schott, 1961);

The Dyer's Hand and Other Essays (New York: Random House, 1962; London: Faber & Faber,1963); republished as *Selected Essays* (London: Faber & Faber, 1964);

About the House (New York: Random House, 1965; London: Faber & Faber, 1966);

The Bassarids: Opera Seria with Intermezzo in One Act, based on "The Bacchae" of Euripides, music by Henze, libretto by Auden and Kallman (Mainz: Schott, 1966);

Collected Shorter Poems 1927-1957 (London: Faber & Faber, 1966; New York: Random House, 1967);

Collected Longer Poems (London: Faber & Faber, 1968; New York: Random House, 1969);

Secondary Worlds (London: Faber & Faber, 1969; New York: Random House, 1969);

City Without Walls (London: Faber & Faber, 1969; New York: Random House, 1970);

A Certain World (New York: Random House, 1970; London: Faber & Faber, 1971);

Academic Graffiti (London: Faber & Faber, 1971; New York: Random House, 1972);

Love's Labour's Lost, music by Nicholas Nabokov, libretto by Auden and Kallman (Berlin: Boat & Bock, 1972);

Epistle to a Godson (New York: Random House, 1972; London: Faber & Faber, 1972);

Forewords and Afterwords, edited by Edward Mendelson (New York: Random House, 1973; London: Faber & Faber, 1973);

Thank You, Fog (London: Faber & Faber, 1974; New York: Random House, 1974);

Collected Poems, edited by Mendelson (London: Faber & Faber, 1976; New York: Random House, 1976);

The English Auden, edited by Mendelson (London: Faber & Faber, 1977; New York: Random House, 1978);

Selected Poems, edited by Mendelson (New York: Vintage, 1979; London: Faber & Faber, 1979).

W. H. Auden was a major English poet, probably the most important English-speaking poet born in the twentieth century. Noted especially for native lyrical gifts and highly developed technical expertise, he also displayed wide reading and acute intelligence in his poems. His life, about which a great deal of detail has come to light in the last two or three years, contains sharp contradictions. His early poems were praised for their political pertinency as well as their aesthetic modernity, and his later poems were condemned for their religious and political orthodoxy. He seems to some a figure of Johnsonian wisdom and good sense; others see a man torn by a homosexuality with which he never came to terms, alcoholism, and domestic unhappiness. Even when he had embraced certain kinds of religious orthodoxy, he continued to live what in many ways was an eccentrically bohemian life; but even in his most revolutionary, his most bohemian, or his least sober moments, he maintained a steady and highly productive work schedule, exemplifying if not always honoring the work ethic of the middle class. As more and more biographical material surfaces, these contradictions are intensified rather than resolved. But contradictions nothwithstanding, he continues to receive recognition as one of the most important poets of the century, and as one of its most representative figures as well.

Wystan Hugh Auden was the son of a nurse and a doctor and the third of three brothers. His father had broad scientific and scholarly interests; his mother was an accomplished musician and devoutly religious; both parents were committed to public service. He was educated at St. Edmund's preparatory school in Surrey (1915-1920); at Gresham's in Holt, Norfolk (1920-1925); and at Christ Church College, Oxford (1925-1928), which he entered on a scientific fellowship, later switching to English. At Oxford, and throughout the decade following his graduation, he was at the center of a group of young writers (including Christopher Isherwood, Stephen Spender, and C. Day Lewis) that his voice especially seemed to define: the Auden Generation, as Sam Hynes describes it in a book by that title.

After being graduated from Oxford with—like other great poets before him—an undistinguished degree (third-class honors), Auden lived for eighteen months in Berlin. Some of his time was devoted to learning German, but more of it to taking full advantage of the excitement and freedom of

W. H. Auden, 1928 (Durham University Library)

Berlin in the last days of the Weimar Republic. Affairs with proletarian German boys helped confirm his sexual nature although he was briefly engaged to a young woman. The music of political cabaret songs, as well as some of Brecht's lyrics, provided him with models for later songs. After he returned to England in late 1929, he taught successively at two schools. He was an enthusiastic, eccentric, inventive, and popular schoolmaster. His first two commercially published volumes—*Poems* (1930) and *The Orators* (1932)—appeared in the years just after his graduation from Oxford and established him, by the age of twenty-five, as an important poet. (The 1928 volume called *Poems* was hand-printed in an edition of approximately forty-five copies by Auden's friend Stephen Spender.) Perhaps no other poet since Keats has shown such precocious brilliance. A posthumously published volume, *The English Auden* (1977), includes virtually all the early poems and prose in order of composition and in the form in which they first appeared (Auden was a continual reviser, rearranger, and even discarder of his early poems). The *revised* versions of the early poems as well as most of his later works appear in *Collected Poems* (1976).

Auden wrote his first major work, *Paid on Both Sides: A Charade*, while still at Oxford. T. S. Eliot accepted it for publication in the *Criterion* in 1928, publishing it in 1930; it also appeared in *Poems* (1930). By charade, Auden meant the kind of elaborate dramatic game played at English country houses; in fact, he originally intended it for performance at that of a friend; the charade, Auden is said to have thought, was one of the few living dramatic forms. *Paid on Both Sides* presents the story of a feud between two families, of an attempt to end the feud, and of the attempt's failure. The work has a complex lineage. Most immediately, it derives from Eliot's *The Waste Land* (1922, which Auden read in 1926, when it became widely known at Oxford, its irony, humor, fragmentary structure, and "unpoetic" verse upsetting the dominant pastoralism of Georgian verse). From *The Waste Land* he probably learned a way of constructing a large work by interweaving diverse threads of material. At Oxford Auden had been reading a great deal of early Germanic literature, especially Anglo-Saxon poetry; and he had known since childhood the Icelandic sagas, which describe in vivid detail complex and bloody feuds. Woven into *Paid on Both Sides* are allusions to, conventions, and scenes from traditional English mummers' plays; John Fuller traces some direct borrowings. *Paid on Both Sides* particularly echoes Anglo-Saxon poetry, with its accentual meter, its organization around a succession of phrases, often appositional, and its concrete, monosyllabic language. The landscape evoked also resembles that of Anglo-Saxon and Icelandic verse. The story takes place at no particular time; some elements seem very much up-to-date; others belong to literary and social antiquity. As several commentators remark, following something Auden said to Christopher Isherwood, the play seems to be partly about some of the bloodier Icelandic sagas, partly about a school officer-training corps; it is meant to suggest a connection between those two worlds.

Serving as structural pillars are a series of choric odes, reminiscent in tone as well as in dramatic and structural function of the odes in Greek tragedy. These odes have a rare beauty and continue today to be published and greatly enjoyed as separate poems, and they lend credence to the Nietzschean notion that tragedy rose out of the Dionysian intensity of the chorus, with plot, character, and action as later additions to the choric expression of a fundamentally lyric impulse. By this blending of the Greek and the Anglo-Saxon, Auden explores the stratum of primitive impulses that lies beneath our common "civil" behavior, a blending that not only helps to explain our behavior but also carries with it the aesthetic power of a social and psychological primacy.

There seems, indeed, to be a psychological allegory in the work. *The English Auden* includes an early version of the poem that Auden had written while still at Oxford. According to Edward Mendelson it is "half the length of the final version, it almost ignores the issue of personal psychology," which in the final version takes the form of an allegorical dream sequence that suggests the possibility of both personal and social regeneration through the innate power of love. In a later poem, "Letter to Lord Byron," Auden attributes the change in the poem to "a chap called Layard," who "fed / New doctrines into my receptive head." He continues:

Part came from Lane, and part from D. H. Lawrence;
Gide, though I didn't know it then, gave part.
They taught me to express my deep abhorrence
If I caught anyone preferring Art
To Life and Love and being Pure-in-Heart.

Lane is Homer Lane, an American psychologist who believed that health comes through reliance on instinct, a view that had much in common with D. H. Lawrence's views as expressed in *Fantasia of the Unconscious* (1922).

In the verse play, Auden means to testify to the primitive powers of love and to suggest that reliance on instinctual love might ameliorate the effects of a feud whose origins have been forgotten but whose effects have been transmitted from generation to generation, and indeed the conflicts in which we all participate. The play, intentionally terse, almost fragmented (though not quite in the manner or to the degree of *The Waste Land* or of *The Orators*), partly suggests the fragmentary quality of the psyche, while at the same time carrying the primitive quality of the Anglo-Saxon, Greek, and Icelandic worlds.

Poems (1930), published on Eliot's recommendation (he was a reader for, but not yet an editor for Faber and Faber), consists of *Paid on Both Sides* and thirty untitled shorter poems, some of which had appeared in *Poems* (1928), identified only by Roman numerals. Many of the thirty shorter poems evoke the Anglo-Saxon world of *Paid on Both Sides*; also discernible are echoes of Laura Riding and Wilfred Owen; of two nineteenth-century poets discovered and revered by the early moderns, Emily Dickinson and Gerard Manley Hopkins; and of Thomas Hardy (Auden's first poetic master), Edward Thomas, and Robert Frost. The poems are terse and use a minimum of exposition. Many read as if taken from a play like *Paid on Both Sides*, as if they would be completely clear if only we knew the plot of the play. Many are dramatic; others, enigmatically narrative. Representative is the first stanza of poem twenty-two (later called "Missing"):

From scars where kestrels hover,
The leader looking over
Into the happy valley,
Orchard and curving river,
May turn away to see
The slow fastidious line
That disciplines the fell,
Hear curlew's creaking call
From angles unforseen,
The drumming of a snipe

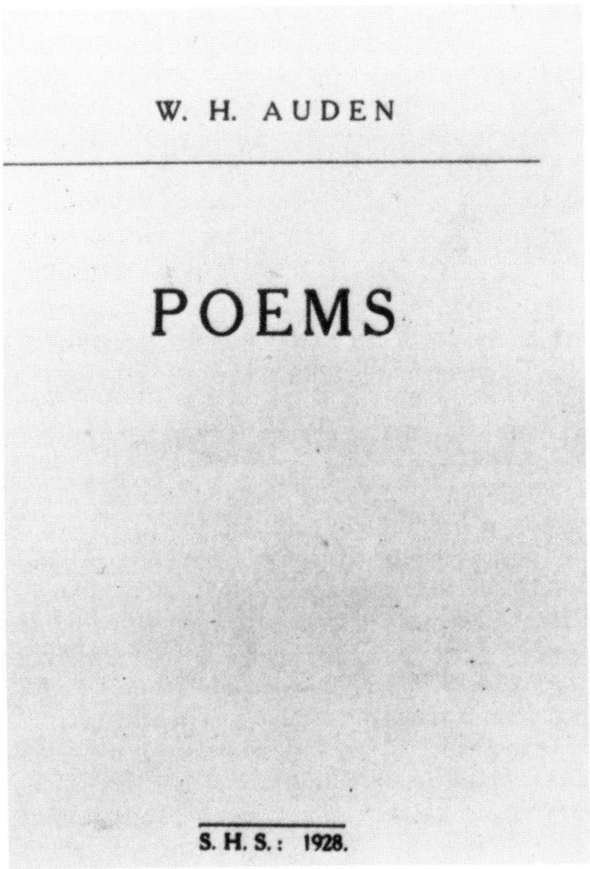

Title page for Auden's first book, printed by Stephen Spender

Surprise where driven sleet
Had scaled to the bone
And streams are arid yet
To an unaccustomed lip.

As in almost all the poems in the volume, the effect of having been torn out of context is central. Without explaining very much, the poem transports the reader quickly into a spare, unadorned world. The landscape's "slow fastidious line / That disciplines the fell" defines the poet's art as well and seems to invite the reader into a disciplined conspiracy with the poet. Cleanth Brooks, in an early essay, noted that "Auden's surest triumphs represent a recovery of . . . archaic imagery." The term *imagery* slightly misses the mark, because the real power here comes from the hardness of words like *scar* and *kestrel*; the reader does not read through the images to find a picture or an abstract meaning, but rather he grasps a unified world and delights in the poet's discovery of words that can create such a sense. The language has amazing vitality, of the sort that comes from its being very much a part of spoken language, and indeed from the more common, earthy part, and yet, often it has an exotic air, from unfamiliarity. So tight is the connection between the landscape and the language that the location seems a verbal one; the language defines the people it depicts.

Other poems from this collection work in analogous ways, using very different materials. Several are poems about love that very often use abstractions in what may seem almost a childish or silly way, in short one- or two-stress lines. For example:

Love by ambition
Of definition
Suffers partition
And cannot go
From yes to no:
For no is not love, no is no.

The poem appears to be an attack on trying too hard to define love, suggesting that when one tries to define love, one divides it; it cannot be turned into a series of simple oppositions. As in "From scars where kestrels hover," however, the reader quickly becomes intrigued by Auden's tantalizing verbal game and especially by the zeal with which Auden works out the details of this playful manner (which, according to Mendelson, came to Auden from Laura Riding, who was making use of methods of Skelton and Emily Dickinson).

The poems discussed do not justly represent the volume, which is notable for considerable variety of manner and technique; one is already aware of what was to characterize Auden's work throughout his life: a breadth of inventiveness quite unequaled by poets of this century and reminding one perhaps of two of the few poets Auden seems genuinely to have disliked, Shelley and Tennyson. Much as *Poems* was read and treasured for its implicit as well as its explicit political and psychological content, and for its general rebelliousness, its real importance was the glimpse it gave of a poet of extraordinary skill and audacity, one who could do almost anything with verse, but also one who would make a career out of trying to adjust his lyrical virtuosity to a changing and developing concern with both public and private values.

During his first years out of Oxford, then, Auden quickly established himself not only as the leading poet but also as a spokesman for his generation. He practiced and extended the techniques of modernism, and yet at the same time he was not fully satisfied with the spiritual content of the modernist tradition. He was always prolific, but the years between *The Orators* (1932), written when he was twenty-six, and *Another Time* (1940), were particularly crowded. With Christopher Isherwood he wrote three plays—*The Dog Beneath the Skin, or, Where is Francis?* (1935), *The Ascent of F 6* (1936), and *On the Frontier* (1938)—and a travel book, *Journey to a War* (1939); and with Louis MacNeice, another travel book, *Letters from Iceland* (1937). The major collection of poems of these years was *Look, Stranger!* (1936; published in the United States in 1937 as *On This Island*).

As John Fuller puts it, "*The Orators* was the work which set the seal on Auden's early reputation. Subtitled 'An English Study' it forms among other things a surrealist anatomy of a country in crisis. The conception is large-scale, the tone exuberantly varied and experimental. Though there is much in the work which is direct and satirical, the predominant allegiance evoked is to the European avant-garde of the 'twenties, to the prose of Stein, Joyce and Wyndham Lewis, to the lingering influence of Baudelaire and Rimbaud, and to more recent poets like St.-J. Perse." In his preface to *The Collected Poetry* of 1945 Auden talked of the work as "a case of the fair notion fatally injured," though he does not say precisely by what; in the preface to a 1966 edition of *The Orators*, Auden wrote that "my name on the title-page seems a pseudonym for someone else, someone talented but near the border of sanity, who might well, in a year or two, become a Nazi." Its central theme, he continued, "seems to be Hero-

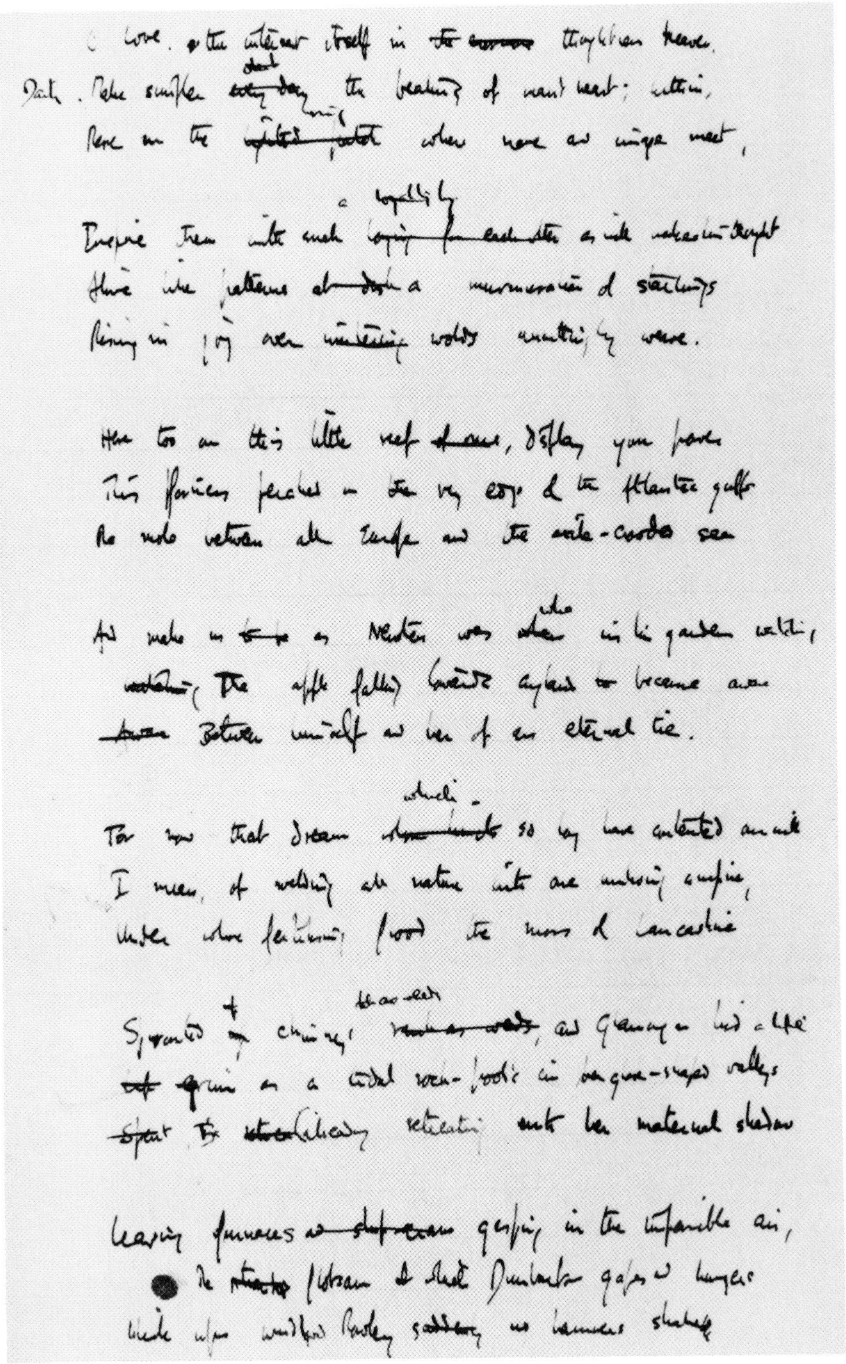

Page from "O Love, the interest itself in thoughtless Heaven," in Auden's 1932 poetry notebook (Houghton Library, Harvard University)

worship, and we all know what that can lead to politically. My guess today is that my unconscious motive in writing it was therapeutic, to exorcise certain tendencies in myself by allowing them to run riot in phantasy."

The Orators is perhaps Auden's most difficult work, the only one, Mendelson argues, that can be read only with a key. On the eve of the work's publication Auden had in fact offered Faber and Faber a prefatory note in which he said: "I felt this book is more obscure than it ought to be. I'm sorry, for obscurity, as a friend once said to me, is mostly swank. The central theme is a revolutionary hero. The first book describes the effect of him and his

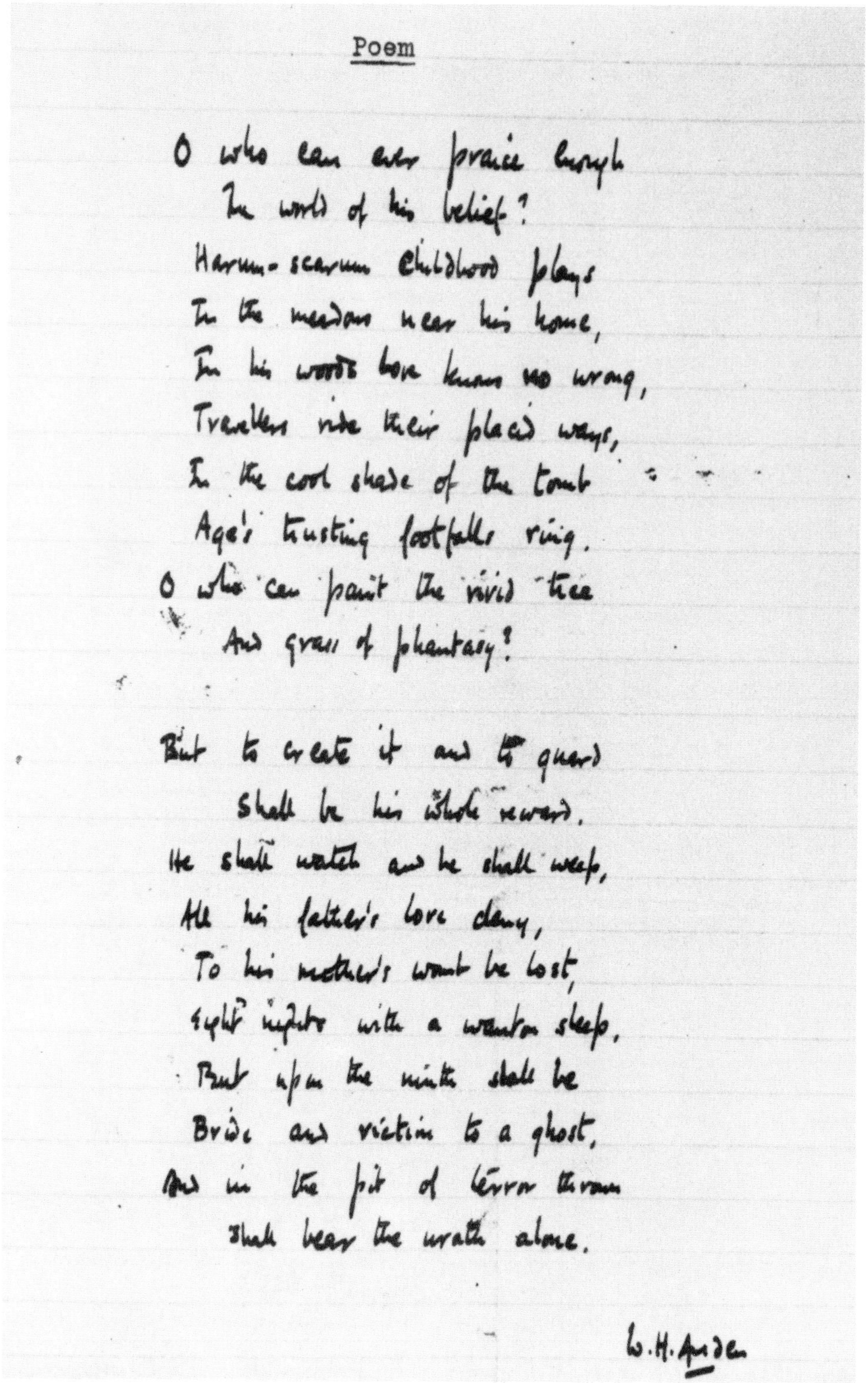
Poem

O who can ever praise enough
The world of his belief?
Harum-scarum childhood plays
In the meadows near his home,
In his woods love knows no wrong,
Travellers ride their placid ways,
In the cool shade of the tomb
Age's trusting footfalls ring.
O who can paint the vivid tree
And grass of phantasy?

But to create it and to guard
Shall be his whole reward.
He shall watch and he shall weep,
All his father's love deny,
To his mother's womb be lost,
Eight nights with a wanton sleep,
But upon the ninth shall be
Bride and victim to a ghost,
And in the pit of terror thrown
Shall bear the wrath alone.

W.H. Auden

Manuscript for "O who can ever praise enough," first published in 1937 (Lockwood Memorial Library, State University of New York at Buffalo)

failure on those whom he meets; the second book is his own account; and the last some personal reflections on the question of leadership in our time." Mendelson goes so far as to suggest that the work's missing key is meant to suggest the missing hero that society longs for; by this view, Auden intends to criticize that longing for a hero, although not necessarily the conditions that give rise to the longing. The number of prefatory warnings Auden has wanted to attach to the work, from before its first publication to its republication almost thirty-five years later, indicates how uncertain Auden was about the form that the poem takes; he seems never, not even when he wrote it, to have been comfortable with its lack of a clear voice of intelligent direction.

No voice from the work tells the reader how to read the work, or what to make of its material, an uncertainty that seems the result of several different impulses. As Hynes, Fuller, and Mendelson have suggested, *The Orators* reflects the obscurity of the whole modernist tradition, Auden's absorption of the lessons of Joyce, Eliot, Stein, and others. But uncertainty also arises because the reader is offered the materials of the work as documents of a deranged or deluded mentality and because, as Auden suggests, the work is the result of incomplete artistic control, a failure to realize an artistic impulse.

Besides the poetic prologue and epilogue, *The Orators* comprises three books: "The Initiates" and "The Journal of an Airman," which are prose, and "Six Odes," in verse. These sections cover a great range of oratory, from the public modes of the first part, which parodies various kinds of inspirational rhetoric such as that addressed to schoolchildren on prize days, through the intensely private "The Journal of an Airman," to the celebratory odes of the third book. A rough-hewn logic lurks behind this organization: England is in trouble, and one can sense it in the windblown rhetoric of her traditional orators. As Fuller suggests, "the Ciceronian political ideal mirrored in the British educational and diplomatic system, may have provided an ironical structure for the work." With the decay of believable public rhetoric, the need for a leader, a reviving force, becomes clear. But, as "The Journal of an Airman" indicates, the place to which the young of 1932 might most reasonably turn offers no real hope and is in itself dangerous; as Auden wrote to his friend Naomi Mitchison, "in a sense the work is my memorial to Lawrence; i.e., the theme is the failure of the romantic conception of personality."

To the extent that there is an answer to the quandary created by this double failure of both tradition and revolution, it is not yet fully manifest although it is suggested in exuberant odes and the epilogue that close the volume. While the answer cannot be stated fully, it is embedded in a kind of spiritual health that for now can only be expressed poetically. The epilogue is perhaps the best summary of Auden's poetic response to political, rhetorical, and personal bankruptcy:

> 'O where are you going?' said reader to rider,
> 'That valley is fatal when furnaces burn,
> Yonder's the midden whose odours will madden,
> That gap is the grave where the tall return.'

All four stanzas of the epilogue contrast an agent with a patient: reader with rider, fearer with farer, and hearer with horror; the half-rhymes carry the weight of meaning.

Where the rider, the farer, the hearer will go is not clear; *The Orators* ends only with the repeated phrase, "As he left them there, as he left them there" ("he" is the rider-farer-hearer, "them" is reader, fearer, and horror). In artistic terms, the journey is away from modernism, at least in its purest forms. For Auden, the rest of the 1930s was an irregular time of questing—questing indeed became one of the dominant motifs of his poetry—conducted against the background of political turmoil and uncertainty: Hitler's rise to power; worldwide economic depression; the Spanish Civil War; the beginning of World War II. Auden's relation to these events is paradoxical. On the one hand, the political upheavals are at least in part responsible for his revolt against the subjectivism and the obscurity that marked, without completely dominating, his earliest works. Auden was regarded as a spokesman for the left; he went to Spain (13 January-2 March 1937) and to China (26 February-12 June 1938) to see wars in action; and his epigrammatic brilliance made his words among the most quoted by the British left. On the other hand, Auden's participation in political movements did not completely absorb him and absorbed him decreasingly as the 1930s progressed. Like other writers who participated in politics, he was shocked by some of the harsher realities of political life. Also, something else was beginning to happen in his life; perhaps the event to date it from was a mystical experience that occurred in 1933, when he had a vision of the power of love. More and more his poems came to center not on power, but on love. His homosexuality, although he appeared to many to be happily licentious, troubled him; his primary concern was not power but love in all its physical, emotional, and spiritual complexity. Finally, toward the end of the decade, he began to move back toward the orthodox Christianity of his youth.

Look, Stranger! (1936; published in the United

States in 1937 as *On This Island*, the title Auden preferred) collects thirty-one lyrics written between 1933 and 1936. The volume is dedicated to Erika Mann, Thomas Mann's daughter, whom Auden had married in 1935 in order to provide her with British nationality so that she would be allowed to leave Germany. Four brief dedicatory lines summarize his new concerns:

> Since the external disorder, and extravagant lies,
> The baroque frontiers, the surrealist police;
> What can truth treasure, or heart bless,
> But a narrow strictness?

One sees here the beginning of a process that has been perhaps best described by Clive James: "always in Auden, ethics and techniques were bound up together. Barely out of his teens, he was already trying to discipline, rather than exploit, the artistic equivalent of a Midas touch. . . . The moral struggle in Auden was fought out between what was possible to his gift and what he thought allowable to it. . . ." The dedicatory lines nicely illustrate just this struggle. Their logic is familiar: external disorder, especially of a political sort, requires "narrow strictness," discipline of thought, feeling, and expression. Auden underscores the point by using artistic terms—*baroque* and *surrealist*—to describe fascism and war, as if to suggest a link between the kind of art he had practiced in his early work and the disorders of the time.

By this logic, formalism, directness, and clarity become political gestures, or at least parts of a large-scale ethical undertaking. It would not be accurate, however, to say that Auden suddenly converted to classicism after an intense early dalliance with modernism. One needs instead a complex sense of a young poet, at once brilliant and troubled, living in tumultuous times, at first immersing himself in the churning waters of modernism, and then beginning a long, zigzagging path that ultimately led to a new artistic creed. What perhaps most distinguishes Auden is that he never stopped producing brilliant poetry as he made his way; and poems that were for him way stations were often for his readers jewels to be treasured. Already in the 1930s readers saw Auden's steps forward as rejections of positions that his earlier poems had almost magically embodied.

The second poem in *Look Stranger!*, later called "A Summer Night 1933," stands both as an example of the new accessibility of Auden's poems and as the record of the mystical experience referred to earlier. It was only much later, in 1964, in his introduction to *The Protestant Mystics*, edited by his friend Anne Fremantle, that it became clear that the poem was based on a vision that Auden himself had had. Like Blake's visionary poems, the simplicity is perhaps the most striking aspect of Auden's poem, the first stanza of which reads:

> Out on the lawn I lie in bed,
> Vega conspicuous overhead
> In the windless nights of June;
> Forests of green have done complete
> The day's activity; my feet
> Point to the rising moon.

The combination of lightness of tone, directness and simplicity of manner, clarity of meaning, and exactness of expression is a harbinger of what became a central pole in Auden's career; poems similar to this one appeared throughout his life and are among his most durable kinds of art.

With modern poetry dominated by Yeats and Eliot, to champion light verse was indeed a revolutionary—or counterrevolutionary—act; and many of the poems in *Look, Stranger!* may seem light not only in the descriptive but in the negative sense as well. Yet many have great power, stemming from Auden's formal mastery and control of tone, as well as from his extraordinary phrasemaking and his sharp eye for the telling detail. A good example is the title poem of the British edition (also in a sense the title poem of the American edition):

> Look, stranger, on this island now
> The leaping light for your delight discovers
> Stand stable here
> And silent be,
> That through the channels of the ear
> May wander like a river
> The swaying sound of the sea.
> . . . .
> Far off like floating seeds the ships
> Diverge on urgent voluntary errands,
> And the full view
> Indeed may enter
> And move in memory as now these clouds do,
> That pass the harbour mirror
> And all the summer through the water saunter.

The poem illustrates Auden's ability not only to adapt form to purpose but also to create something richer than either form or purpose promises. Auden uses a rhymed version of the syllabic stanza of Marianne Moore, whose work he had recently read with great pleasure. This form isolates individual words, because, as with the Anglo-Saxon line, syllables do not merge into a flowing musical pattern. In this case, Auden uses the form to dramatize the traditional empiricist mode of perception, as described by Locke, according to which ideas are built up from individual sense impressions. Implicitly, then, Auden disputes the idealist premises of romanticist poetry, with its emphasis on "the shaping power of the imagination," on the way in which the activities of the mind create or alter reality.

This poem then, details a way of "seeing" that is richly poetic but is the product of a clear-eyed, unshaping response to reality, one that in turn produces clear ethical imperatives. In effect the poem consists of a series of instructions for establishing a properly fruitful relationship with reality and for avoiding overimaginative editing of reality.

All the poems in *Look, Stranger!* may be taken as a new kind of experiment for the young Auden (at its publication, he was twenty-nine and already regarded as an established poet), as parts of a quest for a postmodern form that would embody a sane, clear-eyed view of the world. A good example and record of this quest is a long poem written in 1936, "Letter to Lord Byron." The occasion for the poem was Auden's trip with Louis MacNeice to Iceland for the purpose of writing a travel book. The project attracted Auden partly because his family traced its origins to Iceland.

W. H. Auden, 1938 (BBC Hulton)

The aristocratic Byron may seem an unusual poet for a young radical of the 1930s to choose as imagined recipient of a letter, but the choice is one by which Auden clarified his evolving poetic personality. His turning away from some of the assumptions of modernism resembles Byron's move from the orthodox romanticism of *Childe Harold* and *Manfred* to the brilliant satire and wit of *Don Juan*. Why Auden chose *Don Juan* as a model—and how successfully he imitated it—will be clear from the following:

I like your muse because she's gay and witty,
Because she's neither prostitute nor frump,
The daughter of a European city,
And country houses long before the slump;
I like her voice that does not make me jump:
And you I find sympatisch, a good townee,
Neither a preacher, ninny, bore, nor Brownie.

Such lightness of touch contrasts with the leadenness of what Auden calls "The Poet's Party," the romantically individualistic group of artists that sprang up in response to the Industrial Revolution. Byron, then, is attractive as the continuer of the tradition of Dryden and Pope into the new circumstances that saw the beginning of the romantic traditions against which Auden is now reacting.

But if Auden found such a form as the Byronic epistle momentarily useful, he adopted neither it nor any other fixed form. These years established him only as a persistent and inventive eclectic. The three plays Auden wrote with Isherwood—*The Dog Beneath the Skin or, Where is Francis?*; *The Ascent of F 6*; and *On the Frontier*—cannot be called complete artistic successes. All three attempt to deal with pressing questions of the mid-1930s: *The Dog Beneath the Skin*, whose buoyant spirits echo those of *The Orators*, with the state of Europe; *The Ascent of F 6*, with the myth of the romantic hero who moves toward fascism, another echo of *The Orators*; and *On the Frontier*, with the now advanced growth of fascism. In general Auden wrote verse passages, Isherwood the prose, and both worked on the original conceptions and the revisions. In all three plays Auden was attempting to address a combination of political and psychological questions directly. Confusion within the three plays reflects not only imperfect collaboration but also continued groping, with changing focus, for a living form in which to express valid reactions to the deteriorating scene in Western Europe. It is increasingly clear that Auden was finding either the witty commentary of Byronic light verse or the deft simplicity of formal lyrics more authentic than the overtly political dramas. At the same time it would be inaccurate to write the plays off as failures; all of them are at least interesting to read, and *Dog Beneath the Skin* can still be staged; all three provide excellent insight into the 1930s.

Auden's most overtly political action was to go to Spain in 1937 during the civil war; and "Spain," the poem he wrote just after his return, became one of the best-known political poems ever written. The story of Auden's six weeks in Spain has never been made completely clear; the best account is in Humphrey Carpenter's *W. H. Auden: A Biography* (1981). Auden himself spoke little about his experiences, evidently torn between his continuing loyalty for the Loyalist, anti-Fascist cause, and his dismay, and even shock, at the confusion, the anticlericalism, and the brutality on the Loyalist side. His ostensive reason for going was to drive an ambulance, which, for reasons that are still not clear, he was never allowed to do. He felt he was prevented because he was not a Communist; others suggest it was sheer bureaucratic ineptitude; others still that the Loyalists wanted only to use him for propaganda purposes; and at least one commentator says that he was prevented because officials recognized how bad a driver he was. Perhaps the most useful comment on why Auden went appears in a letter to his friend the classicist E. R. Dodds: "I am not one of those who believe that poetry need or even should be directly political, but in a critical period such as ours, I do believe that the poet must have direct knowledge of the major political events."

The poem "Spain" was composed immediately after his return to England in March 1937. George Orwell, writing in 1940, saw the poem as "one of the few decent things that have been written about the Spanish Civil War," although he also saw Auden as a somewhat mindless dupe of Communist orthodoxy, one of those writers who could "swallow totalitarianism *because* they have no experience of anything except liberalism." He quotes these stanzas—

> To-morrow for the young the poets exploding like bombs,
> The walks by the lake, the weeks of perfect communion;
> To-morrow the bicycle races
> Through the suburbs on summer evenings: but today the struggle.
>
> To-day the inevitable increase in the chances of death:
> The conscious acceptance of guilt in the necessary murder;
> To-day the expending of powers
> On the flat ephemeral pamphlet and the boring meeting—

and comments: "The second stanza [quoted] is intended as a sort of thumbnail sketch of a day in the life of a 'good party man.' In the morning a couple of political murders, a ten-minutes' interlude to stifle 'bourgeois' remorse, and then a hurried luncheon and a busy afternoon and evening chalking walls and distributing leaflets. All very edifying. But notice the phrase 'necessary murder.' It could only be written by a person to whom murder is at most a *word*. . . . Mr. Auden's brand of amoralism is only possible if you are the kind of person who is always somewhere else when the trigger is pulled." Orwell's comments are both acute and subtly misleading, and to follow their implications is to sense the crucial changes occurring in Auden's life, poetry, and beliefs at this time. Auden himself later found not foolish but "wicked doctrine" the poem's last stanza:

> The stars are read. The animals will not look.
> We are left alone with our day, and the time is short, and
> History to the defeated
> May say Alas but cannot help nor pardon.

Auden crossed out these closing lines from Cyril Connolly's copy in the 1950s, writing "This is a lie." in the margin. He excluded the poem from the *Collected Shorter Poems* of 1950. Most readers today find the poem neither an unabashed piece of partisanship nor dishonest, but rather a powerful poem not about the war but about the dreadful moral choice war evokes. Much of what Orwell argues should be in Auden's poem, is in fact there; Auden was dealing with the moral as well as political complexity of the war. And yet he himself was later uncertain about its idioms.

The years between Auden's return from Spain (in March 1937) and the outbreak of war in Europe (in September 1939) are crowded with political

W. H. Auden and Christopher Isherwood after their return from China (BBC Hulton)

events, travel, changes in outlook and ideas, and magnificent poems. Out of this period came two major books, *Journey to a War* (1939, with Christopher Isherwood) and *Another Time* (1940). Random House, Auden's American publisher, persuaded Faber and Faber, his British one, to join in commissioning a travel book about the Far East, with the precise locale to be left to the authors; the outbreak of hostilities between China and Japan in the summer of 1937 determined China as their objective. They left England in January 1938, traveling eastward through Suez by boat, and returned through America about six months later. The resultant book consists of poems and photographs by Auden and a travel diary that Isherwood compiled, after they returned, from the diaries both men kept during their trip. Of primary interest is "In Time of War," a sequence of twenty-seven sonnets that Mendelson calls "Auden's most profound and audacious poem [*sic*] of the 1930's, perhaps the greatest English poem of the decade." In it and the accompanying "Verse Commentary" Auden attempts to construct an intellectual framework within which to comprehend the crumbling of Europe and the outbreak of world war. As Samuel Hynes describes the sonnet sequence, "the first thirteen sonnets compose a parable-history of mankind, from the creation and the exclusion from the Garden, through the phases of differentiation of social function, into actual history—the establishment and failure of the Church, the end of the Age of Faith, and the beginning of the Age of Economic Man." The second half deals with the present: first with the war in China, then with more general questions of war and morality. Auden was forging a mature style, a mature view of war, and a mature view of politics and history. The sonnet sequence is perhaps the first major fruit of this maturity. The dedicatory poem to E. M. Forster, whom Auden had known for six or seven years and had grown increasingly fond of, illustrates what had been happening to his verse:

> Here, though the bombs are real and dangerous,
> And Italy and King's are far away,
> And we're afraid that you will speak to us,
> You promise still the inner life shall pay.
>
> . . . .
>
> For we are Lucy, Turton, Philip, we
> Wish international evil, are excited
> To join the jolly ranks of the benighted
>
> Where Reason is denied and Love ignored:
> But, as we swear our lie, Miss Avery
> Comes out into the garden with the sword.

The poem succinctly summarizes the position—

liberal humanism—Auden had endorsed in the years immediately before the outbreak of general war. Critics on both sides expressed considerable unhappiness with his stance. During the 1930s Auden had been a hero to a great many literary and political partisans for whom Forster's liberal humanism was anathema; it is easy enough to fault such a poem for lacking either the passion of Yeats, the irony of Eliot, the experimental vigor of Pound, the metaphysical suggestiveness of Stevens, or the classicized colloquial vigor of Frost. Nor is the position behind the poem one that Auden long maintained. But in the context of Auden's growth during the 1930s, one who is fully aware of Auden's mastery and rejection of either the Yeatsian or the Eliotic mode reads this dedicatory poem not as a facilely shallow exercise but as a hard-won achievement.

Another Time (1940), published after Auden's move to the United States in January 1939, gathers together the poems written during Auden's last years in Europe, a period during which he was creating something quite new to modern poetry, a civil style. His reputation at the time was for a certain casualness in his writing; as he put it in "New Year Letter": "Time and again have slubbered through / With slip and slapdash what I do. . . ." Or, as Cyril Connolly said in *Enemies of Promise*, published in October 1938, "We have one poet of genius today, Auden, who is able to write prolifically, carelessly and exquisitely, and who does not seem to have to pay any price for his inspiration. It is as if he worked under the influence of some mysterious drug, which gives him a private vision, a mastery of form, and of vocabulary." It was at about this time that Auden began taking drugs both to wake himself up for work in the morning and to put himself to sleep at night; but in fact, in the midst of personal and social turmoil, Auden was taking a great deal of time to work on his poems carefully, spending four weeks in Brussels, for example, in December 1938 and January 1939, to get away from the English literary scene. "The English," he said some years later, "have a greater talent than any other people for creating an agreeable family life; that is why it is such a threat to their artistic and intellectual life. If the atmosphere were not so charming, it would be less of a temptation." Whether or not such an observation accounts at all for Auden's decision to leave England for the United States, it should be noted that Auden was throughout his life an extremely hard worker and that, although he at times had works published before they were fully ripened, he was in the late 1930s becoming more and more scrupulous about revising and about working steadily. The poems in *Another Time* were the product of the period during which these habits were becoming more pronounced.

Another Time is full of memorable poems: elegies on Freud and Yeats, "As I Walked Out One Evening," "Musée des Beaux Arts," "Lay Your Sleeping Head, My Love," "The Unknown Citizen," and "September 1, 1939." Many are about writers: Housman, Pascal, Melville, Arnold, Yeats, and Voltaire, and there are poems on "the novelist" and "the composer" as general types. It is clear that Auden was plotting his own position and course, that these poetic essays, beginning perhaps with "Letter to Lord Byron," and followed by essays on Pope and Byron, constitute a record of Auden's creation of his own poetic stance. To many eyes, of course, this new position was a betrayal of modernism: traditional forms and meters were increasingly used, the poems are discursive and reflective rather than imagistic and organic; they are reasonable and accessible. For readers who accept the central premises of romanticism and modernism, the poems may seem tepid. But for others, the poems mark one of the balance points of Auden's career, where lyrical gift, formal discipline, and ethical impulse come together, with considerable vitality, and in an idiom almost unique in modern poetry. Such ordering indeed becomes the central subject of the poems in *Another Time*, and Auden's view is anything but simple. "Matthew Arnold," for example, is the story of a poetic gift, as well as a psychological depth, that goes unrecognized, as Arnold tried too hard to please his Liberal father's "fond chastising sky." The gift

> would have gladly lived in him and learned his ways,
> And grown observant like a beggar, and become
> Familiar with each square and boulevard and slum,
> And found in the disorder a whole world to praise.

Finally, Arnold "thrust his gift in prison till it died, / And left him nothing but a jailer's voice and face," which became "the clear denunciation / Of that gregarious optimistic generation." The psychologizing, which may well seem facile now, is characteristic of almost all Auden's poems of this period, especially those dealing with other writers. Read in aggregate, these poems suggest a great deal of insight into both the writers and Auden himself. They give evidence of a rich struggle between gift and psyche, on the one hand, and formal and ethical commitment, on the other. Another poem of this period, "Nietzsche," published as one of the notes to "New Year Letter" (published in *The Double Man*, 1941), gives another side to the question: Nietzsche is the "masterly debunker of our liberal fallacies," who has turned out to be right about their insufficiency:

> In dim Victorian days you prophesied a
> reaction,
> And how right you've been. But tell us, O tell
> us, is
> This tenement gangster with a sub-machine
> gun in one hand
>
> Really the superman your jealous eyes
> imagined,
> That dark Daemonic One whose voice would
> cleave the rock open
> And offer our moribund era the water of life?

Another Time also includes the first poems Auden wrote in America. His emigration has long been an issue in England, because he—and Isherwood, who left with him—seemed to some to be fleeing the war. In fact, both Isherwood and Auden had made plans to emigrate as much as two years earlier (the exact time is uncertain), and had settled on America after their stop in New York on the way back to England from China in 1938. Auden elaborated his reason for staying in a letter to E. R. Dodds, written a year after his arrival, in which he called America "a terrifying place and I daresay I'm no tougher than the rest, but to attempt the more difficult seems to me the only thing worth while. At least I know what I am trying to do, which most American writers don't, which is to live deliberately without roots. I would put it like this. America may break one completely, but the best of which one is capable is more likely to be drawn out of one here than anywhere else." Auden had intentionally uprooted himself not only from English literary and political life, with which he had had, from the beginning, an uncertain relationship, but also from his family, to whom he had been close. Put positively, he was making himself into an émigré, undergoing self-imposed alienation, as if to adopt the role of a central modern literary figure, the exile, which had fascinated him for years. Perhaps he had instinctively come to recognize that, for him, there was a curious security in exiled status. Both in his poems and his life, throughout the 1930s exile had been a continual theme, the exile a continually present figure. With his move to America he was making it a permanent part of his life.

One of Auden's best-known and most controversial poems, "September 1, 1939," emerges from the early days of this new exile:

> I sit in one of the dives
> On Fifty-Second Street
> Uncertain and afraid
> As the clever hopes expire
> Of a low dishonest decade:
> Waves of anger and fear
> Circulate over the bright
> And darkened lands of the earth,
> Obsessing our private lives;
> The unmentionable odour of death
> Offends the September night.

The date, of course, is that of the German invasion of Poland, and hence of the outbreak of World War II. For many, the poem not only commented on an event but crystallized an emotional response, that of the committed yet skeptical literary intellectual. Controversy came because Auden later repudiated the poem's last stanza:

> Defenceless under the night
> Our world in stupor lies;
> Yet dotted everywhere,
> Ironic points of light
> Flash out wherever the Just
> Exchange their messages:
> May I, composed like them
> Of Eros and of dust,
> Beleaguered by the same
> Negation and despair
> Show an affirming flame.

Later, in the introduction to B. C. Bloomfield's 1964 bibliography of his early works, Auden made this comment: "Rereading a poem of mine, *1st September, 1939*, after it had been published, I came to the line 'We must love one another or die' and said to myself: 'That's a damned lie! We must die anyway.' So, in the next edition, I altered it to 'We must love one another and die.' That didn't seem to do either, so I cut the stanza. Still no good. The whole poem, I realized, was infected with an incurable dishonesty—and must be scrapped." As Charles Osborne points out, Auden has the sequence of events wrong; actually, he cut the last stanza out of the *Collected Poetry* of 1945, then restored it with the alteration "We must love one another and die," and finally removed the whole poem in *Collected Shorter Poems* (1966). The issue here becomes complicated because Auden's many revisions, deletions, rearrangements, retitlings, and the like, are often thought to be a result of his defection from the radical left-wing politics of the 1930s, his emigration, and his return to Christianity. Auden's own position was that he revised or discarded poems not in terms of later orthodoxies but in the interest of authenticity; he did not object to the theology of "September 1, 1939," but to its inauthenticity; it seemed to bear someone else's signature, and whether it was a good poem or a bad one, it seemed to him like a forgery. In an influential general study of political poetry Thomas Edwards suggests that "September 1, 1939" "is one of Auden's poorest" poems. Its problem, he argues, is that "The language of juvenile conspiracy and fantasy is in fact what is most alive in the poem, much more interesting and expressive than the rhetoric that points to international crisis and war. . . . He has no terms that can firmly link personal concerns and public issues." By this view, Auden's sense of artistic flaw in the poem seems to have been accurate, and the flaw appears to have arisen precisely because Auden was struggling to find an idiom that would express the complex view he was shaping, one that was at once personal, political, and religious.

Whatever its effect on specific poems, Auden was indeed undergoing a religious conversion that affected his life and his poems in major ways. Although he grew up in a devout home, he had lost interest in religion at fifteen, and his mystical experience of agape in 1933 had led him in no particular religious direction. In Spain, he was surprised to find himself shocked that the cathedrals were closed (in fact, most had been destroyed, and priests had been tortured and executed by the thousands). Surely Auden's growing disenchantment with secular religions, whether Lawrentian or Marxist, is another source of his return to Christianity. Another source is Auden's meeting (just after his return from Spain) Charles Williams, an editor at Oxford University Press. Williams, a novelist, poet, and sometime theologian, had a stunning effect on Auden: "for the first time in my life [I] felt myself in the presence of personal sanctity. I had met many good people before who made me feel ashamed of my own shortcomings, but in the presence of this man—we never discussed anything but literary business—I did not feel ashamed. I felt transformed into a person who was incapable of doing or thinking anything base or unloving. (I later discovered that he had had a similar effect on many other people.)" In talking about his conversion, Auden also referred to an experience which forced him "to know in person what it is like to feel oneself the prey of demonic powers, in both the Greek and the Christian sense, stripped of self-control and self-respect, behaving like a ham actor in a Strindberg play." According to Carpenter, what Auden is referring to here is his discovery that Chester Kallman, a young American with whom he had fallen in love just after coming to America, and had been close to for two years, "had taken another lover. Auden went completely to pieces." Evidently, Auden had even contemplated murder over the infidelity. Ultimately, he was reconciled to Kallman again; their lives were intertwined as long as Auden lived, and, as far as one can tell, Auden thought of their life together as a marriage, a lasting emotional commitment, that, although it gripped him completely, continued to cause him unhappiness, owing to Kallman's continuing infidelities.

Despite such personal crises that precipitated Auden's conversion, intellectual elements played a major role. Auden discovered Kierkegaard, probably through Charles Williams's writings, and became an avid reader of Kierkegaard's works. They presented him with a different kind of Christianity from any he had experienced, intellectually daring. Kierkegaard writes that belief comes as an answer to personal crisis rather than as an imposition from parents and the established authority of an institution. Kierkegaard describes a dialectical movement through aesthetic and moral stages to a religious one, and Auden could readily see in this sketch the stages of his own career to date, which moved from embracing aesthetic modernism in his first poems, in the early 1930s, to the "narrow strictness" and political involvement of the middle 1930s. Kierkegaard provided him with an accurate description of his own life; and the obvious next step, one that Auden could see had been brewing within himself for years, was to declare his belief.

Auden's first major American work was *The Double Man*, which contains "New Year Letter," a long epistle in iambic tetrameter couplets, as well as a number of notes in verse, prose notes, a sequence of twenty sonnets called "The Quest," and a prologue and epilogue. "New Year Letter" is a natural step from "Letter to Lord Byron" and the shorter pieces in *Another Time*. It includes references to a good deal of what Auden had been reading and thinking about in connection with his conversion, and also includes his reflections on the current state of civilization. The most obvious thing about the work is its Augustan form: it is striving to be discursive, pertinent, nonpersonal in the sense that Pope's and Dryden's poems are so; it is unashamedly intellectual: the volume even contains a bibliography. Oddly enough, considering all these trappings of the age of reason, the clearest prototype for the poem is "a book of aphorisms and reflections" called "The Prolific and the Devourer" (modeled on Blake's *The Marriage of Heaven and Hell*) that Auden wrote during 1939 and 1940, but which was published only recently in *The English Auden* (1977). Auden wants both Blake and Dryden in his "New Year Letter," both a sense of the insufficiency of reason, of its dangerousness as a sole determinant of the human condition, and at the same time a sense of the dangers of cults of irrationalism. The poem is an attempt to define the situation confronting the world on 1 January 1940: war had started, and with it came the last dawning of an awareness that something had gone wrong for civilization in a major way. The poem works from Auden's awareness of the decisiveness of the exact moment at which it was written; and as the poem widens its focus outward from the moment, through the whole preceding decade, and into the historical era that began with the Renaissance and the Reformation, one sees this moment as a turning point in the history of civilization.

The poem is at the same time a personal letter, addressed to Elizabeth Mayer, a German emigre who had befriended Auden and other exiled artists in New York. Even as the epistle inquires into the causes of the decay of civilization that led to the poem's present moment, it develops a counter theme that affirms art and individual human relations as antidotes to the general decay. The two parts of this counter theme are summarized in the person of Elizabeth Mayer and hence in the personal tone of what is essentially a nonpersonal poem.

"New Year Letter" has always seemed an oddity, a series of contradictions, even, to some, the symptom of Auden's decline as a poet. At the same time, it has some of the ingredients of major status: command of its own idiom, intellectual breadth, timeliness, and what Matthew Arnold called high seriousness. To those who see Auden as a poet without a large and substantial vision of the world, "New Year Letter" is a pertinent refutation: it is in fact one particularly clear manifestation of an inquiring spirit that lay behind Auden's verse from the beginning and was rarely so fully or clearly expressed. The poem was, in fact, the first of four large works that dominated his work during his early years in America.

During these first years, Auden divided his time between New York (for a while he acted as a kind of "house mother" of a boardinghouse for artists in Brooklyn and evidently did an excellent job) and various colleges and universities; from 1942 until 1945 he taught at Swarthmore College, near Philadelphia, and also at nearby Bryn Mawr. During this period he composed two major works, "For the Time Being," subtitled "A Christmas Oratorio," and "The Sea and the Mirror," subtitled "A Commentary on Shakespeare's *The Tempest*." These two works were published in a single volume entitled *For the Time Being* in 1944.

"For the Time Being" is among Auden's most overtly religious works, and perhaps the one that most clearly reflects his conversion. It was originally intended for a musical setting by Benjamin Britten, with whom Auden had collaborated on a number of works, including an opera, *Paul Bunyan*, that opened in 1941. The collaboration never occurred, both because Britten returned to England while Auden was still writing and because of a complicated series of personal and professional conflicts between Auden and Britten.

Auden intended the work partly as a memorial to his mother, who had died in August 1941; the work is dedicated to her, and its overt Christian subject, unusual in Auden and somewhat against his view that art should not be directly religious, is thought to be a specific tribute to Mrs. Auden's religious temperament and her influence on Auden. Woven into the work are concepts that echo Kierkegaard and the American theologian Reinhold Niebuhr, who had become Auden's friend. Equally important as an influence is a little-known work by a Canadian scholar, C. B. Cochrane, *Christianity and Classical Culture*. Cochrane treats changing views of history, the state, and the human self from Homer, Herodotus, Plato, and Thucydides, through the establishment and decay of the Roman imperium down to their complete revaluation by St. Augustine, and thus their transformation into the intellectual framework of the Church. The work may be read as an explanation of how classical culture, in all its brilliance, sophistication, and power, proved insufficient for a great worldly intelligence like Augustine's and as a description of the intellectual and spiritual edifice Augustine erected in its place.

It would not be accurate to suggest that Cochrane's or any other text was decisive in the growth of Auden's thought, but Cochrane's book provides evidence of the intellectual as well as the spiritual depth of Auden's emerging view of the world, and of the parallel Auden had in mind, in writing "For the Time Being," between the crisis that beset the ancient world in late antiquity and the crisis now threatening the modern world.

"For the Time Being" combines the naive representationalism of pageant or tableau with the agile intellect of an updated religious belief; it ends up being something like a blend of Kierkegaard with *The Second Shepherd's Play*. Shepherds, Wise Men, Mary, Joseph, Simeon, and Herod all speak in an idiom that is psychologically up-to-date, a little as if there had been periodic seminars in Freud and Jung during the actual nativity; and yet they do not give the feeling of a facile contemporaneity. To Auden the nativity exposed the fundamental problems of existence that we strive to understand in our modern way, problems to which the truths of Christianity are the best available answer. Thus Mary looks at the baby and says,

> Sleep. What have you learned from the womb that bore you
> But an anxiety your Father cannot feel?
> Sleep. What will the flesh that I gave do for you,
> Or my mother love, but tempt you from His will?
> Why was I chosen to teach His Son to weep?
> Little One, sleep.

The oratorio completely dissolves if we apply to it a principle of realism: no one, and certainly not Auden, imagines a Mary who fully understands the theology of the Incarnation, the dangers of possessive love, and our modern sense of anxiety. Once again, Auden is striving to create a kind of art that is inimical to the romanticist and modernist credos. Perhaps the most important point to be made is that the blend of naiveté and sophistication, of shepherd's play and existential theology, quite precisely summarizes modern man's intellectual skepticism and spiritual needs.

"The Sea and the Mirror," a secular companion to "For the Time Being," also makes no attempt at being a realistic representation, and even parades its parasitic nature by calling itself not a version of Shakespeare's work but a commentary on it. Many have found it to be Auden's most brilliant and, paradoxically, most creative work. Its self-advertised commentarial status should not be minimized: Auden wanted, in fact, to suggest that reading another work was a creative act. In "Criticism in a Mass Society," an essay published in 1941, Auden had suggested the potential of universal allegorizing: works of literature, like biblical texts, might properly be read in any of a number of contexts, and, indeed, inevitably will be; almost any work can become a text illustrating, for example, the importance of forgiveness and charity. In "The Sea and the Mirror," then, Auden is not so much claiming a "right interpretation" of *The Tempest* as presenting one available mode of interpretation, universal in its widespread applicability.

He presents his reading of the play in three sections. In the first section Prospero, speaking to Ariel, explains why he has decided to give up his use and pursuit of magic. In the second, the "Supporting Cast," each speaking in an appropriate verse form, gives a brief comment that explains his or her individual governing passions. In the third, Caliban, speaking in a style that echoes Henry James's late prefaces, presents the fullest exposition available of Auden's religious and aesthetic positions. (Auden, perhaps ironically for a great lyric poet, thought of this speech as his finest individual work.)

The terms of the title refer to life and art, and through the work Auden brilliantly displays and develops the skills of the artist, while at the same time indicating the limitations of art and an artistic mentality. But "life" and "art" suggest an oversimple polarity between two clear-cut categories, and neither is sufficient to convey Auden's sense of the true subject of poetry, "existence" itself. Thus, at the very beginning of the work, the Stage Manager addresses the Critics:

> Well, who in his own backyard
> Has not opened his heart to the smiling
> Secret he cannot quote?
> Which goes to show that the Bard
> Was sober when he wrote
> That this world of fact we love
> Is unsubstantial stuff:
> All the rest is silence
> On the other side of the wall;
> And the silence ripens,
> And the ripeness all.

Ripeness corresponds here to existence, not just our existence but the existence of anything. Great art, at best, gives a feeling of contact with existence; at its worst—that is, when misused or misread—it leads us astray from the fundamental sense of existence. There is, then, a quality to existence that defies even the most brilliant verbal formulation of it; indeed, the more brilliant the formulation, paradoxically, the more misleading it may be, precisely because it can pass for life. This inability to describe reality fully is a condition not simply of literary art but of all attempts to construe existence, and Auden established not simply an aesthetic but also a theological starting point for his inquiry.

Auden's answer to the quandary is that truly great art—for example, Shakespeare's art—possesses within itself a powerful principle of disenchantment, a point Auden makes partly through his own interpretation of *The Tempest*. In that reading, Caliban represents the principle of existence, the presence of life that existential philosophers see formal philosophy, philosophy concerned with essences, as ignoring or even betraying. Shakespeare's greatness, then, lies partly in his ability to use the artistry of enchantment to promote a recognition of life in all its intransigent presence. He does so not simply by creating such a character as Caliban but also by making his dramatic constructions extend our perception of the "staginess" of both life and art. As Caliban says in the third section:

> Beating about for some large loose image to define the original drama which aroused his imitative passion, the first performance in which the players were their own audience, the worldly stage on which their behaving flesh was really sore and sorry. . . , the fancy immediately flushed is of the greatest and grandest opera rendered by a very provincial touring company indeed.
>
> Yet, at this very moment when we do at last see ourselves as we are, neither cosy nor playful, but swaying out on the ultimate wind-whipped cornice that overhangs the unabiding void—we have never stood anywhere else,—when our reasons are silenced by the heavy huge derision,—There is nothing to say. There never has been,—and our wills chuck in their hands—There is no way out. There never was,—it is at this moment that for the first time in our lives we hear, not the sounds which, as born actors, we have hitherto condescended to use as an excellent vehicle for displaying our personalities and looks, but the real word which is our only *raison d'être*. Not that we have improved; everything, the massacres, the whippings, the lies, the twaddle, and all their carbon copies are still present, more obviously than ever; nothing has been reconstructed; our shame, our fear, our incorrigible staginess, all wish and no resolve, are still, and more intensely than ever, all we have: only now it is not in spite of them but with them that we are blessed by that Wholly Other Life from which we are separated by an essential emphatic gulf of which our contrived fissures of mirror and proscenium arch—we understand them at last—are feebly figurative signs, so that all our meanings are reversed and it is precisely in its negative image of Judgment that we can positively envisage Mercy; it is just here, among the ruins and the bones, that we may rejoice in the perfected Work which is not ours.

The point of the magnificent long speech from which these lines are taken comes to us through both their content and the wonderfully incongruous picture of Caliban addressing the audience in the manner of Henry James and expounding doctrines that echo Kierkegaard and Reinhold Niebuhr. Caliban is, in fact, an image of ourselves: the "behaving flesh," a histrionic animal. Caliban refutes, both in his meaning and in his very presence, the "spiritualizing fallacy" against which Auden is arguing, what Auden goes so far as to call a species of Manichaean heresy existing in Shakespeare's original, the belief that sin comes from the flesh—that is, from Caliban—and goodness from spirit, from Ariel. Caliban presents and represents the opposite view: that we are fleshly creatures most likely to be misled by the magic of our own imagination. "The Sea and the Mirror" is both a celebration of art and a warning against its dangers.

Auden's next major work was a collection of poems, which he finished in late 1943. It was not, however, published until 1945, partly because of wartime paper shortages, and partly because of slowness on the part of Random House. In fact, by the time they were ready to publish it, he had finished "The Sea and the Mirror" and was able to include it and "For the Time Being" in the collection. According to Humphrey Carpenter, Auden did not like the title chosen by Random House, *The Collected Poetry*, because it implied finality in what he regarded, correctly of course, as a still developing career; although he wished the work to be definitive, he wanted the title to be simply "Poems 1928-1945." The volume was reprinted at least twenty times and sold over 50,000 copies. Subsequent collections have almost completely superseded this volume, and many readers will now find it confusing, incomplete, even capricious. Yet it remains an important source of information about Auden, as well as an important volume in the history of modern poetry. Perhaps Auden's most striking kind of revision was to arrange the poems in alphabetical order according to opening lines, with "Songs and Other Musical Pieces" in a separate section; plays and such early works as *The Orators* are dismantled: "Letter to a Wound" from *The Orators* and a speech from *Dog Beneath the Skin* (retitled "Depravity: A Sermon") receive separate sections, as do five longer works: "The Quest," "In Time of War," "New Year Letter," "For the Time Being," and "The Sea and the Mirror." Untitled poems from the 1930s are given titles, some of them flippant ones that appear to contradict or diminish the original intentions. Auden revised some of the poems and omitted others.

All of these changes brought considerable criticism, most of it to the effect that Auden had edited out of his works his early political, psychological, and aesthetic passions, that he was trying to Christianize his early works, that he was ashamed of his Marxist past. In *The Making of the Auden Canon* (1957), Joseph Warren Beach presented a detailed case against the revisions, one that ultimately was unpersuasive. Beach was not completely accurate in his scholarship, and he clearly believed that Auden was wrong to be a Christian. More persuasive, or in any case more damaging, were two articles by the young Randall Jarrell, reprinted in his *Criticism: The Third Book* (1969). They focus on the relation of changes in Auden's beliefs to changes in his style, particularly from the "tough" language, so concrete and uncompromising, of the early poems to the far more abstract language of the poems in *Another Time*, "New Year Letter," and other works of the 1940s. Throughout the rest of Auden's career, one set of readers held that he had fallen off radically in his poetic powers or his poetic principles as a result of his immigration and his conversion; to those holding this view, the revisions of *The Collected Poetry* are an attempt to substitute the later style for the early style, and the totally unchronological arrangement of poems is an attempt to cover his tracks. Auden was a relentless reviser throughout his career and often quoted with approval Paul Valéry's remark that "A poem is never finished, only abandoned." Auden told his friend Stephen Spender that he had scrambled the works' chronology to defeat readers who came to poems with a fixed paradigm of development in their minds; he wanted to make sure that they read the poems on their own terms. It should perhaps be added that he was doing precisely what critical orthodoxy of the time suggested one should do, allowing his poems to be read without a convenient biographical, historical, ideological, or developmental context to shape the reader's responses.

Whatever their feelings about the issues raised by the revisions and deletions, almost everyone recognized the great talent represented in the volume. It showed Auden's work in a bulk and variety that suggested major talent and called for comparison with the collected works of earlier modernist poets like Yeats, Eliot, Stevens, and Frost. Of the 168 poems and songs in *Collected Poetry*, only 21 were written since the publication of *Another Time* in 1940, a statistic that indicates how much time Auden was devoting to the several longer works. Among the most notable of the new poems is one that first appeared in *Horizon* in 1941, "At the Grave of Henry James." It was published in the *Collected Poetry*, was not included in some of the volumes of selected poems that appeared later in the 1950s and 1960s, then reappeared in a substantially revised form, less than half as long as the original, in *Collected Shorter Poems 1927-1957* (1966). The poem is a long meditation on the artist's calling, using what Monroe Spears has called a "sympathetic parody" of James's style. We may take it as a part of that series of place-finding poems that includes "Letter to Lord Byron" and the poems about artists in *Another Time* and extends through the reconsideration of James and Shakespeare in "The Sea and the Mirror." In all these poems Auden is, as modern critical jargon would have it, finding his literary fathers, and defining his vocation and his artistic manner in terms of them. Paradoxically, Auden the convert, the brilliantly skilled poet, the English immigrant to America defines his vocation in terms of James the religious skeptic, the prose writer, the American immigrant to England. In "At the Grave of Henry James" Auden purposely submerged his own poetic style and manner in the imitation of James's prose, as an act not only of homage but of discipleship, as if to expand the implications of the Jamesian sobriquet "Master." Such submission has a religious dimension; and in its last stanza the poem echoes the Anglican *Book of Common Prayer*, taking, indeed, the form of a prayer:

> All will be judged. Master of nuance and scruple,
> Pray for me and for all writers, living or dead:
> Because there are many whose works
> Are in better taste than their lives, because there is no end
> To the vanity of our calling, make intercession
> For the treason of all clerks.

"The treason of all clerks" echoes the title of Julien Benda's *La Trahison des Clercs* (1927), which charged European intellectuals—clerks in the medieval sense, the term suggesting the original religious, that is "clerical" calling of intellectuals—with selling out to political powers. Here Auden, much criticized for his artistic and spiritual independence,

W. H. Auden and Chester Kallman in Venice, 1949 (photo by Stephen Spender)

honors James as someone true to his own craft and intelligence and thus a fit model for young artists. The poem also suggests, in its style, a continuing attempt to find blends of poetry and prose that would bring into verse ethical content without sacrifice of artistic integrity.

At the very end of World War II Auden was given a job with the U.S. Strategic Bombing Survey as a civilian researcher with the honorary rank of major. In this capacity he returned to Europe for the first time since 1939. Thus also ended his longest stint of teaching in the United States, three years at Swarthmore. For almost the rest of his life he was centered in New York City, distinctly a part of that city's intellectual and artistic life and widely recognized not only as a major poet but also as a man of letters. He lectured frequently, spent short stints teaching at various colleges, edited books, reviewed widely, and became increasingly involved in musical affairs. He and Chester Kallman collaborated on the libretto and lyrics for Igor Stravinsky's opera *The Rake's Progress*, which opened in 1951. He was judge and editor of the Yale Younger Poets Series from 1947 until 1959, each year choosing a manuscript of a poet whose work had previously been unpublished in book form. Through his editing, his literary journalism, his teaching, lecturing, and readings, his influence on younger poets spread; much of it was in the interest of formalism, even traditionalism, and a whole generation of American poets shows the mark of his influence (although his choices for the Yale series indicate a great range of taste). With Jacques Barzun and Lionel Trilling, both professors at Columbia University, he selected new books for an intellectual book club, the Mid-Century, writing short notices and occasional longer essays for a monthly newsletter the club put out.

His first major work after the war and after publication of *Collected Poetry* was *The Age of Anxiety*, published in 1947 and winner of the Pulitzer Prize for 1948. Leonard Bernstein designed his Second Symphony from it (Auden, however, disliked the symphony and the Jerome Robbins ballet based on it). Despite its fame and its aphoristic title that quickly became part of the language, the book was not a great success with critics and has continued to have an ambiguous reputation. Subtitled *A Baroque Eclogue, The Age of Anxiety* takes place in a Third Avenue bar; the external action is described in prose, but the real subject is the inner consciousnesses of four characters with the suggestive names

Quant, Emble, Rosetta, and Malin. The characters talk at first to themselves, then to each other, finally joining in an exploration of their communal psychic landscape. To portray these actions Auden uses the alliterative accentual line of Anglo-Saxon verse, a form he had not used since early in his career; other forms appear in the last part of the poem.

The return to the early verse form is appropriate because this book is Auden's most intense exploration of the inner life since his earliest poems; and it is perhaps his last attempt to represent psychological states comprehensively. Is the work a contradiction of the long movement away from the Lawrentian subjectivism of his earliest work, which so much of the 1930s and even early 1940s verse seems to be trying to exorcise? One answer to this question is to note that in *The Age of Anxiety* Auden is understanding subjectivism within a religious framework. Auden follows Kierkegaard and other existentialist theologians in seeing a necessity to assert the peculiarly subjective truths of the human situation. It is not the passionate or heroic aspect of the inner life that primarily interests Auden, however, but rather the unpredictable, the ordinary, the aspects of the inner self that define individuality without claiming transcendence. Like Joyce in *Ulysses* and Eliot in "The Love Song of J. Alfred Prufrock"—to take two defining works of the modernist sensibility—Auden thoroughly explores small details of his characters' inner lives. But unlike Joyce and Eliot (in "The Love Song of J. Alfred Prufrock," at least), Auden understands these insignificant trivia theologically as the stage on which the actions of grace can be seen. Each of us, Kierkegaard said—in a phrase that Auden liked to use—may be "a knight of the infinite"; and *The Age of Anxiety* is an attempt to fashion a heroic poem out of the ordinary and unspectacular spiritual existences of four obviously fallen humans. Thus understood, the work is considerably more audacious than most of its critics have recognized. John Bayley, in *The Romantic Survival*, had written with particular insight into the poem, saying that Auden "is a Symbolist of the common fate, the humdrum situation." Bayley adds that Auden's "first fascination was to make a myth out of the everyday, to join by the links of private connection the symbols that excited and intrigued him. In *The Age of Anxiety* this process is still going on: indeed it reaches its climax and its masterpiece. . . . Empirically, at least, what emerges from the poem is that the remedy against Anxiety is the slightly absurd richness of the human consciousness, its capacity for protecting itself with a colorful cocoon of myth and invention." Or, as John Fuller puts it, "*The Age of Anxiety* is rich not only in noble despair, but in a kind of inner glee and inventive response to the conditions of life which is the mark of great literature."

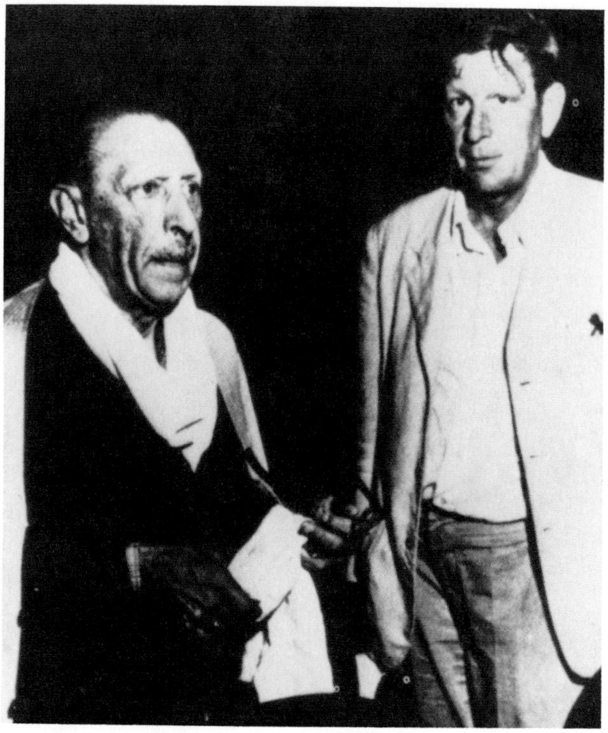

Igor Stravinsky and W. H. Auden during rehearsals for The Rake's Progress *(photo by Robert Craft)*

Despite such appreciations, *The Age of Anxiety* remains a problematic work, as challenging to readers, perhaps, though for different reasons, as *The Orators*. An interesting work to read alongside it is *The Enchafèd Flood or, The Romantic Iconography of the Sea* (1950), a series of lectures delivered at the University of Virginia in 1949. The lectures are a dense treatment of romantic imagery; E. M. Forster's review remarked that the book is "in itself a poem." At the end, Auden expresses preference for the Builder over the Romantic Wanderer, although he regards both as necessary to the goal of building the Just City. From the point of view of Auden's evolving ideas, this work gives evidence that Auden continued to think about a problem that had been with him for years: how is the rich heritage of verse centering on the individual consciousness to be put to use in service of communal goals?

Auden's next book of poems was *Nones*, published in 1951. The volume appears to be a grab bag; the title poem, "Nones," and the first poem, "Prime," are both parts of a series that did not appear as such until the next volume. There is no overall order to the other poems; and many of the poems have the same deceptive casualness that the whole volume has. In fact *Nones*, along with its successor volume, *The Shield of Achilles* (1955), represents Auden's mature style at its best. The variety and haphazardness of the volume are illusory; almost all the poems express the vocation that Auden had hewn out of his gifts, his experiences, his reading, his conversion, and mostly out of his own continual allegiance to making poems. What emerges in these volumes is perhaps best described as Horatian; and the Horatian ode, an apparently relaxed but in fact carefully constructed meditation on almost any subject, becomes a favorite mode. The volume contains the poem that, according to Charles Osborne, was in later years Auden's favorite of all his poems, "In Praise of Limestone":

> If it form the one landscape that we, the inconstant ones,
> Are consistently homesick for, this is chiefly
> Because it dissolves in water. Mark these rounded slopes
> With their surface fragrance of thyme and, beneath
> A secret system of caves and conduits; hear the springs
> That spurt out everywhere with a chuckle,
> Each filling a private pool for its fish and carving
> Its own little ravine whose cliffs entertain
> The butterfly and the lizard. . . .

Such poems are almost completely engaging: the reader is drawn into them, rather than being forced back by them to admire their mastery or the brilliance of their talent. They seem almost effortless, but are in fact the fruit of a technical concentration that was a constant throughout Auden's early career. It is ironic that *Nones* was not received particularly well.

Auden's next volume, *The Shield of Achilles*, not only added a new stock of fine poems but also drew two of the poems from *Nones* into a brilliant series, "Horae Canonicae," and presented another complete series, "Bucolics." Any suggestion of frivolity or randomness was dispelled, although *The Shield of Achilles* was also greeted without particular warmth and with some severe criticism. The poems in "Horae Canonicae," which contains "Prime" and "Nones" as its first and fourth poems, correspond to daily services in the medieval church, still observed in some religious communities; they also correspond roughly to events on Good Friday. The poems vary in form, but the dominant mode is the long-lined meditation that makes so effective an appearance in both *Nones* and *The Shield of Achilles*. Like so much of Auden's work, their most insistent subject is the relation between our internal existence and the world in which we find ourselves: the poems are in fact powerful meditations on human existence, with the philosopher Martin Heidegger dimly in the background. The poems once again discover Christian terminology, applied with a very light touch, to be a useful way of discussing existence. The fall, the Crucifixion, and the redemption are all aspects of experience, rather than of doctrine.

"Prime," corresponding to the first liturgical office of the day, is a meditation on the moments of awakening; it finds within those moments a first definition of our place in the world. It begins

> Simultaneously, as soundlessly,
> As, at the vaunt of the dawn, the kind
> Gates of the body fly open
> To its world beyond. . . .

Throughout the sequence, we see both an ordinary day and Good Friday superimposed on each other; the implication is clearly typological: we recreate the biblical events in our daily actions, just as theologians have for centuries believed that biblical events were types of later history. Seldom, however, do the poems become directly religious; as John Fuller points out, Auden lets the framework of the canonical hours carry most of the burden of religious reference.

The other major sequence in *The Shield of Achilles*, "Bucolics," is also a series of seven poems, these based on different kinds of nature: "Woods," "Winds," "Mountains," "Lakes," "Islands," "Plains," and "Streams." They represent Auden's appreciation of the pastoral mode, and not in merely an idle sense. Pastoral, being a highly artificial, civilized, court mode that portrays "natural" life, in its unrefined aspects, immediately raises questions Auden had been exploring for years, including that raised in "The Sea and the Mirror": how can art, whose essence is refinement and order, portray life, whose essence is disorder, without distortion? The first lines of the second poem, "Sylvan meant savage in those primal woods / Piero di Cosimo so loved to draw," echo sentences in an essay by art historian Ernst Panofsky on painter di Cosimo. In the essay and elsewhere, Panofsky draws a distinction between hard and soft primitivism that may well lie behind Auden's conception of this sequence. Pastoral in the popular sense of "sylvan," suggesting sweet scenes of soulful shepherds, belongs to soft primitivism. In contrast an older sense, represented by "savage" and by the paintings of di Cosimo, recognizes the toughness of nature and of the evolutionary struggle. Moreover, Panofsky shows how a number of now scattered paintings by di Cosimo must have been meant to fit together in a room as a depiction of "the early history of man." It is easy to imagine Auden thinking of his poems in some analogous arrangement, a series of panels that depict the evolution of man. Auden's series, in effect, holds the soft and the hard versions of pastoral together and ultimately presents in the soft pastoral mode—as it emerges in the last poem, "Streams"—a figurative picture of redemptive grace. Such a description may well make the sequence sound more argumentative than it is; such an impression would be misleading. Auden has created in this sequence a fine blend of artistic gracefulness and serious content, ample scope for his technical expertise as well as his intellectual concerns.

Of the other poems in *The Shield of Achilles* the most impressive is probably the title poem. According to Carpenter, it (like another impressive poem in the volume, "Memorial for the City") arose partly out of Auden's experiences viewing the desolation and destruction of Europe at the end of World War II. The poem imagines Thetis looking for classically reassuring images on the shield Hephaistos made for Achilles (as described in book eighteen of the *Iliad*). Instead, Hephaistos has placed on the shield images of the postwar world—barbed wire, a great mass of aimless people standing on a plain, a kind of mock crucifixion—and suggestions of a bureaucratic nightmare world, a combination of a Kafka novel, the streets of New York, Dachau, and the Kremlin. Hephaistos held considerable fascination for Auden as a type of the truth-telling artist, and the poem, like others of this time, is itself meant as a kind of shield of Achilles, another variation on the theme of the mirror of art. There is great grandeur in the poem; it is austere and even magnificent, despite the depressing picture it presents. One is aware, even if reading the poem without much sense of Auden's religious position, of the implied need for some principle of love to redeem the picture of the modern world presented on the shield.

Auden's next major volume of poems, *Homage to Clio*, was published in 1960. As much as *The Shield of Achilles*, the volume is built around a theme, which, as the title makes clear, is history. *History* is a rich word to Auden; it brings together at least two different ideas. First, history is a definition of human existence in time. For Auden our experience is imperfect, in that sense "fallen," but our experience is also redeemable; we are responsible for our conduct and even for the shape of the future. Second, history is, in the popular sense of the term, the record of all events. As with *Nones* and *The Shield of Achilles*, it is convenient to link this volume with another one whose roots are in a poem first published separately from the sequence of which it eventually became a part. One of the poems in *Homage to Clio*, "On Installing an American Kitchen in Austria," became the center of another sequence of poems called "Thanksgiving for a Habitat," published as a group in *About the House* (1965).

To understand the "habitat" described, one needs to go back momentarily to the late 1940s, when Auden began spending part of his year on the Mediterranean island of Ischia, near Naples; signs of his years there appear in *Nones* and *The Shield of Achilles*, where poems specifically treat the island or its surrounding neighborhood. In 1957, Auden received news at Oxford (he was serving a five-year term as Oxford Professor of Poetry, 1956-1961) that he had won an Italian prize for poetry amounting to the equivalent of thirty-three thousand dollars; and he decided to apply it toward the purchase of a house near Vienna, Austria, in a town called Kirchstetten. There were a variety of reasons for the move, among them his wanting to be near the Viennese opera and to be in a more Northern and German-speaking culture.

Working from the poem about the kitchen from *Homage to Clio*, Auden wrote poems about every room in the house. At first reading, the sequence seemed to many a fussy collection of poems about the lives of two middle-aged homosexuals who cared about music, wine, and regular hours. Nor do the poems need to be anything in addition to that in order to be successful. In fact, however, the sequence is as carefully planned as "Horae Canonicae" or "Bucolics" and as carefully thought out. Their domestic fussiness is in fact a synecdoche for an aspect of the modern human condition, the shrinking of our sense of action from the public to the private sphere. Auden expresses rueful acceptance, domestic pleasure, and moral pain over this shrinkage, so well represented not only by the domestic scene pictured in the house but also by the running comparison between poetry and architecture. The poem stems in part from Auden's reading of philosopher Hannah Arendt's *The Human Condition*, which attempts to trace the modern triumph of the active over the contemplative life, but also the

W. H. Auden, John F. Kennedy, John O'Hara, and Herbert Kubly at the 1956 National Book Awards ceremony (Associated Press)

modern loss of a sense of publicly significant action. In the modern world, she says, there is no real equivalent to the Greek polis, where the citizen enjoyed his fullest sense of humanness in his words and actions toward other citizens. Auden offers the life of the artist—himself—as an instance of the modern sense of action: the artist, acting with words, has some of the public integrity of statesman and citizen in Greece; and yet the artist's life is ultimately a sadly private one.

In such a manner does the sequence acquire a much larger scope of reference than the poems seem at first glance to have. In fact, the entire range of human functions and activities is represented. Particularly moving are "The Cave of Making," a poem about writing that is also an elegy for Auden's friend Louis MacNeice, and "Tonight at Seven-Thirty," a poem about eating that contrasts the elaborate ritual of a well-cooked meal eaten by friends with various kinds of animal consumption of food.

Perhaps Auden's other most significant books of the 1960s were his essays and collected poems. In 1962 he produced a collection of critical essays, *The Dyer's Hand*. The title is from Shakespeare's sonnet 111: "My nature is subdu'd / To what it works in, like the dyer's hand," suggesting more than anything else a craftsman's devotion to art. The real subject of the volume, Auden told Stephen Spender, was Christianity and Art; and in fact, the essays, which date from 1948 but were mostly delivered later at Oxford, are far more thematic than formal, and especially display Auden's continuing adeptness at reading literature allegorically. Although he tended to play down his abilities as a critic, the volume in fact had the effect of making it clear that he was a worthy successor to Eliot in the great line of poet-critics that stretches from Sydney and Ben Jonson, through Dryden, Pope, and Samuel Johnson, Coleridge, Keats, and Arnold.

Several selections of Auden's poems had appeared since *The Collected Poetry* of 1945, but no collected edition. In 1966, *Collected Shorter Poems 1927-1957* appeared. As noted in connection with "At the Grave of Henry James," Auden made some revisions; some poems were left out (for example, "Spain" and "September 1, 1939"). He arranged the poems in a general though not an exact chronological order and added a brief preface commenting on the revisions, omissions, and order. Two years later, a companion volume, *Collected Longer Poems*, appeared containing *Paid on Both Sides* and "Letter to

Auden in Peck Quad, Christ Church College, Oxford, 1972 (Camera Press, photo by Billett Porter)

Lord Byron" (neither of which were at that time widely known, especially in America) as well as the four long poems from the 1940s. *The Orators* was republished separately in 1967.

Auden died on 29 September 1973, in a hotel in Vienna; he was sixty-six. In his last years he produced two volumes of poems, *City Without Walls* (1969) and *Epistle to a Godson* (1972); a third volume on which he was working when he died, *Thank You, Fog* (1974), appeared posthumously. Several important collections and prose works also appeared either during these last years or immediately after his death. *Secondary Worlds* (1969, the T. S. Eliot memorial lectures) is an uneven but revealing series, especially interesting for its last chapter, "Words and the Word," a further treatment of Christian art. *A Certain World* (1970) is a commonplace book, a collection of passages copied from a vast variety of sources, with, in many cases, accompanying comments; one can learn as much about Auden, particularly in his later years, from this as from almost any other source. *Forewords and Afterwords* (1973) collects Auden's best review articles, introductions to works, and the like, dating back to 1943; it too reveals a great deal about Auden's mind and makes clear his preeminence as an occasional critic. Finally there were three late collections of poems, all of them edited by Auden's literary executor, Edward Mendelson: *Collected Poems* (1976), which presents the poems as Auden wanted them finally to be read and is the most comprehensive volume available; *The English Auden* (1978), Auden's early poems; and *Selected Poems* (1979), which adds poems to a 1968 selection (including some, like "September 1, 1939," that Auden had omitted from various collections) and restores others to the forms in which they first appeared.

Clive James's comments on Auden's last three volumes of new poems are worth recording:

> It is a common opinion among the English literati that Auden's later work is a collapse. I am so far from taking this view that I think an appreciation of Auden's later work is the only sure test for an appreciation of Auden. . . . You must know and admire the austerity which Auden achieved before you can take the full force of his early longing for that austerity—before you can measure the portent of his early brilliance. . . . Famed stranger and exalted outcast, Auden served a society larger than the one in which he hid. In his later work we see not so much the ebbing of desire as its transference to the created world, until plains and hills begin explaining the men who live on them. Auden's unrecriminating generosity towards a world which had served him ill was a moral triumph. Those who try to understand it too quickly ought not to be trusted with grown-up books.

The Horatian ode, still in these last volumes among Auden's favorite forms, provides a convenient test case for James's contentions about the last poems. The ode lacks ostentation; its power lies in our reaction to the fineness of word choice, phrasing, tone, and intelligence to its austerity. In "The Horatians," written in 1968 and collected in *City Without Walls*, Auden works within the form to describe those who might be considered contemporary followers of Horace (he clearly means those whose way of life is Horatian, not those who simply write in the manner of Horace):

> Among those I really know, the
> British branch of the family, how many have
> found in the Anglican Church
> your Maecenas who enabled
>
> a life without cumber, as pastors adjective
> to rustic flocks, as organists in trollopish
> cathedral towns.

How one reacts to words like *cumber*, *adjective*, and *trollopish* will probably determine one's general reaction to the poem. One might find it fussy, slightly pedantic, a little silly; certainly, in its quaintness it draws a clear picture of what kinds of lives those Horatians, in their trollopish towns, live. *Adjective* in the general sense means not simply "attached," but "dependent," or "subordinate." A pastor depends on his flock to an extent, especially if the church is a Maecenas (the Roman patron of the arts, friend to Augustus, to whom Horace dedicated his first three books of odes and Vergil his *Georgics*). At the same time, awareness that the root sense of *adjective* is "dependent" may throw us back to its grammatical sense and sharpen our sense of what an adjective really is, finally making us aware of the grammatical bonds that hold language together; similarly the "rustic flocks" on whom he underscores the root sense of "pastor," and the connection between this pastoral Horatian and the poetic Horatians, masters of pastoral verse. Such are the kinds of pleasure that a Horatian reader might find in these poems: a certain exactness as well as a certain playfulness of language and a growing knowledge of how language works. Indeed, one of the major themes of Auden's later work was the poet's special responsibility as a guardian and craftsman of language. The ode's peroration, read in contrast to the passage just quoted, is an indication of how much tonal variation is possible:

> You thought well of your Odes, Flaccus, and believed they
> Would live, but knew, and have taught your descendants to
> say with you: "As makers go,
> compared with Pindar or any
>
> of the great foudroyant masters who don't ever
> amend, we are, for all our polish, of little
> stature, and, as human lives,
> compared with authentic martyrs
>
> like Regulus, of no account. We can only
> do what it seems to us we were made for, look at
> this world with a happy eye
> but from a sober perspective."

The understatement of the last lines is perhaps considerable: a sober perspective will seem to many a large accomplishment, just as the unamending foudroyant masters and the martyrdom of Regulus, who was martyr to his own harsh peace terms against the Carthaginians, may seem more than a little ambiguous.

A good final example of Auden's late manner, also in the Horatian manner, is "Ode to Terminus," written in 1968. Terminus is the Roman god of limits, boundaries, and landmarks, and he was Erasmus's personal god. Such severe self-limitation as Terminus suggests has a profound side: limita-

Allen Ginsberg and W. H. Auden, 1973 (BBC Hulton, photo by John Minihan)

tion is a fundamental aspect of humanism; to know one's place, one's limits, can be the basis of morality. The ode begins:

> The High Priests of telescopes and cyclotrons
> keep making pronouncements about
> happenings
> on scales too gigantic or dwarfish
> to be noticed by our native senses,
>
> discoveries which, couched in the elegant
> euphemisms of algebra, look innocent,
> harmless enough but, when translated
> into the vulgar anthropomorphic
> tongue, will give no cause for hilarity
> to gardeners or housewives: if galaxies
> bolt like panicking mobs, if mesons
> riot like fish in a feeding-frenzy,
>
> it sounds too like Political History
> to boost civil morale, too symbolic of
> the crimes and strikes and
> demonstrations
> we are supposed to gloat on at breakfast.
>
> How trite, though, our fears beside the
> miracle
> that we're here to shiver, that a Thingummy
> so addicted to lethal violence
> should have somehow secreted a placid
>
> tump with exactly the right ingredients
> to start and to cocker Life, that heavenly
> freak for whose manage we shall have to
> give account at the Judgement, our
> Middle-
> Earth, where Sun-Father to all appearances
> moves by day from orient to occident
> and his light is felt as a friendly
> presence not a photonic bombardment.

The opening lines refer to scientists and technologists; "high priests" suggests the veneration in which they are held (even with such digs at science, Auden knew a great deal about it and respected many of its discoveries). The central term in the poem, perhaps, is "Middle-Earth," an allusion that goes back to the surviving poem of, at least by legend, the first English poet. "Middle-Earth" is the "middangeard" of "Caedman's Hymn," the home created specifically for humans. Auden's concern is with human scale, which exists between the infinite and the microscopic worlds examined by scientists. To define and create such a human scale is one of the functions of poetry; it has political as well as aesthetic value, particularly in our present world of "colossal immodesty." In this ode, Terminus becomes "God of walls, doors and reticence," who gives us "games and grammar and metres." Terminus has something of a religious function as well:

> By whose grace, also, every gathering
> Of two or three in confident amity
> repeats the pentecostal marvel,
> as each in each finds his right translator.

The first echo is to a prayer of St. Chrysostom, from the *Book of Common Prayer*; and the pentecostal marvel is the miracle of total comprehension: everyone spoke in a different language, but there was complete understanding among the speakers. Such limitation as Auden is practicing, expressed in games, grammar, and meters, becomes the means of mutual understanding, which, indeed, is among his poems' highest goals.

To some critics, such a poem is clear evidence of Auden's long decline from the great achievements of his earliest poems; to others, like James, it represents the hard-won austerity that is in fact Auden's great moral and artistic achievement. Critics of Auden divide into those who adopt a decline paradigm, to use historians' jargon, and those who do not. To different critics the decline dates from various points; for example, F. R. Leavis, the champion of Lawrence and Eliot, saw Auden as a brilliant poet in his very first poems, but, as soon as Auden abandoned his Lawrentian manner and views, Leavis attacked him, partly because he mistakenly thought Auden was a Marxist. Randall Jarrell's influential articles put forward a somewhat similar case in a more thoroughgoing manner: Auden gave up direct apprehension of life for an abstract style, and did so as he moved "from Freud to Paul," from psychologism to Christianity. Joseph Warren Beach dates the onset of Auden's decline a little later; to him Auden's high-water mark is the liberal humanism of *Look, Stranger!* and *Another Time*, and the falling away sets in when Auden returns to Christianity. Many others see a decline beginning with *The Age of Anxiety* (1948) or with the meditative manner in *Nones* and *The Shield of Achilles* or with the last three volumes. In fact, "the decline of Auden" became a critical commonplace during the last thirty or even forty years of Auden's life, with different critics vying like so many historians of Rome to pinpoint precisely the date, the cause, and the worst consequences.

Perhaps the first important counter to the decline theory came in Monroe K. Spears's *The Poetry of W. H. Auden* (1963), which presents a view of Auden as a serious, intelligent, growing poet, and had special importance because of the thoroughness with which it handled Auden's texts, correcting a number of false impressions left by Beach and others. One immediate effect of Spears's work was to prompt studies of Auden's later work on its own terms, with the subsequent claim that later works hold their own solidity. Books like John G. Blair's *The Poetic Art of W. H. Auden* (1965), Herbert Greenberg's *Quest for the Necessary* (1968), and George Bahlke's *The Later Auden* (1970), and essays by Robert Bloom and Edward Callan, among others, led readers to consider the postemigration, postconversion work more seriously than they had. Other books that helped establish the largeness of Auden's achievement are B. C. Bloomfield's bibliographies (1964; and, with Edward Mendelson, 1971) and John Fuller's *Reader's Guide To W. H. Auden* (1970).

John Bayley, in *The Romantic Survival* (1957), came at Auden from a different angle: beneath the formalism and rationalism of Auden's later work, beneath the socialism and psychological analysis of the earlier work, Bayley found that Auden had an "exuberance of particularity" that links him with the romantics and with novelists like Dickens. This view shows particularly well in *The Age of Anxiety*: the work that a great many critics regard as one of Auden's worst, is, to Bayley, his very best. A somewhat parallel, but ultimately different view emerges in Peter Conrad's *Imagining America* (1980). To Conrad, Auden came to America for its existential freedom, and his conversion was to a brand of Christianity that celebrates temporariness, rootlessness, anonymity; in Christianity and America Auden found a framework in which to realize the freedom that he lusted for in his early Lawrentian days and that he thought was no longer possible in collapsing Europe: "American literature [is] a charter of aliens' rights, a defense of deviant freedoms," even "a charter for homosexual rights . . . Auden turns homosexual one-night stands into existential tests or theological reminders . . . of the fragility and imperfection of all human couplings." Conrad also sees *The Age of Anxiety* as an important work and offers interesting, if ultimately perverse,

John Betjeman at the unveiling of the Auden memorial stone in Poets' Corner, Westminster Abbey, October 1974 (photo by Mark Gerson)

readings of "New Year Letter" and *Paul Bunyan*.

To accept Auden as a major writer who continued to produce interesting poems throughout his career does not necessarily mean to denigrate his brilliant beginnings, and two recent works have been particularly useful in defining that achievement. Samuel Hynes, in *The Auden Generation* (1977), traces Auden's early development in the specific context of literary and political events of the 1930s. Edward Mendelson, in *Early Auden* (1981), provides both the richest detail and the fullest explanation of Auden's early development. Mendelson's paradigm is one of growth, and a companion volume that will trace the later years, based, like *Early Auden*, on Mendelson's unique knowledge of sources, should complete the fullest picture we have of Auden's career. In the meantime, probably the most challenging sketch of Auden's development is Clive James's. To James, Auden's special importance is that he applied to his extraordinary gifts a severe moral discipline. What various critics see as evidence of decline, James argues to be the product of the most exciting and enlightening poetic career in modern literary history, that of a brilliant lyric poet who sought and created channels to make his gift ethically pertinent to a confused modern era. For the time being, to use an Auden phrase, Mendelson's and James's are the most persuasive accounts of Auden that we have.

Other:

The Poet's Tongue, edited by Auden and John Garrett (London: Bell, 1935);

Oxford Book of Light Verse, edited by Auden (Oxford: Clarendon Press, 1938);

"Criticism in a Mass Society," in *The Intent of the Critic*, edited by Donald A. Stauffer (Princeton: Princeton University Press, 1941), pp. 125-147;

A Selection from the Poems of Alfred, Lord Tennyson, edited, with an introduction, by Auden (Garden City: Doubleday, Doran, 1944);

Henry James, *The American Scene, Together with Three Essays from "Portraits of Places,"* edited, with an introduction, by Auden (New York: Scribners, 1946);

Joan Murray, *Poems*, Yale Younger Poets Series, volume 45, edited, with a foreword, by Auden (New Haven: Yale University Press, 1947);

Charles Baudelaire, *Intimate Journals*, translated by Christopher Isherwood, introduction by Auden (Hollywood: Marcel Rodd, 1947);

"Squares and Oblongs," in *Poets at Work*, edited by Charles Abbott (New York: Harcourt, Brace, 1948), pp. 163-181;

Charles Abbott (New York: Harcourt, Brace, 1948), pp. 163-181;

Robert Horan, *A Beginning*, Yale Younger Poets Series, volume 46, edited, with a foreword, by Auden (New Haven: Yale University Press, 1948);

The Portable Greek Reader, edited, with an introduction, by Auden (New York: Viking, 1948);

Rosalie Moore, *The Grasshopper's Man*, Yale Younger Poets Series, volume 47, edited, with a foreword, by Auden (New Haven: Yale University Press, 1949);

Poets of the English Language, 5 volumes, edited by Auden and Norman Holmes Pearson (New York: Viking, 1950);

Selected Prose and Poetry of E. A. Poe, edited, with an introduction, by Auden (New York: Rinehart, 1950);

Adrienne Rich, *A Change of World*, Yale Younger Poets Series, volume 48, edited, with a foreword, by Auden (New Haven: Yale University Press, 1951);

W. S. Merwin, *A Mask for Janus*, Yale Younger Poets Series, volume 49, edited, with a foreword, by Auden (New Haven: Yale University Press, 1952);

"Presenting Kierkegaard," in *The Living Thoughts of Kierkegaard*, edited by Alfred O. Mendel (New York: McKay, 1952), pp. 3-22;

Frederick Jacobi, Jr., ed., *Tales of Grimm and Anderson*, introduction by Auden (New York: Modern Library, 1952);

Edgar Bogardus, *Various Jangling Keys*, Yale Younger Poets Series, volume 50, edited, with a foreword, by Auden (New Haven: Yale University Press, 1953);

Daniel G. Hoffman, *An Armada of Thirty Whales*, Yale Younger Poets Series, volume 51, edited, with a foreword, by Auden (New Haven: Yale University Press, 1954);

An Elizabethan Song Book, edited by Auden, Noah Greenberg, and Chester Kallman (Garden City: Doubleday, 1955);

John Ashbery, *Some Trees*, Yale Younger Poets Series, volume 52, edited, with a foreword, by Auden (New Haven: Yale University Press, 1956);

Essay in *Modern Canterbury Pilgrims and Why They Chose the Episcopal Church*, edited by James A. Pike (New York: Morehouse-Goreham, 1956);

Charles Williams, *The Descent of the Dove: A History of the Holy Spirit in the Church*, introduction by Auden (New York: Meridian, 1956);

The Faber Book of Modern American Verse, edited by Auden (London: Faber & Faber, 1956);

James Wright, *The Green Wall*, Yale Younger Poets Series, volume 53, edited, with a foreword, by Auden (New Haven: Yale University Press, 1957);

John Hollander, *A Crackling of Thorns*, Yale Younger Poets Series, volume 54, edited, with a foreword, by Auden (New Haven: Yale University Press, 1958);

William Dickey, *Of the Festivity*, Yale Younger Poets Series, volume 55, edited, with a foreword, by Auden (New Haven: Yale University Press, 1959);

Rae Dalven, trans., *The Complete Poems of Cavafy*, introduction by Auden (New York: Harcourt, Brace & World, 1961);

Johann von Goethe, *Italian Journey*, translated by Auden and Elizabeth Mayer (London: Collins, 1962);

The Viking Book of Aphorisms, edited by Auden and Louis Kronenberger (New York: Viking, 1962);

Anne Fremantle, ed., *The Protestant Mystics*, introduction by Auden (Boston & Toronto: Little, Brown, 1964);

Dag Hammarskjöld, *Markings*, translated by Auden and Leif Sjöberg (New York: Knopf, 1964);

19th Century British Minor Poets, edited, with an introduction, by Auden (New York: Delacorte, 1966);

Selected Poetry and Prose of Byron, edited by Auden (New York: New American Library, 1966);

The Elder Edda: A Selection, translated by Auden and Paul B. Taylor (London: Faber & Faber, 1969);

"In the Year of My Youth," in "W. H. Auden's 'In the Year of My Youth . . .,' " by Lucy McDiarmid, *Review of English Studies*, new series 29 (August 1978): 281-309;

"The Prolific and the Devourer," *Anteus*, 42 (Summer 1981): 1-65.

Bibliographies:

B. C. Bloomfield and Edward Mendelson, *W. H. Auden: A Bibliography, 1924-1969*, second edition (Charlottesville: University Press of Virginia, 1972);

Martin E. Gingerich, *W. H. Auden: A Reference Guide* (Boston: G. K. Hall, 1977).

Biographies:

Charles Osborne, *W. H. Auden: The Life of a Poet* (New York: Harcourt Brace Jovanovich, 1979);

Humphrey Carpenter, *W. H. Auden: A Biography* (Boston: Houghton Mifflin, 1981);

Charles H. Miller, *Auden: An American Friendship* (New York: Scribners,1983).

References:

Alfred Alvarez, "W. H. Auden: Poetry and Journalism," in his *Stewards of Excellence* (New York: Scribners, 1958), pp. 87-106;

George W. Bahlke, *The Later Auden* (New Brunswick: Rutgers University Press, 1970);

John Bayley, "W. H. Auden," in his *The Romantic Survival* (London: Constable, 1957), pp. 127-185;

Joseph Warren Beach, *The Making of the Auden Canon* (Minneapolis: University of Minnesota Press, 1957);

John G. Blair, *The Poetic Art of W. H. Auden* (Princeton: Princeton University Press, 1965);

Robert Bloom, "The Humanization of Auden's Early Style," *PMLA*, 83 (May 1968): 443-454;

Bloom, "W. H. Auden's Bestiary of the Human," *Virginia Quarterly Review*, 42 (Spring 1966): 207-233;

John R. Boly, "Auden and the Romantic Tradition in the Age of Anxiety," *Daedalus*, 111 (Summer 1982): 149-171;

Cleanth Brooks, *Modern Poetry and the Tradition* (Chapel Hill: University of North Carolina Press, 1939), pp. 125-135;

Frederick Buell, *W. H. Auden as a Social Poet* (Ithaca: Cornell University Press, 1973);

Edward Callan, "Allegory in Auden's 'The Age of Anxiety,' " *Twentieth Century Literature*, 10 (January 1965): 155-165;

Callan, *Auden: A Carnival of Intellect* (New York: Oxford University Press, 1983);

Callan, "Auden's Goodly Heritage," *Shenandoah*, 18 (Winter 1967): 56-68;

Callan, "Auden's Ironic Masquerade: Criticism as Morality Play," *University of Toronto Quarterly*, 35 (January 1966): 133-143;

Callan, "W. H. Auden: The Farming of a Verse," *Southern Review*, new series 3 (April 1967): 341-356;

Cyril Connolly, *Enemies of Promise and Other Essays* (London: Routledge & Kegan Paul, 1938);

Peter Conrad, "Theological American: W. H. Auden in New York," in his *Imagining America* (New York: Oxford University Press, 1980), pp. 194-235;

Malcolm Cowley, "Virtue and Virtuosity: Notes on W. H. Auden," *Poetry*, 65 (January 1945): 202-209;

Cecil Day Lewis, *The Buried Day* (London: Chatto & Windus, 1960), pp. 25, 176-179, 185-186, 216-217;

E. R. Dodds, *Missing Persons* (Oxford: Clarendon Press, 1977);

François Duchene, *The Case of the Helmeted Airman* (London: Chatto & Windus, 1972);

Richard Ellmann, "Gazebos and Gashouses," in his *Eminent Domain* (New York: Oxford University Press, 1967), pp. 97-126;

G. S. Fraser, "Auden as the Young Prophet," "Auden in Midstream," and "Auden's Later Manner," in his *Vision and Rhetoric* (London: Faber & Faber, 1959), pp. 149-178;

John Fuller, *A Reader's Guide to W. H. Auden* (New York: Noonday, 1970);

Herbert Greenberg, *Quest for the Necessary* (Cambridge: Harvard University Press, 1968);

Stuart Hampshire, "W. H. Auden," in his *Modern Writers and Other Essays* (London: Chatto & Windus, 1969), pp. 19-29;

Barbara Hardy, "The Reticence of W. H. Auden," *Review*, 11-12 (1964): 54-64;

Hardy, "W. H. Auden, thirties to sixties: a face and a mask," *Southern Review*, new series 5 (July 1969): 655-672;

Richard Hoggart, *Auden: An Introductory Essay* (London: Chatto & Windus, 1951);

Hoggart, "The Long Walk: The Poetry of W. H. Auden," in his *Speaking to Each Other* (London: Chatto & Windus, 1970), II: 56-94;

Samuel Hynes, *The Auden Generation* (New York: Viking, 1977);

Christopher Isherwood, *Lions and Shadows* (London: Hogarth, 1938);

Clive James, "Auden's Achievement," *Commentary*, 56 (December 1973): 53-58;

James, "On *Epistle to a Godson*" and "Farewelling Auden," in his *First Impressions* (New York: Knopf, 1980), pp. 141-164;

Randall Jarrell, "Changes of Attitude and Rhetoric in Auden's Poetry" and "From Freud to Paul: The Stages of Auden's Ideology," in his *Criticism: The Third Book* (New York: Farrar, Straus & Giroux, 1969), pp. 115-187;

Richard A. Johnson, "Auden and the Art of Clarification," *Yale Review*, 61 (Summer 1972): 496-516;

Johnson, "Auden's Architecture of Humanism," *Virginia Quarterly Review*, 48 (Winter 1972): 95-116;

Johnson, *Man's Place: An Essay on Auden* (Ithaca: Cornell University Press, 1973);

F. R. Leavis, in his *New Bearings in English Poetry* (London: Chatto & Windus, 1950), pp. 226-229;

Lucy S. McDiarmid and John McDiarmid, "Artifice and Self-Consciousness in Auden's *The Sea and the Mirror*," *Contemporary Literature*, 16 (Summer 1975): 353-377;

Lucy S. McDiarmid, "Auden and the Redeemed City: Three Allusions," *Criticism*, 13 (Fall 1971): 340-350;

Edward Mendelson, *Early Auden* (New York: Viking, 1981);

Donald Mitchell, *Britten and Auden in the Thirties* (London: Faber & Faber, 1981);

Marianne Moore, *Predilections* (New York: Viking, 1955), pp. 84-102;

New Verse, special Auden issue, 26-27 (November 1937);

Richard Ohmann, "Auden's Sacred Awe," *Commonweal*, 78 (31 May 1963): 279-281;

Peter Porter, "The Achievement of Auden," *Sydney Studies in English* (1978-1979);
Justin Replogle, *Auden's Poetry* (Seattle: University of Washington Press, 1969);
Karl Shapiro, *Essay on Rime* (New York: Reynal & Hitchcock, 1945), pp. 18-19, 41-44;
Shapiro, "The Retreat of W. H. Auden," in his *In Defense of Ignorance* (New York: Random House, 1960), pp. 115-141;
Shenandoah, special Auden issue, 18 (Winter 1967);
Monroe K. Spears, ed., *Auden: A Collection of Critical Essays* (Englewood Cliffs: Prentice-Hall, 1964);
Spears, "The Nature of Modernism: The City," in his *Dionysus and the City* (New York: Oxford University Press, 1970), pp. 82-90;
Spears, *The Poetry of W. H. Auden* (New York: Oxford University Press, 1963);
Stephen Spender, "The Airman, Politics and Psychoanalysis," in his *The Destructive Element* (London: Cape, 1935), pp. 251-277;
Spender, "The Theme of Political Orthodoxy in the Thirties," in his *The Creative Element* (London: Hamilton, 1953), pp. 140-158;
Spender, ed., *W. H. Auden: A Tribute* (New York: Macmillan, 1975);
Spender, *World Within World* (London: Hamilton, 1951);
Igor Stravinsky and Robert Craft, *Themes and Episodes* (New York: Knopf, 1966);
Julian Symons, *The Thirties* (London: Cresset, 1960);
Raymond Williams, "Auden and Isherwood," in his *Drama from Ibsen to Brecht*, revised edition (London: Chatto & Windus, 1968), pp. 199-206.

Papers:
The Berg Collection at New York Public Library has the principal collection of Auden's papers. The Humanities Research Center at the University of Texas, Austin, also has extensive holdings. The Bodleian Library, Oxford University; the British Museum, London; the Butler Library, Columbia University; the Lockwood Memorial Library, State University of New York at Buffalo; and the Swarthmore College Library also have collections of Auden's papers.

George Barker

(26 February 1913-)

Jo Marie Gulledge
Louisiana State University

BOOKS: *Thirty Preliminary Poems* (London: Parton Press, 1933);
Alanna Autumnal (London: Wishart, 1933);
Janus (London: Faber & Faber, 1935);
Poems (London: Faber & Faber, 1935);
Calamiterror (London: Faber & Faber, 1937);
Elegy on Spain (Manchester: Contemporary Bookshop, 1939);
Lament and Triumph (London: Faber & Faber, 1940);
Selected Poems (New York: Macmillan, 1941);
Sacred and Secular Elegies (Norfolk, Conn.: New Directions, 1943);
Eros in Dogma (London: Faber & Faber, 1944);
Love Poems (New York: Dial Press, 1947);
The Dead Seagull (London: Lehmann, 1950; New York: Farrar, Straus & Young, 1951);
News of the World (London: Faber & Faber, 1950);
The True Confession of George Barker (Denver: Swallow, 1950; London: Fore Publications, 1950; London: Parton Press, 1957; enlarged edition, New York: New American Library, 1964; London: MacGibbon & Kee, 1965);
A Vision of Beasts and Gods (London: Faber & Faber, 1954);
Collected Poems, 1930-1955 (London: Faber & Faber, 1957; New York: Criterion, 1958);
Two Plays (London: Faber & Faber, 1958);
The View from a Blind I (London: Faber & Faber, 1962);
Collected Poems 1930-1965 (New York: October House, 1965);
Dreams of a Summer Night (London: Faber & Faber, 1966);
The Golden Chains (London: Faber & Faber, 1968);
At Thurgarton Church (London: Trigram Press, 1969);

George Barker

Runes and Rhymes and Tunes and Chimes (London: Faber & Faber, 1969);
Essays (London: MacGibbon & Kee, 1970);
What is Mercy and a Voice (London: Poem-of-the-Month Club, 1970);
To Aylsham Fair (London: Faber & Faber, 1970);
Poems of Places and People (London: Faber & Faber, 1971);
The Alphabetical Zoo (London: Faber & Faber, 1972);
III Hallucination Poems (New York: Helikon Press, 1972);
In Memory of David Archer (London: Faber & Faber, 1973);
Dialogues, etc. (London: Faber & Faber, 1976);
Seven Poems (Warwick: Greville Press, 1977);
Villar Stellar (London & Boston: Faber & Faber, 1978).

Yvor Winters once remarked that "poetry is not a career. One will make one's living elsewhere." But the prolific writer George Barker has defied that notion for the past fifty years, aspiring toward the life of the true poet. Barker has traveled from continent to continent, writing poetry and prose. In 1973, Barker's neglected career was honored by tributes from friends in *Homage to George Barker on His 60th Birthday*, a collection of essays acknowledging the achievements of this humorous and often puzzling man. Previously overshadowed by Dylan Thomas in the 1930s and considered merely one of W. H. Auden's followers, Barker has become recognized for his satirical nature, vivid images, and religious concerns.

George Granville Barker was born in Loughton, Essex, the son of George Barker, a constable, whom he refers to as "a little low / In the social register" in his autobiographical poem *The True Confession of George Barker* (1950). His mother, Marion Frances Taaffe Barker, admired by Barker for her gentleness and quick mind, was an Irish peasant and daughter of a marine pilot from Drogheda. He describes her in his much anthologized poem "To My Mother":

> Under the window where I often found her
> Sitting as huge as Asia, seismic with laughter
> Gin and chicken helpless in her Irish hand,
> Irresistible as Rabelais, but most tender for
> The lame dogs and hurt birds that surround her.

When Barker was quite young, his family left Loughton and moved to Chelsea in London. Barker attended the Regent Street Polytechnic, a secondary school, until the age of fourteen. Working at various odd jobs, from "wallpaper designer to a garage mechanic," Barker drifted about after he dropped out of school. In his desolate state, he at times slept "on Putney Common with newspapers wrapped around the body for warmth."

Although Barker came from a meager background, his education in literature began early, when at age nine, he read Byron. By the time he was fifteen, he was familiar with the writings of T. S. Eliot and James Joyce, but his inspiration came from poets such as William Empson, who had drifted away from their influences. Barker's first novel, *Alanna Autumnal*, and his first collection of poetry, *Thirty Preliminary Poems*, were published when he was twenty.

Thirty Preliminary Poems (1933) gives an early view of the themes that Barker carried throughout his career: man's spiritual loss, frustration, sexuality, and death. The attitude of many writers during the 1930s was one of despair, with a concern for social conditions, and Barker, strongly influenced by such contemporaries as Louis MacNeice, was enmeshed in the attitudes of the era. His "Elegy Number 1" concludes:

> Lovers on Sunday in the rear seats of the cinemas

Kiss deep and dark, for is it the last kiss?
Children sailing on swings in municipal parks
Swing high into the reach of the sky,
Leave, leave the sad star that is about to die.
Laugh, my comedian, who may not laugh again—
Soon, soon,
Soon Jeremiah Job will be walking among men.

In "Memories of George Barker" (published in *Homage to George Barker*) Maurice Carpenter describes the origin of *Thirty Preliminary Poems*. On a spring day in 1933, Barker and David Archer, a bookstore owner, were sitting in a coffee shop in London. In a corner alone "sat a man with a magnificent head" known as Colonel Lawrence. On his menu Barker scratched the following words, which later became the introduction to his book, later published by Archer's Parton Press in 1933:

O to us speak
Bleak snow
With you mellifluous smooth voice.

Barker, "an imperious young man with a Roman nose, a sensual rather feminine mouth," was burdened with thoughts of death, the despair in life, and the uselessness of man. These themes, introduced in *Thirty Preliminary Poems*, have continued throughout his work. Impressed by both *Alanna Autumnal* and *Thirty Preliminary Poems*, David Muir sent him to the offices of the *Criterion* to meet with T. S. Eliot, who later helped him get *Poems* (1935) into print. While Barker may have been unconsciously attempting to detach himself from the "Auden school," his work still remained within the framework of such major modern British writers as Stephen Spender and C. Day Lewis in tone and style.

Disgusted with life "gone sour, and times gone awry," Barker moved in 1935 with his wife Jessica Woodward, whom he married that same year, from London to a little cottage in Plush Bottoms, on a hill overlooking Piddletrenthide. Sitting in the comforts of his new cottage in front of a roaring fire and sipping apple cider from the surrounding orchards, Barker was still discontent. Constantly possessed by thoughts of suicide and death, he caused Archer and Carpenter great concern.

Barker's preoccupation with death was evident in *Poems*, a collection of his best verse to date, and in *Calamiterror* (1937). Even though these books were published by a large publishing house, Faber and Faber, Barker's following remained small as his work went practically unnoticed. Francis Scarfe finds in these earlier works "innumerable Miltonic latinisms and barbarisms" and calls Barker "so unsophisticated as to use such quaint words as 'hark' to set one's teeth on edge." Allowing sensation to dominate caused his message—man's battle between materialism and self-knowledge—to lapse into emotional and violent disarray. But, according to Scarfe, "the most important thing about [*Poems*] is the fact that, at that date, a young poet could be so self-contained as to ignore the stifling but necessary influences of the Eliot and Auden generations."

Scarfe calls the poems in *Thirty Preliminary Poems* and *Poems* "awkwardly grandiose" because of their complex, flowing syntax and heavyhanded rhetorical style. But Barker's next book, *Calamiterror*, despite certain stylistic flaws, was well received by critics. Here Barker's tendency toward romanticism is controlled by his adopting the techniques of the French symbolists. The themes of the title poem are birth, the act of suffrage, and the inevitability of death. While these themes are not new in this poem, it gained Barker recognition from the critics. He was able to continue his work through grants received from his publisher Faber and Faber and the Royal Society of Literature.

Barker's "Elegy on Spain," the title poem of his book published in 1939, reflects his feelings about the Spanish civil war. The poem was inspired by a photograph of a child killed in the air raid over Barcelona. Along with Auden's "Spain," "Elegy on Spain" was hailed as one of the best poems about that war. But Barker, unlike Auden and Spender, took an ambivalent point of view toward the war and remained independent.

In the same year that *Elegy on Spain* was published, Barker went to Japan as a visiting professor of English literature at the Imperial Tohaku University at Sendai. In his self-imposed exile, he distanced himself from the turmoil in Europe, which he recalls in "Pacific Sonnets" (collected in *Eros in Dogma*, 1944). His isolation is apparent in the opening lines of the first sonnet:

Between the wall of China and my heart
O exile is. Remember the tremendous
Autumnals of nations threatening to end us all,
I speak of the things nearest to my heart.
These space cannot alienate, or time part
From me. . . .

Barker later told Anthony Thwaite (whose essay appears in *Homage to George Barker*) that during this time of hostility that preceded the outbreak of war between Britain and Japan he "was followed

George Barker, 1951 (BBC Hulton)

everywhere by a tiny spy in white gloves, and that the calligraphy was upsetting." Prior to leaving Japan six months after his arrival, he composed the lengthy poem "View of England" in honor of his distant homeland. Influenced by visits to foreign places, Barker's style frequently became a surrealistic collage of images. He seemed unable to restrict his imagery to specific geographical places.

While he felt isolated from his own culture, Barker moved to the United States instead of returning to England. The alienated wanderer found solace not in his Catholic heritage but in his poetry, after "informally leaving the Roman Catholic Church and ending his marriage in 1940." While he was in the United States, Barker's two most successful books of verse, *Lament and Triumph* (1940) and *Eros in Dogma* (1944) were published. The poems in these books acknowledge external forces with less emphasis on the internal self. The last poem in *Eros in Dogma*, "To Any Member of My Generation," expresses the burdens of war placed on his generation and the influential poets of the 1940s, such as

David Gascoyne, Kathleen Raine, Vernon Watkins. Malcolm Cowley has said that "Barker has the talent for making final statements," as he does in this poem:

> Whenever we kissed we cocked the future's rifles
> And from our wild-oats words, like dragon teeth,
> Death under foot now arises: when we were gay
> Dancing together in what we hoped was life,
> Who was it in our arms but the whores of death
> Whom we have found in our beds today, today?

During his years in the United States, Barker wrote book reviews for the *Nation*, had poems published in the *New Republic*, and recorded poetry for the Harvard library.

While maintaining his rebellious attitude and continuing to use erotic images, Barker began to contain his abstractions in powerful and meaningful poetry. His obsession with rebellion and eroticism was obvious in *News of the World* (1950), but his verse was disciplined with a mature technical control. As in earlier books, pessimism and thoughts of death overshadowed the theme of love in *News of the World*. In the same year, Barker's most controversial book, *The True Confession of George Barker*, was published. A long autobiographical poem with various personae, including François Villon and Charles Pierre Baudelaire, the poem was omitted from *Collected Poems, 1930-1955* (1957) at the request of both his British and his American publishers. Considered as some of the best rhetoric in modern poetry, *Collected Poems* was also found by the *Manchester Guardian* to be a "combination of some of the finest as well as some of the worst poetry of our time."

After the publication of *Collected Poems*, Barker ended his wanderings around the western United States and returned to New York City. He then spent two years traveling throughout the United States, giving poetry readings, sometimes visiting twelve campuses in twelve weeks. He returned to England in 1959, only to leave again for

Dust jacket for the 1965 enlarged edition of Barker's long autobiographical poem. The 1950 edition of this poem aroused so much controversy that his publishers asked him to omit it from his 1957 Collected Poems.

Italy in 1960. Barker's *The View from a Blind I* was published in 1962 during a period when he was dividing his time between London and Rome. In these poems a lighter tone replaced the previous heavy rhetoric. He returned once again to the United States as a visiting professor at the State University of New York at Buffalo in 1965, bringing with him his wife Elspeth Langlands, whom he married in 1964. (Little is known about Barker's second marriage.) After one year, Barker returned to London and began work on his next book, *The Golden Chains* (1968), a collection of 104 poems, each consisting of two rhymed quatrains.

During the 1950s and 1960s, Barker was the recipient of various honors for his poetry and prose: a Royal Society of Literature bursary in 1950, the Guiness Prize in 1962, *Poetry* magazine's Levinson Prize in 1965, the Borestone Mountain Poetry Prize in 1967, and an Arts Council bursary in 1968. But most of his poetry of the 1970s, his most productive years—*Poems of Places and People* (1971), *III Hallucination Poems* (1972), *In Memory of David Archer* (1973), *Dialogues, etc.* (1976), *Seven Poems* (1977), and *Villar Stellar* (1978)—went virtually unnoticed. *Contemporary Poetry* remarked that "their tone was often one of puzzled plain questioning, of the past and of past mistakes, of human mistakes of human frailty and absurdity, relieved with something more sardonic and ironical." Barker's last book of the 1970s, *Villar Stellar*, was considered by most critics to be hollow with numerous worn-out phrases. But of his most recent work, Barker says: "It has two purposes, the first to record biographical instances and the second to record the frames of the mind in which these incidents and instances were recollected. I have tried to describe the changing colours of the memory, as the dolphin might, if it could, try to describe the altering colours of its skin as it dies."

Whether one finds Barker's poetry "plain-speaking" or marred by obscurity, honest or blasphemous, the astonishing images will last. The entry on Barker in *The Oxford Companion to English Literature* says: "His poems are marked by a rhetorical and Dionysiac style and a preoccupation with human suffering and guilt." Barker commented that this statement was very true but hoped "one day to write in an unrhetorical and Apollonian style about human joy and innocence." After an extended visit to Greece, Barker returned to his home at Norfolk, England, in December 1981 in order to complete his next book, "A Fragment of Anno Domini."

Other:

Alfred, Lord Tennyson, *Idylls of the King and a Selection of Poems*, edited by Barker (Garden City: Doubleday, 1961);

Penguin Modern Poets, Number Three, includes poems by Barker, Charles Causley, and Martin Bell (London: Penguin, 1962);

"Tennyson's Two Voices," in *Master Poems of the English Language*, edited by Oscar Williams (New York: Trident, 1966), pp. 654-657.

Periodical Publications:

"16 Comments on Auden," *New Verse*, 26-27 (November 1937): 23;

"A Note on the Dialectics of Poetry," *Purpose*, 10 (January-March 1938): 27-30;

"Notes from the Largest Imaginary Empire," *New Republic*, 105 (8 December 1941): 791-792;

"A Note on André Gide," *Life and Letters Today*, 60 (February 1949): 117-119;

"The Opinion of George Barker on Some Modern Verse," *Life and Letters Today*, 64 (February 1950): 131-133;

"Poet as Pariah," *New Statesman and Nation*, 40 (8 July 1950): 37-38.

References:

Audrey Beecham, "George Barker," *Life and Letters Today*, 25 (April-June 1940): 273-281;

Harvey Breit, "View of the World," *Poetry*, 59 (December 1941): 159-162;

Anthony Cronin, "Poetry and Ideas: George Barker," *London Magazine*, 3 (September 1956): 44-52;

David Daiches, "The Lyricism of George Barker," *Poetry*, 69 (March 1947): 336-346;

Cecil Day Lewis, *The Poetic Image* (London: Cape, 1947), pp. 128-130;

Martha Fodaski, *George Barker* (New York: Twayne, 1969);

Fodaski, "Three Memorial Sonnets," in *Master Poems of the English Language*, edited by Oscar Williams (New York: Trident, 1966), pp. 1032-1036;

John Heath-Stubbs and Martin Green, eds., *Homage to George Barker on His 60th Birthday* (London: Brian & O'Keeffe, 1973);

Francis Scarfe, "George Barker, A Pure Poet," in his *Auden and After* (London: Routledge, 1942), pp. 118-130;

C. H. Sisson, "The Forties," in his *English Poetry 1900-1950* (London: Hart-Davis, 1971).

John Betjeman

John Clarke
University College, London

BIRTH: London, 28 August 1906, to Ernest Edward and Mabel Bessie Betjeman.

EDUCATION: Magdalen College, Oxford, 1925-1928.

MARRIAGE: 1933 to Penelope Valentine Hester Chetwode; children: Paul, Candida.

AWARDS AND HONORS: Heinemann Award for *Selected Poems*, 1949; Foyle Poetry Prize for *A Few Late Chrysanthemums*, 1955; Loines Award for Poetry, 1956; Duff Cooper Memorial Prize for *Collected Poems*, 1958; Foyle Poetry Prize for *Collected Poems*, 1959; Queen's Gold Medal for Poetry for *Collected Poems*, 1960; Commander, Order of the British Empire, 1960; Knight Commander of the British Empire, 1969; Honorary Fellow, Royal Institute of British Architects, 1971; Honorary Fellow, Keble College, Oxford, 1972; Poet Laureate, 1972; Honorary Fellow, Magdalen College, Oxford, 1975.

John Betjeman

SELECTED BOOKS: *Mount Zion* (London: James Press, 1931);

Ghastly Good Taste: a depressing story of the rise and fall of English architecture (London: Chapman & Hall, 1933; New York: St. Martin's, 1971);

Continual Dew: A Little Book of Bourgeois Verse (London: Murray, 1937);

An Oxford University Chest (London: Miles, 1938);

Antiquarian Prejudice (London: Hogarth Press, 1939);

Old Lights for New Chancels (London: Murray, 1940);

Vintage London (London: Collins, 1942);

English Cities and Small Towns (London: Collins, 1943);

John Piper (Harmondsworth, U.K.: Penguin, 1944);

New Bats in Old Belfries (London: Murray, 1945);

Slick But Not Streamlined: Poems & Short Pieces, selected and introduced by W. H. Auden (Garden City: Doubleday, 1947);

Selected Poems (London: Murray, 1948);

The English Scene (London: Cambridge University Press, 1951);

First and Last Loves (London: Murray, 1952; New York: Musson, 1952);

A Few Late Chrysanthemums (London: Murray, 1954);

Poems In The Porch (London: S.P.C.K., 1954);

The English Town In the Last Hundred Years (Cambridge: Cambridge University Press, 1956);

Collected Poems (London: Murray, 1958; Boston: Houghton Mifflin, 1959; enlarged edition, London: Murray, 1962; enlarged again, London: Murray, 1970; Boston: Houghton Mifflin, 1971);

Summoned By Bells (London: Murray, 1960; Boston: Houghton Mifflin, 1960);

Ground Plan to Skyline, as Richard M. Farren (London: Newman Neame Take Home Books, 1960);

A Ring of Bells (London: Murray, 1962; Boston: Houghton Mifflin, 1963);

The City of London Churches (London: Pitkin Pictorials, 1965);

High and Low (London: Murray, 1966; Boston: Houghton Mifflin, 1967);

A Pictorial History of English Architecture (London: Murray, 1972; New York: Macmillan, 1972);

London's Historic Railway Stations (London: Murray, 1972);

A Nip In The Air (London: Murray, 1975; New York: Norton, 1976);

The Best of Betjeman, selected by John Guest (London: Murray, 1978).

John Betjeman is a unique figure in twentieth-century English poetry, enjoying a degree of fame and success unequaled by any poet since Byron. His *Collected Poems* of 1958 reputedly sold more than 100,000 copies, and they are read by millions of people who normally never read poetry, while he has become a household name through his many appearances on television panels and on programs about architecture. He is also quintessentially English, a pillar of the so-called establishment and the friend of royalty (Princess Margaret's affection for his poetry is well known), and he has, during a long and diverse career, accumulated several honorary doctorates, a CBE, and a knighthood before being created the Poet Laureate in 1972.

Despite such public recognition (or perhaps partly because of it) Betjeman's stature as a poet has remained singularly hard to assess. Some critics have always maintained that he is a poet of mediocre talents, a competent versifier whose adroit exploitation of the television medium in its early years enabled him to carve out for himself a reputation he does not deserve. The appearance of his poetry in Sunday newspaper supplements and the like, together with the popular image he has always cultivated as what Derek Stanford has called "the sort of poet you expect to read about in a woman's magazine under the drier," has also aroused the distrust of purists. Others—of whom Philip Larkin is an important example—regard Betjeman as a major living English poet and accord him a place in a central poetic tradition that would also probably include Tennyson, Hardy, and Kipling. Less controversial is the widespread recognition that Betjeman's contribution to the appreciation of nineteenth-century English architecture—through a large number of books and broadcasts—has been deeply significant. Some have even described Betjeman as an architect manque, though he prefers to be considered primarily a poet. It would be careless, however, to try to distinguish too sharply between the two roles: Betjeman's poetry and his architectural and topographical writings often share not only a similar subject matter, but can be seen to form a coherent body of attitudes to English society and so continually comment upon each other. Most important for an understanding of Betjeman's artistic importance is a knowledge of the facts of his early life. Few other poets so openly recognize, or unashamedly describe, the formative experiences of their childhood.

John Betjeman was born in London in 1906, the only child of Ernest Betjeman, a prosperous manufacturer of Dutch origin. The discreet opulence of the North London suburbs in which Betjeman spent his childhood is captured most memorably in a stanza from his poem "St. Saviour's, Aberdeen Park, Highbury, London, N." (1948):

> These were the streets my parents knew when they loved and won—
> The brougham that crunched the gravel, the laurel-girt paths that wind,
> Geranium-beds for the lawn, Venetian blinds for the sun,
> A separate tradesman's entrance, straw in the mews behind,
> Just in the four-mile radius where hackney carriages run,
> Solid Italianate houses for the solid commercial mind.

Betjeman's obsession with class, visible throughout all his poetry, derives in part from his early intuitions of the subtle snobbery permeating this polite childhood environment; while the terror of death, equally important to his poetry, was instilled in him at an early age by a Calvinistic nursery maid ("Hating to think of sphere succeeding sphere / Into eternity and God's Dread Will / I caught her terror then. I have it still.") The same nursery maid's alleged cruelty to Betjeman ("Lock'd into cupboards, left alone all day") may have been the origin of the deep sensitivity to pain and the fear of loneliness which are almost obsessive qualities in his later poetry.

This early sense of loneliness was to increase during Betjeman's adolescence, when his realization that he could not continue in the family business slowly estranged him from his father. "For myself," he wrote, "I knew as soon as I could read and write / That I must be a poet." At his preparatory school in Highgate, London, one of his teachers was the newly arrived T. S. Eliot, to whom the precocious schoolboy presented his first poetic attempts: "I bound my verse into a book / 'The Best

John Betjeman, circa 1933

of Betjeman' and handed it / To one who, I was told, liked poetry— / The American master, Mr. Eliot." Betjeman did not record Eliot's opinion.

From 1917 to 1920 John Betjeman attended the Dragon School, Oxford, where, under the influence of a teacher, Gerald Haynes, he first developed an interest in architecture. In 1920 Betjeman left this school for Marlborough public school in Wiltshire, where the fear of being bullied added to feelings of vulnerability and isolation in an already oversensitive mind.

After the "Doom! Shivering doom!" of Marlborough, Betjeman went up to Magdalen College, Oxford, in 1925. Here his poetic talents and already remarkable knowledge of English architecture earned him the admiration of the scholar C. M. Bowra, while his neglect of academic work—"While we ate Virginia hams, / Contemporaries passed exams"—earned the scorn of his tutor C. S. Lewis, whom Betjeman later satirized in some of his poems. At Oxford Betjeman became part of the fashionable undergraduate set that was to provide material for the early novels of Evelyn Waugh, whose long friendship with Betjeman dates from this time. As an undergraduate Betjeman maintained his now well-known indifference to sport ("I still don't know where the playing fields are. . . .") and cultivated instead a deliberate aestheticism. An early photograph shows him in dreamy contemplation under a pseudo-Gothic archway, and the poem "The Arrest of Oscar Wilde at the Cadogan Hotel," written at Oxford, reflected this pose in a similar manner.

Betjeman has been as responsible as anyone for creating the popular image of this Oxford generation as one of rich mindlessness, notably through poems like "The 'Varsity Students' Rag" (written while he was at Oxford):

> But that's nothing to the rag we had at the college the other night;
> We'd gallons and gallons of cider—and I got frightfully tight.
> And then we smash'd up ev'rything, and what was the funniest part
> We smashed some rotten old pictures which were priceless works of art.

Perhaps unsurprisingly, Betjeman left Oxford having failed to receive a degree. After a short spell of teaching at Heddon Court School, in Barnet, Hertfordshire (where, typically, he obtained the job by masquerading as an expert on cricket), he became in 1931 the assistant editor of the *Architectural Review*, a post which brought him into contact with leading architects and historians of architecture: "In my own unpleasant occupation of architectural journalism I am continually meeting architects," he wrote. Nineteen thirty-one also saw the publication of Betjeman's first book of poems, *Mount Zion*.

The spirit in which this book was conceived is suggested by Betjeman's description of it as a "precious, hyper-sophisticated book" and by the dedication of it to Mrs. Arthur Dugdale, mistress of Sezincote, an English country house to which Oxford's most fashionable undergraduates were frequently invited. Although *Mount Zion* smacked of affectation—not least in its highly ornate binding and blue leaves—it contained in embryo themes and preoccupations that recur throughout Betjeman's poetic oeuvre.

Notable among these were an interest in topography, particularly that of English suburbia ("Croydon," "Camberley"); nineteenth-century architecture; religion ("Hymn," "The Wykehamist"); and death ("Death in Leamington"), several of these

Evelyn Waugh and John Betjeman, circa 1935

elements often being present within a single poem, such as "For Nineteenth-Century Burials." Most obvious in *Mount Zion*, however, was Betjeman's early talent for comic verse and gentle satire, at its most extreme in "The 'Varsity Students' Rag," but creeping into virtually every other poem in the volume. "Prolonged solemnity is not in his nature," a friend of Betjeman's once remarked; the comment is certainly applicable to *Mount Zion*.

In 1933 Betjeman left his post on the *Architectural Review* and began to edit the Shell series of topographical guides to Britain. In the same year he married Penelope, daughter of Sir Philip (later Lord) Chetwode, Commander-In-Chief, India. (Of his relationship with her daughter, Lady Chetwode is said to have retorted, "We ask people like that to our houses but we don't marry them"), and in the following year Betjeman became the film critic to Lord Beaverbrook's *Evening Standard*. He was sacked within a year for writing overenthusiastic reviews, but there survives an anecdote from this time which typifies the humor and eccentricity for which he has since become well known. As Derek Stanford reports, "On one occasion, he had been asked to interview the star Myrna Loy. 'I took her out to lunch' he recollects, and asked her would she mind if he wrote that she 'was very interested in English Perpendicular' [an architectural style] 'Not at all' replied Miss Loy, whereupon Mr. Betjeman duly reported his little witticism."

Betjeman's second volume of verse, *Continual Dew*, appeared in 1937. Its subtitle—*A Little Book of Bourgeois Verse*—pinpointed the emergence of what was to become a favorite poetic subject: the upper-middle-class milieu of the English home counties. In "Love In A Valley" he portrayed this milieu with a characteristic blend of irony and affection:

Deep down the drive go the cushioned rhododendrons,
Deep down, sand deep, drives the heather root,
Deep the spliced timber barked around the summer-house,
Light lies the tennis-court, plantain underfoot.
What a winter welcome to what a Surrey homestead!
Oh! the metal lantern and white enamelled door!
Oh! the spread of orange from the gas-fire on the carpet!
Oh! the tiny patter, sandalled footsteps on the floor!

The complexity of tone apparent in a poem like "Love In a Valley" was not recognized by the first readers of *Continual Dew*. As with Betjeman's first volume, a disproportionate degree of attention was given to his comic and light-verse poems, of which "Slough," appearing first in *Continual Dew* and since highly anthologized, was the most notorious: "Come friendly bombs, and fall on Slough / It isn't fit for humans now / There isn't grass to graze a cow." Betjeman's desire to be taken seriously as a poet has frequently suffered through the popularity of poems in this mode at the expense of his more serious endeavors. Referring specifically to "Slough" and the earlier "The 'Varsity Students' Rag," he later complained that "they now seem to me merely comic verse and competent magazine writing, topical and tiresome." Although *Continual Dew* showed only limited improvement on *Mount Zion*, one poem in it did indicate the stirrings of a far maturer poetic vision. In "Death of King George

V," inspired by the newspaper headline "New King Arrives in Capital By Air," Betjeman crystallized in a potent image the troubled sense of a passing era which the tone of postwar England was to confirm: "Old men who never cheated, never doubted, / Communicated monthly, sit and stare / At the new suburb stretched beyond the runway / Where a young man lands hatless from the air." Betjeman's doubt about modernity—with its implied disrespect for tradition, its faith in material progress and the kind of landscape and people produced by it—was to become overt pessimism in future volumes of verse.

During World War II Betjeman continued to work largely in the media, serving variously in the Admiralty, as the United Kingdom press attache to Dublin, as a broadcaster with the BBC (1943), and in the books department of the British Council (1944-1946). The war period also saw the publication of *Old Lights for New Chancels* in 1940, followed by a further collection of poems, *New Bats in Old Belfries*, in 1945. Although both these volumes were well received and sold well, in the mid-1940s Betjeman was still better known as a writer of books on topography and architecture than as a poet, and he had already made a reputation for himself as an expert on (and champion of) the Victorian Gothic revival in architecture. His first book on architecture, *Ghastly Good Taste: a depressing story of the rise and fall of English architecture*, had appeared as early as 1933, when Betjeman was still at the *Architectural Review*. It was shortly after followed by *An Oxford University Chest* in 1938, and *Antiquarian Prejudice* (1939), which contained the early expression of what was to become a familiar argument: "Architecture has a wider meaning than that which is commonly given to it. For architecture means not a house, or a single building or a church . . . but your surroundings; not a town or a street, but our whole over-populated island. It is concerned with where we eat, work, sleep, play, congregate, escape. It is our background, alas, often too permanent." Betjeman's fascination with the relationship between people and surroundings—the social history of architecture—forms the basis of all of his topographical writings, from *Vintage London* (1942) to *English Cities and Small Towns* (1943), the popularity of which was eclipsed only by *First and Last Loves* (1952), perhaps the most representative of his prose writings. A list of some of its chapter headings indicates the nature and variety of its author's topographical interests: "Aberdeen Granite," "Leeds—A City of Contrasts," "London Railway Stations," "Nonconformist Architecture." The title itself—*First and Last Loves*—is indicative of Betjeman's approach to his subject: invariably enthusiastic, partisan, celebrating the places he likes, excoriating the things he detests. In *First and Last Loves* appeared a description of a Cornish church which has become a famous example of Betjeman's idiosyncratic style: "Saint Endellion! Saint Endellion! The name is like a ring of bells . . . on the top of the hill was the old church of St. Endellion. It looked, and still looks, just like a hare. The ears are the pinnacles of the tower and the rest of the hare, the church, crouches among wind-slashed firs." A reviewer of *First and Last Loves* wrote, "Any industrious fool with a good reference library can docket and classify a work of art, but to transmit it as an experience shared is an infinitely rare gift." This "gift" was invaluable in Betjeman's increasing popularity as a television broadcaster following World War II, a period which witnessed his influence in changing the British public's attitude to the Victorian achievement in the visual arts. Despite this activity, Betjeman has always insisted that he is a poet first and foremost, even claiming that his topographical works are merely a means of gaining the financial freedom which allows him to pursue poetry.

Betjeman at work in his flat, 1951 (BBC Hulton, Picture Post*)*

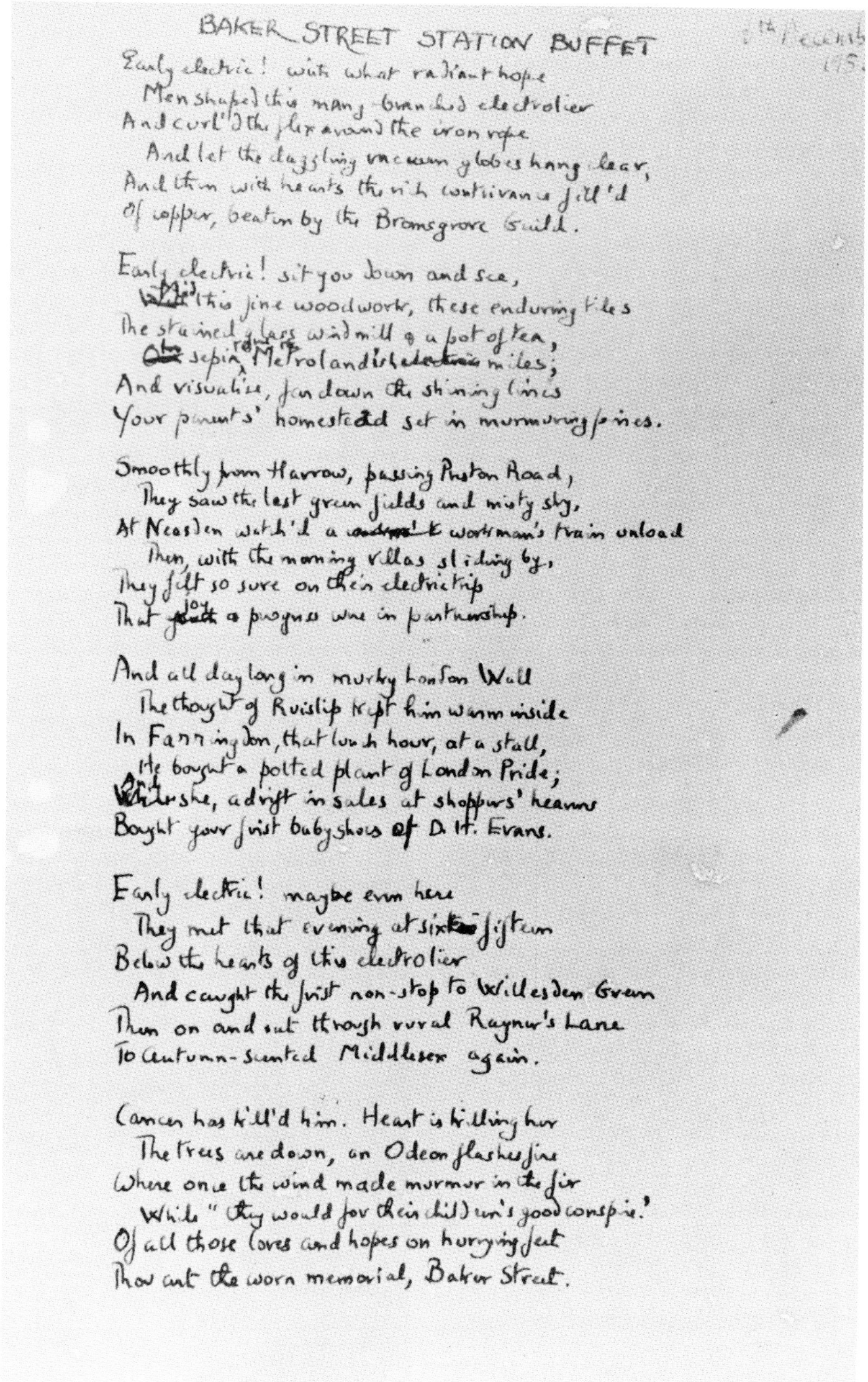

BAKER STREET STATION BUFFET

th Decemb
195

Early electric! with what radiant hope
  Men shaped this many-branched electrolier
And curl'd the flex around the iron rope
  And let the dazzling vacuum globes hang clear,
And then with hearts the rich contrivance fill'd
Of copper, beaten by the Bromsgrove Guild.

Early electric! sit you down and see,
  'Mid this fine woodwork, these enduring tiles
The stained glass windmill & a pot of tea,
  ~~Or~~ sepia rural Metrolandish ~~electric~~ miles;
And visualise, far down the shining lines
Your parents' homestead set in murmuring pines.

Smoothly from Harrow, passing Preston Road,
  They saw the last green fields and misty sky,
At Neasden watch'd a ~~[illegible]~~ workman's train unload
  Then, with the morning villas sliding by,
They felt so sure on their electric trip
That ~~faith~~ joy & progress were in partnership.

And all day long in murky London Wall
  The thought of Ruislip kept him warm inside
In Farringdon, that lunch hour, at a stall,
  He bought a potted plant of London Pride;
~~While~~ And she, adrift in sales at shoppers' heavens
Bought your first baby shoes at D. H. Evans.

Early electric! maybe even here
  They met that evening at six~~teen~~ fifteen
Below the hearts of this electrolier
  And caught the first non-stop to Willesden Green
Then on and out through rural Rayner's Lane
To autumn-scented Middlesex again.

Cancer has kill'd him. Heart is killing her
  The trees are down, an Odeon flashes fire
Where once the wind made murmur in the fir
  While "they would for their children's good conspire."
Of all those loves and hopes on hurrying feet
Thou art the worn memorial, Baker Street.

A late draft for the poem published in 1953 as "The Metropolitan Railway Station" (collection of H. Bradley Martin)

The publication of *Old Lights for New Chancels* in 1940 seemed to justify Betjeman's insistence that serious attention be paid to his poetry. The poems that make up this collection show a marked advance in metrical subtlety and a more profound treatment of familiar themes—rather than any radical departure from his earlier poems. Indeed, Betjeman has never been an experimental poet, differing from most of his contemporaries by remaining immune—even in the 1920s—to the pressures of modernism. Philip Larkin wrote that for Betjeman "there has been no symbolism, no objective correlative, no T. S. Eliot or Ezra Pound, no rediscovery of myth or language as gesture, no *Seven Types* or *Some Versions*. . . ." Instead Betjeman has always preferred to create within the limitation of preexisting metrical forms, particularly those of nineteenth-century poets, some of whom remain quite obscure. Betjeman described his selection and adoption of these poetic models in an unpretentious manner: "I am a traditionalist in metre and have made few experiments. The rhythms of Tennyson, Crabbe, Hawker, Dowson, Hardy, James Elroy Flecker, Moore and Hymns Ancient and Modern are generally buzzing about in my brain, and I choose one from these which seems to me to suit the theme." Betjeman's affection for the nineteenth century is common both to his topographical writings and his poetry, where it is revealed not only stylistically in pastiche, parody, or straightforward adoption of a particular stanza form, but in subject matter too. There is, in Betjeman's poetry, a high incidence of narrative or anecdotal poems in nineteenth-century settings. The whole tenor of Betjeman's imagination has even been described as Victorian: his fondness for the quaint and the grotesque, his wistful piety, and his unashamed sentimentality.

In *Old Lights for New Chancels* and *New Bats in Old Belfries* there emerged for the first time a lyrical poetry of a power and delicacy which surprised its early readers. In "Trebetherick" Betjeman discovered in memories of his childhood a previously untapped source of inspiration. The poem is one of several based on memories of holidays on the Cornish coast: "But when a storm was at its height, / And feathery slate was black in rain, / And tamarisks were hung with light / And golden sand was brown again, / Spring tide and blizzard would unite / And sea came flooding up the lane." "Trebetherick" ushered in Betjeman's poetic maturity, achieved in those poems which directly express personal experience. In another fine poem, "Ireland with Emily," he drew again on memories of undergraduate holidays spent in a country whose melancholy beauty ("Stony hills poured over space") never ceased to fascinate him.

As had been the case with earlier volumes, it was the lighter verse in *Old Lights for New Chancels* which was to receive the most attention, and the emergence of the "Betjeman heroine" received particular notice. Beginning with "Pam, you great big mountainous sports girl / Whizzing them over the net with the strength of five," this rather fearsome, asexual heroine reappeared in *New Bats in Old Belfries* as Myfanwy, "Ringleader, tom-boy and chum to the weak," before reaching its apotheosis (also in *New Bats in Old Belfries*) in "Miss J. Hunter Dunn, Miss J. Hunter Dunn / Furnish'd and burnish'd by Aldershot sun, / What strenuous singles we played after tea, / We in the tournament—you against me." When asked whether he really found this kind of woman attractive, Betjeman admitted that, yes, he did like such "great dominating creatures," and added characteristically, "Anyone who has been to a Public School is a masochist."

Old Lights for New Chancels also contained a preface in which Betjeman described some of his poetic interests: "I love suburbs and gaslights and Pont St. and Gothic Revival Churches and mineral railways, provincial towns and garden cities." The importance of topography to Betjeman's poetry is reflected even by the number of his poems which take their titles from the names of places. But as W. H. Auden wrote in his introduction to *Slick But Not Streamlined* (1947), "Wild or unhumanized nature holds no charms for the average topophile because it is lacking in history." Betjeman delights in describing places and buildings not for their intrinsic value but for their human associations. Starting with the premise that architecture is the outward and visible manifestation of a society's spiritual condition, the body of Betjeman's prose and poetry from the 1940s onward has reiterated the conviction that happiness is difficult to achieve in a world growing uglier. In the early poem "Death of King George V," Betjeman had registered an uncertain response to a new era; this attitude was replaced by a more articulate criticism of the spiritlessness and physical ugliness of postwar English society. His early satire on town planners, bureaucrats, speculators, and their victims had been essentially comic, and his portraits of modern living, in such poems as "Slough" (1937), too crude and extravagant: "In labour-saving homes, with care / Their wives frizz out peroxide hair / And dry it in synthetic air / And paint their nails." Such lightly worn attitudes were absorbed into a more comprehensive crusade against certain kinds of environmental change and their effect on society. Some commentators, including John Press, have for this reason placed Betjeman "in the direct line of descent from . . . Ruskin and Morris, whose love of the arts was linked with their desire for the regeneration of society." Others have been less impressed with Betjeman's aesthetic conservatism. His reputation has frequently suffered through what has been sometimes regarded as a lack of awareness of, and sympathy with the life-style of the masses. It is true that Betjeman's professed disgust with much of modernity is sometimes indistinguishable from a rather unspecific, aristocratic disgust of the ordinary people who have to live in it. His appeal to the English people, in a 1951 lecture, to raise their eyes "from the privet hedge to the hills" is not free from condescension, and in his poetry he is often at pains to dissociate himself from what A. Alvarez has called the "post-war Welfare State Englishman: shabby . . . poor . . . underfed, underpaid, overtaxed, hopeless." One can see in Betjeman's descriptions of working-class and lower-middle-class people the influence of T. S. Eliot's *The Waste Land* (1922).

Both critics and devotees of Betjeman would find some truth in Philip Larkin's descriptions of him as one who is "insular and regressive, against the dominant trends of today"; one who proclaims "a benevolent class system the best of all political worlds." Although Larkin writes partly in approval, others have been more critical, and Betjeman has, in his journalism and his poetry alike, defended himself against criticism of this kind. He has declared his attitude to modernity as one of reluctant acceptance ("Dear old, bloody old England / Of telegraph poles and tin"), while his deepened religious faith has forced him to recognize his kinship with those whom he would have formerly satirized: "Our Creator is with us yet, / To be worshipped by you and the woman / Of the slacks and the cigarette." His proverbial nausea at contemporary suburban life is at least ambiguous: "I see no harm in trying to describe overbuilt Surrey in verse. But when I do so I am not being satirical but topographical." Affection and mockery are usually combined in Betjeman's finest poems about suburban living.

The 1950s and onward have seen little reduction in Betjeman's output. In the fields of architecture and topography he has written prolifically, establishing his reputation internationally as a historian of English—especially nineteenth-century—architecture. A further collection of poems, with the rather premature title of *A Few Late Chrysanthemums*, appeared in 1954 and reinforced growing convic-

John Betjeman, 1955 (BBC Hulton, photo by Kurt Hutton for Picture Post*)*

tions that Betjeman had to be regarded as a serious artist. Four years later appeared the best-selling *Collected Poems*, following a year of regular BBC broadcasts. It was typical of Betjeman's style that *Collected Poems* was introduced not by a fellow poet or by a critic, but by a member of the English aristocracy. (The critic Bernard Bergonzi later described this introduction as "inept and unnecessary.") Since 1958 two more collections of poetry have appeared, *High And Low* (1966) and *A Nip In The Air* (1975), as well as the blank-verse autobiographical poem *Summoned By Bells* (1960), a modest account of the poet's life from first memories until his departure from Oxford in 1928. Since large sections of *Summoned By Bells* merely seemed to repeat—and in a more pedestrian fashion—material already made familiar through the *Collected Poems*, it received only a quiet reception at its publication. But as an account of the growth of a disturbingly self-conscious mind ("Deep, dark and pitiful I saw myself / In my mind's mirror") it sheds light on the introspective qualities of Betjeman's later poetry.

This introspection first became evident in *A Few Late Chysanthemums*. Early readers were struck by its predominant gloominess. The fear of death, always present in Betjeman's work, became a major obsession in poems like "The Cottage Hospital," where the poet pictures his own death: "And say shall I groan in dying / as I twist the sweaty sheet? / Or gasp for breath uncrying / as I feel my senses drown'd?"

Related to these were a number of poems expressing the loss and displacement felt by a generation who have been discarded by the march of "progress." "The Metropolitan Railway" was typical: "Cancer has killed him. Heart is killing her. / The trees are down. An Odeon flashes fire / Where stood their villa by the murmuring fir / When 'they would for their children's good conspire.' " In such poems Betjeman's affinities to Philip Larkin could be discerned. The two poets have admired in each other's writing the properties they hold in common: a traditionalism in form dictated by the need for simple, direct expression; an instinctive conservatism which struggles to accept contemporaneity; and a pervasive spiritual questioning. Betjeman's own tenaciously held Anglicanism was seen to offer

John Betjeman wearing Henry James's morning clothes (photo by Hans Beacham)

little to ameliorate the deep pessimism that characterizes *A Few Late Chrysanthemums*. In an important article, "John Betjeman Replies," which appeared in the *Spectator* (October 1954), Betjeman accounted for the pervasive gloominess of this volume of poems. Speaking first of his earlier verse, he admitted that "in those days my purest pleasure was the exploration of suburbs and provincial towns, and my impurest pleasure the pursuit of the brawny athletic girl," and went on to add that "fear of death (a manifestation of the lack of faith I deeply desire) remorse and a sense of man's short time on earth and an impatience with so-called 'progress' did inform many of the poems in my latest volume." He then described quite candidly the inadequacy of his religious faith: "the only practical way to face the dreaded lonely journey into Eternity seems to me the Christian one. I therefore try to believe that Christ was God, made man and gives Eternal Life, and that I may be confirmed in this belief by the sacraments and by prayer." Betjeman is a Christian because he has no choice, finding faith more easy to wear in public (in 1952 he was appointed governor of the Oxford Anglican Study Centre, Pusey House) than in private, and easiest to accept in its outward forms: "Eternity Contained In Time and coloured glass." Betjeman's later poetry has only reiterated this struggle to believe.

How is Betjeman's achievement to be judged? Despite his immense popular following and the scholarly respect paid to his prose writings, Betjeman's poetic stature has remained for a long time in doubt. The personality of the man looms so large (we are told, for instance, that he likes to order champagne by the tankards; that he owns, and wears, clothing that once belonged to Henry James) that criticism of his poetry has always been partisan or of a limited and ad hoc nature. Although his work has been praised at different times by writers as diverse as Edmund Wilson and W. H. Auden (who dedicated *The Age of Anxiety* to Betjeman), most critics would concur that he is a poet of considerable importance who has yet narrowly failed to reach the front rank of modern English poetry.

To this failure is attributed a number of reasons, one of them being the limitations of his peculiarly English sensibility. In 1947 Philip Larkin felt forced to write, almost apologetically, that "His poetry, with its wealth of local allusion and local sentiment, its high-pitched titter, does shut a door in the face of American or European visitors," adding that it is a "Special, English thing."

The more serious consequence of such insularity is reflected in the frequent criticism that

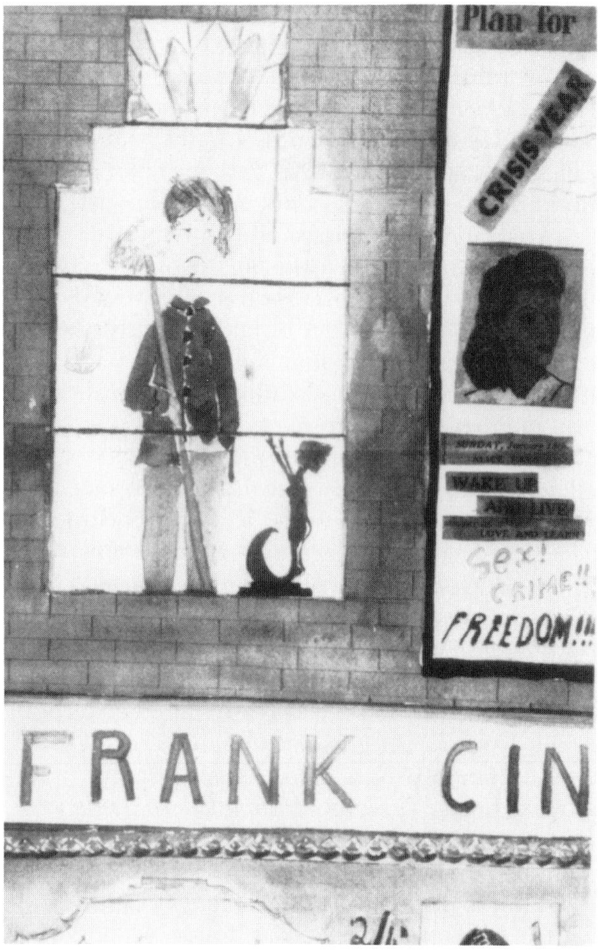

Crisis Year, *watercolor by Betjeman*

Betjeman's poetic sympathy is either restricted to the experience of the class to which he belongs, or is exclusively personal. Certainly, it is true of his later poems about death that they are usually expressions of Betjeman's fear of his own death, or the deaths of close friends, and that they lack any universal application, just as his poems on the loss of innocence refer exclusively to John Betjeman's loss of innocence.

Again, his poetic response to World War II was also of this wholly personal nature: the elegies he wrote to friends killed in war are quite untroubled by the wider moral problems most poets encountered in trying to frame a response to an evil whose enormity disabled poetry's attempt to be sincere. John Press wrote in 1974 that Betjeman "does not, for all his variety and keenness of social observation, give us a powerful and comprehensive vision of society, or a sustained argument about the nature of man," a sentiment which has been echoed by Bernard Bergonzi, who distrusts the unintellectual temper of Betjeman's writing: "One can only regret the association of so much cleverness with so little real intelligence." Bergonzi has also criticized the sentimentality of Betjeman's religious faith (as he expresses it in his poetry) and his inability to defend it from any clear intellectual position. Indeed, Betjeman's poetry has often been deliberately unintellectual, and he has differed from most modern poets by eschewing doctrine, adopting no aesthetic, joining no movement, and making no excessive claims for the importance of his art. But it would be incorrect to conceive of him as one who has created for himself a large popular audience at the expense of a poetry which fails to engage life at its deepest level. W. H. Auden argued that we should not associate Betjeman's frequent lack of earnestness with triviality. It *could* be said of his poems about the sea that their theme of human impermanence measured against the vastness and endurability of nature is only tentatively suggested before Betjeman

Sir John Betjeman, 1971 (BBC Hulton)

switches into a lighter mood. But it may be that his unwillingness to explore such ideas is deliberate, and that his humor provides a necessary bulwark against "a nature already prone to bouts of depression," and thus against what might be the natural conclusion to such poetic explorations.

More sophisticated biographical criticism, such as Press's, has gone on to suggest that the topographical accuracy and precision of period detail evident in Betjeman's poetry is born of this same need to allay restlessness and to stabilize an excessively gloomy imagination. In this need he has been compared to Tennyson, whose influence on Betjeman's poetry is considerable. Future attempts to evaluate Betjeman's importance as a writer are likely to find such psychologically oriented approaches among the most rewarding. Betjeman's position within the mainstream of English poetry yet remains to be ascertained, though it will be related to the value placed on the reaction against modernism. Since his important self-explanatory article in 1954 Betjeman has offered few further insights into himself. His personal life has become a mystery even as his public esteem has led him to be regarded as much a part of English heritage as that which he defends in his poetry and prose.

Recordings:

The Poems of John Betjeman: The Golden Treasury of John Betjeman, Spoken Arts 710, 819, Volumes 1 and 2;

Summoned By Bells, Argo PLP 1069.

Other:

Devon: Shell Guide, edited by Betjeman (London: Architectural Press, 1936);

Shropshire: A Shell Guide, edited by Betjeman and John Piper (London: Faber & Faber, 1951);

Collins' Guide to English Parish Churches, edited, with an introduction, by Betjeman (London: Collins, 1958); republished as *An American's Guide to English Parish Churches* (New York: McDowell, 1959);

A Hundred Sonnets by Charles Tennyson Turner, selected, with an introduction, by Betjeman and Sir Charles Tennyson (London: Hart-Davis, 1960);

Cornwall: A Shell Guide, edited by Betjeman (London: Faber & Faber, 1964);

Victorian And Edwardian London from Old Photographs, edited, with introduction and commentaries, by Betjeman (London: Batsford, 1969);

Victorian And Edwardian Oxford from Old Photographs, edited by Betjeman and David Vaisey (London: Batsford, 1971);

Victorian And Edwardian Brighton from Old Photographs, edited by Betjeman and J. S. Grey (London: Batsford, 1972).

Periodical Publications:

"Lord Mount Prospect," *London Mercury*, 21 (December 1929): 113-121;

"The Death of Modernism," *Architectural Review*, 70 (December 1931): 161;

"Victorian Architecture," *World Review*, new series 23 (January 1951): 46-52;

"John Betjeman Replies," *Spectator*, 193 (8 October 1954): 441;

"City and Suburban," *Spectator*, 193 (15 October 1954) - 200 (10 January 1958);

"A Century of English Architecture," *Spectator*, 209 (24 August 1962): 252-254;

"A Tribute to Wystan Auden," in "Five," by Robert Lowell and others, *Shenandoah*, 18 (Winter 1967): 45-57.

Bibliography:

Margaret L. Stapleton, *Sir John Betjeman: A Bibliography of Writings By And About Him* (Metuchen, N.J.: Scarecrow Press, 1974).

References:

W. H. Auden, Introduction to *Slick But Not Streamlined* (Garden City: Doubleday, 1947);

Bernard Bergonzi, "Culture and Mr. Betjeman," *Twentieth Century*, 165 (February 1959): 130-137; (May 1959): 520;

Earl of Birkenhead, Introduction to *Collected Poems* (London: Murray, 1958; Boston: Houghton Mifflin, 1959);

C. M. Bowra, *Memories 1898-1939* (Cambridge: Harvard University Press, 1967), pp. 165-172;

Jocelyn Brooke, *Ronald Firbank and John Betjeman* (London: Longmans, Green, 1962);

Tim Devlin, "Sir John Betjeman, the new Poet Laureate," *Times* (London), 11 October 1972, p. 16;

John Hollander, "John Betjeman: Almost Uniquely Qualified," *New York Times*, 11 October 1972, p. 18;

Frank Kermode, "Henry Miller and John Betjeman," in his *Puzzles & Epiphanies* (New York: Chilmark Press, 1962), pp. 140-154;

Philip Larkin, "The Blending of Betjeman," *Spectator*, 205 (2 December 1960): 913;

Larkin, Introduction to *Collected Poems* (Boston:

Houghton Mifflin, 1971);
John Press, *John Betjeman* (Harlow: Longman, 1974);
John Sparrow, "The Poetry of John Betjeman," in his *Independent Essays* (London: Faber & Faber, 1963), pp. 166-179;
Stephen Spender, "Poetry for Poetry's Sake and Poetry beyond Poetry," *Horizon* (London), 13 April 1946, pp. 221-238;
Derek Stanford, *John Betjeman: A Study* (London: Spearman, 1961);
John Wain, "Four Observer Pieces: John Betjeman," in his *Essays On Literature And Ideas* (London: Macmillan, 1963; New York: St. Martin's, 1963), pp. 168-171.

Papers:
The library of the University of Victoria, British Columbia, has the major collection of Betjeman's papers.

Edmund Blunden

(1 November 1896-20 January 1974)

Vincent B. Sherry, Jr.
Villanova University

(BBC Hulton)

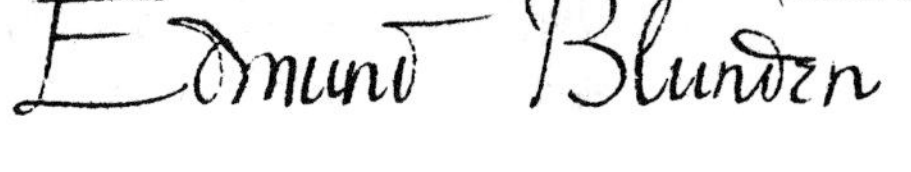

SELECTED BOOKS: *Poems, 1913 and 1914* (Horsham: Price, 1914);
The Barn (Uckfield: Privately printed, 1916); bound with [Three Poems] as *The Harbingers* (1916);
[Three Poems] (Uckfield: Privately printed, 1916); bound with *The Barn* as *The Harbingers* (1916);
The Harbingers (Uckfield: Privately printed, 1916);
Pastorals: A Book of Verses (London: Macdonald, 1916);
The Waggoner, and Other Poems (London: Sidgwick & Jackson, 1920; New York: Knopf, 1920);
The Shepherd and Other Poems of Peace and War (London: Cobden-Sanderson, 1922; New York: Knopf, 1922);
The Bonadventure: A Random Journal of an Atlantic Holiday (London: Cobden-Sanderson, 1922; New York: Putnam's, 1923);
Christ's Hospital: A Retrospect (London: Christophers, 1923);
Masks of Time (London: Beaumont, 1925);
English Poems (London: Cobden-Sanderson, 1926; New York: Knopf, 1926);
Lectures in English Literature (Tokyo: Kodokwan, 1927);
Retreat (London: Cobden-Sanderson, 1928; Garden City: Doubleday, Doran, 1928);
Undertones of War (London: Cobden-Sanderson, 1928; Garden City: Doubleday, Doran, 1929; revised edition, London: Cobden-Sanderson, 1930);
Nature in English Literature, Hogarth Lectures in Literature, 9 (London: Hogarth Press, 1929;

New York: Harcourt, Brace, 1929);
Near and Far (London: Cobden-Sanderson, 1929; New York: Harper, 1930);
Leigh Hunt: A Biography (London: Cobden-Sanderson, 1930); republished as *Leigh Hunt and His Circle* (New York: Harper, 1930);
The Poems of Edmund Blunden (London: Cobden-Sanderson, 1930; New York: Harper, 1932);
Votive Tablets: Studies Chiefly Appreciative of English Authors and Books (London: Cobden-Sanderson, 1931; New York: Harper, 1932);
The Face of England in a Series of Occasional Sketches (London & New York: Longmans, Green, 1932);
Halfway House (London: Cobden-Sanderson, 1932; New York: Macmillan, 1933);
We'll Shift Our Ground; or, Two on a Tour, by Blunden and Sylvia Norman (London: Cobden-Sanderson, 1933);
Charles Lamb and His Contemporaries (Cambridge: Cambridge University Press, 1933; New York: Macmillan, 1933);
The Mind's Eye (London: Cape, 1934);
Choice or Chance (London: Cobden-Sanderson, 1934);
Keats's Publisher: A Memoir of John Taylor (1781-1864) (London: Cape, 1936);
An Elegy and Other Poems (London: Cobden-Sanderson, 1937);
On Several Occasions (London: Corvinus, 1939);
Poems 1930-1940 (London: Macmillan, 1940; New York: Macmillan, 1941);
Thomas Hardy (London: Macmillan, 1941; New York: Macmillan, 1942);
Cricket Country (London: Collins, 1944);
Shells by a Stream (London: Macmillan, 1944; New York: Macmillan, 1945);
Shelley: A Life Story (London: Collins, 1946; New York: Viking, 1947);
Shakespeare to Hardy (Tokyo: Kenkyusha, 1948);
After the Bombing and Other Short Poems (London: Macmillan, 1949; New York: Macmillan, 1949);
Addresses on General Subjects Connected with English Literature (Tokyo: Kenkyusha, 1949);
Sons of Light: Lectures on English Writers (Hosei: Hosei University Press, 1949);
Poetry and Science and Other Lectures (Osaka: Osaka Kyoiku Tosho, 1949);
Influential Books (Tokyo: Hokuseido Press, 1950);
Edmund Blunden: A Selection of His Poetry and Prose, edited by Kenneth Hopkins (London: Hart-Davis, 1950; New York: Horizon, 1951);
Chaucer to "B.V." (Tokyo: Kenkyusha, 1950);
Essayists of the Romantic Period, edited by Ichiro Nishizaki (Tokyo: Rodokwan Press, 1952);
Poems of Many Years (London: Collins, 1957);
A Hong Kong House: Poems 1951-1961 (London: Collins, 1962);
Eleven Poems (Cambridge: Golden Head, 1965).

The controversy over Edmund Blunden's appointment as Professor of Poetry at Oxford in 1966 continued the critical debate waged through his entire poetic career. Hailed as a master of stanzaic and prosodic art, praised for reinstating a traditional formal elegance in verse, Blunden was also labeled a slave of dead conventions, charged with abandoning the ambitions of literary modernism. Blunden was doubtless a "silver" and "occasional" poet. Indeed, his skill with the elegant occasional piece might have gained him the laureateship far more easily than the Oxford professorship, but years of teaching in the Orient had removed him from national fame. Blunden can now be regarded as a major poetic talent, but it is commonly agreed that he failed to achieve his full potential, probably because he failed to experiment in the spirit of his age.

Edmund Charles Blunden was born in London but grew up in the village of Yalding, Kent. His parents, both of whom were schoolteachers, helped to shape the boy's studious temperament. He won a scholarship to Christ's Hospital, London, where he excelled in Latin and won the senior classics scholarship to Queen's College, Oxford. But in 1915 he withdrew from university to join the army. He served as a lieutenant with the Royal Sussex Regiment in France and Belgium from 1916 to 1918, winning the Military Cross as an Intelligence and Field Works officer. He was also nominated for a captaincy, but was refused on account of his age; the rejection was appropriate, he might later admit ruefully, since in 1917 he was "still too young to know" war's "depth of ironic cruelty." Gas attacks increasingly aggravated his asthma, and he was finally evacuated in March 1918. Shortly after returning to England, he married Mary Davies and attempted for a while to resume his studies at Oxford. But he left college in 1919, feeling separated from other students by his war experience. Lady Ottoline Morrell introduced him into her circle at Garsington Manor, where he met John Middleton Murry, Katherine Mansfield, Desmond MacCarthy, and Aldous Huxley. The connection with Murry developed into a position as subeditor and regular contributor for the *Athenaeum* in 1920, when he began to move freely in London literary society.

Edmund Blunden (seated at right) with a group of his fellow officers, circa 1917 (Imperial War Museum)

Blunden's affinity with the prewar Georgian poets had begun with his childhood in Kent. His descriptions of nature and rural culture were precise, keenly objective. To order his rural detail he required a good measure of formal definition. His metrical art was highly disciplined. Rarely experimenting with free verse, he found models outside stanzaic forms in the tightly controlled verse paragraphs of eighteenth-century pastoral meditations. But his lyric skills worked to evoke external reality better than mental process. Likewise, the poems may seem deficient in intellectual interest. For the most part, his rural subjects prescribe and limit his ideas: the continuity and longevity of rural traditions, time, and the cycles of the seasons.

Soon after Blunden arrived in London in 1920, Sidgwick and Jackson published his first major volume of poetry, *The Waggoner, and Other Poems*, which included selected early verse from three privately printed chapbooks. His pictures of country people evoke their personalities through the objective details of their culture. Likewise, he strives to free his natural topics from his own subjectivity. In the last line of "The Pike," for example, he shifts perspective from within to above the pond, in one stroke projecting the distance and difference of the world beneath the surface: "And the miller that opens the hatch stands amazed at the whirl in the water." But the two longest poems—"The Silver Bird of Herndyke Mill" and "The Barn"—are poetic fables, whose enchantments contrast with his typically objective notation. An interest in detail alone could not sustain his more ambitious longer poems; already his objective poetic was displaying its limitations.

But the limitations appeared as strengths to early reviewers. Annabel Williams-Ellis accepted Blunden as "one of those poets who succeed largely by reason of their willingness to limit their province." "Better short than long," echoed J. C. Squire, but he proclaimed that Blunden was "already consciously in possession of a field which he knows and loves and about which nobody else is writing so surely as he." This conservative poet, "in the main English tradition," drew fire only for his experiments. Robert Bridges could not fully approve the use of dialectal words, and Squire disliked the verbal inventiveness, the "passion for exact, if need be coined, epithets," which produced "grotesque words."

Blunden maintained his editorial position when the *Athenaeum* merged with the *Nation* under H. W. Massingham in 1921. Still ailing as a result of the war, he sailed to South America later in the same year. He recorded the journey in his first prose book, *The Bonadventure: A Random Journal of an Atlantic Holiday* (1922). He also finished writing and arranging the poems for *The Shepherd and Other Poems of Peace and War* (1922), published by Cobden-Sanderson when he returned to England. A final group of war poems, arranged as a sequence, made an important addition to the familiar nature verse. J. C. Squire perceived the ambitious structure of the book, finding the paradox of a "country parish" and an "inimical war" to make for a volume "very much more impressive" and "even better than *The Waggoner*." But Squire also recognized that the poems relied too much on detail, too little on thought. For a poet whose nature could not wear the "garment of the eternal," he had to qualify his praise: "a universal poet he may never be." But Edmund Gosse expressed "no doubt" that Blunden would "rise much further yet," while H. W. Massingham saw his protégé "fast arriving at a recognized place in English poetry, to attain eventually, it may be, a place among its classics."

Edmund Blunden, captain of the authors' cricket team, watching their match against members of the National Book League, 30 June 1951 (BBC Hulton, photo by Bert Hardy for Picture Post*)*

In 1924, Blunden went as Professor of English to the Imperial University at Tokyo, where he would remain until 1927. To his teaching, says Alec M. Hardie, Blunden "brought a sympathy and toleration that allowed him to make friends quickly with a people shy and easily rebuffed; they found his sincerity easy to trust." The university environment was equally congenial to him. The Japanese reverence for English traditions, "the passion for our literature . . . our imaginative inheritance," appealed naturally to his own traditional literary temperament. His wife had not accompanied him to Japan due to a strain in their relationship, and Blunden developed a liaison with a Japanese teacher of English. Aki Hayashi, his "Dearest Autumn," evidently lessened the loneliness, and he was able to write several important volumes while in Japan.

The pieces in *English Poems* (1926) fall under four headings: "Village," "Field," "Mind," and "Spirit." The "Mind" and "Spirit" poems have as their occasions the same rural scenes as the "Village" and "Field" poems, and as such promise an intellectual content and coherence for the rural subjects. The eighteenth-century graveyard meditation, a disquisition on nature and death in the country churchyard, is a genre especially suited to his intellectual purposes. Time is the motif he deals with most often, variously in the cyclical form of the seasons, the linear form of human life, and the Keatsian form of the infinite moment of art. The reviewer E. G. Twitchett praised the time poems in the volume. He admired especially the moments of aesthetic "standstill," for example the Keatsian "Masks of Time," where, as the lark sang, "the woods as sharp and carved as Parthenon / Stood before charmed eyes forever."

Masks of Time (1925), published shortly before *English Poems*, contained the Keatsian piece as its title poem. The volume also included a series of war poems. Blunden continued to expand this series while writing his prose memoir *Undertones of War* (1928), which he completed in Tokyo, but it was not published until after his return to England in the autumn of 1927. He then collected the war verse in a "Supplement of Poetical Interpretations and Variations" for the prose book.

The "undertones" of war are the quiet internal meanings of the experience. Blunden demonstrates an admirable capacity for paradox as he meditates on his conflicting emotions: a public schoolboy's loyal nationalism, a young infantry officer's disenchantment, a disenchantment that builds like an anthem through the book. Irony likewise structures the best poems in the supplement. He balances two opposing images of man, who can "at once be animal and angel," in a paradox of redemption: the suffering body, that "poor unpitied Caliban, / Parches and sweats and grunts to win the name of Man." Blunden's ability to control his suffering through such positive irony won critical praise. F. J. Harvey Darton found him "more master of himself than any other of the young men who had a like experience. There is even a serenity in his anger." H. W. Tomlinson likewise acclaimed his controlled energy: "This poet's eye is not in a fine frenzy rolling. There is a steely glitter in it." Now in German and Japanese as well as English and American editions, *Undertones of War* has remained a popular success since 1928.

The critical success of *Undertones of War* eclipsed *Retreat* (1928) and *Near and Far* (1929), whose poems, in any case, were inferior to those in *Undertones of War*. The war book had, in fact, taken the best part of Blunden's personal energy. He was tired and disoriented when he returned to England in 1927. Moreover, his marriage had not survived his absence. He withdrew to his home village in Kent, where he resumed work as editor for the *Nation*. Here he also composed *Nature in English*

Edmund Blunden, Miss Laidler, and Michael Martin Harvey at Kensington Art Gallery, 9 April 1953 (BBC Hulton, Evening Standard *Collection)*

Literature (1929), originally delivered in the new Hogarth Lectures in Literature series.

In 1930, Blunden was elected fellow and tutor at Merton College, Oxford. Before leaving Kent, he compiled his first major collection, *The Poems of Edmund Blunden* (1930), a stroke of ambition which F. R. Leavis quickly checked. In the early verse Leavis perceived an interesting tension between the "frank literary quality" and the "homespun texture" of Blunden's detailed rural world, but in the verse of the later 1920s that "peculiar poise . . . proved difficult to maintain." Leavis judged him a poet of failed promise. The strengths of the early poems had become weaknesses, because Blunden had never developed or experimented with them. "A poet serious enough to impose his pastoral world on us," Leavis complained, "could hardly rest in it."

By the time Blunden moved into Oxford in 1931, he had recovered his health at Yalding, and university life, which appealed deeply to him, activated all his energies. "Edmund was constantly at work," recalls a former student, "editing old poets, assisting young poets, preparing papers, writing his own poems and books, reading new novels in proof copies for the Book Society. He was indefatigable and indomitable." Here Blunden researched his studies, *Keats's Publisher: A Memoir of John Taylor (1781-1864)* (1936) and *Thomas Hardy* (1941); he continued to write the essays and "appreciations" collected in *Votive Tablets* (1931) and *The Mind's Eye* (1934). He also collaborated with Sylvia Norman, whom he married in 1933 and later divorced, in his single attempt at a novel: *We'll Shift Our Ground; or, Two on a Tour* (1933).

Blunden remained at Oxford through the 1930s, and the poems of the decade reflect his university circumstances. He acquired a bookish habit of addressing poems to literary, historical, and re-

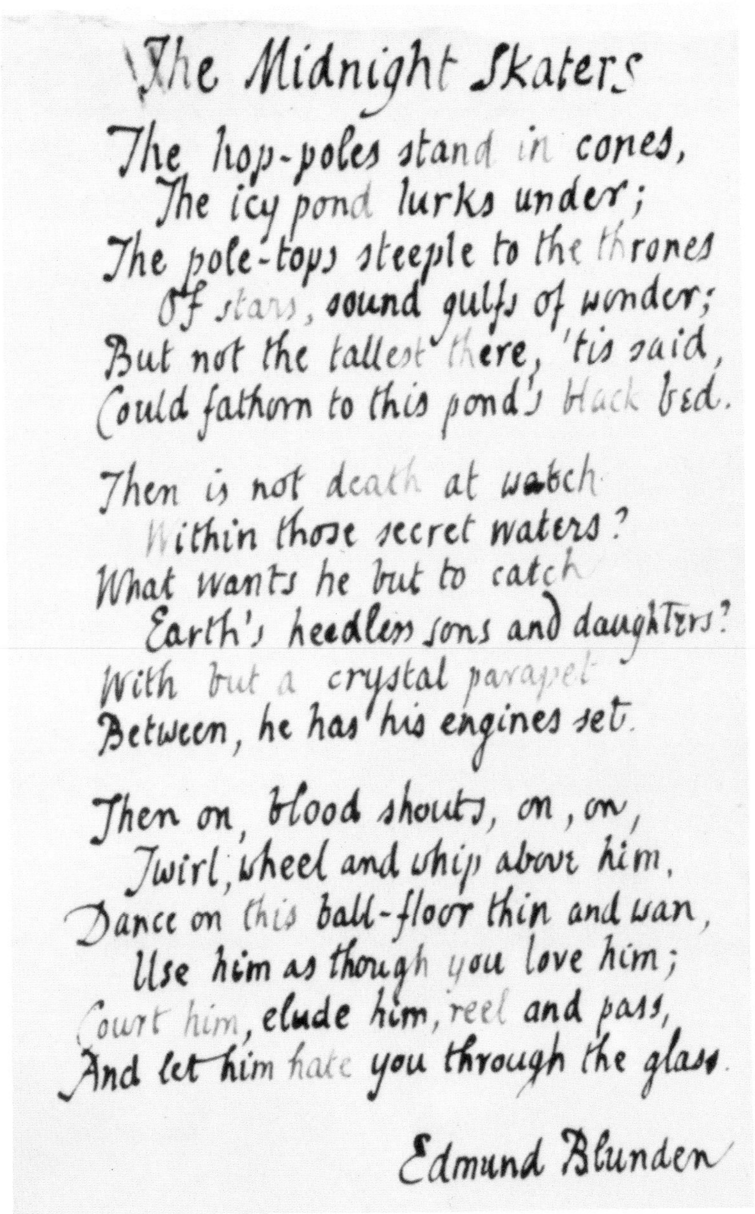
The Midnight Skaters

The hop-poles stand in cones,
The icy pond lurks under;
The pole-tops steeple to the thrones
Of stars, sound gulfs of wonder;
But not the tallest there, 'tis said,
Could fathom to this pond's black bed.

Then is not death at watch
Within those secret waters?
What wants he but to catch
Earth's heedless sons and daughters?
With but a crystal parapet
Between, he has his engines set.

Then on, blood shouts, on, on,
Twirl, wheel and whip above him,
Dance on this ball-floor thin and wan,
Use him as though you love him;
Court him, elude him, reel and pass,
And let him hate you through the glass.

Edmund Blunden

Manuscript for "The Midnight Skaters"

ligious figures; a new donnish wit enlivens the verse; there is also an ambition to be more toughly intelligent. Three poems from *Choice or Chance* (1934) indicate the range of his university style. "An Ominous Victorian," a ballad in rollicking limerick rhythms about an obscure Victorian figure, is pure donnish showmanship. "Reflections" more soberly considers the discrepancies between life and art. "To One Long Dead," written "on reading *Harriet*, a novel by Elizabeth Jenkins, founded on the Penge Murder of 1877," typifies his poems on literary occasions. The first and last pieces of *An Elegy and Other Poems* (1937) have political subjects—a commemoration of George V and a warning about appeasing Hitler—but most poems follow the university style of this decade. Unfortunately, his verse was becoming increasingly occasional, and he could not always disguise its contrivance. *On Several Occasions* (1939) contains many poems as rigged as "And Then": "Inconstancy, too rarely / The theme of verse, a verse to you."

When collected in *Poems 1930-1940* (1940), the verse of the Oxford decade demonstrated not so much Blunden's university wit as his growing reliance on contrived occasions. "After Any Occasion" was inserted as an apology: "See what lovely hours you lost," he admits, "While with a half-triumphant mind you crost / Lath-swords of words on some uncertain matter." Less forthright were the apologies from Blunden's loyal critics, who saw the need now to vindicate an endangered reputation. Against the "young derisionists" who "sneered at his 'nature' poetry," Richard Church strenuously defended its simple occasions: "Blunden has always valued so passionately the 'tiny circumstances' of the world, and found in them a joy so abundant that it overflows his heart and saturates every phrase." Blunden's detailed precision and metrical skills continued to draw high praise. But for L. Aaronson, Blunden's technical perfections left a "deadly correct dullness," while his occasions lacked a "real power to awaken interest, they lacked dynamism." Most important, these occasional poems measured a growing lack of personal involvement in Blunden's verse, an absence which Aaronson perceived as the clue to the poet's "decline": "Mr. Blunden seems to have reversed the usual current of a poet's growth; his later verse belongs less and less to himself—and therefore less and less to us. He seems to have cut himself off from the living flow and becomes a ghost in his poetry."

After the outbreak of World War II, Blunden served as instructor in the University Senior Training Corps at Oxford, where he remained until 1943. He then joined the staff of the *Times Literary Supplement* in London, where he continued and completed work on his most important literary biography, *Shelley: A Life Story* (1946). With his third wife, Claire Margaret Poynting (whom he married in 1945), he returned in 1948 to Japan, where they remained until 1950, while he served as a member of the United Kingdom Liaison Commission. He regarded himself as a cultural ambassador, his mission a kind of moral embassy. In two years he delivered over two hundred lectures on various literary and cultural topics. In 1950 he was elected (with

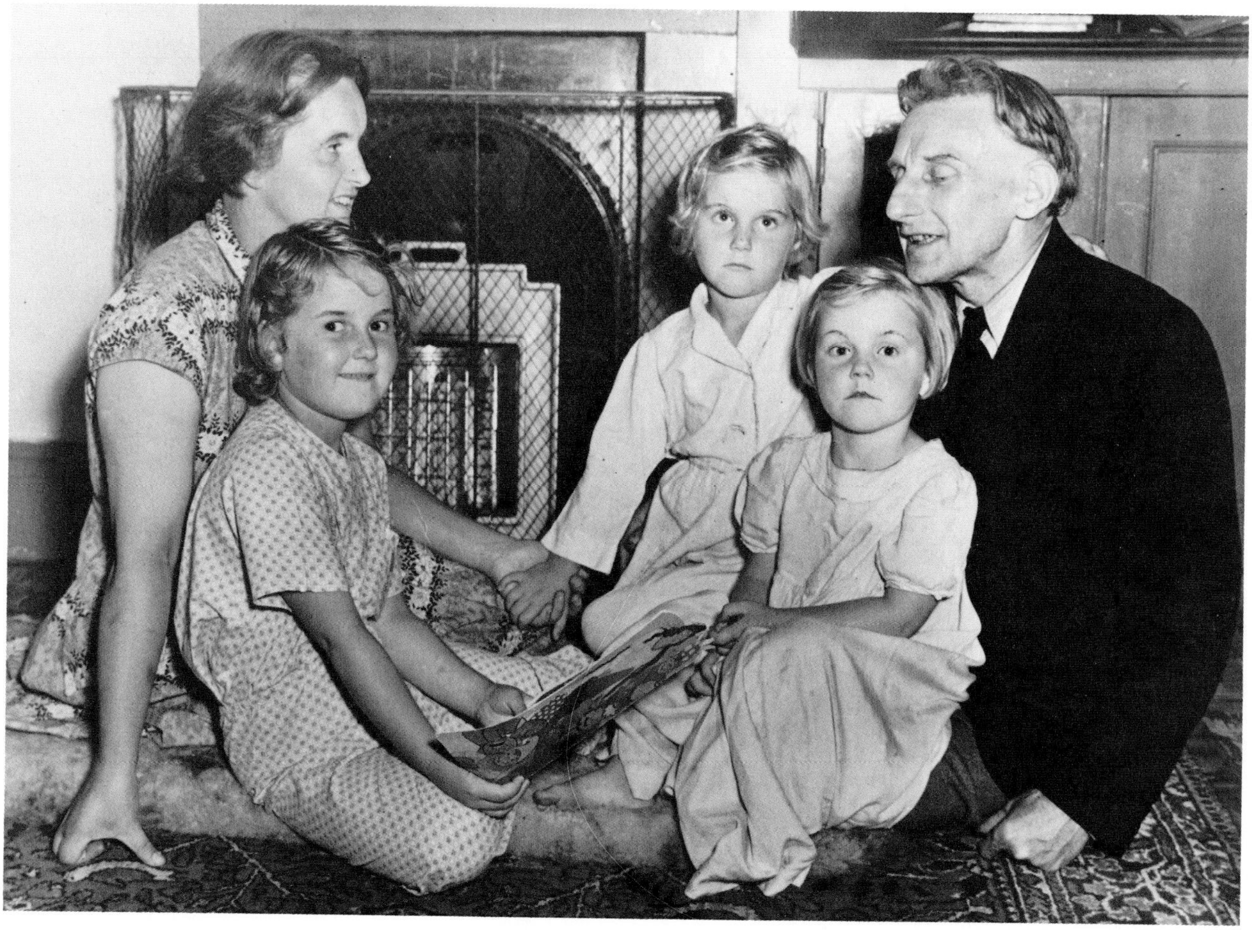

Claire and Edmund Blunden with their children, Margaret, Lucy, and Frances, in August 1953, just before they sailed for Hong Kong (BBC Hulton)

Einstein) an honorary member of the Japan Academy.

Blunden's various commitments limited his poetic output through the 1940s; he produced only two thin volumes of verse: *Shells by a Stream* (1944) and *After the Bombing and Other Short Poems* (1949). The first includes tributes to "older friends"—his poetic tutors and colleagues—in an interesting variety of techniques: an imitation of Hardy's dramatic colloquies, a lofty ode sustained in Coleridge's style, a personal appreciation of Lascelles Abercrombie. The war poems display the same knack for paradox as the verse in *Undertones of War*. "A Prospect of Swans," for example, mixes images of insular English peace and peripheral global war. The best poems of *After the Bombing* develop the same paradox. Just as peace has followed war, beauty might emerge from squalor: "The slough and swamp of nature yields this wild / Royal extravagance." The same redemptive spirit is represented, in a larger sense, by the contents of the volume: a reinstatement of Blunden's characteristic subjects, the peaceful world of traditional English rural culture.

Blunden's brand of tradition was praised highly by Hugh l'Anson Fausset in his important essay "Edmund Blunden's Later Poetry." Unlike the literary modernists, who were neurotically "using fragments of the past . . . in a despairing attempt to shore the ruins of the present," Blunden, who was "in the true tradition" of English rural culture, drew strength naturally from "the mellow grace of the past." His tradition provided a continuity, a stability synonymous with "the timeless quality of poetry" itself.

In 1950, Blunden resumed work at the London office of the *Times Literary Supplement*. But in 1953 he returned to the East as Professor of English at the University of Hong Kong. Cut off from English literary society, he wrote far fewer poems. For his major collection, *Poems of Many Years* (1957), he added a small number of new pieces. Many of these are retrospective; a chief concern is the passage of time; along the same lines, he includes several elegies and historical meditations.

A reviewer of Blunden's last chapbook, *Eleven Poems* (1965), proposed that, despite the "slight and occasional" nature of his later poetry, Blunden's "very best work" was comparable with that of Auden, Graves, and Hardy. Like them, to be sure, he was a skillful practitioner in traditional forms. But, unlike the major poets, he never restored these poetic forms, never renewed them through serious intellectual thought; he remained largely a poet of external things. His best poems paradoxically prescribe both their excellence and their limitation: these are occasions of rare elegance, but mere occasions. Blunden's stature remains debatable, a point demonstrated all too clearly in 1966 by the controversy over his appointment to the poetry chair at Oxford.

Symbolic, unfortunately, of Blunden's tenuous position at Oxford, ill health forced him to resign the chair in 1968. He subsequently limited himself to editorial work, and died on 20 January 1974.

Other:

John Clare, *Poems Chiefly from Manuscript*, edited by Blunden and Alan Porter (London: Cobden-Sanderson, 1920; New York: Putnam's, 1921);

Clare, *Madrigals and Chronicles*, edited, with a preface and commentary, by Blunden (London: Beaumont, 1924);

Shelley and Keats as They Struck Their Contemporaries, edited by Blunden (London: Beaumont, 1925);

The Autobiography of Leigh Hunt, introduction by Blunden (Oxford: Oxford University Press, 1928);

The Poems of Wilfred Owen, edited, with a memoir, by Blunden (London: Chatto & Windus, 1931; New York: Viking, 1931);

Charles Lamb: His Life Recorded by His Contemporaries, compiled, with a preface, by Blunden (London: Hogarth Press, 1934).

Interviews:

Ichiro Nishizaki, Interview with Blunden, *Youth's Companion*, 7 (July 1949): 28-32;

Nishizaki, "On Life and Reading," *Study of English*, 52 (November 1963): 4-9;

Dom Moraes, "A Dream of Violence Among the Spires: Edmund Blunden," *Nova* (London), (May 1966): 128-129, 131;

John Press, Interview with Blunden, in *The Poet Speaks*, edited by Peter Orr (London: Routledge & Kegan Paul, 1966), pp. 33-37.

Bibliography:

Brownlee Jean Kirkpatrick, *A Bibliography of Edmund Blunden*, Soho Bibliographies, 20 (Oxford: Clarendon Press, 1979).

References:

L. Aaronson, "Edmund Blunden," *Nineteenth Century and After*, 129 (June 1941): 580-585;

Francis Barker, "The Poetry of Edmund Blunden," *Nineteenth Century and After*, 109 (January 1931): 115-124;
Bernard Bergonzi, *Heroes' Twilight: a Study of the Literature of the Great War* (London: Constable, 1965), pp. 68-72;
Robert Bridges, *The Dialectal Words in Blunden's Poems* (Oxford: Society for Pure English, 1921);
Richard Church, "Edmund Blunden: Agonist," *Fortnightly Review*, 154 (October 1940): 377-384;
F. J. Harvey Darton, *From Surtees to Sassoon: Some English Contrasts 1838-1928* (London: Morley & Kennerley, 1931), pp. 153-160;
Hugh l'Anson Fausset, "Edmund Blunden's Later Poetry," in his *Poets and Pundits* (New Haven: Yale University Press, 1947), pp. 192-201;
Paul Fussell, *The Great War and Modern Memory* (New York: Oxford University Press, 1975);
Alec M. Hardie, *Edmund Blunden*, Writers and Their Work, 94 (1958; revised edition, London: Longmans, Green, 1971);
John H. Johnston, *English Poetry of the First World War* (London: Oxford University Press, 1964; Princeton: Princeton University Press, 1964), pp. 113-154;
F. R. Leavis, *New Bearings in English Poetry* (1932; enlarged edition, London: Chatto & Windus, 1950), pp. 65-68;
Charles Morgan, "Edmund Blunden's 'Thomasine,'" in his *Reflections in a Mirror: Second Series* (London: Macmillan, 1946), pp. 131-140;
J. C. Squire, "Mr. Edmund Blunden," in his *Essays on Poetry* (1923; reprinted, Freeport, N.Y.: Books for Libraries, 1967), pp. 171-181;
Michael Thorpe, *The Poetry of Edmund Blunden* (Kent: Bridge Books, 1971);
E. G. Twitchett, "The Poetry of Edmund Blunden," *London Mercury*, 14 (October 1926): 621-631;
Charles Williams, "Edmund Blunden," in his *Poetry at Present* (Oxford: Clarendon Press, 1930), pp. 207-216;
Annabel Williams-Ellis, "Edmund Blunden," in her *An Anatomy of Poetry* (Oxford: Blackwell, 1922), pp. 281-283;
Frederick T. Wood, "On the Poetry of Edmund Blunden," *Poetry Review*, 23 (July-August 1932): 255-274.

Papers:
The Humanities Research Center, University of Texas at Austin, has the manuscripts of *Undertones of War*, poems, and letters; the Department of Manuscripts, British Library Reference Division, and the Berg Collection, New York Public Library, have manuscripts of poems.

Ronald Bottrall

(2 September 1906-   )

Terence Diggory
Skidmore College

BOOKS: *The Loosening and Other Poems* (Cambridge: Gordon Fraser / Minority Press, 1931);
Festivals of Fire (London: Faber & Faber, 1934);
The Turning Path (London: Barker, 1939);
Farewell and Welcome (London: Editions Poetry, 1945);
Selected Poems (London: Editions Poetry, 1946);
The Palisades of Fear (London: Editions Poetry, 1949);
Adam Unparadised (London: Verschoyle, 1954);
The Collected Poems of Ronald Bottrall (London: Sidgwick & Jackson, 1961);
Rome, Art Centres of the World series (London: World, 1968; Cleveland: World, 1968);
Day and Night (London: London Magazine Editions, 1974);
Poems 1955-1973 (London: Anvil Press Poetry, 1974);
Reflections on the Nile (London: London Magazine Editions, 1980).

Since the appearance of his first volume of verse in 1931, Ronald Bottrall has been identified with the immensely influential school of criticism

Ronald Bottrall

that was establishing itself at Cambridge University during the 1930s. F. R. Leavis, who is now recognized as sharing with I. A. Richards the leadership of that school, singled out Bottrall as the poet to watch for confirmation of the course that Leavis charted in *New Bearings in English Poetry* (1932). In the pages of the journal *Scrutiny*, founded the same year, Leavis and his colleagues watched Bottrall all too closely, with the result that, in Bottrall's case at least, a flourishing school of criticism offered scant nourishment for a poet.

The man who was to achieve such early notoriety through Leavis's boosting came from the obscurity of the Cornish mining town of Camborne, where he was born Francis James Ronald Bottrall, the only child of working-class parents, Francis John and Clara Jane Rowe Bottrall. Though his poems frequently recall the Cornish coast with affection, Bottrall's initial literary impulses seemed to have formed out of a desire to escape from a society that was economically depressed, after the exhaustion of the tin mines at the end of World War I, and emotionally restrictive. The restriction was enforced at home by Bottrall's father, who was a lay preacher in the Methodist church. At mealtimes, Bottrall baited his father by countering citations from scripture with references to H. G. Wells. Alone in bed, Bottrall found an outlet for adolescent sexuality through reading about Renaissance Italy and peopling an imaginary Italian landscape with cavorting nymphs and satyrs.

If emotionally frustrating, the environment of Bottrall's childhood home did not lack encouragement for the intellect. Bottrall's father deeply regretted having to leave school at the age of fourteen. He clung to the knowledge of Greek, Latin, and French that he had acquired by that time and stocked his study not only with the Bible and Cruden's concordance but also with works by Longfellow and Emerson. Thus, when Bottrall went up to Pembroke College, Cambridge, on a scholarship in 1925, he was fulfilling not only his own desire for escape but his father's desire for education.

Bottrall's desire to write poetry, which had emerged with disappointing results during his years at Redruth County School, was deliberately kept in check while he was a student at Cambridge. He claims to have written no verse as an undergraduate, with the exception of a brief poem that was published in the anthology *Cambridge Poetry 1929*, along with six poems by Bottrall's friend and fellow student William Empson. Bottrall's years at Cambridge were a time of great ferment in English literary studies, which were just gaining recognition as a legitimate academic discipline. English was still administered jointly with modern languages, a circumstance well suited to Bottrall's linguistic talents. Men like I. A. Richards and E. M. W. Tillyard were busy inventing an English syllabus that would allow candidates for the B.A., for the first time, to sit for the final honors examination (the Tripos) solely in the modern period (since Chaucer). More informally, F. R. Leavis was holding Friday "At Homes" at which he recruited the corps of young critics who became regular contributors to *Scrutiny*. Amid all the excitement Bottrall performed with brilliance, becoming one of five students to receive top honors (first class with distinction) in the new part two (modern) of the English Tripos in 1929.

After receiving his B.A. from Cambridge, Bottrall began a series of foreign sojourns that have provided the imagery for poems throughout his career. During a vacation from Cambridge he had already traveled to the Italy of his adolescent dreams, where he was disillusioned by an unhappy love affair that he later recorded in the poem "Love in Umbria" (*Poems 1955-1973*). Either this or another affair, together with the experience of living alone in a strange country, precipitated his first serious attempts to write poetry while he was serving as lecturer in English at the University of Helsinki from 1929 to 1931. To help him give shape to his experience, Bottrall discovered a poetic model through the advice of F. R. Leavis. Bottrall had already read Leavis's hero, T. S. Eliot, but Eliot's example did not immediately stimulate Bottrall as a writer. Now Leavis sent Bottrall Eliot's selection of the poems of Ezra Pound (1928), with the recommendation that Bottrall pay particular attention to Pound's sequence *Hugh Selwyn Mauberley*. "As I read 'Mauberley,' " Bottrall later recalled, "and I saw, or thought I saw, how contemporary verse should be written, I worked through Pound's poetry and I tried to discover how he had arrived at the perfection of 'Mauberley.' "

The results of Bottrall's study are clearly evident in *The Loosening and Other Poems* (1931), published appropriately from what had already become Bottrall's cultural base, Cambridge. One of the poems in the volume, "The Thyrsus Retipped," from which Leavis took part of the epigraph to *New Bearings in English Poetry*, alludes to a period of "understudying" Joyce and Valéry but assigns that period to a "bewildered" youth who must be buried, as Pound buried his fin de siècle persona in *Hugh Selwyn Mauberley*. "The Thyrsus Retipped" forms part of a sequence entitled "Arion Anadyomenos," which acknowledges a debt to *Hugh Selwyn Mauberley* in its title, recalling Pound's Venus Anadyomene, and in its structure, which arranges several separate poems into a single long poem. Like Pound, also, Bottrall deftly arranges his lines to end in thoughtful, ironic pauses, frequently clinched by multisyllable rhymes made possible by ultrasophisticated diction. Pound's model for this technique, Théophile Gautier, was shared by Eliot, whose influence is also apparent in Bottrall's sequence in, for instance, the echoes of Eliot's "A Cooking Egg" in "Salute To Them That Know": "We do not lack our testament and creed, / We have our umbrellas and our A.B.C.'s."

Furnished with such equipment, Bottrall was well prepared to write the social satire which constituted a major poetic mode during the 1930s. For Leavis, Bottrall was closer to Eliot than Pound in his depiction of "a world in which the traditions are bankrupt, the cultures uprooted and withering, and the advance of civilization seems to mean death to distinction of spirit and fineness of living." Such a vision was a prerequisite for any contemporary poet who wanted to be taken seriously, as far as Leavis was concerned, but Bottrall's confidence in confronting this vision seemed to take him beyond either Pound or Eliot. As Leavis concluded in *New Bearings in English Poetry*, "Bottrall's work clinches felicitously the argument of this book, and sanctions high hopes for the future," because Bottrall himself maintained some hope. The evidence lies in the "positive energy" generated by Bottrall's impressive control of rhythm—a feature to which Leavis directed special attention—but also in the movement of imagery in his longer poems. Both "Arion Anadyomenos" and "The Loosening," a sequence less Poundian in structure than later, move toward a vision of love that, like the vision of sympathy at the end of *The Waste Land*, might bind together the fragments of the modern world but that, unlike the vision of sympathy in *The Waste Land*, is unmistakably regarded as a hope for the future, rather than a lost opportunity of the past.

Both of Bottrall's sequences connect their hope to the image of the sea, and "The Loosening" identifies the sea as that which Bottrall had known as a boy: "Not for nothing was I born / Within earshot of that iron sea." Bottrall's ambivalence toward Cornwall, reflected also in the depiction of landscape in "Cornish Dawn," lends a complexity to his use of sea imagery that persisted throughout his career (see "Cornish Sea" in *Poems 1955-1973*). In *The Loosening and Other Poems*, the sea represents inexhaustible power. As the "iron sea," its power can be destructive, but its destruction is part of creation, part of that process invoked in the title poem by the self, who, in the light of Eliot and the Cambridge anthropologists, sees himself as the hanged god whose sacrifice is necessary for life's renewal. Throughout this volume Bottrall understands life in terms of patterns of renewal, the flux of the sea's tides. Death as the opposite of life is a fixity associated not with the Cornwall of Bottrall's past but with the Finland of his recent exile, represented in "the frozen sea" of the arctic north ("A December Harbour in Exile") or in the mechanical motion of parading Finnish soldiers, "static against mobility of ideas" ("Miles Ingloriosus").

The World War I veteran portrayed in "Miles Ingloriosus" deplores the transformation of a Finland threatened by skyscrapers and automobiles, in short, the Americanization of a Finland "Run by Chicago time." If Cornwall were becoming for Bottrall the center of a natural harmony that was elsewhere drowned out by the blaring discords of modern life, America seemed to be the capital of cacophony, an image confirmed by firsthand experience after Bottrall left Finland to spend the years 1931-1933 as a Commonwealth Fund Fellow at Princeton University. His impressions of America as a paradoxical mixture of violence and anesthesia constitute a pattern of imagery that runs throughout his second volume, *Festivals of Fire* (1934), in the title poem as well as in such shorter pieces as "A Corollary (Empire State Building, 102nd Floor)," "Broadway," "The Olympic Games, Los Angeles, 1932," and "Road Accident in Idaho."

Festivals of Fire was published by Faber and Faber, probably at the recommendation of T. S. Eliot, a director of the firm, who in a 1932 interview listed Bottrall as one of the four most important poets of the younger generation, along with W. H. Auden, Stephen Spender, and Louis MacNeice. Within Bottrall's volume, however, the guiding spirit remains Ezra Pound, though in the title poem Bottrall's study of *Hugh Selwyn Mauberley* has been supplemented by the close reading of *A Draft of XXX Cantos* (1930) that Bottrall undertook in preparation for a review-essay published in *Scrutiny* in 1933. The presence of the *Cantos* in the title poem of *Festivals of Fire* somewhat dampened the enthusiasm of F. R. Leavis, who thought that Pound had written nothing worth reading since *Hugh Selwyn Mauberly* and who now detected in Bottrall's poetry the willful assertiveness that, in Leavis's view, prevented the *Cantos* from developing as poetry.

In reviewing *Festivals of Fire* for *Scrutiny* in 1934, Leavis approached the title poem from a direction that Bottrall had held to be the wrong approach for understanding Pound's *Cantos* and that would seem equally inapplicable, presumably, to work influenced by the *Cantos*. Bottrall's extensive use of the myth of Balder led Leavis to interpret "Festivals of Fire" according to "the anthropological methods of the *Waste Land*" rather than Pound's different method, which Bottrall termed "the method of scenario." In Bottrall's opinion, the *Cantos* remained fragmented because Pound had neglected the demands of his own method, but Bottrall's intention of developing a connected scenario in "Festivals of Fire" is evident in the reference within the poem to the techniques of the Russian filmmaker Sergei Eisenstein:

> Gesture (as in Eisenstein) wipes out
> Gesture, is renewed in the renewal
> Of pattern, furling limits and
> Lineations within a complex switch
> Of reference.

In Pound's *Cantos* and Eisenstein's films, Bottrall had found additional models for the patterns of renewal that *The Loosening and Other Poems* had discovered in the Cornish sea.

Besides poetry and film, the art which plays the greatest role in the structuring of "Festivals of Fire" is one which has always greatly interested Bottrall, the art of music. Each section of Bottrall's poem, as in a piece of music, is marked with indications of dynamics and expression. In this regard, Leavis rightly objected that the poem lacks the rhythmic variety, and hence the progression, promised by the section headings. Given such lack of progression, the promise of a return of power at the poem's conclusion lacks the persuasiveness of similar promises at the end of "Arion Anadyomenos" and "The Loosening," though the curiously mechanistic imagery with which Bottrall portrays power at the end of "Festivals of Fire" makes it doubtful whether this is a power that he hopes to see. Whether or not he intended it as such, *Festivals of Fire* is Bottrall's least optimistic volume.

Leavis excused the shortcomings of *Festivals of Fire* as the consequence of Bottrall's growing ambition, and he remained confident that Bottrall would someday be able to fulfill that ambition. Meanwhile, the list of Bottrall's influential admirers continued to grow. In a letter written in 1934, before the publication of *Festivals of Fire*, Ezra Pound agreed with T. S. Eliot's assessment that Auden and Bottrall were in the forefront of the younger generation. In a belated review of *Festivals of Fire* in 1936, Edith Sitwell, an object of scorn among the *Scrutiny* critics, discovered in Bottrall "the most remarkable technique of any of the younger poets." Acclaim for Bottrall was no longer confined to a small coterie. Publishers of such different status as the Poetry Bookshop and Pelican Books were including his poems in anthologies.

During this period, from 1933 to 1937, Bottrall was removed from English literary centers, heading the department of English at the University of Singapore, but he managed to keep in touch nevertheless. He supplied Edith Sitwell with notes to aid her in interpreting "Festivals of Fire." He corresponded with the editors of *Scrutiny* about L. C. Knights's article on Shakespeare's sonnets. With his wife Margaret Florence Saumarez Smith, an Australian-born, Oxford-educated woman whom he married in 1934, Bottrall arranged a literary luncheon in honor of his Cambridge friend William Empson, who was living not too far away in Japan. (Empson could not face the luncheon after the previous night's tour of Singapore's bars.)

In 1937 Bottrall returned to Europe and spent a year as acting director of the British Institute in Florence. He was in Cambridge in November to deliver a paper to the Cambridge University English Club on "Byron and the Colloquial Tradition in English Poetry," later published in the last issue of T. S. Eliot's journal, the *Criterion*. The colloquialism of Bottrall's verse had been commended as early as the appearance of *The Loosening and Other Poems*, so Bottrall's tracing of a colloquial tradition from Byron back to Pope and Dryden is significant for his implication that he is one of Byron's descendants. When he discusses contemporary poetry, however, he refers not to his own poetry but to that of W. H. Auden, who had just published his "Letter to Lord Byron" in *Letters from Iceland* (1937).

Despite the linking of Auden and Bottrall in the minds of Eliot and Pound, Auden's preeminence as the Poet of the Thirties was by this time taken for granted in most of the British periodicals concerned with contemporary literature. The outstanding exception was *Scrutiny*, where Auden was commonly regarded as a precocious youth whose evident promise was spoiled by his readiness to indulge technical facility for the sake of being fashionable. This view is evident in Bottrall's comments on Auden, but his recognition of Auden's talent is apparent in his willingness to place Auden in a tradition in which he would include himself and in his adaptation of Auden's style in his next volume, *The Turning Path* (1939). Auden's influence can be located in *The Turning Path* in specific types of poems (the set of instructions for a vaguely defined but darkly threatening "mission" offered in the ironic "Preamble to a Great Adventure"), and in characteristic imagery of action (mountain climbing in "Prologue" and "Uncertain Footholds") or of landscape (the quasi-allegorized island and fountain in "Darkened Windows").

In a letter published as preface to *The Turning Path*, Robert Graves interpreted Bottrall's landscape as an allegorical representation of "the personal and immediate hell of living unfulfillment: the vast, muddled, choking region of waste activities." The fertile realm that Bottrall had opposed in earlier poems to this wasteland is also pointed to in this volume, but, like its opposite, it is less clearly identified with a specific locale than had been the case in the past. Instead of idealizing Cornwall, Bottrall refers to universal biological processes, further guarding against idealization by couching his references in scientific terminology reminiscent of Empson's verse: "Intense vitality of infusoria / Multiplying by fission, adjusts the scale" ("Counterpoise"). The climax of this vitality, in a volume in which the poems are arranged to read as a sequence, arrives in the final poem, "New Birth," inspired by the birth of Bottrall's son, Anthony. The poem's final lines link it to the series of hopeful proclamations that began in "Arion Anadyomenos," though here it is Venus herself who, in substantiation of the Greek epithet, rises from the sea: "From cradling waves foams the Mother of Love, / Subduing earth and sea in naked utterance."

"New Birth" is unusual for Bottrall because its combination of the birth of a son and the vision of Venus has aspects of the real and ideal worlds, which are more often left separate, even in open conflict, in Bottrall's other work. Obviously, to a poet for whom love was the supreme ideal, an opportunity to ground that ideal in reality might seem to be offered by marriage. However, in Bottrall's next volume, *Farewell and Welcome* (1945), there are signs that marriage has fallen short of his ideal, just as the real Italy fell short of his youthful dreams. The title sequence of the volume, written in the first person, turns on the speaker and his wife the cold scalpel of *Hugh Selwyn Mauberley*, sharpened in the series of exercises entitled "Variations on a Theme of Pound." Bottrall, who held it to be a weakness of the pre-Pisan *Cantos* that Pound was willing to consign others to hell while letting himself go free, was careful to avoid that weakness in such lines as these from "Nearness Has Terrors," the third section of "Farewell and Welcome":

> The analysis and censorship
> Of every spontaneous surge of feeling
> Led to badinage and the cutting short at the
> lip
> Of the longed-for word and the spirit's
> welling.

Though Bottrall has not lost his faith in ideal love, his treatment of it throughout this volume is hampered by the suppression of "every spontaneous surge of feeling." Since Bottrall cannot realize love, he defines it—one section of "Farewell and Welcome" is entitled "Definition of Love"—and his poems suffer from "discursiveness," to use the term applied by *Scrutiny's* reviewer, A. I. Doyle.

A superficial indication that Bottrall was attempting to impose a shape that was external to the experience recorded in *Farewell and Welcome* is his new interest in the Provençal fixed forms, inspired perhaps by Empson's and Auden's experiments with these forms. Bottrall's volume contains examples of the sestina, the ballade, the rondeau (dedicated to Edith Sitwell), the villanelle, and their Italian relations, the sonnet and terza rima. It is not surprising that someone who acquired such an early facility in the handling of verse would be attracted by another opportunity for virtuoso display, and Bottrall has since insisted that such formal discipline constitutes an essential part of a poet's training, but he has generally been more successful with the looser patterns derived from Pound and Eliot than he has been with the fixed forms, perhaps because they occur to him, as in *Farewell and Welcome*, at moments when the ideal and the real are felt to be furthest apart.

Such separation has its advantages, of course. The notable advantage in *Farewell and Welcome* is that the real world is allowed to stand on its own, without the allegorization that so transformed that world in *The Turning Path*. Specific images that can be traced to Bottrall's extensive travels—to Singapore, China, Japan—return to this volume. Cornwall is treated more realistically than ever before in the best poem of the volume, a memorial to a primitive painter entitled "One Cornishman to Another—Peace Alfred Wallis!" Such realism, and probably his father's death, allowed Bottrall to admit his father directly into his verse for the first time, both in the Wallis poem and in "A Valediction."

Despite the gain in realism in *Farewell and Welcome*, the event that one would expect to demand attention from such a sensibility, World War II, remains curiously in the background in Bottrall's volume. The explanation seems to be that most of the poems of *Farewell and Welcome* were composed while Bottrall was living in a neutral country, Sweden, having begun, after brief service with the Air Ministry in 1940-1941, a long association with the British Council. The perspective that Sweden offered on the war is recorded in "A Nocturnal," which finds its occasion in the Swedish celebration of Saint Lucy's Day, when the poet finds himself "thinking in lights of / The lands without light." Although a note to the poem refers to Donne's "Nocturnall for S. Lucies Day," a more immediate influence is T. S. Eliot's *Four Quartets* (completed in 1942), from which Bottrall has derived his juxtaposition of meditative and lyric sections.

With Gunnar Ekeloef, Bottrall edited a volume of Eliot's verse for a Swedish publishing firm in 1942. This began a series of editing projects, including two verse anthologies prepared in collaboration with his wife, the first for another Swedish publisher (1945) and the second for the London firm of Sidgwick and Jackson (1946). Also in 1946, Bottrall, now representing the British Council in Italy, edited his own *Selected Poems*, published with a preface by Edith Sitwell.

Bottrall's *Selected Poems*, though it contains no new work, marks a decline in his career that is evident first in his reception by critics but more and more clearly in the poems themselves. While earlier reviewers in *Scrutiny* balanced their scrupulous criticism of Bottrall with statements of confidence in his future development, H. A. Mason, the reviewer of *Selected Poems*, stated bluntly that "Mr. Bottrall is not developing further." That view was shared by Peter Lienhardt, who reviewed *The Palisades of Fear* (1949) in 1950, and by Leavis himself, who in 1950 wrote a "Retrospect" to be appended to *New Bearings in English Poetry*, in which he admitted that Bottrall's development had not fulfilled the high hopes that Leavis had expressed in the first edition. Two main criticisms emerge from these assessments: first, that Bottrall's failure in part reflected the disintegration of the intellectual community as well as the larger social order that contained it; second, that Bottrall had failed to uncover a depth of personal emotion beneath the sophisticated, overintellectualized surface of his poetry.

Not only the first but both of these criticisms are colored by the despair of the war years, for the war had driven even the champion of impersonal poetry, T. S. Eliot, to seek a firmer foundation in personal experience in the autobiographical second section of *Little Gidding* (1942). Similarly, not only the first but both of these criticisms can be attributed as much to the failure of the project that had inspired *Scrutiny*, which ceased publication in 1953, as to the individual failure of Bottrall. Bottrall had composed his slickly impersonal surfaces to Leavis's prescription, a fact which makes the fervor in Leavis's early praise of Bottrall less surprising than it might otherwise seem. The danger inherent in Leavis's prescription was recognized by Bottrall from the start. In "Salute To Them That Know," published in his first volume, he had warned:

> But perhaps our academic few
> Have chosen overmuch to refute
> Themselves. Why cannot beauty dwell where
> it pleases. . . ?

Still, if the academic few determined the rules, it was Bottrall's choice to accept them.

The two volumes which Bottrall was writing while his critics undertook their reassessment record the disintegration of the imagined order toward which his earlier volumes had moved. The central principle of that order, love, is reexamined in general terms in *The Palisades of Fear*, whose "Prolegomena" flatly declares "Love is not enough."

Love is unraveled within a more personal context in *Adam Unparadised* (1954), published in the year of Bottrall's divorce from his first wife. "He and She" records a failed love affair undone partly by a failure of language: "the words cracked." Having returned from Italy to London to serve as Controller of Education for the British Council, Bottrall finds himself, in "Natural Order," "kept awake by trams" and dreaming not only of natural order but of the cultural order of Renaissance Italy. He feels excluded from both orders. Such honest self-appraisal comes close to supplying the personal depth that the *Scrutiny* critics were now looking for in Bottrall's work, but the affirmative ending had become so much a part of a poem's structure for Bottrall that he could not resist tacking on such endings where they do not belong, in "Natural Order," for instance, or in the poems "Tenebrae" and "Letter to a Friend" in *The Palisades of Fear*.

In Bottrall's version of the Fall in *Adam Unparadised*, the forbidden fruit grows on the "Tree of too much knowledge" ("He and She"), a further indication that he was aware of the threat that the intellect posed for his poetry. This and the preceding volume show Bottrall consciously developing strategies for countering that threat. He entitles a section of *The Palisades of Fear*, "Occasional Poems," and a section of *Adam Unparadised*, "Asides," as if to deflect the powers of judgment installed at Cambridge and in his own mind from engagement with work ostensibly unworthy of their attention. Another section of *The Palisades of Fear* is called "Poems for Music," again an attempt to limit the claims made for the poems, but also an attempt to invoke emotion rather than intellect as the inspiriting power. One of these poems, "Variant on Campion," pleads, "Grant me a little quiet from the involute brain." Besides Campion, and probably Blake, another guide to the lyric impulse in these volumes is a new influence for Bottrall, Dylan Thomas, who received high praise from Edith Sitwell but little more than condescension from the critics of *Scrutiny*.

As often happens, the decline in Bottrall's poetry coincided with a period of official recognition. He was made an officer of the Order of the British Empire in 1949, received a Coronation Medal in 1953 and the city of Syracuse's Theocritus International Poetry Prize in 1954, and was admitted as a fellow of the Royal Society of Literature in 1955. In the twelve years between 1952 and 1964, Bottrall wrote scarcely more than twelve poems. From 1964 to 1971 he wrote none. He has explained, "as one goes on, I find, myself, that the technique is there and the themes get rarer and the situations do not seem to crop up." In the last poem Bottrall wrote in 1964, he seems to be drained of all inspiration save the "names of poets and hidden quotations" around which, he acknowledges, the poem was built. It is called, significantly, "The Ancient Enemies."

Dust jacket for Bottrall's 1974 collection

During this dry period for poetry, Bottrall continued work for the British Council, "putting over British culture," as he termed it, in Brazil (1954-1956), Greece (1957-1959), and Japan (1959-1961). A new job as chief of the fellowships and training branch for the United Nations Food and Agriculture Organization (1963-1965) took him back to Rome. Bottrall kept up some literary activity, contributing translations to a collaborative version of Dante's *Inferno* commissioned by the BBC in 1963 and writing reviews for the *Times Literary Supplement* from 1965 to 1974. Suddenly, in the early morning of 13 December 1971, the same date and time that he had composed "The Ancient Enemies" seven years earlier, the poem "Prisoner's

Round" came to him, and Bottrall entered a new period of productivity that has lasted up to the present.

The work of the most recent period in Bottrall's career has been collected in two volumes. *Poems 1955-1973* (1974) includes the seven poems from *The Collected Poems* (1961) that had not appeared in earlier volumes as well as all the poems from *Day and Night* (1974). *Reflections on the Nile* (1980) includes work written since June 1974. Bottrall's thematic preoccupation in these poems is the recognition, though not always the acceptance, of limitation. The poem from which the new period arose, "Prisoner's Round," considers what might happen "If we could only learn to live in shade / Tilling our gardens, leaning on a spade," but insists nonetheless on tunneling toward the light, on breaking out of the limitation that is here sensed as imprisonment. Bottrall evidently feels that he has escaped the restrictions of the intellect at least in a group of poems written rapidly at night, when intellectual faculties lay dormant. These poems recall the Blakean impulse detectable in *The Palisades of Fear*, but the impulse remains unfulfilled because Bottrall lacks a visionary imagination. He suggests a transcendent world much more powerfully when he writes from the perspective of the human society he knows so well and arranges images of that superficial existence to hint at some underlying mystery, as in two poems from his Brazilian experience, "Copacabana 1955" and "Amazonian Scene" (*Poems 1955-1973*).

Reflections of Bottrall's more recent travels are registered disappointingly in poems that seem thoroughly superficial and banal, an extreme development of the other strategy that Bottrall had explored earlier in his attempt to escape the demands of intellect. Bottrall views Cairo, London, and Rome, the three principal locales of his most recent poems, from the perspective of a tourist, scribbling postcards that do not even qualify as light verse rather than inditing the sophisticated social satire of his early work. Nor has Bottrall's second marriage in 1954 to Margot Pamela Samuel, a personnel assistant from London, occasioned the probing self-criticism of *Farewell and Welcome* or *Adam Unparadised*. Cornwall remains the locale that elicits the richest response from Bottrall, especially when the landscape combines with the most potent personal influence in Bottrall's life, that of his father. That combination produces striking results in the long poem "Talking to the Ceiling" (*Poems 1955-1973*) or in "My Father as Poem" (*Reflections on the Nile*). The recognition of limitation appears as a moving farewell to Cornwall in "The Old Blowing-house": "I have lost my land, lying castaway / On sand counted out and outnumbered."

Edith Sitwell concluded her preface to Bottrall's *Selected Poems* with an allusion to the poem "Icarus" (*Farewell and Welcome*), claiming that Bottrall had matched Icarus's achievement yet escaped his doom. If Bottrall is granted a fuller identification with this poem, it can still stand—though more modestly—as an emblem of Bottrall's career. "In his father's face flying," Bottrall is the Icarus who soared over many cities but who, when his inspiration proved "unable / To sustain its presumptuous mood," fell to an extinction that went almost unnoticed. In his recent work, however, Bottrall has relocated himself as one of "the hard-handed peasants" who, oblivious of Icarus, "go their round / Turning the soil," each content to cultivate his garden.

Other:

T. S. Eliot, *Dikter*, edited by Bottrall and Gunnar Ekeloef (Stockholm: Albert Bonniers, 1942);

The Zephyr Book of English Verse, edited by Bottrall and Margaret Bottrall (Stockholm: Zephyr, 1945);

Collected English Verse, edited by Bottrall and Margaret Bottrall (London: Sidgwick & Jackson, 1946);

Terence Tiller, ed., *Dante's Inferno*, cantos 1-3 translated by Bottrall (London: British Broadcasting Corporation, 1966; New York: Schocken Books, 1966).

Periodical Publications:

"XXX Cantos of Ezra Pound (An Incursion into Poetics)," *Scrutiny*, 2 (September 1933): 112-122;

"Byron and the Colloquial Tradition in English Poetry," *Criterion*, 18 (January 1939): 204-224; republished in *English Romantic Poets: Modern Essays in Criticism*, first edition, edited by M. H. Abrams (London & New York: Oxford University Press, 1960), pp. 210-227;

"The Achievement of Ezra Pound," *Adelphi*, new series 28 (May 1952): 618-623; republished in *Ezra Pound: The Critical Heritage*, edited by Eric Homberger (London: Routledge & Kegan Paul, 1972), pp. 415-421.

References:

G. S. Fraser, *The Modern Writer and His World* (London: Verschoyle, 1953), pp. 254-256;

F. R. Leavis, "Auden, Bottrall and Others," *Scrutiny*,

3 (June 1934): 70-83;

Leavis, *New Bearings in English Poetry* (London: Chatto & Windus, 1932);

H. A. Mason, "Room for Doubt? Mr. Bottrall's Selected Poems," *Scrutiny*, 14 (Spring 1947): 217-222;

Peter Orr, Interview with Bottrall, in *The Poet Speaks*, edited by Orr (New York: Barnes & Noble, 1966), pp. 39-44.

Papers:

The State University of New York at Buffalo has manuscripts of twenty poems, mostly from *The Turning Path*, and 17 letters by Bottrall. The University of Texas at Austin has ninety-three manuscripts, 80 letters by Bottrall, 341 letters addressed to Bottrall, and forty-four miscellaneous manuscript items. The British Library, London, has manuscripts of five poems.

Basil Bunting

(1 March 1900-)

Barbara E. Lesch
Sonoma State University

BOOKS: *Redimiculum Matellarum* (Milan: Privately printed, 1930);

Poems 1950 (Galveston: Cleaner's Press, 1950); revised as *Loquitur* (London: Fulcrum Press, 1965);

First Book of Odes (London: Fulcrum Press, 1965);

The Spoils (Newcastle: Morden Tower Book Room, 1965);

Briggflatts (London: Fulcrum Press, 1966);

Collected Poems (London: Fulcrum Press, 1968; enlarged edition, London & New York: Oxford University Press, 1978).

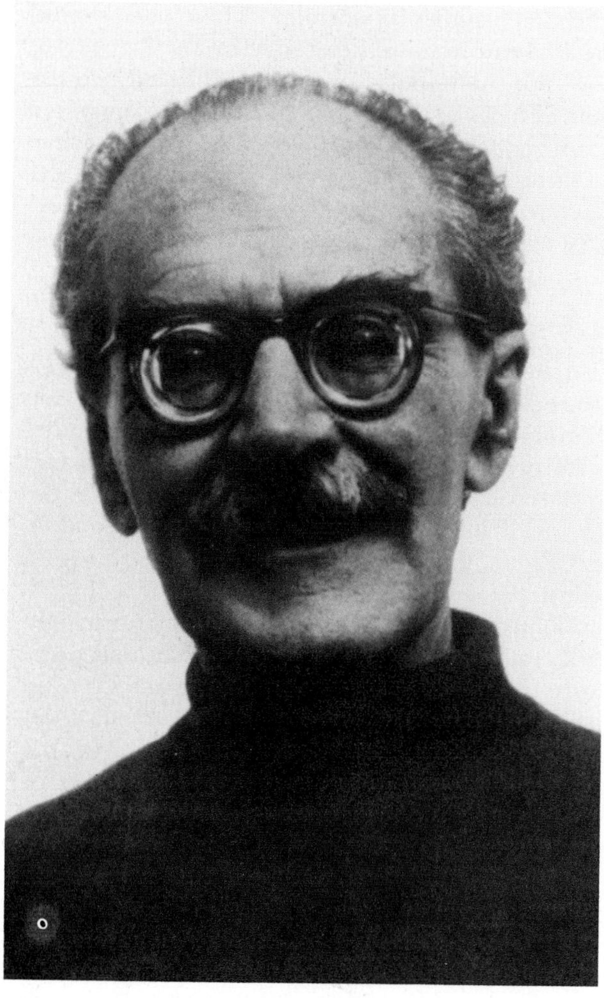

Basil Bunting, 1966 (photo by Jonathan Williams)

The work of Basil Bunting refutes the long-held contention that modernism is an exclusively American phenomenon which began on British soil. Integrally connected with Ezra Pound, this movement in poetry began in England in 1908. Not only does the form of Bunting's poetry show a similarity in its lucidity and spareness with Pound's and that of other modernists such as T. S. Eliot, but the themes with which it concerns itself are typical of those associated with modernism. Bunting was first attracted to Pound's and Eliot's work in 1919 because he felt that he shared with them a concern with adapting music to poetry. In fact, Bunting suggests that his only *unique* contribution to poetry is his adaptation of the sonata form to a poetic structure.

At the very core of Bunting's approach to life is an acceptance of many of the tenets of Quakerism which he learned as a child. These beliefs appear most clearly in his longest work, *Briggflatts* (1966), but they are also implicit in many of the other poems. It is partially as a result of the reflection of these beliefs in his poetry, among them a perception of the integral connection of all aspects of the chain of existence, that Bunting achieves a highly individual view of reality and a distinctly personal voice which makes him more than a follower of Pound and the modernist mode.

It is exactly Bunting's stance as a distinctly British modernist that may mark his special achievement in modern poetry. The language used in Bunting's verse, particularly that written after 1950, is markedly different from that of the American modernists. Not only does it reveal an interest in etymology and the stresses of the Old Britonic and Welsh languages, but it captures the flavor of a British perception of existence. There is in his work an ability to capture language and place that distinguishes Bunting, not only as a poet who was born in England but as one whose work illuminates various aspects of the character of England and its inhabitants.

Basil Bunting, who was born near Newcastle in 1900, has remained a poetic enigma for far too long. After attending Newcastle Royal Grammar School, Bunting was sent to a Quaker boarding school at Ackworth and then to one at Leighton Park in Berkshire. His only other formal education was a year and a half at the London School of Economics (1919-1920).

A gentle man, whose speech reflects his Northumbrian upbringing, Bunting contends that his commitment to the craft of poetry dates back to his early childhood. It was after Bunting's release from prison in 1919, where he had been sent as a conscientious objector during World War I, that he began to pursue his poetic career. Bunting says that, when he discovered the work of Pound and Eliot (Eliot's "Preludes" in particular), he "was delighted to discover that there were actually people doing what I had merely worked out in my head was the kind of thing that ought to be done. This was a revelation, that it really could be done, that it wasn't a hopeless trade."

From 1924 to 1930, Bunting traveled extensively. In 1924, after leaving London, he moved to Paris, where earlier, in 1922, he had first met Pound. On this second trip Pound started Bunting's literary career by introducing him to Ford Madox Ford and by helping him to secure a post as a subeditor of Ford's *transatlantic review*. Bunting's earliest extant works are an ode dated 1924 (which did not appear in print until 1930) and a review of Conrad's *The Rover*, which appeared in the July 1924 issue of the magazine.

On a brief trip to Rapallo in late 1924, Bunting visited Pound, and it is from this encounter that Bunting dates the start of his friendship with the older poet. Although Bunting returned to London soon after and did not see Pound again until five years later, he says that "there were letters every six months or so, and I never lost touch with him again." In London, Bunting struggled to support himself as a writer until he landed a position as the music editor for the *Outlook* in 1926. It was during this time as a music editor that Bunting honed his knowledge of that art, a knowledge which would serve him well when he was writing his "sonatas."

When the *Outlook* stopped publication in 1928 rather than face a libel suit, Bunting set out again with financial assistance from Margaret de Silver. He first went to Northumberland, where he lived in a shepherd's cottage for six months. (The visit provided him with material that was ultimately incorporated into part five of *Briggflatts*.) Then, after a brief trip to Germany (which provided him with the impetus and knowledge to write "Aus dem zweiten Reich"), he returned to Rapallo. Except for a brief visit to America in 1929-1930, when he visited Louis Zukofsky (another poet who was acquainted with and influenced by Pound) and married his first wife, Marion (whom he had met in New York), Bunting remained in Rapallo with Pound from 1929 until 1933.

Bunting began submitting his work to *Poetry* magazine in 1926, but it was not until 1930 that his work appeared in print. That year Bunting's first sonata "Villon" (written in 1925) not only appeared in *Redimiculum Matellarum* (a collection of Bunting's work that was privately printed in Milan with Pound's help) but also in the October 1930 issue of *Poetry* magazine, where it had been sent by Pound the previous year. The volume of Bunting's poetry went unnoticed, except for a review by Zukofsky in *Poetry*. *Redimiculum Matellarum*, whose title Bunting translates as "a necklace of chamberpots," contains twelve short poems (odes) as well as "Villon." In the preface to the volume, Bunting says that "these poems are byproducts of an interrupted and harassed apprenticeship." The short poems in the volume are called "carmina," after the Latin title for Horace's work. In their subsequent appearances, they are assigned numbers rather than titles and in *Poems 1950* are collected together as odes.

According to Bunting, Pound "did for my 'Villon' exactly what he'd done for Eliot and *The Waste Land*. He took a blue pencil and scratched out about half of the poem." In addition, Pound's interest in the poetry of François Villon and in the relationship of poetry to music appears to have had a profound impact on both the form and the content of Bunting's "Villon."

Bunting's sonata is based, in part, on poet François Villon's *Le Grand Testament* (1461) and uses, as thematic material, details related to the life and work of the poet. In "Villon," Bunting uses a shifting point of view, with some sections of the sonata narrated from a perspective conjecturally like that of the fifteenth-century poet and others articulated by a more modern figure whose life at times strangely parallels both Bunting's and Villon's. Throughout the poem, actual events, artifacts, and people reflect Bunting's concerns with the relationship of artifice to reality and the relationship of the artificer to the raw materials of his trade. The other major theme explored in the sonata is the legacy of the artisan's work, which endures beyond his mortality:

> our doom
> is, to be sifted by the wind,
>
> heaped up, smoothed down like silly sands.
> We are less permanent than thought.
> The Emperor with the Golden Hands
>
> is still a word, a tint, a tone,
> insubstantial-glorious,
> when we ourselves are dead and gone
> and the green grass growing over us.

Throughout the sonata, Bunting's skill at capturing the flavor of a long-dead poet in a modern idiom, which was also one of Pound's fortes, is evident. Bunting feels that by only translating the work of another one cannot preserve the past: "The poetry has to preserve it or it's forgotten. Your attempts to do something of that sort of thing only get across what you can make of it in the twentieth century." Obviously Villon's poetry preserved a sense of his age, and Bunting shares with his readers the concerns, the conditions, and the music of Villon's age as he "translates" it into a contemporary voice.

In Bunting's second sonata, "Attis: Or, Something Missing," his use of material from the work of others is quite different than that in "Villon." Direct quotations and allusions do not produce a reflection of the past upon the present as much as they are a mocking of the past when it is contrasted with the present situation. The sonata, written in 1931, did not appear in print in its entirety until the publication of *Poems 1950*, although its third section appeared in *Poetry's* October 1931 "Objectivist" issue (edited by Zukofsky).

"Attis: Or, Something Missing" is informed by the myth of Attis and Cybele, which functions in much the same way as the life and work of François Villon in the first sonata. However, the work has far more literary analogues than the first, including Catallus's "Carmen 63," Lucretius's *De Rerum Natura*, and works by Pound, Eliot, Dante, Milton, and Çino de Pistoia. These analogues add to both the irony and the ironic deflation which begins with the title and continues throughout the entire sonata. Bunting's notation for the form, "sonatina," is also ironic, because this is one of the most completely developed of his early sonatas.

"Attis: Or, Something Missing" is not only thematically related to "Villon," but its structure is also comparable as both follow the three-part development of the musical sonata with coda. In addition, Bunting's use of rhythms shows a significant advance over the earlier sonata, as does his mastery of literary and mythological allusions.

The sonata opens with a description of a modern-day Attis, whose impotence is defined in terms of his weak moral fiber and character, rather than in terms of his sexuality:

> Out of puff
> noonhot in tweeds and gray felt,
> tired of appearance and
> disappearance;
> warm obese frame limp with satiety;
> slavishly circumspect at sixty;
> he spreads over the ottoman
> scanning the pictures and table trinkets.

By the end of the sonata, Attis also symbolizes the artistic sterility and failure of the contemporary poet. Throughout, the sonata indicates that belief in the power of Cybele, and by implication in the gods and most organized religion, is a sham which cheats men and enslaves them. However, the power of the muse of art, which allows men to create without placing restrictions upon them, ultimately refutes this belief. Art is seen as a true religion and a form of immortality to which men can genuinely aspire. Bunting implies that something is missing in modern man, not only when his procreative energy is denied but when man can no longer exercise his creative potential. As in "Villon," the doubt and pessimism regarding the progress of civilization and man's powerless position is refuted by the act of poetic creation, of which the sonata is an example.

If "Attis: Or, Something Missing" is a statement about the condition of modern civilization which reflects the work of past and present authors, then the other sonata which Bunting wrote during 1931, "Aus dem zweiten Reich," can be seen as an evocation of that modern civilization in one country at one particular point in history. The sonata is the fruit of Bunting's brief stay in Germany in 1928 and mirrors his dislike for the legacy of the Second Reich to the German people and their culture. The sonata, which, because of its relative brevity, should more appropriately be called a sonatina, is tight and compact with none of the extensive thematic development or changing points of view that characterized the two previous sonatas.

The entire sonata is an evocation of the ambience of Berlin in the 1920s, with each section presenting a vignette of that society and the final stanza functioning as a commentary upon the whole. Although the sonata, when compared to Bunting's other works, seems slight, it is far from unsuccessful, and it is far more accessible to the reader or listener. It is an excellent evocation of the poet's judgment of the Berlin which he visited at the end of the 1920s:

> Hour and hour
> meeting against me,
> efficiently whipped cream,
> efficiently metropolitan chatter and snap,
> transparent glistening wrapper
> for a candy pack.
>
> Automatic, somewhat too clean,
> body and soul similarly scented,
> on time,
> rapid, dogmatic, automatic and efficient,
> ganz modern.

The sonata's tight, self-contained structure has a certain crystalline beauty. "The Well of Lycopolis," Bunting's next sonata, is a more complex work, but the poetic line is not always as clear nor the thematic strands as cleanly woven as in "Aus dem zweiten Reich."

Although Bunting was able to support himself in part while in Rapallo by writing articles for newspapers and magazines, particularly *Il Mare's Supplemento Letterrario*, the rising cost of living in Italy eventually forced him to leave for the Canary Islands at the end of 1933. Bunting and his family, which included two young daughters, Bourtai and Roubada, stayed in the Canary Islands until several days before the outbreak of the Spanish civil war in 1936. Bunting's experiences while living in the Canary Islands were transformed into "The Well of Lycopolis." As Bunting says, "I got very gloomy in the Canaries and wrote a poem called 'The Well of Lycopolis,' which is about as gloomy a poem as anyone would want." Although the sonata was written in 1935, it did not appear in print until it was published in *Poems 1950*. It is the last of Bunting's sonatas written prior to World War II and is more highly dependent on the works of others than are his later sonatas. "The Well of Lycopolis" is also the first of Bunting's long works to be sent to Zukofsky in manuscript form with explanatory notes, although Bunting had previously sent Zukofsky copies of his odes and translations.

From the beginning of the sonata, Bunting's subject is clearly an examination of love in the modern world. It is, by inference, concerned with those who have literally drunk from a well like that in Lycopolis and have lost their innocence. Because Lycopolis is described as being a modern city, the reader can infer that Bunting's message applies to the contemporary situation, rather than being based on a contrast between an older age and the modern one, as was the case in "Villon" and "Attis: Or, Something Missing."

The sonata chronicles the essential failure of modern man in terms of his relationship with love, and its muse Venus, and poetry, and its muse Polymnia. By implication it condemns not only modern man in general but also poets who have tried and failed to capture an understanding of the modern world in their works. In spite of what is described as a debased experience of love, at the end of the sonata there is a "sighing" of hope for which no explanation is given:

> I want you to know for certain
> there are people under the water. They are sighing.
> The surface bubbles and boils with their sighs.
> Look where you will see it.
> The surface sparkles and dances with their sighs
> as though Styx were silvered by a wind from Heaven.

There is something ultimately unconvincing about this conclusion, which may well be a reflection of the despair of a man who grasps for a reason to believe that life can be better but remains unpersuaded.

In "The Well of Lycopolis" Bunting is experimenting with the use of multiple voices rather than using an omniscient narrator who presents a spectrum of voices as in "Attis: Or, Something Missing." Although this is an essential stylistic development for Bunting, it often clouds the focus of the sonata. Bunting is attempting a sonata whose scope and style far outreach those in his earlier sonatas and look forward to the more successfully developed longer sonatas written after World War II. If this particular sonata is less successful, it is also a step forward in terms of its more complex structure, which Bunting manipulated with greater facility in "The Spoils" and in *Briggflatts*.

Shortly after he wrote "The Well of Lycopolis," Bunting and his family left the Canary Islands and returned to London. Not long after their return, his wife, who was pregnant with their son, Rustam, left him and returned to New York with their daughters. Bunting spent most of 1938 living on a small boat, *The Thistle*, and going out with the herring fishermen off the coast of Devon. After selling the boat, he went to New York and then to Los Angeles, in part to seek work and in part, as his letters to Zukofsky suggest, to seek a reconciliation with his family. He returned to England the next year, where he lived with his mother until he enlisted in 1940.

Many of Bunting's letters to Zukofsky during the late 1930s and early 1940s deal with his despair over his inability to visit his children, as well as his economic difficulties. He wrote several short odes before the war but became too involved during the war years to devote his energy to the writing of verse. In 1945 Bunting wrote to Zukofsky, "I have been on almost every British front worth being on except Dunkirk, travelled through every rank from Aircraftsman First Class to Squadron-Leader. . . , seen huge chunks of the world that I wouldnt otherwise have visited, been sailor, balloon-man, drill instructor, interpreter, truck driver in the desert, intelligence officer of several kinds, operations officer to a busy fighter squadron, recorder of the doings of nomadic tribes, labour manager. . . ."

After the war, Bunting served briefly as vice-consul at the British Embassy in Isfahan. After a nine-month visit to England, he returned to Iran in 1947 to take a position with the British Embassy in Teheran. It was there, during the next year, that he married his second wife, Sima.

While Bunting was in Iran, *Poems 1950* was compiled and published by Dallas Simpson, a disciple of Pound's who had founded *Four Pages* magazine and The Cleaner's Press in Galveston, Texas, in 1948 in order to disseminate Pound's economic and political theories. It seems that Pound, who was at St. Elizabeths mental hospital in Washington, D.C., was more closely involved with the project than Bunting. Reviewers praised *Poems 1950*, but, because it was available only in a limited edition, it was not widely distributed.

Poems 1950 contains not only the sonatas but many of the odes and several translations which had not appeared in *Redimiculum Matellarum*. Bunting stresses the musical aspect of his odes and says that his "odes are called odes because Horace called his odes. An ode is essentially a sonnet to be sung, not all of mine are meant to be sung; most of them are." Yet, Horace's concern with the range of human experience and the foibles of man, as reflected in his odes, is a concern which Bunting shares. The odes explore several broad themes, all of which show Bunting's concern for man—as individual, in relationship with other individuals, and in society—concerns which can be traced throughout his entire canon.

In the odes written after 1930, there is a development toward a simpler line whose music depends less on the conventions of rhyme. In many there is a concern with patterns of stress and an experimentation with non-Western poetic forms such as the haiku and the *rubai*. The skill in these odes is not so much in musical structuring or complexity of images as in the art of observation and commentary. It is this advance in skill which also marks the sonata written during the 1950s, "The Spoils."

After leaving the embassy in 1949, Bunting took a job as a foreign correspondent for the London *Times*. Paid poorly and, increasingly unable to support his wife and baby daughter (Sima Maria), Bunting finally left Iran in 1951 and took a position as a journalist in Italy. There, in 1951, "The Spoils," whose working title was "The Fifth Sonata," was completed. Several draft versions of the sonata that were sent to Zukofsky are preserved in the Humanities Research Center at the University of Texas at Austin. "The Spoils," which more than any other of Bunting's works shows the impact of his experiences in Persia, was accepted for publication immediately and appeared in the November 1951 issue of *Poetry* magazine.

While writing "The Spoils," Bunting indicated to Zukofsky that he was trying to show that the priorities which Westerners value and assume are universal, including physical comfort, are not necessarily shared by other cultures. From the title on, the work shows that other priorities are valued in the East and that perhaps this Eastern set of attitudes toward life may allow man to appreciate his existence and its significance in a fuller and richer manner. "The Spoils" is concerned with the way in which men cope with the restraints their society places upon them and the way in which society's rules allow men a fullness of experience in which they express themselves, are creative, and, most important, deal with life and death. In the course of the sonata, which is a journey through life, one acquires not only a familiarity with death but a familiarity with the wonder and dazzle which is a part of the experience of war:

> Have you seen a falcon stoop
> accurate, unforeseen
> and absolute, between
> wind-ripples over harvest? Dread
> of what's to be, is and has been—
> were we not better dead?
>
> His wings churn air
> to flight.
> Feathers alight
> with sun, he rises where
> dazzle rebuts our stare,
> wonder our fright.

In terms of the way in which the material is treated, the number of intersecting thematic strands which are manipulated, the number of poetic voices which are introduced, and the sheer length of the sonata, "The Spoils" is a step forward from the earlier sonatas. But Bunting's own hesitancy about the structural lopsidedness of this sonata was one of the major impetuses behind the creation of *Briggflatts*, a poem which was specifically planned to achieve the musical balance which he felt was lacking in "The Spoils."

Bunting returned to Iran briefly in 1953 as a correspondent for the *Times* but was expelled nine months later because he refused to allow the Iranian government to censor his news releases. When he returned to England, the *Times* was unable to employ him, and he barely subsisted for the next year and a half with his family, including his son Thomas, who was born in 1952. In 1953 he started the type of taxing work (ultimately as subeditor of the Newcastle *Morning Chronicle*) which was his sole means of support for the next decade.

Because his work for economic survival so consumed him during the 1950s and early 1960s, Bunting's poetic output was nonexistent. It was not until Bunting came into contact with a young Newcastle poet, Tom Pickard, that he and his work came out of "retirement." Pickard republished "The Spoils" and persuaded Bunting to give readings at the Morden Tower on the Newcastle city wall (which Pickard had transformed into a poetry bookstore). The Morden Tower Book Room published a limited edition pamphlet containing "The Spoils" in 1965. For so small a distribution, Bunting's sonata received a significant amount of critical attention (including articles by Cyril Connolly and reviews in the *New Statesman*, *Poetry*, and the *Times Literary Supplement*). In addition, Bunting's connection with Pickard enabled him to reach an entirely new audience, one which he felt truly appreciated his verse even when they did not understand it. After his readings at Morden Tower, Bunting regained a desire to write, and from 1964 to 1966 he produced the eight odes, which originally composed the "Second Book of Odes" section of *Collected Poems*, and began work on *Briggflatts*. The eight odes can be seen as necessary exercises in the renewal of Bunting's poetic craft which made possible the composition of *Briggflatts*.

Each of the odes in the "Second Book of Odes" has a simple focus; it is as if the poet were using them to sharpen his tools of observation. Although the themes and poetic concerns in the "Second Book of Odes" are comparable to those in the odes of the first book, the tone is less weary, more life-affirming and, in many respects, indicative of the stance of a mellower and maturer poet viewing life from a different vantage point.

In 1965, Fulcrum Press, a small venture of a fellow poet and admirer of Pound's, Stuart Montgomery, began to republish Bunting's work in several volumes. The first was an edition of the *First Book of Odes*, which includes the odes from *Poems 1950*. It was followed by *Loquitur*, a lightly revised edition of the complete *Poems 1950*. In the preface to *Loquitur*, Bunting indicates that he has given "the book a title to replace the off-hand label by which it has been known or unknown for fifteen years." In view of his faith in the value of poetry, Bunting's title for the volume is profoundly ironic; it derives from the Latin verb meaning "to chatter."

Notwithstanding the critical reception which these volumes received, it is Bunting's major sonata, *Briggflatts*, that is primarily responsible for the recognition which he now enjoys, both in England and America. *Briggflatts* originally appeared in *Poetry* magazine in 1966 and was published by Fulcrum Press the same year. If the critical attention given to *Loquitur* was substantial (including commentary by A. Alvarez and reviews in the *Guardian*, the London *Tribune*, *Poetry*, and the *Sunday Times*), then that given to *Briggflatts* (including articles by Cyril Connolly, Donald Davie, Hugh Kenner, and Tom Pickard) was overwhelming. The popularity of the sonata, both in England and America, permanently changed Bunting's status as an unknown or as a "poet's poet."

In 1953 Bunting, upon rereading "The Well of Lycopolis" and "The Spoils," said that "they arent good enough . . . Rhone wine when I wanted Mouton. . . . " He sought to prove that poetry could approximate musical form at its purest. He was looking forward to *Briggflatts* when he said, "I shall have to try again to write a QED sonata to earn the hatred of all the tasteful critics and a few centuries of misrepresentation *but* convince all candid listeners and so survive." By 1964, Bunting felt a sense of urgency to create this ultimate sonata and in a letter to Zukofsky indicated that he owed a "longish" poem "to Peggy Greenbank and her whole ambience, the Rawthey valley, the fells of Lunedale, the viking inheritance all spent save the faint smell of it, the ancient Quaker life accepted without thought and without suspicion that it might seem eccentric: what happens when one deliberately thrusts love aside as I did then—it has its revenge. . . ."

Bunting contends that the sonata grew out of a diagram to which he attached several Latin mottoes and that the work is informed by Scarlatti's B minor fugato sonata. After establishing the structure, Bunting wrote it at a furious pace, mainly while commuting back and forth to work. The sonata is dedicated to Peggy Greenbank, his childhood sweetheart, from whom he was separated by his imprisonment during World War I and to whom he never returned. Although Bunting marks the sonata "An Autobiography," he says it is not factual. Rather, he sees it as following the "phases of a lifetime in line with the phases of a year without any attempt to bring in historical facts." The sonata begins in spring around the village of Briggflatts:

> Brag, sweet tenor bull,
> descant on Rawthey's madrigal,
> each pebble its part
> for the fells' late spring.
> Dance tiptoe, bull,
> black against may.
> Ridiculous and lovely
> chase hurdling shadows
> morning into noon.
> May on the bull's hide
> and through the dale
> furrows fill with may,
> paving the slowworm's way.

It ends on the Northumberland coast in winter. The coda, which questions the quality of existence in the face of death, points to the way in which the past can and must vitally inform the present:

> A strong song tows
> us, long earsick.
> Blind, we follow
> rain slant, spray flick
> to fields we do not know.
>
> Night, float us.
> Offshore wind, shout,
> ask the sea
> what's lost, what's left,
> what horn sunk,
> what crow adrift.
>
> Where we are who knows
> of king who sup
> while day fails? Who,
> swinging his axe
> to fell kings, guesses
> where we go?

In essence, *Briggflatts* can be seen as a carefully selected and emotionally charged ordering of what Bunting saw, read, and experienced in the sixty-four years prior to its composition, mixed with a sprinkling of imaginings.

In the wake of Bunting's increased reputation, Fulcrum Press published a collected edition of his work in 1968 and a second edition and paperback version two years later. In 1978, Oxford University Press republished the *Collected Poems*, at which time four short works were added. Thus, the volume contains all of Bunting's work which he has chosen to preserve—six sonatas, forty-eight odes, fourteen short translations, and one long translation (or overdraft).

If one were to identify the sources of Bunting's achievement they would have to be in the way in which he controls and uses language, the way in which his poetry captures a particular time and place, the way in which he uses the work of other writers to enhance one's understanding of the present age, the way that he perceives the past informing the present, and the way in which he has adopted the sonata form to poetry. Throughout his work, there is a continual growth in mastery of the poetic line, in manipulation of varied thematic material, and in handling of increasingly larger and more cohesive forms.

Yet, it may well be his imaginative range and control that stand out most clearly when one attempts to assess the value of his work. Bunting's themes are essentially universal: the relationship of life and art, of past and present, of ideal form and physical manifestation, of memory and artifact, of love and human existence. It is the way he manipulates these thematic concerns, interweaving them throughout his poetic canon and finding points of resolution within the cyclical nature of his sonatas, that shows a man whose mind truly controls the verse he creates out of his experience of reality. Such exploration is one of the marks of a major writer. Bunting's struggle with memory and regret cannot help but elicit a response in his audience, even if all they hear is a "pattern of sound that may sometimes . . . be pleasing."

Periodical Publications:

POETRY:

"Villon," *Poetry*, 27 (October 1930): 27-33;

"Chomei at Toyama," *Poetry*, 242 (September 1933): 301-307;

"The Spoils," *Poetry*, 79 (November 1951): 84-97;

Briggflatts, *Poetry*, 107 (January 1966): 214-237.

NONFICTION:

"Basil Bunting Talks About 'Briggflatts' " and "The Poet's Point of View," *Georgia Straight Writing Supplement*, 6 (18-24 November 1970): n. pag.

Interviews:

Jonathan Williams, *Descant on Rawthey's Madrigal: Conversations with Basil Bunting* (Lexington: Gnomen Press, 1968);

Dale Reagan, "An Interview with Basil Bunting," *Montemora*, 3 (Spring 1977): 68-80;

Williams and Tom Meyer, "A Conversation with Basil Bunting," *St. Andrew's Review*, 4 (Spring / Summer 1977): 21-32.

References:

A. Alvarez, "New Poetry," review of *Loquitur*, *Observer*, 24 October 1965, p. 27;

Jim Burns, "Poem like a Symphony," review of *Briggflatts*, *Tribune* (London), 3 March 1967, p. 14;

Thomas Clark, "New Lines," review of *Loquitur*, *Poetry*, 109 (November 1966): 110-112;

Alasdair Clayre, "Recent Verse," review of *Briggflatts*, *Encounter*, 29 (November 1967): 74-79;

Cyril Connolly, "Critics Choice of the Year," review of *Briggflatts*, *Sunday Times* (London), 3 December 1967, p. 29;

Connolly, "The Nature of Poetry," review of *The Spoils*, *Sunday Times* (London), 26 September 1965, p. 47;

Kenneth Cox, "The Aesthetic of Basil Bunting," *Agenda*, 4 (Autumn 1966): 20-28;

Cox, "A Commentary on Basil Bunting's 'Villon,' " *Stony Brook*, 3-4 (Fall 1969): 59-69;

Donald Davie, "Privately Published," review of *Briggflatts*, *New Statesman*, 72 (4 November 1966): 672;

Sister Victoria Forde, "Music and Meaning in the Poetry of Basil Bunting," Ph.D. dissertation, University of Notre Dame, 1973;

Anthea Hall, "Basil Bunting Explains How a Poet Works," *Journal* (Newcastle), 17 July 1965, p. 7;

Francis Hope, "The Authentic," review of *The Spoils*, *New Statesman*, 70 (17 December 1965): 976;

Richard Howard, "British Chronicle," review of *The Spoils*, *Poetry*, 110 (June 1967): 195-198;

Richard Kell, "Extension and Structure," review of *Loquitur*, *Guardian* (Manchester), 18 February 1966, p. 8;

Hugh Kenner, "Never a Boast or a See-Here," review of *Briggflatts*, *National Review*, 19 (31 October 1967): 1217-1218;

Barbara E. Lesch, "Basil Bunting: A Major British Modernist," Ph.D. dissertation, University of Wisconsin-Madison, 1979;

Tom Pickard, "Bunting's Power and Delicacy," review of *Briggflatts*, *Evening Chronicle* (Newcastle), 26 February 1966, p. 4;

John Raymond, "Matters of Voice and Vision," review of *Loquitur*, *Sunday Times* (London), 19 June 1966, p. 29;

Anthony Suter, " 'Attis: Or, Something Missing': A Commentary on the Poem by Basil Bunting," *Durham University Journal*, new series 24 (1972-1973): 189-200;

Suter, "Basil Bunting, Poet of Modern Times," *Ariel: A Review of International English Literature*, 3 (October 1972): 25-32;

Suter, "The Sea in the Poetry of Basil Bunting," *Forum for Modern Language Studies*, 9 (July 1973): 293-297;

Suter, "Time and the Literary Past in the Poetry of Basil Bunting," *Contemporary Literature*, 12 (1971): 510-526;

Charles Tomlinson, "Experience into Music: The Poetry of Basil Bunting," *Agenda*, 4 (Autumn 1966): 11-17;

Gael Turnbull, "An Arlespenny: Some Notes on the Poetry of Basil Bunting," *King Ida's Watch Chain: A Moving Anthology: Link One* (1965): n. pag.;

"Unfortified," review of *The Spoils* and *Loquitur*, *Times Literary Supplement*, 17 February 1966, p. 119.

Papers:

Drafts of "The Spoils," uncollected poems, translations, and articles, as well as letters to Marion Bunting, Edward Dahlberg, T. S. Eliot, Sisley Huddleston, Edward Lucie-Smith, Ezra Pound, and Louis Zukofsky are at the Humanities Research Center, the University of Texas at Austin. Letters to the editor, James Leippert, Karl Shapiro, Harriet Monroe, and Morton Dauwen Zabel are held at the University of Chicago Library.

Roy Campbell

(2 October 1901-23 April 1957)

D. S. J. Parsons
University of Saskatchewan

SELECTED BOOKS: *The Flaming Terrapin* (London: Cape, 1924; New York: Lincoln MacVeagh/Dial, 1924);
The Wayzgoose (London: Cape, 1928);
Adamastor (London: Faber & Faber, 1930; New York: Lincoln MacVeagh/Dial, 1931);
The Georgiad (London: Boriswood, 1931);
Taurine Provence (London: Harmsworth, 1932);
Flowering Reeds (London: Boriswood, 1933);
Broken Record (London: Boriswood, 1934);
Mithraic Emblems (London: Boriswood, 1936);
Flowering Rifle (London, New York & Toronto: Longmans, Green, 1939);
Sons of the Mistral (London: Faber & Faber, 1941);
Talking Bronco (London: Faber & Faber, 1946; Chicago: Regnery, 1956);
Collected Poems, volume 1 (London: Bodley Head, 1949); republished as *Selected Poems* (Chicago: Regnery, 1955);
Light on a Dark Horse (London: Hollis & Carter, 1951; Chicago: Regnery, 1952);
Lorca: An Appreciation of His Poetry (Cambridge: Bowes & Bowes, 1952; New Haven: Yale University Press, 1952);
The Mamba's Precipice (London: Muller, 1953; New York: Day, 1954);
Portugal (London: Reinhardt, 1957; Chicago: Regnery, 1958);
Collected Poems, volume 2 (London: Bodley Head, 1957; Chicago: Regnery, 1957);
Collected Poems, volume 3 (London: Bodley Head, 1960; Chicago: Regnery, 1960).

Roy Campbell (photo by Jane Bown)

The paradox of Roy Campbell fascinates. As a poet he can be both superb and despicable. In technique and outlook ostensibly an isolated anachronism, he yet in a subordinate but distinctive way joins the ranks of Eliot, Pound, Yeats, and the Sitwells. In personality he could be humble and inward, but was also well known for swashbuckling exhibitionism and mischief. Once, having journeyed with friends to visit the Grand Old Man Thomas Hardy at Max Gate, he remained in the car, too awed to go in. In London, after World War II, he used to parade around in a King's African Rifles bush hat, carrying a knobkerrie, or in a bullfighter's cape and headgear. On one occasion, when he entered a busy pub in bullfighter's garb to meet his wife and a few friends, a whole roomful of strangers spontaneously rose to their feet. This story, unlike many about Campbell, mostly told by himself, is verifiable.

The son of Samuel George and Margaret Wylie Dunnachie Campbell, Ignatius Roy Dunnachie Campbell was born and grew up in Durban, Natal, South Africa, at a time when southern Africa was still largely untamed and unspoiled. Although much of his childhood was idyllic, his circumstances and character early determined the restless and otherwise limiting features of his life and art. His father, a prominent doctor and a hero of the Zulu War, was one of the sons of a founder of the city of Durban, and the talented family had prospered and gained local importance. As a boy Roy Campbell hunted and rode in the subtropical bush surrounding Durban and stayed on his uncle's huge sugar estates or at the family cottage by the sea. His school holidays he spent in Rhodesia, on the farm of another uncle. Campbell proudly described his family as one of "soldiers, scholars, athletes, poets, doctors and farmers." His sense of superiority made him contemptuous of the narrow parochialism of the shopkeeping citizenry, and he felt alienated from much of the society. Throughout his days at Durban High School he suffered a persecution he never forgot from the headmaster, who had a feud with his father. When he was fifteen Campbell ran away from school in an attempt to join the army.

His first ambition was to be a painter. From an early age he sketched wildlife and wrote verse with precocious skill. His parents encouraged him, and his father gave him a generous allowance with which to buy books. Though an indifferent scholar at school, he immersed himself to good effect in Latin, English, and French poetry, especially the Parnassians and Baudelaire. In 1918, with his father's support, he left for Oxford University. Once there, however, he soon abandoned his attempt to satisfy the entrance requirement in Greek and devoted his time to reading what then mattered to him, principally the Elizabethans and the metaphysical poets. He joined one of the literary groups and met, among others, T. S. Eliot, Aldous Huxley, and Edith Sitwell. He became a close friend of William Walton, the composer, and was taken up with enthusiasm by T. W. Earp, then president of the Oxford Union, who was the first to recognize his talent.

In 1920 Campbell accompanied Earp to Paris and then went on his own to Provence. The experience was to be doubly fruitful. In Paris Campbell acquired the poems of Paul Valéry; having already been introduced to the symbolists, notably Rimbaud, by Earp and having greeted the 1919 volume of *Wheels* (a series of anthologies of new verse that the Sitwells had begun editing in 1916) with great excitement, he now began to come under the influence of a number of modern French poets. In Provence he found an environment very much to his liking, and over the next two years he revisited it when not working as a deckhand on coastal vessels or living in London. It was Provence, in some ways like the South Africa he had known, that eventually helped persuade him to become a European. Being by the Mediterranean and on ships reminded him of the sea at Durban and, more particularly, of his love of shipboard life gained from the time he went as a youth on a whaler to the Kerguelen Islands. Not surprisingly, maritime imagery dominates in some of his best poems, notably in *The Flaming Terrapin* and "Tristan da Cunha," and in some of his best prose.

When in London Campbell met Wyndham Lewis, who was to have considerable influence on him and who made him the model for several of his characters. He became an habitué of the Café Royale, knew Augustus John and Jacob Epstein, and met T. E. Lawrence. Generally, for his intellectual friends, Campbell preferred painters or sculptors and men of action. In November 1922 after a wildly romantic courtship, Campbell married Mary Garman, a beautiful dark-haired art student. Because he married without parental consent and while under age, his father showed his disapproval by cutting off his allowance for a time.

As a result, the couple had to find a means of living cheaply. They left London and rented a converted stable in Carnarvonshire, North Wales, at a point opposite Bardsey Island. During the year they lived there their daughter Teresa was born, and Campbell wrote *The Flaming Terrapin*. When this "narrative" poem of 1,300 lines in six parts was published in 1924, its primeval vision, imaginative sensuousness, and overwhelming vitality created a great stir. Between 1924 and 1935 the English edition went through five impressions. The American edition was reprinted in 1970.

In *The Flaming Terrapin* Campbell refashioned the story of the Flood and Noah's Ark by superimposing upon it his own myth of the great terrapin which tows the Ark about the world before finally beaching it. Within the framework of the myth the Flood is made to symbolize the chaos and disruption wrought by the Fiend, aided by Corruption, Mediocrity, Plutocracy, and other evils. To a world still recovering from World War I the myth proclaims the terrapin and the Noah family, together with the animal world in their keeping, to represent the forces of creative energy and regenerative power. The poem, itself youthful, calls upon the youth of the world to be inspired by their triumph. In his review Edward Garnett wrote: "The poet's achievement lies in the leaping fountain of imagination, in its profusion of invention, in its lavish exuberance, and wealth of emotion. Its pictures are so concentrated and its transitions so abrupt that it is not easy to grasp the effect of the whole, even at a second reading." An often quoted section of the poem is

> His was the crest that from the angry sky
> Tore down the hail: he made the boulders fly
> Like balls of paper, splintered icebergs, hurled
> Lassoes of dismal smoke around the world,
> And like a bunch of crisp and crackling straws,
> Coughed the sharp lightning from his craggy jaws.

The poem was almost universally praised. However, complaints, of a kind to be repeated about Campbell's later work, were expressed—about his exaggerations, excesses, and repetitiveness, his sometimes rough metrics undercutting his fecund rhyming, his overloaded lines. Campbell's habit, to be lifelong, of drawing from other poets was widely sensed, and attempts were made to suggest the poem's indebtedness to a diversity of influences. The actual model, Rimbaud's *Le Bâteau ivre* (1871), was scarcely noted at that time. More lately Campbell's skillful adaptations from it have been stressed. Immediate causes of enthusiasm, such as the tonic value of *The Flaming Terrapin* in the years following World War I and the exhaustion of Georgian poetry, have long since receded, but Campbell's first reaction in poetry to the contrast he discovered between the Africa he had known and a world-weary Europe still has power.

The convictions underlying this early poem are ones from which Campbell never deviated, though sometimes he was to apply them undesirably. For Campbell, Noah and his family, like the other mythologized figures of his poetry—the cowboy, the poet, the bullfighter, and the soldier—are superior as men and have the power to survive because they possess hard-won skills, strength, endurance, and courage. They are part of "the clean / System of active things." Campbell's heroes reflect his belief that the true man resists every force that seeks to reduce his energy, to rob him of his independence and dignity. Such a viewpoint, of course, lies at the heart of romanticism. What caused the ferment in Campbell's mind was a passionate conviction that the pursuit of peace or happiness or profit, and concern with power or possessions, is a contemptible betrayal of the true end of human life: the attempt to make something worthy of survival. In "Autumn" (first published in periodicals in 1929) he was to write

> I love to see, when leaves depart,
> The clear anatomy arrive,
> Winter, the paragon of art,
> That kills all forms of life and feeling
> Save what is pure and will survive.

Campbell's roots are in the early nineteenth century and, at times, the eighteenth. At moments in the poem he speaks almost the language of Blake. More often, with the enthusiasm of Nietzsche, he dwells on the idea that when one cycle of history has ended in moral weakness and decadence, a new one, barbarian, fresh, and strong, begins the story again. He is fascinated by examples of resolute moral resistance to decay or mediocrity, of those who protect the sublime and the heroic. All that "The Man, clear-cut against the last horizon!" truly possesses he owes to his own unflagging labor and his hunger for beauty. The only thing of absolute value in the universe is the "sudden strength that catches up men's souls." In *The Flaming Terrapin*, as elsewhere, Campbell reveals a complex of attitudes whose heritage can be traced to the romantics, to Herbert Spencer, and to Nietzsche.

Following the success of *The Flaming Terrapin* Campbell returned to Durban. He seems to have wanted to establish himself as a leading literary light in his native country. However, events and his own temperament were to prevent this. In 1926, after he had met two other young South African writers, William Plomer and Laurens van der Post, he decided to start a magazine with them as coeditors. Its name, *Voorslag* ("Whiplash"), is suggestive of the trouble that soon arose. From the outset the journal was boldly provocative, but it was Campbell's ardent championing of Plomer's novel *Turbott Wolfe* and its sympathetic treatment of an interracial love affair, and his more thoroughgoing assault in a subsequent essay on racial inequality in South Africa, which brought matters to a head. The financial backer of the magazine insisted on a change of policy and control by a new managing editor, and many let Campbell and his associates know they had transgressed. Campbell resigned dramatically and the others withdrew. The eventual effect of the episode was that Campbell was to leave South Africa; the immediate effect was that he wrote *The Wayzgoose*, his first major satiric poem.

The Wayzgoose possesses a wit and a sophisticated élan largely absent from his rather haranguing, self-consciously intellectual prose in *Voorslag*. But his subject matter is the same: the wrong of racial prejudice and discrimination, the absurdities of South African politics, colonial prudery and cultural anemia, the dullness and triviality of Durban journalists and literati. Though obviously modeled on *The Dunciad*, the poem successfully subordinates its debt to Pope, and also Dryden, to its own spirited if egotistical originality, especially in the memorable portrait of Polybius Jubb.

Not surprisingly, Campbell was unable to find anyone in South Africa willing to print the poem. After he and his family had returned to England in December 1926, it was published there in 1928 and enjoyed only a succes d'estime. Its subject matter was too remote, and, while its dexterity was admired, the venom it expended at length on minor and unfamiliar targets was thought misplaced. Other, briefer satires Campbell wrote during his sojourn in South Africa contain less wit and lightheartedness and give first notice of elements of rancor and a fierce intolerance in his outlook. These appear to have been bred out of a wounded ego and a deep-seated bitterness, the origin of which has not been altogether established.

Fortunately, though such blemishes are not absent from it, Campbell's second major satire, *The Georgiad* (1931), does say things worth saying, often in an extremely clever and amusing way, despite the fact that parts of it have caused him, with some justice, to be accused of gross lapses in taste. As elsewhere, Campbell is sometimes the victim of imperfectly controlled anger and a lack of emotional restraint.

In the poem Campbell once again revives the methods of Pope and Dryden; but as often his ingeniously rhymed couplets and careless technique recall Byron or Charles Churchill. His attack on J. C. Squire and other neo-Georgians, as well as on some of the lesser Bloomsburyites, has its own freshly insouciant force, however. The poem's chief weakness, as in *The Flaming Terrapin*, is in its meandering and changeable narrative framework, but even on the purely narrative level, Campbell, typically, can provide very effective sections; for instance, the fabliau vignette in the last of the poem's three parts is extremely funny and done with great vigor and panache. Otherwise, the satire is at its best in the cruelly clever dissections of several of J. C. Squire's poems and of Victoria Sackville-West's *The Land*. It becomes less meaningful and persuasive when it adopts views previously expressed by Wyndham Lewis and attempts to suggest that a conspiracy existed among members of the literary establishment to suppress the talents of dissenting outsiders like Lewis and Campbell himself. Its harping on the vitiating prevalence of homosexuality in the literary world becomes tiresome.

William Plomer, Roy Campbell, and Mary Campbell, 1926

Campbell's sense of himself as an outsider most often in the right when others were in the wrong, already engendered by what had happened to him in South Africa, was intensified and made permanent both by events that inspired *The Georgiad* and by the mainly hostile response to it on publication. After the Campbells (a second daughter, Anna, had been born in South Africa) had returned to England, Sir Harold Nicolson and his wife, Victoria Sackville-West, invited them to live for as long as they wished in a cottage on their property at Longbarn, near Sevenoaks in Kent. In this way it came about that Campbell was introduced to various literary figures with whose values, manners, and morals he found himself at odds. After several months the Campbells packed up and went to live in Provence, where in due course *The Georgiad* was written. Henceforth, in a selective fashion, Campbell was to regard himself as a European, even though during and after World War I he was to live in England again for some years and to revisit South Africa, periods when he especially restored the image of himself as a South African.

Before *The Georgiad*, *Adamastor* (1930), the collection of Campbell's poems which became his most popular work and the one upon which his reputation chiefly rests, was published. Poems from this collection have been the ones most frequently anthologized, and many of them reappeared in *Sons of the Mistral* (1941; reprinted seven times, most recently in 1958). The first English edition of *Adamastor* went through three impressions within two months of publication, and new editions were published in 1932 and 1950, the latter being reprinted in 1954. It was the second work of Campbell's also to be published in America, where it was reprinted in 1971. Translations into French of some of the poems appeared in 1936 and again in 1958. Fourteen of them are in Aquilino Duque's Spanish translation of selected poems by Campbell, published in 1958.

Many of the *Adamastor* poems were first printed in the *New Statesman*. Most reflect either Campbell's African experience or his new life in Provence. The best known and the most often praised include "Rounding the Cape," "The Serf," "The Zulu Girl," "The Zebras," "Tristan da Cunha," "The Sisters," "African Moonrise," "Mass at Dawn," "Horses on the Camargue," "The Palm," and "Autumn." On the whole, criticism has not been kind to the satirical pieces, though Campbell is perhaps best known for that corrosive epigram "On Some South African Novelists." Thinking primarily of the lyrical poems, the *Times Literary Supplement* reviewer wrote: "He is rich to the point of embarrassment in learning, not perhaps the academic kind, but the learning of a curious ardour ranging the geographical and mythological worlds; his vocabulary is magnificent in its swift provision of words of every grade and opportunity; his versification is athletic, finely strung, quick turning." Concerning these poems much comment has been devoted to Campbell's debts to Baudelaire, Rimbaud, Valéry, and other French poets. In a discussion of Campbell's lifelong immersion in the French symbolists and his borrowings from them, Rowland Smith concluded: "In some cases Campbell merely borrows from a Romance poem a mood, and the pattern of imagery which created that mood. In other cases he molds a poem by another poet into an original work which becomes distinctly his. . . . consistently the more intangible Gallic material becomes direct and concrete. . . ."

Campbell's first books of prose, as he admitted, were written for money and were hurried productions. Nevertheless, both *Taurine Provence* (1932) and *Broken Record* (1934), his first autobiography, reveal a good deal about the direction in which he was moving as a poet and personality. The poems of *Flowering Reeds* (1933) surpass in evocation of Provençal life and landscape the best descriptions of these in *Taurine Provence*, and the political and social values pervading *Mithraic Emblems* (1936) are the ones first enunciated in *Broken Record*. These prose works are dramatic proof of the intense effect on Campbell of both the outcome of the *Voorslag* episode and the stay with the Nicolsons. In violent reaction against many manifestations of contemporary society, he at the same time rejected the reigning literary and cultural values to which for a while he had himself subscribed. With great effort of will Campbell had been developing his aggressively flamboyant persona, the leading characteristic of which was to be as un-English as possible. By extolling bullfighting in *Taurine Provence* and describing his own exploits in the arena in *Broken Record*, he established a position from which to hurl banderillas at anything and everything Anglo-Saxon that he disliked. Having painfully felt himself to be an outsider when in England, he now deliberately confirmed that exclusion by identifying himself with the cattlemen and fishermen of Provence and with the cultural and literary milieu of Mistral, Daudet, de Montherlant, and Maurras. Accordingly, he set out in his prose his "vision of the salvation of civilization from tradesmen and pedestrians by equestrians and cattlemen." In doing so, he evoked his South African background in order to explain his incompatibility with much in the modern world, as in, "I am presenting an outsider's point of view: you may take it as that of the previctorian man, or of a pagan who was never put through any mill except that of the pre-industrial European culture of an equestrian, slightly feudal type."

As a reactionary, Campbell expounds in these books what he regards as the human value of tradition and time-honored ways that lead to a natural expertness and doing things well. He delights in tracing the history of the bullfighting and nautical games in which he himself learned to participate honorably. The one goes back to Mithraism and the other to the Roman naumachia. What is important to him in such traditional activity is the harmonious balance achieved in it between mind and body. Combined with this emphasis on tradition is Campbell's liking for what is aristocratic. "Aristocracy, culture and wealth have always been associated with equestrianism," and with "a sense of style." Whether detailing his boyhood exploits as a hunter and student of the wild or his abilities in gaining acceptance by seamen, horsemen, farmers, sportsmen, or divers as someone proficient in their métier, Campbell continually stresses the importance of traditional skills as intrinsic to genuine culture.

Even Wyndham Lewis, from whom Campbell acquired some of his more pugnacious ideas in these books, mocked his rhapsodic mystagogy concerning bullfighting and Mithraism by portraying him in *Snooty Baronet* (1932) as Rob McPhail, a comic bullfighter who gets killed as a result of trying to act upon his theories. The dangerous silliness of some of *Taurine Provence* and *Broken Record* is undeniable, in particular the expressions of arrant contempt for the ordinary city dweller (Campbell's "pedestrian," or, more opprobriously, "Charlie"), the anti-Semitic and racist comments, and the wilder remarks on literature, journalism, modern art, and science. But what makes these books still readable, apart from the light they shed on Campbell's poetry and personality, is a disarming quality. He makes it clear that he is seldom to be taken literally, that his mode is an entertaining and emotive overstatement and constant imaginative embellishment. His autobiography is full of tall stories and transformations of events and facts, as much for his own credit as the reader's delight.

Understandably, these first prose works have received little notice. But what is harder to understand, and unfortunate, is the neglect of *Flowering Reeds*, Campbell's next major collection of poems following *Adamastor*. Not for the first or last time did a sudden change in his language, technique, and subject matter cause caution, if not bewilderment. The poems in *Flowering Reeds* possess a quiet, intellectually controlled intensity and quite often employ startling metaphysical conceits. None is satiric, and the poems' lyricism depends on a much stricter concern for form, precision, and clarity. In them Campbell turns away from the posture of defiant Byronic victim to deal more objectively with classical themes. Perhaps, too, the poems largely failed to strike a responsive chord because, unlike the socially engaged poetry then becoming fashionable, they dealt with love, beauty and mutability, heroic triumph and suffering.

With the exception of some French criticism, it is only recently that studies have undertaken to compensate for this neglect. Reappraisals have recognized that much of the excellence of *Flowering Reeds* is due to Campbell's success in freely adapting from Valéry's *Charmes* and some of Baudelaire's poems. "The Secret Muse," which may be compared with Valéry's "Les Pas," is one of several poems employing the metaphysical conceit effectively. In "Overtime" Campbell imposes his own playful wit upon more uniformly somber Baudelairean material. In "The Olive Tree" poems and "Choosing a Mast" he freshly invokes classical motifs and blends them with the Provençal landscape. Some of the octosyllabic poems sink into a confusion of Pre-Raphaelite detail, but a number of the sonnets revivify even that well-tried form. "The Road to Arles" reworks the myth of Actaeon with a powerful deftness—

> Along the cold grey torrent of the sky
> Where branch the fatal trophies of his brows,
> Actaeon, antlered in the wintry boughs,
> Rears to the stars his mastiff-throttled cry.

Unhappily for Campbell, the idyllic side of his life in Provence was not the only one. By 1933 he was in financial straits, and conflict had developed between him and the local people. The Campbells, though destitute, found it necessary to leave and moved to Spain. After some miserable months in a Barcelona slum, Campbell was able to rent a farm near Alicante. There they stayed for a year, during which time they decided to become Roman Catholics and took instruction from the local priest, whom they found to be an impressive person. In his second autobiography, *Light on a Dark Horse* (1951), Campbell tells us, "From the very beginning my wife and I understood the real issues in Spain. There could be no compromise in this war between the East and the West, between Credulity and Faith . . . now was the time to decide whether . . . to remain half-apathetic . . . or whether we should step into the front ranks of the Regular Army of Christ." From 1935 until the outbreak of the civil war, they lived happily in Toledo, the city that henceforth was to have the greatest significance for Campbell as the traditional center of Catholic Spain, associated with Saint John of the Cross and Saint Teresa of Avila, and with the religious paintings of El Greco. But during "the Terror" preceding the outbreak of hostilities, the Campbells' lives were often in danger. Despite this danger, Campbell agreed to take custody of the Carmelite archives when that order was threatened. Soon after, at the height of the disorders, Campbell managed to arrange the evacuation of his family and himself by fleeing to Valencia and boarding a British warship. Back in England, filled with a sense of outrage at what he had witnessed in Spain, he was forced to stay with his Communist in-laws, surrounded by their kind, and found their viewpoint galling.

Campbell's conversion was in part politically motivated, but unquestionably there were deep personal reasons as well. Much in his temperament, past thinking, and experience led him to take the step. That this was so becomes plain from the religious poems forming a unit at the beginning of *Mithraic Emblems*. With their fusion of Mithraic and Christian allusiveness and startling, but obscure color symbolism, these cryptic sonnets play variations on the themes of sacrifice, purgation, and redemption. Most overtly refer to Campbell's own experience of conversion; others treat spiritual experience more generally. At least one, "The Sixth Sword," in its clear allusion to the struggle in Spain, is ostensibly political. The earlier version of this short-line sonnet, however, was quite different. The experience of "the Terror" in Toledo appears to have crystallized Campbell's pro-Franco sympathies and to have been behind the composition of the more violent and unfeelingly partisan poems in the rest of the collection. In them Campbell directly aligns his equestrian-aristocratic outlook with the cause of the Spanish Nationalists and, too often, with a sickeningly messianic fervor predicts wholesale destruction and bloodletting as the solution for the ills of Western civilization. Some poems have terrible implications and show where Campbell's reactionary, anachronistic dream of an old, unchanging Spain was leading him. Such was Campbell's capacity to rise above his worst poetic self, however, that there are worthier individual poems. These are invariably the ones in which he avoids a public rhetoric and writes out of his own deeply felt and keenly observed experience. "The Sling," "After the Horse-fair," "Toledo, July 1936," "The Fight," and "Posada" are among them. Of Toledo he could write

> When I saw you die
> . . . .
> I heard the silence of your bells
> Who've left these broken stones behind
> Above the years to make your home,
> And burn, with Athens and with Rome,
> A sacred city of the mind.

For a short time in 1937 Campbell returned to Spain as a war correspondent. The relief by Franco's forces of the heroic garrison of Toledo's Alcázar fortress affected him profoundly and became a central event in his treatment of the war. With unreserved and uncritical fervor he espoused the Nationalist cause as a Christian crusade against Bolshevism and what were to him its dupes—the western democracies, the British left, and the Anglo-Saxon press. When he said he wished to join Franco's army, the authorities asked him to support their cause with his pen instead—"There are enough rifles but not enough pens," he was told. So it was that he came to write *Flowering Rifle* and other poems on the war.

In Portugal in the course of about a year he poured out the 5,000 lines of his monstrous six-part "epic," the 1939 version of *Flowering Rifle*. In his review of the poem Stephen Spender described it as "a kind of three-decker sandwich consisting of one layer of invective against the intellectuals of the Left, the International Brigade, the Spanish Republican Army, etc.; a second layer of autobiography concerning the exploits of Mr. Campbell and his flowering rifle; and a top layer of rhapsody about Franco and his colleagues, who are treated as nothing less than angels." He goes on to say that beneath "ignoble sweepings of every kind of anti-Semitic and atrocity propaganda," there are buried "stones of a certain lustre," but adds, "There are several passages in this book which make me feel physically sick." Campbell did not put *Flowering Rifle* into his 1949 *Collected Poems*, but a revised version of it was included with those poems published posthumously. Fair-minded and sympathetic critics have drawn back from accusing Campbell of fascism, but he came perilously close to being guilty of it.

After having indulged in so much coarse rhetoric Campbell never fully recovered his poetic virtues, and his endless involvement in polemics and personal quarrels occasioned by his stance on Spain almost fatally diverted his energies. Had it not been for World War II and its effect on him he might well have been finished as a poet.

In 1939, after Franco's victory, Campbell returned to Toledo and remained there until deciding in 1941 to go to Britain. At first he acted as an air-raid warden in London, and then he joined the British army. Because of his knowledge of African

Roy Campbell, circa 1946 (BBC Hulton, photo by K. Hutton)

languages, he was sent to Kenya and Somalia; in 1944 he was invalided out and returned to England. It seems that what prompted him to fight for the democracy he had vilified was a new admiration for the English in wartime and perhaps a belated recognition of the true nature of fascism. However, his best war poems, to appear in *Talking Bronco* (1946), present a sober and realistic, at times a surreal and satiric, picture of the war in North Africa from the point of view of a seasoned, sometimes cynical NCO. Poems like "The Skull in the Desert," "Dreaming Spires," "Heartbreak Camp," "Nyanza Moonrise," and "Monologue" suggest that the suffering and comradeship of the war helped to endow Campbell's verse with a new humanity and poetic resource. Nor can one forget the more personal and moving sonnet "Luis de Camões." But otherwise there is much dross in the collection and evidence of a general slackening, repetitiveness, and dependence on formulas, characteristics to be found in other verse in the second volume of *Collected Poems* (1957). The vices to which Campbell's verse was now prone—including resort to colloquialism and army slang, but without his former ability to give them aptness and sting—are especially evident in the title poem, "Talking Bronco."

For some years following the war's end Campbell produced only a few poems, most of them translations, and spent his time, when not acting as a talks producer for the BBC, writing journalism and giving lectures. But the good reception of his *Collected Poems* in 1949 seems to have renewed his creative energy. In the next few years he produced his translation of the poems of St. John of the Cross (1951; for which he was awarded the William Foyle Poetry Prize), his second autobiography (1951), his translation of Baudelaire's *Fleurs du Mal*, and his book on Lorca (1952).

Undoubtedly Campbell's translation of St. John of the Cross made many more people aware of a body of great religious poetry. Campbell's attempt—frequently not altogether successful—to capture something of St. John's diction, imagery, and rhythms led the way for several other verse translations. These have improved upon Campbell's in many respects, but none has excelled its best moments of poetry as poetry. Besides "Upon a Gloomy Night," one thinks of "Songs between the Soul and the Bridegroom" and "Verses written after an ecstasy of high exaltation." Between 1951 and 1968 the translation went through five hardcover editions in the United States, and appeared in two paperback editions, one of them reprinted. But after its first publication attention shifted for a time to *Light on a Dark Horse*.

This richly anecdotal autobiography, along with his study of Lorca, contains Campbell's best prose. In many ways it seems a deliberate improvement on *Broken Record*: it covers much the same ground, but with infinitely more solidity and detail and with the intemperate views either eradicated or muted; its descriptions often bring one close to Campbell's poetry, and the narrative is frequently dramatic and well managed. Throughout the book shines his love for his family. But not all is gain. It has been agreed that, judged as an account of exotic adventures and a display of a prankish, exuberant, passionately intense personality, the book greatly succeeds, but that as autobiography it almost totally fails. So intent is Campbell upon impressing, astonishing, or amusing us that when we do occasionally glimpse the real man, it is by accident. We learn next to nothing about the inner self or the growth of a near-great poet. In the second part of the book especially, the boasting and unauthentic showiness contrast with the direct simplicity and manifest leg-pulling of much of *Broken Record*. It almost seems that Campbell set out to write a best-seller,

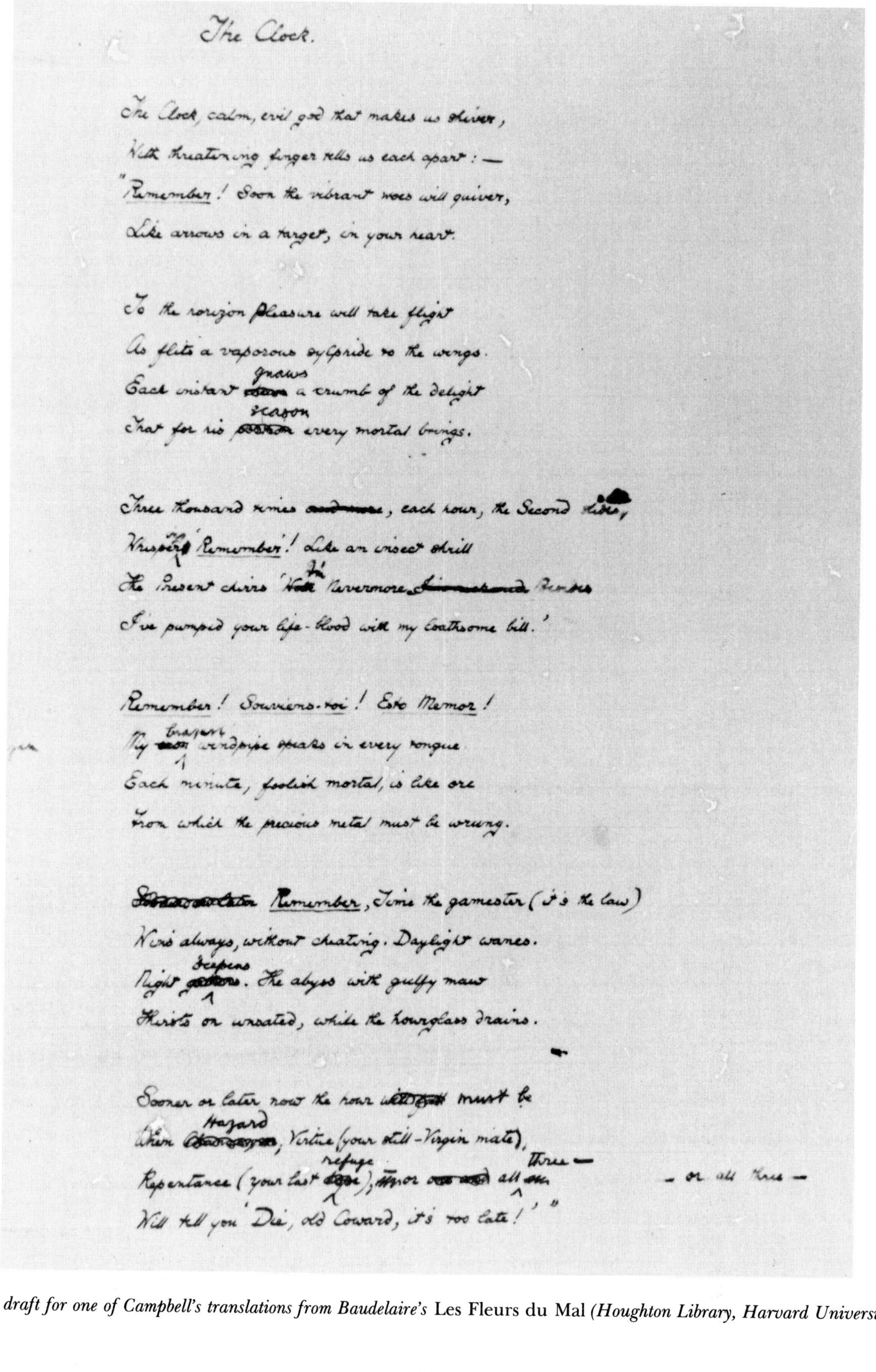
The Clock.

The Clock, calm, evil god that makes us shiver,
With threatening finger tells us each apart:—
"Remember! Soon the vibrant woes will quiver,
Like arrows in a target, in your heart.

To the horizon Pleasure will take flight
As flits a vaporous sylphide to the wings.
Each instant gnaws a crumb of the delight
That for his season every mortal brings.

Three thousand times, each hour, the Second slides,
Whispers 'Remember'! Like an insect shrill
The Present chirps 'I'm Nevermore
I've pumped your life-blood with my loathsome bill.'

Remember! Souviens-toi! Esto Memor!
My brazen windpipe speaks in every tongue.
Each minute, foolish mortal, is like ore
From which the precious metal must be wrung.

Remember, Time the gamester (it's the law)
Wins always, without cheating. Daylight wanes.
Night deepens. The abyss with gulfy maw
Thirsts on unsated, while the hourglass drains.

Sooner or later now the hour must be
When Hazard, Virtue (your still-Virgin mate),
Repentance (your last refuge), or all three —
Will tell you 'Die, old Coward, it's too late!'"

— or all three —

A late draft for one of Campbell's translations from Baudelaire's Les Fleurs du Mal *(Houghton Library, Harvard University)*

and in fact the book sold well, was reprinted, went into a second edition, and became a Penguin paperback.

Campbell's strange reticence about his literary self is the more to be regretted considering his overcrowded, but subtle and exciting exploration of his subject in *Lorca*. This book, too, went into a paperback edition and has been twice reprinted—as the result, one believes, of its incandescent intellectual analysis and sensibility, and the presence in it of some of Campbell's best translations, including "Song of the Horseman" and "Lament for the Matador."

Though a short work, *Lorca* demonstrates not only Campbell's deep immersion in his subject and in Spanish poetry generally, as well as in the French symbolists, but his ability to order what he had absorbed. This same provision of a well-based perspective is to be found in his praiseworthy survey of Portuguese literature in *Portugal* (1957), which also contains translations. Whenever Campbell bestowed his love, as against his hate, the outcome could be remarkable.

Since he had a lifelong attachment to the poetry of Baudelaire, it is not surprising that it should have provided him with his most sustained triumph in translating. After the initial appearance in Britain and America of Campbell's rendering of the complete poems in 1951, a popular edition of selections came out in 1960. In *The Flowers of Evil* (1955), as selected and edited by M. and J. Mathews, thirty-one of the translations are Campbell's; six were included in *The Penguin Book of Modern Verse Translation* (1966). After having expressed some reservations, J. G. Weightman summed up one of his two reviews of the poems by saying, "Hardly anyone could do better, and most of us would do far worse."

In 1952 the Campbells went to live on a farm near Sintra in Portugal. Campbell in the next several years undertook two North American lecture tours, revisited South Africa in order to receive an honorary D.Litt. degree from the University of Natal, Durban, and made a trip to Rome. He was killed in an automobile accident in Portugal.

Campbell will likely be remembered for his lyric gift as displayed in some twenty of his earlier, much anthologized poems and in a number of translations, above all those of St. John of the Cross and García Lorca. As for the rest of his work, it is uncertain whether its more than occasional excellence will cause any of it to survive the dimming of the memory of his personality and the effect of too much technical unevenness and adherence to unacceptable ideas.

Other:

"Contemporary Poetry," in *Scrutinies by Various Writers*, collected by Edgell Rickword, volume 1 (London: Wishart, 1928);

"The History of a Rejected Review," in *Satire and Fiction*, by Wyndham Lewis (London: Arthur Press, 1930).

Translations:

The Poems of St. John of the Cross (London: Harvill, 1951; New York: Pantheon, 1951);

Poems of Baudelaire (London: Harvill, 1952; New York: Pantheon, 1952);

José Maria de Eça de Queiróz, *Cousin Bazilio* (London: Reinhardt, 1953; New York: Noonday, 1953);

Eça de Queiróz, *The City and the Mountains* (London: Reinhardt, 1955; Athens: Ohio University Press, 1960);

Eric Bentley, ed., *The Classic Theatre. Volume Three: Six Spanish Plays*, includes five plays translated by Campbell (Garden City: Doubleday, 1959);

Pedro Calderón de la Barca, *The Surgeon of His Honour* (Madison: University of Wisconsin Press, 1960).

Periodical Publications:

"Fetish Worship in South Africa," *Voorslag*, 1 (July 1926): 3-19;

"A Decade in Retrospect," *Month*, new series 3 (May 1950): 319-333;

"Poetry and Experience," *Theoria* (University of Natal, Pietermaritzburg), 6 (1954): 37-44;

"The Poetry of Luiz de Camões," *London Magazine*, 4 (August 1957): 23-33.

Bibliography:

D. S. J. Parsons, *Roy Campbell: A Descriptive and Annotated Bibliography* (New York: Garland, 1981).

Biography:

Peter Alexander, *Roy Campbell: A Critical Biography* (Oxford: Oxford University Press, 1982).

References:

Alan Paton, "Roy Campbell," in *Aspects of South African Literature*, edited by Christopher

Heywood (London: Heinemann, 1976), pp. 3-23;
John Povey, *Roy Campbell* (Boston: Twayne, 1977);
Rowland Smith, *Lyric and Polemic: The Literary Personality of Roy Campbell* (Montreal & London: McGill-Queen's University Press, 1972).

Papers:
The University of Texas at Austin has manuscripts of *The Poems of St. John of the Cross*, of half of the *Poems of Baudelaire*, and of an unpublished translation of García Lorca's *The House of Bernarda Alba*, as well as many letters and fragments. The University of Saskatchewan Library has manuscripts of translations of Spanish plays and of *The City and the Mountains*; a lightly annotated copy of *Collected Poems*, volume 1; and a lightly annotated manuscript of *Collected Poems*, volume 2; many prose drafts, letters, and research notes. The National English Literary Museum, Rhodes University, South Africa, has extensive correspondence, numerous files of journal and newspaper clippings, the late Dr. W. H. Gardner's research notes, and his preliminary draft of a biography.

Austin Clarke
(9 May 1896-19 March 1974)

Mary FitzGerald
University of New Orleans

See also the Clarke entry in *DLB 10, Modern British Dramatists 1900-1945*.

BOOKS: *The Vengeance of Fionn* (Dublin: Maunsel, 1917);
The Fires of Bäal (Dublin: Maunsel & Roberts, 1921);
The Sword of the West (Dublin & London: Maunsel & Roberts, 1921);
The Cattledrive in Connaught and Other Poems (London: Allen & Unwin, 1925);
The Son of Learning: A Poetic Comedy in Three Acts (London: Allen & Unwin, 1927);
Pilgrimage and Other Poems (London: Allen & Unwin, 1929; New York: Farrar & Rinehart, 1930);
The Flame: A Play in One Act (London: Allen & Unwin, 1932);
The Bright Temptation: A Romance (London: Allen & Unwin, 1932; New York: Morrow, 1932);
The Collected Poems of Austin Clarke (London: Allen & Unwin, 1936; New York: Macmillan, 1936);
The Singing Men at Cashel (London: Allen & Unwin, 1936);
Night and Morning: Poems (Dublin: Orwell Press, 1938);
Sister Eucharia: A Play in Three Scenes (Dublin: Orwell, 1939; London: Williams & Norgate, 1939);

Austin Clarke (BBC Hulton)

Black Fast: A Poetic Farce in One Act (Dublin: Orwell Press, 1941);
The Straying Student (Dublin: Gayfield Press, 1942);
As the Crow Flies: A Lyric Play for the Air (Dublin: Bridge Press, 1943; London: Williams & Norgate, 1943);
The Viscount of Blarney and Other Plays (Dublin: Bridge Press, 1944; London: Williams & Norgate, 1944);
First Visit to England and Other Memories (Dublin: Bridge Press, 1945; London: Williams & Norgate, 1945);
The Second Kiss: A Light Comedy (Dublin: Bridge Press, 1946; London: Williams & Norgate, 1946);
The Plot Succeeds: A Poetic Pantomime (Dublin: Bridge Press, 1950; London: Williams & Norgate, 1950);
Poetry in Modern Ireland (Dublin: Three Candles Press for the Cultural Relations Committee of Ireland, 1951; revised edition, Cork: Mercier, 1962; Folcroft, Pa.: Folcroft Editions, 1974);
The Sun Dances at Easter: A Romance (London: Melrose, 1952);
The Moment Next to Nothing: A Play in Three Acts (Dublin: Bridge Press, 1953);
Ancient Lights: Poems and Satires (Dublin: Bridge Press, 1955);
Too Great a Vine: Poems and Satires (Dublin: Bridge Press, 1957);
The Horse-Eaters: Poems and Satires (Dublin: Bridge Press, 1960);
Later Poems (Dublin: Dolmen, 1961);
Forget-Me-Not (Dublin: Dolmen, 1962);
Six Irish Poets: Austin Clarke, Richard Kell, Thomas Kinsella, John Montague, Richard Murphy, Richard Weber, edited by Robin Skelton (London: Oxford University Press, 1962);
Twice Round the Black Church: Early Memories of Ireland and England (London: Routledge & Kegan Paul, 1962);
Collected Plays (Dublin: Dolmen, 1963);
Flight to Africa and Other Poems (Dublin: Dolmen, 1963);
Poems: A Selection, by Clarke, Tony Connor, and Charles Tomlinson (London: Oxford University Press, 1964);
Mnemosyne Lay in Dust (Dublin: Dolmen, 1966; London: Oxford University Press, 1966; Chester Springs, Pa.: Dufour Editions, 1966);
Old Fashioned Pilgrimage and Other Poems (Dublin: Dolmen, 1967; Chester Springs, Pa.: Dufour Editions, 1967);
The Echo at Coole and Other Poems (Dublin: Dolmen, 1968; Chester Springs, Pa.: Dufour Editions, 1968);
A Penny in the Clouds: More Memories of Ireland and England (London: Routledge & Kegan Paul, 1968; Chester Springs, Pa.: Dufour Editions, 1968);
Two Interludes (Dublin: Dolmen, 1968);
A Sermon on Swift and Other Poems (Dublin: Bridge Press, 1968);
The Celtic Twilight and the Nineties (Dublin: Dolmen, 1969);
Orphide and Other Poems (Dublin: Bridge Press, 1970);
Tiresias: A Poem (Dublin: Bridge Press, 1971);
The Impuritans: A Play in One Act, adapted from Nathaniel Hawthorne's "Young Goodman Brown" (Dublin: Dolmen, 1973);
Collected Poems, edited by Liam Miller (Dublin: Dolmen, 1974; London, Oxford & New York: Oxford University Press, 1974);
The Third Kiss: A Comedy in One Act (London & New York: Oxford University Press, 1974; Dublin: Dolmen, 1976);
Selected Poems, edited by Thomas Kinsella (Dublin: Dolmen, 1976; Winston-Salem, N.C.: Wake Forest University Press, 1976);
Liberty Lane: A Ballad Play of Dublin in Two Acts with a Prologue (Dublin: Dolmen, 1978).

Among the generation of poets who came to prominence in Ireland after William Butler Yeats, Austin Clarke is possibly the finest. Although he is less well known outside Ireland than Louis MacNeice and less obviously an influence on younger poets than Patrick Kavanagh, his metrical complexity and thematic integrity mark him as an important writer of the period. Poet, playwright, novelist, and literary critic, he was born Augustine Joseph Clarke in Dublin. His father, Augustine Clarke, was a civil servant whose nationalism he came to share, and his mother, Ellen Patten Browne Clarke, was a dominating personality whose scrupulous and narrow religiosity inculcated in him an abiding sense of guilt which produced severe mental trauma in his young manhood and haunted him most of his life.

Like James Joyce and Patrick Kavanagh, but unlike most of the more famous figures of the Irish revival, Clarke was Catholic and Celtic, rather than Protestant and Anglo-Irish, and his poetry derives much of its content from these twin aspects of his heritage. His early education had much in common with Joyce's: he too attended Belvedere College (1903-1909, 1910-1912), which Joyce immortalized in *A Portrait of the Artist as a Young Man* (1916), and

Clarke claimed that he identified with Stephen Dedalus when he read the novel years after. Like Stephen, Clarke felt himself the social inferior of his classmates, chafed under parental control, experienced a guilt-ridden adolescence, and struggled with the history, religion, politics, and language of his native land.

During a brief attendance at another Jesuit school, Mungret College (1909-1910) in County Limerick, Clarke discovered poetry—especially what he described as "the evocative power of verbal rhythm." Hearing poetry read aloud in his classes there, the adolescent Clarke responded intellectually and emotionally to the balance of imaginative freedom and controlled expression which such patterned language made possible. He decided that he wanted to write, and he felt that in poetry he had found a major shaping force for his life. Another, less positive shaping force awaited him on his return to Belvedere, however; he suffered his first serious attack of depression, which manifested itself in an uncharacteristic lethargy and an uneasy confusion of mind. These symptoms gradually faded, although they would recur from time to time in the years to come, and he turned eagerly to his metier and began reading the poetry and plays of Yeats. He found himself disliking Yeats's early symbolism and his metrical irregularities, but he greatly admired the lyricism of Yeats's poetic line, and he was even more attracted by Yeats's verse dramas as he read them and saw them performed at the Abbey Theatre.

He took his B.A. at University College, Dublin, and while there discovered the language and literature of Gaelic-speaking ancient Ireland, learning Irish well enough to read the old tales in the original language, something Yeats never had learned to do. Partly in an attempt to "correct" Yeats's versions of the stories and partly in imitation of the long narrative poems of Samuel Ferguson and Herbert Trench, he began to write his own adaptations of the major tales of the mythological cycles. To make them more his own, he turned to imitating the rigorous formal intricacies and the vividly precise description of old Irish prosody and technique within the confines of English narrative form.

Clarke finished his B.A. in the tumultuous year of 1916, not long after his friend and mentor, Thomas MacDonagh, was executed by the British government for his part in the Easter Rising. Though shocked by this turn of events, Clarke continued at University College for his masters degree in English (1917), as MacDonagh had urged him, and found himself appointed to MacDonagh's vacant teaching post for a three-year term in 1917. In the same year, through the influence of George Russell (AE), he produced his first volume of poetry, *The Vengeance of Fionn*, an epic retelling of the most famous love story from the Fenian cycle of Irish mythology. The poems, written in rhymed and unrhymed iambic pentameter but employing metrical conventions from early Irish verse, recount the marriage of Fionn to the beautiful Grainne, her elopement with his younger comrade Diarmuid, Fionn's pursuit of the lovers, and the final treachery by which he destroys Diarmuid and regains Grainne. Although it is overburdened with sensory detail, the poem was well received as an impressively ambitious first attempt, and it earned Clarke an early audience.

Following upon this success, however, came the death of Clarke's father and his own hospitalization for nervous breakdown. References to this dark period of his life appear in several poems, until in *Mnemosyne Lay in Dust* (1966), his late poem, he chronicles his terrifying loss of memory and its slow return. During the period immediately prior to his hospitalization—and for some time after his release—he spent long hours talking with the young novelist and playwright Geraldine Cummins, and in 1920 he married her. She was older than he was, had published more than he had, and was active in the women's suffrage movement. They were apparently drawn together rather more by what they both disliked in the world than what they liked in each other and by Clarke's need of her. Whether for these reasons or for others (Clarke suggests in his autobiographies that their marriage was not consummated), the marriage lasted only ten days. To this burden of failure was added a further shock: in 1921 Clarke was denied reappointment at the university, apparently because his civil marriage displeased his academic superiors. His teaching career suddenly behind him, he thought of immigrating to London and working as a literary reviewer there, while continuing to work on his poems. By year's end he had produced *The Fires of Bäal*, begun as an attempt at a religious theme but rather more an allegory of Irish history told in terms of the struggles of the Israelites, and *The Sword of the West*, a retelling of the stories about the hero Cuchulain from the Ulster cycle of mythological tales. The books indicate the different lines of his future thematic development: a concern with public events, which would become the dominant theme of his later poetry, and the continuing attempt to retell the old Irish tales in a modern English poetry with echoes of the complex assonantal patternings of the original Irish.

Clarke left for England in 1922, the year in

which Ireland was divided by treaty into North and South. Although he returned home at intervals to see family, attend the Abbey Theatre, and visit archaeological sites—a growing interest—Clarke spent the next fifteen years largely in England, earning his living by writing reviews for major newspapers and journals. The poetry written in England turns toward what he called the "Celtic Romanesque" period in Irish art and letters, leaving behind the ancient pagan-hero tales for a more medieval milieu. Although his poetry of the period is still firmly rooted in Ireland, it deals with the varieties of individual lives—both indulgent and ascetic—lived in Christian Ireland before the Elizabethan wars and the Williamite plantations. In 1925 he published the last of his poems drawn from early Irish legend, *The Cattledrive in Connaught*, based on the most famous Irish epic of the Ulster cycle, and soon began work on his first verse play, set in the Celtic-Romanesque era.

The Son of Learning, a pungent play based on a medieval poem, was rejected by the Abbey Theatre but accepted for performance at the Cambridge Festival Theatre in 1927. It recounts the cure of an insatiably hungry king by a poet who lures the "hunger demon" out of the king by conjuring an unbelievably gluttonous feast for him. When the play was performed in Dublin at Micheal Mac Liammóir and Hilton Edwards's Gate Theatre in 1930, the name was changed to *The Hunger Demon*. Witty and satirical, it proved popular with both audiences and provided Clarke with the impetus he needed to devote himself to verse drama, which became his major literary preoccupation during the 1930s, though *Pilgrimage and Other Poems*, a volume of Celtic Romanesque poems, appeared in 1929. The medieval Irish world continued to provide the source of his settings for verse plays, as he was more at home where faith and reason had been one and where religion had not been altogether joyless. Placing his characters in such a time allowed him to imply comparison with the less satisfactory state of things in present-day Ireland.

He continued his journalistic work while writing plays, serving as assistant editor of *Argosy Magazine* for a time in summer 1929, and in 1930 he met Nora Walker, who became his wife. The first of their three sons was born in 1931. Feeling himself more intimately involved in life, Clarke began to experiment with nature poetry and also tried a new genre, the prose romance. The first of his romances, *The Bright Temptation* (1932), ushers in a new era of self-confidence for Clarke. He had finally, it seems, vanquished his own demons. Set in the middle ages, the story follows the picaresque and Dantesque adventures of a young monk who travels through Ireland in the company of a beautiful woman, and it mixes fantasy with satiric commentary on the puritanism of the Catholic teachings of his childhood. The book was banned in Ireland within three weeks of its publication—testimony to the success of its satirical intent—but the first edition had completely sold out before the ban went into effect. Clarke sent a copy to Yeats, who praised it as a "charming and humourous defiance of the censorship and its ideals." Pleased with that and with the success of his play *The Flame* (1932), which was greeted well on its production in Edinburgh, Clarke faced middle age—he was turning forty—with some sense of satisfaction. Once again, as they had done after the publication of his first poem, people were acclaiming him as Yeats's successor, and when the Irish Academy of Letters was founded in November 1932, Yeats and George Bernard Shaw invited Clarke to be a charter member.

His reputation continued to grow, and in 1933 he was invited to serve as a judge at the Oxford Festival of Spoken Poetry, the event founded by John Masefield, Lawrence Binyon, and Walter de la Mare. Trained in verse speaking—he had studied under Frank Fay—Clarke found his experience with the group a pleasant one, and it probably served as the inspiration for the verse-speaking society which he founded himself in Ireland upon his eventual return to Dublin.

In 1936 Clarke turned forty. The British Drama League Festival produced *The Flame*, he brought out a volume of collected poems and a second prose romance, *The Singing Men at Cashel*. The romance, which was banned like its predecessor, further developed the form he had already used: in addition to telling a medieval love story—this time the sad tale of the poet-queen Gormlai, who is wed first to the celibate King Cormac and then to his lustful foster brother before she is free to marry her childhood friend—there is also a Rabelaisian subplot, which the censors found offensive. As before, the mixture of fantasy and invective makes an uneasy combination, and the subplot does not really blend into the story line. There are beautiful passages, as always, and its notoriety won it other admirers, but on the whole it was becoming clear that prose fiction was less Clarke's genre than drama or verse.

In the same year Clarke decided to try literary biography and approached Yeats about the possibility of writing his life. Their interview, recounted in Clarke's autobiographies, did not go smoothly: Clarke abandoned the project and Yeats, despite his earlier praise, left Clarke out of the *Oxford Book of Modern Verse* (1936). His omission of Clarke did not help the younger man's reputation.

As his oldest son reached school age, Clarke became increasingly restless in England, and in 1937 the family returned to Ireland, settling in Bridge House, Templeogue, Dublin. Although the change of residence did not affect his journalistic activities—he continued reviewing for British papers and returned to London for regular visits—it did contribute to a change in his poetry. The slim volume *Night and Morning* (1938), his only collection of verse during this long period of playwriting, marks a significant departure from his earlier poetry. In it, Clarke moved from the public or bardic voice to an intensely personal and private one. The poems are less accessible to the reader, but they are unmistakably universal in their stringent self-examination and precision of phrase.

Living in Ireland, Clarke became familiar with the younger generation of Irish poets, as he had done with the English poets, and he attended the Abbey Theatre with growing frequency. He was generally accepted warmly—within a year of returning to Ireland he was awarded the Casement Prize for Poetry and Drama—but he also became a target for the wit of Samuel Beckett, who parodied him viciously as Austin Ticklepenny of the Magdalen Mental Mercyseat in *Murphy*. Clarke, who had successfully sued for libel in England, winning the retraction of a remark attributed to him in Arnold Bennett's diaries, declined Oliver Gogarty's suggestion that he sue Beckett, because he felt that the book had a sufficiently limited audience appeal, and possibly also because his own satiric impulses had taught him the importance of poetic license: *Murphy* is ostensibly fiction.

Yeats died in January 1939, and with his passing, Clarke seemed even more his successor than before: the year became something of an annus mirabilis for him. He was elected to the presidency of the Irish chapter of P.E.N., began to contribute autobiographical essays to the *Dublin Magazine* at the invitation of Seumus O'Sullivan, became a regular reviewer for the *Irish Times*, and started to broadcast regularly on Radio Eireann. Dublin writers of note began to attend his literary evenings on Sundays. His new play, *Sister Eucharia*, was performed at the Gate to good reviews. A miracle play set in modern times, its moral is that religious authority misjudges the truly saintly, and it seems more than a little indebted to Yeats's *The Countess Cathleen* in structure and theme.

In 1940 he founded the Dublin Verse-Speaking Society with Robert Farren. Its stated aim was to preserve and continue the verse drama which Yeats had begun, and it organized readings of poems and plays, performing them on radio and at the Abbey Theatre. Again with Farren, he started the Lyric Theatre troupe, which performed regularly at the Abbey and became a primary outlet for his own plays after 1944. His primary interest in the 1940s was drama, and he wrote, had published, and staged *Black Fast*, *The Kiss*, *The Viscount of Blarney*, *The Plot Is Ready*, and *The Second Kiss*. There were revivals of his older plays as well, and the new dramas continued in much the same vein as their predecessors. In action or in theme they are usually Celtic Romanesque; they nearly always explore sin and guilt; their primary purpose seems didactic: they teach repeatedly the lesson that authority is often misguided or simply wrong and that the individual is the proper arbiter of morality. Although they were reasonably well received, they had a limited audience appeal as verse drama, and they made the absence of his poetry more obvious. His contemporaries refer to the fifteen-year hiatus in his poetic output as his long "silence"—as though he were not writing plays and review articles the whole time.

Ireland in the 1940s and early 1950s was not particularly hospitable to writers, and part of the explanation for Clarke's "silence" and for the fact that he began to have his plays published in private-press limited editions of 200 copies is the same phenomenon which drove other writers into exile: censorship. Upon the death of F. R. Higgins, his close friend, in 1940, Clarke accepted nomination to the Irish Academy of Letters, an honor which made him a spokesman of sorts for Irish writers, particularly in the battle against censorship. In the early 1940s, Clarke helped organize and sponsor a meeting of the Council of Action against Censorship in Dublin. In the closing years of the decade, he was again elected president of the Irish chapter of P.E.N. and was frequently a guest of honor at P.E.N. conferences after his term expired as well. In 1952 he became president of the Irish Academy of Letters, but this honor did not make him proof against the censorship, and his next prose romance, *The Sun Dances at Easter* (1952), which integrates a strong plot with two subplots and is the best of his efforts in the genre, also was banned in Ireland. This ban especially rankled, and although his next play, *The Moment Next to Nothing* (1953), was produced successfully on radio, he wrote a stinging article on censorship for the *New Statesman*. Within the year the twenty-two-year ban on *The Bright Temptation* was lifted. Although a subsequent appeal of the ban on *The Sun Dances at Easter* failed, this positive sign, together with some traveling he did in the west of Ireland, appeared to revitalize Clarke's purely poetic instincts, and he began to experiment with satiric poetry, one of the oldest prerogatives of Irish poets. A new, more public voice is heard with the publication of his three volumes of satires: *Ancient Lights* (1955), *Too Great a Vine* (1957), and *The Horse-Eaters* (1960). The poems are vigorous and fiercely worded, expressing a public anger across a broad range of social concerns, from religious and political hypocrisy to the sale of horses for food. In technique they are often tightly structured and knotted with imagery so dense as to be sometimes impenetrable, as if Clarke had been storing sounds and ideas for fifteen years and they had all demanded expression simultaneously. There is no mistaking the authority of the voice.

Now in failing health—he had suffered a heart attack in 1959—Clarke began to look back across his career. He put together *Collected Plays* (1963) and a volume of poems written between 1929 and 1960, *Later Poems* (1961), incorporating his private-press editions and revising some early poems. As private-press publication had obscured his recent development for all but a very small audience, the wider public brought by *Later Poems* reawakened interest in his work. He began to write his autobiography, finishing two volumes, *Twice Round the Black Church* (1962) and *A Penny in the Clouds* (1968). Although they manifest his customary obsessions with guilt-inducing religious authority, they are illuminating and well done, and they brought him even greater recognition. Warmed by the renewed approbation, Clarke turned again to the writing of poems for more than satiric purposes. In 1963 he brought out *Flight to Africa*, usually considered the best of his last volumes of poetry. It earned him the Denis Devlin Memorial Award as the best book of poems to appear in Ireland for three years. Other awards followed in recognition of his life's achievement: from the Arts Council of Britain in 1965, a literary award; from Trinity College in 1967, D.Litt; from the Irish Academy of Letters in 1968, the Gregory Award; from the American Irish Foundation in 1972, a generous cash award. Clarke was nominated a candidate for a Nobel Prize, and he was invited to lecture at University College, Dublin, and at the State University of New York at Buffalo—both of which invitations he accepted.

In 1966 he produced *Mnemosyne Lay in Dust*, the long poem describing his mental breakdown of forty years earlier. In eighteen sections of varying meters, Clarke traces the descent of his persona, Maurice Devane, into the nightmare of himself with a precision of description and a violence of poetic texture that are riveting. Pushed to his farthest limits, Devane, like Coleridge's Ancient Mariner, blesses nature: he comes to accept the inherent sexuality of the natural world and imagines himself worshiping in a grove of trees, the "holy ictyphalli." Immediately the mood changes, the spell of madness is broken, and Devane sees a vision of preternaturally innocent children running and playing in moonlight: "Love / Fathered him with their happiness." This newfound knowledge allows him to confront his other guilty obsessions, among them Margaret (his "pale protectress") and his mother, and to work his way back slowly to an acceptance of himself and sanity. The poem is courageous in its scrupulous honesty, a uniquely personal statement that is both autobiography and metaphor.

The last years of his life saw a great outpouring of poetry, usually on social issues, usually piercing satire of his countrymen. The tone is less angry than before, however, and has been replaced by a mordant wit. Responding to a bishop's statement that the children killed in a tragic fire in a church school had at least the consolation that their suffering had earned them an immediate union with God, Clarke fired off a bitter poem ending "Those children, charred in Cavan / Passed straight through hell to heaven," a paraphrase of the bishop's words which demolishes the pious sentiment with irony. If there is a fault in Clarke's poetry of these years, it is that it frequently responds directly to the news of the day rather than meditates upon universal themes. In some senses, of course, Clarke had earned the right to his role as a public conscience, and the journalistic element in such immediately responsive verses makes them an appropriate fusion of the creative and the critical aspects of his life's work. But even when they are most effective, as for example in a poem castigating Catholic members of the Irish government for standing outside the church during the Protestant funeral of Douglas Hyde, first president of Ireland and the founder of the language movement, they have a limited applicability beyond their immediate frame of reference, and their formal design is not often memorable in itself, the result of going too quickly into print under the pressure of time.

Clarke wrote more than satire in his final years, however. He also went over old themes, as in "The Healing of Mis," which celebrates the importance of sexual self-acceptance (and perhaps pays implicit tribute to his wife and family) in retelling the folk legend of a girl who is rescued from madness by a sympathetic poet's loving instruction in the facts of life. The darker side of sexual fantasy is elaborated in "Orphide," the title poem of a 1970 collection, which uses the nightmarish goat figure from Bernadette Soubirous's dreams as its point of departure for a rationalist approach to the phenomenon of Lourdes. And like Yeats's, his late poetic voice is often that of a "wild old wicked man."

All in all, from 1966 to nearly the end of his life, Clarke produced one—and sometimes two—volumes of poetry a year, together with the final volume of his autobiography in 1968, whose title, *A Penny in the Clouds*, may be an oblique answer to Beckett's early caricature of him. Although the poetry is not the same quality as *Flight to Africa* and earlier collections, it has more than simply biographical interest, as in much of it he experimented with rime riche, trying yet again to invigorate modern English prosody with infusions from non-English traditions.

In 1974, Dolmen Press, which had published many of his later poems, brought out his *Collected Poems*, under the editorship of Liam Miller, its founder. Clarke died just as the book became available. A *Selected Poems*, edited by the poet Thomas Kinsella, appeared in 1976. Since then, Clarke has gradually garnered more attention from literary critics, and the assessment of his career is presently underway. There have been two full-length studies of his work and critical examinations of shorter lengths as well. It seems clear that he will be regarded as an important innovator in modern metrics: although he was not the first to incorporate Celtic assonantal patterns in an English line, he was the first to do so memorably, and some of his successors have followed his example in a subtler way. As with Yeats, the immediate consensus after his death was that his poetry would stand better than his plays, but more recent studies have begun to rehabilitate the verse dramas.

As a personal poetry and as a public poetry, his work deserves further study. It is different from most of the poetry of his contemporaries. Although Clarke is traditional in his harkening back to a simpler time and to an older form of metrics, he is modern in his intention to forge something new out of the old. He is also, with Yeats and T. S. Eliot, one of the few modern exponents of verse drama. His adherence to locale and his insistence that form echo content are modern too, as is his relentless self-examination. Although the poems from his earliest days are perhaps too richly endowed with clusters of images and with deliberately complex metrical patterning, and although his latest poems are almost too bitterly narrow in their tone and theme, his overall achievement is considerable. When he is in relaxed control of his material and his form, as he is in "Mabel Kelly" or "Martha Blake at Fifty-one" or "The Straying Student," where the intricate Celtic assonances merge imperceptibly into a flowing English line, Austin Clarke is unsurpassed.

Other:

The Poems of Joseph Campbell, edited, with an introduction, by Clarke (Dublin: Allen Figgis, 1963);

Francis MacManus, ed., *The Yeats We Knew*, includes an essay by Clarke (Cork: Mercier, 1965), pp. 74-94;

"The Poetry of Swift," in *Jonathan Swift 1667-1967: a Dublin Tercentenary Tribute*, edited by Roger McHugh and Philip Edwards (Dublin: Dolmen, 1967), pp. 94-115;

The Plays of George Fitzmaurice, volume 1, includes an introduction by Clarke (Dublin: Dolmen, 1967);

Two Interludes: Adapted from Cervantes: The Student from Salamanca / La cueva de Salamanca and The Silent Lover / El viejo celoso, translated and adapted by Clarke (Dublin: Dolmen, 1968);

"Gaelic Ireland Rediscovered," in *Irish Poets in English: the Thomas Davies Lectures on Anglo-Irish Poetry*, edited by Sean Lucy (Cork: Mercier, 1973): 30-43;

The Wooing of Becfola (After the Irish), translated and adapted by Clarke (London: Poems of the Month Club, 1973).

Periodical Publications:

"The Problem of Verse Drama To-day," *London Mercury*, 33 (November 1935): 34-38;

"Verse-speaking and Verse Drama," *Dublin Magazine*, new series, 12 (October-December 1937): 9-17;

"Poetry in Ireland To-Day," *Bell*, 13 (November 1946): 155-161;

"Verse Speaking," *Bell*, 15 (December 1947): 52-56;

"Irish Poetry Today," *Dubliner*, no. 7 (January-February 1963): 64-68;

"W. B. Yeats and Verse Drama," *Threshold*, no. 19 (Autumn 1965): 14-29;

"The Visitation: a Play," *Irish University Review*, 4 (Spring 1974): 74-90.

References:

Raymond B. Browne and others, eds., *The Celtic Cross: Studies in Irish Culture and Literature* (West Lafayette, Ind.: Purdue University Press, 1964);

Susan Halpern, *Austin Clarke, His Life and Works* (Dublin: Dolmen, 1974);

Irish University Review: Austin Clarke Special Issue, edited by Maurice Harmon, 4 (Spring 1974): 74-90;

John Jordan, *Austin Clarke* (Lewisburg, Pa.: Bucknell University Press, 1970);

J. C. C. Mays, "Mythologized Presences: *Murphy* in its Time," in *Myth and Reality in Irish Literature*, edited by Joseph Ronsley (Waterloo, Ont.: Wilfrid Laurier University Press, 1977);

Vivian Mercier, "The Verse Plays of Austin Clarke," *Dublin Magazine*, new series, 19 (April-June 1944): 39-47;

G. Craig Tapping, *Austin Clarke: A Study of His Writings* (Totowa, N.J.: Barnes & Noble, 1981).

Elizabeth Daryush

(5 December 1887-7 April 1977)

John Finlay

BOOKS: *Charitessi 1911* (Cambridge, U.K.: Bowes & Bowes, 1912);

Verses by Elizabeth Bridges (Oxford: Blackwell, 1916);

Verses (London: Oxford University Press, 1930);

Verses: Second Book (London: Oxford University Press, 1932);

Verses: Third Book (London: Oxford University Press, 1933);

Verses: Fourth Book (London: Oxford University Press, 1934);

The Last Man and Other Verses (London: Oxford University Press, 1936);

Verses: Sixth Book (Oxford: Privately printed, 1938);

Selected Poems, edited by Yvor Winters (New York: Swallow / Morrow, 1948);

Verses: Seventh Book (South Hinksey, U.K.: Carcanet Press, 1971);

Selected Poems (South Hinksey, U.K.: Carcanet Press, 1972);

Collected Poems (Manchester: Carcanet New Press, 1976).

Elizabeth Daryush has been one of the most neglected poets writing in English in this century. She stubbornly held on to certain traditional poetic procedures and maintained a diction that frequently was criticized as archaic. The literary revolutions effected by Ezra Pound and T. S. Eliot never touched the somewhat insular attitude she had toward poetry. Consequently, she has been dismissed as belonging more to the discredited world of the late Victorians than to the poetically more authentic movements of the twentieth century. Yet such an assessment is slowly being recognized as both unjust and inaccurate. American poet-critic Yvor Winters championed her from the beginning of her career; Donald E. Stanford sought her out in her old age and published several of her last poems in the influential *Southern Review*. In her native England such important poets as Roy Fuller and Donald Davie have recently "discovered" her and commented on the power and integrity of her best poems, and Michael Schmidt, the director of the Carcanet Press, has brought most of her work back into print. The writer of Daryush's obituary in the London *Times* speaks of Schmidt's having become "devoted to the Edwardian formality of the Daryushes—their 'magnificent humanity and dignity and ready complex of humour and wit.' " The emerging picture is that of an isolated figure who does not repeat tradition in an artificial manner but who uses traditional forms to create a vision of her own. Ironically, in view of her reputation as an extreme traditionalist, her future reputation might well rest on the experiments she conducted, following the lead of her father, Robert Bridges, in syllabic meter. Roy Fuller, for instance, penetrated behind the standard estimation of her work to see her as the forerunner in syllabic experimentation in this century, anticipating Marianne Moore and W. H. Auden, and he paid generous homage to her in the 1969 lecture he gave as Oxford Professor of Poetry.

She was born on 5 December 1887 to Robert Seymour Bridges, the poet laureate, and Mary Monica Waterhouse Bridges, the daughter of the famous nineteenth-century architect Alfred Waterhouse. There is a story that she was seen in her cradle by her father's friend Gerard Manley Hopkins, and if true it would imply a kind of continuity in English poetry. She lived much of her childhood at Chilswell, the house on Boar's Hill, overlooking Oxford, where the family moved in 1907, and was acquainted with John Masefield and Robert Graves when they lived on Boar's Hill. She also met Thomas Hardy. Her background was that of the privileged upper classes of the Victorian and Edwardian eras, a background she later criticized in her poetry and against which she rebelled. In the early 1920s she met Ali Akbar Daryush, who was introduced to her by Margery Fry, the sister of the Bloomsbury painter Roger Fry. She married Daryush on 29 December 1923. The couple went to Persia and lived there until 1927, when they returned to England. For the rest of her life she and her husband lived alone in their house Stockwell on Boar's Hill, close to Chilswell. She died on 7 April 1977, a few months before her ninetieth birthday. Those who visited her in her last years remember her as a strong, compelling figure with an acerbic streak to her conversation and a devotion to poetry undisturbed by the neglect and isolation she suffered all her life. She was almost totally blind during her last years and wore dark glasses even inside the house; yet one felt nothing went by her unobserved.

Her first book, *Charitessi 1911* (1912), and her second, *Verses by Elizabeth Bridges* (1916), are unobtainable today, but judging from *Verses* (1930) to the final poems, there is little dramatic development as such in her poetry; those conversions and often violent unheavals so frequently found in the lives and work of other twentieth-century poets are absent from her career. Instead, there is a deepening and surer investigation of a reality she never beguiled herself into thinking was other than it was. She thought the supposed powers of the romantic imagination hopelessly exaggerated. There are two exceptions to this generalization, one concerning subject matter, the other technique. Her early poetry is preoccupied with rather conventional subject matter and owes a great deal to the Edwardians, but *The Last Man* (1936) suggests a new awareness on her part of the anguish and pain caused by the profound changes that transformed English social life during the 1930s. Yvor Winters, writing in a 1936-1937 issue of the *American Review*, commented that "she appears to be increasingly conscious . . . of social injustice, of the mass of human suffering." This consciousness is presented ironically and indirectly in two of her best poems, "Still-Life" (*The Last Man*) and the conventional sonnet beginning "Children of wealth . . ." (*Verses: Sixth Book*, 1938). The focus in both these poems is on the privileged and the advantaged, whose wealth and social position protect them from and keep them ignorant of the knowledge of "elemental wrong" existing outside their narrow world. There is an unmistakable note of protest and outrage beneath each of these poems' polished and apparently undisturbed surfaces.

The other quite noticeable development she underwent concerns the experiment in syllabic meter which she inherited from her father. She once quoted him as saying that the traditional accentual-syllabic meter of English poetry had been almost exhausted, that a limited number of things could be said in such a meter and most of them had already been said. Consequently, a new meter, but one not formless and indeterminate like free verse, was needed to effect a new music in verse and to accommodate subject matter generally considered inappropriate in the conventional meter. Both Daryush and her father saw syllabics based on just the number of syllables in a line and leaving accent out of account as the solution to this problem. Daryush improved on her father's experiments by correcting their one error: he often gave syllabic identity to written but unpronounced clusters of letters in a line of verse. She gives such identity only to those syllables that are actually pronounced. And by always employing tight rhyme schemes she saved such a meter from the prosiness to which it is liable in the absence of an accentual regularity. "Still-Life" is one of the best examples of the subtle kind of music she was able to achieve in syllabic meter. It ends:

She comes over the lawn, the young heiress,
from her early walk in her garden-wood,
feeling that life's a table set to bless
her delicate desires with all that's good,

that even the unopened future lies
like a love-letter, full of sweet surprise.

Elizabeth Daryush at her home in Persia, circa 1925

But by and large her poetry pursues a steady course with no deviations or conversions invalidating what has gone before. The one theme that emerges most prominently in her work is the danger that imagination might beguile one into disregarding those tragic facts she considered inevitable and unavoidable in human life. She possessed a mind that insisted, almost at times to the point of bitterness, on disillusioning truth. For her, as for Thomas Hardy, poetry dealt with the "stubborn fact" of life as it is, and the only consolations it offered were those of understanding and a kind of half-Christian, half-stoical acceptance of the inevitable. Neither for her could poetry ever become merely an aesthetic experience centered around the cult of the beautiful that was so widespread and influential during the first decades of the twentieth century, the time she first began writing poetry. The flowers she alludes to in "Song: Throw Away the Flowers," published in *Verses: Fourth Book* (1934), are surely the rhetorical ones of such an aestheticism—they are found to be inadequate in an age preparing for war:

Throw away the flowers,
    fetch stubborn rock;
    build for the hours
Of terror and shock;
    go to timeless fact
    for what beauty lacked.

But her subject matter is not always so tragic. Scattered throughout all her books are the poems Yvor Winters and others consider her best work, poems dealing with the moral resources found in one's own being, a quiet stoicism mitigated by the Christian conception of charity, and a recognition of the beauties in the immediate, ordinary world around us. They are classical in the best sense of the word in that they possess "the sanity of self-restraint," to use Matthew Arnold's phrase, and they have the moral dignity of a person in conscious command of his life. One of the best examples of this type of poetry is "Faithless Familiars" (*Verses: Second Book*, 1932), which ends:

Now the still hearth-fire
    intently gloweth,
now weary desire
    her dwelling knoweth,

now a newly-lit
    lamp afar shall burn,
the roving spirit
    stay her and return.

The language is seemingly bare and straightforward, with little or no ambiguous or connotative overtones to it, and its thematic content, the rejection of fulfillment through change and emotional abandonment, is counter to contemporary preoccupations. Donald Davie, in his introduction to the 1976 *Collected Poems*, suggests as a "useful starting point" for an appreciation of Daryush's poetry Yvor Winters's "confession" concerning the merits of such poetry: "The quality which I personally admire most profoundly . . . is the ability to imbue a simple expository statement of a complex theme with a rich association of feeling, yet with an utterly pure and unmannered style."

The defects of her poetry are a diction often unnecessarily archaic and a frequently melodramatic use of personified abstractions. But these defects will irritate only those readers so committed to the Pound-Eliot revolution in poetic style that they refuse to see virtue in any other poetry than that modern and imagistic. For readers who wish to explore the full range of English poetry, such defects should not blind them to the obvious excellencies of the poetry of Elizabeth Daryush, its thematic sturdiness and the subtle kind of music she was able to achieve in syllabic meter. Minor poets who stay at home and do solid good work often have a greater chance for survival of their work than those whose poems are flashier and more pretentious. One can well conceive of Elizabeth Daryush's surviving for this very reason.

References:

Donald Davie, "The Poetry of Elizabeth Daryush," introduction to *Collected Poems* (Manchester: Carcanet New Press, 1976), pp. 13-23;

Roy Fuller, Preface to *Verses: Seventh Book* (South Hinksey, U.K.: Carcanet Press, 1971);

Yvor Winters, Foreword to *Selected Poems* (New York: Swallow / Morrow, 1948);

Winters, *Forms of Discovery* (Denver: Swallow, 1967), pp. 347-348;

Winters, *In Defense of Reason* (Denver: Swallow, 1947), pp. 148-149;

Winters, "Robert Bridges and Elizabeth Daryush," *American Review*, 8, no. 3 (1936-1937): 353-367.

C. Day Lewis

Robert H. Canary

University of Wisconsin, Parkside

See also the Day Lewis entry in *DLB 15*, *British Novelists, 1930-1959*.

BIRTH: Ballintubbert, Queen's County, Ireland, 27 April 1904, to Reverend Frank Cecil and Kathleen Blake Squires Day-Lewis.

EDUCATION: B.A., Wadham College, Oxford, 1927.

MARRIAGES: 27 December 1928 to Constance Mary King, divorced; children: Sean Francis, Nicholas Charles. 27 April 1951 to Jill Angela Henrietta Balcon; children: Lydia Tamasin, Daniel Michael Blake.

AWARDS AND HONORS: Clark Lecturer, Trinity College, Cambridge, 1946-1947; Charles Eliot Norton Lecturer, Harvard University, 1964-1965; Poet Laureate of England, 1968-1972.

DEATH: Hadley Common, Hertfordshire, England, 22 May 1972.

SELECTED BOOKS: *Beechen Vigil and Other Poems* (London: Fortune Press, 1925);

Country Comets (London: Hopkinson, 1928);

Transitional Poem (London: Hogarth Press, 1929);

From Feathers to Iron (London: Hogarth Press, 1931);

The Magnetic Mountain (London: Hogarth Press, 1933);

Dick Willoughby (Oxford: Blackwell, 1933);

A Hope for Poetry (Oxford: Blackwell, 1934);

A Question of Proof, as Nicholas Blake (London: Collins/Crime Club, 1935; New York: Harper, 1935);

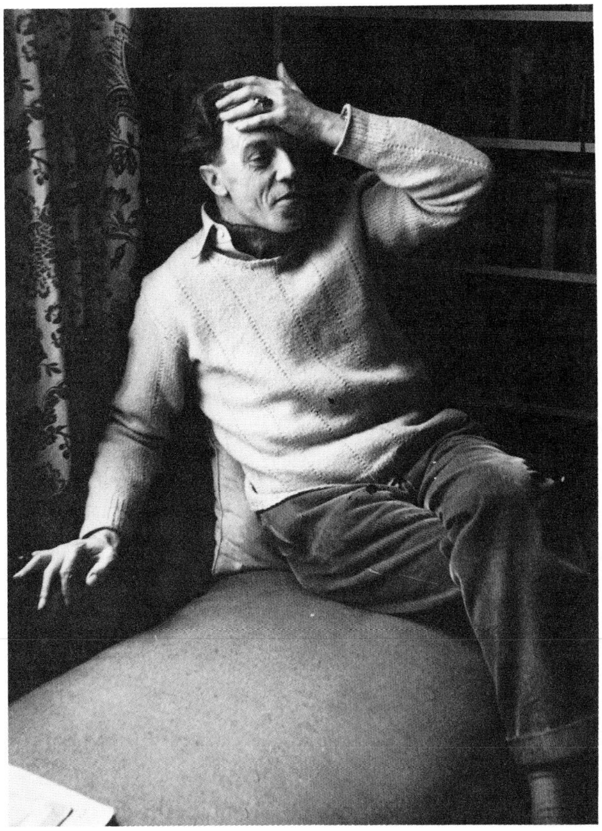

C. Day Lewis, circa 1951 (BBC Hulton)

Collected Poems 1929-1933 (London: Hogarth Press, 1935);
Collected Poems 1929-1933 and A Hope for Poetry (New York: Random House, 1935);
A Time to Dance and Other Poems (London: Hogarth Press, 1935);
Revolution in Writing (London: Hogarth Press, 1935);
Noah and the Waters (London: Hogarth Press, 1936; New York: Transatlantic Arts, 1947);
A Time to Dance: Noah and the Waters and Other Poems; With an Essay, Revolution in Writing (New York: Random House, 1936);
Thou Shell of Death, as Blake (London: Collins/Crime Club, 1936); republished as *Shell of Death* (New York: Harper, 1936);
The Friendly Tree (London: Cape, 1936; New York: Harper, 1937);
There's Trouble Brewing, as Blake (London: Collins/Crime Club, 1937; New York: Harper, 1937);
Starting Point (London: Cape, 1937; New York: Harper, 1938);
Overtures to Death and Other Poems (London: Cape, 1938);
The Beast Must Die, as Blake (London: Collins/Crime Club, 1938; New York: Harper, 1938);
The Smiler with the Knife, as Blake (London: Collins/Crime Club, 1939; New York: Harper, 1939);
Child of Misfortune (London: Cape, 1939);
Poems in Wartime (London: Cape, 1940);
Selected Poems (London: New Hogarth Library, 1940);
Malice in Wonderland, as Blake (London: Collins/Crime Club, 1940); republished as *The Summer Camp Mystery* (New York: Harper, 1940);
The Case of the Abominable Snowman, as Blake (London: Collins/Crime Club, 1941); republished as *The Corpse in the Snowman* (New York: Harper, 1941);
Word Over All (London: Cape, 1943);
Short is the Time, Poems 1936-1943 (New York: Oxford University Press, 1945);
The Poetic Image (London: Cape, 1947; New York: Oxford University Press, 1947);
Minute for Murder, as Blake (London: Collins/Crime Club, 1947; New York: Harper, 1948);
The Otterby Incident (London: Putnam's, 1948; New York: Viking, 1949);
Poems 1943-1947 (London: Cape, 1948; New York: Oxford University Press, 1948);
Head of a Traveller, as Blake (London: Collins/Crime Club, 1949; New York: Harper, 1949);
The Poet's Task (Oxford: Clarendon Press, 1951);
Selected Poems (Harmondsworth, U.K.: Penguin, 1951);
An Italian Visit (London: Cape, 1953; New York: Harper, 1953);
The Dreadful Hollow, as Blake (London: Collins/Crime Club, 1953; New York: Harper, 1953);
The Whisper in the Gloom, as Blake (London: Collins/Crime Club, 1954; New York: Harper, 1954);
Notable Images of Virtue (Toronto: Ryerson Press, 1954);
Collected Poems (London: Cape/Hogarth Press, 1954);
A Tangled Web, as Blake (London: Collins/Crime Club, 1956; New York: Harper, 1956);
End of Chapter, as Blake (London: Collins/Crime Club, 1957; New York: Harper, 1957);
The Poet's Way of Knowledge (Cambridge: Cambridge University Press, 1957);
Pegasus and Other Poems (London: Cape, 1957; New York: Harper, 1958);
A Penknife in My Heart, as Blake (London: Collins/Crime Club, 1958; New York: Harper, 1959);
The Widow's Cruise, as Blake (London: Collins/

Crime Club, 1959; New York: Harper, 1959);
The Buried Day (London: Chatto & Windus, 1960; New York: Harper & Row, 1960);
The Worm of Death, as Blake (London: Collins/Crime Club, 1961; New York: Harper & Row, 1961);
The Gate and Other Poems (London: Cape, 1962);
The Deadly Joker, as Blake (London: Collins/Crime Club, 1963);
Requiem for Living (New York: Harper & Row, 1964);
The Sad Variety, as Blake (London: Collins/Crime Club, 1964; New York: Harper & Row, 1964);
The Room and Other Poems (London: Cape, 1965);
The Lyric Impulse (Cambridge: Harvard University Press, 1965; London: Chatto & Windus, 1965);
The Morning After Death, as Blake (London: Collins/Crime Club, 1966; New York: Harper & Row, 1966);
Selected Poems (New York: Harper & Row, 1967);
The Private Wound, as Blake (London: Collins/Crime Club, 1968; New York: Harper & Row, 1968);
The Whispering Roots (London: Cape, 1970);
The Whispering Roots and Other Poems (New York: Harper & Row, 1970);
Poems of C. Day-Lewis, 1925-1972, edited by Ian Parsons (London: Cape/Hogarth Press, 1977).

Cecil Day Lewis has two contrasting claims on our attention. The first is as an archetypal poet of the 1930s, the first-born, last-named member of the Auden-Spender-Day Lewis triad, and the only one of those three friends whose commitment to Marxism extended to joining and working for the Communist party. His second claim to recognition, at least for literary historians, is as the Poet Laureate of England from 1968 until his death in 1972. For critics and biographers, he poses the intriguing problem of reconciling the radical poet of the 1930s with the traditional poet of later decades.

The most obvious answer to the seeming paradox of Day Lewis's career is that his native poetic temperament was always romantic, even Georgian, and that the ideological overtones of his work in the 1930s were even then at war with a talent more at home with nature poetry and personal lyrics. But this answer leads only to another paradox, for his poetry was at its most vital in a period when he was least true to his natural inclinations. The answer to this may be that Day Lewis always felt the need to discipline the lyric impulse. The discipline imposed by his Marxist commitment in the 1930s produced the kind of internal conflicts that give life to poetry; the formal poetic disciplines imposed on his later poetry produced too often a perfect but lifeless verse.

The roots of Day Lewis's vocation and inhibitions as a poet lie in his childhood. He was born in Ireland of Anglo-Irish parents; the family name had originally been Day, but his grandfather added the surname of an uncle and called himself Day-Lewis. The poet's inverted snobbery in dropping the hyphen in his name on his publications (beginning in 1927) has been a source of trouble for librarians and bibliographers ever since. The family moved to Malvern, Worcestershire, in 1905 and to Ealing, West London, in 1908, when the poet was four years old. His mother died soon after the move, leaving Day Lewis, an only child, to bear the full brunt of his father's love and need for love, mixed with unpredictable spurts of paternal discipline. The father was a clergyman, and it was assumed that Day Lewis would follow in his steps. Educated at home until he was eight, he says in his autobiography, *The Buried Day* (1960), that he began by writing verses, "short stories and sermons with a fine impartiality." It was an atmosphere of high expectations and high demands, and Day Lewis's later memories of it seem dominated by guilt over his failure to meet the expectations and his inability to respond to the emotional demands.

Day Lewis's account of his schooling is dominated by a pattern of early promise followed by failure and disappointment. At his first school, Wilkie's in London, he began well but was humiliated by repeated failures to pass the Mathematics Certificate. At Sherborne School in Dorset, which he entered in 1917, he rose to be head boy in his house but had to stay on an extra year after failing in his first attempt to secure a university scholarship. At Wadham College, Oxford, he found himself less and less able to concentrate on his studies, ending, he said later, with "A fourth in Greats—and it is a mystery to me why the examiners did not fail me altogether." Day Lewis may have somewhat exaggerated this pattern in the interest of heightening the contrast of his eventual return to Oxford as elected Professor of Poetry in 1951—he actually secured a third in Greats—but the pattern seems real enough.

The disappointments of his academic career encouraged him to seek other ways of gaining self-esteem. At Sherborne he was active in sports and in singing, interests which he retained through life. His chief consolation, however, was a romantic image of himself as a poet, and at Oxford this identity was confirmed, though with many variations based on changing ideas of just what a poet should be. In 1925, he took a £25 legacy and paid for the publication of his first volume of verse, *Beechen Vigil and Other Poems*. He says in *The Buried Day* that "The publication of this book, and the inclusion of two of my poems in *Oxford Poetry 1925* were quite enough to assure a young man with a temperament as sanguine as mine that he was a poet of accepted achievement," though he continued to have difficulty in persuading anyone else to publish his verse. A second collection of undergraduate poems, *Country Comets*, was not published until 1928.

The tendency toward Georgian nature verse suggested by the title of *Beechen Vigil* reflects both the derivative character of Day Lewis's early verse and the possible influence of his first deep love, Mary King. Two years older than Day Lewis, she was the daughter of one of the masters at Sherborne, part of a large family in which Day Lewis found a surrogate household that partially compensated for his increasing alienation from his father and the stepmother his father married in 1921. Mary King was a "nature-worshipper" then, and Day Lewis "took up nature worship because it was a poetic thing and because it would bring me closer to Mary." Thus awakened, his love of nature soon became quite sincere, though the resulting poems are poor. Getting closer to Mary King proved more difficult. Theirs had begun as a brother-sister relationship, and Day Lewis's feelings were transformed into romantic love several years before his importunities persuaded her to yield her love to him. They were finally married during the Christmas holidays in 1928.

Country Comets (1928) is a somewhat more mature volume than its predecessor, with lyrics which reflect his love for Mary and his philosophical studies at Oxford. It is, however, clearly a volume of juvenilia, and Day Lewis was justified in excluding the poems in both *Beechen Vigil* and *Country Comets* from later collections of his verse.

In his last year at Oxford, Day Lewis met and came under the influence of Wystan Hugh Auden, whose ideas were to transform Day Lewis's poetry for the next decade. Like many others, Day Lewis was fascinated by Auden's restless energy, formidable intelligence, and air of authority. Auden and Day Lewis served as joint editors of *Oxford Poetry 1927*, for which they wrote a manifestolike preface, which combines dogmatic overstatement and burlesque in ways that make it clear that Auden was the dominant partner. Tossing together ideas from Eliot, the new psychology, and socialism, they call for a new kind of poetry whose exact lineaments are hard to discern in their prose.

Rex Warner and C. Day Lewis, 1928

Day Lewis's own ideas about the shape of the new poetry are embodied in *Transitional Poem* (1929). Most of this volume was written during the winter of 1927-1928, when he was teaching at Summer Fields, a preparatory school in Oxford. It is a lyric sequence organized into four parts and utilizing a variety of stanza forms; when first published, it was accompanied by learned and not terribly useful notes in the manner of T. S. Eliot's notes to *The Waste Land*. The unity of the whole and of each part is thematic rather than narrative, and the volume does not so much develop a theme as circle around it. In his notes, Day Lewis identifies the theme as the pursuit of wholeness. The various parts, he says, take up in turn the metaphysical, ethical, psychological, and aesthetic aspects of this pursuit.

Transitional Poem is a remarkable advance on Day Lewis's two previous volumes, and it is, in part, a celebration of his progress to maturity as a poet. The opening lines announce that the poet has "come to reason / And cast my schoolboy clout," and part two opens with the declaration that "It is becoming now to declare my allegiance." His "allegiance" is given to those who have helped him find his way: to Mary; to his friend Rex Warner; to an older woman friend who had helped him through some of the difficult passages of adolescence; and to Auden. New poetic allegiances, to Eliot and to Auden, coexist with the older models evident in such lines as "Or as the little lark / Who veins the sky with song."

Looking back on *Transitional Poem* in *The Buried Day*, Day Lewis describes it with some amusement as "a relentlessly and unexpectedly *highbrow* poem." Part one presents man as cut off from nature, which he must somehow reduce to order through words. In part two, the poet is torn one way and another by desires, ambitions, love of knowledge, and love of nature—a conflict more difficult to resolve in a world from which the old certitudes have flown. The lyrics of part three rehearse the same dilemmas, while part four offers hints, if nothing more, that the poet may be able to live with, if not resolve, the antinomies of his existence.

Despite its intellectual pretensions, *Transitional Poem* is in many respects a love poem to the poet's wife-to-be. Much of its interest derives from the collision of its conventional romantic sentiments with the ideas Day Lewis was struggling to make his own. One lyric, for example, begins with memories of a time when "Her beauty walked the page / And it was poetry," but ends with the admission "that beauty is / A motion of the mind." The confusions and contradictions which the verse mirrors make acceptable the frequent awkwardness of the rhythms.

The most clearly innovative aspect of *Transitional Poem* is its imagery, which at its best can blend the modern and scientific with the traditional and poetic, as in "I think love's terminals / Are fixed in fire and wind." In using imagery drawn from the modern urban world, Day Lewis was following the examples of Eliot and Auden, but such imagery acquires a special savor when used to express Day Lewis's own romantic sensibility. Despite the derivative character of his ideas and manner, *Transitional Poem* is the volume of a poet with a distinctive voice. Its acceptance by Leonard and Virginia Woolf at the Hogarth Press marked Day Lewis as a poet to be reckoned with as the 1930s opened.

Day Lewis had now achieved some of that recognition as a poet which he had long craved, but poetry was not a career on which he could expect to support his new wife. His mediocre results at Oxford did not open many doors to him, but friends secured him a series of posts as a schoolmaster. He entered the teaching profession with a sense of defeat and a positive distaste for the work he was entering upon. After a year at Summer Fields, he found a new post as a master at Larchfield School in Helensburgh, Dunbartonshire, Scotland. He left Larchfield in 1930—his successor was Auden—and moved to Cheltenham Junior School, Gloucestershire, "a highly conventional public school," where he never felt entirely at home, despite making one or two close friends on the staff. Although he came to have a better feeling toward his work as a teacher and to feel some affection for his young charges, Day Lewis continued to define himself as a poet. One of his superiors found the mildly erotic implications of some lyrics in *Transitional Poem* disturbing, and not everyone at Cheltenham was happy with Day Lewis's increasing, quite open Marxism.

The poet found no inspiration in his teaching. Instead, his next volume, *From Feathers to Iron* (1931), is a lyric sequence inspired by the birth of his first son. The birth itself is the climax of the volume; most of the lyrics are meditations by the poet or poems addressed to his wife or the unborn child. The first four lyrics introduce the metaphor of the journey; it is the child's journey toward life, but it resolves into an image of his parents' sexual love. Their union "is love's junction, no terminus," for it will engender life. The coming child means a new journey for his parents, who have been "Two years marooned on self-sufficiency." The father-to-be is no longer fully part of the process, however; he

Mary and Cecil Day Lewis, 1930

pauses on "the frontier," where he must "wait between two worlds," between "conception and fruition." The father's mind is on his unborn child, who must come from the feathery world of the womb to an iron material world. He wonders what sort of world the child will find or help to build. The time passes slowly, but at last the child is born, and the father can invite him to "Come out into the sun!" He issues the same invitation to the world at large, that they might celebrate this birth. The volume ends with "Epilogue: Letter to W. H. Auden," which again summons up the imagery of journey and exploration, this time applied to the poet's task.

In his autobiography, Day Lewis says that in writing *From Feathers to Iron*, "I found that my own excitements and apprehensions linked up quite spontaneously with a larger issue—the struggle and joy in which our new world should be born—and derived strength from it, so that I could use naturally for metaphors or metaphysical conceits the apparatus of the modern world, the machinery which, made over for the benefit of all, could help this world to rebirth." Earlier, in *A Hope for Poetry* (1934), Day Lewis indicated that he was "quite unconscious" of some of the poem's political implications and complained that "the critics, almost to a man, took it for a political allegory; the simple, personal meaning evaded them." *From Feathers to Iron* is certainly not a political allegory; even political imagery is relatively rare in this volume. Nevertheless, Day Lewis's growing political commitment is part of the background of the poem, and the poem's strength is that the birth of his son evoked from the poet verses which pull together all that mattered most to him at that time.

From Feathers to Iron was an important book for Day Lewis as a poet. Held together by a simple narrative line, it had the kind of unity *Transitional Poem* only sought. The influence of Auden is apparent, but seems healthy—stiffening Day Lewis's rhythms and sharpening his diction. When Day Lewis's work appeared the next year alongside that of Auden and Stephen Spender in the *New Signatures* (1932) anthology, edited by Michael Roberts, it bore the comparison surprisingly well, and the legend of an Auden-Spender-Day Lewis "group" was born.

Day Lewis may not have intended *From Feathers to Iron* as a political allegory, but his next volume, *The Magnetic Mountain* (1933), is just that. The mountain itself is a rather cloudy symbol of an ideal world which lies just beyond the horizon, the promise of a new beginning and of a new world in which body and spirit can be as one. The volume celebrates the mountain's attraction for the pure of heart in thirty-six lyrics, arranged in four parts. In part one the poet summons his readers to join him on the difficult journey but says that he himself is "taking a light engine back along the line / For a last excursion, a tour of inspection." This tour takes up the next two parts of the poem. In part two, four defendants speak on behalf of the old world and its values of nature, schooling, church, and domesticity; each is dismissed with a lyric of rebuke—responses anticipated by the sonnet of prejudgment which opens this section of the volume. In part three, we hear from four enemies of the quest, speaking on behalf of sensuality, journalism, science, and poetry itself, and their temptations are rejected. Part four rounds off the poem, not with an account of the journey, but with a miscellaneous group of lyrics celebrating the new world to come and inviting the reader to turn to its promise.

The merits of *The Magnetic Mountain* are mainly structural. It has an oddly static structure for a poem which says so much about journeys, but the sequence does not fall apart into separate lyrics until the last section. The middle sections are given unity by the use of the defendants and enemies. The influence of Auden is apparent throughout the poem and is a mixed blessing. Rhythmically, Day Lewis is often most effective when borrowing from Auden, particularly in lines like "Consider these, for we have condemned them" or "You who go out alone, on tandem or on pillion." Day Lewis's attempts to capture Auden's jocular tone, however, show that he lacked Auden's natural high spirits and talent for light verse.

In retrospect, any comparison of *The Magnetic Mountain* with *From Feathers to Iron* is bound to suggest that Day Lewis was better at writing political allegories when he was not conscious of doing so. In *The Magnetic Mountain*, the political concerns which had given depth to its predecessor overwhelm the poem. Although epigraphs chosen from William Blake, D. H. Lawrence, and Gerard Manley Hopkins suggest that the allegory might have had more than purely political significance, other meanings tend to be drowned out by its noisy rhetoric. The immediate effect of the publication was to confirm Day Lewis's standing as one of the revolutionary young poets of the "Auden group," though the poet's own efforts to sing the joys of such comradeship are rather embarrassing—e.g., "Look west, Wystan, lone flyer, birdman, my bully boy!"

When he came to write his first book of critical prose, *A Hope for Poetry* (1934), Day Lewis could fairly claim that the recent "boom" in poetry "has been connected in certain quarters with the names of Auden, Spender and myself." Day Lewis himself expressed only the modest hope that his generation might yet produce a poet with the stature of Yeats, the integrity of Hardy, or even the technique of de la Mare. The names are significant; *A Hope for Poetry* was a manifesto for the 1930s because it assumed the political correctness of communism, but its underlying aesthetic is more romantic than Marxist.

A Hope for Poetry begins with the observation that poetic revolutions are quite usual in English poetry and that they are not incompatible with the deepest reverence for certain "ancestors." As ancestors for his own generation, Day Lewis singles out Hopkins, Wilfrid Owen, and Eliot, who have given new life to poetry. The modern poet, though, faces special problems, for the growth of industrial civilization has cut him off from both the tradition and the kind of "compact, working social group" within which the heightened communication of poetry is possible. Invoking D. H. Lawrence's analysis of the sickness of society, Day Lewis argues that the poet needs a healthy society to function as a poet, which is why he is likely to be sympathetic to communism. It is the lack of a clearly defined audience which makes postwar poetry seem obscure, and it is the effort to substitute a small group of friends for the missing audience which accounts for the clubbiness and private jokes which some object to in the poetry of Day Lewis and his friends. The poet must be faithful to himself and his own situation; he must not become a propagandist, and he cannot make himself over into a proletarian. The poet may, however, help call into being the new world through his "poetic vision," whose nature it is "to perceive those invisible truths which are like electrons the basis of reality," the effects of which we can sense by the almost physical response it elicits in us.

The claims Day Lewis makes for poetry are more exalted than those he makes for communism. The role of communism in *A Hope for Poetry* is functional; it offers one way of creating a society in which the poet can recover his lost solidarity with his fellow men. It is natural, then, that when the claims of poetic truth and politics conflict, the poet must choose poetic truth. Communism does not appear as a social duty, and it is with a tone of regret that Day Lewis observes that in a world of social conflict "the lyric irresponsibility of the artist is hard to achieve." The limitations of Day Lewis's own social commitment are obvious, and his later withdrawal from political activism was not inconsistent with the aesthetic of *A Hope for Poetry*.

As *A Hope for Poetry* appeared, Day Lewis was becoming more active in such left-wing endeavors as the Friends of the Soviet Union, and he was under increasing pressure to take the decisive step of joining the Communist party. In 1935 he did so, and for several years he was extremely active in party activities. Membership "gave me what from time to time I have needed—the sense of being part of a close community," the kind of group described as necessary for poetry in *A Hope for Poetry*. As a bourgeois poet in a proletarian movement, Day Lewis was subject to a certain amount of fraternal backbiting, but he did not change his critical position.

Joining the party did require a change in Day Lewis's career. In the spring of 1935, he had managed to get himself on the agenda of Cheltenham's governing body by giving a talk on collective farming to a local group, an offense apparently more serious than writing revolutionary poetry and literary criticism. Although he had been retained on the staff, he could hardly become an open party member and expect to stay. Although he had a wife and two children to support, he resigned his position to become a free-lance writer.

Day Lewis's decision to become a full-time writer was eased by a contract from the publishing house of Jonathan Cape guaranteeing him £ 300 a year for three years to write novels. Earlier in 1935, he had had a detective novel, *A Question of Proof*, published under the pseudonym Nicholas Blake. He had written the book out of a fondness for detective fiction and the need to raise money to repair the roof of his cottage. On the basis of its success, his agent had persuaded Cape that Day Lewis might become a popular serious novelist. The three resulting novels published under his own name—*The Friendly Tree* (1936), *Starting Point* (1937), and *Child of Misfortune* (1939)—did not confirm this estimate. *Starting Point* has some interest for its picture of life on the Left, but its politics are muddled and its tone excessively earnest.

Although Day Lewis was not destined to become an important novelist, he was able to repeat the success of his detective novel. As Nicholas Blake, he became one of England's most popular and well-regarded detective novelists, producing a book a year through 1941 and at a somewhat reduced rate in the years after World War II. His detective novels are still available in paperback, and he probably stands higher today among lovers of detective fiction than among lovers of poetry. The detective novels are simply better than his serious novels,

C. Day Lewis and J. I. M. Stewart (BBC Hulton)

displaying a wit and ingenuity not much found in any of Day Lewis's serious work. In a curious sort of way, his detective novels are also sometimes more personal than his poetry, drawing on areas of his experience hardly touched upon in his verse. According to Day Lewis, his first such novel, whose schoolmaster hero "was having a love-affair with the golden-haired wife of the headmaster," got him gossiped about in the village and denounced at a meeting of the school's governing body. Although Day Lewis was innocent of any such affair himself, it is worth noting that his most revolutionary verses never became indecorous enough to stir such reactions.

While 1935 marked only the beginning of Day Lewis's steps toward fame as a detective novelist, it may have been the highwater mark of his reputation as a poet. Hogarth Press brought out *Collected Poems 1929-1933* (1935), which was also published with *A Hope for Poetry* by Random House in New York, the first of Day Lewis's volumes of poetry to achieve American publication. A new volume of verse, *A Time to Dance and Other Poems* (1935), received some respectful critical attention and sold notably better than his previous books. Nor was this favorable reception unearned, for the poems of *A Time to Dance* showed that Day Lewis was still growing as a poet. This volume was his most successful to date in balancing his bourgeois romanticism with his proletarian politics.

While *The Magnetic Mountain* externalizes Day Lewis's internal conflicts through the defendants and enemies and ends by dismissing them without resolution, a number of the poems in *A Time to Dance* make poetry out of his dilemmas. The poet uses images of warfare to depict the conflict between the claims of past and future, "heir and ancestor," in the poem "In Me Two Worlds." In "The Conflict," the poet sees himself as a bird of song caught in a conflict which allows for no neutrality—"only ghosts can live / Between two fires." The most original of these poems, though its ballad manner derives from Auden, is "Johnny Head-in-the-Air." In this poem, a crowd of travelers has come through harsh terrain to a mysterious crossroads, where the signpost is an electrified man, arms "stretched to the warring poles," pointing east and west. To the right is fair but dying land, whose gold will make them ghosts; to the left is a harder road to a better world. They ask him to come down and join them, but he cannot do so while men are still kept apart, for he is "here to show / Your own divided heart." The ballad rhythms give the tone a light air, desirable when the poet presents himself as a Christ figure, and the poem represents an advance in self-knowledge over *The Magnetic Mountain*.

The lyric sequence which gives its title to *A Time to Dance* is an elegy to L. P. Hedges, who had been a friend and colleague of Day Lewis's at Cheltenham. The poet's grief over his friend's death is somehow connected with his anger at a world in which workers can find no work and children starve. The guilt felt by the living appears in the poem as guilt toward those who have taken a firmer political stand than the poet. The most explicit connection made is between the poet's need to find grounds for affirmation in the face of death and a sick society. His affirmations are most convincing in a long section devoted to a narrative of the flight of Pater and M'Intosh, two young Australian aviators in World War I who managed to fly back to Australia from England after the war in an obsolete aircraft. In this lyric the narrative provides a natural home for Day Lewis's familiar images of flight and journeys. Their heroism is a metaphor for the poet's praise of his friend's indomitable will; their brotherhood in the face of danger is a metaphor for the comradeship of the political struggle; their return home from the skies echoes hopes Day Lewis had expressed in other poems for the poet as songbird or hawk. As individual lyrics, the poems of the "A Time to Dance" sequence vary from the effective to the embarrassing. Day Lewis's subsequent excisions have improved the average level of the verse; in downplaying the social dimensions of the poem, these revisions have also deprived the poem of much of its resonance and excitement.

Day Lewis could not maintain the balance of poetry and politics found in *A Time to Dance*. His next book returned to the political allegory of *The Magnetic Mountain*. *Noah and the Waters* (1936) was begun as the basis for a choral ballet and evolved into an unstageable poetic drama. It represents Day Lewis's contribution to the efforts at revival of poetry for the theater as called for by Eliot and joined in by his coevals Auden, Spender, and Louis MacNeice. Even more static than Eliot's *Murder in the Cathedral* (1935), *Noah and the Waters* gives little hint of the ingenuity in plot construction Day Lewis was capable of in his detective fiction.

In this play the biblical flood waters become the rising waters of revolution, futilely opposed by the liberal-capitalist burgesses of the world. Noah, a burgess himself, nevertheless has the option of joining with the waters. The debate between the burgesses and the waters is mirrored by a debate between Noah's own inner voices. In the end, Noah casts his lot with the waters and sets off on his ark.

Noah's dilemma is Day Lewis's, and his final decision is like the poet's decision to join the party. The principal difficulty is that the author loads the dice to the point where Noah's decision seems the only possible one. The burgesses are objects of satire, and the waters are objects of admiration; the play is less concerned with presenting Noah's dilemma than with justifying his decision. Since Day Lewis had by no means resolved all of his own doubts in joining the party, those passages which affirm solidarity with the watery masses ring less true than those which lament the lost land, pillaged by townsfolk. One should note, however, that Noah cannot really become one with the waters, so that his escape to the ark is as much of a retreat to nature as it is a decision to join the struggle.

The true rising tide of the late 1930s was fascism. The poems of *Overtures to Death and Other Poems* (1938), Day Lewis's next volume, were written in years dominated by Mussolini's attack on Ethiopia, Hitler's march into the Rhineland, and Franco's successes in the Spanish civil war. The party line became the Popular Front, and the death and destruction warned of in such monitory poems as "The Bombers" and "Newsreel" are the coming war. These two poems are among Day Lewis's most effective political lyrics, perhaps because he was more wholehearted in fearing the horrors of war than in praising the revolutionary violence anticipated in *Noah and the Waters*.

The longest political poem in this volume is "The Nabara," a narrative of a sea fight in the Spanish civil war in which a fascist cruiser intercepted and destroyed a government flotilla bringing supplies to the Basques. The poem celebrates heroic self-sacrifice, sticking close to the action described and pointing the political moral only in the opening and closing passages. Like the account of the Australian aviators in "A Time to Dance," the poem employs an epic hexameter line, with frequent variations for emphasis. In "The Nabara," however, the poet keeps his distance from his subject, which does not have for him the symbolic connotations of flight; as a result, the rather flat narrative lines are not charged with the energy which heightens the impact of the earlier narrative. Such interest as "The Nabara" has come from the incident itself rather than any poetic transformation of it.

For Day Lewis, the most significant death in this period may have been the death of his father in the summer of 1937. For the poet, this death brought feelings of guilt over their long estrangement, and he reports in *The Buried Day* that "For many years after my father's death" he had recurring dreams about their broken relationship. A father's death is also a son's reminder of his own mortality, and this may help account for the personal tone of the death visions in *Overtures to Death*. The lyric sequence which gives its title to the volume had its origin in his father's death and represents the poet's own attempts to come to terms with death's inevitable triumph. More directly than in *From Feathers to Iron*, the author's personal reflections are placed in the context of a world in which death has all too many allies. At a personal level the poet cannot hope to defeat his grim antagonist—"the fight's framed: for this I blame not you / But the absentee promoter." For society, however, there is some hope in their battle with "your damned auxiliaries," for "Our war is life itself and shall not fail." It is this hope which makes personal death acceptable.

In the best poems of *Overtures to Death* the poet's personal concerns and political commitments are united. Elsewhere in the volume, the poet's divided will leads to poems animated by only part of his being—a political impulse in "The Nabara" and a lyric impulse in "Spring Song." "Overtures to Death" itself is as good as anything in *A Time to Dance*, but the volume as a whole suggests retreat rather than continued growth.

In the years since his decision to join the party, Day Lewis had taken his responsibilities as a party member seriously. He was in charge of political education for his local party group and did his best to lead his fellows through the intricacies of theories he barely understood himself. He passed out leaflets, spoke at public meetings, felt guilty over not going to fight in Spain, and served on committees of intellectuals formed to advance one or another good cause. He wrote essays reproaching intellectuals who had not come as far left as himself and defending himself against critics who felt that his

C. Day Lewis with his sons Sean and Nicholas, circa 1940

own commitment was so far insufficient. In the summer of 1938 he abandoned both his party membership and his political activities.

Day Lewis's motives for leaving the party, like his reasons for joining, were more personal than political. Unlike those intellectuals who left the party earlier over the Moscow Trials or a little later over the Nazi-Soviet pact, Day Lewis felt and expressed no dramatic revulsion from Communist theory or practice. The primary motive seems to have been the increasing incompatibility between his party work and his needs as a poet. In his autobiography, Day Lewis cites an Edwin Muir review of *Noah and the Waters* as having forced him to see that his poetry was suffering from the time he devoted to politics, but the lyrics of *A Time to Dance* show that he was already aware of the conflict. Earlier in the 1930s, politics had given life to his verse. When it no longer seemed to be doing so, it was inevitable that Day Lewis would choose poetry over politics.

Other, less rational elements may also have entered into Day Lewis's decision to leave the party. His father's death, the approaching end of his novel contract, the defeat of his ambitions as a novelist and dramatist, his stalled career as a poet—all of these made him ready for new beginnings. In 1938 he and his wife sold their home in Cheltenham and purchased a house in the small village of Musbury in Devon. That a certain emotional restlessness lay behind this move and his abandonment of politics is suggested by Day Lewis's soon entering into a passionate love affair with Edna Elizabeth ("Billie") Currall, a young married woman in Musbury. The openness with which he conducted this affair gave a great deal of pain to his wife. Day Lewis himself speaks of it as "sowing my first wild oats—at the age of thirty-five." A thinly disguised account of the affair can be found in his last Nicholas Blake novel, *The Private Wound* (1968).

The retreat to Musbury was also a retreat to nature worship. The most significant immediate poetic result of this was not in Day Lewis's own verse but in his translation of the *Georgics of Virgil* (1940). Like the other public-school poets of his generation, Day Lewis had grown up with Virgil's verses drummed into his ear, and the modified epic line he used in "The Nabara" and portions of "A Time to Dance" comes from Virgil. The nostalgic escapism of Virgil's hymns to the countryside in the *Georgics* was well suited to Day Lewis's mood. As a translator of Virgil—he later translated *The Aeneid* (1952) and *The Eclogues* (1963)—Day Lewis suffers somewhat from his own lack of natural musicality, but his identification with the original makes the *Georgics* a satisfying translation.

Day Lewis moved to Musbury in the year of Munich, and World War II came the following year, but the war had relatively little effect on either Musbury or Day Lewis's poetry. His next major collection was *Word Over All* (1943), which incorporated the handful of verses published earlier as *Poems in Wartime* (1940). Those few poems which deal directly with wartime subjects are wholly conventional. There is no reason to doubt the patriotic sincerity of poems such as "Watching Post" and "Lidice," but they express widely shared sentiments rather than the poet's own unique feelings. Properly proud of his countrymen and enraged by the enemy, the poet does not make the kind of linkages which give life to his best poetry in the 1930s. His patriotism is in a separate compartment from his own pride as a man and a poet; he cannot recognize the enemy as his darker self; and so the war remains a thing apart from the turmoil in the poet's own life.

The poet was doing his best to create such turmoil, displaying in his romantic life the "lyric irresponsibility" he had praised in *A Hope for Poetry* and the artistic ruthlessness not always applied to his verse. He ended his affair with Mrs. Currall on a graceless note and soon began a long affair with the novelist Rosamond Lehmann, to whom *Word Over All* was dedicated. His wife did not believe in divorce, and for many years the poet was divided between his home and times spent with Rosamond Lehmann. His situation found vent in love lyrics and poems of marital discord, but these are timeless topics. Although his autobiography attributes his affair with Mrs. Currall partly to the "desparate irresponsibility and the fatalism which had been in the air since Munich," the shadow of Munich does not fall across his love lyrics; although his autobiography's only reference to his affair with Rosamond Lehmann speaks of "a heart at war with itself," the war seems far away in his poems.

The closest Day Lewis comes in *Word Over All* to making the connection between himself and the larger world is in a sequence of nine sonnets, "O Dreams, O Destinations." A meditation on the child's fall into a world of time, this sequence combines in its seventh sonnet the imagery of war and journeys to speak of man's fight for wholeness. The poem returns, however, to more abstract concerns and to imagery which might have been used by any poet in the past three centuries.

Of all the poets of the 1930s, Day Lewis had been the most deeply engaged in politics, but he shared the general failure of the 1930s poets to make poetic sense of the war they had warned against. The war scarcely appears in *Poems 1943-1947* (1948); this volume is preoccupied with his own marital situation. His models are no longer his contemporaries but late Victorians such as George Meredith and Thomas Hardy, but his poems of marriage do not attempt the sustained analysis of Meredith's *Modern Love*, and nothing in the volume approaches Hardy's attempts to make sense of history in Hardy's *The Dynasts*. As personal lyrics, a number of these poems are attractive, as are many of the Georgian lyrics they rather resemble. For a poet of Day Lewis's initial promise, though, such poems are emblems of defeat. In one of the volume's long poems, "New Year's Eve," the poet says that his "todays are / Repetitive, dull, disjointed"; he can only "practise them over and over / Like a five-finger exercise" in hopes that passion will one day redeem them and bring harmony to his life. The grander hopes of the 1930s are gone.

The most ambitious of Day Lewis's postwar poems is *An Italian Visit* (1953), a lyric sequence in seven parts evidently inspired by a trip to Italy several years earlier with Rosamond Lehmann, to

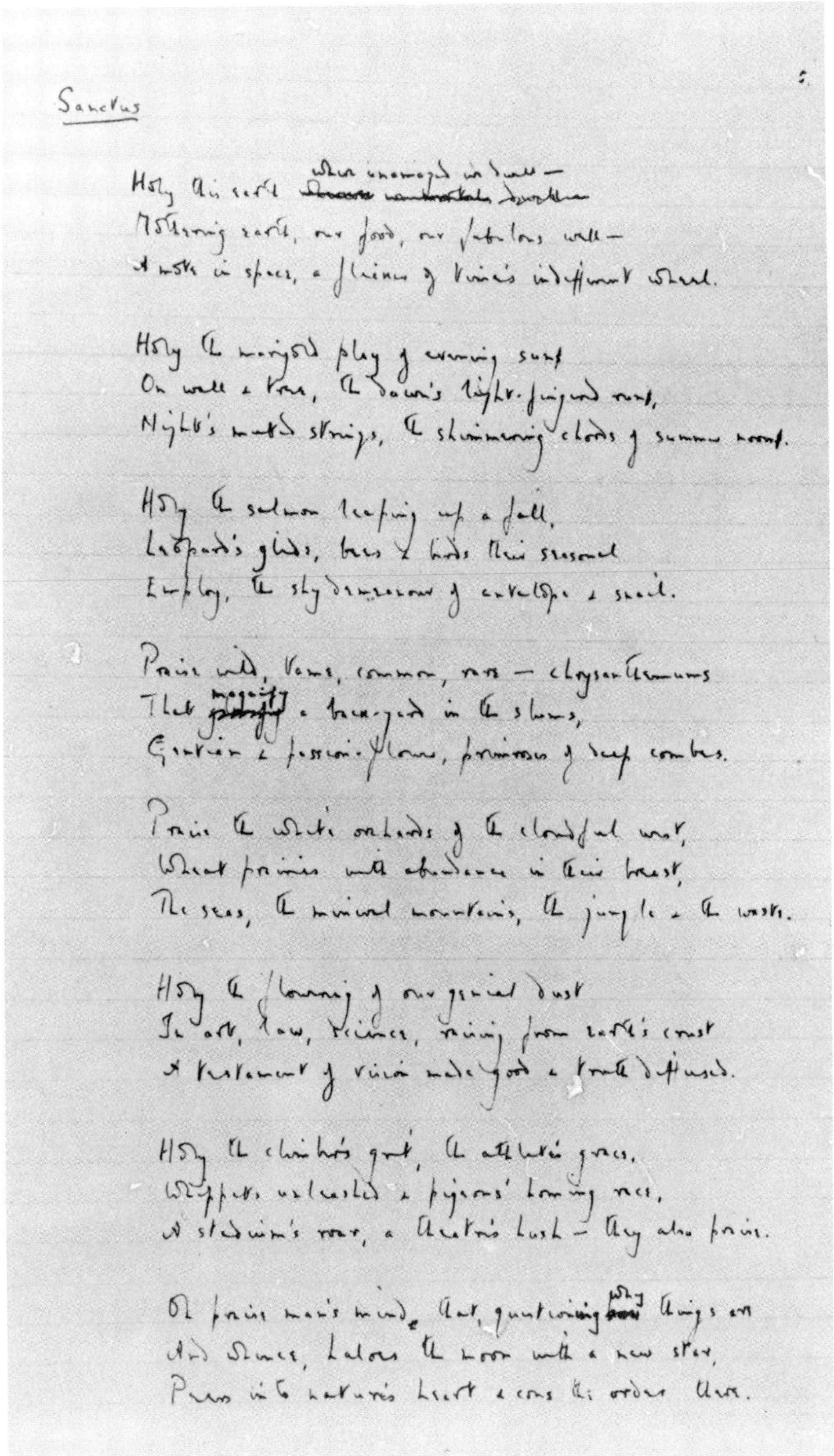

Sanctus

Holy this earth when enwrapped in [illegible] —
Mothering earth, our food, our fabulous well —
A mote in space, a flicker of Time's indifferent wheel.

Holy the marigold play of evening sun
On wall & tree, the dawn's light-fingered run,
Night's muted strings, the shimmering chords of summer noon.

Holy the salmon leaping up a fall,
Leopard's glide, bees & birds their seasonal
Employ, the shy dimension of antelope & snail.

Praise wild, tame, common, rare — chrysanthemums
That majesty & braggart in the slums,
Gentian & passion-flower, primroses of deep combes.

Praise the white orchards of the cloudful west,
Wheat prairies with abundance in their breast,
The seas, the mineral mountains, the jungle & the waste.

Holy the flowering of our genial dust
In art, law, science, rising from earth's crust
A testament of vision made good & truth diffused.

Holy the climber's grit, the athlete's grace,
Whippets unleashed & pigeons' homing race,
A stadium's roar, a theatre's hush — they also praise.

Oh praise man's mind, that, questioning why things are
And [illegible], labours the moon with a new star,
Press into nature's heart & construe its order there.

Page from the final draft for "Requiem for Living" (Humanities Research Center, University of Texas at Austin) whom one of the poem's sections is dedicated. Like most journeys in Day Lewis's work, this one is intended to be a voyage of self-discovery and self-renewal. The poem opens with a "Dialogue at the Airport" among the poet's various selves. Sensual Tom will grasp at the sensations of the present; the romantic Dick will look for lessons from the past; and the intellectual Harry will seek a better future. Their "Flight Toward Italy" is thus a flight toward rebirth. After posting a "Letter from Rome," the tourist takes a "Bus to Florence." The fifth section, "Florence: Works of Art," includes a set of parodies in which Thomas Hardy, William Butler Yeats, Robert Frost, W. H. Auden, and Dylan Thomas respond to famous Renaissance masterpieces. In "Elegy Before Death: At Settignano," the poet imagines his loved companion dead and writes his praises, renewing his love. Flying home in "The Homeward Prospect," Tom, Dick, and Harry react in characteristic ways to their visit, each finding reasons to praise Italy.

An Italian Visit suggests at times the traveler's poetry of Auden and MacNeice's *Letters from Iceland*, especially in the chatty "Letter from Rome." As a pleasant travel diary in verse, it has some charm, but the tourist impressions are insufficiently assimilated by the poem's efforts to say something about the nature of art and love. The backbiting and chitchat of Tom, Dick, and Harry goes on too long for the amount of amusement it affords, and the visit brings no real reconciliation of these differing selves. The circular character of the poem's movement made it an appropriate close for Day Lewis's *Collected Poems* (1954), for the poet's career had brought him back to the divided self he had sought to overcome in *Transitional Poem* and back to the poetic influences he had left behind with that poem.

When Day Lewis's wife finally agreed to a divorce in 1951, he quickly married again. His bride was not Rosamond Lehmann but Jill Balcon, a young BBC actress. They had met at a poetry reading in 1948, met again by accident in 1949, and become lovers in 1950. Settling down to renewed domesticity with his new wife, Day Lewis led a more tranquil life in his last two decades.

Day Lewis's reputation as a poet declined fairly steadily in the postwar years, at least among poets and literary critics. This decline did not keep him from becoming increasingly respectable as a poet. In the postwar years, Day Lewis received the kind of academic and official laurels reserved for poets who live long enough to be regarded as

Cecil and Jill Day Lewis with their children, Daniel and Tamasin, reading letters of congratulations on his appointment as poet laureate (Daily Telegraph)

tamed. At Cambridge, he gave the Clark Lectures in 1946-1947; at Oxford, he was made Professor of Poetry in 1951; and at Harvard, he gave the Charles Eliot Norton lectures for 1964-1965. In 1968 he was made Poet Laureate of England. His Clark Lectures were published as *The Poetic Image* (1947) and his Harvard lectures as *The Lyric Impulse* (1965). Both volumes preach the only faith left to Day Lewis, a romantic faith in poetry itself. The poem as an "image" creates order and harmony out of our jumbled perceptions of a disordered world; the "lyric" impulse is a spontaneous welling-up of song, which must, however, be contained by form. Neither volume has much original to say; their interest lies in Day Lewis's incidental comments, as a practicing poet, on his predecessors and on his own poetry.

So completely was Day Lewis now the poet that many of his better poems in his later volumes are reflections on the nature of poetry. Poetry is the subject, for example, of the title poems of his three collections after the 1954 *Collected Poems: Pegasus and Other Poems* (1957), *The Gate and Other Poems* (1962), and *The Room and Other Poems* (1965). In "Pegasus" the poet masters the poem with the golden bridle, which is both the gift of the gods and a kind of discipline—the image recurs in both *The Lyric Impulse* and *The Poet's Way of Knowledge* (1957), a pamphlet reprinting a lecture delivered at Cambridge. "The Gate" gives order to the world it separates. And in "The Room," the poet finds a world in retreating into his room of self.

Day Lewis's own retreats into memories are another frequent topic in his later poetry, particularly in his last volume, *The Whispering Roots* (1970). His most important prose work of the postwar years is his autobiography, *The Buried Day* (1960), which is at its best in its account of his childhood; it is highly selective in dealing with his life in the 1930s, and it ends altogether in about 1940.

Day Lewis may have had prudential reasons for ending his autobiography in 1940, but for many critics he ceased to be a poet of any real interest at about that time. The poet himself may have shared that feeling at times, for he says of himself that he was in all ways "fated to be a good starter but a poor finisher." It seems probable that his leftist verse of the 1930s was overrated because it suited the fashion of the times, and it may be that his neo-Georgian verse of later decades has been underrated because it did not suit the dominant fashions then. It is hard, however, to disagree with the consensus that holds that his verse of the 1930s has a vitality and complexity which makes it superior to his later work. The lyric impulse he valued is present in his later poetry, but the golden bridle of poetic form is applied too strictly and proves more of a burden than the ideological baggage carried by his poetry in the 1930s.

In the years since his death, Day Lewis has not been the object of much independent critical attention. When his work is discussed at all, it is as part of the work of the Auden group or of the 1930s as a period. Given the almost universal critical tendency to neglect minor figures and to exaggerate the gap between their work and that of "major" poets, it seems likely that Day Lewis's reputation will continue to be linked with that of Auden and the Auden generation. It would take a major revolution in critical taste to win any kind of recognition for his later poetry.

Other:

Oxford Poetry 1927, edited by Day Lewis and W. H. Auden (Oxford: Blackwell, 1927);

The Mind in Chains, edited by Day Lewis (London: Muller, 1937);

The Chatto Book of Modern Poetry 1915-1955, edited by Day Lewis and John Lehmann (London: Chatto & Windus, 1956).

Translations:

The Georgics of Virgil (London: Cape, 1940; New York: Oxford University Press, 1947);

The Aeneid of Virgil (London: Hogarth Press, 1952; New York: Oxford University Press, 1952);

The Eclogues of Virgil (London: Cape, 1963).

Bibiliography:

Geoffrey Handley-Taylor and Timothy d'Arch Smith, *C. Day Lewis, the Poet Laureate: A Bibliography* (Chicago: St. James Press, 1968).

Biography:

Sean Day-Lewis, *C. Day-Lewis; An English Literary Life* (London: Weidenfeld & Nicolson, 1980).

References:

Clifford Dyment, *C. Day Lewis* (London: Longmans, Green, 1955);

D. E. S. Maxwell, *Poets of the Thirties* (London: Gollancz, 1975), pp. 175-191;

J. N. Riddel, *C. Day Lewis* (New York: Twayne, 1971);

Derek Stanford, *Stephen Spender, Louis MacNeice, Cecil Day Lewis* (Grand Rapids, Mich.: Eerdmans, 1969), pp. 37-44.

William Empson

(27 September 1906-   )

Peter MCMillan
University of South Carolina

SELECTED BOOKS: *Letter IV* (Cambridge: Heffer, 1929);

Seven Types of Ambiguity (London: Chatto & Windus, 1930; New York: Harcourt, Brace, 1931; revised edition, London: Chatto & Windus, 1947; New York: New Directions, 1947; revised again, London: Chatto & Windus, 1953; Norfolk, Conn.: New Directions, 1953);

Poems by William Empson (Tokyo: Privately printed, 1934);

Some Versions of Pastoral (London: Chatto & Windus, 1935); republished as *English Pastoral Poetry* (New York: Norton, 1938);

Poems (London: Chatto & Windus, 1935);

Shakespeare Survey, by Empson and George Garrett (London: Brendin, 1937);

The Gathering Storm (London: Faber & Faber, 1940);

Collected Poems (New York: Harcourt, Brace, 1949; enlarged edition, London: Chatto & Windus, 1955);

The Structure of Complex Words (London: Chatto & Windus, 1951; New York: New Directions, 1951);

Milton's God (London: Chatto & Windus, 1961; Norfolk, Conn.: New Directions, 1962; revised edition, London: Chatto & Windus, 1965).

William Empson

Even if William Empson had never written a word of poetry, his name would be important in any overall evaluation of twentieth-century letters. For Empson first became well known, not for his poetry, but for his contribution to literary criticism. In each of his four major critical works, beginning with *Seven Types of Ambiguity* (1930) and spanning three decades to *Milton's God* (1961), Empson has made an important, if highly controversial, contribution to our way of reading and understanding literature. It is only in the last three decades that his poetry has been treated with the seriousness it deserves. William Empson has a unique and memorable voice which, when put together with his commensurate technical skills, makes him an important poet.

As a poet Empson is a traditionalist, saying once, "I am in favour of rhyme and metre in English poetry." He also brings to his verse a commitment to the power of conventional but complicated themes. Many of his poetic tenets, such as ambiguity of statement and complex analogies, are closely related to his critical credo. Argument is one of Empson's favorite forms, as he considers it to be truly poetic. For Empson, argument demands and guarantees a strict logical control of the subject matter and the technique. It may be said that the intellect takes precedence over the muse in Empson's case. His poetry is rational and self-conscious, and rhythm, rhyme, and meter are always at the service of intellect. He is in many senses a twentieth-century "metaphysical" poet, much more so than Eliot. But he has renewed both their subject matter and their verse patterns in his distinct and original voice.

Empson descends from a family of landed gentry. His roots are steeped in the history of Yorkshire with family records going back at least to Oliver Cromwell. Some time in the eighteenth century his ancestors took up residence at Yorkefleet Hall, an estate of some 4,000 acres bordering the river Ouse. It was here that William Empson was born in 1906, the youngest of the five children of Arthur Reginald and Laura Micklethwait Empson. Yorkefleet is remote, and perhaps the underlying theme of isolation and indeed alienation in Empson's verse may be traced to his upbringing in the diminishing world of landed aristocracy. In 1920, after preparatory school in Folkestone, Empson entered Winchester College in Winchester, Hampshire, on a scholarship. (Among his classmates was the future political writer and British Labour party politician Richard Crossman.) There is little record of Empson's activities at Winchester, but by 1924 he had secured a scholarship to read mathematics at Magdalene College, Cambridge, and he went there in the autumn of 1925.

The atmosphere of Cambridge in the 1920s was of crucial importance to the development of Empson's poetry. Indeed his poetry might have been quite different had he been mixing with W. H. Auden, Stephen Spender, and other contemporaries who at this time were reading English at Oxford. Cambridge was the right place for Empson's intense and highly rational outlook. Not only was it an important center of scientific discovery and dissemination (Nobel Prize winner Ernest Rutherford was the director of the Cavendish Laboratory and Sir Arthur Eddington was professor of astronomy), it was also the base for the important and influential literary critics I. A. Richards and F. R. Leavis. A post-Einsteinian view of physics and astronomy pervaded the intellectual life of the university both with a feeling that man's possibilities were limitless and with a profound sense of humility at the sheer size and complexity of the universe, attitudes that are captured in Eddington's *The Nature Of The Physical World* (1928). In *Science and Poetry* (1925) Richards, who was a psychologist before he was a critic, tried to justify poetry on a scientific basis: its ability to organize "impulses" in significant ways, and for Empson, at least, the study of literature was consistent with an awareness of the scientific discoveries of the day. Such essays as T. S. Eliot's "The Metaphysical Poets" placed an emphasis on poetry that was complex and difficult, and this interest in intricate verse was shared by Leavis and I. A. Richards, who became Empson's tutor. Thus while the newly discovered areas of science provided an imaginative framework, the critical emphasis outlined by Eliot and others determined the density of Empson's thought. The importance of life in Cambridge to the shaping of Empson's poetry becomes apparent when one considers that half of it was written during the years that he was an undergraduate (1926-1929) and that all his poetry bears the unmistakable stamp of his Cambridge experiences.

Empson responded to the intellectual challenges of Cambridge with great gusto, earning first-class degrees in both mathematics and English in 1929. He began studying English in 1926, and in June 1927 his first poem was published anonymously in the college magazine. "Poem about a Ball in the Nineteenth Century," is a charming piece, which employs repetition and alliteration to subtly convey a witty and ironic effect. The following year was to be his single most important year as a poet. In 1928 he wrote twenty poems, fifteen of which were later to appear in the *Collected Poems* (1949). One of these poems, "To an Old Lady," conveys Empson's attitude of respect for his mother:

> Ripeness is all; her in her cooling planet
> Revere; do not presume to think her wasted.
> Project her no projectile, plan nor man it;
> Gods cool in turn, by the sun long outlasted.

The opening words, "Ripeness is all," are from *King Lear*, where they are spoken by Edgar to his father, Gloucester, a parallel that reinforces the thematic content. Fusing images from astronomy and entomology, Empson pays tribute to his mother. In the bulk of the early poems the sciences of biology, astronomy, and entomology are conjoined with allusions to Shakespeare and the metaphysical poets, especially John Donne. In "To an Old Lady," for example, the word "precession" brings together both the astronomical term and the Victorian sense of dignity which Empson's mother stands for and which is so highly praised in this poem.

"Arachne," another of these early poems, demonstrates Empson's mastery of traditional verse forms, in this case terza rima. Despite all its somewhat extraneous philosophizing, it is essentially a love poem. The image of Arachne, the proud spider queen, determines the tone of the poem, which is open to much interpretation, partly arising from the complexity of syntax, an aspect of Empson's verse that his contemporaries at Cambridge admired. A vision of man is outlined in the opening stanza:

> Twixt devil and deep sea, man hacks his caves;
> Birth, death; one, many; what is true and seems;
> Earth's vast hot iron, cold space's empty waves.

Man's condition is seen as precariously placed between dichotomies. His condition is philosophically Pre-Socratic in that Empson employs the Heraclitean and Parmenidean notions of man as caught between the One and the Many, between truth and illusion. Man may successfully walk on a tightrope "between void and void," but the balance is easily disturbed. Within this framework the derogatory metaphor of the spider also evokes a complex vision of courage, virtue, and pride in a modulated tone which refuses absolute condemnation. Basing his poem on the myth of Arachne, who challenged the goddess Athene for destroying her tapestry and was turned into a spider for her presumption, Empson rehumanizes Arachne and suggests that, like a female spider, she will probably devour her lover before, during, or after sexual intercourse. "Arachne" is a brilliant but difficult poem in which Empson manages to combine myth with contemporary science to disclose profound feelings of apprehension and fear in the face of this awesome yet destructive beauty. The majority of these early poems display great technical skill with a definite sense of structure and an ability to renew traditional verse patterns with a modern inflection. Despite the many influences, his voice is always original and transcends the echoes that ring throughout his poems.

Other of Empson's 1928 and 1929 poems, including "Dissatisfaction with Metaphysics," "Letter I," and "Camping Out," appeared in a new magazine, *Experiment*, whose first issue was published in November 1929. Its three active editors, Empson, Jacob Bronowski, and Hugh Sykes Davies, derived their critical standards largely from I. A. Richards's lectures. Between 1929 and 1931 Empson published eight more of his poems in this magazine, which apparently ran to seven numbers. In 1929, the year of Empson's graduation, the Hogarth Press published six of his poems in *Cambridge Poetry*. These poems far outshone anything else in the volume and were singled out for high praise by F. R. Leavis, who wrote in the *Cambridge Review* (1 March 1929), "He is an original poet who has studied the right poets . . . in the right way. His poems have a tough intellectual content . . . and they evince an intense preoccupation with technique."

In 1930 Chatto & Windus published Empson's *Seven Types of Ambiguity*, which defines ambiguity as "any verbal nuance, however slight, which gives room for alternative reactions to the same piece of language." Empson analyzes, under seven categories, major works in English poetry which he deems to be ambiguous. It was immediately recognized as a landmark in English literary criticism, and on the basis of this book I. A. Richards recommended him for the post of professor of English literature at the Tokyo University of Literature and Science. Empson went there via the Trans-Siberian railway in August of 1931 and remained there for the three years of his contract. Only one new poem appeared during this period: "Aubade," which contains the beautiful refrain "The heart of standing is we cannot fly"; but before he left Japan he brought out a little book called *Poems by William Empson*, containing fourteen poems and printed for private circulation by the Fox and Daffodil Press.

Empson spent the years 1934 to 1937 in England, where his first commercially published collection of poetry, *Poems* (1935), and his second critical work, *Some Versions of Pastoral* (1935), were published. In 1937 he again set out for the Orient, this time China, where he had a position as professor of English at the Peking National University. The Sino-Japanese war had just begun, and he arrived in Peking by Japanese troop train after the city had fallen. Empson spent the first term teaching some eighty miles from Peking, in Nan-Yeuh, a mountain village where the students had been advised to reassemble. In China he wrote four poems about his Chinese experience and completed "Bacchus," an extraordinarily complex poem. Read aloud it is always rhythmically stimulating and encourages rereading:

> The laughing god born of a startling answer
> (Cymbal of clash in the divided glancer
> Forcing from heaven's the force of earth's desire)
> Capped a retort to sublime earth by fire
> And starred round within man its salt and glitter
> (Round goblet, but for star—or whirled—map fitter?
> Earth lost in him is still but earth fulfilled),
> Troubled the water till the spirit' stilled
> And flowered round tears-of-wine round the dimmed flask
> The roundest ones crack least under this task;
> It is the delicate glass stands heat, better than stone.
> This is the vessel could have stood alone
> Were it not fitted both to earth and sky),
> Which trickled to a sea, though wit was dry,
> Making a brew thicker than blood, being brine,
> Being the mother water which was first made blood,
> All living blood, and whatever blood makes wine.

William Empson, circa 1946 (BBC Hulton)

This long first stanza demonstrates the true "metaphysical" quality of Empson's work. He makes universal judgments on the condition of man and on such transcendental qualities as desire. As this poem is about Bacchus, the god of wine, it may be seen, in some senses at least, as a meditation on either the fallen nature of man or, at least, on his natural vulnerabilities and weaknesses. Yet there is, as in metaphysical poetry, a sense that flawed human nature is somehow being celebrated by virtue of its being captured in beautiful and living verse.

In 1939 Empson returned to London, where he worked for the British Broadcasting Corporation in their Far Eastern section. It was here that he met Hester Henrietta Crouse, a South African, who at that time was also employed by the BBC. The two were married in 1941 and have two sons. Empson's second collection, *The Gathering Storm*, was published in 1940. Like those in *Poems*, the poems in *The Gathering Storm* are accompanied by copious notes (an example of Eliot's influence). In his preface Empson says of these notes: "No doubt the notes are partly needed through my incompetence in writing. . . . they had better have been worked into the text. I do the best I can. But partly they are meant to be like answers to a crossword puzzle; a sort of puzzle interest is part of the pleasure you are meant to get from the verse, and that I get myself when I go back to it."

The poems in this collection do full justice to the conventional forms Empson prefers. Not only has he mastered a wide range of subject matter, but he is also adroit and skillful in his use of traditional verse forms for contemporary ends. One of these forms is the villanelle, of which he has written three—"Villanelle," "Missing Dates," and "Reflection from Anita Loos." "Villanelle" is a good example of his technical expertise:

It is the pain, it is the pain, endures.
Your chemic beauty burned my muscles through.
Poise of my hands reminded me of yours.

The poem may be seen as a dramatization of three forces: beauty which causes pain, pain which endures, and poise which reminds the poet of beauty. The girl's beauty is at once a "poison draught" and a "deep beauty," a polarity. Like most of Empson's love poetry, this poem expresses aspects of his sense of loss in love:

You are still kind whom the same shape immures.
Kind and beyond adieu. We miss our cue.

As in "Arachne," where Empson dramatizes his fear of women, here too he confronts his incompetence before those he loves most.

In another memorable poem, "Legal Fiction," Empson dramatizes man's illusions: "Law makes long spokes of the short stakes of man," he argues, and though man's existence is enclosed by matter his mind must nevertheless strive to control and make sense of the external world. Yet if this poem is about Empson's view of the mind's pretensions and man's predicament, then his attitude is by no means clearcut. Elements of satire and quiet admiration are the components of Empson's tone in this complex and intricate poem. For though one has a "well fenced out real estate of mind" which reaches down to where "all owners meet, in hell" nevertheless:

Earth's axis varies; your dark central cone
Wavers, a candle's shadow, at the end.

The poem highlights Empson's predicament as a poet. Highly intelligent and highly aware of the absurdities of modern life, he is finally unable, or

William Empson and Louis MacNeice, 1952. MacNeice produced an Empson reading for BBC Radio (BBC Hulton).

unwilling, to condemn man to "Hell's/Pointed exclusive conclave, at earth's centre." There are two senses, then, in which Empson speaks of the end. It is the end of the poem signifying his ultimate skepticism—or ignorance—in the face of death and thus his refusal to condemn; and it is also an agnostic belief that the only hell there is, is firmly placed at "earth's centre," that is, in everyday life. One is left with the conclusion that if false beliefs are deeply held, they are at least as true as other beliefs and have accordingly their own proper status.

The Gathering Storm contains only twenty-one poems, of which ten were published for the first time. Between 1940 and 1947 Empson had only three poems published, and from 1947 to 1952, while he was once again in China, teaching at Peking National University, his only output was a translation of "Chinese Ballad," a section of a longer ballad by Li Chi, a communist poet. Apart from a masque—"The Birth of Steel," a mock-heroic work written at Sheffield and first published in the 1955 edition of *Collected Poems*—his canon has not been added to.

Until the end of the 1940s most responses to Empson's poetry took the form of short reviews. According to Richard Eberhart, Empson's contemporaries at Cambridge were fascinated by his verse: "Empson was considered a startling poet by the learned. . . . His poems challenged the mind, seemed to defy the understanding, they amused and they enchanted. . . . the shock and the impact of this new kind of poetry were so considerable that people at times had no way to measure its contemporary or its timeless value. They were amazed by it." Other early responses were not so sympathetic. Louis MacNeice called Empson's poetry "inhuman." Julian Bell dismissed his poetry as "Another useless obscurity," and said it was "setting ingenious puzzles for old maids to solve in The Spectator." Yet just a year after the publication of *Poems* (1935), William Butler Yeats included "Arachne" in *The Oxford Book of Modern Verse* (1936), and Michael Roberts included six of Empson's poems in one of the most important anthologies of the decade, *The Faber Book of Modern Verse* (1936). In the early 1950s there appeared not only articles on Empson's verse but also chapters on his works in books. The revival of interest in Empson's work had begun, spurred on

William Empson (photo by Hans Beacham)

partly by his return to England to accept the chair of English at the University of Sheffield (1953), partly by the publication of his critical work *The Structure of Complex Words* (1951), and partly by John Wain's influential article "Ambiguous Gifts" in *Penguin New Writing 1950*. This revival of interest in Empson's poetry in England was preceded by the publication of Empson's *Collected Poems* in the United States in 1949. An enlarged edition was published in England in 1955.

William Empson has described himself as a minor poet, and in terms of his output and the sales of his books this is certainly how he must be judged. The total number of his poems is sixty-three, most of which are in *Collected Poems*. By 1942, when an air raid destroyed the remaining copies, only 600 of the 1,000 copies in the first and only edition of *Poems* (1935) had been sold. *The Gathering Storm* fared about the same. Four hundred copies were sold the first year, but the remaining 600 copies were sold off sporadically in the next ten years. Even with the British edition of *Collected Poems*, the total sales from 1955 to 1975 averaged only 200 copies per year. Yet Empson is represented in most major anthologies of modern English poetry and has exercised considerable influence on such poets as John Wain, Anthony Thwaite, and A. Alvarez.

Though his verse is difficult and demands consistent rereading, Empson has to his favor a sharply committed perspective, and his fundamental message, "how to learn a style from a despair," rings true to the modern reader.

Whatever the controversy surrounding his verse, Empson has been much honored in his own country. He has received honorary doctorates from the University of East Anglia (1968), the University of Bristol (1971), Sheffield University (1974), and his alma mater, Cambridge (1977). He is a fellow of the British Academy, and in 1979 he was knighted for his services to arts and letters in England.

References:

A. Alvarez, *The Shaping Spirit* (London: Chatto & Windus, 1958), pp. 73-86;

Richard Eberhart, "Empson's Poetry," *Accent*, 4 (Summer 1944): 195-208;

Philip and Averil Gardner, *The God Approached* (London: Chatto & Windus, 1978);

Roma Gill, ed., *William Empson: The Man and His Work* (London: Routledge & Kegan Paul, 1974);

Angelo Morelli, *La Poesia di William Empson* (Catania: Niccolo Giannotta, 1959);

John Wain, "Ambiguous Gifts," in *The Penguin New Writing*, volume 40, edited by John Lehmann (Harmondsworth: Penguin, 1950), pp. 116-128.

Roy Fuller

(11 February 1912-   )

Allan E. Austin
University of Guelph

See also the Fuller entry in *DLB 15, British Novelists, 1930-1959*.

BOOKS: *Poems* (London: Fortune, 1939);
The Middle of a War (London: Hogarth Press, 1942);
A Lost Season (London: Hogarth Press, 1944);
Savage Gold: A Story of Adventure (London: Lehmann, 1946);
With My Little Eye: A Mystery Story for Teenagers (London: Lehmann, 1948; New York: Macmillan, 1957);
Epitaphs and Occasions (London: Lehmann, 1949);
The Second Curtain (London: Verschoyle, 1953; New York: Macmillan, 1956);
Counterparts (London: Verschoyle, 1954);
Fantasy and Fugue (London: Verschoyle, 1954; New York: Macmillan, 1956);
Image of a Society (London: Deutsch, 1956; New York: Macmillan, 1957);
Brutus's Orchard (London: Deutsch, 1957; New York: Macmillan, 1958);
The Ruined Boys (London: Deutsch, 1959); republished as *That Distant Afternoon* (New York: Macmillan, 1959);
The Father's Comedy (London: Deutsch, 1961);
Collected Poems 1936-1961 (London: Deutsch, 1962; Philadelphia: Dufour, 1962);
The Perfect Fool (London: Deutsch, 1963);
Buff (London: Deutsch, 1965; Chester Springs, Pa.: Dufour, 1965);
My Child, My Sister (London: Deutsch, 1965);
Catspaw (London: Ross, 1966);
New Poems (London: Deutsch, 1968; Chester Springs, Pa.: Dufour, 1968);
Off Course (London: Turret, 1969);
To an Unknown Reader (London: Poet-of-the-Month Club, 1970);
The Carnal Island (London: Deutsch, 1970);
Owls and Artificers (London: Deutsch, 1971; New York: Library Press, 1971);
Seen Grandpa Lately? (London: Deutsch, 1972);
Song Cycle from a Record Sleeve (Oxford: Sycamore, 1972);
Tiny Tears (London: Deutsch, 1973);
Professors and Gods: Last Oxford Lectures on Poetry (London: Deutsch, 1973; New York: St. Martin's, 1974);
An Old War (Edinburgh: Tragara, 1974);
From the Joke Shop (London: Deutsch, 1975);
The Joke Shop Annexe (Edinburgh: Tragara, 1975);
An Ill-Governed Coast (Sunderland, U.K.: Ceolfrith, 1976);
Poor Roy (London: Deutsch, 1977);
Re-Treads (Edinburgh: Tragara, 1979);
The Reign of Sparrows (London: London Magazine Editions, 1980);
Souvenirs (London: London Magazine Editions, 1980);
More About Tompkins (Edinburgh: Tragara, 1981);
Vamp Till Ready: Further Memoirs (London: London Magazine Editions, 1982);

House and Shop (Edinburgh: Tragara, 1982).

Roy Broadbent Fuller came to prominence as an English poet during World War II with *The Middle of a War* (1942) and *A Lost Season* (1944). His first book, *Poems* (1939), is apprentice work influenced by W. H. Auden and other 1930s poets. Wartime experience as a service man in East Africa enabled him to establish his individuality. In 1961 Robert Conquest included work by Fuller in his collection *New Poetry*, placing him with the loosely associated group of poets known as The Movement, the predominate British poets of the 1950s and 1960s. Accordingly, Fuller serves as the bridge between prewar and postwar English poetry. He is also a notable novelist, a writer of children's fiction, and a prolific essayist and reviewer, recognized as a significant voice in recent decades for his urbane insistence upon high literary standards. Throughout his writing career, until his retirement in 1968, he worked full-time as a corporate lawyer. In 1968 the students at Oxford University elected him the Professor of Poetry at Oxford. Fuller's literary career marks him as one of England's most distinguished men of letters in the past half century.

Fuller was born into a lower-middle-class Failsworth, Lancashire, home in 1912. His father, Leopold Charles Fuller, was works manager of a rubber-proofing mill. When Fuller was eight, his father died, and his mother, Nellie Broadbent Fuller, took him and a younger brother to live in Blackpool. At sixteen Fuller articled with a solicitor, and at twenty-one he passed his qualifying law exams. He joined a firm of solicitors in Ashford, Kent, in 1935 and the following year married Kathleen Smith. Just before the outbreak of World War II, the Fullers and their infant son, John, moved to London when Fuller joined the Woolwich Building Society, a home-mortgage company. Excluding wartime service with the Royal Navy (1941-1945), he remained with this firm until his retirement. In 1968 he was named a governor of the BBC and served for more than ten years.

Throughout his career, Fuller has spoken as a gentleman. Capable of anger, of high seriousness, and of insouciance, he is most typically thoughtful, clear-sighted, urbane, witty, and wry. He is Arnoldian in his belief in poetry's seriousness; yet too worldly and skeptical to become excessively serious in his own writing. This essential ambivalence is both his strength and, some critics say, a limitation as well. His poetry can be moving, but it is not marked by intensity. Always he seeks to combine honesty and clarity in serving the humane. His social background and formative years account for his socialist sympathies (as a young man he was briefly active in left-wing intellectual groups, but after 1935, he reports, his sympathies became largely theoretical). His social mobility and intellectual concerns make him an elitist. This uneasy combination leads to frequent expressions of guilt. His poetic personae are unfailingly human in their honesty, doubts, frustrations, and firm assertion of life's worth. All these qualities find overt expression in "Obituary of R. Fuller" (*Epitaphs and Occasions*, 1949), in such lines as,

> Between, his life had all been spent
> In the small-bourgeoise element,
> Sheltered from poverty and hurt,
> From passion, tragedy and dirt.
> His infant traumas somewhat worse,
> He would have written better verse,
> His youthful prudence not so guided
> His politics more decided.
> . . . .
> Part managerial, part poetic—
> Hard to decide the more pathetic.
> . . . .
> If any bit of him survives
> It will be that verse which contrives
> To speak in private symbols for
> The peaceful caught in public war.
> For there his wavering faith in man
> Wavers around some sort of plan.

Fuller performs the archetypal poetic act of perception, seeing remarkable conjunctions and relationships. To do so is to make the quotidian and the cosmos more habitable. The smallest notation of nature may lead to striking insights into the human condition. He observes as well the disfiguring manifestations of human power seeking and time-serving emptiness. He is especially fond of commenting on the contemporaneous by invoking history and employing witty anachronism. Fuller has over the decades displayed remarkable ability to diversify his narrow range of personae. Almost from the start, his has been an older voice, middle-aged, avuncular, and worldly. The range of tone has been narrow, with the voice never raised and eschewing always self-pity. The stance is most often self-deprecating and sardonic. Fuller has a fondness for an omniscient viewpoint which invariably yields ironies. As he has grown older Fuller has not so much caught up with his personae as advanced them as well. Roy Fuller and Anthony Powell are both good friends and great admirers of one another's work; Powell dedicated the eighth volume

Roy Fuller

of his *A Dance to the Music of Time, The Soldier's Art* (1966) to Fuller. This mutual admiration is unsurprising given the proximity of their temperaments and ways of viewing the world. For both writers remarkable observation takes precedence over literary mannerism. Their originality and wit must be traced to this root.

In a general way all but the first three of Fuller's volumes of poetry have a typicality. Perhaps the archetypal poem is located in the speaker's urban garden (Fuller has lived for many years in Blackheath, a district in Greater London) and commences with an observation on the life of the local birds or on the season of the year. The garden, where man and benign Nature meet, is a world unto itself; it is as well a buffer zone between the great world beyond the enclosing hedges and the domestic realm, two zones of high drama. At the pinnacle of the Fuller pantheon is the female, who is regularly hymned. A considerable portion of poems concerns creative work: the lives of writers, painters, musicians; the recurring problems of creativity; the celebrations of notable works; the relationship of creator and audience; the distinctions between literal and created worlds; the impact of change and of influences. Fuller has never eschewed the autobiographical and often takes a wryly detached view of libidinous desires, of ill health, of aging, of being a creative person. The converse of these autobiographical views are broader statements of social concern about the great mass of men and the conditions under which they suffer and endure and the most biting of Fuller poems prompted by flashy, trendy pop culture. These principal motifs have continued over the decades, with each succeeding volume demonstrating the poet's resourcefulness, and they have provided the context for the inevitable surprises which have punctuated virtually every collection. Fuller has displayed a dedication to the poetic art and, as with his mentor Auden, has employed a wide variety of verse forms and line patterns. He has, for instance, sustained an interest in syllabics.

Fuller's first slight volume, *Poems* (1939), appeared just before the outbreak of war. Its debt to 1930s poetry is evident both thematically and metaphorically. The war in Spain, tension along borders, and the foreboding of doom are typical concerns. The imagery, which melds politics and predators, is fashionably Audenesque: "The open hungry jaw/Of Breslau and Vienna" ("August 1936"). Fear is the dominant note. But one striking personal poem, "To My Brother," transcends the influences. The speaker, gripped by expectations of war and thinking of his brother working on the Continent, has been reading the poems of Pope, which offer reassurance of man's innate urge for order. A sequence of counterpointing expands the implications, and strained syntax conveys the extreme tension. The movement between the general and the specific culminates in "The centre land mass breathes a tragic wind."

Early in his Royal Navy career, Fuller was selected to study the new field of radar, and he spent 1942 to 1944 stationed in Kenya as a radar technician. This time spent in East Africa proved doubly fortunate for the emergent poet: it gave him an abundance of fresh and provocative material; it provided ample time for writing. *The Middle of a War* (1942) is concerned largely with a man going to war. Thoughts of violence and death ("Soliloquy in an Air Raid"), basic training ("ABC of a Naval Trainee"), loneliness ("The End of a Leave"), departure from loved ones ("Goodbye for a Long Time"), and travel and boredom ("Troopship") are typical. The concluding stanza of "The End of a Leave" conveys the pervasive mood. In a cavernous

London terminal in the midst of hundreds of military personnel saying goodbye, the speaker is with the woman he loves. His detached ability to balance the personal and the general moves yet abrogates self-pity:

> Suddenly our relation
> Is terrifyingly simple
> Against our wretched times,
> Like a hand which mimes
> Love in this anguished station
> Against the whole world's pull.

The timeliness of such utterance clearly underwrote the reception of his work and made Fuller's a familiar name for the first time.

The second wartime collection, *A Lost Season* (1944), includes numerous military poems, but the striking poems record Africa's impact upon the poet. "The Giraffes" suggests that meaningful lessons are to be learned by studying these animals. "The Plains" and their inhabitants stir primordial memories. The impact of Western civilization on "The Green Hills of Africa" leaves the speaker with divided feelings. The poet's own journeys to the heart of darkness are expressed in the powerful "Sadness, Theory, Glass" and the disturbing "What Is Terrible," in which life's potential horrors are "like cavities / Of surgery or dream." The most powerful poem, "The Statue," juxtaposes the common individual, in all his helplessness and fragility, and the ego driven powerful dedicated to dramatic history. The concluding poems reflect the fact that Fuller was recalled to London and a post at the Admiralty late in 1944. In such poems as "During a Bombardment of V-Weapons" he continues his chronological recording of the unfolding drama. Fuller's was one of the two significant contributions to English war poetry of the period. Keith Douglas, who gave his life, spoke in a more personal and subjective voice for the fighting men. Fuller, eight years his senior and sounding even older, spoke for those who served, whether in the forces or on the bomb-torn home front, behind the fronts. Douglas, in appropriately shorter poems, is more immediately moving; Fuller, inclined to the diffident, is more thoughtful and comprehensive.

In the immediate postwar period Fuller wrote three books including his first two works of fiction. Though modest, they represent a significant stage of transition. Like many other writers who served in the forces, Fuller returned to civilian life feeling drained yet wanting to keep the creative powers alive. He took the opportunity to pursue a persistent desire to try his hand at fiction. The results were two boys' adventure stories. *Savage Gold* (1946), whose narrative centers on hidden treasure, exploits the author's acquaintance with Kenya, and the book's strength is evocation of place. More impressive both in characterization and story is *With My Little Eye* (1948), about crime detection.

The fourth collection of verse, *Epitaphs and Occasions* (1949), draws inspiration chiefly from the eighteenth century. This source of inspiration suggests a thoughtful symmetry when one recalls the immediate prewar "Poem to My Brother," which acknowledges the need to set aside the civilized world Pope represents as the struggle for survival looms. With the end of the war it is appropriate to reassert the aims of Pope and Wordsworth. The opening "Dedicatory Epistle" concludes with a determination to write the kind of verse urged by Wordsworth, verse which "ought to speak on all occasions / In language which has no evasions." Appropriately employing couplets, this poem attacks contemporary follies and aberrations: "raving, grubby oracles," "aspirin art," and "mad generals." The assault is extended in several other poems. Retrospectively, it can be seen that the volume's chief significance resides in the first of a sequence of garden poems, "The Divided Life Re-Lived," and "1948," which begins with a motif to be sounded with numerous variations in coming decades,

> Reading among the crumbs of leaves upon
> The lawn, beneath the thin October sun,
> I hear behind the words
> And noise of birds

It is a poem about the scarring impact of the war years, "grotesque interlude," upon the consciousness. Another type of poem that is to recur is represented by "Chekhov" and "Emily Dickinson" in which the essence of these writers is succinctly captured. The Freudian, to be another recurring motif, provides the basis for several personal, near confessional, works: "To My Son" deals with the father-son relationship; "Sleeping and Waking" with the implication of dreams.

The lull in literary activity in England's immediate postwar years was inevitable. The process of getting the social machinery going took time and, indeed, the nation experienced an additional transformation with Clement Atlee's Labour government's institution of sweeping changes in such areas as education and industry. Equally inevitable was the burst of fresh activity in the early 1950s, largely fueled by the class issues raised by the welfare-state

Laurie Lee and Roy Fuller at a British P.E.N. Club party, February 1949 (BBC Hulton)

policies. The provocative dramas of Samuel Beckett and John Osborne led the way, followed by the novels of Iris Murdoch, Kingsley Amis, John Braine, and Anthony Powell. The poetic scene was likewise busy, and more confusing. Fuller was a prominent participant in this 1950s renaissance with two collections of verse and four novels. As the process of clarification asserted itself, the central body of poetic activity became known as The Movement. The poets associated with this acquired unofficial formulization by having their work published in *New Lines: An Anthology* (1956), edited by Robert Conquest, and again in Conquest's *New Lines II: An Anthology* (1963). Fuller was represented along with, among others, Philip Larkin, Donald Davie, D. J. Enright, Elizabeth Jennings, and Thom Gunn. These writers shared a sense that poetry ought to be commonsensical and robust in content, ironical, nonsentimental, and skillful in versification. The bywords were clarity and honesty. Given the fact that Fuller was something of an elder statesman in the group and that the criteria perfectly described his work, it is appropriate to view him as The Movement's father figure. Fuller's position is thus clear: he is the linking figure between England's most representative verse of the 1930s and the 1950s.

Assurance, above all, marks Fuller's poetry collections of this decade, *Counterparts* (1954) and *Brutus's Orchard* (1957). *Counterparts* includes two of Fuller's most anthologized pieces, "The Image" and "Translation." They disclose two distinctive sides of the poet. "The Image," about responsibility toward the infirm, is minutely observed and understated. It moves quietly from the specific and incidental, the spider in the bathtub, to the normally unexamined motivation for compassionate care. This poem presents the domestic Fuller; "Translation" casts him in his public role. The persona, a crotchety, seemingly retired, civil servant, is sourly dismissive of contemporary pop culture. Similar material, handled routinely in *Epitaphs and Occasions*, is managed with real panache in "Translation." The poem concludes typically with the speaker wryly observing himself. The voice of "The Image," contemplative, honest and humane, is Fuller at his most characteristic; but the more assertive and dramatic voice of "Translation" is employed increasingly in his later poetry, the voices in counterpoint enriching his volumes.

The dramatic fully asserts itself in *Brutus's Orchard*, a rich and vital collection that is arguably Fuller's finest. Where the ambience of *Epitaphs and Occasions* is Augustan and Wordsworthian, in *Brutus's Orchard* it is Renaissance and Yeatsian. The title poem is a soliloquy by Fuller's Brutus, standing in his darkened garden awaiting the arrival of fellow conspirators—a very human figure contemplating his mixed feelings, his ultimate motivation for the impending political murder. At the heart of the collection are nineteen "Mythological Sonnets," in which the omniscient observer looks down upon representative moments in history, the significance of which is unsuspected by the depicted participants. In some instances the sonnets employ a split-screen effect, the dual situations producing an ironic statement. A sense of amplitude pervades the many poems which evoke the immensity of the cosmos, the fecundity of nature, and the galaxies of the libido. Especially accomplished are "The Perturbations of Uranus" and "Night Piece," which explore conjunctions between the heavens and the heart. Implicitly the book celebrates the energy of the universe. The stance of the poet is suggested in the distinguished poem "The Final Period." The aging writer at his study desk, watching his youthful daughter beyond his window, draws together thoughts on the relationship between experience and art. Wisdom, desire, and facts contend endlessly. One stanza delineates the volume's essence:

Bermuda or Byzantium—
To some utopia of forgiving
And of acceptance I have come.
But still rebellious, still living.

During the 1950s Fuller wrote four novels. *The Second Curtain* (1953) is an effective mystery story because the protagonist George Garner is so well realized. A heavy-set, middle-age writer, he becomes inadvertently involved in the machinations of a shadowy corporate operation. His thoughts on writers and writing enrich the narrative. In *Fantasy and Fugue* (1954), Fuller set himself the challenge of writing a thriller from the viewpoint of a young man who is being victimized and on the edge of mental collapse. In essence the story is a race between the unveiling of the villain and the narrator's breakdown. *Image of a Society* (1956) draws upon the author's business experience; the title refers to a building society. Which of two rivals will succeed the newly deceased general manager is the question at issue. Fuller reveals a fine gift for creating lifelike characters and gradually, through developing action, disclosing their determining dimensions. The fourth novel, *The Ruined Boys* (1959), is among Fuller's two or three best. It centers on the friendship of two boys in contact with authority at a marginal public school. Only gradually do the insensitivity and moral ambivalence of the admired headmaster—and the destructive threat he represents—emerge. It should be noted that Fuller has considered himself equally a poet and a novelist, though critics tend to think of him as primarily a poet. Yet Fuller's writing of fiction seems to have enhanced his writing of poetry. The increasingly dramatic element in his verse may well be attributed to his fictive thinking.

Collected Poems 1936-1961 (1962) is divided into seven sections, the first six including most of the work from the first six collections and the seventh Fuller's latest verse. This verse carries on from the dramatic impetus of *Brutus's Orchard*. Included are two sequences. The eleven "Faustian Sketches" rework aspects of the Faust story and are mostly the thoughts of various of the participants. The themes of desire and fulfillment are treated both poignantly and humorously. More ambitious are the twenty-one sixteen-line "Meredithian Sonnets," which chart the thoughts of a middle-age peripatetic who ponders the sights of London and reflects on life's disappointments. Three of the remaining poems are among Fuller's finest and provide a strong conclusion to one of the most notable books of poetry published in England in recent decades. "Versions of Love," overtly about a Shakespearean textual problem, covertly concerns middle-age desire, painfully real, painfully unrealizable. "On the Mountain" is a dignified restatement of "Translation," the persona now older and, albeit distressed by the state of society, not unhopeful about its future. The lengthy "Monologue in Autumn," a miniature verse novel in its suggestiveness, explores a marital relationship in the context of privilege and social responsibility.

The 1960s saw two additional collections. Both *Buff* (1965) and *New Poems* (1968) display Fuller's dexterity with his masks and themes. *Buff* contains his third sonnet sequence, "The Historian," twenty-five English sonnets which relate to the earlier "Mythological Sonnets" in allowing the poet to range across the recurrences and ironies of history. The appealing persona is an aging scholar who treats of matters in a worldly manner, sardonically yet tolerantly. Mindful that the barbaric hordes, in one form or another, never cease, he is at times gloomy; but at others he is delightfully astute on such various issues as why Paris chose Venus for the prize and the relationship between the evolution of engineering and the female shape. Such lines as these illustrate the Fullerian bias of the historian persona:

even at the stadium I—
Unlike the rearing mass—admire the skills

Dust jacket for Fuller's 1975 collection, structured like a one-year diary in which the poet examines society's and his own state of health

> Impartially. In fact, my hope is only
> That blood will not be spilt and that each side
> Will with defeat be somehow satisfied.

One of the poet's masterworks is "To X," a narrative made up of twenty-one roundels—that is, thirteen ten-syllable iambic lines with line one repeated as the seventh and thirteenth, line two recurring as the eighth, and the whole poem restricted to two rhymes. This tour de force relates how the older bachelor, who is recalling the experiences, became involved with a younger married woman and chose not to consummate the relationship though opportunity was not wanting. Intricacy of narration, explanation, and form strikingly meld.

New Poems, which won the Duff Cooper Memorial Prize in 1968, displays a new concern for the metaphysical. The possibility of other beings cohabiting man's space stimulates the poet, and in "The Visitors," "Orders," and "Those of Pure Origin" the subject is handled with an effective blend of thoughtfulness and skeptical wit. An epigraph by Friedrich Holderlin introduces the book, and his speculations about the interplay of divine and mortal have been a fructifying source. Most impressive is the autobiographical "In Lambeth Palace Road." With remarkable ease, the speaker, sitting in a tea shop while allowing the effects of a radiation treatment to wear off, draws together a heterogeneous confluence of thoughts. The world is filled with contrasts, the beautiful and squalid, the sophisticated and crude—"Strange companions"—both the tangible and the sublime. The art of living rests largely on the endless balancing of compassion and distress over the human condition and human conduct. Similar material is deployed in "Last Sheet" from the viewpoint of poet as speculator. It is an attractive restatement of the gap, seemingly never to be fully straddled by the artist, between conception and realization.

During the 1960s Fuller wrote three novels and a children's story, *Catspaw* (1966). *The Father's Comedy* (1961) traces out the reorienting of the relationship between a father and son. Set in London and Africa and involving a murder charge, this novel is a well-realized and moving book. *The Perfect Fool* (1963), the author's most ambitious novel, never rises above the routine because the material, particularly the vacuous protagonist, does not lend itself to Fuller's gifts for subtle characterization and tasteful handling of occasions of crises. In contrast, *My Child, My Sister* (1965) is a novel of real distinction and Fuller's best. The protagonist-narrator is a sixty-year-old don-novelist who tells about primarily his friendship with the teenage stepdaughter of his former wife's second marriage—the daughter he himself never had. This story about family relationships is about loss and gain. In this most Powellian of Fuller's novels the narrator's mature wit is a source of strength.

Fuller's considerable productivity eased up marginally in the 1970s as he experienced health problems. He was just past sixty when his tenth collection of poems, *Tiny Tears* (1973), appeared. This book contains no fresh surprises but keeps abreast of his advancing years. The poet apparently is spending more time at home, judging by the number of garden poems, such as "Robins and Woodlice" and "The Lawn, Spring and Garden." Typically a specific observation leads into speculation about the relative roles of birds and human beings and about the great chain of being. Characterizing such flights of fancy as "half-baked," the poet is at once thoughtful and humorous. "At T. S. Eliot's Memorial Service" is an elegant tribute to the poet, which employs an evocation of the interior of Westminster Abbey. The title poem, about finding the remains of a doll on the seashore, is a forceful contribution to the writer's poems in praise of women.

From the Joke Shop (1975) is at once a unique Fuller collection and the most Fullerian. Its sixty-three poems of widely varying length are all made up of three-line stanzas. The book is totally personal. Structured like a diary covering one year, the poet's basic concerns are the state of health in both his society and himself, the world of nature in his garden, the passing away of friends, and the fact of approaching death. The title comments upon both his present appearance and his continuing libidinous yearnings. The three-line stanza is perfect for Fuller's short and shifting flights of thought. An invigorating effect is achieved by the flow of rumination. For example, "XXVII," concerned with what makes life bearable, moves effortlessly from the gods to ill-health to sparrows to retirement to cooking eggs to "the swan" to Auden's death to drink to sleep. Though plagued by insomnia—many of these are night pieces and, indeed, Edward Young, author of the long poem *Night Thoughts on Life, Death and Immortality* (1742-1746), is saluted at one point—and by ill-health, the poet recurringly celebrates the life spirit. Indeed, the poet is bemused to find himself a carrier of "sanguine news."

Fuller's only novel of the 1970s, *The Carnal Island* (1970), may be characterized as poetic. Set on the southwest coast of England and on an offshore island, it is richly evocative of place. The setting befits both the protagonist, a well-known, aging poet Daniel House, and the mystical theme. Unbeknown to him and in an unusual but properly inevitable way, the young writer-narrator, who comes as a publisher's emissary to House, is to become the "son" and successor to House's literal and figurative kingdom. At the climax House dies, but not before bestowing the secret sources from which he drew his poetic inspiration upon his successor.

The 1970s witnessed the publication in two volumes of Fuller's lectures as Professor of Poetry at Oxford. *Owls and Artificers* (1971) opens with "Philistines and Jacobins" which reconsiders in contemporary terms the issues posed by Matthew Arnold in *Culture and Anarchy* (1869). This lecture appropriately establishes the general position Fuller will pursue in the remaining fourteen. His primary concern is with the downward drift of his culture and the need to reassert and sustain responsible literary standards. Most of the essays concern poetry and imply the position from which Fuller produced his own work. Arguably the finest lecture is a tribute to Wallace Stevens, "Both Pie and Custard." As another man who pursued a full-time professional career in tandem with his creative work, Stevens holds an obvious attraction. An admirer of the poetry, Fuller also praises Stevens's letters which, he argues, compose "one of the great books of the twentieth century." Two years later came *Professors and Gods*. The title essay expands Fuller's attack on fashionable but transitory trends in modern literature. Elsewhere he thoughtfully anatomizes the C. P. Snow-F. R. Leavis "two-cultures" controversy. Two valuable contributions to literary history are "English Poetry of the Two World Wars" and "Poetic Memories of the Thirties." Fuller used his final lecture, "The Planet on the Table," to remind the Oxford students of their literary heritage, Shakespeare especially.

Fuller produced two books in 1980. *The Reign of Sparrows*, his twelfth collection of poetry, is Hardyesque in tone as thoughts of dwindling powers and death dominate. Most notable, and one of his finest poems, is "On His Sixty-Fifth Birthday," based on Arnold's "Rugby Chapel." Echoed are both the anguished sense of lost powers and the affirmation of life. *Souvenirs* is a memoir of his childhood and adolescence in Lancashire.

Roy Fuller has had an exemplary career as a man of letters. Over more than forty years he has written poetry of merit, several fine novels, and a large body of thoughtful criticism. This accomplishment is the more astonishing given his lengthy career as a lawyer in a demanding corporate world; and indeed he has contributed as well to the literature of his profession. His bridging of the 1930s and the 1950s assures his place in the tradition of British poetry. Though he has, for periods of his career, been associated with central literary movements, first with the Auden generation and later with The Movement, he has maintained an independent voice which has sustained itself with undiminished force. Adverse criticism has faulted him for being unadventuresome and prone to straddle issues. Not without foundation, these charges represent the price this most diffident of individuals has willingly paid to be a highly representative spokesman. If his concerns over more than four decades have been narrow, they have been significant and have allowed the poet to display great resourcefulness and a remarkable versatility. Always, speaking as an individual, this most humane of writers has sought to speak for mankind.

Other:
Robert Conquest, ed., *New Lines: An Anthology*, includes poems by Fuller (London: Macmillan, 1956);
Conquest, ed., *New Lines II: An Anthology*, includes poems by Fuller (London: Macmillan, 1963).

References:
Allan Austin, *Roy Fuller* (Boston: Twayne, 1979);
A. A. Cleary, "Roy Fuller—What the Poetry Didn't Say," *Thames Poetry*, 2 (February 1981): 27-39;
Roger Garfitt, "Intimate Anxieties," *London Magazine*, 15 (December 1975-1976): 102-109;
Peter Orr, ed., *The Poet Speaks* (London: Routledge & Kegan Paul, 1966);
Anthony Thwaite, *Contemporary English Poetry* (London: Heinemann, 1964);
George Woodcock, "Private Images of Public Ills: The Poetry of Roy Fuller," *Wascana Review*, 4, no. 2 (1969): 21-34.

David Gascoyne

(10 October 1916-)

Philip Gardner
Memorial University of Newfoundland

BOOKS: *Roman Balcony* (London: Lincoln Williams, 1932);
Opening Day (London: Cobden-Sanderson, 1933);
A Short Survey of Surrealism (London: Cobden-Sanderson, 1935);
Man's Life is this Meat (London: Parton Press, 1936);
Hölderlin's Madness (London: Dent, 1938);
Poems, 1937-1942 (London: Nicholson & Watson/ Editions Poetry London, 1943);
A Vagrant, and Other Poems (London: Lehmann, 1950);
Thomas Carlyle (London & New York: Longmans, Green, for The British Council, 1952);
Night Thoughts (London: Deutsch, 1956; New York: Grove, 1956);
Collected Poems, edited by Robin Skelton (London: Oxford University Press/Deutsch, 1965; New York: Oxford University Press, 1965);
The Sun at Midnight (London: Enitharmon Press, 1970);
Three Poems (London: Enitharmon Press, 1976);
Paris Journal 1937-1939 (London: Enitharmon Press, 1978);
Journal 1936-37, Death of an Explorer, Léon Chestov (London: Enitharmon Press, 1980);
Early Poems (Warwick, U.K.: Greville Press, 1980);
Antennae (San Francisco: City Lights, 1982).

David Gascoyne

Precocity is the first element in David Gascoyne that the literary historian notices. Gascoyne brought out his first volume of poetry when he was sixteen, and by the age of twenty he had had three further books published. Two of these, *A Short Survey of Surrealism* (1935) and *Man's Life is this Meat*

(1936), embody his response, unusually wide and deep for an English writer, to European literary movements and particularly to the poetry of twentieth-century France, a great deal of which he has translated. Awareness of French poetry influenced him to become, for a time in the mid-1930s, a surrealist: in 1942 Francis Scarfe described him as "the only English writer who integrally accepted Surrealism and abandoned himself to its tender mercies." But by then Gascoyne had already emerged from surrealism, and in the following year he produced *Poems, 1937-1942*, which is among the most distinguished and powerful collections of the last fifty years. It entirely justifies Lawrence Durrell's recent description of Gascoyne as "one of the finest and purest metaphysical poets of the age." The intensity of vision implied by this description, however, was hard-won in terms of psychological strain, and has proved to be fitful in its recurrence. Two further volumes appeared, in 1950 and 1956, but almost no work subsequent to then is found in Gascoyne's *Collected Poems*, published in 1965. In recent years, Gascoyne has produced very little poetry, but the publication of two journals which he kept in the 1930s has fed the interest deservedly aroused, and maintained, by the fine poetry he wrote between the ages of twenty-one and forty. Gascoyne now participates, a welcome and honored guest, in poetry festivals in various parts of England. A selected poems, entitled *Antennae*, was published in the United States by City Lights in 1982.

David Emery Gascoyne was born in October 1916 in the small Middlesex town of Harrow, on the northwest edge of London. His mother, Winifred Isabel Emery Gascoyne, has been described by Gascoyne as "a frustrated actress"; she had been brought up by her aunt, Winifred Emery, a well-known actress married to the actor-manager Cyril Maude. Gascoyne's father, Leslie Noel Gascoyne, of possibly Huguenot descent, worked first in the Pall Mall, London, branch of the Midland Bank, and as a result of his various transfers and promotions his son's childhood and youth were peripatetic. Gascoyne lived successively near Edinburgh, in Bournemouth, in Salisbury, and in the small Hampshire town of Fordingbridge, where his father had been appointed manager of the Midland Bank. At the age of eight he went as a boarder to the Choir School at Salisbury, remaining a chorister at Salisbury Cathedral until 1930, when his voice broke. The experience gave Gascoyne a lifelong love of music: he learned to play the piano; one of his earliest poems is a tribute to the composer Bernard van Dieren; and the antiphonal, multivocal patterning of his long poem for broadcasting, *Night Thoughts* (1956), may be seen to derive in part from his years of choral singing.

By 1930 Gascoyne's father, not the most successful of bank managers, had been transferred to the Midland Bank's head office in London (he eventually became chief cashier there), and the family was living in East Twickenham, a southwestern suburb of London across the Thames from Richmond. Gascoyne returned from Salisbury to live with his parents, attending for his secondary education the Regent Street Polytechnic in central London and preparing for his matriculation examinations. By 1932, however, it seemed clear to his headmaster that he would never pass any examinations, and to his "great relief" he was removed from school at the age of sixteen. Henceforth he received no more formal education and dedicated himself to self-fulfillment as a writer by way of a life-style of an old-fashioned "bohemian" sort: hand-to-mouth, alternating between hope and despair, gregarious on the surface but inwardly solitary. The Irish-Canadian poet Paul Potts described him, very aptly, as "a poet of man's loneliness."

Gascoyne has stated that his parents never objected to the life of the artist which he took up. It was perhaps easier for them to accept it because Gascoyne had already achieved some small success as a writer. While still at school in 1932, he had used £25 from a small legacy to have published a collection of forty-three poems which he entitled *Roman Balcony*. Only one of the poems had previously appeared in a magazine; none was reprinted in Gascoyne's *Collected Poems*, edited by Robin Skelton; and only one ("The Netsukés of Hottara Sonja") was included in his recent volume *Early Poems* (1980). Yet for a poet in his mid-teens *Roman Balcony* demonstrates talent. Largely imagist and "aesthetic" in technique and flavor, with titles such as "Mood," "Rain Clouds," "Lucubration," and "Vista," the poems reveal an awareness of T. S. Eliot's free verse in *The Love Song of J. Alfred Prufrock*, the poetry of the fin-de-siècle ("Vista" begins: "A clatter of geese / fantastically waddling / across the jade silk lawn"), and possibly some influence of Richard Aldington, whose *A Dream in the Luxembourg* (1930) Gascoyne had read. Highly impressionistic, introspective, and word-conscious, the collection also embraces the realistic and demotic in, for instance, the observation of "New Cut Market" ("fish silvery-glittering / In the light of the naptha flares"). A few passages point forward to Gascoyne's maturer manner. In "Mood" occurs the best single line in the volume—"An ashen silence overpowers the wood"—which anticipates Gascoyne's later verbal and rhythmical density. "The New Isaiah," dedicated to Oswald Spengler, already holds in it the germ of Gascoyne's historical prescience in "Snow in Europe" (1938) and his visionary response to metropolitan landscape in *Night Thoughts*:

> The sun has gone. The City's lights
> shine out with fevered brilliance.
> When at the last these brilliant lights shall fail
> how dark and terrible the Winter night!

While at school, Gascoyne had also completed a "semi-autobiographical" novel entitled *Opening Day*. With the help of Alida Monro (the wife of Harold Monro), this book was published in 1933 by Cobden-Sanderson, a highly reputable firm whose authors included Edmund Blunden. *Opening Day* chronicles, with great sensitivity but almost excessive detail, a single day in the life of Leon, an adolescent who longs to escape from the stifling meanness of middle-class suburban existence to the wider intellectual and artistic life of central London, represented by the congenial Bloomsbury flat of his Aunt Sue, who is a portrait of an old friend of Gascoyne's mother. Leon, long-legged and "very tall for his age," is a close physical portrait of Gascoyne himself and shares with his creator a childhood in Hampshire and school days as a chorister at Salisbury. Leon's family circumstances, however, differ from Gascoyne's: Leon has lost his mother and lives with a detested father who has no sympathy with his literary ambitions. (It may be significant that, undergoing psychoanalysis in Paris in 1938, Gascoyne uncovered "a masochistic attitude towards my father, whom I imagine to be punishing me all the time"; and Leon, an unusual name, happens to be the inversion of Noel, the name of Gascoyne's father.)

Much of the novel, influenced by the method of Dorothy Richardson, painstakingly notes Leon's observations and feelings: a sizeable chunk of it describes a bus ride from Richmond Bridge to Twickenham and back and Leon's careful choice of books at the public library. As in the work of Virginia Woolf, it also makes frequent use of parentheses in order to punctuate the flow of Leon's consciousness and relate it to time's passing in the world outside him. The novel's conclusion, rather surprisingly, shifts into melodrama, or subconscious wish-fulfillment: Leon at last nerves himself to tell his father he intends to leave home, and their consequent quarrel causes the father to have a fatal heart attack.

As a portrait of the artist as a young man, *Opening Day* lacks the vividness and poetry of James Joyce; but as a portrait of the artist by a young man, Gascoyne's novel is variously impressive: in its sheer perseverance, in the polish and efficiency of its prose, and in its ability to make use of pioneering literary techniques. It also displays that remarkable combination of self-absorption and unsentimental detachment which characterizes Gascoyne's later work and which is so fully displayed in his journals.

Among the books in Leon's room is "an anthology of French verse, in French." Gascoyne's knowledge of French, which has led to his many translations of contemporary French poetry, was largely self-taught, and his advance royalties for *Opening Day* financed the first of his many sojourns in Paris, in autumn 1933. In Paris he visited the studio of the surrealist painter Max Ernst and also fell in love with an English girl, Kay Hime. In 1933 Gascoyne also began to meet and make friends with English contemporaries and near-contemporaries who figured in literary and artistic life: the painter Julian Trevelyan, who later drew the evocative jacket illustrations for *Night Thoughts* and Gascoyne's two journals; Cyril Connolly, future editor of *Horizon*; Geoffrey Grigson, who edited *New Verse* and there published Gascoyne's earliest translations (of Albert Giacometti, Georges Ribemont-Dessaignes, and Pierre Unik) as well as his "first longish surrealist poem"; the poet Kathleen Raine, who has remained a close friend and written the best essay on his work; and her then husband, the poet and sociologist Charles Madge. Through Madge, and his friend Humphrey Jennings, Gascoyne eventually became involved, in 1936, in "Mass-Observation," the brainchild of a number of social anthropologists, notably Tom Harrisson, who wanted to study the group behavior of ordinary people.

Kathleen Raine later recollected the impression Gascoyne made on her in 1933: "Tall, possessed . . . of the androgynous beauty of adolescence, his blue eyes expressive of great depth of feeling and imagination, . . . he had, even then, a dignity, a presence, as if of a being from another world." Lawrence Durrell, who first met him in Paris in 1937, described him more briskly but in essentially the same terms: "Underneath his charm and good looks David always convinced us all that he had that mysterious 'thing' which was the hallmark of the realised artist." These descriptions make it easy to understand Gascoyne's facility in making friends, while also suggesting the intense, lonely introspection which his writing expresses. The mid-1930s were for Gascoyne the crucible in which his best work was shaped, with slow concentration and in moods of alternating elation and depression.

Influenced first by 1890s aestheticism and by imagism (both fashions international, and particularly French, in their affiliations), Gascoyne turned in 1933 toward surrealism, which seemed to him "to correspond to certain instincts of non-conformism and revolt which I had always recognised in myself." This phase in his development lasted until about the middle of 1936, when he was one of the organizers of the International Surrealist Exhibition in London. In 1935, commissioned by Cobden-Sanderson, he revisited Paris to collect material for *A Short Survey of Surrealism* and met prominent French surrealists such as the poet and theoretician André Breton, with whose definition of surrealism—"Pure psychic automatism, by which it is intended to express . . . the real process of thought"—he agreed. For Gascoyne surrealism was "a restatement of the ancient and supposedly discredited notion of inspiration," serving to link dreams with waking life and (though this aim may seem strange when one reads actual surrealist poems) to make "the special domain of poets" into "the acknowledged common property of all." Gascoyne's book, illustrated and with an appendix of translations by himself and others, is a lively and still useful study, tracing the evolution of surrealism from the writings of nineteenth-century figures such as Arthur Rimbaud, Lautréamont, and Alfred Jarry, through the dadaist movement started in 1916 by Tristan Tzara and Hans Arp, to the flourishing "revolution of ideas" implemented by Breton, Salvador Dali, Paul Eluard and Benjamin Peret, further examples of whose work Gascoyne translated in separate volumes published in 1935 and 1936.

Nineteen thirty-six also saw the appearance of Gascoyne's own volume of surrealist poems (described as such in his introductory note), *Man's Life is this Meat*. This book was published by David Archer's short-lived Parton Press, which had already brought out collections by Dylan Thomas and George Barker, who later became a close friend of Gascoyne's and occasionally accommodated him in wartime London. Some of the poems, such as "The Very Image," dedicated to René Magritte, and "Salvador Dali," simply transcribe the dislocated images of paintings. Others, such as "Lozanne" and "Phenomena," are prose poems couched, for all the oddity of their juxtaposed impressions, in correct and elaborate sentences. A few, including "The Cubical Dome," "The Diabolic Principle," and "The Rites of Hysteria," display the kind of unpunctuated, nonlogical sequence that seems as likely to represent a willed suspension of logic as an irrepressible outflowing of subconscious material ("The flatfooted heart of memory opened its solitary eye / Till the freak in the showcase was smothered in mucus and sweat"; or, "its vast pink parachutes full of underdone mutton / Its tableaux of the archbishops dressed in their underwear").

These outpourings seem now as much of a convention as what they rebel against. It is in poems such as "Unspoken," "Educative Process," and "Antennae," where emerging logic and a subtler rhythm combine with language both imagist and emotive, that Gascoyne achieves memorableness: in phrases like "The full breasts of eternity awaiting tender hands" and "Negotiations with the infinite / Upon the empty beach." Here, and in the resonance of "The Unattained," which is not at all surrealist, Gascoyne begins also to suggest the sense of a higher plane of existence, reached for and occasionally experienced, that gives his best work its emotional power.

In September 1936 Gascoyne sweepingly rejected all his earlier work in a journal entry: "*Nothing* I have written so far is of the least value." He had just joined the Communist party, like so many writers of about his generation, and was also beginning to make new friends: Humphrey Jennings, later a director of documentary films; and the novelist Antonia White (author of *Frost in May*), with whom his relationship gradually became intimate. His idealistic espousal of the party was not lasting: in October, with £ 20 from Cobden-Sanderson, he went to Spain, for a while broadcasting in English for the propaganda ministry in Barcelona, and was disillusioned by Communist hostility to the anarchists and the Trotskyite P.O.U.M. In Barcelona he also met the ex-dadaist Tristan Tzara—whose development by 1938 of a personally humanist view of life in some ways resembles Gascoyne's own movement toward an essentially religious outlook: indeed, "Am I really a religious?" is a question he was asking himself in April 1937.

From summer 1936 to autumn 1937 Gascoyne wrote almost no poetry, though he struggled with a novella entitled "April" and some short stories about English insularity and genteel inertia which he intended to call "A Quiet Mind." During this period he felt that poetry was "a dishonest occupation." However, in October 1936 he produced a long poem called "Elegiac Stanzas in memory of

Alban Berg"; and in September 1937, a month after going to live in Paris, where he stayed until March 1939, he wrote the sequence of "free adaptations" from poems by Friedrich Hölderlin and four interpolated original poems which was published in 1938 under the title *Hölderlin's Madness.*

The idea for this book was suggested by his discovery, on a bookstall by the Seine, of *Poèmes de la Folie de Hölderlin*, the 1930 translation by Pierre-Jean Jouve. Jouve was a poet with whom Gascoyne soon made friends (he was also psychoanalyzed by Jouve's wife) and whose mystical religious intensity greatly influenced him. The language Gascoyne uses in his many translations of Jouve has sometimes a marked resemblance to his own densely packed lines in *Poems, 1937-1942*. Certainly Gascoyne's mastery of the alexandrine—a difficult line length to manage in English—derives from his knowledge of French poetry, and one often feels the aptness, in terms of both form and content, of Philippe Soupault's remark to Kathleen Raine, describing Gascoyne as "a French poet writing in English."

Gascoyne's long stay in Paris made him aware of his differences from the Auden/Spender generation, though he admired Spender for his "passion," and just occasionally sounds like him. He realized that "the values I believe in are European values and not English ones." Reading Christopher Isherwood's *Lions and Shadows* (1938) early in 1939, he concluded that "one cannot properly deal with existence simply by being continually bland and matter-of-fact." Like Hölderlin, the type of seer who gains a vision of what André Gide called "Paradise," the true poet must be prepared "to risk madness, despair and death for the sake of a possibility of redeeming existence by the secret power of the Word." Gascoyne risked all three during the poverty and relentless self-examination of his life in Paris, though for a short time he was sustained by a love affair with a young Dane named Bent von Müllen (to whom he dedicated the poem "Jardin du Palais Royal") and by his response to music, painting, poetry, and ideas. However, by the time he returned to England and faced the inevitability of war, he was beginning to emerge from a sense of futility and despair—life seen as "a long and painful operation performed without an anaesthetic"—into "a desolate clarity": the consciousness of his "prophetic" role and his need to speak out of the "universal anguish" and "spiritual crisis" of modern man and express a "total vision." "My life has passed on to another plane," he declared on his twenty-third birthday.

In September 1939 Gascoyne was hoping for a favorable decision from T. S. Eliot, who had been considering a collection of his poems for publication by Faber and Faber; at this time he added to Eliot's dossier some recent poems—"The Open Tomb," "The Three Stars," and "Artist," the last written on 11 September 1939. Eliot declined the collection, which (substantially augmented) eventually came out in 1943, not with Faber but under the imprint of Editions Poetry London, whose editor, the Singhalese poet Tambimuttu, was perhaps the most celebrated, and percipient, figure in British poetry publishing during the 1940s.

Geoffrey Thurley has incorrectly described Gascoyne as taking no part in the war on the grounds of pacifism. In fact, Gascoyne expected to be conscripted but was found unfit for military service for medical reasons and graded C3. (He has subsequently had three serious nervous breakdowns in the course of his life.) Instead, having in 1941 played a couple of roles as an amateur actor and hoping to learn playwriting, he did some repertory acting, first with actress Joan Greenwood, later for ENSA, the organization formed to entertain the troops, and finally in the West End.

Critical response to the publication, in 1943, of Gascoyne's *Poems, 1937-1942*—a handsome volume, despite the economies of wartime publishing, with five illustrations by Graham Sutherland—was summarized in 1947 by Derek Stanford: Gascoyne was variously called "an Ernest Dowson between two wars, an aesthetic Christian, a religious Rimbaud, a decadent seer." No one of these phrases, by itself, does justice to the volume; taken together, they give some idea of its range, though not of its force and penetration, nor of its density of language and its almost Miltonic grandeur of sound ("The Ural and the Jura now rejoin / The furthest Arctic's desolation," for instance, from "Snow in Europe"). For Stanford, the collection was "the most significant recent work in verse, after Auden and *Four Quartets*," and his judgment is a just one.

The volume consists of fifty-seven poems, together with five translations of poems by Pierre-Jean Jouve and, placed at the end, an adaptation of a poem by Jules Supervielle. Gascoyne's own poems had originally been planned as two sequences entitled "The Open Tomb" and "The Conquest of Defeat," but he rearranged them in five generic, rather than chronologically ordered, groups. The central section, a revised version, in French, of his elegy for Alban Berg, is preceded by the dark, brooding eight-part "Miserere"—with its final magnificent invocation of a "Christ of Revolution and of

David Gascoyne, circa 1951 (BBC Hulton, Picture Post*)*

Poetry"—and a group of "metaphysical" poems which present Gascoyne's spiritual odyssey from the nihilistic vision of "Bottomless depths of roaring emptiness" ("Inferno") through "the too-long-suffered tyranny and / Celebrated scandal of man's life" ("Insurrection") to "that Bethlehem beyond despair / Where from the womb of Nothing shall be born / A Son" ("The Three Stars"). These visionary, inner-directed poems are balanced by the visionary, outer-directed poems of the last two sections which, though entitled "Personal" and "Time and Place," are not essentially separate. Among the "Personal" poems, for instance, is "Noctambules," a description of prewar Paris by night in skillfully handled short iambic lines; and in "Time and Place" occurs "An Autumn Park," which could be in any city, in which Gascoyne apprehends "the true / And imminent glory breaking through man's circumstance." Gascoyne's relieved, buoyant goodbye to the "grim Thirties," "Farewell chorus" is in "Time and Place"; but a similar retrospect, given an edge of pathos, is found in the "personal" poems in his elegy for his friend and exact contemporary Roger Roughton, who edited *Contemporary Poetry and Prose* during the mid- and late-1930s and gassed himself in Dublin in 1941.

Kenneth Allott, compiling his Penguin anthology *Contemporary Verse* (1950), chose to represent Gascoyne by "A Wartime Dawn," written in April 1940. Though full of minute and sometimes almost neurotic impressionism (waking, Gascoyne registers "a moist-tinged black / Sky like the inside of a deaf-mute's mouth"), the poem relates this, ultimately, to the atmosphere of an external, real world in which "one more day of War starts everywhere." This fine poem lacks, however, the quality of radiance—the ability to transcend the world without forgetting it—which is Gascoyne's particular hallmark in this volume. It is found—though to single out one poem from so many is invidious—in full measure in "The Gravel-Pit Field," written in spring 1941, which begins by describing, with attentive, compassionate gravity, a "nondescript terrain" near Gascoyne's suburb of Teddington, and ends in a luminous glimpse of

> the fields'
> Apotheosis: No-man's-land
> Between this world and the beyond,
> Remote from men and yet more real
> Than any human dwelling-place:
> A tabernacle where one stands
> As though within the empty space
> Round which revolves the Sage's Wheel.

Poems, 1937-1942 was twice reprinted, in 1944 and 1948. After the war, Gascoyne lived briefly again in Paris, where in his poem "A Vagrant" he described himself as "although anxious still just sane," leading a life of "quasi-dereliction" in which he strayed "slowly along the quais towards the ends of afternoons / That lead to evenings empty of engagements." In a psychological trough again, after the intense peak of his wartime poems, he chose to remain outside a society of "sleepysickness-rotted sheep," yet was unsure whether "the strain of doing nothing is too great / A price to pay for spiritual integrity." The Atlantic Award for Literature which he won just after the war may have provided some reassurance that the uncertainties of the self-defined life were worthwhile.

"A Vagrant" became the title poem of Gascoyne's fourth (and to date his last) collection, published in 1950. Only one poem in it, the splendidly taut, symmetrical, Hopkinsesque "September Sun: 1947," recaptures the mystical fire of the preceding volume; the rest, facing a postwar world of disappointing mediocrity, accommodate in the fluid intricacy of their sometimes rambling lines a range of feelings from indignation through self-doubt to a resigned gentleness. Ever-renewed hope for the second coming of a "Puer Aeternus," "whose swordlike Word comes not to bring us peace" is balanced by a milder longing for a childlike "Rex Mundi," whose smile will pardon "morals, classes, business, war." Two poems, "Eros Absconditus" and "The Goose-girl," printed in sequence, present Gascoyne's personal, bisexual search for two contrasting kinds of love: one, apparently homosexual, like "a new kind of electricity"; the other, union with "a lonely, silent girl" to whom he will be father, brother, and husband. Other poems were prompted by Gascoyne's friendships, with Lawrence Durrell ("The Other Larry"), Kathleen Raine ("A Little Zodiak for K.J.R.") and George Barker. The last of these poems, the slow-paced meditation "The Sacred Hearth," conveys both the loneliness of the poet, a vagrant and outsider whistling in the dark, and his counteracting belief

> That there can be for us no place quite alien and
> unknown,
> No situation wholly hostile, if somewhere there still
> burns
> The faithful fire of vision still awaiting our return.

Like "The Sacred Hearth," many poems in *A Vagrant* transmit a quiet inner beauty one would call mellow, if that word did not carry overtones of a temperament too easily satisfied. Perhaps one may suggest their spiritual quality by saying that they convey a new acceptance of human limitation, a reconciliation—as shown in "After Twenty Springs," addressed to the shade of D. H. Lawrence—with the need for patience in the quest for "life, more life, new life." If there is, in this volume, a certain relaxing of emotional tension—and, in poems such as "Three Venetian Nocturnes," a tendency to overelaborate verbalizing—it is in the main compensated for by new subtleties of rhythm, especially in the deft handling of long colloquial lines, and by a wry, half-smiling tolerance of self and others, which argues an advance in maturity. A final section entitled "Makeweight Verse" (omitted from the *Collected Poems*) even essays humor: an affectionate, if elephantine, parody of Wallace Stevens and his "poignantly quince-flavoured lute," entitled "With a Cornet of Winkles," and a number of epigrams, notably a self-portrait of Gascoyne called "Toujours dans les Nuages": "I'm such an impractical dreamere / I seem to have mislaid my chimère." Clumsy as this couplet is, the touch of kindly self-mockery is welcome: it offsets Gascoyne's habitual seriousness, while humanizing and reinforcing it.

In 1951 Gascoyne's achievement as a poet won him election as a fellow of the Royal Society of Literature. In the same year, he visited and gave readings in the United States and Canada in company with Kathleen Raine and the Scottish poet W. S. Graham—with whom he was appropriately linked in volume seventeen of the *Penguin Modern Poets* series in 1970. In 1952 the British Council

Series *Writers and Their Work* published his essay on Thomas Carlyle, which characteristically concentrates not on chronological biography but on a wide-ranging discussion, and advocacy, of Carlyle's ideas, as a "national prophet" and prose-poet who denied the efficacy of Victorian materialism and offered the world a message of "genuine hope" based on "a long and courageously searching look at the worst." It is not hard to see affinities here between Carlyle and Gascoyne himself.

This almost "official" period in Gascoyne's life was rounded out when the BBC commissioned from him a work for broadcasting on its Third Programme. *Night Thoughts*, which for some critics represents the high point of Gascoyne's career (Geoffrey Thurley called it "the culminating poem in the European *avant garde* movement"), was broadcast on 7 December 1955 and published in 1956.

Night Thoughts, despite its superficial likeness, in genre, to Dylan Thomas's "play for voices" *Under Milk Wood* (1954), is really a very different kind of work. It does not so much offer a verbal evocation of character and place, directing the listener to imagine a created world outside himself; rather it evokes the listener's innermost thoughts and feelings about himself and his existential predicament, and uses the medium of radio to establish a link between poet and listener and between individual listeners and all those "other beings like themselves" who are listening at the same time. The three-section poem for voices, set in the night of a modern metropolis which is both real London and a place of dream and nightmare, is Gascoyne's largest-scale treatment of two motifs which have always been at the heart of his writing: the city, with its contrasting crowdedness and loneliness, and night, which can be seen as either the frightening nothingness which extinguishes personality or as a pregnant silence out of which may come "the command: Lift up your heart!"

Presenting, in sequence, the doubts and fears of postwar man, the siren cries of materialist "megalometropolis," and all the tiny sounds that distract the ear from the contemplation of eternal silence, Gascoyne displays great technical and verbal skill, both in verse and in a prose poetry of more than merely descriptive accuracy ("The City blaring with electricity just over the horizon flings its glare-reflection like a continual exclamation of astonishment into the sky, emitting intermittently a high-pitched filtered rumour of its roar"). At the end, Gascoyne's vision, expressed with moving simplicity, is of a world of isolated individuals who, in realizing that their isolation is in common, are united in a kind of hope: "Greetings to the solitary. Friends, fellow beings, you are not strangers to us. We are closer to one another than we realize. Let us remember one another at night, even though we do not know each other's names."

Dust jacket for Gascoyne's 1956 radio play, which Geoffrey Thurley called "the culminating poem in the European avant garde *movement"*

Gascoyne has had little creative work published since *Night Thoughts*. From 1954 to 1964 he lived in Paris and Aix-en-Provence, "dispirited" and suffering from the side effects of the amphetamines to which he had become addicted during the war: these side effects, he said in 1970 in *The Sun at Midnight*, had reduced his poetic output "to the strict minimum of work on which a poet's reputation may plausibly rest." (They also caused him to try to approach both Buckingham Palace and the Elysée Palace with "a great spiritual message" which kindly policemen and uncomprehending *barbouzes* dissuaded him from delivering.) In 1964, after a severe mental breakdown, following which he was told he could no longer live alone, he returned to England to live with his retired parents in the Isle of Wight. His *Collected Poems*, published in 1965, contains only two new poems, a conversation in unusually limpid and regular blank verse called "Sentimental Colloquy" and a longish elegy in memory of Paul Eluard. His *Collected Verse Translations* appeared in 1970, along with *The Sun at Midnight*, an aphoristic journal employing a title he had long wanted to use (in *A Short Survey of Surrealism* he had spoken of "that other plane of existence where stones fall upwards, and the sun shines by night, if it chooses"); the book contains a few Blakean stanzas of a "Poem in Progress," which has not yet been added to.

In 1973, after a further breakdown, brought on by depression caused by his parents' death, Gascoyne went into a hospital in the Isle of Wight. Here he met Judy Tyler Lewis, who was doing part-time work "cheering up mental patients" by reading them poetry. (She and Gascoyne both now do this work regularly.) They married in 1975, and in 1979, in the introductory note to his *Journal 1936-37*, Gascoyne felt able to say that he had "completely, and, hopefully, permanently recovered" from what he once listed as manic depression, schizophrenia, and paranoia. On 18 May 1981 Gascoyne's European reputation was appropriately celebrated when The British Council and the Centre Georges Pompidou in Paris collaborated in presenting an evening of readings of his poetry, in English and French, under the title "Homage to David Gascoyne."

Gascoyne's two journals of the 1930s, published in 1978 and 1980, lay open with total and engaging honesty both the intensity of his commitment to the vocation of poetry and his spiritual struggle—renewed in subsequent years—"from dark to light." Even had this struggle produced little poetry, these two books would still be fascinating historical and psychological documents. As the record of three crucial years in the development of one of this century's most important British poets, they are especially valuable. Sporadic in its appearance, limited in its quantity (though there is far more than any "strict minimum"), Gascoyne's poetry possesses at its frequent best, in the words of John Press, "splendid force, penetration and energy." In terms of externals, it is memorable in rhythm, word choice, and sensitivity to combinations of sound; and few poets of this century have been able to handle abstract terms (those big words so distrusted by Hemingway) with such felicity and conviction as Gascoyne. The conviction is not mere rhetoric; it comes from within and has been earned by a rare concentration on the fundamentals of man's life as "a spiritual being": in the themes he has attempted and the intensity with which he has conveyed them, Gascoyne belongs in the company of modern poets like Yeats, Eliot, and Edwin Muir. In the words of another visionary poet, Kathleen Raine, his gift "has been rather genius than talent."

Other:

Poets of Tomorrow, includes poems by Gascoyne (London: Hogarth Press, 1942);

Kenneth Patchen, *Outlaw of the Lowest Planet*, edited, with an introduction, by Gascoyne (London: Grey Walls, 1946);

Penguin Modern Poets No. 17, includes poems by Gascoyne, Kathleen Raine, and W. S. Graham (Harmondsworth, U.K.: Penguin, 1970);

"Whales and Dolphins," in *A Garland of Poems for Leonard Clark on his 75th Birthday* (London: Lomond Press/Enitharmon Press, 1980).

Translations:

Salvador Dali, *Conquest of the Irrational* (New York: J. Levy, 1935);

Paul Eluard, *Thorns of Thunder*, translated by Gascoyne and others (London: Europa/Nott, 1936);

Benjamin Peret, *A Bunch of Carrots*, translated by Gascoyne and Humphrey Jennings, *Contemporary Poetry and Prose Editions*, no. 1 (London: Roger Roughton, 1936); republished as *Remove your Hat* (London: Roger Roughton, 1936);

Contemporary Poetry and Prose, no. 2, Surrealist Double Number, contains translations by Gascoyne and others (June 1936);

André Breton, *What is Surrealism?*, translated by Gascoyne (London: Faber & Faber, 1936);

Collected Verse Translations, edited by Alan Clodd and Robin Skelton (London & New York: Oxford University Press, 1970).

Periodical Publications:

"The Sun at Midnight," *Two Rivers* (Winter 1969): 15-21;

"Antonia White: A Personal Appreciation," *Literary Review*, no. 21 (25 July-8 August 1980): 12-13.

References:

Kathleen Raine, "David Gascoyne and the Prophetic Role," in her *Defending Ancient Springs*

(London & New York: Oxford University Press, 1967), pp. 35-65;
Francis Scarfe, *Auden and After: The Liberation of Poetry 1930-1941* (London: Routledge, 1942), pp. 145-154;
Michael Schmidt, Essay on David Gascoyne, in *Fifty Modern British Poets* (London: Heinemann, 1980);
Derek Stanford, *The Freedom of Poetry* (London: Falcon Press, 1947), pp. 40-73;
Stanford, *Inside the Forties: Literary Memoirs 1937-1957* (London: Sidgwick & Jackson, 1977), pp. 106-111;
Geoffrey Thurley, "David Gascoyne: Phenomena of Zero," in his *The Ironic Harvest* (London: Arnold, 1974), pp. 98-120.

W. S. Graham

(19 November 1918-)

Diane D'Amico
Western Illinois University

SELECTED BOOKS: *Cage Without Grievance* (London: Parton Press/David Archer, 1942);
The Seven Journeys (Glasgow: Maclellan, 1944);
2ND Poems (London: Editions Poetry, 1945);
The Voyages of Alfred Wallis (New York: Wittenborn / London: Froshaug, 1948);
The White Threshold (London: Faber & Faber, 1949; New York: Grove, 1952);
The Nightfishing (London: Faber & Faber, 1955; New York: Grove, 1955);
Malcolm Mooney's Land (London: Faber & Faber, 1970);
Implements in Their Places (London: Faber & Faber, 1977);
Collected Poems 1942-1975 (London: Faber & Faber, 1979);
Selected Poems (New York: Ecco Press, 1980).

W. S. Graham began publishing his poetry in the early 1940s. The twisted syntax and crowded, shifting imagery so characteristic of his first volumes quickly led to his being termed a Scottish Dylan Thomas. However, despite this reliance upon Thomas as a model, he was a truly gifted poet. In fact, this early period later proved to be an apprenticeship leading to a more original style, one distinguished especially by its rhythmic qualities. One of the first products of this successful apprenticeship was "The Nightfishing," the title poem of Graham's fifth volume of verse. A long narrative poem employing a vital and forceful sea-imagery, "The Nightfishing" is the best known and most often praised of his works.

Born in Greenock to Alexander Graham, an engineer, and Margaret Macdiarmid Graham, William Sydney Graham spent his childhood on the west coast of Scotland, and his poems are often included in anthologies of Scottish verse. However, he does not consider himself "in any way as characteristic of Scots poetry," although some readers do find the physical environment reflected in his poems more typical of Scotland than England. At fourteen he was apprenticed to a firm of engineers in Glasgow. While an apprentice, he studied philosophy and literature at university night classes. (His firm apparently expected him to study mathematics and physics, subjects more typical of an engineering student.) After a five-year apprenticeship, he became a journeyman engineer. About this same time Graham was awarded a bursary to Newbattle Abbey College near Edinburgh, where he continued to study philosophy and literature. During World War II, he worked as an engineer in a torpedo factory on Clydeside and also as a casual laborer, crofter, and fisherman in Cornwall, where he now lives with his wife, Nessie Dunsmuir, whom he married in 1954. They have one daughter, Rosalind. In 1947 he received the Atlantic Award for Literature, and from 1947 to 1948 he lectured at New York University. Throughout his career he has had his work published in numerous periodicals and given readings in the United States, Canada, and Great Britain.

In 1942, Graham's *Cage Without Grievance*, a collection of fifteen poems with drawings by Benjamin Creme and Robert Frame, appeared. The imagery of these early poems has been compared to Thomas, the use of alliteration and full lines to Hopkins, and echoes of an archaic pantheism have been linked to Blake. However, if one sets aside possible influences and acknowledgments, Graham's own poetic voice can certainly be heard. "Here Next The Chair I Was When Winter Went" prefigures a major theme of Graham's mature poetry, the inadequacies of language:

My tongue is a sick device.
Fear evening my boot says. The chair sees iceward
In the bitter hour so visible to death.

Although when this volume first appeared it received little attention, later critics have found a distinctive lyricism in such poems as "O Gentle Queen of the Afternoon," and a laudable search for a system of value in such verses as "Endure No Conflict. Crosses Are Keepsakes."

Cage Without Grievance was followed in 1944 by *The Seven Journeys* (again with drawings by Robert Frame), supposedly written during rest periods at the torpedo factory. Although these narrative poems still resemble Thomas in their reliance upon the effects of twisted syntax, their dreamlike qualities have been compared to Rimbaud's *Les Illuminations* (1886), a work Graham has read in all available English translations. Fellow poet William Montgomerie provided an introduction, which encourages the reader first to respond to the rhythm of the language and second to consider the meaning in metaphysical terms. With the structure of each journey based on a dominant series of images—in the third water images, in the fourth images of ice and snow—Graham takes his reader not to specific geographical places, but to places of inward experience. Throughout these poems, there is emphasis on the poet's inner resources for perceiving and then for creating: "I build an Iliad in a limpet dome." Preceding the first of these journeys is "The Narrator," a poem apparently favored by Graham, for it is the only verse from this volume he has included in later collections. "The Narrator" concludes with questions echoing both Blake and Job and serving as the poet's introduction to the inward journeys which follow:

Who knows the rose or quotes her holy somersaults
Preached from a dangled spinner on a maypole thread.
What summer eyes perched deep within a dream
Could bring the god the child and the rose to speak.
What tongue like a stamen stemmed on a kiss or a grave
Is yet enchanted into form.

Soon after *The Seven Journeys*, Graham produced his third volume, *2ND Poems* (1945). Again it received little immediate response; however, by the end of the decade, when Graham was beginning to be recognized as a serious poet worthy of consideration, some attention was given to *2ND Poems* by such critics as Vivienne Koch. Although many of these poems were seen as too obscure, too full of directionless words and images, "Many Without Elegy," a lament for "the washed-away dead" was praised for its lyrical qualities and its deepening realization of mortality. It is still recognized as one of the best of Graham's early poems. Another poem in this volume that now seems significant is "My Glass World Tells of Itself," in which a ship in a bottle functions as a symbol of the timeless and static world of art, an image Graham used again in later poems.

Graham's next collection of verse, *The White Threshold* (1949), was the first of his works to receive critical attention immediately upon publication. The thirty-one poems in this volume had all been written between 1944 and 1946, and most had appeared in various periodicals in the United States, Canada, and Great Britain. (*The Voyages of Alfred Wallis*, also in this collection, had been published in a limited edition of 200 copies in 1948.) The sea imagery which is present occasionally in Graham's previous work becomes even more predominant in this volume. Graham draws upon the sea not merely for descriptive purposes but for images to embody philosophical inquiries. Often physical death by drowning is a metaphor for spiritual salvation: the old self dies only for a new to be born. In poems such as "The White Threshold," the sea is a crossing place, a threshold, where the self must confront the essential mysteries of identity:

Very end then of land. What vast is here?
The drowning saving while, the threshold sea
Always is here. You may not move away.

Although Graham's style had by the late 1940s become more concise and lucid, some poems in *The White Threshold* were still open to criticism for "tortured verbiage"; however, even amid these accusations of obscurity, there was a general acceptance of Graham as a genuine poet.

At this time, critics such as Edwin Morgan accorded Graham especially high praise for his interest in and experimentation with the relationship between poet and reader. He was hailed as one striving "to light up the imaginative dialogue of poet and reader without resort to well-laid fuses of moral or social response and without the adoption of any attitude . . . towards personal experience except the bedrock attitude of acceptance, of patience, interest, exploration, wonder, and vigilance." Graham's views on poetry and its relationship to the reader appeared in the essay "Notes on a Poetry of Release," written at approximately the same time as the poems of *The White Threshold*. Both Graham's concern for the ambiguity of words and his knowledge of their power are apparent in his statement that the poet "must face it that words are ambiguous, but realise that this has to do with the fundamental force of poetry and is to be used to a positive end. The poem is not a handing out of the same packet to everyone, as it is not a thrown-down heap of words for us to choose the bonniest. The poem is the replying chord to the reader. It is the reader's involuntary reply."

Recognition of Graham as a significant poet was further increased with the publication of *The Nightfishing* in 1955. In such poems as "Letter II," Graham continued to pare down his language to a forceful but concise expression: "Burned in this element / To the bare bone, I am / Trusted on the language." The difficulty of communicating from a constantly changing identity, a theme which had appeared in several earlier poems, becomes Graham's dominant concern in this volume. In the long narrative title poem, a night of herring fishing provides metaphors for an examination of the changing self, of death and rebirth and language's part in that process:

The keel in its amorous furrow
Goes through each word. He drowns, who but ill
Resembled me.

Primarily because of Graham's original and tactile handling of sea imagery, Robert B. Shaw (*Nation*, 8 November 1980) has said that "The Nightfishing" "may be the best sea poem" in the language. American poet James Dickey has also praised this poem.

After a fifteen-year silence, just about the time such critics as Edwin Morgan were suggesting that perhaps Graham the poet had little more to say, *Malcolm Mooney's Land* (1970) appeared. Language and its difficulties is the major theme. In the title poem a polar traveler tries to send messages out of the white silence of ice and snow:

From wherever it is I urge these words
To find their subtle vents, the northern dazzle
Of silence cranes to watch.

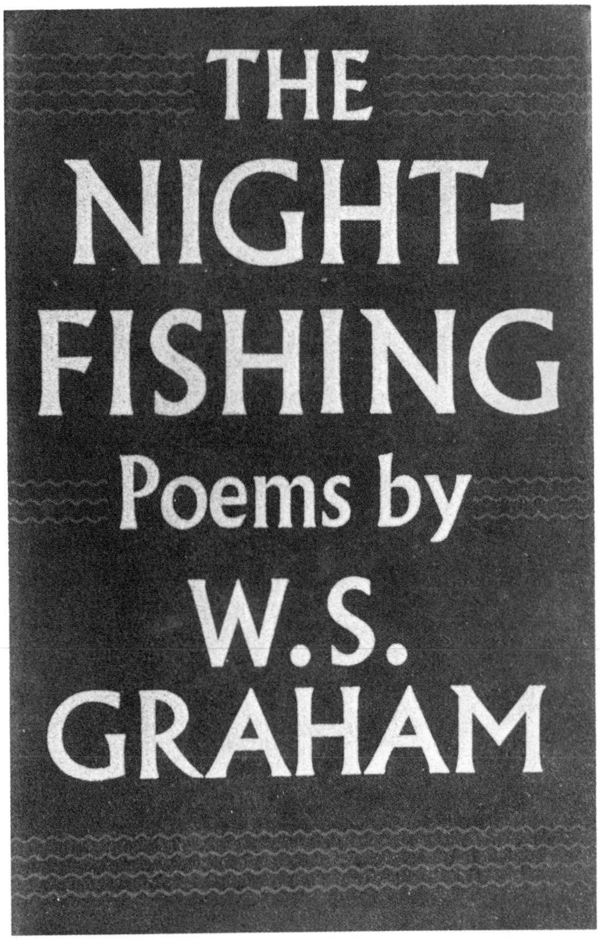

Dust jacket for Graham's 1955 collection. Robert B. Shaw said that the long title poem "may be the best sea poem in the language. . . ."

At first this collection received some harsh reviews, especially in the *Times Literary Supplement* (31 July 1970) and from Alan Brownjohn in the *New Statesman* (1 May 1970) and John Fuller in the *Listener* (8 October 1970). Graham was accused of being too obsessed with the theme of language. However, later critics have found various qualities to single out for praise such as dramatic skill and reserved pathos. A poem considered excellent even by his severe critics is "Thermal Stair," an elegy for the painter Peter Lanyon:

Remember me wherever you listen from.
Lanyon, dingdong dingdong from carn to carn.
It seems tonight all Closing bells are tolling
Across the Duchy shire wherever I turn.

In 1977, a second new collection, *Implements in*

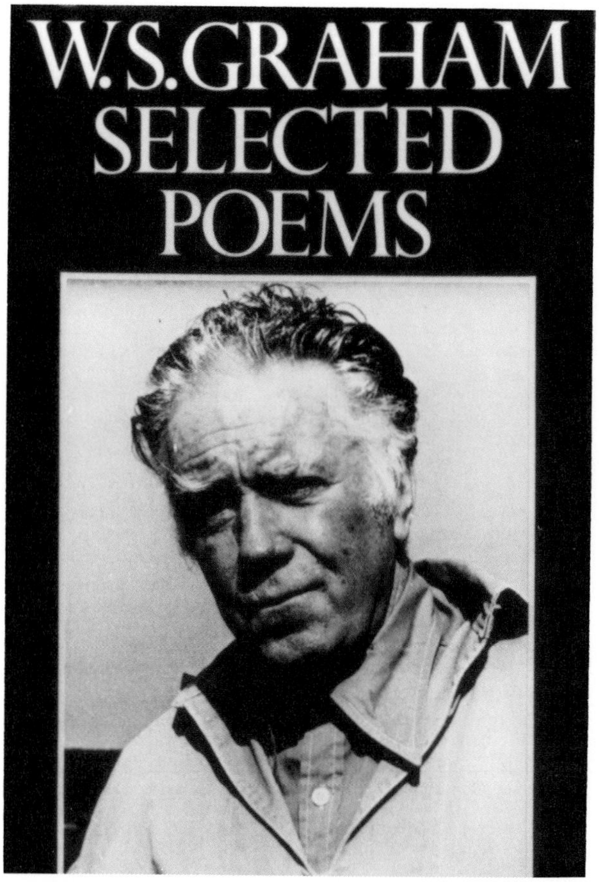

Dust jacket for Graham's 1980 collection, his first book to be published in the United States since 1952

Their Places, was published. This volume of twenty-six poems was well received and helped to reestablish Graham's reputation as one of the most original and entertaining of contemporary poets. Again, as in "Language Ah Now You Have Me," one of the main themes is the difficulty but necessity of communicating:

Language ah now you have me. Night-time tongue,
Please speak for me between the social beasts
Which quick assail me. Here I am hiding in
The jungle of mistakes of communication.

Among these poems on the dark jungles of language are several, such as "Dear Bryan Winter" and "Lines on Roger Hilton's Watch," which convey with impressive clarity the sorrow of loss. Although there are similarities to the earlier work, the linguistic style of these twenty-six poems is decidedly more condensed than that of Graham's first volumes. The title poem is a sequence of seventy-four short poems, some epigrams, on art and life: "It is only when the tenant is gone / The shell speaks of the sea." The fifth section of this sequence offers Graham's depiction of his poetic development:

When I was a buoy it seemed
Craft of rare tonage
Moored to me. Now
Occasionally a skiff
Is tied to me and tugs
At the end of its tether.

Since *Implements in Their Places*, two volumes of Graham's previously published poems, simply entitled *Collected Poems 1942-1975* (1979) and *Selected Poems* (1980), have been published. Both have been seen by such critics as Andrew Motion (*New Statesman*, 11 January 1980) and Robert B. Shaw (*Nation*, 8 November 1980) as representing an important contribution to twentieth-century poetry.

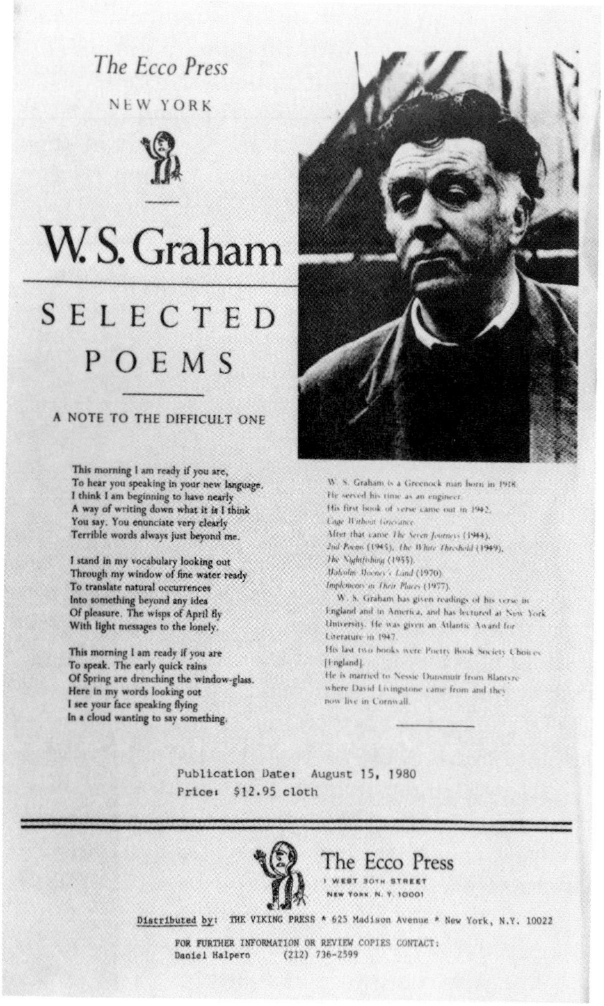
The Ecco Press
NEW YORK

W. S. Graham

SELECTED
POEMS

A NOTE TO THE DIFFICULT ONE

This morning I am ready if you are,
To hear you speaking in your new language.
I think I am beginning to have nearly
A way of writing down what it is I think
You say. You enunciate very clearly
Terrible words always just beyond me.

I stand in my vocabulary looking out
Through my window of fine water ready
To translate natural occurrences
Into something beyond any idea
Of pleasure. The wisps of April fly
With light messages to the lonely.

This morning I am ready if you are
To speak. The early quick rains
Of Spring are drenching the window-glass.
Here in my words looking out
I see your face speaking flying
In a cloud wanting to say something.

W. S. Graham is a Greenock man born in 1918.
He served his time as an engineer.
His first book of verse came out in 1942,
Cage Without Grievance.
After that came *The Seven Journeys* (1944),
2nd Poems (1945), *The White Threshold* (1949),
The Nightfishing (1955),
Malcolm Mooney's Land (1970),
Implements in Their Places (1977).
W. S. Graham has given readings of his verse in England and in America, and has lectured at New York University. He was given an Atlantic Award for Literature in 1947.
His last two books were Poetry Book Society Choices [England].
He is married to Nessie Dunsmuir from Blantyre where David Livingstone came from and they now live in Cornwall.

Publication Date: August 15, 1980
Price: $12.95 cloth

The Ecco Press
1 WEST 30TH STREET
NEW YORK, N. Y. 10001

Distributed by: THE VIKING PRESS * 625 Madison Avenue * New York, N.Y. 10022

FOR FURTHER INFORMATION OR REVIEW COPIES CONTACT:
Daniel Halpern (212) 736-2599

Publicity release for Graham's 1980 collection

Although much of Graham's early work has been criticized for its obscurity, it has nevertheless been praised for its musical quality, and, despite the view that his poetic world is a narrow one, concentrating too often on the theme of language, he has been praised for the intensity of his verse and for his poetic determination to speak against the silence, to "endure the sudden affection of language."

Other:

Penguin Modern Poets No. 17, includes poems by Graham, David Gascoyne, and Kathleen Raine (Harmondsworth, U.K.: Penguin, 1970).

Periodical Publication:

"Notes of a Poetry of Release," *Quarterly Review of Literature*, 3 (1947): 345-348.

References:

Calvin Bedient, *Eight Contemporary Poets* (London: Oxford University Press, 1974), pp. 159-180;

James Dickey, *Babel to Byzantium* (New York: Farrar, Straus & Giroux, 1968), pp. 41-45;

Damian Grant, "The Poetry of W. S. Graham," in *British Poetry Since 1970: A Critical Survey*, edited by Peter Jones and Michael Schmidt (New York: Persea, 1980), pp. 22-38;

Vivienne Koch, "A Note on W. S. Graham," *Sewanee Review*, 56 (1948): 665-670;

Edwin Morgan, "Graham's Threshold," *Nine*, 3 (Spring 1950): 100-103.

Papers:

The National Library of Scotland, Edinburgh, has typescripts, some annotated, of several poems, and thirty-six letters.

Robert Graves

Patrick J. Keane
LeMoyne College

BIRTH: Wimbledon, 24 July 1895, to Alfred Perceval and Amalie von Ranke Graves.

EDUCATION: B. Litt., Oxford University, 1925.

MARRIAGES: 23 January 1918 to Nancy Nicholson, divorced; children: Jenny, David, Catherine, Samuel. May 1950 to Beryl Pritchard Hodge; children: William, Lucia, Juan, Tomas.

AWARDS AND HONORS: Bronze Medal for Poetry (Paris Olympics), 1924; Hawthornden Prize for *I, Claudius*, 1935; James Tait Black Memorial Prize for *I, Claudius* and *Claudius the God*, 1935; Femina-Vic Heureuse Prize for *Count Belisarius*, 1939; Russell Loines Poetry Award, 1958; Gold Medal of the Poetry Society of America, 1959; Prince Alexander Droutzkoy Memorial Award for Services to Poetry, 1960; William Foyle Poetry Prize for *Collected Poems*, 1960; honorary M. A., Oxford University, 1961; Arts Council Poetry Award, 1962; Gold Medal for Poetry (Mexico City Cultural Olympics), 1968; Queen's Gold Medal for Poetry, 1968; honorary member, American Academy of Arts and Sciences, 1970.

SELECTED BOOKS: *Over the Brazier* (London: Poetry Bookshop, 1916);

Goliath and David (London: Chiswick Press, 1916);

Fairies and Fusiliers (London: Heinemann, 1917; New York: Knopf, 1918);

Treasure Box (London: Chiswick Press, 1919);

Country Sentiment (London: Secker, 1920; New York: Knopf, 1920);

The Pier-Glass (London: Secker, 1921; New York: Knopf, 1921);

On English Poetry: Being an Irregular Approach to the Psychology of This Art, from Evidence Mainly Subjective (New York: Knopf, 1922; London: Heinemann, 1922);

Whipperginny (London: Heinemann, 1923; New York: Knopf, 1923);

The Feather Bed (Richmond: Hogarth Press, 1923);

Mock Beggar Hall (London: Hogarth Press, 1924);

The Meaning of Dreams (London: Palmer, 1924; New York: Greenburg, 1925);

Robert Graves

Poetic Unreason and Other Studies (London: Palmer, 1925);
John Kemp's Wager: A Ballad Opera (Oxford: Blackwell, 1925; New York: French, 1925);
My Head! My Head!, Being the History of Elisha and the Shunamite Woman (London: Secker, 1925; New York: Knopf, 1925);
Contemporary Techniques of Poetry: A Political Analogy, Hogarth Essays, series 1, no. 8 (London: Hogarth Press, 1925);
Welchman's Hose (London: Fleuron, 1925);
The Marmosite's Miscellany, as John Doyle (London: Hogarth Press, 1925);
Another Future of Poetry, Hogarth Essays, series 2, no. 17 (London: Hogarth Press, 1926);
Impenetrability, or The Proper Habit of English, Hogarth Essays, series 2, no. 3 (London: Hogarth Press, 1926);
Lars Porsena, or The Future of Swearing and Improper Language (London: Paul, Trench, Trübner, 1927; New York: Dutton, 1927; revised edition, London: Paul, Trench, Trübner, 1936);
Poems (1914-1926) (London: Heinemann, 1927; Garden City: Doubleday, Doran, 1929);
Poems (1914-1927) (London: Heinemann, 1927);
Lawrence and the Arabs (London: Cape, 1927); republished as *Lawrence and the Arabian Adventure* (Garden City: Doubleday, Doran, 1928); republished as *Lawrence and the Arabs, Concise Edition* (London & Toronto: Cape, 1934);
A Survey of Modernist Poetry, by Graves and Laura Riding (London: Heinemann, 1927; Garden City: Doubleday, Doran, 1928);
A Pamphlet Against Anthologies, by Graves and Riding (London: Cape, 1928; Garden City: Doubleday, Doran, 1928);
Mrs. Fisher, or The Future of Humour (London: Paul, Trench, Trübner / New York: Dutton, 1928);
The Shout (London: Elkin Mathews & Marrot, 1929);
Good-Bye to All That (London: Cape, 1929; New York: Cape & Smith, 1930; revised edition, Garden City: Doubleday, 1957; London: Cassell, 1957);
Poems, 1929 (London: Seizin Press, 1929);
Ten Poems More (Paris: Hours Press, 1930);
But Still It Goes On: An Accumulation (London & Toronto: Cape, 1930; New York: Cape & Smith, 1931);
Poems, 1926-1930 (London: Heinemann, 1931);
To Whom Else? (Deyá, Majorca: Seizin Press, 1931);
No Decency Left, by Graves and Riding, as Barbara Rich (London: Cape, 1932);
Poems, 1930-1933 (London: Barker, 1933);
I, Claudius (London: Barker, 1934; New York: Smith & Haas, 1934);
Claudius the God and His Wife Messalina (London: Barker, 1934; New York: Smith & Haas, 1935);
'Antigua, Penny, Puce' (Deyá, Majorca: Seizin Press/London: Constable, 1936); republished as *The Antigua Stamp* (New York: Random House, 1937);
Count Belisarius (London, Toronto, Melbourne & Sydney: Cassell, 1938; New York: Random House, 1938);
Collected Poems (London, Toronto, Melbourne & Sydney: Casseli, 1938; New York: Random House, 1939);
No More Ghosts: Selected Poems (London: Faber & Faber, 1940);
Sergeant Lamb of the Ninth (London: Methuen, 1940); republished as *Sergeant Lamb's America* (New York: Random House, 1940);

The Long Week-End: A Social History of Great Britain, 1918-1939, by Graves and Alan Hodge (London: Faber & Faber, 1940; New York: Macmillan, 1941);

Proceed, Sergeant Lamb (London: Methuen, 1941; New York: Random House, 1941);

The Story of Marie Powell, Wife to Mr. Milton (London, Toronto, Melbourne & Sydney: Cassell, 1943); republished as *Wife to Mr. Milton, The Story of Marie Powell* (New York: Creative Age Press, 1944);

The Reader Over Your Shoulder: A Handbook for Writers of English Prose, by Graves and Hodge (London: Cape, 1943; New York: Macmillan, 1943);

The Golden Fleece (London, Toronto, Melbourne & Sydney: Cassell, 1944); republished as *Hercules, My Shipmate* (New York: Creative Age Press, 1945);

King Jesus (New York: Creative Age Press, 1946; London, Toronto, Melbourne & Sydney: Cassell, 1946);

Collected Poems (1914-1947) (London, Toronto, Melbourne & Sydney: Cassell, 1948);

The White Goddess: A Historical Grammar of Poetic Myth (London: Faber & Faber, 1948; New York: Creative Age Press, 1948; revised and enlarged edition, London: Faber & Faber, 1952; New York: Vintage, 1958; revised and enlarged again, London: Faber & Faber, 1961);

Watch the North Wind Rise (New York: Creative Age Press, 1949); republished as *Seven Days in New Crete* (London, Toronto, Melbourne, Sydney & Wellington: Cassell, 1949);

The Common Asphodel: Collected Essays on Poetry, 1922-1949 (London: Hamilton, 1949);

The Islands of Unwisdom (Garden City: Doubleday, 1949); republished as *The Isles of Unwisdom* (London, Toronto, Melbourne, Sydney & Wellington: Cassell, 1950);

Occupation: Writer (New York: Creative Age Press, 1950; London: Cassell, 1951);

Poems and Satires, 1951 (London: Cassell, 1951);

Poems, 1953 (London: Cassell, 1953);

The Nazarene Gospel Restored, by Graves and Joshua Podro (London: Cassell, 1953; Garden City: Doubleday, 1954);

Homer's Daughter (London: Cassell, 1955; Garden City: Doubleday, 1955);

The Greek Myths, two volumes (Harmondsworth: Penguin, 1955; Baltimore: Penguin, 1955);

Collected Poems 1955 (Garden City: Doubleday, 1955);

Adam's Rib and Other Anomalous Elements in the Hebrew Creation Myth (London: Trianon Press, 1955; New York: Yoseloff, 1958);

The Crowning Privilege: The Clark Lectures 1954-1955, Also Various Essays on Poetry and Sixteen New Poems (London: Cassell, 1955); republished, with new essays and without the poems, as *The Crowning Privilege: Collected Essays on Poetry* (Garden City: Doubleday, 1956);

¡ Catacrok!: Mostly Stories, Mostly Funny (London: Cassell, 1956);

Jesus in Rome: A Historical Conjecture, by Graves and Podro (London: Cassell, 1957);

They Hanged My Saintly Billy (London: Cassell, 1957; Garden City: Doubleday, 1957);

5 Pens in Hand (Garden City: Doubleday, 1958);

The Poems of Robert Graves (Garden City: Doubleday, 1958);

Steps: Stories, Talks, Essays, Poems, Studies in History (London: Cassell, 1958);

Collected Poems, 1959 (London: Cassell, 1959);

Food for Centaurs: Stories, Talks, Critical Studies, Poems (Garden City: Doubleday, 1960);

Greek Gods and Heroes (Garden City: Doubleday, 1960); republished as *Myths of Ancient Greece* (London: Cassell, 1961);

The Penny Fiddle: Poems for Children (London: Cassell, 1960; Garden City: Doubleday, 1961);

More Poems, 1961 (London: Cassell, 1961);

Collected Poems (Garden City: Doubleday, 1961);

Oxford Addresses on Poetry (London: Cassell, 1962; Garden City: Doubleday, 1962);

The Big Green Book (New York: Crowell-Collier, 1962);

New Poems, 1962 (London: Cassell, 1962; Garden City: Doubleday, 1963);

The Siege and Fall of Troy (London: Cassell, 1962; Garden City: Doubleday, 1963);

Hebrew Myths: The Book of Genesis, by Graves and Raphael Patai (Garden City: Doubleday, 1964; London: Cassell, 1964);

Collected Short Stories (Garden City: Doubleday, 1964; London: Cassell, 1965);

Man Does, Woman Is (London: Cassell, 1964; Garden City: Doubleday, 1964);

Ann at Highwood Hall: Poems for Children (London: Cassell, 1964);

Love Respelt (London: Cassell, 1964; Garden City: Doubleday, 1966);

Mammon and the Black Goddess (London: Cassell, 1965; Garden City: Doubleday, 1965);

Majorca Observed (London: Cassell, 1965; Garden City: Doubleday, 1965);

Collected Poems (London: Cassell, 1965; Garden City: Doubleday, 1966);

Two Wise Children (New York: Quist, 1966; London: Allen, 1967);

17 Poems Missing from 'Love Respelt' (London: Rota, 1966);

Colophon to 'Love Respelt' (London: Rota, 1967);

Poetic Craft and Principle: Lectures and Talks (London: Cassell, 1967);

Poems, 1965-1968 (London: Cassell, 1968; Garden City: Doubleday, 1968);

The Poor Boy Who Followed His Star (London: Cassell, 1968; Garden City: Doubleday, 1969);

The Crane Bag and Other Disputed Subjects (London: Cassell, 1969);

On Poetry: Collected Talks and Essays (Garden City: Doubleday, 1969);

Beyond Giving (London: Rota, 1969);

Poems About Love (London: Cassell, 1969; Garden City: Doubleday, 1969);

Love Respelt Again (Garden City: Doubleday, 1969);

Poems, 1968-1970 (London: Cassell, 1970; Garden City: Doubleday, 1970);

Poems, 1970-1972 (London: Cassell, 1972; Garden City: Doubleday, 1973);

Difficult Questions, Easy Answers (London: Cassell, 1972; Garden City: Doubleday, 1973);

Timeless Meeting: Poems (London: Rota, 1974);

At the Gate: Poems (London: Rota, 1974);

Collected Poems, 1975 (London: Cassell, 1975); republished as *New Collected Poems* (Garden City: Doubleday, 1977).

Robert Graves may well be remembered as the preeminent minor poet of the twentieth century. He would not be disturbed by the label. "Nothing," he said in his sixties in a lecture on the legitimate criticism of poetry, "is better than the truly good, not even the truly great," and, again, "minor poetry, so called to differentiate it from major poetry, is the real stuff." At the same time, Graves did almost all those things major poets do. He wrote a great deal of verse (more than fifty volumes) and, through revision and a winnowing that was judicious until his later years, he established a canon. An occasionalist in many tones and modes—love poems, recollections of childhood and war, psychological studies and more detached "observations," satires, grotesques, epigrams—Graves eventually found a central focusing theme in his devotion to a muse-goddess who inspires, comforts, and ultimately destroys her chosen acolyte. That "one story and one story only / That will prove worth your telling" provides a sustaining context for many of the hundreds of skillfully crafted lyrics that make up Graves's canon.

Graves's poetic phases, emblematical of love and war, were largely shaped by the two world conflicts and by his literary and emotional partnership with the American poet and theorist Laura Riding. The poetry ranges from the early bucolic yet war-haunted lyrics (1916-1923), through the more analytic work of the mid-1920s and the rich, resilient poems of the Laura Riding period (1926-1939), to the "magical" White Goddess poems and those added after 1959, a year that saw the emergence of the White Goddess's more benign black sister, under whose spell Graves wrote lapidary poems marked less by emotional conflict than by a "miraculous certitude in love."

What for Graves was a central theme may seem to others eccentric; what to him was the persistent survival of a timeless motif may strike others as an atavistic aberration. And yet, despite his obsession with the arcana of the past—with love magic and poetic magic, with dragons and dreams and rites of blood, with ancient Welsh prosody, Sufi mysticism, and Celtic romance—Graves remained a man of the modern world: a primitivist who was sophisticated, a soldier who fought in that war which has itself come to seem a zigzag trench cutting through this century, dividing the old from the "modern" consciousness.

A man with one foot in the past, one in the present, Graves was also a poet in four traditions: the Classical and the British, the romantic and the Anglo-Irish. The mixture helps to explain his paradoxical relationship to visionary romanticism. While the great nineteenth-century romantics maintained an imaginative balance that was more than rational without being irrational, some of their twentieth-century followers have been tempted to yield themselves up to the occult. Graves's version of Yeats's *A Vision* and D. H. Lawrence's *Fantasia of the Unconscious* is, of course, *The White Goddess* (1948), subtitled *A Historical Grammar of Poetic Myth*. But whatever his attraction to the mysteries and primitivistic rites surrounding that fatal muse, Graves had, in addition to British common sense, a post-renaissance mind and a passionately skeptical Anglo-Irish temperament that combined to keep his magical-shamanistic tendencies in balance.

In its particular interplay of tradition and individual talent, Graves's poetry seems to some both a record of considerable achievement and a falling short of the heights attained by the great romantics, his precursors in devotion to the muse and as mythmakers. For others, his accomplishment stands, as in so many ways Graves himself always stood, on its own, part of no "ism," uncatalogable but worthy of honor. Certainly, the qualities that make so many of his poems admirable—meticulous verse craft, clarity, flexibility of tone and diction, syntactical and verbal precision, ironic wit, and a genuine balance between wildness and civility—ought to insure him a permanent audience.

From the time he began to write seriously, as a schoolboy of thirteen, Graves, writing in "a romantic vein," was also engaged in "technical experiments" in prosody and phrasing. That combination of craftsmanship and emotion, allied to the harnessing of imagination by reason, remained characteristic of his best poetry. Even after Graves's attraction to the irrational and mystical was solemnized in his official bewitchment by the White Goddess, that ecstatic allegiance did not preclude experimentation with sophisticated techniques of alliteration and assonance, meter and rhyme; nor did it overwhelm intelligible communication: the lucidity and almost-Horatian impassioned plainness that mark Graves's work in both poetry and prose. That work first appeared in print in 1913 (in the July issue of *Green Chartreuse*); by the mid-1970s the long struggle to write well was over. A 1979 visitor to Deyá, Graves's retreat on the island of Majorca, reported that by then the old man's life was "a rest from all that arduous, honorable toil." But in the six decades (1916-1975) between the publication of Graves's first and final volumes of poetry, there was little or no rest from that toil.

Graves's list of publications is staggering—in variety, quantity, and, for the most part, quality. One of the most accomplished poetic craftsmen of the century, he was also a master of what he called "clean" English prose. He produced the most widely known and generically influential historical novel of his time, *I, Claudius* (1934); a mythographic study, *The White Goddess*, exceeding even the Yeatsian system in its fertile and idiosyncratic learning; and perhaps the most memorable, certainly the most moving yet ironically funny, account of men in modern war, *Good-bye to All That* (1929). Embracing Blake's dictum that prudence is a rich, ugly old maid courted by incapacity, Graves's work can be outrageous, but never unreadable. His critical iconoclasm, flaunted in the 1950s in the Clark Lectures and in the 1960s in his Oxford addresses, can be sampled in *On Poetry* (1969), while the blend of erudition and intuitive audacity that understandably infuriates scholars is displayed in his biblical and historical "reconstructions" and in *The Greek Myths* (1955), a retelling of the old stories buttressed by Gravesian glosses that are intriguing even when they are most dubious.

At the turn into the final quarter of the twentieth century, Robert Graves was more than ever a household word. The international fame first achieved with his autobiography, reinforced by *I, Claudius* and revived by the British poets of The Movement in the late 1950s, was then riding the crest of the superb BBC dramatizations of the Claudius novels. But for all his fame as autobiographer, historical novelist, and scholar-vassal of the White Goddess, Graves presented the final edition of his *Collected Poems* in 1975, only to be greeted by something approaching critical neglect. The irony was that, for much of the preceding half century, Graves had insisted that his prose was merely the day labor of a poet hymning his goddess by the raging moon. But he had also, perhaps, defensively armed himself against neglect. "I write poems for poets," he announced in 1945, "and satires and grotesques for wits. For people in general I write prose, and am content that they should be unaware that I do anything else." His prose works were his "show dogs," bred to support his "cat," poetry. The show dogs fared well enough to make Graves a rarity: a professional writer who supported himself, and not only one but two families, with his pen alone. Nevertheless, it was on the poetry that he took his stand and as a poet that he wanted to be judged and to be remembered in the history of English literature.

Since lyric, not "insufficient" prose, was the medium of "emotional crises," Graves declared in 1951, "a volume of collected poems should form a sequence of the intenser moments of the poet's spiritual autobiography." A dozen years later he told a student of his work that he had "never known a poet whose poetry had not been an accurate self-portrait." The accuracy of the details of Graves's self portrait is blurred by his reticence regarding certain of the "intenser moments" in his autobiography and by his lifelong habit of reassessing and revising his poetic canon. Though the final *Collected Poems* was intended by Graves to supersede not only the earlier individual volumes but the preceding seven collections as well, no one volume should have canonical status, especially given Graves's disservice to his own accomplishment: his overvaluation of the work of his final two decades in relation to his poetry as a whole. In explaining the "Legitimate Criticism of Poetry" to the young women at Mount Holyoke College in the 1960s, Graves enjoined them to "keep hold of that critical cold-chisel, and strike it home without mercy: on my work too, if you please." In order to liberate the clean outline of Graves's true poetic canon, it will be necessary for future readers to chip away mercilessly at this late encrustation. Most of what remains will prove worthy of their passionate attention.

Robert von Ranke Graves was born at Wimbledon, just outside London, on 24 July 1895. His mother, Amalie von Ranke, forty at the time, was the second wife of his father, nine years older than she. Alfred Perceval Graves, an inspector of schools for the Southwark district of London, was a Gaelic scholar and minor Irish poet, author of the well-known toast to Father O'Flynn, the "Kindliest creature in ould Donegal." His father's avocation, Graves noted in his autobiography, preempted any "false reverence" for poets. "I sing some of his songs while washing up after meals, or shelling peas, or on similar occasions." His parents had married, it later seemed to their son, so that Mr. Graves, a widower, might have help in raising his five motherless children.

Graves made much of the difference between the precise, puzzle-solving Graveses and the imperious but generous-hearted von Rankes. He was particularly impressed by his mother's combination of *gemütlichkeit* and command, and the future devotee of the White Goddess remembered her cryptic saying that there was once a man "who died of grief because he could never become a mother." Though Graves preferred his mother, he recognized the psychological and poetic usefulness of his hereditary balance: the Gravesian coldness, "anti-sentimental to the point of insolence," provided "a necessary check" to the von Ranke expansiveness. His poetry displays a related balance: a wild civility mingling precision and passion, artistry and emotion; imagination checked by reason and argument.

Though he checked it at Charterhouse and in the trenches, Graves otherwise took justifiable pride in his distinguished German ancestors. They include the historian Leopold von Ranke, who, to Graves's delight, scandalized his contemporaries by declaring, "I am a historian before I am a Christian; my object is simply to find out how things actually occurred." Graves inherited his great-grand-uncle's priorities. Despite an Anglican upbringing of evangelical fervor and his own sentimental attachment to the image of Jesus as the perfect man, Graves's allegiance to Christianity began to fade as early as age sixteen when, to his astonishment, he first encountered people who did not accept Christ's divinity. The much-anthologized "In the Wilderness," the only poem from his first volume retained in Graves's canon, was his "last Christian-minded poem," and it was written when he was eighteen. As for finding out how things actually occurred: that was the avowed object of Graves's own historical reconstructions and textual "restorations"; and, though his results were rather different, he always claimed that he owed to his great-grand-uncle his historical method.

Graves's early childhood was happy. Even the two-generation gap between him and his parents made for an amicable relationship; he was able to think of them as generous and kindly grandparents. The household was conventional and comfortable in the best Victorian way. There were servants, and a nurse to tend the children—the second marriage yielded five, Robert being the middle child, to balance the five of the first. There was also a library containing several thousand books: scholarly works once owned by his grandfather, Robert's namesake, buttressed by his father's collection, the pride of which was a cabinet of Anglo-Irish literature. Later, Graves, a poet in the romantic tradition, would also insist that he had always remained faithful to the Anglo-Irish tradition into which he had been born: a shared heritage which helps explain the anxiety and hostility he always displayed toward Yeats, the

Robert Graves (center) with a group of his fellow officers, September 1917

colossus bestriding these two traditions in modern poetry.

The big house at Wimbledon straddled city and country living. There were also spring and summer excursions to Harlech in North Wales, where Graves's mother had built a house, and summer trips—five between his second and twelfth years—to southern Germany to see his maternal grandfather and other relatives.

In the desolate, rocky hill country of Harlech, where he found "a personal peace independent of history or geography," Graves got his first taste of rock-climbing, training himself to overcome his fear of heights as part of a deliberate regimen continued in later life: "I have," he has written, "worked hard on myself in defining and dispersing my terrors." The Harlech hills, subject of a childhood poem, were later celebrated, from a perspective made cold-eyed by the war, in one of his best-known poems, "Rocky Acres." There, Harlech's "wild land, country of my choice, / With harsh craggy mountain, moor ample and bare," a land of "rocks and lank heather" presided over by a predatory bird who seeks out and destroys small hidden things and "tears them in pieces," looms forth as a "Sempiternal country" of soldierly, even Nietzschean, unsentimentality—"Nursing no valleys for comfort or rest," a "Stronghold for demigods when on earth they go, / Terror for fat burghers on far plains below."

There were eerier but less alienating experiences in pre-World War I Germany. On these summer trips ("easily the best things of my early childhood"), the family visited Amalie's father, who lived at Deisenhofen, near Munich; two nearby uncles who kept a peacock farm; and, occasionally, Graves's Aunt Agnes, the Baronin von Aufsess. Her ancestral keep high in the Bavarian Alps was an imposing ninth-century building to which a medieval castle had been added. Aufsess boasted amazing treasures of plate and armor, a mysterious locked chest containing nobody knew what, and "an underground river" yielding trout "white from the darkness, of extraordinary size, and stone-blind." Naturally, a ghost walked the halls. Laufzarn, his grandfather's restored manor house, though it could not compare with Aufsess in tradition, did have its compensations: in addition to a secret passage, "two ghosts went with the place." These Gothic impressions haunt the best of the early ghost-raddled poems: "The Haunted House," "A Frosty Night," "The Pier-Glass," "Down," "The Castle," and others. Though "The Castle" records the fear of getting locked up in Harlech Castle at nightfall while "we were playing hide-and-seek in its towers and dungeons," the castle, mysterious passage, and "violent subterrene flow / Of rivers" in the powerful dream poem "Down" unmistakably reflect childhood experiences in Germany.

Of course, this obsessive imagery of entrapment, though grimly reinforced by Graves's experience in the trenches, is no less unmistakably sexual. Sexual fear is, indeed, a pervasively dark theme running through the childhood chapters of *Good-by to All That*. His religious training developed in him both "a great capacity for fear" and "a sexual embarrassment" from which Graves found it "very difficult" to free himself; just how difficult, many of the poems attest. At Penrallt, one of six preparatory schools he attended, he was terrified by the inordinate interest in his anatomy on the part of the headmaster's little daughter and her girl friend. On another frightening occasion, ten-year-old Graves had to wait for his older sisters in the cloakroom of the girl's high school. The girls coming and going giggled and whispered, and his sisters, when they arrived, "looked ashamed of me and seemed quite different from the sisters I knew at home. I had blundered into a secret world." The incident occasioned nightmares for a long time to come, and Graves acknowledged that his "normal impulses were set back for years by these two experiences." Even during World War I Graves did not avail himself of French prostitutes, remaining "puritanical except in language" throughout his overseas service; and when at the age of twenty-two he married eighteen-year-old Nancy Nicholson, both were virgins.

Graves's way station between boyhood and war and marriage was Charterhouse, a public school he hated so much (though one detects a certain relish in the hatred) that he later refused to send his own boys there, "on principle." The procession of schools leading to it included Rugby and Copthorne, where he "learned to keep a straight bat at cricket, and to have a high moral sense." It was from Copthorne that he went on scholarship to Charterhouse, a place which filled him with "an oppression of spirit" he hesitated to recall in its full intensity in his autobiography.

The public school Graves encountered was conventional, antiintellectual, and preoccupied with athletics and "romantic friendships." Young Graves's scholarly nature, sexual naiveté (he had "remained as prudishly innocent as my mother had planned"), and German heritage combined to make him unpopular; and his defensive insistence on his Irish paternity merely earned him the enmity of an older Irish boy who resented the claim. He was sufficiently badgered to sham madness; left to his own devices, he began to write poems, thus providing his tormentors with "stronger proof of insanity." At the suggestion of a friend, Graves discovered a more effective method of dealing with those who periodically wrecked his room and spattered his exercise books with ink. He began boxing, "seriously and savagely," eventually winning the grudging respect of his house, and two silver cups, by knocking out several opponents in his fifth year. (When he tried after World War I to sell the cups, they turned out to be only plated. The same was true of the Prince Alexander Droutzkoy medal awarded him a half century later for services to poetry. But the Queen's Gold Medal for Poetry, which he received at a private audience in Buckingham Palace in 1968, was, he reported, eighteen karat.)

The crucial events of Graves's final years at Charterhouse were his growing passion for poetry, his friendship with George Mallory (then a young master at the school), and his romantic attachment to George Johnstone, the boy he calls "Dick" in his autobiography. In English preparatory and public schools, romance was, as Graves reminds the reader, "necessarily homosexual," involving a hatred of the opposite sex from which many English schoolboys "never recover." In a sentence which appears only in the 1929 edition of *Good-bye to All That*, Graves admitted, "I only recovered by a shock at the age of twenty-one," a reference to news that reached him at the front to the effect that Dick had made "a certain proposal" to a Canadian soldier stationed near Charterhouse. While he was unconscious of any sexual desire for Dick, Graves did fall "in love" with this spirited and intelligent boy three years younger than himself, an infatuation whose after-effects lasted into 1917. On convalescent leave that year, Graves fell in love with a pianist and probationer nurse named Marjorie but said nothing. His heart had remained "whole, if numbed, since Dick's disappearance from it," yet he felt difficulty in adjusting himself "to the experience of woman love." When he met Dick for the last time, at Oxford in 1920, Graves found him so changed that it "seemed absurd to have ever suffered on his account."

In his last years at Charterhouse, however, "poetry and Dick were still almost all that mattered." Almost; for apart from this attachment, the most important thing that happened in these years was that he got to know George Mallory, who introduced him to modern literature and to Edward Marsh, then secretary to Winston Churchill, the First Lord of the Admiralty, but more influential as the editor of the Georgian poets anthologies. Marsh liked Graves's poems, shown him by Mallory, but pointed out, as he had with many of the Georgians' verses, that they were written in an outmoded poetic diction; whatever the poetry's intrinsic quality, readers might be prejudiced, Marsh suggested, "against work written in 1913 according to the fashions of 1863."

In addition to taking an active interest in his work and lending him books, Mallory, the great mountaineer later to die on Everest, took Graves climbing on Mount Snowden during school vacations. The sport, Graves observed in a school essay, seemed to make all others trivial. It allowed a man to stand somewhere where nobody else had stood before, and—a remark applicable to his later feelings about the sacramental bond uniting the soldiers of a regiment—"to be alone with a specially chosen band of people—people in whom a man can trust completely."

The young essayist's description of rock climbing suggests that he may also have seen the sport as analogous to the writing of poetry. Climbing was challenging and dangerous, though it becomes reasonably safe if one "keeps to the rules," stays fit, keeps one's "apparatus" properly overhauled, advances with "no hurry, anxiety, or stunts," and, above all, keeps a "sense of balance." When Geoffrey Young, a superb climber, told Graves that he had "the finest natural balance" he'd ever seen, the compliment pleased Graves "far more than if the Poet Laureate had told me that I had the finest sense of rhythm he had ever met in a young poet." Balance, adherence to rules, a challenge accepted: all characterize Graves's best poetry, in conception as well as execution. "His strict forms, though variable, are chosen," says one critic, "as a climber chooses a rockface to prove himself on a problem judged to be just within his prowess." Graves's mature work—characterized by a lucid, uncannily balanced awe in the face even of the phantasmagoria he himself evokes—is poetry of the British middle ground, its climate of thought generally located in the temperate zone, content to be native and traditional in both technique and theme. "*Vers libre* could come to nothing in England," Thomas Hardy assured an admiring Graves in the early 1920s. "All we can do is to write on the old themes in the old styles, but try to do it a little better than those who went before us." Graves always maintained a traditionalist belief that certain principles could not be violated without poetry turning into something else. Whether climbing a rockface or writing a poem, one keeps to the rules, advances deliberately, eschews stunts, and maintains one's balance.

Graves ends his account of his schooldays with a description of his "worst climb." On Lliwedd, the most formidable of the Snowdon precipices, at just the point requiring most concentration, "a raven circled round the party in great sweeps. I found this curiously unsettling, because one climbs only up and down, or sideways, and the raven seemed to be suggesting diverse other possible dimensions of movement—tempting us to let go our hold and join him." One senses here the tension, present in Graves's life and poetry alike, between order and chaos, reason and unreason, holding on and letting go. There may even be an implicit contrast between Graves's "limited" traditionalist conception of poetry and the diverse other possible dimensions suggested by the work of those poets of the modernist movement he later excoriated: Pound, Eliot, and Yeats.

The whirl he felt compelled to join was considerably more unsettling than the vertiginous movement of birds or of modernist poetry. A week out of Charterhouse, Graves was visiting Harlech before going up to Oxford when England declared war on Germany. He was about to enlist when the secretary of the Harlech golf club suggested taking a commission. On 11 August 1914 Graves began training with the Royal Welch Fusiliers, an old and distinguished regiment proud of its twenty-nine battle honors. Young Graves soon "caught the sense of Regimental tradition," but (he says in the foreword to *Collected Poems 1955*) it was "getting caught up in the First World War" itself that "permanently changed my outlook on life." At least one in three of Graves's generation at school died in the war, at some stages of which an infantry subaltern on the Western Front could expect to last three months before being killed or suffering incapacitating wounds.

After brief training at Wrexham (the tactics were as outmoded as the diction of his Charterhouse poems), nineteen-year-old Second Lieutenant Graves arrived in France, a replacement officer posted not to the Royal Welch but to the undistinguished Welsh Regiment. Soon under fire, he was also exposed to the nightmare of gas and the arrogance of staff officers, as well as to the standing jokes about rats and lice (see his poem "The Trenches"). The ubiquitous rats flourished by gorging on the plentiful corpses; one story about two of them tussling on a new officer's blankets for possession of a severed hand "circulated as a great joke." There is plenty of this sort of description in *Good-bye to All That*. "We all laughed" is a repeated formula in Graves's series of dramatized "caricature scenes" of black comedy; and, as he later said in describing the rhetorical strategy of his memoir, "the most painful chapters have to be the jokiest."

When Graves finally joined the Royal Welch in the summer of 1915, he was posted to the Second Battalion, which—because its swaggering officers reminded him of the Charterhouse snobs—he contrasted unfavorably to the more humane First Battalion. But both lived up to regimental tradition—making it a point of honor to dominate no-man's land from dusk to dawn, always insisting on getting fire ascendancy on arrival in a new sector. Graves valued, and never ceased to value, courage and soldierly virtues; however he hated the war, he shared the fusiliers' belief that "regimental pride remained the strongest moral force that kept a battalion going as an effective fighting unit," contrasting it particularly with "patriotism and religion." The absence of religion was notable in the trenches, while patriotism was a remote sentiment fit only for civilians on the despised "home front." When, on leave in August 1915 in a London "unreally itself," Graves professed himself merely "surprised" by the "general indifference to, and ignorance about, the War," he was understating that detestation of civilian complacency universal among the trench soldiers of World War I.

Nothing, not even the "bloody balls-up" at Cambrin known as the Battle of Loos (15 September-13 October 1915), a murderous farce in which everything conceivable went wrong, could break the sacramental bond uniting the regiment. Going out at dusk to rescue the wounded, Graves, one of only six surviving company officers, was struck by the attitudes in which the dead had stiffened—"bandaging friends' wounds, crawling, cutting wire." One riddled corpse was that of a man his comrades had made several attempts to rescue during the battle. Graves found that he had "forced his knuckles into his mouth to keep himself from crying out and attracting any more men to their death"—an incident less movingly recreated in "The Dead Fox Hunter" in *Over the Brazier* (1916). That the attack scheduled for the next day was cancelled at the last moment was fortunate; Graves was singing nursery rhymes aloud just before he was to lead his men over the top.

In November 1915, having served six months in the trenches and on the verge of a breakdown, Graves, to his delight, received orders to join the

First Battalion. In the company mess he noticed a copy of Lionel Johnson's essays, the first work of literature he had seen in France aside from his own copies of Keats and Blake. He introduced himself to the book's owner, Siegfried Sassoon, and the two men talked of poetry. When Graves showed him drafts of some of the poems soon to be published in his first book, Sassoon frowned and said that war should not be written about "in such realistic terms." Nothing in *Over the Brazier* (1916) or *Fairies and Fusiliers* (1917) approaches the effective realism of the later poems of Wilfred Owen, Isaac Rosenberg, or of Sassoon himself, who began writing what he thought were "genuine trench poems" only in 1916. They make the war unforgettable; Graves, though almost as fascinated as he was repelled by the mud and blood of the trenches, utilized every device—whimsy, nursery rhymes, Keatsian doggerel, schoolboy jocularity (the first volume included several Charterhouse poems), and understandable but regressive pastoralism—to *forget* the war. For a long time he hoped, through the remembered joys of simple bucolic experience, to escape "these soul-deadening trenches." But as one might expect from the poetic inertness of that last phrase (from "1915" in *Over the Brazier*), forgetfulness required a preliminary stage more profound than literary evasion.

Sassoon, too, had a long way to go. At this first meeting he showed Graves some of his own poems, one of which began with a typically euphemistic reference to the "woeful crimson of men slain." Sassoon had not yet been in the trenches; he would, Graves assured him, "soon change his style." He did, and not only poetically. Soon after, Second Lieutenant David Thomas, Sassoon's close friend and by then a close friend of Graves's as well, was killed in action. Graves felt Thomas's death keenly and wrote of it ("Goliath straddles over him") in the war poem "Goliath and David." But he did not share Sassoon's anger. Whereas he "just felt empty and lost," Sassoon went out on patrol night after night "looking for Germans to kill." He was soon to become known, after his heroic feats on the Somme, as "Mad Jack."

That great slaughter was at hand. In March 1916 Graves and Sassoon were on the Somme with the First Battalion; a month later Graves was back in England for an operation enabling him to breathe through his boxer's broken nose in the new-style gas helmet. During his leave he met his future wife, Nancy Nicholson, and pleased his parents by going to church and receiving the sacrament on Good Friday, "the last occasion on which I ever attended a church service." The furlough, followed by temporary duty in England, caused Graves to miss being with his battalion when the Somme offensive began. His friend Sassoon survived, but sixty percent of their fellow officers in the First Battalion were killed. They were not alone. As Paul Fussell writes in *The Great War and Modern Memory* (1975), "the Somme affair, destined to be known among the troops as the Great Fuck-Up, was the largest engagement fought since the beginnings of civilization." It may rank as the most stupid as well. At precisely 7:30 on the sunlit morning of 1 July 1916 a week-long bombardment was shifted to more distant targets, "and the attacking waves of eleven British divisions climbed out of their trenches on a thirteen-mile front and began walking forward." By 7:31, the German defenders "had carried their machine guns upstairs from the deep dugouts where during the bombardment they had harbored safely—and even comfortably—and were hosing down the attackers walking toward them in orderly rows or puzzling before the still uncut wire. Out of the 110,000 who attacked, 60,000 were killed or wounded on this one day, the record so far. Over 20,000 lay dead between the lines, and it was days before the wounded in No Man's Land stopped crying out." There had been a delusion that the war would soon be won. By the end of this day most rational men realized that neither side had won, or could win. As Graves's friend the soldier-poet Edmund Blunden later observed, "The War had won, and would go on winning."

Graves, now a captain temporarily posted to the Second Battalion, arrived on 14 July at the original Somme front line. It was shell-pitted, shrouded in gas, and littered with bodies, one of them the bloated green-faced corpse described in "The Dead Boche" in *Fairies and Fusiliers* (1917). Their mission was to reinforce a point secured at High Wood on the Somme. The Germans, however, put down so formidable a barrage along the Royal Welch position that a third of the battalion was lost before the show started. "I," Graves reports laconically, "was one of the casualties."

Graves had been hit by fragments of an eight-inch shell that burst three paces behind him. He was nearly blinded by chips of flying stone—one, lodged under his right eyebrow, remained a lifelong souvenir. One shell fragment went through his left thigh, "high up, near the groin; I must have been at the full stretch of my stride to escape emasculation." The most severe injury was a lung wound, the result of a piece of shell that had "gone in two inches below the point of my right shoulder blade and came out through my chest two inches above the right nipple." Unconscious for twenty-four hours, Graves was officially reported to have "died of wounds." A few days later, on his twenty-first birthday, he was able to follow up his colonel's letter of condolence by assuring his mother that he was alive.

In the prose account of his near-fatal wounding the reader feels, beneath the characteristic matter-of-factness, the poignant vulnerability of flesh. In his poem "Escape" Graves says, "I *was* dead, an hour or more." But past "the door / That Cerberus guards and half-way down the road / To Lethe," he woke on his stretcher to discover, bending over him, "Dear Lady Proserpine." However interesting as a personalizing of myth, even an adumbration of the goddess, "Escape," with its jaunty tone and classical baggage, is a transparent ritualizing of terror, an attempt to mythologically distance himself from his own reported death. It has less in common with D. H. Lawrence's ostensibly similar underworld journey in "Bavarian Gentians" than with Graves's interpretation of Keats's jocularity, in the letter to his brother accompanying "La Belle Dame sans Merci," about shutting the lady's eyes with "kisses four." Two of the kisses being "more properly pennies laid on the eyes of the dead," Graves writes in *On English Poetry* (1922), Keats's trivial "light heartedness . . . can carry no possible conviction"—a remark echoing his emphasis, earlier in this book, on the trench soldiers' fear, "hidden under a false gaiety, of the horrible death that threatened them all."

In that sense "Escape" is escapist—another of those distancings, rather than objectifications, of horror characteristic of Graves's war poems. One often has to read between the lines of Graves's wartime volumes to realize the depth of the generating experiences, and over the years Graves has even removed those poems, along with virtually all subsequent poetry dealing directly with the war, from his canon. Even *Good-bye to All That*, written more than ten years after the military experiences it recounts, is at once brutally direct and bemusedly distanced: a money-making theatrical performance by a master farceur which is both a personal exorcism and a dismissal of the very audience that paid to have Graves scorn it. A similar disdain informs the much later poem in which Graves reminds the reader how he became one of the privileged few enrolled by Fortune among "the second-fated / Who have read their own obituaries in *The Times*, / Have heard 'Where, death, thy sting? Where, grave, thy victory?' / Intoned with unction over their still clay." It was, Graves goes on in "The Second-Fated," but a "brief demise," rising from which the imperial "we" learned to "scorn your factitious universe / Ruled by the death which we had flouted."

Graves survived, but less intact than "flouted" suggests. Sassoon, expressing his joy at learning that Graves was still alive, wrote that he himself "felt nine parts dead from the horror of the Somme fighting." For though Graves did survive the war—mentally, physically, and poetically—something in him died on the Somme. A. Alvarez, who admires Graves's poetry but does not think the poet survived the war, finds his case summed up in D. H. Lawrence's description in *Aaron's Rod* of an officer in whom there was "a lightness and an appearance of bright diffidence and humour." But beneath was "the hot, seared burn of unbearable experience, which did not heal. . . . The experience gradually cooled on top: but only with a surface crust. The soul did not heal, did not recover." If Graves had his own doubts, they were resolved in a peculiarly Gravesian way. The postwar poems are filled with web-hung spirits, revenants who refuse to stay dead. The autobiographical genesis of those survivals, of the resurrection of the destroyed beast in the poem "Saint," and of the human survival of Calvary by Graves's Christ (in *Jesus in Rome*, 1957), was surely the poet's survival of his own "death" on the Somme in 1916.

In September, two months after the Somme fighting, Graves and Sassoon spent a brief leave together in Harlech. Both were getting poems in order for publication; Sassoon was happy to accept the corpse's amendments to the premature obituary he had written on Graves's death. Before boarding the train they had read the casualty list in the *Times*: practically every officer in the First Battalion was listed as killed or wounded. Graves, still in a weakened condition, "could not help weeping all the way to Wales." Though they were soon back at the front, Graves's damaged lungs (the diagnosis was "bronchitis") sent him home again—first to Somerville College, Oxford, which had been converted into a hospital, then on to Osborne, on the Isle of Wight.

He was recuperating there when Sassoon sent him a copy of his famous *non serviam* of July 1917, his open letter "Finished with the War: A Soldier's Declaration." Despite his magnificent war record, Sassoon expected to be tried and imprisoned for his self-described "act of wilful defiance of military authority." Graves agreed completely with the declaration's position regarding the "political errors and insincerities" which, in prolonging the war, were sacrificing a generation, and on "the callous complacence with which the majority of those at home regard the continuance of agonies which they do not share, and which they have not sufficient imagination to realize." But Graves felt that Sassoon's gesture was as naive and futile as it was courageous; that nobody would follow his example, in either England or Germany. Above all, he was filled with anxiety about the risk his friend was taking. Without Sassoon's knowledge, Graves began to pull strings. He contacted Evan Morgan, private secretary to one of the coalition ministers and a recent canoeing partner, asking him to do "everything possible to prevent republication of, or comment on, the letter," and explaining that Sassoon should not be allowed to become "a martyr to a hopeless cause in his present physical condition." He then arranged for Sassoon to face a medical board rather than a court martial. In the course of his testimony—appearing, against his will, in "the role of a patriot distressed by the mental collapse of a brother-in-arms," a collapse directly attributable to Sassoon's exploits in the trenches—Graves himself broke down in tears three times.

Though both men *were* near mental collapse, it was a rigged scene. And it worked: instead of facing probable imprisonment, Sassoon was sent to a convalescent home for neurasthenics at Craiglockhart, Scotland, where he came under the care of the prominent Cambridge psychologist W. H. R. Rivers, a specialist in treating "shellshock." "Cured," and driven by a sense of loyalty to the men under his command, Sassoon returned, after a brief tour of duty in Palestine, to the trenches of France. The famous episode remains, moving yet somehow troubling. Graves had saved Sassoon, but at the cost of annulling his courageous war against the war. By first getting Morgan to minimize publicity, then convincing Sassoon (by falsely swearing on the Bible) that the War Office had no intention of allowing him to become a martyr, and, finally, giving false testimony to the medical board, Graves had spun what Sassoon called in *Memoirs of an Infantry Officer* (1930) "a very successful lie"—though, he added immediately, "no doubt I should have done the same for him if our positions had been reversed."

Graves had told Sassoon that, given the general mania, their only recourse was "to keep on going out until we got killed," but his lungs had finally invalided him out of the fighting war. While on garrison duty in Wales, he fell in love with Nancy Nicholson, a young woman of seventeen "as sensible about the War as anybody at home could be." They decided to marry at once. Nancy, an ardent feminist disgusted by the sexist wording of the marriage service, almost refused to go through with the wedding. But it did come off—on 23 January 1918, with George Mallory acting as best man. The description of the wedding day is prime Graves: "Another caricature scene to look back on: myself striding up the red carpet, wearing field-boots, spurs and sword; Nancy meeting me in a blue-check silk wedding-dress, utterly furious; packed benches on either side of the church, full of relatives; aunts using handkerchiefs; the choir boys out of tune; Nancy savagely muttering the responses, myself shouting them in a parade-ground voice." At the reception, after some champagne, Nancy "went off and changed back into her land-girl's costume of breeches and smock." Later, "the embarrassments of our wedding night (Nancy and I being both virgins) were somewhat eased by an air-raid: Zeppelin bombs dropping not far off set the hotel in an uproar." After a week's honeymoon, Graves was back on duty; Nancy joined him in February when he was transferred to a Cadet Battalion at Rhyl.

In July 1918 Sassoon was shot through the head but not killed; that "happy warrior and bitter pacifist" was finally invalided home. In the same month, Nancy's mother died of influenza and, two months later, her brother Tony was killed in France. More ghosts for the "haunted" mirrors in the Nicholson's Tudor house near Harlech, where Graves and Nancy (pregnant with their first child) spent time during his final leave. Graves tried to forget about the war by working on the romantic poems and ballads later published in *Country Sentiment* (1920). In November came the Armistice and, at the same time, news that a friend who had gone back just before the end had been killed—as had Wilfred Owen, who had met Sassoon at Craiglockhart and who had been sending Graves poems from France. The end of the war did not bring the universal "delight" promised in Sassoon's poem on the Armistice, "Everyone Sang." Not quite everyone—it sent Graves out "walking alone along the dyke above the marshes of Rhuddhan (an ancient battlefield, the Flodden of Wales), cursing and sobbing and thinking of the dead."

It was no short-lived state of mind. In "A Boy in Church," the most original poem in *Fairies and Fusiliers*, the preacher's "gabble-gabble" and the credulous, complacent congregation safely seated in pews that never "sway or lurch" are suddenly disturbed by a "dumb blast" that "sets the trees swaying / With furious zeal like madmen praying." Beyond the usual baiting of religion and civilians, the poem is a rare acknowledgment of terror, of

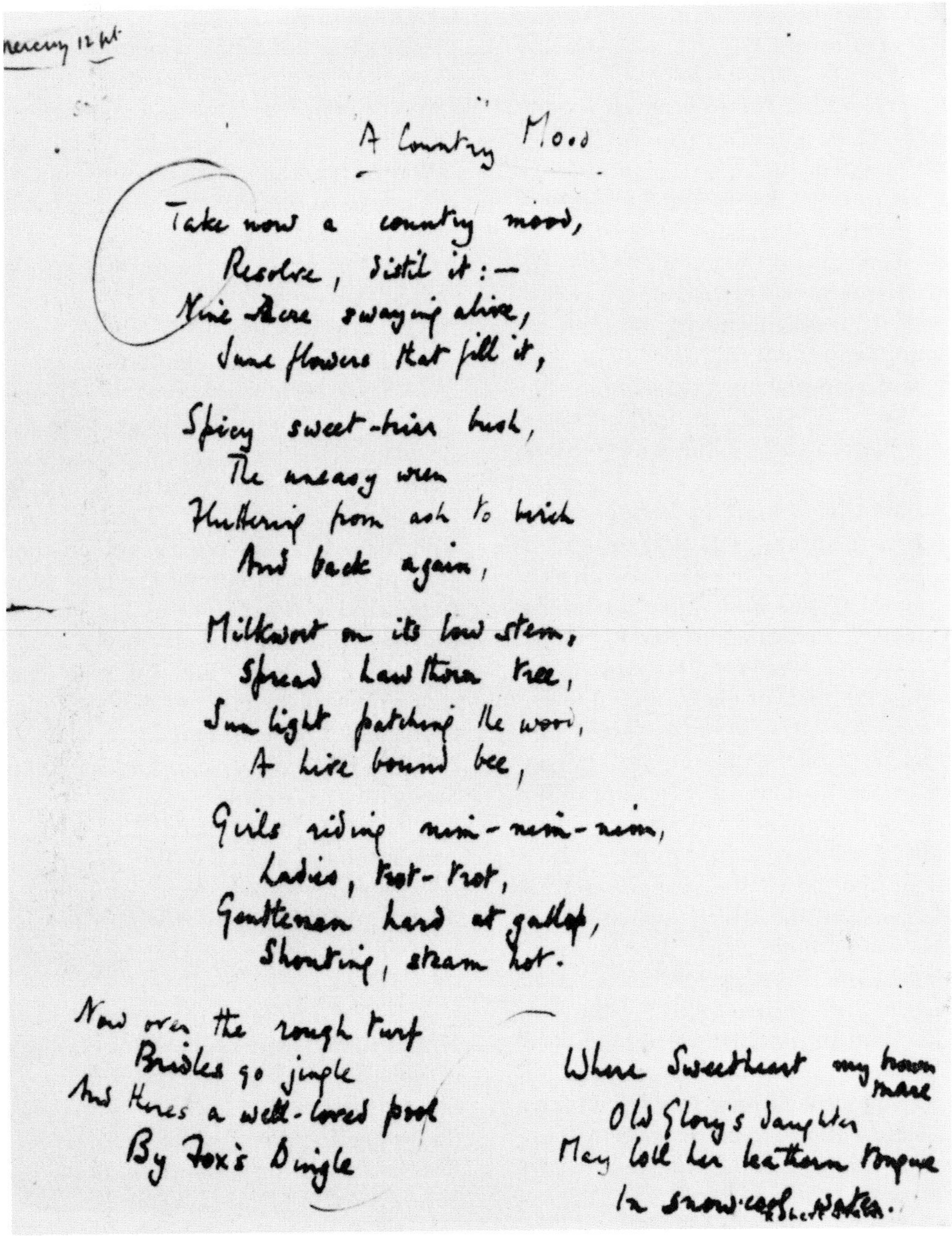
Mercury 12 pt.

A Country Mood

Take now a country mood,
Resolve, distil it:—
Nine Acre swaying alive,
June flowers that fill it,

Spicy sweet-briar bush,
The uneasy wren
Fluttering from ash to birch
And back again,

Milkwort on its low stem,
Spread hawthorn tree,
Sunlight patching the wood,
A hive bound bee,

Girls riding nim-nim-nim,
Ladies, trot-trot,
Gentlemen hard at gallop,
Shouting, steam hot.

Now over the rough turf
Bridles go jingle
And there's a well-loved pool
By Fox's Dingle

Where Sweetheart my brown mare
Old Glory's daughter
May loll her leathern tongue
In snow-cool water.

Robert Graves

Manuscript for "A Country Mood," first published in 1920

the irrational fury Graves experienced as a personal threat. Like the more familiar lines in his later masterpiece "Sick Love"—about the "cry / That soars in outer blackness dismally, / The dumb blind beast, the paranoic fury"—this poem reflects the shellshock, neurasthenia, paranoia (Graves uses all three terms) he experienced in the postwar years. Demobilized and living in Harlech in a house lent them by Nancy's father, Graves was "still mentally and nervously organized for War. Shells used to come bursting on my bed at midnight, even though Nancy shared it with me; strangers in daytime would assume the faces of friends who had been killed." When strong enough to climb the hill behind Harlech, he could not help seeing his favorite country as a prospective battlefield in which he would find himself working out elaborate tactical problems. Some of these symptoms lasted for years.

The hallucinations, nightmares, and obsessions became, with the help of his friend W. H. R. Rivers, *materia poetica*. Though frequently referred to as having received psychiatric treatment, Graves, unlike Sassoon, Owen (and, for that matter, "Dick"), was never a patient of Rivers. For a time he accepted the general theory of a "subconscious self" as expounded by Rivers and Dr. Henry Head. It was, he added with typical pride in his German forebears, a theory "first formulated" by his great-grandfather Gotthilf von Schubert, "the friend of Goethe, Schiller, and the Brothers Grimm." He never accepted Freud's "deformation of it." Characteristically, what attracted Graves was the balance of Rivers, who presented Freudianism with "English reserve and common sense," not regarding sex as "the sole impulse" in dream-making or assuming that dream symbols were "constant." In that modified form, the theory appealed to Graves as "reasonable."

Rivers became the shaping influence on Graves's postwar criticism and, significantly but less consistently, on his poetry, which was frankly "therapeutic." In *On English Poetry*, that intriguing hodgepodge of 1922, dedicated to Rivers and to T. E. Lawrence, Graves synopsized his view of the "use" of poetry as a form of psychotherapy. By transforming into dream symbolism some "disturbing emotional crisis in the poet's mind," poetry has the power of "homeopathically healing other men's minds similarly troubled" by presenting to them an allegorical solution of the trouble. "Once the allegory is recognized by the reader's unconscious mind as applicable the affective power of his own emotional crisis is diminished." The alternating volumes of criticism and poetry published during the "reconstructive" period following the war were colored, he said in the 1949 introduction to *The Common Asphodel*, by the "contemporary view of humanity as convalescent after a serious nervous breakdown," a state with which it was "easy to identify myself closely." His hope at the time was "to help the recovery of public health of mind, as well as my own."

The postwar year in Harlech was not conducive to the health of Graves's mind. The writing of therapeutic poems was accompanied by a variety of family tensions. Graves's parents, having sold the house at Wimbledon, were then living permanently in Harlech. Though proud of Robert, the only member of the family to have seen active service, they were scandalized by his politics and lack of religion—and by Nancy, who kept her own name for all purposes and was always clad in breeches and farmer's smock. Neither Graves nor his wife attended church; they refused to baptize their daughter Jenny, born in January 1919; and they distributed birth-control material in the village. Graves expressed sympathy with the humane aspects of the Bolshevik revolution and Nancy, too, thought of herself as a socialist, though her politics seemed to Graves a means to a single end, judicial equality of the sexes. Gradually, "male stupidity and callousness became such an obsession with her that she began to include me in her universal condemnation of men." Nancy's feminist ideas strained the relationship but seem, in retrospect, to have adumbrated the coming of the White Goddess. The marriage's loss was the myth's gain: one example of what to make of a diminished thing.

To expedite his demobilization, Graves had expressed his intention to become a student. In October 1919, five long years after he was originally scheduled to do so, he went to Oxford, financed by a government grant of £ 200 a year. John Masefield, who liked Graves's poetry, rented them a nearby cottage on Boar's Hill, at the time something of a poetic colony. There Graves met, besides Masefield, the poet laureate Robert Bridges, W. H. Davies, Walter de la Mare, and Edmund Blunden, who called himself another of "War's People" struggling to "dispel / The scene and action that was learned in hell." In his Oxford years Graves met many poets, including Thomas Hardy, whose quirky traditionalism he admired; T. S. Eliot, to whom he had first been introduced in 1916 and with whom he was briefly scheduled to collaborate on a critical book; and Ezra Pound, to whom he was introduced by T. E. Lawrence, who accurately predicted that they would not hit it off.

The Graveses ran a general store on Boar's Hill. It folded after six months, leaving them £ 300 in debt, a third of which was repaid by Nancy's father, the rest by Lawrence, who generously gave the struggling poet four chapters of *Seven Pillars of Wisdom* to sell for serial publication in the United States. In 1921 Graves, having failed to sit for his Oxford degree, moved his family—a second child, David, had been born the previous year—to a cottage in Islip purchased by his mother and rented to them for ten shillings a week. For the next five years Graves fitfully pursued his Oxford degree, sharing the housework and childcare with Nancy. Two more children—Catherine, born in 1922, and Sam, 1924—completed the symmetrical family Nancy had planned. Amid the crises of neurasthenia and short finances, teething and diaper changing, he kept working. They needed the money, and nothing ever stopped Graves from writing. Between 1920 and 1925 he produced—in addition to three critical studies, a ballad opera, a novel, and a satire on contemporary poets—a half-dozen volumes of poetry, in which can be traced a movement from the "anodynic" through the analytic and abstract to a promising fusion of emotion and discipline.

Graves himself characterized the poems in *Country Sentiment* (1920) as products of the "desire to escape from a painful war neurosis into an Arcadia of amatory fancy." The bucolic fancy is less compelling than the unexorcised vestiges of war—not in the explicit war group entitled "Retrospect," but in the volume's finest, if rather alienating, poem, "Rocky Acres," and in "The Haunted House." Even more haunted, *The Pier-Glass* (1921), a book whose mood he described as "aggressive and disciplinary," contains two riveting poems of nightmarish guilt, the title poem and "Down." No less cryptic and guilt-ridden is "The Children of Darkness," the most memorable poem in *Whipperginny* (1923), a volume marked by a deliberate lessening of emotional stress, intensity gradually yielding to sardonic detachment. Emotion and cynicism combine in *The Feather Bed* (1923), dominated by the title poem, an interior monologue in which a neurotic man, whose lover has deserted him to enter a nunnery, dreams that the Mother Superior comes naked to his bed to practice earthbound wiles—Boccaccio without the exuberance. That quality is notable by its absence in the theory-raddled *Mock Beggar Hall* (1924), from which Graves included only one poem, the plangent "Full Moon," in the final *Collected Poems*. But *Welchman's Hose* (1925) opens with the exuberant "Alice," a gay and thoughtful celebration of Lewis Carroll's balanced heroine, and includes successful poems as different as "The Clipped Stater," a longish narrative poem about Alexander the Great, whose actions are based on the postwar life of T. E. Lawrence; "Vanity," a brilliantly rhymed satire on naive optimism; and the impersonal yet deeply moving "Love Without Hope," a flawless quatrain fusing fantasy and poignance in a typically Gravesian celebration of doomed love. At the same high level are "The Cool Web" and "Pure Death," two poems written at this time but not published until two years later in Graves's first winnowed selection, *Poems (1914-1926)* (1927). Both exhibit emotion and fear disciplined rather than merely dismissed or subjected to aloof analysis.

Graves was awarded the Bronze Medal for Poetry at the 1924 Paris Olympics, and there was an explosion of work in 1925. But neither his poetry nor his other writings proved financially successful. With four children to support and his wife's health somewhat precarious, he needed a job. Teaching seemed the least objectionable option. To that end he vigorously pursued and finally attained an Oxford degree, submitting as a B.Litt. thesis his recently published *Poetic Unreason and Other Studies* (1925), an attempt to develop "soberly" what he admitted were the "wayward notes on poetic psychology" published three years earlier as *On English Poetry*. Both books, reflecting the modified Freudianism of Rivers, distinguish between irrational associative thought and logical "secondary elaboration," the first of which Graves identifies with romantic poetry, the second with classical. But these facile distinctions blur, and *Poetic Unreason and Other Studies*, for all its incidental insights, remains, as Graves himself later observed, "a tangle of contradictions or difficult evasions of contradiction."

Despite the disciplined romanticism triumphantly achieved in a handful of superb recent poems, Graves was looking for guidance out of his theoretical and critical tangle. He had discussed poetry with Sassoon, Blunden, Hardy, and others; and he had been even more influenced by such nonpoets as Mallory, Rivers, Lawrence, and Basanta Mallik, the Bengali intellectual whose metaphysics inform the theological poems in *Mock Beggar Hall*. Mallik had warned Graves against "being dominated by any . . . individual." But in 1924-1925, Mallik was back in India, Blunden had gone to teach in Japan, Lawrence was with the Royal Tank Corps, Mallory had disappeared on Everest, and Graves, who thought Mallik's advice "agreed well with my practice," was about to have that practice changed.

His domination by another individual began when a friend visiting Graves at Islip in 1924 drew to his host's attention a poem entitled "The Quids" in the February issue of the *Fugitive*, a periodical edited by Graves's American friend John Crowe Ransom and others. The poem was by the extraordinarily self-assured Laura Riding Gottschalk—a typically unsensuous, if atypically playful, cerebration on the similarity underlying differentiation, the quids being the "atoms" within the universal whole, the unchanging "Monoton." Graves thought it a satire on "traditional metaphysics" and on what he took the Monoton to symbolize: modern society's "dreary standardization." As impressed as Ransom and his Nashville colleagues had been (Riding had won a $100 prize offered by the *Fugitive*), Graves, with the concurrence of his wife, wrote to the poet and, finding their exchanged views congenial, extended an invitation for her to join them in England. Three years later, in the rhapsodic epilogue dedicating the first edition of *Good-bye to All That* to Laura Riding, Graves pictured "your coming" as something written in the stars; he tells how his wife and he, "happening by seeming accident upon your teasing *Quids* were drawn to write to you, who were in America, asking you to come to us. . . ."

If it is hard to believe that this breathless prose (later expunged) comes from the author of the splendidly taut memoir that precedes it, it is easy to perceive in it the predisposition which so quickly turned Graves into an adoring acolyte. For Riding, by then divorced, had come to England—and then joined Graves, Nancy, and the children when, in 1926, the poet took the one salaried position of his life: teaching literature at the new Royal Egyptian University, Cairo, a position for which he had been recommended by Lawrence, E. M. Forster, and Arnold Bennett, among others. Despite the substantial remuneration (the year's salary plus passage money came to £ 1,400), Graves resigned after one year. It is hard to know which irritated him most: the heat, the curriculum, the faculty, or the student papers. The best thing he had seen in Egypt was "the noble face of old Pharaoh Seti the Good, unwrapped of its mummy-cloths in the Cairo Museum"; the funniest, a French bedroom farce played in Arabic by men and women who had, for religious reasons, to keep on opposite sides of the stage. The audience talked through the performance, while munching on "peanuts, oranges, sunflower-seeds and heads of lettuces." This is among the last of the caricature scenes recorded in *Good-bye to All That*. Some of the scenes in Graves's life between 1926 and 1929 were even more bizarre but, as he says in the final paragraph of the book, "unpublishable."

Less than a year after the entourage returned from Egypt, Graves and Riding moved into a flat at 35A St. Peter's Square in London. Nancy and the children established residence on a nearby barge in the Thames, though all three adults took a hand in caring for the children. The literary collaborators were busy. Graves and his *domina* finished *A Survey of Modernist Poetry* (1927) and, the following year, their even more strident *A Pamphlet Against Anthologies* (1928). They also established the Seizin Press. In addition to two more critical books, Graves wrote a successful hero-worshipping biography, *Lawrence and the Arabs* (1927); his eerie and powerful short story "The Shout" (made, half a century later, into a prize-winning film directed by Jerzy Skolomowski and starring Alan Bates and Susannah York); and two closely overlapping volumes of collected verse: *Poems (1914-1926)* (1927) and *Poems (1914-1927)* (1927). Then, on 27 April 1929, Riding stepped out of a fourth-floor room of the flat—"by the window, of course." In the "Dedicatory Epilogue" to the 1929 edition of his autobiography, Graves, doubtless recalling his own experience on the Somme, reminds Riding of how "you . . . survived your dying" and, sounding still more like the author of *Good-bye to All That*, quotes the doctor who is said to have observed to those about him in the operating theater: "It is rarely that one sees the spinal-cord exposed to view—especially at right-angles to itself."

Riding was pieced together, and with the help of various sources, the same can be done for the events preceding her famous leap. What it comes down to is a case of "tragedy posing as farce"—to borrow Frank O'Connor's apt synopsis from the portion of his autobiography dealing with his friend, the Irish journalist and poet Geoffrey Phibbs. Phibbs, it seems, had left his wife to move into the flat with Graves and Riding, whom he described to O'Connor as his favorite modern poet. Soon under her rigorous tutelage, but uneasy with communal life, he asked Riding to leave with him. When she refused, citing her commitment to the Graveses, Phibbs reconciled with his wife and went off to France—only to be pursued by Graves, Laura, and Nancy, all of them urging him to return, and all in vain. Riding soon discovered that she could not work without him; and when Phibbs finally did return to London and visited the flat, Riding felt the only way to end the paralyzing impasse was to jump from the window in the room in which the four principals were gathered. She only intended, she said later, to die for awhile.

During Laura Riding's three-month hospitalization for a compound spinal fracture, Nancy permanently broke with Graves—on 6 May 1929 keeping the children and barge—and Graves himself wrote most of *Good-bye to All That*, his "bitter leave-taking of England where I had recently broken a good many conventions; quarreled with, or been disowned by, most of my friends; been grilled by the police on a suspicion of attempted murder, and ceased to care what anyone thought of me." When Riding was released from the hospital, she and Graves departed—first to France, and then, at the suggestion of Gertrude Stein, who called it a paradise if one could stand it, on to Majorca. They went, Graves informed Nancy's dubious father in a postcard, "to stop time," a reflection of Laura Riding's notion that "historic Time had effectively come to an end." Nancy and the four children remained on the houseboat, where, soon after, she was joined by—Phibbs (or "Taylor," for he had by then changed his name by deed-poll). A farcical tragedy indeed, but not without fruit. The complex tonality of some of Graves's middle poetry and of

Good-bye to All That—its mingled horror, sangfroid, black humor, and farce—seems to have its genetic roots entangled in the eccentricities of more than World War I.

Graves and Riding spent seven productive years (1929-1936) in Deyá, a small fishing, sheep-raising, and olive-producing village on the northwest coast of Majorca. The Seizin Press was reestablished, and they formed a literary enclave consisting, at various times, of poets James Reeves, Norman Cameron, and Alan Hodge; scientist Jacob Bronowski; painter John Aldridge; Honor Wyatt, a novelist; Len Lye, the film maker; and American journalist T. S. Matthews. Though dominated by Riding, the enclave was supported by Graves's pen. The critical and monetary triumph of his autobiography was capped five years later by the historical novels *I, Claudius* and *Claudius the God* (both 1934). They brought fame, awards (the prestigious Hawthornden and James Tait Black prizes) and the income needed to underwrite the colony and Graves in his own chosen vocation of poet.

Hart Crane had found Laura "engrossing," and the American Fugitives thought her both impressive and pushy; Graves considered her indispensable. His description of himself as partner "to" Riding in the Seizin Press; the female joint pseudonym (Barbara Rich) under which they published their unsuccessful novel *No Decency Left* (1932); the pieces she and Graves printed in *Focus*, the Deyá newsletter, and in their periodical, *Epilogue*—all these, not to mention Riding's letters and books, reveal a relationship of dictatorial instructress and submissive ephebe (or pupil), a case of thralldom to a woman whose intellectual powers and capacity to dominate a small group have become legendary. More than protective of Riding, Graves seemed to T. S. Matthews, "in a constant swivet of attention to please her, to forestall her every wish, like a small boy dancing attendance on a rich aunt of uncertain temper. And she treated him—like a dog. There was no prettier way to put it." Matthews came to the conclusion that Riding was "not so much his mistress as his master; he was *in statu pupilari* to her."

Matthews was closer to the truth than he could have known at the time. For what makes Graves's devotion all the more remarkable is not only the fact that he was the better-known writer of the two, but that by this time Riding had limited their relationship to that of working friends. "Bodies have had their day," she declared in 1933, adding the following year in response to a question about Freud that she thought sex "disgusting." Graves, whose own dualistic nature was torn between simultaneous attraction to and revulsion from sexuality, may have agreed. In any case, his devotion was unabated. Riding believed that she and Graves were remarkable human beings; that, as a unique repository of truth, she was entitled to be in command of their partnership; and that he, her "closest" associate and beneficiary of the intensive care she applied to his "writing problems and ambitions," had made "his own," as much as he could, her "processes of word, mind, moral feeling." Graves in effect concurred.

While critics may differ regarding the effects of Laura Riding's influence, Graves himself—in the foreword to the volume that marks the end of the Riding years, the 1938 *Collected Poems*—has humbly recorded his indebtedness to her poetic and critical principles. She gradually caused him "to revise his whole attitude to poetry," and he concludes: "I have to thank Laura Riding for her constructive and detailed criticism of my poems in various stages of composition. . . ."

If the poetry written in the wake of World War I under the influence of Rivers had been the expression of a shared neurosis requiring cure, that written under the aegis of the arrogant but incorruptible Laura Riding sought a reality external to the haunted self—a truth attainable only through poetry, defined by Riding in the preface to her *Collected Poems* (also published in 1938) as nothing less than "an uncovering of truth." Fusing her ethic with his own aesthetic, Graves moved beyond the therapeutic to what he called "self-humbling honesties," addressed both to himself and to the values (or lack of them) in the world around him. If Graves and Riding, islanded on Majorca, saw themselves as surrounded by ignorant and mendacious armies clashing by night, they could at least be true to one another—which meant being true to the values oracularly pronounced by the sibylline Laura Riding.

Graves's important 1938 collection was preceded in 1931 by *Poems, 1926-1930* (consisting of *Poems, 1929* and *Ten Poems More*, plus the nine poems added to the second of his 1927 collections) and *Poems, 1930-1933*, the 1931 Seizin Press *To Whom Else?* supplemented by thirteen additional poems. Reading through these overlapping collections and the rigorously winnowed 1938 volume, it seems clear that Graves's terseness, disciplined control, excision of sentimentality, and developing moral certainty reflect, or at the very least were reinforced by, Laura Riding's emphasis on the precise definition of each "Word uttered" (to quote his poem "History of the Word"), as well as by her central conception of the poetic function: the relentless stripping down of reality to a hard core of truth, what she and Graves had called in *A Survey of Modernist Poetry* that "hard, matter-of-fact skeleton" under the flesh.

In one of his more Ridingesque poems, Graves tells the reader over his shoulder: "I am a clean spirit / And you for ever flesh." Riding's divided feelings about sexuality probably coincided with rather than shaped Graves's. Such brilliant, quintessentially Gravesian poems about the relationship of mind and body, love and lust as "The Succubus," "Ulysses," "Down, Wanton, Down!," "Certain Mercies," "Saint," and "Sick Love" are, however tautly controlled, written out of emotional conflict, not out of the sexless rationalism and cold lucidity characteristic of Laura Riding. Similarly, though gnomic and ingenious, such familiar poems as "The Legs," "It Was All Very Tidy," "Warning to Children," and "The Terraced Valley" avoid that unmetaphoric flatness typical of her intellectual exercises. And, unlike hers, even his ostensibly antiromantic poems are not devoid of exuberance or aloofly remote from the conflict that produces poetic tension.

Her ideas and sheer presence are another matter—even if they were of greater significance to Graves than to subsequent literary and critical history. For example, despite what has become a critical commonplace, it was not essentially to the notorious Riding-Graves exegesis of Shakespeare's Sonnet 129 that *Seven Types of Ambiguity* was indebted. William Empson's influential notion of ambiguity was based on Graves's earlier observations (in *On English Poetry* and *Poetic Unreason and Other Studies*) on latent associations, "combined poetic meanings" (or "congruity"), and subtextual patterns. "Modern literary criticism was invented by a number of people, but by Graves as much as any other individual," Empson insisted in 1955—a remark worth noting since Graves's more eccentric and cranky critical pronouncements (especially the reckless bombardeering of Virgil and Milton, and the iconoclastic attacks on Yeats, Pound, Eliot, and the other idols of the modernist pantheon in the calumnious Clark and Oxford Lectures in the 1950s and 1960s) have tended to obscure the more penetrating aspects of his criticism. In reaffirming his debt in 1966, Empson noted that he had not meant to slight Riding; it was simply that "Robert Graves had used the method of analysis by recognizing ambiguity" in a book prior to *A Survey of Modernist Poetry*, "not collaborating with anyone."

On the other hand, there was much Riding could teach and Graves gladly learn. His assertion of the moral strength and superiority of woman, peripheral in "Down, Wanton, Down!" and "A Jealous Man," and at the heart of "The Great-Grandmother," echoes Laura Riding's dictum that in the fundamental relation, which is between the male and female mind, "the female mind is the judge, and the male mind the subject of judgment." There is a loved woman in "Through Nightmare," one of those who "carry / Time looped so river-wise about their house / There's no way in by history's road / To name or number them." Though Laura Riding is apparently not the beloved of this poem, obviously her theories about historical time influenced Graves's conception, fundamental to the methodological procedures of *The White Goddess* and of his historical reconstructions, that time can be "suspended" or bound into a "manageable ring" through the use of "proleptic" and "analeptic" methods of thought. To illustrate the theory in a 1970s essay, Graves quoted his own 1931 poem "On Portents," written, he said, "of a woman genius." The genius in that poem is of course Laura Riding, and since "On Portents" is the forerunner of the White Goddess poems, one cannot diminish or localize her impact upon Graves—even if she herself subsequently disclaimed any "involvement in a pokerfaced muse or goddess game of poetic didactics."

It is significant that "On Portents," so proleptic of Graves's future direction, was placed in the fifth and final section of the 1938 *Collected Poems*, part of a small group of lyrics which, according to Graves's foreword, express "a more immediate sense of poetic liberation," achieved, Graves added, "not by mysticism but by practical persistence." In "On Portents," that persistence takes the form, first, of the goddess's own efforts to overcome resistance. But it is the poet-lover who is caught up in the turbulence made by "the strong pulling of her bladed mind" through the ever-reluctant element of time. Clearly, service to the goddess—then incipiently incarnate in Laura Riding, who had as bladed a mind as even Graves could wish—must take the form of a freedom to be achieved only after considerable difficulty, and pain, on the part of her acolyte. Indeed, the more-than-metaphoric significance of that bladed mind is stressed in the final stanza of "End of Play," in this same concluding section of the 1938 volume. Surviving "lies" and "bestial sensuality," love is carved on a sill "Under antique dread of the headsman's axe; / It is the echoing mind, as in the mirror / We stare at our dazed trunks at the block kneeling." The primal scene established in these lines would become stan-

Robert Graves, circa 1941 (BBC Hulton, Picture Post*)*

dard in Graves's mythology; for this is decapitation by a headsman proleptic of the White Goddess: that archetypal ax wielder whose bladed mind pulls strongly deep in the reader's, or at least in Robert Graves's, echoing mind.

Still, Laura Riding's presence in the poems of the 1930s does seem, above all, liberating. The 1938 *Collected Poems* opens with "The Haunted House"; the phantoms are exorcised in the volume's penultimate poem "No More Ghosts," in which the haunted bed is "cut to wholesome furniture for wholesome rooms," and we are "free / From cramps of dark necessity." In this restored simplicity and ordered ease, "No new ghosts can appear. Their poor cause / Was that time freezes, and time thaws; / But here only such loves can last / As do not ride upon the weathers of the past."

That restored serenity, though a genuine accomplishment and a tribute to the benign aspects of Laura Riding's museship, had been disturbed even before the publication of the 1938 collection. The Majorcan years had come to an abrupt end in July 1936. With the outbreak of the Spanish civil war, that dress rehearsal for what was soon to come, British subjects were officially advised to leave Spanish territory. Given two hours notice and limited to what they could cram in a single suitcase each, Graves, Riding, their secretary Karl Gay, and Alan Hodge were evacuated on a British destroyer. The Seizin's huge Albion handpress had to be abandoned, as had almost all personal belongings and papers (all to be recovered, intact, when Graves returned to the island ten years later). Graves and Riding traveled from Majorca to France to England; over the next three years they wandered to Switzerland, back to England, to Brittany, and again to England. The gathering storm of a second world conflict stimulated two poems, included in Graves's

1938 collection, which stand out as his finest on the subject of war.

Beneath the late-Roman trappings, "The Cuirassiers of the Frontier" reveals Graves's old regimental pride as well as his contempt for what he later called "the whole demonic machinery officially sanctioned by a corps of regular padres." Improving on Housman's fine poem on an army of noble mercenaries, "The Cuirassiers of the Frontier" scorns corrupt civilians safe at home (cutthroats, "pederastic senators," and the eunuchs of the metropolis's "draped saloons") and that other corruption, Christianity. It seems an unqualified affirmation of the soldierly bond Graves (both in this poem and in his prose on the war) designates a "sacrament." But then comes the kind of final "surprise" compared in *On English Poetry* to the "shock of a broken electric circuit." The speaker, one of the barbarian guards protecting Roman civilization, concludes that there is "no faith nor truth, / Nor justice" in either the Roman state or in "Peter's Church." "We, not the City, are the Empire's soul: / A rotten tree lives only in its rind." The wonderful last line goes beyond the simple contrast of decadence and vitality to raise a question: If the sick Roman civilization is being supported only by the solid virtues and barbarian virility of its frontier guards, are not they, however admirable, part of the corruption? After all, that which is falling, says Nietzsche's Zarathustra, one should also push—not prolong.

As this poem is meant to remind the reader, the pride and courage of men bound to one another by a suicidal sacrament had been exploited and misdirected in more recent history. Gallantry and romanticism had themselves become suspect, especially after the adoption of universal conscription in 1916, "when every man was a compulsory hero, when love of battle in prospect had become loathing in retrospect." The allegedly distanced retrospect finally came twenty years later in Graves's definitive war poem.

"Recalling War" begins with wounds, surgery, vestigial pain, the legacy of World War I—all seen from the perspective of a backward glance whose distancing is belied by anger posing as a series of paeans to the healing art. "What, then, was war?" the second stanza asks—at a time when it was clear that the 1914-1918 conflict was about to lose all claim to being the war to end war. The mimicry of philosophic detachment and the ironic use of the past tense (as if war were a quaint anachronism safely relegated to the museum of the past) trigger recollections of the actual "infection" of those years. Though oppressed by the "stupidities" of nationalism, the soldiers are described as responding to the pseudoromanticism of war in images of adolescent male sexuality. They had "thrust out / Boastful tongue, clenched fist and valiant yard" (here, as in "Ogres and Pygmies," an appropriately obsolescent word for penis), "dying" in a "premature fate-spasm." The penultimate stanza, the strongest in the poem, recaptures the subtle ambivalence of the opening movement of Yeats's "Nineteen Hundred and Nineteen," a poem obtusely ridiculed in *A Survey of Modernist Poetry*. In both poems, genuine anguish for what has been destroyed by war is complicated by insight into the naiveté and blind deluded pride which went before a fall that begins to seem, if not just, at least what Graves calls a "return" of a brutal reality that men, babbling of logic or of love, had tried to gloss over or repress. The ultimate theme of both poems is synopsized in Yeats's original manuscript title: "The Things That Come Again."

Whatever his possible indebtedness to "Nineteen Hundred and Nineteen," Graves noted in his diary, "with considerable satisfaction," the death of Yeats in January 1939. The "Yeatsian Spectre" (to borrow the term he revealingly used to describe the Yeats anthology to which he and Riding had refused to contribute in 1936) was at last laid to rest. But a considerably more disturbing event was imminent: a personal trauma coinciding with the onset of the world's trauma in 1939.

In the spring of that year Graves and Riding wrote to T. S. Matthews, who had long been urging them to come to America to meet his best friend, Schuyler Jackson. They had decided they would. Matthews put up $25,000 to rebuild Nimrod's Rise, a ruined eighteenth-century farmhouse on Jackson's property in New Hope, Pennsylvania. There, remnants of the Deyá enclave (Graves, Riding, Alan and Beryl Hodge, and David Reeve, James's brother) were to join Tom and Julie Matthews and Schuyler and Kit Jackson. The group came together that spring for weeks of almost continuous meetings, the avowed purpose of which was to carry out an obsession of Laura's. This was the drawing up of a "Protocol" which, as Matthews later put it, "by the sternness of its thought and the authority of its language would arrest the drift of the world into the war we saw coming. Believe it or not. The Protocol was never finished; instead, three of the families in our group broke up."

In New Hope, the thirteen-year association of Riding and Graves ended in harrowing circumstances resembling those that had threatened it a decade earlier. The old role of Geoffrey Phibbs was played now by the more formidable Schuyler Jackson, with whom Laura fell in love. Once his wife, declared a witch and exorcised by Riding, had divorced him, she and Schuyler Jackson were married. By then a shattered Graves had returned to England. Matthews, who accompanied him to New York where he boarded ship in August 1939, described Graves as "desperate and wretched, near the end of his tether," an assessment later confirmed by Graves himself, when he wrote Matthews in 1960 to say that, regarding those days and the alliance of Riding and Jackson, he preferred "to let it go into the bottomless gulf where Laura knowingly cast herself, and into which she nearly dragged me and indeed all of us."

Graves stayed at first with friends in Essex, but he was soon joined by Beryl Hodge. (In May 1950, by which time Nancy had finally agreed to a divorce, they married—a marriage that lasted.) While Beryl's divorce was pending, her husband collaborated with Graves on *The Long Week-End* (1940), a social history of England between the wars. As remarkable as the amicable collaboration was the book's admiring appraisal of Laura Riding—the "one poet of the time," we are told, "who spun, like Arachne, from her own vitals without any discoverable philosophical or literary derivations: and the only one who achieved an unshakable synthesis." None were intended, but one may half create reservations. Athena, after all, turned Arachne into a spider, the insect she hated most, and Riding's synthesis was "unshakable" *provided* "the premise of her unique personal authority were granted, and another more startling one—that historic Time had effectively come to an end." One thing was certain: Riding was, as Graves and Alan Hodge concluded, "a perfect original."

The war the "Protocol" had been designed to stop was not an original, merely the second round of what had begun in 1914. Graves, who tried to volunteer for infantry service but was turned down because of his age, wounds, and fine record in the first war, spent the duration of the second with Beryl Hodge in the Devonshire village of Galmpton, near Brixton, to "avoid getting bombed unnecessarily." The couple had three children in England: William, Lucia, and Juan (a fourth, Tomas, was later born on Majorca). In March 1943, Graves's first son, David, was killed in action, fighting with the First Royal Welch on the Arakan peninsula in Burma. "Shot through the head" while trying singlehandedly to take a Japanese strong point, David Graves was recommended for a posthumous Victoria Cross. The War Office turned it down on the ground, Graves drily reports, that the general attack "had failed." Readers of *Good-bye to All That* will not fail to remember that a quarter century earlier, on the Hindenburg Line, Sassoon, "shot through the throat," had fought on until he collapsed. His recommendation for a Victoria Cross had also been refused "on the ground that the operations had been unsuccessful." Historic time had apparently not come to an end; there was no saying good-bye to *all* of all that.

During his wartime sojourn in South Devon, Graves produced his two Sergeant Lamb novels, accounts of a Royal Welch Fusilier during the American Revolution, and an iconoclastic novel in which he allowed Milton's first wife to borrow his pen in order to rectify the great poet's "prejudiced" account of their marriage. As the supposed authoress, "Marie Powell" exposes an idol with feet of clay, the brutal oppressor of a lively and bright young woman capable of holding her own with him intellectually. When to *The Story of Marie Powell, Wife to Mr. Milton* (1943) is added Graves's 1949 description of Milton as a "renegade" who soon "abandoned his half-hearted allegiance to the Muse," one realizes that Graves has been moving all along toward worship of the White Goddess. It was in fact in Galmpton in early 1943 while he was working on *The Golden Fleece* (1944; republished in the United States as *Hercules, My Shipmate*, 1945) that Graves was interrupted by "a sudden overwhelming obsession." His reconstruction of the adventures of Jason and the Argonauts became dominated by the White Goddess, whose cult he repeatedly encountered in his research. Within three weeks he had written 70,000 words, the first draft of what became *The White Goddess*, his erudite and eccentric, bewildering and exhilarating grammar of poetic myth. The book was completed two years later on Majorca, to which Graves brought his new family soon after the war.

It is not to cast doubt on "the sudden obsession that overcame me at Galmpton," or to reduce her to a surrogate for Laura Riding, to suggest that—whatever the Goddess's roots in his classical, Celtic, and romantic reading—Laura Riding's rejection of him in 1939 gave Graves the necessary distance to judge their relationship objectively and to discern in it the archetypal pattern of inspiration, love, and ultimate destructiveness he later associated with the Triple Muse. Graves's White Goddess is, in fact, experience mythologized and myth made personal, a weaving of what Yeats called "an always personal emotion . . . into a general pattern of myth and

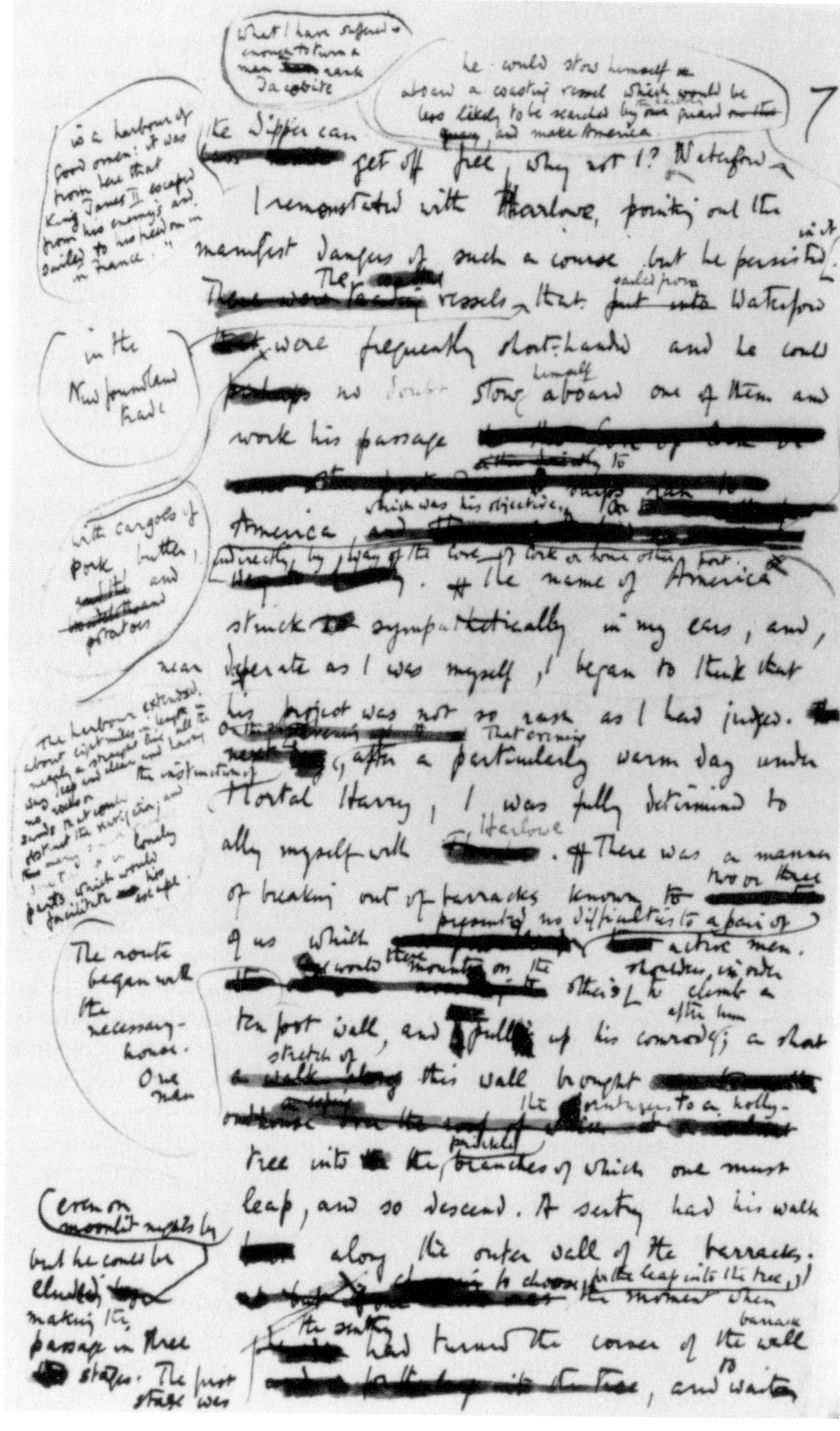

Page from the manuscript for Sergeant Lamb of the Ninth

symbol." Graves's own personal emotions disposed him to be open to "the ancient Mediterranean Moon-Goddess whom Homer invoked in the *Iliad*," whom Apuleius encountered as Isis in *The Golden Ass*, and whom Sir James Frazer, Jane Harrison, and J. J. Bachofen discussed in their anthropological investigations. As the obsession of a poet in the romantic tradition, Graves's goddess is a sublime femme fatale, a creature related to Blake's female figure in "The Mental Traveller," Coleridge's harlot dicer with death in "The Rime of the Ancient Mariner," and Keats's fairy temptress in "La Belle

Dame sans Merci"—especially since, as Graves says in *On English Poetry* and in *The White Goddess*, "Keats was writing under the shadow of death about his Muse, Fanny Brawne." On the level of myth, the Sacred King is "the Moon-Goddess's divine victim," and "every Muse-poet must, in a sense, die for the Goddess whom he adores, just as the King died." On the personal level, therefore, "being in love does not, and should not, blind the poet to the cruel side of woman's nature—and many Muse-poems are written in helpless attestation of this by men whose love is no longer returned."

These tensions, rooted in Graves's earlier poetry of emotional conflict involving love and death but rationally suppressed during the Laura Riding years, seem reconciled in the few but impressive poems written between 1938 and 1944. "A Love Story" and "Mid-Winter Waking," two of his most beautiful lyrics, indicate the direction in which Graves was moving. The first poem's eerie setting and dominant icons—moon, owls, snow—look back to the 1924 "Full Moon" and ahead to the symbolic system to be encountered in the "magical" White Goddess poems. "A Love Story," in which a lunar queen teaches her presumptuous lover a lesson, ends with the chastened man serenely submitting to his fate as vassal. The reward for that service which is perfect freedom comes in "Mid-Winter Waking," where, stirring from "long hibernation" and knowing himself "once more a poet," the speaker finds "her hand in mine laid closely / Who shall watch out the Spring with me."

By 1944 the muse and the White Goddess were one, and all "true" poetry "necessarily" an invocation of her powers of inspiration and destruction. The muse poems printed in *The Golden Fleece* and *The White Goddess*, and in the three volumes of verse published between 1944 and the enlarged edition (1952) of *The White Goddess*, embodied "the Theme," that "antique story" of birth, death, and resurrection presided over by a "capricious and all-powerful Threefold Goddess," man's archetypal "mother, bride, and layer-out." Drawn—by mythic and poetic precedent, and by his own experience and temperament—to the crueller aspects of her ambivalent nature, Graves tended to depict the White Goddess as "the ancient power of fright and lust—the female spider or the queen-bee whose embrace is death."

Even within this restrictive monomyth, the White Goddess runs a limited gamut of emotions. Stirred by vengeful "Gusts of laughter," she is at her most sardonic in "The Destroyers" and in "Dethronement," in which the lover's "true anguish / Is all that she requires." But she can be winning. In that splendid exposure of male egotism and self-deception, "Theseus and Ariadne," in which the deserted woman emerges a triumphant moon goddess, Ariadne is "Playing the queen" to the "nobler company" (the god Dionysus) who succeeded ignorant Theseus when he abandoned her on Naxos. She is also the sought perfection at the end of an exacting ordeal: the Persephone of "Instructions to the Orphic Adept," one of Graves's most rhythmically compelling performances. She is a demythologized but real presence in four fine poems from the 1951 *Poems and Satires*: "Counting the Beats," "The Portrait," "The Survivor," and "The Young Cordwainer." The fullest mythic description of the goddess—encountered at "full moon," her "long hair streaming," her Cretan ax "propped idly on a stone"—occurs in "Darien," but the most memorable of the mythical-archaic poems remain "To Juan at the Winter Solstice" and "The White Goddess." The truly "magical" thing about the first—Graves's best-known poem and the most distilled synopsis of his myth—is that despite the thematic reduction of everything to "one story and one story only," the poem itself is a triumph of incantatory resonance, its music transcending both the myth and the glosses Graves and others have supplied.

Following a description of the archetypal victim's unfaltering tread of the "never altered circuit of his fate," the royal bartering of "life for love," and the portents of death in the penultimate stanza, the poet's son Juan is instructed to ponder the ambivalence of the goddess herself, that smiling bearer of the "leafy quince" who is also the destroyer. "Dwell on her graciousness," Juan is told, "dwell on her smiling, / Do not forget what flowers / The great boar trampled down in ivy time." Ivy time is October, the anniversary of the death of boar-hunting Adonis and the time of the revels of the Maenads, the frenzied priestesses of Dionysus who chewed ivy as an intoxicant and who tore to pieces any man who interrupted their autumnal rites. Nevertheless, Juan is to dwell on the goddess's graciousness and smiling. At least temporarily: for while Yeats ends "A Prayer for My Daughter," as Coleridge does "Frost at Midnight," with a prayer that his child may enjoy a serene fate very different from his own, Graves's inexorable myth compels him to warn his son that whatever aspect of the goddess he may concentrate on, she will inevitably turn as murderous as the Maenads. Nevertheless, during the time of allotted union, she shall bring her devotee love and inspiration—until the time comes for the ax to

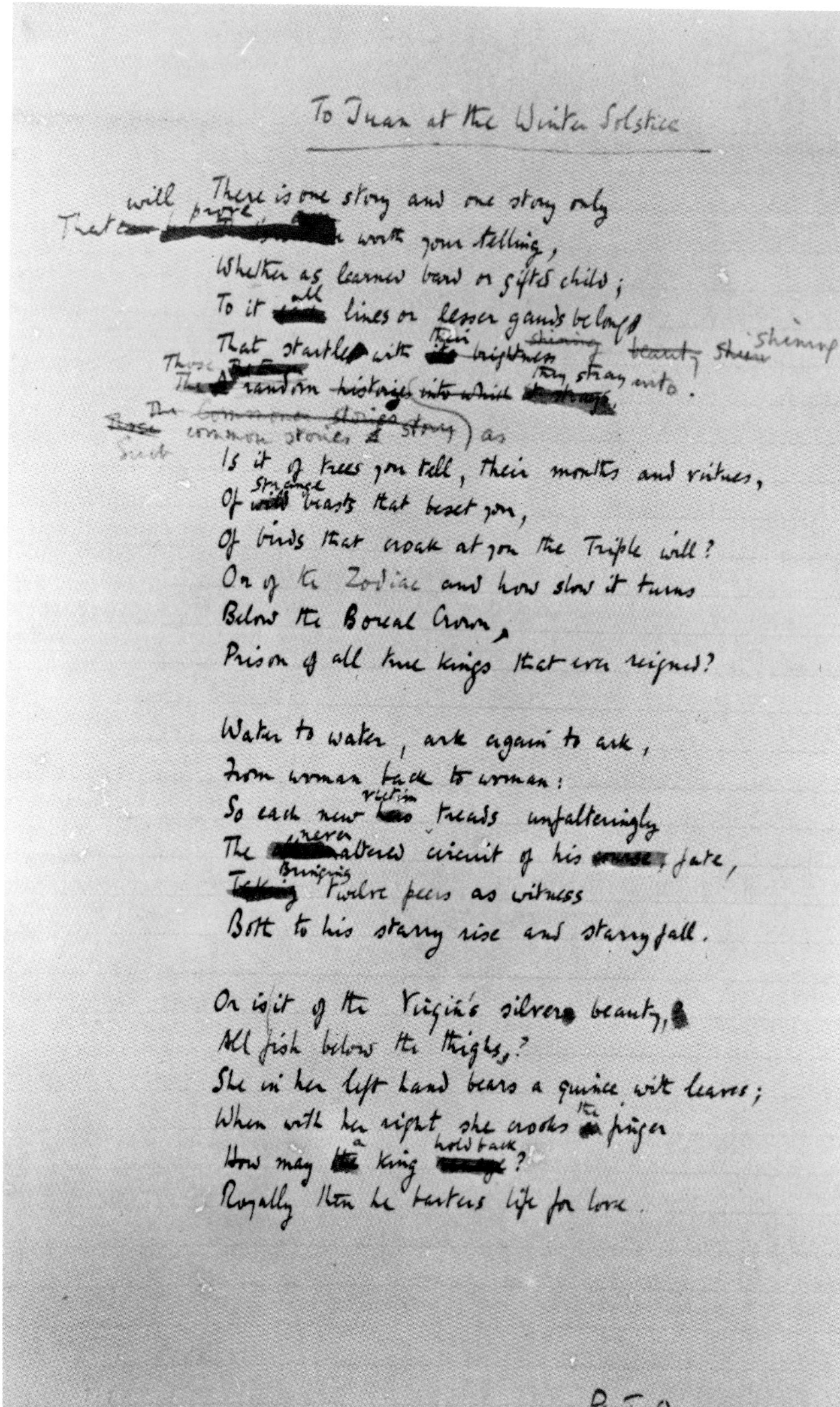
To Juan at the Winter Solstice

There is one story and one story only
That will prove worth your telling,
Whether as learned bard or gifted child;
To it all lines or lesser gauds belong
That startle with their shining
Such common stories as they stray into.

Is it of trees you tell, their months and virtues,
Of strange beasts that beset you,
Of birds that croak at you the Triple will?
Or of the Zodiac and how slow it turns
Below the Boreal Crown,
Prison of all true kings that ever reigned?

Water to water, ark again to ark,
From woman back to woman:
So each new victim treads unfalteringly
The never altered circuit of his fate,
Bringing Twelve peers as witness
Both to his starry rise and starry fall.

Or is it of the Virgin's silver beauty,
All fish below the thighs?
She in her left hand bears a quince with leaves;
When with her right she crooks the finger
How may a king hold back?
Royally then he barters life for love.

P.T.O

Page from a draft for Graves's poem to his son (Lockwood Memorial Library, State University of New York at Buffalo)

fall, as fall it must. Hence the negative construction of the final affirmation: "But nothing promised that is not performed."

In the context of the poem the bargain with the goddess seems worth it; we may suspend disbelief in the myth, allowing Graves's architectural skill and hypnagogic rhythms to persuade us that we are attending a sacred drama—ultimately, a divine comedy—in which individual agony is subsumed. And yet, even though the poem is addressed to his own son, Graves does seem to lose sight of the reality of human suffering. Or is it that, like Nietzsche, he longs to circumscribe suffering within a fuller glory, what Nietzsche calls in *The Birth of Tragedy* a "higher, overmastering joy" an order so transforming terror that "lamentation itself becomes a song of praise?"

That transformation of terror occurs in "The White Goddess," a quest poem and song of praise ending on a note of *sprezzatura* reminiscent of Nietzsche or Yeats. Scorning Apollonian saints and sober men who revile the goddess, "we sailed to find her / In distant regions likeliest to hold her / Whom we desired above all things to know." The "headstrong and heroic" enterprise is rewarded by a vision of the goddess, blue-eyed and berry-lipped, "With hair curled honey-coloured to white hips." The poem ends in a magnificent incantation celebrating the goddess—despite her brow "white as any leper's," and despite awareness of the inevitable "bright bolt" which, balancing the sap that rises in the spring, shall fall in the fall:

> Green sap of Spring in the young wood a-stir
> Will celebrate the Mountain Mother,
> And every song-bird shout awhile for her;
> But we are gifted, even in November
> Rawest of seasons, with so huge a sense
> Of her nakedly worn magnificence
> We forget cruelty and past betrayal,
> Heedless of where the next bright bolt may fall.

Temporary amnesia notwithstanding, the questor knows that he must die at the hands of she whom he desired above all things to "know." This emphasis on knowledge is deliberate. The birds and flowers celebrate her in season; "we," who have struggled through hardship to find her and are alone conscious of what is to come, hail the goddess proleptically, confident in raw winter of both her spring generosity and her destructive autumnal blow.

"The White Goddess" was originally published as the dedicatory poem to the volume of that title. "I am not eager to rehearse / My thoughts and theory," says the Yeatsian ghost in Eliot's *Little Gidding*. "These things have served their purpose: let them be." Whatever Robert Graves "really" believed about the goddess—whatever the ontological status he conceived her to occupy, or the various scholarly and psychological sources of his matriarchal theories—the primary interest in *The White Goddess* is not those sources and theories. As in similar cases (Yeats's system-making in *A Vision*, Wordsworth's employment of Platonic myth in the Immortality Ode, Joyce's use of Viconian cycles in *Finnegans Wake*), what matters is the artistic use to which the theories are put. If they enabled Graves to hammer his thoughts into unity and to write such poems as "To Juan at the Winter Solstice," and "The White Goddess," the mythographic expeditions recorded in *The White Goddess* served their purpose by bringing rare treasure to port. This aspect of the situation has been summed up by Randall Jarrell, a skeptical admirer for whom Graves's goddess worship is no more (or less) than a projection upon the universe of his own unconscious. But it was a projection that brought into efficient and creative "symbiosis" the antagonistic halves of the poet's nature. "Because of the White Goddess," Jarrell concluded, "some of the most beautiful poems of our time have come into existence."

By the time *The White Goddess* was published in 1948, Graves was back on Majorca, his permanent home for the remainder of his life. In his final decades he was a famous man. A rhapsode of the matriarchal who was himself the patriarch of an island, he devoted himself to writing poetry inspired by several incarnate muses, venturing forth only to honor and be honored, or to deliver his refreshingly iconoclastic if often outrageously wrongheaded lectures. Though he had displayed a reckless audacity in the 1954 Clark Lectures at Cambridge, this most anti-Apollonian of poet-critics found himself elected Professor of Poetry at Oxford—a tenure stretching from 1961 to 1966, though he spent most of even those years on Majorca. He also traveled to Hungary, Israel, and the United States, where, in 1970, he was made one of the few honorary members of the American Academy of Arts and Sciences.

Until his very latest years, Graves has seemed indefatigable. The books poured forth: historical novels, translations, biblical reconstructions, criticism (collected in *On Poetry*, 1969), and, of course, poetry itself. His persistence, craftsmanship, and balance recommended him to The Movement poets in England, and his verse was repeatedly honored:

the Russell Loines Award in 1958, the William Foyle Prize in 1960, and, in 1968, both a gold medal at the Mexico City Cultural Olympics and, in a private audience, the Queen's Gold Medal for Poetry. In 1966 Graves made his film debut, playing, at the age of seventy-one, Merlin the Magician in *Deadfall*. Graves has lived long enough to see *I, Claudius* (a film partially made in the 1930s by Alexander Korda was never released) brilliantly produced by the BBC; long enough, too, to see both his island retreat and his most esoteric speculations domesticated by cultural tourists. He also came, in time, to experience the goddess in a more benign aspect, though the poetic consequences were mixed.

In one of the Oxford lectures, Graves described poetry as passing through three distinct phases: "first, the poet's introduction, by Vesta, to love in its old-fashioned forms of affection and companionship; next, his experience of death and recreation at the White Goddess's hand; and lastly a certitude in love, given him by the Black Goddess, his more-than-Muse." Graves's later love poems were written largely under the mythological sign of the Black Goddess. Though this figure, quarried out of Sufism and Orphic and Judaic mystery cults, still ordains that the poet who seeks her must pass

Robert Graves at his home in Majorca, circa 1954 (BBC Hulton, photo by Daniel Farson for Picture Post*)*

uncomplaining through all the passionate ordeals to which her exacting white sister may subject him, she is a more benevolent deity, the representative of a mystical and pacific bond between men and women.

One might be reassured by this late arrival of a kindly muse, finding in it evidence that Graves has at last found a wisdom deeper than that implied by mutual rendings concluding in masochistic submission to the ax. Poetically, too, a burst of color and vitality accompanied the coming of the Black Goddess: "At sunset, only to his true love, / The bird of paradise opened wide his wings / Displaying emerald plumage shot with gold / Unguessed even by him." This unexpected display at sunset (the poet was almost seventy when he wrote "Bird of Paradise") also fills the "more-than-Muse" with astonishment; trembling, she asks herself: "What did I do to awake such glory?"

What incarnate muse had awakened this late glory? Graves, like Yeats, steered between the extremes of Eliotic extinction of personality and name-naming confessionalism. In his foreword to *Poems About Love*, a 1969 collection of love lyrics chosen from more than twenty of his books published over the preceding half-century, Graves noted that while each of the poems "commemorated a secret occasion and was written solely for whoever inspired it," he had refrained from "marking the large groups with names of the women who inspired or provoked them." That, he concluded, would "lead only to mischief." Besides, "poetry should not be confused with autobiography." Graves prefers, for example, that the reader not know whose eyes have been immortalized in the poem entitled "The Black Goddess," where "your black agate eyes, wide open, mirror / The released firebird beating his way / Down a whirled avenue of blues and yellows."

Whatever its genesis, this new-won sense of liberation and fecundity had its poetic limitations. The muse had always been, in Graves's mythology, the perpetual other woman, never the poet's wife. Standing between the unadventurous, submissive domesticity of Vesta and the bittersweet, unpredictable vagaries of the Triple Muse, the Black Goddess had seemed to unify the vision of woman. After a while, however, the hymns in her honor sacrificed the primitivistic excitement of the White Goddess poems to a tranquillity as tiresome poetically as—in Graves's bardic view—wedlock itself. Judging from his dotage on the poetry of his last two decades—much of which does not, in the veteran's own soldierly phrase, "pass muster"—Graves did not rec-

Robert Graves in Palma, Majorca, circa 1954 (BBC Hulton, photo by Daniel Farson for Picture Post*)*

ognize the falling off others find perceptible in his work. The late poems have not lacked defenders, but Graves himself was more than kind to these children of his prolific old age. His post-1965 corpus, nearly three hundred lyrics, constitutes fully forty percent of the poems he chose as his final canon, filling 160 of the 403 pages of *New Collected Poems* (the 1977 American edition of the final *Collected Poems*). Despite Graves's insistence that the poet alone is qualified to establish his final testament, most critics—those "old-clothes-men of literature," as Graves calls them—would probably agree that his overvaluation of the later work, combined with his elimination over the years of a number of fine poems, has served to distort his accomplishment as a whole.

The slackening of tension actually predated the coming of the Black Goddess; Graves admitted in a preamble to a reading in the mid-1950s that some of his recent poems were so "cunning" that they lacked exuberance. For all his attunement to archetypal mysteries, Graves had always been fascinated by the minutiae of craftsmanship and insistent on the need for poems to make "good sense." But by the mid-1960s he was, he wrote his friend James Reeves, "writing nothing but songs of obsessional perfectionism." That perfectionism was technical. Though his employment of Anglo-classical and Welsh tricks (*cynghanedd* and allied techniques of alliteration, assonance, and internal rhyming) has been justly praised, Graves himself had warned against their dangerous potential back in 1922. Modern poets were not the first, he said in *On English Poetry*, to have confused poetry with "ingenious Alexandrianisms," trying, "for lack of any compelling utterance," to beat the critics by "piling an immense number of technical devices on their verses, killing what little passion there was, by the tyranny of self-imposed rules," the most restrictive being those invented by the Irish and Welsh bards. "The way out for poetry does not lie by this road, we may be sure," Graves concluded. "But neither on the other hand do we need to call in the Da-da-ists." With his characteristic balance between Alexandrianism and Dadaism, Graves had generally avoided the pitfalls at either extreme; technical cunning and obsessional perfectionism almost succeeded, however, in killing what passion there was in many of the late poems. More than one reader of later Graves has been reminded of Roy Campbell's "They use the snaffle and the curb all right, / But where's the bloody horse?"

There is no guarantee that an intricately crafted poem will not be trivial or, worse, bloodless. Much of the lesser, thinner work of Graves's old age sacrifices passionate intensity to a love "magic" and "togetherness" more tedious than serene. The words *magic* and *togetherness* appear again and again in the late poems. The most obvious of "surface faults" among poets, Graves had also remarked in *On English Poetry*, was a "bias towards running to death" a particular "set of words." We can apply to Graves's use of *magic* and *togetherness* Graves's own complaints about Shelley's "queer obsession" with caves, abysses, and chasms. In the same book he had published, under the heading "Sequels Are Barred," his grimly hilarious epitaph on an unfortunate artist who had found a successful "formula for drawing comic rabbits," only to discover that "in the end he could not change the tragic habits / This formula for drawing comic rabbits made." In the end, Graves, repeating his conjuring tricks, did tend to write semiformulaic sequels. His characteristic failures come when he is too rationally or technically reined in or when he succumbs to repetition and abstraction. Too often he tells rather than shows, so that despite his deserved reputation as a love poet, the later lyrics only sporadically make the reader feel the passion Graves asserts. And whereas he had, in *On English Poetry*, noted that the truth of poetry "flashes out with the surprise and shock of a broken electric circuit," and made surprise a notable element in his early and middle poems, the later ones seem sometimes so predictable that their end is in their beginning.

And yet, even granted this falling off, Graves remained a craftsman rather than a mere technician. Such late pieces as "Tilth" and "A Poisoned Day"—two poems having only brevity and flawlessness in common—remind the reader that Graves has, in every period, written mini-lyrics as unimprovable as any in the language: "Love Without Hope" and "Sick Love" in the 1920s, "Thief" and "On Portents" in the 1930s, "She Tells Her Love While Half Asleep" in the 1940s, "A Plea to Boys and Girls" in the 1950s. To be sure, the second half of the final collection contains too many short, repetitive poems, dozens of which could and should have been sacrificed to make room for the best of the poems deleted over the years: "Recalling War," "Saint," "The Clipped Stater," "Virgil the Sorcerer," "The Worms of History," "The Challenge," "The Felloe'd Year," "Hotel Bed," and "The Destroyers," to mention several of the most regrettable decanonizations. Fortunately, a variorum edition of Graves's poetry is planned. In the meantime, not even his own distortion of his canon can diminish Graves's genuine accomplishment. If we can meaningfully speak of "Lycidas" as a "long short poem," then it can also make sense to conclude that Robert Graves is likely to be remembered as a "major minor poet"—a craftsman who often succeeded in fusing his experience of love and his love of art into what a minor major poet, Hart Crane, once called the silken, skilled transmemberment of song.

Robert Graves, 30 May 1973 (BBC Hulton)

Recordings:

Robert Graves Reading His Own Poems (Argo and Listen);

Robert Graves Reading His Own Poetry and The White Goddess (Caedmon);
The Rubáiyát of Omar Khayyám (Spoken Arts).

Other:

The English Ballad, edited, with an introduction and critical notes, by Graves (London: Benn, 1927; revised edition, Melbourne, London & Toronto: Heinemann, 1957); republished as *English and Scottish Ballads* (New York: Macmillan, 1957);

John Skelton (Laureate), edited, with a note, by Graves (London: Benn, 1927);

The Less Familiar Nursery Rhymes, edited, with a foreword, by Graves (London: Benn, 1927);

The Real David Copperfield, condensed by Graves (London: Barker, 1933); republished as *David Copperfield, by Charles Dickens, Condensed by Robert Graves*, edited by Merrill P. Paine (New York & Chicago: Harcourt, Brace, 1934);

Frank Richards, *Old Soldiers Never Die*, rewritten by Graves (London: Faber & Faber, 1933);

Richards, *Old-Soldier Sahib*, rewritten by Graves (London: Faber & Faber, 1936; New York: Smith & Haas, 1936);

The Comedies of Terence, edited, with a foreword, by Graves (Garden City: Doubleday, 1962; London: Cassell, 1963).

Translations:

Georg Schwartz, *Almost Forgotten Germany*, translated by Graves and Laura Riding (Deyá, Majorca: Seizin Press / London: Constable, 1936);

Lucius Apuleius, *The Transformations of Lucius, Otherwise Known as The Golden Ass* (Harmondsworth: Penguin, 1950; New York: Farrar, Straus & Young, 1951);

Manuel de Jesús Galván, *The Cross and The Sword* (Bloomington: Indiana University Press, 1955; London: Gollancz, 1956);

Pedro Antonio de Alarcon, *The Infant with the Globe* (London: Trianon Press, 1955; New York & London: Yoseloff, 1955);

George Sand, *Winter in Majorca*, with José Quadrado's *Refutation of George Sand* (London: Cassell, 1956);

Lucan Pharsalia, *Dramatic Episodes of the Civil War* (Harmondsworth: Penguin, 1956; Baltimore: Penguin, 1957);

Suetonius, *The Twelve Caesars* (Harmondsworth: Penguin, 1956; Baltimore: Penguin, 1957);

The Anger of Achilles: Homer's Iliad (Garden City: Doubleday, 1959; London: Cassell, 1960);

The Rubáiyát of Omar Khayyám, translated by Graves and Omar Ali-Shah (London: Cassell, 1967);

The Song of Songs (New York: Potter, 1973; London: Collins, 1973).

Letters:

In Broken Images: Selected Letters of Robert Graves, edited by Paul O'Prey (London: Hutchinson, 1982).

Bibliographies:

Fred H. Higginson, *A Bibliography of the Works of Robert Graves* (London: Vane, 1966; Hamden, Conn.: Archon, 1966);

John Woodrow Presley, "Addenda to F. H. Higginson's *Bibliography of the Works of Robert Graves*," *Papers of the Bibliographical Society of America*, 69 (1975): 568-569;

A. S. G. Edwards and Diane Tolomeo, "Robert Graves: A Check-List of His Publications, 1965-74," *Malahat Review*, 35 (1975): 168-179;

Anthony S. G. Edwards, "Further Addenda to Higginson: The Bibliography of Robert Graves," *Papers of the Bibliographic Society of America*, 71 (1977): 374-378; 75 (1981): 210-211;

Ellsworth Mason, "Emendations and Extensions of the Bibliography of Robert Graves," *Analytical and Enumerative Bibliography*, 2 (1978): 265-315.

Biography:

Martin Seymour-Smith, *Robert Graves, A Literary Biography* (London: Hutchinson, 1982).

References:

J. M Cohen, *Robert Graves* (Edinburgh: Oliver & Boyd, 1960; New York: Grove, 1961);

Douglas Day, *Swifter Than Reason: The Poetry and Criticism of Robert Graves* (Chapel Hill: University of North Carolina Press, 1963);

D. J. Enright, *Robert Graves and the Decline of Modernism* (Singapore: University of Malaya, 1960); republished in *Essays in Criticism*, 2 (1961): 319-336;

Jean-Paul Forster, *Robert Graves et la dualité du réel* (Berne: Herbert Lang / Francfort: Peter Lang, 1975);

G. S. Fraser, "The Poetry of Robert Graves," in his *Essays on Twentieth Century Poets* (Leicester: Leicester University Press, 1977);

Ronald Gaskell, "The Poetry of Robert Graves," *Critical Quarterly*, 3 (1961): 213-222;

Daniel Hoffman, *Barbarous Knowledge: Myth in the Poetry of Yeats, Graves, and Muir* (New York:

Oxford University Press, 1967);
Randall Jarrell, "Graves and the White Goddess," in his *The Third Book of Criticism* (New York: Farrar, Straus & Giroux, 1966);
Patrick J. Keane, *A Wild Civility: Interactions in the Poetry and Thought of Robert Graves* (Columbia & London: University of Missouri Press, 1980);
Michael Kirkham, *The Poetry of Robert Graves* (New York: Oxford University Press, 1969);
Malahat Review, special Graves issue, edited by Robin Skelton and William David Thomas, 35 (1975);
James S. Mehoke, *Robert Graves: Peace-Weaver* (The Hague: Mouton, 1975);
Sydney Musgrove, *The Ancestry of "The White Goddess"* (Auckland, New Zealand: University of Auckland Press, 1962);
Martin Seymour-Smith, *Robert Graves* (London: Longmans, Green, 1956);
Seymour-Smith, "Robert Graves," in his *Guide to Modern World Literature* (New York: Funk & Wagnalls, 1973), pp. 244-247;
Shenandoah, special Graves issue, 13 (1962);
Katherine Snipes, *Robert Graves* (New York: Ungar, 1979);
Monroe K. Spears, "The Latest Graves: Poet and Private Eye," *Sewanee Review*, 73 (1965): 660-678;
George Stade, *Robert Graves* (New York: Columbia University Press, 1967);
George Steiner, "The Genius of Robert Graves," *Kenyon Review*, 22 (1960): 340-365;
John B. Vickery, *Robert Graves and the White Goddess* (Lincoln: University of Nebraska Press, 1972).

Papers:

An extensive collection of papers—letters, worksheets, and a 1,546-page autograph diary covering 1935-1939—is housed in the Graves Manuscript Collection at the University of Victoria, British Columbia. Other Graves papers are in the Lockwood Memorial Library, State University of New York at Buffalo; the Berg Collection of the New York City Library; the Humanities Research Center of the University of Texas, Austin; and the University of Southern Illinois, Carbondale.

David Jones

(1 November 1895-28 October 1974)

Vincent B. Sherry, Jr.
Villanova University

BOOKS: *In Parenthesis* (London: Faber & Faber, 1937; New York: Chilmark, 1962);
The Anathemata: fragments of an attempted writing (London: Faber & Faber, 1952; New York: Chilmark, 1963);
Epoch and Artist: Selected Writings, edited by Harman Grisewood (London: Faber & Faber, 1959; New York: Chilmark, 1963);
The Fatigue (Cambridge: Rampant Lions, 1965);
The Tribune's Visitation (London: Fulcrum, 1969);
An Introduction to the Rime of the Ancient Mariner (London: Clover Hill, 1972);
The Sleeping Lord and other fragments (London: Faber & Faber, 1974; New York: Chilmark, 1974);
The Kensington Mass (London: Agenda Editions, 1975);
Use & Sign (Ipswich: Golgonooza Press, 1975);
The Dying Gaul and other writings, edited by Grisewood (London & Boston: Faber & Faber, 1978);
Introducing David Jones: a selection of his writings, edited by John Matthias (London & Boston: Faber & Faber, 1980);
The Roman Quarry and other sequences, edited by Grisewood and Rene Hague (London: Agenda Editions, 1981).

David Jones seemed to enter the company of major modern poets when, at a 1937 reception for the publication of his first work, the book-length poem based on his experience in World War I, William Butler Yeats rose from the crowd and in-

David Jones, 1 November 1965 (Mark Gerson)

toned: "I salute the author of *In Parenthesis*." Later T. S. Eliot, in a "Note of Introduction" to the second edition (1961) of *In Parenthesis*, included David Jones with Ezra Pound, James Joyce, and himself in the inner circle of modernist writers. But as late as 1980 it was necessary to entitle a selection of his poetry *Introducing David Jones*. As the youngest member of his literary generation, and the slowest to have his work published, Jones has been late in gaining popular recognition. He lived largely apart from the public literary world, pursuing in seclusion his other crafts of painting and engraving and lettering, illustrating his books, and writing theoretical essays on history and religion, art and literature. But he is increasingly regarded as an important, innovative poet, who has extended and refined the techniques of literary modernism.

David Michael Jones was born outside London at Brockley in Kent, the youngest of three children to an English mother, Alice Ann Bradshaw Jones, and Welsh father, James Jones, who instilled in his son an enthusiasm for Welsh culture and history. He left grammar school in 1909 and entered Camberwell School of Art, which, if nothing else, reinforced his aversion to becoming a "commercial artist." But the outbreak of war took away the immediate need of earning a living. He first tried to enlist in the Artists' Rifles, "was rejected as deficient in expansion of chest," and subsequently joined the Royal Welch Fusiliers. Siegfried Sassoon and Robert Graves served as officers in the same regiment, but Jones, who remained at the rank of private throughout the war, never made their acquaintance. He served in Flanders from December 1915 through June 1916 and received a leg wound at the Somme in July 1916. He returned in October to the northern front, where he remained until March 1918, when he was evacuated with a severe case of trench fever. As a soldier he labeled himself "a knocker-over of piles, a parade's despair," but the war was undoubtedly the most important experience of his life. Later he felt that "the particular Waste Land that was the forward area of the West Front had a permanent effect upon me and has affected my work in all sorts of ways"—for example, a painting strategy taken from positional warfare: "I like looking out on to the world from a reasonably sheltered position."

Jones reentered art school at Westminster on a government grant in 1919. Lacking direction, for a while he considered reenlisting for the Archangel expedition against the new Bolshevik regime. In January 1921 he visited Ditchling Common in Sussex, a guild of Catholic artists and workmen under the direction of Eric Gill, the polemical essayist and sculptor. His regimen of work and prayer, and the religious, sacramental importance given to art at Ditchling, appealed deeply to Jones. He entered the Catholic church in September 1921 and joined Ditchling Common in January 1922. Gill hoped to "knock some corners off him," but Jones was unable to acquire the workmanlike behavior of the guild. Gill thought of the artist's table as an altar for an offering to God, but on his table Jones mounted a heap of books, discarded brushes, and paint cans with crushed cigarette ends in them. He failed to learn carpentry, and he kept chaotic accounts. But he finally learned and mastered the trade of engraving, which admitted him to Ditchling Common and earned the greater part of his living until 1933. He lived with the Gill family (he was engaged for a while to Gill's second daughter) until 1924 at Ditchling, then until 1927 at Capel-y-ffin in the Black Mountains on the Welsh border. Here he met René Hague, master printer and typesetter for his books, commentator on his work, correspondent, and later editor of his letters. Periodically he would visit a Benedictine monastery at Caldey Island, Pembrokeshire, and his parents' cottage by the sea at Portslade, Sussex.

Jones's poetry is thoroughly modernist in practice: highly allusive, discontinuous, a juxtaposition of "fragments" drawn from history and literary culture and his own experience. And, following his experience, the poetry pictures man in the two images of soldier and artist. Although soldiers inflict and endure unreasonable hardships, they possess a fundamental dignity based on a Christian acceptance of suffering. But man is first of all a maker of art (*maker* is a term from Gill's workshop). Art, as Jones's impractical temperament would have it, is essentially gratuitous, intransitive; it serves no social purpose; it is, ideally, a free hymn of praise to God, and as such resembles the gift offerings of sacrament.

Jones began writing *In Parenthesis* while visiting his parents' cottage in 1928. In early 1929, he rejoined the Gill family at Pigotts, a large farmhouse in Buckinghamshire, where he worked with Gill on printing and engraving until 1933. Few letters survive from these years; it was a fertile but feverish period; he completed sixty paintings in 1930 alone. Straining to finish *In Parenthesis* brought on the first of his nervous breakdowns in the early autumn of 1933. A London neurologist diagnosed the problem as "shell-shock," a delayed reaction to the war; to Jones it evinced the "neurasthenia" of the war generation. The doctor sent him on a Mediterranean cruise to Cairo and Jerusalem in the spring of 1934. Improvement was surprisingly quick; by the second day out of port he was playing shuffleboard and deck tennis and enjoying the sea air.

He returned to England in the summer of 1934 to complete *In Parenthesis*. His income was less secure since, in 1933, he had abandoned engraving. The only regular paycheck Jones had in fact ever drawn was from the army; he could never force himself to work for money alone. His parents now regularly supplemented the small amount he earned from the occasional sale of a painting. He lived alternately as a guest at the Yorkshire home of Helen Sutherland, an art collector and later his personal patron, and in Sidmouth at the Fort Hotel.

In Sidmouth Jones received regular visits from Prudence Pelham, daughter of Lady Chichester. His relationship with her was undoubtedly the most important relationship with a woman in his life. Her vivacity remedied his depressions. She darned his socks, made him gifts ranging from money to filched pewter teapots, supplied him with books, and gave suggestions for the final revisions of *In Parenthesis*. Jones had drawn a map of the Flanders front to aid his memory in writing; it bears page references to the manuscript before and after revisions, and shows that nearly fifty pages were deleted in 1935. He also saw the need now to provide notes for the text, in the manner of Eliot's *The Waste Land*. These thirty-four pages of notes discuss esoteric details of trench warfare or explain the allusions and symbolism. He rewrote his preface several times, and he made drawings for a frontispiece and endpiece. The frontispiece depicts a soldier in a racked, sacrificial posture, his uniform askew and one boot missing—the last detail a comic private reference to the night an artillery attack caught Jones sleeping with one boot off. As late as 1936 he and Hague wished to have the book printed in folio columns, a newspaper format that was probably meant to emphasize its documentary quality. The manuscript was presented to Faber and Faber through Eliot early in 1937, and it was published in June 1937.

The narrative of *In Parenthesis* follows the experience of Jones's platoon from disembarkation in November 1915 to the Somme battle in July 1916, where John Ball, Jones's counterpart, is wounded in the leg and his whole platoon annihilated. The book is divided into seven parts, each bearing a title and a quotation from the sixth-century Welsh heroic poem *Y Gododdin*. The parallel with this earlier work provides a kind of epic perspective on the action and has caused the book to be called "a modern epic" by many critics.

But *In Parenthesis* eludes even the simple categories of novel or poem. Long sections of prose are interspersed with verse—and Jones provided no help by referring to the book only as a "writing." Like a novel, *In Parenthesis* has characters, the members of John Ball's platoon, who live, develop, interrelate, and ultimately die. As in most novels, the narrator occasionally adopts their perspectives to intensify the action, and John Ball adds a special personal dimension through frequent flashbacks and interior monologues. At the same time, *In Parenthesis* is unmistakably poetic in its language, a cadenced prose that breaks naturally into verse. The ritual quality of military life, which suggests a Christian analogy to Jones and thus a whole religious vision to mitigate the suffering of war, lends cadence to the language. The poetry is descriptive and dramatic by turns. The rhythmical evocation of events is punctuated by the dramatic speech of soldiers, whose army cockney, to Jones's ear at least, "reached real poetry." A poetic intensity is achieved by numerous allusions to classical myth, the Bible, and the imaginary heroic literature of the past.

This imaginary past and the present meet at the center of the book, in the middle part of the middle section, where a young infantryman, "Dai Greatcoat," rises to speak a "Boast" in the manner of ancient heroic poetry. His set of adventures includes the major conflicts of Western history, legend, and myth. He is a kind of Universal Soldier, who testifies to the eternal reality of war. But his boast differs from the vaunts of heroes like Achilles and Hector. He sees himself as much a passive instrument as an agent of force—"I was the spear in Balin's hand / that made waste King Pellam's land"—a paradox that reflects the modern soldier's passive role in the new technological warfare.

Several reviews in the popular press joked about the recondite contents of "Davy Jones's Locker," but the first 1500 copies of *In Parenthesis* sold quickly, and a second impression of 1000 was made in 1938. The *Sunday Times* and most literary journals proclaimed it highly. Herbert Read, writing for the *London Mercury* (July 1937), found it "as near a great epic of the war as ever the war generation will reach," displaying "the noble ardour of the *Chanson de Roland* and the rich cadences of the *Morte d'Arthur*." Eliot called it "a work of genius." With the publication of the second British (1961) and first American (1962) editions, Stephen Spender wrote for the *New York Times Book Review* (15 April 1962) that this "monumental elegy of World War I" had been too long neglected. *In Parenthesis* has since remained continuously in print.

Until 1939, Jones continued to live at the Yorkshire home of Helen Sutherland and in Sidmouth at the Fort Hotel. When visiting London, he stayed in Chelsea with his friend Thomas Burns, editor of the *Tablet*. He received small royalties from the sale of *In Parenthesis*, and occasionally there came a windfall like the Hawthornden Prize for *In Parenthesis* (£100) in 1938. But his anxiety about money increased constantly in the years before and during World War II. After the death of his mother in 1937, he depended more and more on the generosity of his friends. By 1939 he was relying on a monthly check from Helen Sutherland, gifts from the collector James Ede, and the proceeds of a fund organized by Kenneth Clark to benefit Jones and several other artists. His stubborn refusal now to sell his paintings—he needed to be surrounded by his work, he claimed, in order to see the "direction" it was taking—lay at the root of his troubles. The news of Prudence Pelham's marriage in early 1939 injected a new tension. "Human relationships are so heart-rending in a way," he confided to James Ede in a letter: "I love her very much and our friendship has meant everything to me. So naturally, however much this may be 'a good thing,' I've naturally had a twisting, trying to get all the tangled delicate emotional bits and pieces tied up and sorted out. I only tell you this because of the intimate friendship we have and I wanted to tell you. *It is all private to you and Helen. I'm sure you'll understand that.*" (Jones's emphasis.) It was probably the radical disorder of his personal life and finances that caused him, in 1939, to flirt briefly with the program for order in *Mein Kampf* (1924). He would later maintain that fellow feelings for the German-front fighters in World War I had led him to dismiss the "reports of Nazi cruelty and nihilism as propaganda, like the stories of soldiers crucified on hay ricks in the Great War." In any case, he perceived the error before the outbreak of war. To correct himself he tried to become absorbed in his art.

Shortly after finishing *In Parenthesis*, Jones had started a work provisionally titled "The Book of Balaam's Ass," a medley of voices and anecdotes in the freewheeling style of soldiers' postwar conversations. It lacked the narrative element of *In Parenthesis*, however, and could not achieve even the coherence of continuity. He abandoned it after struggling with it for several years. At the same time he began his second book-length poem, *The Anathemata*, as a series of experimental "fragments," which would not be completed and published until 1952.

In 1940 Jones returned to London to be near his aging father. Thomas Burns had gone to work at the British embassy in Madrid, and he allowed Jones to live in his Chelsea home until it would be sold. The impermanence and solitude at Chelsea, in addition to his unrelieved financial worries, brought about a relapse of his nervous disorder in 1941. A doctor's certificate disqualifying him from Industrial Service reads:

> In 1932 [1933] he had a nervous breakdown and developed symptoms of mental depression—a depressive psychosis. The condition was severe. The course has been marked by improvement with relapses.
>
> He has been unfit for consecutive work in his own profession for nearly ten years. He is unstable, and under stress of duty would relapse.

He declined treatment for his condition, however, and moved to Sheffield Terrace, in Kensington, where he remained through the duration of the war. His finances continued to be unpredictable. Finally, in June 1944, Ede devised a scheme which, although it did not change the source of his income, at least remedied the uncertainty of its arrival. A number of friends and admirers would pay sums

Frontispiece by Jones for In Parenthesis

regularly into Jones's bank account, and he would reward the donors with paintings or inscriptions at his own discretion. These stipends allowed him to continue work on the fragments of *The Anathemata* through the war.

While staying with Sutherland in the summer of 1946, Jones suffered the last and most serious of his nervous breakdowns. He would later recall that "the main symptom was being frightened. The Bible often mentions men's knees knocking together; it was really like that; it was worse when I was at home; . . ." His friends put him under psychiatric care at Bowden House, a nursing home at Harrow-on-the-Hill, where he remained until late 1947. He seemed to respond quickly and enthusiastically to the "frontal attack" of psychoanalysis. The doctors required him to confront his problems in written form, and he composed long passages on matters related to his condition. He tried to explain his personal neurosis as the problem of every artist in the modern technological world: they must experience a neurotic conflict between utile and gratuitous things. Another cause of neurosis lay in his lack of social status; he was afraid of being an outsider, even an imposter, in the upper-class world of his patrons. But he denied any sexual element in his neurosis, asserting that his failure to marry did not derive from any fear of sex, rather, that the artistic vocation can be a calling to a single life.

By the end of 1947, Jones had recovered sufficiently to move into a room in Northwick Lodge, a residential hotel in Harrow. Here, in a bay window overlooking the hill, his painting flourished. He also drafted many of the essays collected later in *Epoch and Artist* (1959) and *The Dying Gaul and other writings* (1978). He completed the project of writing and rewriting, arranging and rearranging the fragments of *The Anathemata*, which in 1951 Eliot persuaded him to publish with Faber and Faber. Jones composed footnotes, which he now included with the text, and wrote a long preface on the situation of the modern artist. He also supervised the reproduction in halftones of seven inscriptions, one painting, and one woodcut, and he did the inscriptional lettering for the cover.

The Anathemata tells the history of man-as-artist and his artifacts (his anathemata) and in a parallel fashion relates the historical development of British culture. Although history is not treated in linear sequence—there is a modernist mosaiclike organization of fragments—the poem's eight parts interrelate in various ways. Part one follows the development of early man as artist, and part two, in roughly chronological form, views the emergence of the first Mediterranean cultures and traces the voyages of early tin traders to Britain. The motif of the sea voyage then links the middle sections of the poem (parts three-six), where ships reach the site of London variously in Anglo-Saxon, Victorian, late medieval, and early Britonic times. Different world cultures thus penetrate into the island. The last two sections celebrate the activity of the Catholic Mass and return the poem to its thematic center. Man's artifacts resemble sacramental offerings to God; the priest lifting the wafer of bread in the Mass is the supreme artist. The Mass also serves as the unifying occasion of the poem, which begins with the scene of a priest consecrating the bread and ends, 194 pages later, with the elevation of the sacrament. The Mass thus provides a kind of infinite moment; its sacrament is the timeless archetype of all the artifacts catalogued in the poem. Jones always regarded *The Anathemata* as a more sophisticated work than *In Parenthesis*; the conception of art as sacrament dictates the shape of the later poem, whereas the war book follows the simpler pattern of narrative.

The poem's overriding sacramental metaphor also establishes a liturgical tone and incantatory quality for the poetic voice, but the style, like that of *In Parenthesis*, defies simple classification. Prose mingles with verse, and the mode shifts from epic to lyric, from historical chronicle to dramatic monologue. Jones makes a concerted attempt at dramatic immediacy: in the preface he asks the reader to speak the poem aloud; his own lyric voice frequently pierces the text; and there are several dramatic monologues by different historical personages. The longest of the poem's eight parts, the fifth, is the dramatic monologue of "The Lady of the Pool," a lavender seller in late-medieval London, who seems to live in an eternal present, having "entertained" the captains of most of the voyages to the island. Jones felt that the dramatic monologue "showed the way to make the past part of the Now," and the lady, like Dai Greatcoat in *In Parenthesis*, gives her strong speaking presence and character-in-voice to the materials of history and myth. But the poem's subject and vocabulary may seem remote and difficult. The diction bristles with foreign languages, and recondite words can create the impression of verbal density.

None of the poem's initial reviewers failed to notice its difficulty; some could see nothing else. Hayden Carruth, writing for the *Partisan Review* (September-October 1953), labeled it a "devastating conclusion" to the kind of difficult poetry cultivated by the modernists. The *Times Literary Supplement* saw "too many arcane allusions for a reader to grasp the meaning within its magic." Even W. H. Auden and T. S. Eliot, both of whom praised the poem categorically, worried so much about its difficulty that they produced long and detailed (and contradictory) instructions on how to deal with the notes. Most critics, however, echoed Auden's judgment in *Encounter* (February 1954) that "it is one of the most important poems of our time." Winfield Townley Scott, Kathleen Raine, and Emyr Humphreys all accepted its difficulty as necessary, and judged it, with Harman Grisewood, who reviewed the poem for the *Dublin Review* (Autumn 1952), "a major work of poetic innovation." Jones particularly liked Kathleen Raine's assessment, in the *New Statesman* (22 November 1952), of the poem's "obscurity": "Such is the paradox of our time that the more a poet draws on objective tradition, the less on subjective experiences, the more obscure he will seem." A number of misprints resulting from unusual and foreign words were corrected in the second British edition of 1955. *The Anathemata* won the Russell Loines Memorial Award of the American National Institute of Arts and Letters in 1954—the first non-American work to do so—and an American edition followed in 1963.

Jones remained at Northwick Lodge until 1964, when its demolition forced him to move into Monksdene Hotel, also at Harrow-on-the-Hill, where he lived until 1970. No serious nervous relapse occurred in this period, and his financial circumstances were improving. In connection with Ede's financial scheme, he now regularly produced inscriptional poems for the important occasions in his friends' lives, for example, a river-marriage poem in Welsh for the wedding of Welsh friends, a blessing in Latin for a baptism or confirmation. Prudence Pelham left him a legacy at her death (from disseminated sclerosis) in 1952 to supplement the income he received through Ede's plan. In 1964, when Helen Sutherland left him £ 6000, his assets were sufficient for Ede to arrange a guaranteed annuity. At the age of sixty-eight Jones had attained a degree of secure comfort. He received a growing number of visitors in his room at Harrow. Although he welcomed the conversation, his own speech was often painfully deliberate and tentative; he seemed to struggle with "the complication of what he has to say and the desire to get it exactly right." A new visitor had to learn not to fill a pause in the discussion with a new topic (one "asked 'Did you ever meet Chesterton?' between 'ap— ' and '—palling' "). His famous visitors included W. H. Auden, who, Jones would later confide, could never stop talking, and Igor Stravinsky, who would always remember the sight of Jones swaying to and fro in his chair, listening to a Gregorian chant on a portable gramophone he kept beneath his bed. His letters became longer; they took on the decorative quality of his inscriptions, done in different inks to create beautiful polychromatic effects.

The letters were also becoming discursive in a way that reflected his increasing attention to essay writing. Harman Grisewood collected about twenty-five essays under the title *Epoch and Artist* in 1959. These were divided into four subjects: Welsh culture, the religious quality of art, early British history, and contemporary art and literature. The volume drew fire from Frank Kermode, who considered the attempt to view art as sacrament a backward step, "a kind of atavism, an inability to think, however sophisticatedly, in any but primitivistic terms." But Harold Rosenberg of the *New Yorker* (22 August 1964) claimed that the essays were fully alive to contemporary aesthetic problems, judging them "the most acutely relevant writing on contemporary form and value to have appeared in years." Jones's concern about the validity of traditional symbols and the fading awareness of history was, according to Rosenberg, legitimate and necessary. Rosenberg also perceived "the difference between him and the usual elegist of cultural decline: while conscious of being surrounded by modern decadence, instead of devoting himself to denouncing examples of it, he takes pleasure in the questions the decadence raises for him." This acclaim expressed the interest and admiration of an audience that had grown since the republication of *In Parenthesis* in a Viking Compass edition in 1963; the Viking edition of *The Anathemata* in 1965 expanded the readership further. Jones felt increasingly grateful to his American readers, "chaps who are *far* more receptive, willing to worry-out the meaning of a thing, more generous, naive—yes, perhaps, but more open, yes, more perceptive, not so inhibited and

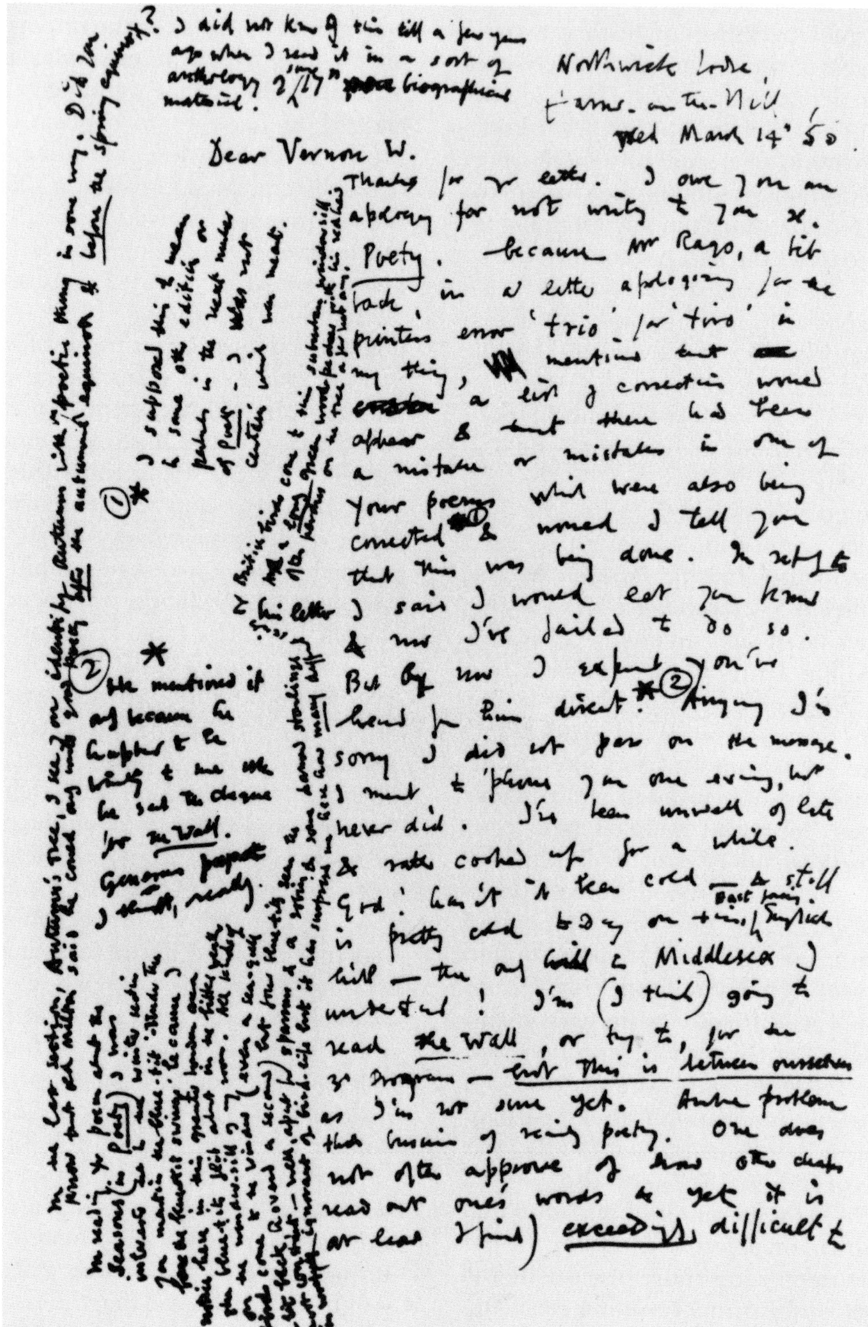
Northwick Lodge, Harrow-on-the-Hill, Wed March 14 '56.

Dear Vernon W.

Thanks for yr letter. I owe you an apology for not writing to you ... Poetry. because Mr Rago, a bit back, in a letter apologizing for the printers error 'trio' for 'tiro' in my thing, mentioned that a list of corrections would appear & that there had been a mistake or mistakes in one of your poems which were also being corrected & would I tell you that this was being done. ... I said I would let you know & now I've failed to do so. But by now I expect you've heard from him direct. Anyway I'm sorry I did not pass on the message. I meant to 'phone you one evening, but never did. I've been unwell of late & rather cooped up for a while. God! hasn't it been cold — & still is pretty cold today on this ... hill — ... in Middlesex I understand! I'm (I think) going to read the Wall, or try to, for the ... programme — but this is between ourselves as I'm not sure yet. Another problem that business of reading poetry. One does not often approve of how other chaps read out ones words & yet it is (at least I find) exceedingly difficult to

Letter from Jones to Vernon Watkins, 14 March 1956

unresponsive as the English— . . ."

In March 1970 Jones fell, broke his leg, and suffered a slight nondebilitating stroke. From the hospital he went to Calvary Nursing Home, also at Harrow, where he continued to write and revise the group of shorter poems collected and published as *The Sleeping Lord* in March 1974. His careful editing and shaping of these pieces becomes clear when one looks at the poetic manuscripts, published in 1981 as *The Roman Quarry and other sequences*, edited by Harman Grisewood and René Hague. Several of the "fragments" in *The Sleeping Lord* (all but the last are complete dramatic or lyric units) date from the early 1940s; others, like the title poem, were written as late as 1967. A special issue of *Agenda* in 1967 had collected six of these poems; two others, published in 1965 and 1969 in limited editions (*The Fatigue* and *The Tribune's Visitation*), and an excerpt from "The Book of Balaam's Ass," completed the collection. As with *In Parenthesis* and *The Anathemata*, Jones supervised the layout and typography of the book, attempting to balance prose and verse on the page. He also designed the cover and reproduced the inscriptions he had made for the two limited editions.

Excluding the introductory lyric and the final piece from "The Book of Balaam's Ass," the poems fall into two contrasting groups: four dramatic monologues by Roman soldiers in Jerusalem, hearkening back to Jones's own visit while recovering in 1934, and three lyric invocations of Celtic antiquity, derived from early Celtic myth and literature. In "The Wall" and "The Dream of Private Clitus," perplexed Roman legionnaires complain from their outpost of the empire about the decay of the founding myths of the Roman republic. In "The Fatigue," a Roman principalis (equivalent to sergeant) directs the military detail for the crucifixion of Christ; although he realizes the implications of the event, the jaded mood of imperial decadence prevails against his conversion. A tribune surprises his soldiers in their garrison in "The Tribune's Visitation"; the officer confesses his private dismay at the corruption of the original innocence of Rome. The speakers in "The Wall" and the audience for the other Roman poems are all legionnaires of mixed provincial recruitment—German and Celtic as well as Roman—and demonstrate as such the heterogeneous nature of the empire, the problems of a political order removed from its local origins. By contrast, the Celtic poems praise the virtues of local, rooted culture. "The Tutelar of the Place" celebrates the spirit of place in the person of a female "tutelar," an earth goddess who protects those of her own "place, time, demarcation, hearth, kin, enclosure" against the encroachment of a Roman Empire or a modern megalopolis. "The Hunt," which is based on the episode of Arthur's chasing the fabulous beast Trywth, invokes the sanctity of Welsh places, viewing Arthur as a Christ who rides and dies for the healing of the land. The longest of the Celtic poems is "The Sleeping Lord," which envisions Arthur asleep beneath the landscape of modern Wales. Like Joyce's Finn asleep beneath Dublin, or Williams's Paterson under the city that bears his name, Arthur waits to be awakened to restore Wales to its ancient inheritance.

The artistry of voice and characterization may be the most striking features of the last poems. The Roman speakers reach a condensed bitter eloquence to fit their disenchantment. A new contemporary accent falls here too; into the Roman monologues Jones dubs the idiom of the modern cockney army. This joking anachronism may be traced back to the cockney speech he heard in the streets of Jerusalem under the British Mandate, but it also conveys the similarity he perceives between the late empire and the twentieth century. The Celtic poems, thick with references to Welsh geography and history and legend, also employ the formulaic language of early Welsh poetry. "The Sleeping Lord," for instance, is spoken in great part through the persona of the Welsh bard stationed in Arthur's household to deliver his funeral eulogy.

The characterization of the old poet in "The Sleeping Lord" might afford an antagonistic critic a portrait of Jones himself as an aging poet:

> But now that he was many winters old, the diverse nature of what he had read had become sadly intermeddled and very greatly confused.

Philip Toynbee, for example, labeled Jones "an eccentric figure on the periphery of English poetry." Critics in the United States and Britain, however, generally welcomed the new work. Peter Scupham, in the *New Statesman* (24 May 1974), praised the new "open dramatic quality running through the book." In the *Spectator* (4 May 1974), Seamus Heaney acclaimed Jones "an extraordinary writer," who has "returned to the origin and brought something back, something to enrich not only the language but people's consciousness of who they have been and who they consequently are." Reviewing the book in *Poetry* (January 1975), John Matthias outlined an intelligent American response to Jones, a response

David Jones, 1964 (Mark Gerson)

"conditioned by an encounter in his work with sheer *otherness*, things otherwise opaque made numinous by the craft of the maker. . . . In remembering, and in encountering things other, we are changed."

In 1973, *Agenda* commissioned Jones to write a poem for a second special issue. He resumed work on "The Kensington Mass," which he had begun in the early 1940s but subsequently lost, and it was published as a "work in progress" in 1974. In 1975, Agenda Editions brought out a soft-cover edition of the poem, including a series of manuscript drafts. These reveal Jones building his repetitive incantatory syntax by layers, draft by draft; the poem takes shape like a clay model built up by a sculptor's hand. He continued to work on the poem until his death on 28 October 1974.

The *Times* obituary of 29 October repeated the comparison frequently drawn between David Jones and William Blake. Both were painters and poets; both were unusual and difficult artists to their contemporaries; both would belatedly receive the fame they deserved. The number of full-length critical studies of Jones steadily grows, and there are chapbooks ranging from personal appreciations to detailed explications. Scholarly articles investigate various aspects of his work. Jones's diversity of interests also invites treatment by historians and theologians, and the very difficulty of closing categories around him allows him to keep company with most major modern writers. Disapproving critics have always been the exception. But as yet there exists no definitive critical work, like Northrop Frye's study of Blake or Richard Ellmann's writing on Joyce, to establish and, at least temporarily, to direct critical interest in the new subject. The title of Jones's last book of poetry is mildly prophetic. Like the Sleeping Lord beneath the treasures of Wales, Jones's achievement waits, under the complex deposits of history and culture and religion, under the many layers of magic and strangeness, to be wakened and fully appreciated.

Recording:

David Jones reading from The Anathemata, In Parenthesis, *and "The Hunt,"* Argo Records (PLP 1093).

Periodical Publications:

POETRY:

"The Narrows," *Anglo-Welsh Review*, 22 (Autumn 1973): 8-12; republished in *Agenda*, 11-12 (Autumn/Winter 1973/4): 12-16.

NONFICTION:

"Langland's 'Piers Plowman,'" letter to the editor, *Listener*, 4 April 1957, pp. 563-564;

"Lost Languages," letter to the editor, *Times* (London), 20 August 1958, p. 9;

"Amends to a Prophet," letter to the editor, *Times* (London), 12 August 1961, p. 7;

"Christianity and Poetry," letter to the editor, *Times Literary Supplement*, 22 July 1965, p. 616;

"Fragments of an Attempted Autobiographical Writing," *Agenda*, 12-13 (Winter/Spring 1975): 98-108.

Letters:

David Jones: Letters to Vernon Watkins, edited by Ruth Pryor (Cardiff: University of Wales Press, 1976);

Letters to William Hayward, edited by Colin Wilcockson (London: Agenda Editions, 1979);

Dai Greatcoat: A Self-Portrait of David Jones in His Letters, edited by René Hague (London & Boston: Faber & Faber, 1980);

Letters to a Friend, edited by Aneirin Talfan Davies (Swansea: Triskele, 1980).

References:

Agenda, special Jones Issue, 5 (Spring/Summer 1967);

Agenda, special Jones issue, 11-12 (Autumn/Winter 1973/4);

Bernard Bergonzi, *Heroes' Twilight: A Study of the Literature of the Great War* (London: Constable, 1965; New York: Coward-McCann, 1965), pp. 198-212;

David Blamires, *David Jones: Artist and Writer* (Manchester: Manchester University Press, 1971; Toronto: University of Toronto Press, 1972);

William Blissett, "David Jones: 'Himself at the Cave Mouth,' " *University of Toronto Quarterly*, 36 (April 1967): 259-273;

Blissett, "*In Parenthesis* Among the War Books," *University of Toronto Quarterly*, 42 (Spring 1973): 258-288;

Blissett, *The Long Conversation: A Memoir of David Jones* (Oxford & New York: Oxford University Press, 1981);

Thomas Dilworth, "The Anagogical Form of *The Anathemata*," *Mosaic*, 12 (Winter 1979):183-195;

Dilworth, *The Liturgical Parenthesis of David Jones* (Ipswich: Golgonooza Press, 1979);

Dilworth, "The Parenthetical Liturgy of David Jones," *University of Toronto Quarterly*, 42 (Spring 1973): 241-257;

Paul Fussell, *The Great War and Modern Memory* (New York and London: Oxford University Press, 1975), pp. 144-154;

René Hague, *A Commentary on The Anathemata of David Jones* (Wellingborough, U.K.: Christopher Skelton, 1977; Toronto: University of Toronto Press, 1977);

Hague, *David Jones* (Cardiff: University of Wales Press, 1975);

Jeremy Hooker, *David Jones: An Exploratory Study of the Writings* (London: Enitharmon, 1975);

John H. Johnston, *English Poetry of the First World War* (London: Oxford University Press, 1964; Princeton: Princeton University Press, 1964), pp. 284-340;

Roland Mathias, ed., *David Jones: Eight Essays on His Work as Writer and Artist* (Llandysul, U.K.: Gomer, 1976);

Samuel Rees, *David Jones* (New York: Twayne, 1978);

Vincent B. Sherry, Jr., "David Jones's *In Parenthesis*: New Measure," *Twentieth Century Literature*, 28 (Winter 1982);

Sherry, "A New Boast for *In Parenthesis*: The Dramatic Monologue of David Jones," *Notre Dame English Journal*, 14 (Spring 1982): 113-128;

Sherry, "*The Roman Quarry* of David Jones: Extraordinary Perspectives," *Agenda*, 21 (forthcoming 1983);

Sherry, "The Roman Quarry of David Jones: Signs and Wonders," *Chesterton Review*, 9 (February 1983): 46-55;

Henry Summerfield, *An Introductory Guide to The Anathemata and the Sleeping Lord Sequence of David Jones* (Victoria: Sono Nis, 1979).

Papers:

The National Library of Wales at Aberystwyth has the manuscripts of *In Parenthesis* and *The Anathemata* as well as Jones's personal library; the Fisher Rare Book Library at the University of Toronto holds the letters to René Hague; and the Beinecke Rare Book Library at Yale University has the letters to Harman Grisewood.

Patrick Kavanagh

(21 October 1904-30 November 1967)

Catherine Cantalupo
Rutgers University

See also the Kavanagh entry in *DLB 15, British Novelists, 1930-1959.*

BOOKS: *Ploughman and Other Poems* (London: Macmillan, 1936);

The Green Fool (London: Joseph, 1938; New York: Harper, 1939);

The Great Hunger (Dublin: Cuala Press, 1942; London: MacGibbon & Kee, 1966);

A Soul for Sale (London: Macmillan, 1947);

Tarry Flynn (Dublin: Pilot Press, 1948; New York: Devin-Adair, 1949);

Recent Poems (New York: Peter Kavanagh Hand Press, 1958);

Come Dance with Kitty Stobling and Other Poems (London: Longmans, Green, 1960; Philadelphia: Dufour, 1964);

Self-Portrait (Dublin: Dolmen Press, 1964);

Collected Poems (London: MacGibbon & Kee, 1964; New York: Devin-Adair, 1964);

Collected Pruse (London: MacGibbon & Kee, 1967);

November Haggard, Uncollected Prose and Verse of Patrick Kavanagh, edited by Peter Kavanagh (New York: Peter Kavanagh Hand Press, 1971);

Complete Poems of Patrick Kavanagh, edited by Peter Kavanagh (New York: Peter Kavanagh Hand Press, 1972);

By Night Unstarred: An autobiographical novel (Curragh, Ireland: Goldsmith, 1977; New York: Peter Kavanagh Hand Press, 1978);

Love's Tortured Headland: A sequel to Lapped Furrows, edited by Peter Kavanagh (New York: Peter Kavanagh Hand Press, 1978).

Patrick Kavanagh (courtesy of Peter Kavanagh)

Patrick Kavanagh is regarded by some as one of the most influential Irish poets after Yeats. Other critics, however, consider him a provincial poet whose main achievement was to give an authentic voice to the peasant culture of rural Ireland after the so-called Irish literary renaissance had exhausted itself in clichés. From the start, Kavanagh opposed what he called the "stage-Irish lie," which seemed to him to perpetuate vulgar, ignorant, and dishonest art. His early poems faithfully represent the native landscape and people, with a jealous ear for local speech and a tremulous passion for the poetic vocation. Critics generally fault his willingness to make statements and praise what Michael Allen has called his " 'parochial' vividness," in which the "ethereal literary voice incarnates itself in the imagery of the actual world," as Seamus Heaney has written. Kavanagh has in fact achieved an intelligent, robust, and ultimately mystical body of work that includes at least one great long poem, *The Great Hunger* (1942), as well as a large body of lyric and satiric poems; a novel, *Tarry Flynn* (1948); and wide-ranging critical prose.

Patrick Joseph Kavanagh was born in Inniskeen Parish, County Monaghan, Ireland, the fourth of ten children, to Bridget and James Kavanagh, a shoemaker and farmer. A second son, Peter, born in 1916, was not only Patrick's closest friend but later his finest critic and his publisher. Patrick's early truancy from school and from the shoemaker's bench, where he began to serve as an apprentice after he quit school in 1916, encouraged his parents to buy an additional piece of farmland in 1926 to ensure him a living. He was to sell it in 1949 after living most deeply off the images it inspired, as exemplified by the early, prescient "Shancoduff" (first published in *Dublin Magazine* in July 1934):

'Who owns them hungry hills
That the water-hen and snipe must have
forsaken?
A poet? Then by heavens he must be poor'
I hear and is my heart not badly shaken?

From the age of twelve he read and wrote poetry as avidly as circumstances permitted since his was the self-described "usual barbaric life of the Irish country poor" where "the real poverty was the lack of enlightenment to get out and get under the moon." By 1928 Kavanagh had achieved his first publication in the *Weekly Irish Independent*, and in 1929 AE (George Russell), then editor of the *Irish Statesman*, published his poem "The Intangible." Considering the hostility and rejection that were to become characteristic of his later reception, Kavanagh's initiation into literary life was ironically easy.

In 1929 Kavanagh's father died, leaving him the head of the family. Yet, because their farming income was supplemented by the working wages of several daughters, it was possible for Kavanagh to take off on foot for Dublin in 1930, ostensibly to visit AE, whose *Irish Statesman* had folded. Kavanagh's desire to be "A fool who eats the leavings of the Wise" (as he says in "Dreamer") was fruitful—he returned with the books of Dostoevski, Hugo, George Moore, Emerson, Melville, Whitman, Frank O'Connor, AE, and others. This visit provided his first taste of a literary culture. AE introduced Kavanagh to the editor of the *Dublin Magazine*, and after several of his poems were published in that magazine and after he made several more visits by train or bicycle, he gained a minor reputation in Dublin as the "peasant poet." By 1935 Kavanagh was writing articles for R. M. Smyllie, editor of the *Irish Times*, as well as farming, cobbling and writing poetry—all while living in Inniskeen.

Ploughman and Other Poems was published by Macmillan in 1936 as part of a new poets' series. The success of this slight book in England and Dublin, though not in Inniskeen, as well as Peter Kavanagh's urgings that he write more poetry, intensified the conflict Patrick Kavanagh had been conscious of ever since his early discovery of a "kink" in his imagination which continually isolated him from clay-mired Monaghan: "For years I had been caught between the two stools of security on the land and a rich-scented life on the exotic islands of literature." Consequently, he visited London in 1937, but the only outcome was an autobiographical account of his life up to the period of his jobless stay in London, *The Green Fool* (1938). He returned to Inniskeen reluctantly and finally moved to Dublin permanently in 1939.

Ploughman and Other Poems consists of thirty-one early lyric poems, devoid of the singsong rhythms and inversions of his apprentice verse but weakened by sentimentality and abstractness. The best poems, such as "Ploughman" and "Beech Tree," are rich in particular details of Monaghan landscape and character:

I turn the lea-green down
Gaily now,
And paint the meadow brown
With my plough.

AE's mystical influence seems to have reinforced Kavanagh's inherent tendency to mythologize the poet and the power of poetry, as in "The Intangible":

Rapt to starriness—not quite
I go through fields and fens of night,
The nameless, the void
Where ghostly poplars whisper to
A silent countryside.

But this poem embodies two tendencies which Kavanagh typically resisted: mystical abstractness, as in the phrase "rapt to starriness" and the modern timidity about making statements, about naming what Beckett called the "unnameable." In "Prelude" (written in 1954) he was to write:

If Platitude should claim a place
Do not denounce his humble face;
His sentiments are well intentioned
He has a part in the larger legend.

By that time he could admit that not every line of verse is poetry and that not all the poet's emotions are fresh, but that they have "a part in the larger legend" that constitutes truth. In *Ploughman and*

Patrick Kavanagh and Frank O'Connor in Dublin, 1931 (courtesy of Peter Kavanagh)

Other Poems "Ascetic" is most typical of Kavanagh's later mystical position, where wisdom has a humble aspect and is achieved only by incessant self-oblation:

> That in the end
> I may find
> Something not sold for a penny
> In the slums of Mind.

With reckless heterodoxy, Kavanagh sprinkled his poems with allusions to Catholic dogma; in later poems he employed religious imagery, always deeply felt, more precisely. In these early poems, however, he considers himself a "passionate pagan" ("Blind Dog"), more concerned to distinguish his ecstatic vision of creation from the conventional religious view than to assert its religious foundation.

Kavanagh had read the work of the imagists with excitement and in their freshness found enticement and discipline for his muse, as in "Tinker's Wife":

> Her face had streaks of care
> Like wires across it,
> But she was supple
> As a young goat
> On a windy hill.

In *Self-Portrait,* Kavanagh writes of this period, "Curious this, how I had started off with the right simplicity, indifferent to crude reason and then ploughed my way through complexities and anger, hatred and ill-will towards the faults of man, and came back to where I started."

Despite Kavanagh's avowal that "only in verse can one confess with dignity," *The Green Fool* (1938) is an important autobiographical novel because it evokes the simplicity of the Monaghan years and the poet's conflicting emotions toward the land. The novel is Kavanagh's most successful objective writing, rich in wit and luxuriously poetic description and lore, interspersed with muted social criticism, "hard facts in soft words." Kavanagh is the decorous yet funny entertainer here, employing the "quaint and bizarre" to good effect. This technique often approaches the Irish clichés, however, for which he later condemned the book. A libel suit brought by Oliver St. John Gogarty suppressed the book immediately (because Kavanagh had innocently written that, when he called on Gogarty, he mistook Gogarty's maid for his mistress), mooting questions of the book's worth just when it seemed capable of becoming a popular and financial success. It was not republished until 1971.

Part of Kavanagh's major long poem, *The*

Great Hunger, first appeared in *Horizon* in 1942. The Cuala Press published 250 copies later in 1942. An abridged version appeared in *A Soul for Sale* in 1947, and complete versions were published in *Collected Poems* in 1964 and *Complete Poems* in 1972. The fourteen-section poem, which Kavanagh wrote in only a few days, is, perhaps, his only major work with modernist affinities, since it tends uncharacteristically toward nihilism. Not surprisingly, it is his best-known work. As Seamus Heaney wrote, *The Great Hunger* "is the nearest Kavanagh ever gets to a grand style, one that seeks not a continuous decorum but a mixture of modes, of high and low, to accommodate his double perspective, the tragic and the emerging comic." Technical power and emotional pressure and insight converge in the poem. Nowhere else but in *Tarry Flynn* are Kavanagh's powers of observation and his intimacy with the land more evident. In the poem's protagonist, Patrick Maguire, Kavanagh created a fully developed figure, a potato farmer tied to the land and to celibacy by stupefying labor, mystifying religious ritual, and accumulating defeats of the will. The incantatory opening line, "Clay is the word and clay is the flesh," announces the engulfing materialism of that life:

> Watch him, watch him, that man on a hill whose spirit
> Is a wet sack flapping about the knees of time.
> He lives that his little fields may stay fertile when his own body
> Is spread in the bottom of a ditch under two coulters crossed in Christ's Name.

The poem works through the seasons of nature and life that find Maguire successively more tyrannized by the land and more sexually repressed. The narrative voice employs half-rhymes, abundant imagery, and symbolic connections to shape a myth of human degradation out of anger, love, and a belief in the spirit.

Introducing the radio broadcast of *The Great Hunger* in 1960, Kavanagh said that "the poem remains a tragedy because it is not completely born. Tragedy is underdeveloped comedy: tragedy fully explored becomes comedy." Indeed, the poem conveys the "twisted and twisting" life of Monaghan with unremitting realism, unbroken by comic relief, and concludes with a bitter, hopeless meditation:

> He stands in the doorway of his house
> A ragged sculpture of the wind,
> October creaks the rotted mattress,
> The bedposts fall. No hope. No lust.
> The hungry fiend
> Screams the apocalypse of clay
> In every corner of this land.

As Kavanagh wrote in an essay on Joyce, "God, through the agency of society, manages to breed a race of artists by the process of starvation and all kinds of indignity due to poverty." Kavanagh viewed his own predicament in this way. While he became increasingly frustrated by the literary opportunism and mediocrity he observed in Dublin, he nonetheless joined the literary scene at the Palace Bar, seeking work and companionship. He was given no work, but he developed a splenetically satiric view of Dublin's literary culture.

In "From Monaghan to the Grand Canal," Kavanagh writes that he had left Monaghan "with my mind filled with the importance-of-writing-and-thinking-and-feeling-like-an-Irishman." This prejudice dominated his criticism and poetry until 1947, resulting in such satiric poems as "The Wake of the Books," "The Paddiad," "Bardic Dust," and "Adventures in the Bohemian Jungle." He describes the enterprise retrospectively in "In the Beginning" as "An intellectual battle waged / Exuding the aura of a spirit outraged." Kavanagh's mastery of technique in his satirical verse is reminiscent of eighteenth-century virtuosity: "He could disburse / A fabulosity of verse" ("Sensational Disclosures!"). He parodies Austin Clarke's verse plays, mimics all sorts of journalese and public voices. Uneven line lengths and frequent counterpointing keep the poems colloquial and lively, while bold rhythms and rhymes drive the wrath and contempt along.

His best satire is intensely engaged with unmasking the moral mediocrity of the local scene, which, he admits, is subtly disguised: "That's Hell's secret, to be the mirror / For a mixture of truth and error" ("Adventures in the Bohemian Jungle"). He creates the "Devil as a Patron of Irish Letters" in "The Paddiad":

> Saintly silvery locks of hair,
> Quiet-voiced as monk at prayer;
> Every Paddy's eye is glazed
> On this fellow mouths amazed
> Quick in all his words of praise.
> O comic muse descend to see
> The devil Mediocrity

The satires are parochial verse, but they strike a universal note in their mocking of human vanity.

Throughout the 1940s and early 1950s,

Kavanagh wrote prolifically for journals and newspapers such as the *Irish Times*, the *Irish Press*, and the *Bell*. He wrote a literary column for the *Standard* in 1943 and film criticism for the same paper from February 1946 to July 1951. *Envoy* published his diary column from December 1949 to July 1951. He became a popular figure with a reputation for eccentricity, largely based on the honesty of his critical views, and was caricatured in the press. Eventually he was reviewing three to four books a week, and he took those opportunities to air his ideas about literature. At its best his criticism is underivative. He writes without pedantry but with the authority of wide reading and the unerring flash of insight. Though the visceral, catholic, and apostolic qualities of his critical prose might never appeal to a literary establishment, a knowledge of this body of work is indispensable for one who is trying to grasp the evolving unity of his thought.

In February 1947 Macmillan published Kavanagh's second book of poetry, *A Soul for Sale*. Although Kavanagh later derided its most famous poem, "Pegasus," for its "whining" tone, the poem is interesting for its technique. Understated rhymes and flattened rhythm are in tension with the inflated epic tone: "My soul was an old horse / Offered for sale in twenty fairs." Several other poems in the book masterfully mold subdued colloquial speech into expressive stanzas, as in "Bluebells for Love," one of several love poems:

> We will have other loves—or so they'll think;
> The primroses or the ferns or the briars,
> Or even the rusty paling wires,
> Or the violets on the sunless sorrel bank.
> Only as an aside the bluebells in the plantation
> Will mean a thing to our dark contemplation.

Here bluebells are a personal symbol of the lovers' hidden passion. The poet takes pleasure in adumbrating the stage when passion is ripe, the senses are reveling, but nonchalance is the true wisdom: "We will not impose on the bluebells in that plantation / Too much of our desire's adulation."

In a 1956 letter to Peter Kavanagh, Patrick Kavanagh describes the poems in *A Soul for Sale* as "Palgravian lyricism, thin and artificial." Several, such as "Memory of Brother Michael" and "A Wreath for Tom Moore's Statue," seem committed to exploring the Irish myth, and lack the "flavour of personality," as he calls it in "Thank You, Thank You." Some poems, such as "Advent," are nostalgic for childhood innocence, which is equated with the seeing power of the imagination: "the newness that was in every stale thing / When we looked at it as children." One of the best poems, "Temptation in Harvest," describes the lush erotic attraction of the land in conflict with the peasant's desire for the poetic vocation. The competition between the familiar, comforting life of the senses and the unknown of spiritual freedom emerges. The poem ends comically with an image of Kavanagh's indecorous brazen muse:

> Now I turn
> Away from the ricks, the sheds, the cabbage garden,
> The stones of the street, the thrush song in the tree,
> The potato-pits, the flaggers in the swamp;
> From the country heart that hardly learned to harden,
> From the spotlight of an old-fashioned kitchen lamp
> I go to follow her who winked at me.

There is not much laughter in *A Soul for Sale*, except in the gay note of acceptance of what is in "Spraying the Potatoes":

> The axle-roll of a rut-locked cart
> Broke the burnt stick of noon in two.
> An old man came through a cornfield
> Remembering his youth and some Ruth he knew.
>
> He turned my way. 'God further the work.'
> He echoed an ancient farming prayer.
> I thanked him. He eyed the potato-drills.
> He said: 'You are bound to have good ones there.'

Hardy's host of timeless, common characters comes to mind, but in Kavanagh's poems Hardy's "satires of circumstance" play no part in dramatizing his characters. Rather, he penetrates to human vulnerability and dignity with great simplicity.

Tarry Flynn (1948) is a drastically revised version of a novel begun in 1938. It was published piecemeal in the *Bell* under the title "Four Picturizations" in 1947. When Pilot Press published the novel in 1948, the Irish Censorship Board banned it for about two weeks, perhaps because of its unflattering depiction of Irish peasant life.

The novel is notable, as critics generally agree, for its documentary realism and its comedy in depicting the peasant life of County Monaghan. While Kavanagh achieves a comic perspective for most of the characters, his supreme creation is Tarry, whose shrewdness, romanticism, and self-irony seem indivisible.

In 1949 Kavanagh sold his farm and had "The Paddiad" published in *Horizon*. He looked for journalism work in London in 1950 without success: "The streets of London are not paved with gold, / The streets of London are paved with failures," he wrote in "Tale of Two Cities." With experience, the objectification and exorcism of his past in *Tarry Flynn*, and his diverse book reviewing, he was expanding his ideological view beyond Irish chauvinism. In "Auden and the Creative Mind," an essay that appeared in the June 1951 issue of *Envoy*, Kavanagh referred to the "anaemic world of petty nationalism" ("Auden and the Creative Mind"). In "Spring Day" (first published in *Envoy*, March 1950), his satire is gently aimed at the modernists and foreshadows his eventual shift to a stance of "not caring":

Peter Kavanagh, 1950 (courtesy of Peter Kavanagh, photo by Paul Radkai)

O come all ye gallant poets—to know it doesn't matter
Is imagination's message—break out but do not scatter.
Ordinary things wear lovely wings—the peacock's body's common.
O come all ye youthful poets and try to be more human.

In August 1951 the Irish Cultural Committee refused to sponsor an American lecture tour for Kavanagh; meanwhile Macmillan was refusing to publish his work. The poems of this low period express his need to divest himself of anger and to pursue some interior truth. "Auditors In" is a precise analysis of the self in two tones: the supple, self-berating of the iambic tetrameter passages and the invocation of the loose iambic pentameter passages. The speaker refers to a mystical movement called the "Return in Departure," from which vantage point, he discovers, praise is infinitely more conscious and complete than before departure:

From the sour soil of a town where all roots canker
I turn away to where the Self reposes
The placeless Heaven that's under all our noses
Where we're shut off from all the barren anger

. . . .

O hunger
Where all have mouths of desire and none
Is willing to be eaten: I am so glad
To come accidentally upon
Myself at the end of a tortuous road
And have learned with surprise that God
Unworshipped withers to the Futile One.

In 1952 Peter Kavanagh returned from a stay of about five years in America, and Patrick Kavanagh persuaded him to write and publish a newspaper with him. The eight-page *Kavanagh's Weekly* was written almost entirely by the two brothers and ran for thirteen weeks until Peter's savings ran out. The paper was trenchant and witty on political and literary subjects; as a result it received almost no outside financial support and a small if enthusiastic following. As Patrick Kavanagh wrote, "Our main problem was two-headed. First, there is the absence of writers and, secondly, the absence of an audience." The last issue ends with a verse of "Having Confessed":

Let us lie down again
Deep in anonymous humility and God
May find us worthy material for His hand.

The wish for anonymous humility was to be shockingly denied. On 11 October 1952 the Irish weekly the *Leader* published an unsigned "Profile" of Kavanagh that he immediately found libelous. In February 1954 Kavanagh took the *Leader* to court. The trial lasted for seven days during which he spent thirteen hours testifying. As Peter Kavanagh describes it, this testimony put aesthetics on trial. The defendant represented the Irish cultural and literary establishment, and Kavanagh was disillusioned and embarrassed when the jury found the article nondefamatory and ordered Kavanagh to pay court costs. Kavanagh appealed, and the case was later decided in his favor.

During the trial Kavanagh wrote "Prelude," which was published in the *Irish Times* along with coverage of the trial. The poem is a song to himself, announcing a new aesthetic as prelude to an outpouring of new poetry. The speaker asserts "That all true poems laugh inwardly / Out of grief-born intensity." He renounces all spiritual and aesthetic fraud: "You have not got a chance with fraud / And might as well be true to God." Self-mockery reposes in the arms of self-assurance. A last satiric fusillade is hurled against

sick-faced whores
Who chant the praise of love that isn't
And bring their bastards to be Christened
At phoney founts by bogus priests
With rites mugged up by journalists

The viciousness seems to justify fully the concise argument that follows:

But satire is unfruitful prayer,
Only wild shoots of pity there,
And you must go inland and be
Lost in compassion's ecstasy,
Where suffering soars in summer air—
The millstone has become a star.

From this point on a guiding principle for Kavanagh would be the search for truths of the deep-lying interior, usually intimated or confirmed by communion with nature.

On 31 March 1955 Kavanagh had a cancerous lung removed; the operation cured him but left him permanently weakened. The two years following his operation was a period of great suffering and finally of conversion to a spiritual outlook whose best testament is the poetry. Kavanagh did a great deal to romanticize what he considered his true birth as a poet, probably out of the motive for writing poetry that he sets down in "Auditors In":

Is verse an entertainment only?
Or is it a profound and holy
Faith that cries the inner history
Of the failure of man's mission?
Should it be my job to mention
Precisely how I chanced to fail
Through a cursed ideal.

In "From Monaghan to the Grand Canal" Kavanagh describes his conversion as a renunciation of chauvinistic and egoistic concerns:

> Previously I had been concerned with Ireland and with my ego, both of which come together often enough. . . .
>
> Then one day as I was lying on the bank of the Grand Canal near Baggot Street having just been very ill in the hot summer of nineteen fifty-five, I commenced my poetic hegira. Without self-pity to look at things. . . . To let experience enter the soul. Not to be self-righteous.

In *Self-Portrait* (1964) he discusses another aspect of this conversion, "the very heart of the matter of human contentment": "This is the secret of learning how not to care. Not caring is really a sense of values and feeling of confidence. . . . The heart of a song singing it, or a poem writing it, is not caring." "Not caring" seems to be Kavanagh's code for intense spiritual devotion to everything but the ephemeral. Whether out of skepticism or humility, he never associated himself with the traditional mystical goal of detachment, although the poems make the connection. For example, "Dear Folks," one of a series of sonnets written from 1957 to 1960, is replete with spiritual and sensual ferment:

The main thing is to continue,
To walk Parnassus right into the sunset
Detached in love where pygmies cannot pin
you
To the ground like Gulliver. So good luck
and cheers.

Kavanagh stopped caring in order "to pray unselfconsciously with overflowing speech" ("Canal Bank Walk"), "For we must record love's mystery without claptrap / Snatch out of time the passionate transitory" ("The Hospital"). Rectitude is made weightless and gay by reliance on "the reality of the spirit, of faith and hope and sometimes even charity," he writes in *Self-Portrait*, and in "Mermaid Tavern" he adds,

In the Name of the Father
The Son and The Mother
We explode
Ridiculously, uncode
A habit and find therein
A successful human being.

However simple or obscure his later poetry seems, at its best its foundation is an intense religious heat, a transformation of suffering into acceptance and praise. The perfect sonnet complexities of "Canal Bank Walk" concentrate lush and exact language to make the crucial "arguments that cannot be proven":

Leafy-with-love banks and the green waters of the canal
Pouring redemption for me, that I do
The will of God, wallow in the habitual, the banal,
Grow with nature again as before I grew.

In this era, Kavanagh wrote several extraordinary sonnets, a form he made his own on rational aesthetic grounds, as he explained in one of his University College lectures, "not merely because it has been the most popular vehicle for the expression of love, but because its strict rules . . . [force] the mind to moral activity but is not itself forced." He had used the form very early and had already achieved dazzling results in his long, posthumously published "Lough Derg," in which various pilgrims speak "prayers shaped like sonnets":

I have sinned old; my lust's a running sore
That drains away my strength. Each morning shout:
"Last night's will's a bone that will not knit."
I slip on the loose rubble of remorse
And grasp at tufts of cocksfoot grass that yield
My belly in a bankrupt's purse.

Compassion and the praise of ordinary things are the strengths of "Lough Derg." Kavanagh's later love poetry breaks through to a praise no longer bound by temperamental attachment to the soil but guided by a divination of the "invisible / In the awful average greenness," as he says in "My Powers." The intuitions of "Ploughman" are confirmed:

I find a star-lovely art
In a dark sod.
Joy that is timeless! O heart
That knows God.

Kavanagh's later poems vacillate between the sensual and the mystical. At the core is the belief that nature is a sacrament of infinite depth: "I do not need to puzzle out Eternity, / As I walk this arboreal street on the edge of town," he writes in "October." The recurrent theme is that God can be known and known only through his creation, as "Miss Universe" suggests:

I learned, I learned—when one might be inclined
To think, too late, you cannot recover your losses—
I learned something of the nature of God's mind,
Not the abstract Creator but He who caresses
The daily and nightly earth; He who refuses
To take failure for an answer till again and again is worn.

This poem is a quintessential expression of conversion: the passionate repetitions draw the reader in; he is invited to admit his own failure in transcendent matters just as the speaker had expected failure, and then he is reassured that the God "who caresses," the elusive God, is also "He who refuses" to let us fail. Compassion and humility are uniformly ascendant in these mystical poems.

The force of intellect hews superfluity and ugliness from spare poems such as "Is," "To Hell with Commonsense," and "The Self-Slaved," whose vitality is in their wit, concision, assertiveness, and play of personality. In "The Self-Slaved" the poet writes:

Me I will throw away.
Me sufficient for the day
The sticky self that clings
Adhesions on the wings
To love and adventure,
To go on the grand tour
A man must be free
From self-necessity.

The rectitude of this stance might be measured by the poem's bareness, as if Kavanagh were willing to throw away the "me" who perceives through rich imagery and thereby risk the nakedness of statement.

In 1957 and 1958 Kavanagh gave a series of

Patrick Kavanagh (right) and his lawyer during his 1954 libel suit against the Leader *(courtesy of Peter Kavanagh and the* Irish Independent*)*

extramural lectures at University College, Dublin, for which he received a sinecure of £ 400 a year for life. These lectures on poetry and poetics were popular; in fact, as Kavanagh put it in a letter to Peter Kavanagh, "it was fame, the rumor going around, in contradistinction to the notoriety of the press." Kavanagh seems to have been sustained by the role of teacher and read at his parting lecture a brilliant poem, "Thank You, Thank You," which shows his fine control of tone. The poem, written in supple tetrameters, moves from witty conversation to didacticism and opens out onto the mystical plane:

I thank you and I say how proud
That I have been by fate allowed
To stand there having the joyful chance
To claim my inheritance
For most have died the day before
The opening of that holy door.

In 1957 Peter Kavanagh built a hand press in his New York City apartment. The next year he published twenty-five copies of Patrick Kavanagh's *Recent Poems*, a collection of a handful of his new kind of poem. By now Kavanagh was reluctant to bring out collections of his past work, so invalid did he consider it in the light of his "rebirth"; nevertheless, in 1960 he collected *Come Dance with Kitty Stobling and Other Poems*, a selection of thirty-four poems, many from the 1940s and 1950s. The book was a popular and financial success and the choice of the Poetry Book Society, leading to a contract for the *Collected Poems* (1964). Kavanagh had no part in making the selections for either the *Collected Poems* or the *Collected Pruse* (1967).

The last seven years of Kavanagh's life were dominated by alcoholism and increasingly bad health. His creative work was uneven, though lack of energy did not divert him from expressing the poetic values that coalesced in the mid-1950s. Furthermore, he made his most incisive autobiographical statement in 1963 in a television film that was subsequently published as *Self-Portrait* (1964). He married Katherine Maloney in April 1967 and died on 30 November of pneumonia. He is buried at Inniskeen.

Paradoxically Kavanagh has been called a provincial poet by both admirers and detractors. His admirers, mainly Irish, value the precise, original vision and language that seem to derive from his "rootedness" in the land, and his detractors point to the limitations of the rooted mind, holding up "cosmopolitanism" as an ideal. It is important to remember that Kavanagh began writing when he was literally mired in clay, and was probably more palpably conscious than any critic that "Clay is the word and clay is the flesh" and that he would have to detach himself from it to achieve the "weightlessness" of poetry. He insisted upon a telling critical distinction: "Parochialism and provincialism are opposites. The provincial has no mind of his own; he does not trust what his eyes see until he has heard what the metropolis . . . has to say on any subject"; and "Parochialism is universal; it deals with the fundamentals." This idea is the kernel of his great poem,"Epic":

I have lived in important places, times
When great events were decided, who owned
That half a rood of rock, a no-man's land
Surrounded by our pitchfork-armed claims.

Kavanagh broke free from provincialism to an extent that critics are hesitant to acknowledge, as he suggests in "Love in a Meadow":

But the critic asking questions ran
From the fright of the dawn
To weep later on an urban lawn
For the undone
God-gifted man.

Kavanagh has not yet gained wide recognition, but his work will endure.

Patrick Kavanagh, 1964 (courtesy of Peter Kavanagh and RTV Guide*)*

Recording:

Almost Everything: Written and Spoken by Patrick Kavanagh (Dublin: Claddagh Records, 1964).

Other:

Peter Kavanagh, *Irish Mythology: A Dictionary*, afterword by Kavanagh (New York: Peter Kavanagh Hand Press, 1959);

The Autobiography of William Carleton, introduction by Kavanagh (London: MacGibbon & Kee, 1962);

W. Steuart Trench, *Realities of Irish Life*, introduction by Kavanagh (London: MacGibbon & Kee, 1966).

Letters:

Lapped Furrows: Correspondence 1933-1967 between Patrick and Peter Kavanagh, with Other Documents, edited by Peter Kavanagh (New York: Peter Kavanagh Hand Press, 1969).

Interviews:

Larry Morrow, "Meet Mr. Patrick Kavanagh," *Bell*, 16 (April 1948): 5-21;

Mairin O'Farrell, "Poetry is Not Really an Art," *Hibernia* (May 1964): 16;

O'Farrell, "Kavanagh's America," *Hibernia* (July 1966): 10.

Bibliographies:

Peter Kavanagh, *Garden of the Golden Apples: A Bibliography of Patrick Kavanagh* (New York: Peter Kavanagh Hand Press, 1972);

John Nemo, "A Bibliography of Materials by and about Patrick Kavanagh," *Irish University Review*, 3 (Spring 1973): 80-106.

Biography:

Peter Kavanagh, *Sacred Keeper: A Biography of Patrick Kavanagh* (Curragh, Ireland: Goldsmith, 1980).

References:

Eavan Boland, Seamus Heaney, Michael Hartnett, and Liam Miller, "The Future of Irish Poetry: A Discussion," *Irish Times*, 5 February 1970, p. 14;

Francis Boylan, "Patrick Kavanagh," *Ishmael*, 1 (Winter-Spring 1972): 26-62;

Hubert Butler, "*Envoy* and Mr. Kavanagh," *Bell*, 17 (September 1951): 32-41;

Douglas Dunn, ed., *Two Decades of Irish Writing, A Critical Survey* (Chester Springs, Pa.: Dufour, 1975);

Peter Kavanagh, *Beyond Affection, An Autobiography* (New York: Peter Kavanagh Hand Press, 1977);

Kavanagh, *The Dancing Flame: A Documentary Drama of the Poet in Society* (New York: Peter Kavanagh Hand Press, 1981);

Brendan Kennelly, "Patrick Kavanagh," *Ariel*, 1 (July 1970): 7-28;

John Nemo, *Patrick Kavanagh* (Boston: G. K. Hall, 1979);

Darcy O'Brien, *Patrick Kavanagh* (Lewisburg, Pa.: Bucknell University Press, 1975);

Basil Payne, "The Poetry of Patrick Kavanagh," *Studies*, 49 (Fall 1960): 279-294;

"Profile: Patrick Kavanagh," *Leader*, 11 October 1952, pp. 8-12;

C. H. Sisson, *English Poetry 1900-1950, An Assessment* (New York: St. Martin's, 1971), pp. 251-254.

Papers:

The National Library of Ireland holds manuscripts of poems, *The Green Fool*, and *The Great Hunger*, as well as other items.

Francis Ledwidge

(19 August 1887-31 July 1917)

Carol M. Dole
Cornell University

BOOKS: *Songs of the Fields* (London: Jenkins, 1916);
Songs of Peace (London: Jenkins, 1917);
Last Songs (London: Jenkins, 1918);
The Complete Poems of Francis Ledwidge (London: Jenkins, 1919; New York: Brentano's, 1919);
The Complete Poems of Francis Ledwidge, reedited by Alice Curtayne (London: Brian & O'Keeffe, 1974).

Part of Francis Ledwidge's slender reputation rests on two biographical facts: he was an Irish peasant with little schooling, and he died fighting in World War I. The fact that he was a soldier actually had little effect on his poetry, for even the verses he wrote at the front are not about war but about the beauties of his homeland and his love for an Irish girl. Although the rudimentary nature of his formal education no doubt delayed his assimilation of the English poetic tradition, his industrious reading ensured that it did not greatly affect his mature verse. And since, as Katharine Tynan insisted, "there was nothing of him peasant. . . . He was born refined," his upbringing caused him little difficulty when he began moving in wider circles. Even the fact of his nationality has only partial relevance; although Ledwidge treated themes popular in Irish literature—the natural world and its seasons, lamentation for what has been lost, and the world of faerie—his poetry owes as much to Keats as to Yeats. The one salient biographical fact is that he died so young, just when the promise of his early poetry seemed about to be fulfilled.

Ledwidge was born in Slane, County Meath. His father, Patrick Ledwidge, a farm laborer, died five years later, leaving his widow to raise their eight children. Although she got little help from the state and had to support the family on the money she earned doing seasonal farm work, Anne Lynch Ledwidge insisted that her children remain in school. Francis proved an apt student; he became interested in literature and, through a Dublin weekly, joined a juvenile literary society from which he acquired a number of books as prizes in the competitions he entered. But he "began to realise that men cannot live by dreams" and left the national school before turning fourteen. His talent for impromptu versifying proved an asset even when he went to work for a local farmer; he amused his fellow laborers with his good-natured rhyming, as he was to do in many subsequent jobs. After he served a brief stint as a houseboy at Slane Castle, Ledwidge's ambitious mother tried apprenticing him to a grocer in Drogheda, eight miles away, with more success. Some months later she sent him on to a grocer in Dublin. The homesick fifteen-year-old lasted only a few days there before setting out on an all-night walk back to his beloved mother; but in the interim he had written "Behind the Closed Eye," a poem marked by juvenile awkwardness but containing lines that later won considerable praise:

Lance-Corporal Francis Ledwidge (BBC Hulton)

And wondrous impudently sweet,
Half of him passion, half conceit,
The blackbird called adown the street.

His mother did not try to send him away again. Over the next four years Ledwidge was a yard boy, a farm laborer, and a road maker—all occupations that gave him an opportunity to sharpen his observation of nature. In 1908 Ledwidge began working in a copper mine that had opened nearby. His volubility made him popular with his fellow miners, one of whom sent a copy of a poem of his to the *Drogheda Independent*. The poem was promptly published, and Ledwidge became a regular contributor to the newspaper. The same year, 1910, he lost his job after organizing a strike to procure better working conditions in the mine. He went back to the roads, soon becoming a foreman.

Throughout these years Ledwidge pursued his studies independently. He read Euclid and the Elizabethans. Longfellow and Tennyson gave way to Swinburne, Shelley, and especially Keats. Ledwidge also joined his brother Joe in a Slane dramatic group.

By 1912 Ledwidge had established a reputation as a poet locally, but he longed for wider recognition. At a friend's suggestion, he wrote for advice to Lord Dunsany, a Meath writer then much in the news. Dunsany responded enthusiastically to the poems of his younger countryman. He gave Ledwidge access to the castle library, advised him on reading, and introduced him to a number of Irish literary figures, including Thomas McDonagh and Oliver St. John Gogarty. By September Dunsany had arranged to have "Behind the Closed Eye" published in the *Saturday Review*, the first of many of Ledwidge's poems to appear there.

Nineteen twelve was an exciting year for Ledwidge in other ways, too. That autumn he was in love with Ellie Vaughey, a local girl he had known for some years. Within a few months, however, the relationship soured. Ellie broke with him, pleading her family's disapproval of their uneven match. (The Vaugheys, though not wealthy enough to prevent Ellie's having to work for a milliner when she finished school, owned a good deal of land in Slane.) Her apparent distress gave him hope that he could eventually win her if he could improve his social position. Their eventual reconciliation seemed more of a possibility when, in 1913, the Slane branch of the Meath Labour Union gave him a one-year post as their secretary. He took advantage of that year to teach himself shorthand and typewriting in the hope that he might later become a reporter for the *Drogheda Independent*.

Francis Ledwidge, 1914

Meanwhile he continued writing poems at such a rate that Dunsany developed "the queer impression that this Irish villager had found some coffer, stored in a golden age, brimful of lyrics and lost long ago." Dunsany chose fifty of these poems and found a publisher for Ledwidge's first book.

Songs of the Fields was scheduled for publication in 1914. That June Dunsany wrote an introduction to the volume, in which he dubbed Ledwidge "the poet of the blackbird" and hoped that "not too many will be attracted to this book on account of the author being a peasant, lest he come to be praised by the how-interesting! school." Herbert Jenkins, the publisher, apparently was less adverse to that type of attraction, for when the volume finally appeared in 1916, he advertised its author—quite inaccurately—as "The Scavenger Poet."

The postponement of his book was not the only unpleasant surprise the poet had to face in 1914. It became apparent that there was to be no reconciliation with Ellie, for she was frequently seen in the company of John O'Neill, a young man no wealthier than Ledwidge. Moreover, although the Drogheda newspaper was glad to pay him for a series of articles on the Boyne Valley, it was unable to take Ledwidge on as a reporter—so he had no real prospects to offer Ellie in any case. A brief romance with another young woman, Lizzie Healy, failed to survive a misunderstanding about some violets that she received anonymously on Valentine's Day and wrongly assumed to be from Ledwidge.

Only his community activities seemed to go well that year. He was elected to the Navan Rural District Council and Board of Guardians, a group that made sure that bread was sent to the poorhouse, that cottages were repaired, and that the people were vaccinated. Election to this council was considered an honor. Additionally, he helped found a Slane branch of the Irish Volunteers, a nationalistic organization formed in response to Ulster's denunciation of the pending Home Rule Bill, and he traveled to Manchester to help organize the volunteers there.

When England declared war on Germany in August 1914, Ledwidge assumed that the Irish volunteers—who had had considerable military training—would be called upon to defend Ireland when British troops were moved to the front. He was dismayed when the Redmondite faction of their leadership called upon the volunteers to enlist in England's army. When the Slane Corps joined up, Ledwidge angrily split with them. But on 24 October, he enlisted in the Royal Inniskilling Fusiliers, a largely Irish unit in which Dunsany was a captain. Ledwidge later explained to Lewis Chase, "I joined the British Army because she stood between Ireland and an enemy common to our civilisation and I would not have her say that she defended us while we did nothing at home but pass resolutions." No

Ledwidge's house in Janeville, Slane

doubt Ledwidge also saw the army as a tempting escape from his increasingly difficult situation in Slane: four months earlier he had written, "I'm wild for wandering to the far-off places / Since one forsook me whom I held most dear."

While in training at Richmond Barracks, Dublin, Ledwidge learned that Ellie had married O'Neill on 25 November. His hopes were now entirely at an end. During his Christmas holidays he renewed his relationship with Lizzie Healy, for whom he wrote "To Eilish of the Fair Hair." He continued corresponding with her when he was moved to Basingstoke, England, in the spring. England proved a congenial environment for writing; Ledwidge took long walks through the Hampshire countryside, and Dunsany provided him with a study in the house he had taken there. The two writers worked together over the page proofs of *Songs of the Fields*, which arrived in June, before Dunsany was sent back to Derry to train recruits.

On the night of 18 June 1915 Ledwidge had a striking dream about white birds flying over the Atlantic. He was a great believer in dreams—his letters and poems are full of them—and this one haunted him. He began working on a poem, "Caoin," recording this vision. Soon afterward he learned that Ellie had died. Rushing to Manchester, where she had been living, he discovered that her marriage had been an unhappy one and that she had died giving birth prematurely. Now, somehow, he developed with Ellie what Alice Curtayne calls a mystical "reunion through death"; she would continue to haunt his poems and his dreams until he died.

In July 1915 Ledwidge's company boarded a ship for the Dardanelles. After a brief stop in Greece, they landed at Suvla Bay, Gallipoli. His two months in the harsh conditions of the Turkish beachhead both appalled and excited Ledwidge; understandably, they produced no poetry. The autumn, which he spent in the mountains of Serbia, was more productive. In October he received a copy of *Songs of the Fields*. He was delighted with the favorable reviews and with the book's popular success (the first printing was rapidly sold out), but he wrote to Dunsany that "my best is not in it. That has to come yet. I feel something great struggling in my soul but it can't come until I return; if I don't return it will never come." This first collection is flawed by what John Drinkwater termed "a manner heavy with self-conscious discovery of English poetry, through which his genius struggles often but brokenly to its own gesture," but it contains such delicate lyrical moments as "The Wife of Llew," a poem based on a Welsh tale from the *Mabinogion*:

They took the violet and the meadow-sweet
To form her pretty face, and for her feet
They built a mound of daisies on a wing,
And for her voice they made a linnet sing
In the wide poppy blowing for her mouth.
And over all they chanted twenty hours.
And Llew came singing from the azure south
And bore away his wife of birds and flowers.

The rheumatism he suffered in the harsh Serbian winter was so bad that Ledwidge asked Dunsany to procure a leave for him. But there was no leave. In December, Ledwidge collapsed during a long march and was sent to a hospital in Egypt to recover from a variety of ailments. Pain and the "Navvy imps in my head" kept him from doing much writing, but he read with interest the new *Georgian Poetry 1913-1915*, a popular anthology in which he was proud to have three of his poems appear.

Given convalescent leave, Ledwidge arrived in England in April 1916 and quickly learned of the Easter Uprising. He was deeply affected by the deaths of the Irish patriots; when he was finally able to make his way to Slane on 10 May 1916, he could talk of little else. The night he arrived he brushed aside his family's questions about the war and read them his new poem, an elegy for his friend Thomas McDonagh, a poet who had been executed after the insurrection. Part of it was later to serve as his own epitaph:

He shall not hear the bittern cry
In the wild sky, where he is lain,
Nor voices of the sweeter birds
Above the wailing of the rain.

Drinkwater identifies "Thomas McDonagh" as the poet's "first encompassing of profound lyric mastery."

During his leave Ledwidge seemed morose and disillusioned. He had longed for home, but "In the fair country of my choice / Nor Peace nor Love again I find." After the events of Easter week and after his own experiences at the front, he was reluctant to return to England's army. When he went to Dublin in May to get his leave extended, he argued with an officer and was refused extra leave; weeks later he was court-martialed and lost his lance-corporal's stripe. He wrote numerous poems commemorating the Easter Uprising. Summer found him in the barracks at Derry, "writing 'potboilers' for English weeklies" and, once again with

Dunsany, selecting and revising poems for his second collection. Dunsany named this volume, which appeared in 1917, *Songs of Peace*—a title that belies that book's melancholy mood. With its deeply felt but controlled grief and its increased mastery of poetic technique, the volume marks an encouraging advance over *Songs of the Fields*.

When Ledwidge was sent to the Somme in the last days of 1916, his state of mind was still far from optimistic; in January he wrote Katharine Tynan, "Death is as interesting to me as life." But he continued writing poems and sending them back to Ireland. That spring, when he read the proofs of *Songs of Peace*, he mentioned to Tynan that "there were several poems I hardly recognised as my own, for I scribble them off in odd moments, and, if I do not give them to some one, they become part of the dust of the earth and little things stuck on the ends of hedges." He also referred in his correspondence to "The Crock of Gold," a one-act play he had written. This play remains unpublished.

In April, a vivid dream provoked him to write "The Lanawn Shee," in which a girl appears and beckons her lover to the "sunny coast" of death. Ledwidge believed the dream to be a portent, and after he had it, the rockets in the night sky seemed to him "like the end of a beautiful world." On 31 July 1917 he was felled by an exploding shell at Boesinghe, near Ypres, Belgium.

Last Songs, selected by Lord Dunsany, appeared the following year. These poems show a promising development of poetic craft, especially in the Irish internal-rhyme technique, in which the last word of the first line rhymes with the word in the middle of the next line. Ledwidge employed this technique skillfully in poems such as "Had I a Golden Pound":

Had I a golden pound to spend,
My love should mend and sew no more.
And I would buy her a little quern,
Easy to turn on the kitchen floor.

Finding *Last Songs* an impressive continuation of Ledwidge's poetic development, some commentators have agreed with Dunsany's evaluation that "here were the makings of a great poet, whom the world will not know now." Although Ledwidge never became more than a minor poet, the "strain of lyric magic" that Conrad Aiken recognized has prevented Ledwidge from being forgotten. His *Complete Poems*, a compilation of the three earlier volumes, sold well in 1919 and was reprinted in 1944 and 1955. A new edition by Alice Curtayne, which added 45 poems to the original 122, came out in 1974, and Curtayne's biography of Ledwidge appeared in 1972. The best of Ledwidge's simple, mellifluous lyrics have continuing appeal.

Ledwidge's grave in Boesinghe, Belgium

Other:

"Desire in Spring," words by Ledwidge and music by Yvor Gurney, in *Chapbook*, 3 (December 1920): 16-23.

Biography:

Alice Curtayne, *Francis Ledwidge: A Life of the Poet* (London: Brian & O'Keeffe, 1972).

References:

Lewis Chase, "Francis Ledwidge," *Century*, 95 (January 1918): 386-391;

John Drinkwater, *The Muse in Council* (London: Sidgwick & Jackson, 1925), pp. 202-217;

Lord Dunsany, *My Ireland* (London: Jarrolds, 1937), pp. 36-46;

Katharine Tynan, *The Years of the Shadow* (London: Constable, 1919), pp. 287-297.

Papers:

Some of Ledwidge's papers are in the National Library, Dublin.

Alun Lewis
(1 July 1915-5 March 1944)

A. T. Tolley
Carleton University

BOOKS: *Raiders' Dawn and Other Poems* (London: Allen & Unwin, 1942; New York: Macmillan, 1942);
The Last Inspection (London: Allen & Unwin, 1942; New York: Macmillan, 1943);
Ha! Ha! Among the Trumpets (London: Allen & Unwin, 1945);
Letters from India (Cardiff: Penmark, 1946);
In the Green Tree (London: Allen & Unwin, 1948);
Alun Lewis: Selected Poetry and Prose, edited by Ian Hamilton (London: Allen & Unwin, 1966).

Alun Lewis

If any poet may be regarded as *the* British "war poet" of World War II, it is Alun Lewis. Though he never saw action, he wrote with great authenticity of the experience of war as encountered by his generation; and it was through the war that his poetry found its real power. He gave classic expression to the experience of being caught up in the machinery of war—to the boredom and waiting, the loves and separations that made up the lives of those in the services. For his last year Lewis was in India, exiled from home in a strange culture, as were many other British soldiers. His poetry is haunted by the central problems of life and death, seen in the perspective that the final purpose of all his activities as a soldier was to kill others. Lewis was characteristic of intellectuals of his generation in contemplating, at the outbreak of war, registration as a conscientious objector. He was characteristic of many poets involved in the war in never seeing action, though he did not survive the war.

Lewis was born on 1 July 1915 in Cwmaman, near Aberdare, in a South Wales coal-mining valley. His father was a schoolteacher—the only one of four brothers never to work in the pits. His grandfather was a miner until his death. A mark of Lewis's work was to be his unpatronizing feeling for the concerns of ordinary people. After study at Cowbridge grammar school, Lewis went on to study history at the University College of Wales at Aberystwyth. After getting his B.A. in 1935, he went to Manchester University to spend two years reading medieval history for his M.A. (obtained in 1937)—work that he found largely uncongenial. Finding no openings for uncertified teachers at the conclusion of his studies, he returned to Aberystwyth in 1937 to work for his teacher training certificate. When he had obtained this certificate, he was still unable to get a job. He contemplated journalism; but in November 1938 he was asked to fill in for the rest of the year at Pengam school, about fifteen miles from Aberdare, where he seems to have been happy until he resigned in 1940.

Throughout these years, Lewis had been writing poetry, though for much of the period publication had been confined to school and college periodicals. While he was studying in Manchester, Helen Waddell, the medieval scholar and translator, suggested that he send some of his poems to the *Dublin Magazine*, where they subsequently appeared. In the winter of 1937-1938, he also had poems published in the *Observer* and in *Time and Tide*.

The coming of war put Lewis into a questioning situation. He took a cottage on the Gower Coast and began work on an autobiographical novel. He foresaw that he would be drawn into the war, and at first considered following his always strong pacifist inclinations. He decided instead to enlist voluntarily so that he might have some say in where he went. He traveled to London in the spring of 1940 with the intention of joining the Merchant Navy. Quite by impulse, he enlisted in the Royal Engineers instead. The ship on which he was to have sailed left without him, was torpedoed, and never returned.

Lewis found himself at Longmoor Depot in Hampshire, where he was put to tasks such as maintaining railway engines. This period provided the material for the title story of his collection of short stories, *The Last Inspection* (1942). After a time, he put in for a transfer to the Army Education Corps, a request that was eventually refused. In the meantime, he was called on to arrange courses for the camp and was given a room of his own with a fire and a typewriter. It was in this period that his development as a poet truly began.

He was twenty-four. Looking back on those days he wrote: "Thinking back on my own writing, it all seemed to mature of a sudden between the winter of 1939 and the following autumn. Was it Gweno or the Army?" (Gweno Ellis was a fellow schoolteacher whom he married in the summer of 1941.) At Longmoor he wrote "All Day It Has Rained," a poem that reflects his early days there, billeted in a tent. It is Lewis's most celebrated poem, and one of the most enduring of World War II:

> All day it has rained, and we on the edge of the moors
> Have sprawled in our bell-tents, moody and dull as boors,
> Groundsheets and blankets spread on the muddy ground
> And from the first grey wakening we have found
> No refuge from the skirmishing fine rain
> And the wind that made the canvas heave and flap
> And the taut wet guy-ropes ravel out and snap.
> . . . .
> And we stretched out, unbuttoning our braces,
> Smoking a Woodbine, darning dirty socks,
> Reading the Sunday papers—I saw a fox
> And mentioned it in a note I scribbled home.

Like so many of Lewis's poems, it is moral in tone and seems to take very decided positions; yet finally it impresses by its undistorted rendering of the experience in which it is rooted. It is a triumph of tone, and achieves the "quietness" that Lewis said he sought in his poetry. There is an interplay between the feeling, so common in the war, of being trapped with oneself or with others, and the sense of the tranquility and melancholy associated with the rain. Lewis must have known Edward Thomas's poem "Rain"; and those who have read Thomas's poetry will recognize a debt to him in the subdued meditative movement of Lewis's poem.

Lewis was at the time stationed in what he called "the Edward Thomas country." He visited Thomas's former house and wrote "To Edward Thomas," which contains a passage that is one of the triumphs of Lewis's poetry:

> I sat and watched the dusky berried ridge
> Of yew-trees, deepened by oblique dark shafts,
> Throw back the flame of red and gold and russet
> That leapt from beech and ash to birch and chestnut
> Along the downward arc of the hill's shoulder,
> And sunlight with discerning fingers
> Softly explores the distant wooded acres,
> Touching the farmsteads one by one with lightness
> Until it reached the Downs, whose soft green pastures
> Went slanting sea- and skywards to the limits
> Where sight surrenders and the mind alone
> Can find the sheeps' tracks and the grazing.

Experience emerges as richly meaningful, yet its meaning remains elusive—elusive with a melancholy that Lewis recognizes, later in the poem, he shared with Thomas: "I knew the voice that called you / Was soft and neutral as the sky / Breathing on the grey horizon / . . . / Till suddenly, at Arras, you possessed that hinted land."

Lewis's first collection, *Raiders' Dawn and Other Poems*, appeared in March 1942. It was divided into five sections: "Poems in Khaki," "Poems in Love," "Songs," "On Old Themes," and "Other Poems." However, the striking division is between the poems written after he joined the army and those written before. Many of the poems in *Raiders' Dawn* are conventional and literary in imagery and sentiment; and, if encountered separately from the mature poems, they would easily be passed over.

In January 1941, Lewis's request to be transferred to the Education Corps was finally turned down, and he decided to apply for a commission in the infantry. He did preliminary training near Gloucester and was married quietly one weekend during that period. From July to October he was with the Officer Cadet Training Unit at Morecombe, after which he was commissioned and given a month's leave, during which he worked on the proofs of *Raiders' Dawn*.

It was during this time that he became involved with Brenda Chamberlain and John Petts in producing the Caseg Broadsheets. The idea was evidently to produce single poems for pennies so that poetry could reach a wider and poorer audience. Lewis believed strongly in this venture, and two of his poems appeared as one of the broadsheets (*Two Poems*, 1941). However, production costs raised the price above an acceptable level, and the scheme was abandoned after a few broadsheets were published.

With *Raiders' Dawn* Lewis emerged as the war poet that British readers had been looking for. By June 1942 the first impression had sold out; the book ran through three impressions that year. By 1946, it had reached a sixth impression, though that printing was still available in the 1970s—a commentary on the sudden decline in interest in war poetry as soon as hostilities ceased.

In a letter to his wife, Lewis wrote protesting: "death doesn't fascinate me half as powerfully as life: you half hinted so . . . but you know really . . . how I turn instantly to more and more life . . . Death is the great mystery, who can ignore him? But I don't *seek* him." Yet, in *Raiders' Dawn* and later, he remains fascinated by death, beyond a questioning of his own role and fate as a soldier; and this probing of the sadness that for him surrounds both life and death was as much his subject as were the experiences of wartime.

At the end of his leave, Lewis joined the 6th Battalion, South Wales Borderers. In November 1942 they embarked for India, arriving in Bombay at Christmas. The experience of India was to bring a new orientation to Lewis's work. He became more deeply interested in the poetry of Rilke. India seemed to draw him to a searching and accepting sense of "that which Is." In one of his last and most extended poems, "The Jungle," he seems to be attempting a statement of his sense of things. Some

Alun Lewis (Bill Brandt)

recent critics have seen these poems from India as Lewis's most important achievement. Yet they do not measure up to those Lewis wrote in his early days in the army, despite his attempts to discipline his earlier adjectival tendencies. They are rhythmically less interesting; and one senses that, for all Lewis's fascination with India, he found himself cut off from the things of Wales that elicited from him such a sensitive response.

Early in 1943, Lewis broke his jaw playing football and found himself in a hospital in Poona. In May he was in the Maharatta Hills, and, during this period, he wrote a large number of poems. In August he was sent to an intelligence course at Karachi, where he made sufficient impression to be asked to stay on as an instructor. He rejected this offer, insisting on going back to his unit. As he was to say of the men he commanded: "They seem to me to have some secret knowledge that I want and will never find until I go into action with them and war really happens to them."

Behind all his activities now lay the promise of that action, and the threat of being involved finally in the business of killing or being killed. This threat had haunted Lewis and his work since the early days of the war. In February his unit moved to the front in Burma. Although as intelligence officer his place was at headquarters, he insisted on going into the forward positions. On his way to them he was killed mysteriously in an accident with his own pistol on 5 March 1944. He was twenty-eight. He was not to see action.

Prior to his death Lewis had put together his new poems to form a second collection. He had sent them to Robert Graves, and in January he had worked on them in the light of Graves's comments. It remained, however, for his wife to bring together *Ha! Ha! Among the Trumpets*, which appeared posthumously in 1945. It was well received and had a second printing in 1946; but, as with the first volume, this postwar impression was still not exhausted by the 1970s.

Lewis was also a writer of powerful short stories, and some critics were of the opinion that his real talent was for fiction. Certainly a story such as "Private Jones" shows a remarkable capacity to project a sense of events as they appear to a largely inarticulate Welshman inducted from the country into the army. Lewis had one book of stories, *The Last Inspection*, published in 1942. A posthumous collection, *In the Green Tree* (1948), contained further stories and a selection of letters home written in India.

It is easy to play down Lewis's achievement as that of the decent, middle-class Welsh boy; but his unironic decency is a mark of the centrality of his response to war. His readiness to give direct expression to widely shared emotions, without the protection of ironic qualification, is what takes the reader back to his best poetry. He himself wrote, "if I get too far away from the *thing*, the thought becomes flabby"; and his poetry does not need the discovery of a hidden philosophical potential to give it stature.

Letters:

"A Sheaf of Letters," *Wales*, 7 (February/March, 1945);

"Alun Lewis to Robert Graves," *Anglo-Welsh Review*, 16 (Spring 1967);

Alun Lewis and the Making of the Caseg Broadsheets, commentary by Brenda Chamberlain (London: Enitharmon, 1970).

Periodical Publication:

Review of *The Trumpet and Other Poems*, by Edward Thomas, *Horizon*, 13 (January 1941): 78.

References:

R. N. Currey, *Poets of the 1939-1945 War* (London: Longmans, Green, 1967);

Ian Hamilton, Introduction to *Alun Lewis: Selected Poetry and Prose* (London: Allen & Unwin, 1966);

Alun John, *Alun Lewis* (Cardiff: University of Wales Press, 1970);

J. S. Williams, "Alun Lewis: A select bibliography," *Anglo-Welsh Review*, 16 (Spring 1967).

Hugh MacDiarmid
(C. M. Grieve)

(11 August 1892-9 September 1978)

Kenneth Buthlay
University of Glasgow

SELECTED BOOKS: *Annals of the Five Senses*, as C. M. Grieve (Montrose: C. M. Grieve, 1923);

Sangschaw (Edinburgh & London: Blackwood, 1925);

Penny Wheep (Edinburgh & London: Blackwood, 1926);

A Drunk Man Looks at the Thistle (Edinburgh & London: Blackwood, 1926; edited by John C. Weston, Amherst: University of Massachusetts Press, 1971);

Contemporary Scottish Studies, First Series, as Grieve (London: Parsons, 1926; enlarged edition, Edinburgh: Scottish Educational Journal, 1976);

Albyn, or Scotland and the Future, as Grieve (London: Paul, Trench & Trübner, 1927);

The Present Position of Scottish Music, as Grieve (Montrose: C. M. Grieve, 1927);

To Circumjack Cencrastus (Edinburgh & London: Blackwood, 1930);

First Hymn to Lenin and Other Poems (London: Unicorn Press, 1931);

Hugh MacDiarmid, May 1936

Second Hymn to Lenin (Thakeham: Valda Trevlyn, 1932);

Scots Unbound and Other Poems (Stirling: Mackay, 1932);

Scottish Scene, by MacDiarmid and Lewis Grassic Gibbon (James Leslie Mitchell) (London: Jarrolds, 1934);

Stony Limits and Other Poems (London: Gollancz, 1934);

At the Sign of the Thistle (London: Nott, 1934);

Selected Poems (London: Macmillan, 1934); enlarged as *Speaking for Scotland: Selected Poems* (Baltimore: Contemporary Poetry, 1946);

Second Hymn to Lenin and Other Poems (London: Nott, 1935);

Scottish Eccentrics (London: Routledge, 1936; New York: Johnson Reprint, 1972);

Scotland, and the Question of a Popular Front against Fascism and War (Whalsay: Hugh MacDiarmid Book Club, 1938);

The Islands of Scotland (London: Batsford, 1939; New York: Scribners, 1939);

Cornish Heroic Song for Valda Trevlyn (Glasgow: Caledonian Press, 1943);

Lucky Poet (London: Methuen, 1943; enlarged edition, Jonathan Cape, 1972);

Poems of East-West Synthesis (Glasgow: Caledonian Press, 1946);

A Kist of Whistles (Glasgow: Maclellan, 1947);

Cunninghame Graham: A Centenary Study (Glasgow: Caledonian Press, 1952);

Francis George Scott: An Essay on the occasion of his Seventy-fifth Birthday (Edinburgh: Macdonald, 1955);

In Memoriam James Joyce (Glasgow: Maclellan, 1955);

Stony Limits and Scots Unbound and Other Poems (Edinburgh: Castle Wynd Printers, 1956);

Three Hymns to Lenin (Edinburgh: Castle Wynd Printers, 1957);

The Battle Continues (Edinburgh: Castle Wynd Printers, 1957);

Burns Today and Tomorrow (Edinburgh: Castle Wynd Printers, 1959);

The Kind of Poetry I Want (Edinburgh: Duval, 1961);

Collected Poems (New York: Macmillan, 1962; Edinburgh & London: Oliver & Boyd, 1962; revised edition, New York: Macmillan/London: Collier-Macmillan, 1967);

The Company I've Kept (London: Hutchinson, 1966; Berkeley: University of California Press, 1967);

A Lap of Honour (London: MacGibbon & Kee, 1967; Chicago: Swallow Press, 1969);

The Uncanny Scot, edited by Kenneth Buthlay (London: MacGibbon & Kee, 1968);

A Clyack-Sheaf (London: MacGibbon & Kee, 1969);

Selected Essays, edited by Duncan Glen (London: Cape, 1969; Berkeley: University of California Press, 1970);

More Collected Poems (London: MacGibbon & Kee, 1970; Chicago: Swallow Press, 1970);

Selected Poems, edited by David Craig and John Manson (Harmondsworth, U.K.: Penguin, 1970);

The Hugh MacDiarmid Anthology, edited by Michael Grieve and Alexander Scott (London: Routledge & Kegan Paul, 1972);

Metaphysics and Poetry (Hamilton: Lothlorien, 1975);

Complete Poems, edited by Michael Grieve and W. R. Aitken, 2 volumes (London: Brian & O'Keeffe, 1978).

Hugh MacDiarmid has long been considered the greatest Scottish poet since Burns. Possibly that might not be the most impressive of distinctions, but his admirers would add that his work has dimensions beyond Burns's, and that in a contemporary context a just appreciation would place it alongside Pound's and Eliot's. If so, the question that immediately confronts us is why MacDiarmid should have received so little attention in comparison with these celebrated names.

Perhaps there are two main reasons for his lack of renown: the extreme unevenness of his output and the fact that much of the best of it is in Scots. To appreciate the latter requires of most readers (even Scottish readers, whose anglicized educational system requires of them little or no knowledge of their native languages) a special effort to extend and sustain their linguistic receptivity. Those who have most influence in matters of literary reputation in Britain have proved unwilling to make such an effort in MacDiarmid's case. Their literature is not, and never has been, British. It is *English* literature—an ambiguous term which can readily lay claim to Irishmen like Yeats and Joyce and Welshmen like Dylan Thomas, but balks at a professedly Anglophobe Scottish nationalist who did his best work in Scots. And that is the case even when they regard that language as a mere dialect of what they call, equally ambiguously, "English." It seems that only an English critic who is himself something of an outsider, Anthony Burgess, is willing to learn much about the historical status of Scots alongside his own language or to approach modern work in Scots in a receptive frame of mind.

C. M. Grieve (photo by Eddie Armstrong)

Burgess, at any rate, has no doubt that MacDiarmid is a major poet.

Hugh MacDiarmid was born Christopher Murray Grieve to James and Elizabeth Graham Grieve in Langholm, Dumfriesshire, near the border with England. His father was a rural postman, and most of his relatives worked in the local tweed mills or on farms. A crucial factor in his boyhood was the happy accident whereby the family found accommodation in the same building as the town library, from which he borrowed books in such quantities that he used a clothes basket to transport them.

He was educated at Langholm Academy, where one of his early teachers was Francis George Scott, the outstanding song composer of his day, who was later to collaborate closely with the poet. From Langholm he went to Edinburgh in 1908 as a pupil-teacher at Broughton Junior Student Centre but turned to journalism in 1910. He was by that time actively involved in socialist politics, having joined the Independent Labour party at the age of sixteen.

After a variety of jobs on local newspapers in Scotland and Wales, he joined the Royal Army Medical Corps in 1915 and served as a sergeant in Greece and France. While on sick leave following bouts of malaria, he married Margaret Skinner in 1918, and when he was demobilized in the following year, the couple made their home in Montrose, Angus.

In the course of the next decade Grieve made this little town the center of what came to be called the Scottish Renaissance movement through his efforts to revive a sense of national identity in cultural and political life. He had returned from a war fought ostensibly for the rights of small nations, and his ultimate aim was to regain for Scotland the place in Europe and the comity of nations which it had lost in the course of assimilation by England. To this end he channeled his formidable energies into a national propaganda movement while earning his living as a reporter on the local newspaper, holding office as town councillor and justice of the peace, and writing a vast amount of prose and the solid body of poetry on which he staked his claim as a creative artist. During this period he became a founder member of the National Party of Scotland and the Scottish center of P.E.N.

Like any other ambitious writer in the Scotland of his day, he began by writing entirely in English, and the first signs of the literary revival that was claimed for Scotland were detected in *Northern Numbers* (1920-1922), a series of three anthologies of contemporary poetry which he edited and to which he contributed verse in English. His own first book, *Annals of the Five Senses* (1923), was likewise in English: a collection of experimental prose pieces, erratic but bearing tokens of extraordinary talents, and a few specimens of his poetry.

His early poems in English were sufficiently impressive to earn him a reputation as the outstanding poet of his generation in Scotland, but, with few exceptions, they have not stood up well to the test of time. Their main interest today is perhaps in the way in which they exhibit his struggle to bring a Georgian-flavored English to terms with tendencies that attracted him in recent European poetry, with which he acquired an extensive acquaintanceship, at any rate in translation.

Grieve first used the name Hugh MacDiarmid in October 1922, in the *Scottish Chapbook*. The immediate reason for this was probably to avoid the charge of writing too much for the magazine of which he was editor, but it was also convenient for him to attribute his work in Scots to MacDiarmid rather than to Grieve, who had achieved a considerable reputation by following the prevailing wisdom and writing entirely in English.

As it happened, one of the factors in his turning to writing poems in Scots was his awareness of the part played by the deployment of neglected linguistic resources of various sorts in recent European literary developments. Hitherto he had been inclined to relegate writing in Scots to the domestic backyard, rather as the Scots speech of his childhood was excluded from the precincts of education. Scots, from being before the union with England a national language with a healthy literature that claimed its place in Europe, had been progressively degraded for politico-religious reasons. The adoption of an English translation of the Bible at the Reformation, the departure of king and court for London at the Union of Crowns in 1603, and the abolition of the Scots parliament in 1707 marked the stages of its decline. It fragmented into regional dialects and was subjected to social prejudices; its prose development was aborted; and its poetic revival in the eighteenth century, culminating in the work of Burns, was inevitably restricted in range. After Burns came too many imitators with minimal literary standards, and by MacDiarmid's time to write in Scots seemed to confine one inescapably to a corner of minor verse.

In 1922, however, he began to explore the language not only in its literature but in dictionaries and other linguistic works and suddenly discovered that his empathy with certain Scots words was re-

Grieve was elected to the Montrose town council as an Independent Socialist in 1922 (photo by A. S. Milne).

leasing a fresh, untapped creative potential. One of his first Scots poems to result from this research, "The Watergaw," which grew around a cluster of unfamiliar expressions encountered in a linguistic study by Sir James Wilson, was immediately recognized as being of exceptional quality by good judges of poetry, including the critic Denis Saurat, who declared it to be a veritable masterpiece and translated it and other early MacDiarmid poems into French.

The standard response of English readers to a poem like "The Watergaw" is to say that some of the vocabulary is so strange to them that they are unable to make anything of the poem. But the vocabulary was quite as unfamiliar to Saurat and to the vast majority of Scottish readers who have, in the subsequent sixty years, shared his high opinion of it.

Perhaps the most useful approach would be to look at some simple-seeming poems in which the language MacDiarmid uses is not so very far removed from "standard" English. In "Empty Vessel," for example, the linguistic problem does not go much beyond recognizing a few Scots cognates of common English words and knowing that a *cairney* is a small heap of stones marking some feature of the landscape or a grave. What is less easily accounted for is the effortless skill in rhythm and image which holds the balance in this tiny poem between a girl singing to her dead child and the music of the spheres, rocked by cosmic winds, while the all-compassing light bends over creation:

I met ayont the cairney
A lass wi' tousie hair
Singin' till a bairnie
That was nae langer there.

Wunds wi' warlds to swing
Dinna sing sae sweet,
The licht that bends owre a'thing
Is less ta'en up wi't.

(*ayont*: beyond; *tousie*: tousled; *wunds*: winds; *warlds*: worlds; *owre*: over; *a'thing*: everything; *ta'en up wi't*: deeply concerned with it)

Or take the poem "Scunner," which is concerned with sexual love. The literal meaning of that familiar, colloquial Scots expression, *scunner*, is "disgust; a shudder betokening physical or moral repugnance." But there is in the poem a suggestion of affection for the "disreputable" Scots word, which subtly conveys the psychological perception on which the poem is based: that the element in the woman's sexuality which from one angle seems repugnant to him, from another angle provides the unique savor which makes him relish the experience. The word *scunner* is so crucial to his meaning, and so patently without an English equivalent, that one feels the poem's existence depended upon that word being available to him. And so the poem acts out one of the theoretical arguments for the value of Scots:

Your body derns
In its graces again
As the dreich grun' does
In the gowden grain,
And oot o' the daith
O' pride you rise
Wi' beauty yet
For a hauf-disguise.

The skinklan' stars
Are but distant dirt.
Tho' fer owre near
You are still—whiles—girt
Wi' the bonnie licht
You bood ha'e tint
-And I lo'e Love
Wi' a scunner in't.

(*derns*: hides; *dreich grun'*: drab ground; *gowden*: golden; *hauf-*: half-; *skinklan'*: glittering; *fer owre*: far too; *whiles*: sometimes; *bood ha'e tint*: should have lost; *lo'e*: love)

This poem also suggests a characteristic of MacDiarmid's use of Scots which he felt linked him with certain avant-garde writers of the time, particularly Joyce: it liberated him from the element of moral censorship which seemed to him to have been built into literary English.

As "Hugh MacDiarmid" took over from C. M. Grieve in the 1920s, a steady flow of poems in Scots followed. In deciding to write in Scots he based himself in the dialect speech of his boyhood—his native tongue—but allowed himself freedom to use any Scots expression that appealed to him, regardless of its historical or geographical distribution. It did not matter to him if a word was categorized as obsolete or obsolescent or extant only in some dialect area remote from his home ground: what mattered was the use he could make of it in a poem. On the theoretical level, he made a strong case for what has been called his "synthetic" Scots, appealing to comparable developments in recent revivals of other long neglected languages and pointing out that his "synthetic" procedure was just an extension of the principle actually followed by Burns, allegedly a model of "naturalness" in language. He also argued for Scots as an expression of national psychology not otherwise available to Scotsmen and deeply rooted in the sound system of the language: "There are certain old Scots words which (apart altogether from their precise original signification) have a significance of sound and shape which may prove infinitely suggestive. . . . I think that if Scottish artists will hunt out all these old words, the mere shapes and sounds of them will suggest to them effects which they cannot at present contrive, and if they set to and secure these effects the results will constitute a Scottish idiom—a Scottish scale of sound-values and physico-psychical effects completely at variance with those of England." But the most persuasive evidence of the value of what he was doing lay in the quality of the poetry he produced. Compared with his earlier work in English, it is much more tightly knit, richer and more powerful in its sound effects, and in its imagery at the same time more concrete and more suggestive—the very thing Pound and the imagists were aiming at. Above all, he rapidly found his own individual voice in Scots and with it a style which rooted the speculative, metaphysical bent of his mind in an earthy, virile vernacular.

Certain deliberate tours de force apart, even the most unfamiliar items in his Scots vocabulary do not, as used by him, give that impression of artificiality associated with a rarefied diction. Some are vivid illustrations of the imaginative life inherent in the process of word formation itself: for example, *yow-trummle* (a late cold spell which comes in a northern summer after the sheep have been shorn—hence the trembling of the ewes), and *how-dumb-deid* (middle of the night), in which the first element in the compound is the *howe* (hollow) occurring in place names. On the other hand a proverbial expression about the weather, "there was nae reek i' the laverock's hoose that nicht" (there was no smoke—hence warmth—in the lark's house that night), in a leap of metaphor conveys that it was a cold, wild night.

MacDiarmid's first two collections, *Sangschaw* (1925) and *Penny Wheep* (1926), consist mainly of short, highly charged Scots poems of which the finest are perhaps "Empty Vessel," "The Bonnie Broukit Bairn," and "The Eemis Stane." These poems show his characteristic sense of the earth, with its earthiness affectionately conveyed through the associations of the vernacular but strongly visualized in a cosmic setting. By far the most difficult, from the lexical point of view, is "The Eemis Stane." The earth is seen as at once a dead star adrift in space and a stone in the cosmic graveyard, inscribed with mysterious words which human history has obscured:

I' the how-dumb-deid o' the cauld hairst nicht
The warl' like an eemis stane
Wags i' the lift;
An' my eerie memories fa'
Like a yowdendrift.

Like a yowdendrift so's I couldna read
The words cut oot i' the stane
Had the fug o' fame
An' history's hazelraw
No' yirdit thaim.

(In the still center of the dead of night, cold at harvest-time, / the world like a loose stone / shakes in the sky, / and my eerie memories fall / like snow driven down by the wind. / / Like snow driven down by the wind, so that I couldn't read / the words cut out in the stone, / had the moss of fame / and the lichen of history / not buried them.)

Along with these short lyrics MacDiarmid began writing longer poems and "suites" of poems in Scots, and his next venture was intended as a major, book-length work which would stake the claim of Scots to regain its place in contemporary European literature. The composer F. G. Scott supplied the title of this poem or poem sequence, *A Drunk Man Looks at the Thistle* (1926), and he also assisted the author in deciding which items in a proliferating mass of material should be eliminated from the work prior to publication and what the order for those retained should be. This assistance suggests a weakness on MacDiarmid's part where the shaping of large-scale forms was concerned, and it was undoubtedly a real weakness which was to bedevil his subsequent determination to turn himself into an epic poet. In the case of *A Drunk Man Looks at the Thistle*, however, he succeeded in organizing an extraordinary variety of material around key images which generate a dynamic symbolism pervading the work as a whole. The whiskey imbibed by the protagonist—the national "spirit," now much adulterated—liberates a stream of consciousness from which separable, fully formed poems, along with much else worthy of interest, emerge as he gazes intently at the thistle in the moonlight. Thistle and moon are the poet's archetypal symbols around which figures of speech and patterns of thought constellate in astonishing profusion. Or perhaps a better suggestion of how they function is to be found in Pound's words: "The image . . . is a radiant node or cluster; it is a *vortex*, from which, and through which, and into which, ideas are constantly rushing."

The thistle is of course the Scottish national emblem, and at one level the problem the Drunk Man sets himself—how to "pluck figs from thistles"—is the problem of writing the poem itself, which is aimed at bringing to fruition the stunted growth of his native Scots tradition. This task involves on the one hand an attempt at scourging contemporary Scotland into awareness of its degenerate condition by a series of scathing satirical attacks and on the other hand an effort toward restoring the international context of the old national tradition by absorbing into the texture of his work Scots adaptations of poems by modern German, French, Belgian, and Russian writers—plus a passage from Dante and a network of literary allusions including a reference to T. S. Eliot's *The Waste Land* (1922), which MacDiarmid confidently set out to rival.

On another level, giving the poem its metaphysical dimension, the thistle embodies prickly philosophical questions confronting all mankind, as the Drunk Man sees in the tension between its jagged leaves and incongruous blossoms an epitome of the human dilemma between matter and spirit and in its unpredicted shape a challenge to the belief that life itself has an intelligible purpose. The fluctuation of the poem from one level to another is related to an idea which runs through a great deal of MacDiarmid's work in addition to *A Drunk Man Looks at the Thistle*. The critic Gregory Smith had diagnosed as the distinguishing feature of Scottish literature a tendency to combine opposites or contraries which he designated "the Caledonian Antisyzygy." What especially excited MacDiarmid about this observation was that he discerned a similar tendency in modern European literatures, and so, if he succeeded in reviving the essential spirit of his national tradition, he would be working in harmony with up-to-date European developments. But the concept of antisyzygy, or the combination of opposites, was in fact an ancient one, going far beyond recent literary tendencies to the function of the human imagination itself (as described for example in Coleridge's and Blake's accounts of that faculty) and informing many European and Eastern philosophies as the principle of *coincidentia oppositorum*, whereby existence itself is a dynamic, creative tension between polar opposites. MacDiarmid's declared philosophical position at the beginning of *A Drunk Man Looks at the Thistle*—"whaur extremes meet"—is another rendering of the same principle, and thus the speculative, metaphysical ramifications of his poem have an underlying connection with his efforts to put into practice a specifically Caledonian aesthetic of antisyzygy.

Around what Gregory Smith had called "the 'polar twins' of the Scottish Muse" MacDiarmid puts into orbit his antinomies of the real and the ideal, passion and intellect, body and soul, lust and love, beauty and ugliness, God and man, life and death, chaos and cosmos, being and essence, oblivion and eternity. The process of the poem is a romantically self-lacerating one, resulting in the total exhaustion of the poet, but it is the speculative stamina he brings to the longer, more sustained passages that ensures that the work is no mere showcase for the more immediately attractive specimens of his art, but that rare thing, a genuine modern long poem. It was written at a time when H. J. C. Grierson's work on Donne (1912) and others was alerting the twentieth century to what its poets could learn from the metaphysicals of the seventeenth. And, using the term in its several senses, MacDiarmid's "metaphysical" anatomy of the thistle may be seen as a splendid celebration of opportunities thus rediscovered for poetry:

Plant, what are you then? Your leafs
Mind me o' the pipes' lood drone
—And a' your purple tops
Are the pirly-wirly notes
That gang staggerin' owre them as they groan.

Or your leafs are alligators
That ha'e gobbled owre a haill
Company o' Heilant sodgers
And left naething but the toories
O' their Balmoral bonnets to tell the tale.

. . . .

The thistle in the wind dissolves
In lichtnin' as shook foil gi'es way
In sudden splendours, or the flesh
As Daith lets slip the infinite soul;
And syne it's like a sunrise tint
In grey o' day, or love and life,
That in a cloody blash o' sperm
Undae the warld to big't again,
Or like a pickled foetus that
Nae man feels ocht in common wi'
—But micht as easily ha' been!
Or like a corpse a soul set free
Scunners to think it tenanted
—And little recks that but for it
It never micht ha' been at a',
Like love frae lust and God frae man!

. . . .

'Let there be Licht,' said God, and there was
A little: but He lacked the poo'er
To licht up mair than pairt o' space at aince,
And there is lots o' darkness that's the same
As gin He'd never spoken
—Mair darkness than there's licht,
And dwarfin't to a candle-flame,
A spalin' candle that'll sune gang oot.
—Darkness comes closer to us than the licht,
And is oor natural element. We peer oot frae't
Like cat's een bleezin' in a goustrous nicht
(Whaur there is nocht to find but stars
That look like ither cats' een),
Like cat's een, and there is nocht to find
Savin' we turn them in upon oorsels;
Cats canna.

(*mind*: remind; *lood*: loud; *pirly-wirly notes*: grace notes; *gang*: go; *haill*: whole; *Heilant sodgers*: Highland soldiers; *toories*: pompoms; *syne*: then; *tint*: lost; *blash*: shower; *big't*: build it; *ocht*: anything; *scunners*: shudders; *a'*: all; *poo'er*: power; *aince*: once; *gin*: if; *spalin'*: guttering; *een*: eyes; *goustrous*: stormy; *nocht*: nothing; *oorsels*: ourselves; *canna*: can't)

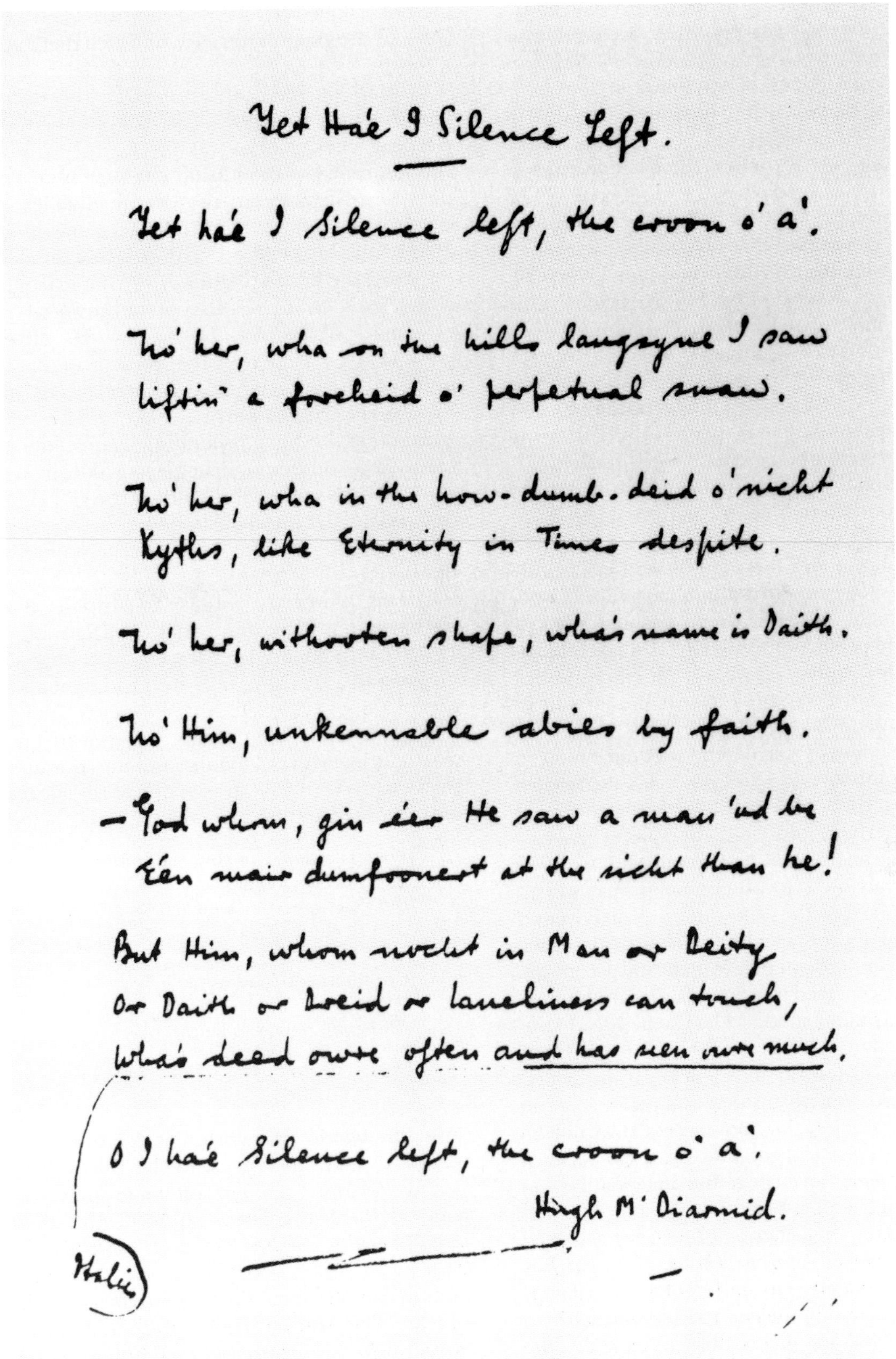

Yet Haé I Silence Left.
Yet haé I Silence left, the croon o' a'.
Tho' her, wha on the hills langsyne I saw
Liftin' a foreheid o' perpetual snaw.
Tho' her, wha in the how-dumb-deid o' nicht
Kyths, like Eternity in Time's despite.
Tho' her, withooten shape, wha's name is Daith.
Tho' Him, unkennable abies by faith.
—God whom, gin e'er He saw a man 'ud be
E'en mair dumfoonert at the sicht than he!
But Him, whom nocht in Man or Deity
Or Daith or Dreid or laneliness can touch,
Wha's deed owre often and has seen owre much.
O I haé Silence left, the croon o' a'.
Hugh M'Diarmid.
Italics

Page from a draft for the conclusion of A Drunk Man Looks at the Thistle

Only quotation on a massive scale could suggest the inventive powers which sustain this astonishing work. *A Drunk Man Looks at the Thistle* is one of the great poems of the century.

MacDiarmid's problem was, inevitably, how to follow it. He struggled for four years before taking the plunge with his next work, a much longer poem in Scots called *To Circumjack Cencrastus* (1930). As the poem reveals, domestic and professional troubles played a large part in his difficulties, acerbated by an ill-fated move to London and then Liverpool. The key factor in his decision to leave Scotland for London in 1929 was the offer of a job on *Vox*, a magazine founded by Compton Mackenzie to cater to the growing interest in the new medium of radio. The magazine was inadequately financed, and MacDiarmid soon had to contend with the scourge of the 1930s, unemployment, along with a succession of personal problems culminating in divorce and separation from his two children.

Mackenzie said of the writing of *To Circumjack Cencrastus* that, under these conditions, it was only by a miracle that any sort of book appeared at all, and it is certainly true that the work shows signs of having been patched together in a desperate attempt to salvage pieces from at least two different projects. One of these projects was the pursuit of Cencrastus on a highly metaphysical level, Cencrastus (the name of a snake the poet encountered in his exploration of Jamieson's Scots dictionary) being conceived as the mythological world-serpent or "the underlying unifying principle of the cosmos," and the meaning of "to Circumjack" being "to lie round or about." The other main project was an attempt at reviving the ethos, not just of Lowland Scotland, but of the ancient Celtic civilization which included Ireland, Scotland, Wales, and Cornwall. This attempt centered on what MacDiarmid hoped would be a dynamic myth, "The Gaelic Idea," conceived as a counterbalance to "The Russian Idea" projected by Dostoevski and radically transformed by Lenin. Since Cencrastus was intended to have an historical dimension, his movements traceable in world history, one can see how these two strands might have been woven together imaginatively in the work, but the poet failed to carry out this integration. Lacking the cohesion of imagery achieved in *A Drunk Man Looks at the Thistle, To Circumjack Cencrastus* obstinately remains full of awkward gaps which MacDiarmid in the end tried to plug with an assortment of bits and pieces, thus ensuring that the work was (as he had said it would be) "a much bigger thing than *A Drunk Man*," but merely in terms of length. Readers may find the bulk of the poem such an indigestible mixture that they are likely to miss some of the good things in it, of which there are not a few.

MacDiarmid's difficulties in the unhappy period which followed were compounded by his political leanings. He was increasingly drawn to communism (a communism cut very much to his own Scottish pattern, though he did become a card-carrying member of the Communist party in 1934), but he believed that the best immediate prospect for his own country, in the existing circumstances, lay in the adoption of the Social Credit economic policies of C. H. Douglas. His efforts to get a Douglas Plan accepted as the economic program of the National Party of Scotland led to his expulsion from that party in 1933, and he was convinced that the forces operating against him in his increasingly desperate struggle to make a living and support his second wife, Valda Trevlyn (whom he married in 1932), and their child, as well as to get his literary work published, were largely political in motivation.

It is, however, a mistake to suppose, as some commentators have done, that MacDiarmid in the 1930s confined his talents as a poet to political propaganda, resulting in hymns to Lenin and that sort of thing. He wrote what he called "Hymns to Lenin," certainly, but they are not what anyone else would be likely to call hymns, and the second of the three, in particular, is an assertion of the supremacy of the work of art over all politics, Lenin's included:

> Your knowledge in your ain sphere
> Was exact and complete
> But your sphere's elementary and sune by
> As a poet maun see't.
>
> Unremittin', relentless,
> Organized to the last degree,
> Ah Lenin, politics is bairns' play
> To what this maun be!

(*ain*: own; *sune by*: soon past; *maun*: must)

The two hymns written at this time were intended to take their place in the first volume of "Clann Albann," a huge autobiographical poem planned for five volumes. Indeed, *First Hymn to Lenin and Other Poems* (1931) and *Scots Unbound and Other Poems* (1932) were presented as interim selections of samples from the first volume—the title of which, "The Muckle Toon," indicated their connection with his birthplace, Langholm—and other material intended for inclusion in it remained for decades forgotten in periodicals. The poems not published in *First Hymn to Lenin and Other Poems* and

Scots Unbound and Other Poems include some excellent longer poems, such as "Whuchulls" and "By Wauchopeside"—a fact which indicated that MacDiarmid was unable to find a place even for some of the best of his poems in the little volumes he did manage to get published.

His first four volumes of poetry had been published by the old Scottish establishment of Blackwood's, but now he had to fall back on the modest resources of the Unicorn Press, for which he worked in London, and a small press in Stirling. A short spell of employment as a public-relations officer in Liverpool was followed by a period of bare subsistence in a borrowed cottage in Surrey, and in 1932 he returned to Scotland in an attempt to eke out a living by journalism in Edinburgh.

The breakup of his first marriage and separation from his children had brought about a return in the poet's imagination to the Langholm of his childhood, with a wry review of his relationships with his kinsfolk and a search for the restorative powers of the images with which the surrounding countryside had first nurtured his inner life. Above all, "a perfect maze of waters is aboot the Muckle Toon," and so the work intended for the first volume of "Clann Albann" is full of the imagery of water, which takes him through the search for the sources of his own creative powers ultimately to the source and evolutionary potential of life itself. "Water Music" is one of the most striking poems which emerged from this search: a verbal tour de force addressed to James Joyce, celebrating the dynamic multifariousness of the rivers Wauchope, Esk, and Ewes in a rhythmic apotheosis of the Scots lexicon:

Wheesht, wheesht, Joyce, and let me hear
Nae Anna Livvy's lilt,
But Wauchope, Esk, and Ewes again,
Each wi' its ain rhythms till't.

Archin' here and arrachin there,
Allevolie or alleman,
Whiles appliable, whiles areird,
The polysemous poem's planned.

Lively, louch, atweesh, atween,
Auchimuty or aspate,
Threidin' through the averins
Or bightsome in the aftergait.

(*wheesht*: hush; *till't*: to it; *archin'*: flowing smoothly; *arrachin*: tumultuous; *allevolie*: volatile; *alleman*: orderly; *appliable*: compliant; *areird*: troublesome; *louch*: downcast; *atweesh*: betwixt; *atween*: between; *auchimuty*: trickling; *aspate*: in flood; *averins*: cloudberries; *bightsome*: ample; *aftergait*: outcome)

The verve of such lines carries the reader along, willing for the sake of the verbal music to forgo his usual semantic sustenance, until

you've me in your creel again,
Brim or shallow, bauch or bricht,
Singin' in the mornin',
Corrieneuchin' a' the nicht.

(*creel*: spell; *brim*: swollen; *bauch*: dull; *corrieneuchin*: gossiping)

In the experiments with dictionary Scots which he made about this time, rhythmic and other relationships in the *sound* of his language are of vital importance in stimulating the reader to respond to the life of the poems. But with his tendency to push experimental techniques to the extreme, as if to find out just how much they could stand, he was beginning, in such works as "Scots Unbound," to lose his rhythmic touch and so to overwhelm the reader with a sense of sheer verbalism. Clearly he could not go much further in that particular direction. And although he could still in 1932 produce one of his most perfect poems, "Milk-wort and Bog-cotton," that was to be the last of his truly great Scots lyrics:

Cwa' een like milk-wort and bog-cotton hair!
I love you, earth, in this mood best o' a'
When the shy spirit like a laich wind moves
And frae the lift nae shadow can fa'
Since there's nocht left to thraw a shadow there
Owre een like milk-wort and milk-white cotton hair.

Wad that nae leaf upon anither wheeled
A shadow either and nae root need dern
In sacrifice to let sic beauty be!
But deep surroondin' darkness I discern
Is aye the price o' licht. Wad licht revealed
Naething but you, and nicht nocht else concealed.

(*cwa'*: come away; *laich*: low; *lift*: sky; *nocht*: nothing; *wad*: would; *dern*: hide; *sic*: such)

MacDiarmid began to write more and more poems in English, as the "Clann Albann" scheme became ever less likely to be carried out, and his reversion to English was made to seem more emphatic when the publisher of his next collection, *Stony Limits and Other Poems* (1934), deleted from the manuscript two of the most substantial works in Scots. (The two poems were restored in *Stony Limits and Scots Unbound and Other Poems*, 1956.) One of these, *Ode to All Rebels*, is his longest sustained achievement in Scots since *To Circumjack Cencrastus*, while the other, "Harry Semen," explores the theme of fascinated revulsion at the human sexual process as powerfully and memorably as anything in that vein in *A Drunk Man Looks at the Thistle*.

The change from Scots back to English, in which language the vast majority of MacDiarmid's later poems were written, accompanied a move which might have been expected to result in some new orientation. In 1933 he left Scotland for Whalsay, in the Shetland Islands, where at any rate physical survival was less of a problem for him, his courageous new wife, and their infant son. In other respects, however, he felt his isolation acutely, and he was to remain there in virtual exile for the next eight years.

The later poems in English suggest a turning away from the lyrical aspects of poetry in a number of directions. There are propaganda pieces—most of the propaganda being Douglasite rather than

JOIN THE

HUGH MACDIARMID BOOK CLUB

Organised to secure publication for a constant stream of revolutionary Scottish Literature, devoted to anti-English separatism.

The majority of the entire Scottish electorate votes for the Left, but this is not only nullified in practice by the English connection but is so far almost entirely unreflected in journalism and publishing. Mr. MacDiarmid's aim is the establishment of a Scottish Workers' Autonymous Communist Republic and a revival of literature in the distinctive Scottish tradition.

SEND NO MONEY, but sign this form and post it to the Secretary, Hugh MacDiarmid Book Club, Whalsay, via Lerwick, Shetland Islands:—

I agree for one year from this date to accept on publication the four or five books to be issued during the ensuing twelve months, at preferential rates to Club members, by the Hugh MacDiarmid Book Club, also the weekly paper, *Red Scotland*, and the monthly *Hammer and Thistle*, at a total inclusive rate, including postage, of 40/- [books to be paid for on delivery, and the *Red Scotland* and *Hammer and Thistle* annual subscriptions (10/- each) on receipt of the first issues of these.]

Name ....

Address ....

.... *Date*.....................

(*Please fill in in clear block letters.*)

HUGH MACDIARMID'S BOOKS INCLUDE:—

Poetry: A Drunk Man looks at the Thistle; Selected Poems; Stony Limits; First Hymn to Lenin; Second Hymn to Lenin, etc., etc.

Criticism: At the Sign of the Thistle; Contemporary Scottish Studies; Scottish Scene, etc., etc.

Biography: Scottish Eccentrics, etc., etc.

Fiction: Annals of the Five Senses; Five Bits of Millar, etc., etc.

Politics: Albyn, or Scotland and the Future, etc., etc.

Music: The Present Condition of Scottish Music.

Agriculture: Rural Reform (with Lord Passfield and others.)

(Thirty titles in all.)

Early Club issues will include *Cornish Heroic Song for Valda Trevlyn* and *The Red Lion* (a poetical gallimaufry of the Glasgow slums). Further Club news in *Red Scotland* weekly.

Circular for the Hugh MacDiarmid Book Club

communist—in which the all-important message is sometimes put across at a crude level of versifying, as in "The Belly-Grip" for example. There are experiments with scientific, technical, or otherwise "recondite" vocabularies, rapidly taken to breaking point as was his wont but achieving some brilliant effects along the way. For example, the first part of "In the Caledonian Forest" is verbalistically supersaturated to a degree which is likely to repel the reader, but in the second part he is lured back against all the odds with the following:

> The gold edging of a bough at sunset, its pantile way
> Forming a double curve, tegula and imbrex in one,
> Seems at times a movement on which I might be borne
> Happily to infinity; but again I am glad
> When it suddenly ceases and I find myself
> Pursuing no longer a rhythm of duramen
> But bouncing in a diploe in a clearing between earth and air
> Or headlong in dewy dallops or a moon-spairged fernshaw
> Or caught in a dark dumosity or even
> In open country again watching an aching spargosis of stars.

There are also much longer, meditative poems which may make use of recondite lexical resources for special effects but which owe their power to the sustained concentration of an endlessly speculative mind coiling itself around the curious, multifarious lore of a lifetime's reading. The most impressive of these is "On A Raised Beach," a sustained meditation on the world of stones, the beginning and end of creation, seen in the hard, clear light of the Shetland Islands. The stones on the raised beach are geological clues to the mystery of the universe, and they are represented at the beginning of the poem by a great pile of recondite words seemingly as hard to penetrate as the stones. But as the poet proceeds to explore the imagery he finds indefatigably for the "barren but beautiful reality" of this bleak world, he does in the end achieve on his own terms the miracle of "bread from stones":

> This is no heap of broken images.
> . . . .
> What happens to us
> Is irrelevant to the world's geology
> But what happens to the world's geology
> Is not irrelevant to us.
> We must reconcile ourselves to the stones,
> Not the stones to us.
> Here a man must shed the encumbrances that muffle
> Contact with elemental things, the subtleties
> That seem inseparable from a humane life, and go apart
> Into a simple and sterner, more beautiful and more oppressive world,
> Austerely intoxicating; the first draught is overpowering;
> Few survive it. It fills me with a sense of perfect form,
> The end seen from the beginning, as in a song.
> It is no song that conveys the feeling
> That there is no reason why it should ever stop,
> But the kindred form I am conscious of here
> Is the beginning and end of the world,
> The unsearchable masterpiece, the music of the spheres,
> Alpha and Omega, the Omnific Word.

In this poem and in "Stony Limits," his noble elegy to a fellow visionary of the desert, Charles M. Doughty, MacDiarmid used his isolation in the wilderness to give resonance to verse of massive dignity. But the strain of his increasingly fanatical demands on himself—"immense exercise of will, / In-

MacDiarmid and his second wife, Valda, outside their cottage in Biggar, 1951

conceivable discipline, courage, and endurance, / Self-purification and anti-humanity"—resulted before long in a mental and physical breakdown. He spent some time in a hospital in 1935 and on his return launched himself into a series of projects for vast, epic works, none of which was ever executed, or at any rate published, on the scale on which they were conceived, though the remainder of his poetic career was largely devoted to them.

Second Hymn to Lenin and Other Poems (1935) strikes one as a clearing of his desk of short poems (including pieces of the rejected *Ode to All Rebels* now recast in English) before committing himself absolutely to these huge projects. The first of them, "Cornish Heroic Song for Valda Trevlyn," seems to have been an attempt to carry out on a much larger canvas what *To Circumjack Cencrastus* had failed to achieve but his long "Lament for the Great Music" had again heralded: a celebration of the unique Celtic contribution to civilization in all its aspects. The other main project was called "Mature Art" or "A Vision of World Language" and was conceived as a "poetry of fact" aimed at presenting as many facets as possible of the world of information and ideas impacting on the mind of a "harbinger of the epical age of Communism." Two of an intended four parts of this work were eventually published as *In Memoriam James Joyce* (1955) and *The Kind of Poetry I Want* (1961).

Meanwhile, MacDiarmid had returned to mainland Scotland, conscripted for war work in 1941. At the age of fifty he worked as a fitter in the copper shell-band department of an engineering works in Glasgow and then moved to service as a ship's engineer until the end of the war, when his job was eliminated, and he rejoined the unemployed.

In 1950 he was awarded a civil-list pension of £ 150 a year for his services to literature and moved soon afterward to the farm worker's cottage near Biggar in Lanarkshire where he stayed until his death from cancer in 1978. An honorary doctorate from Edinburgh University signaled his recognition by the academic establishment in Scotland, and visits to various Communist countries and to North America indicated a growing international reputation. In his own view, the crucial breakthrough occurred in 1962 with the publication in New York of *Collected Poems*, a partial but very substantial collection of his poems. This volume made the range of his work known at last—even in London, though the gradual buildup of critical appreciation occurred elsewhere—and there was now widespread acknowledgment of his public stature as the Grand

Hugh MacDiarmid (photo by Gordon Wright)

Old Man of Scottish literature: a part which he played with great aplomb and a certain subversive relish. Inwardly, he continued in his seventies the pursuit of those unrealized epic schemes which haunted him till almost the end.

The samples of his epic, world-view "poetry of fact" which appeared in 1955 and 1961 contain some pioneering attempts at extending the range of poetry to take in areas long considered to have become foreign to its nature, notably through his use of scientific, technical, and other apparently prosaic materials for purposes of analogy. Although these works have proved stimulating to later poets, particularly Edwin Morgan, they tend to be overwhelmed by an obsessive cataloguing of itemized pieces of information or labeling of specimens. MacDiarmid now conceded only a minimal distinction between poetry and prose, so that the contents of his notebooks and stacks of press cuttings could supply the substance of his epics with little verbal manipulation by the poet himself. He could on occasion do fascinating and imaginative things with passages of prose taken from writers who often had very different purposes in mind, but his determination to project everything onto an epic scale resulted in the erection of a top-heavy tower of Babel which he propped up with some epic wishful thinking.

All of MacDiarmid's poetry has at last become available in the two massive volumes of *Complete Poems* (1978), and it is now a straightforward matter for readers to judge for themselves what part of his total output is worthy of the immense energy and ambition he brought to it. No one could take the risks MacDiarmid repeatedly took and not be vulnerable on a grand scale, but even his disasters have an awesome grandeur about them, and the best of his work is a delight of the highest order which no one who cares for poetry should allow himself to miss.

For you rin coonter to the rhythms o' thocht,
Wrenched oot o' recognition a' words fail
To haud you, alien to the human mind,
Yet in your ain guid time you suddenly slip,
Nae man kens hoo, into the simplest phrase,
While a' the dictionary rejoices. . . .

(*rin coonter*: run counter; *haud*: hold; *kens hoo*: knows how)

Other:

The Golden Treasury of Scottish Poetry, edited, with an introduction, by MacDiarmid (London: Macmillan, 1940);

Harry Martinson, *Aniara*, adapted from the Swedish by MacDiarmid and Elspeth Harley Schubert (London: Hutchinson, 1963);

Bertolt Brecht, *The Threepenny Opera*, translated by MacDiarmid (London: Eyre Methuen, 1973).

Interviews:

Duncan Glen, "A Conversation," *Akros*, 5 (April 1970): 9-72;

George Bruce, "An Interview," *Akros*, 5 (April 1970): 73-77;

Walter Perrie, Interview with MacDiarmid, in *Metaphysics and Poetry* (Hamilton: Lothlorien Publications, 1975);

Alexander Scott, "An Interview with Hugh MacDiarmid," *Studies in Scottish Literature*, 14 (1979): 1-22.

References:

Akros, special MacDiarmid issue, 12 (August 1977);

Kenneth Buthlay, "The Appreciation of the Golden Lyric: Early Scots Poems of Hugh MacDiarmid," *Scottish Literary Journal*, 2 (July 1975): 41-66;

Buthlay, *Hugh MacDiarmid (C. M. Grieve)* (Edinburgh: Oliver & Boyd, 1964; revised edition, Edinburgh: Scottish Academic Press, 1982);

David Daiches, "Hugh MacDiarmid and Scottish Poetry," *Poetry*, 72 (July 1948): 202-218;

Kulgin D. Duval and Sydney Goodsir Smith, eds., *Hugh MacDiarmid a Festschrift* (Edinburgh: Duval, 1962);

Duncan Glen, *Hugh MacDiarmid (Christopher Murray Grieve) and the Scottish Renaissance* (Edinburgh: Chambers, 1964);

Glen, ed., *Hugh MacDiarmid: A Critical Survey* (Edinburgh: Scottish Academic Press, 1972);

Charles I. Glicksberg, "Hugh MacDiarmid the Marxist Messiah," *Prairie Schooner*, 26 (Fall 1952): 325-335;

Edwin Morgan, *Essays* (Cheadle Hulme: Carcanet New Press, 1974), pp. 194-221;

Morgan, *Hugh MacDiarmid* (Harlow: Longman, 1976);

P. H. Scott and A. C. Davis, eds., *The Age of MacDiarmid Essays on Hugh MacDiarmid and his Influence on Contemporary Scotland* (Edinburgh: Mainstream, 1980);

Scottish Literary Journal, MacDiarmid memorial number, 5 (December 1978).

Papers:

Most of MacDiarmid's papers are in Edinburgh University Library and the National Library of Scotland, Edinburgh. Others are in the libraries of Yale University; the State University of New York, Buffalo; and the University of Delaware, Newark.

Louis MacNeice

(12 September 1907-3 September 1963)

Robert H. Canary
University of Wisconsin, Parkside

See also the MacNeice entry in *DLB 10, Modern British Dramatists, 1900-1945.*

SELECTED BOOKS: *Blind Fireworks* (London: Gollancz, 1929);

Roundabout Way, as Louis Malone (London & New York: Putnam's, 1932);

Poems (London: Faber & Faber, 1935; New York: Random House, 1937);

Out of the Picture (London: Faber & Faber, 1937; New York: Harcourt, Brace, 1938);

Letters from Iceland, by MacNeice and W. H. Auden (London: Faber & Faber, 1937; New York: Random House, 1937);

Poems 1937 (New York: Random House, 1937);

The Earth Compels, Poems (London: Faber & Faber, 1938);

I Crossed the Minch (London, New York & Toronto: Longmans, Green, 1938);

Modern Poetry (Oxford: Oxford University Press, 1938; New York: Haskell House, 1969);

Zoo (London: Joseph, 1938);

Autumn Journal (London: Faber & Faber, 1939; New York: Random House, 1940);

Selected Poems (London: Faber & Faber, 1940);

The Last Ditch (Dublin: Cuala Press, 1940);

Poems 1925-1940 (New York: Random House, 1941);

The Poetry of W. B. Yeats (London, New York & Toronto: Oxford University Press, 1941);

Plant and Phantom (London: Faber & Faber, 1941);

Meet the U. S. Army (London: His Majesty's Stationery Office, 1943);

Christopher Columbus (London: Faber & Faber, 1944);

Springboard, Poems 1941-1944 (London: Faber &

Louis MacNeice (BBC Hulton)

Faber, 1944; New York: Random House, 1945);

The Dark Tower and Other Radio Scripts (London: Faber & Faber, 1947);

Holes in the Sky, Poems 1944-1947 (London: Faber & Faber: 1948; New York: Random House, 1949);

Collected Poems 1925-1948 (London: Faber & Faber, 1949; New York: Oxford University Press, 1963);

Ten Burnt Offerings (London: Faber & Faber, 1952; New York: Oxford University Press, 1953);

The Penny That Rolled Away (New York: Putnam's, 1954); republished as *The Sixpence That Rolled Away* (London: Faber & Faber, 1956);

The Other Wing (London: Faber & Faber, 1954);

Autumn Sequel: A Rhetorical Poem (London: Faber & Faber, 1954);

Visitations (London: Faber & Faber, 1957; New York: Oxford University Press, 1958);

Eighty-Five Poems (London: Faber & Faber, 1959; New York: Oxford University Press, 1961);

Solstices (London: Faber & Faber,1961; New York: Oxford University Press, 1961);

The Burning Perch (London: Faber & Faber, 1963; New York: Oxford University Press, 1963);

The Mad Islands and The Administrator (London: Faber & Faber, 1964);

Astrology (London: Aldus Books, 1964; Garden City: Doubleday, 1964);

The Strings Are False, An Unfinished Autobiography, edited by E. R. Dodds (London: Faber & Faber, 1965; New York: Oxford University Press, 1966);

Varieties of Parable (Cambridge: Cambridge University Press, 1965);

The Collected Poems of Louis MacNeice, edited by Dodds (London: Faber & Faber, 1966; New York: Oxford University Press, 1967);

One for the Grave (London: Faber & Faber, 1968; New York: Oxford University Press, 1968);

Persons from Porlock and Other Plays for Radio (London: British Broadcasting Company,1969).

Louis MacNeice was widely regarded in the 1930s as a junior member of the Auden-Spender-Day Lewis group: MacNeice and Stephen Spender were contemporaries and friends at Oxford, serving as joint editors of *Oxford Poetry, 1929*. MacNeice became a friend of Wystan Hugh Auden's and collaborated with him on *Letters from Iceland* (1937). And in *Modern Poetry* (1938), MacNeice provided the best critical statement of the poetic aims and achievements of his friends. Despite these personal and professional ties, MacNeice did not share the ideological commitments of the "Auden group." From first to last, his own work reflects a melancholy skepticism too honest to give final assent to any fixed system. MacNeice might sympathize with, and even envy, those who believed, but he remained a detached outsider.

Born in Belfast Frederick Louis MacNeice was an outsider almost from the beginning. His family moved to Carrickfergus, County Antrim, soon after his birth. His father, John Frederick MacNeice, although a minister and eventually a bishop of the Anglo-Irish Church of Ireland, favored Home Rule, believed in ecumenical cooperation, and spoke out against the Protestant bigotry and violence in Northern Ireland. When MacNeice was six, his mother, Elizabeth Margaret MacNeice, who was suffering from severe depression, entered a nursing home in Dublin; he did not see her again, and she died in December 1914 of tuberculosis. His father remarried when young MacNeice was ten, and thereafter MacNeice was educated at English schools. At Sherborne Preparatory School in Dorset and later at Marlborough College, he found the promise of a wider and more colorful world than the puritan rectory of his father and stepmother. He lost his Irish accent and abandoned his baptismal first name of Frederick and his father's faith. He could never again feel entirely at home in his father's house or in Ireland, but he never lost a sense of himself as an Irishman in England, and his imagination returned again and again to childhood fears and memories.

MacNeice was raised among books and began writing poetry at the age of seven. By the time he went up to Merton College at Oxford in 1926, his reading included such modern poets as Edith Sitwell and T. S. Eliot. Troubled by his "lack of belief or system," he studied metaphysics without advancing much beyond the "vague epicureanism" with which he had begun. It is mainly as a young aesthete that he appears in the four poems he contributed to *Oxford Poetry, 1929* and his undergraduate collection, *Blind Fireworks* (1929). His foreword to *Blind Fireworks* compares its poems to Chinese fireworks, "artificial and yet random; because they go quickly through their antics against an important background, and fall and go out quickly." The poems invite us to admire the poet's versatility in versification and cleverness in imagery. Except in some poems reflecting childhood and family experiences, the sharp observations of the everyday world which is one of MacNeice's later strengths is not much in evidence, despite the con-

Louis MacNeice at Oxford

temporary flavor of the diction. The underlying melancholy which characterizes much of his work is already in evidence, but it sometimes seems melodramatically heightened. More than most young poets, MacNeice had assimilated his influences so that his poetry does not seem derivative in manner, but one is left with a bright young man who can speak in his own voice but has not yet settled what he is to speak about.

MacNeice was certainly bright enough to master his studies, though he affected to be bored by them. He took a first in Honors Mods. in 1928. His further studies took second place to his courtship of the stepdaughter of an Oxford scholar, Giovanna Marie Therese Babette Ezra, to whom he dedicated *Blind Fireworks*. At one point he was forced to wire his teetotaling rector father "that I had been put in gaol for drunkenness and was engaged to marry a Jewess," but the authorities allowed him to remain at Oxford, his parents were reconciled to his prospective bride, and MacNeice took another first in Greats. In 1930, he married his Mary and took a position as an assistant lecturer in classics at Birmingham University.

MacNeice was less pleased with teaching than he had anticipated; the students of Birmingham were not the students of Oxford, and he found more congenial the workingmen he drank with in pubs. He admired his colleague E. R. Dodds, but felt no inclination to become a scholar. His time as a classicist and his friendship with Dodds did, however, bear fruit later in MacNeice's translation of *The Agamemnon of Aeschylus* (1936), produced by the experimental Group Theatre in 1937 with music by Benjamin Britten. This translation remains one of the best modern poetic translations of any Greek drama; as such, it is probably more widely read currently than MacNeice's original work.

MacNeice's early married life was idyllic—too much so, by his own account, for the poet in him: "To write poems expressing doubt or melancholy, an anarchist conception of freedom or nostalgia for the open spaces (and these were the things that I wanted to express), seemed disloyal to Mariette. Instead I was disloyal to myself, wrote a novel which purported to be an idyll of domestic felicity." This novel, *Roundabout Way* (1932), was a failure. He may have written another novel in the 1930s; if so, it was never published. Casting about for writing outlets, he also wrote *Station Bell* (unpublished), a surreal farce about Irish politics produced by the Birmingham University Dramatic Society in 1937.

Whatever uncertainties may have afflicted MacNeice as a poet in the early 1930s, *Poems* (1935) shows a real advance in his work. In Birmingham, the urban imagery which he had learned to admire in Eliot became part of his own felt experience. In poems such as "Belfast," "Birmingham," "Sunday Morning," and "An Eclogue for Christmas," the poet speaks as a city dweller in an unforced way, observing the scene with detached but sympathetic irony. This characteristic detachment also marks his political stance. MacNeice's personal sympathies were with the Left, but "To a Communist" responds to one whose "thoughts make shape like snow" with reminders of the intractable particularity and variety of the earth and its weather. "An Eclogue for Christmas" offers some images of violent revolution—"sniggering machine guns in the hands of the young men"—but MacNeice's love is for "ephemeral things" rather than "pitiless abstractions." He seems identified with the voice of "The Individualist Speaks," who hopes to "escape, with my dog, on the far side of the Fair."

Poems (1935) helped establish MacNeice as one of the bright new poets of the 1930s. T. S. Eliot accepted the volume for Faber & Faber, who were to remain MacNeice's English publishers for his poetry. In "Postscript 1936," written for a new edition of his *A Hope For Poetry* (1934), C. Day Lewis described MacNeice's book as "in some ways the most interesting of the poetical work produced in the last two years," a comparison which took into account important works by Eliot, Auden, Spender, Empson, and Day Lewis himself.

But 1935 was also the year in which MacNeice's personal world fell apart. His wife suddenly left him and their year-old son, running away with a young American graduate student who had been staying with them in Birmingham. The MacNeices were formally divorced in 1936. MacNeice eventually wrote more and better poetry about the loss of his wife than he had ever written about their marital bliss, but it took him some time to recover from the blow. He plunged himself into his work and sought other distractions, vacationing in Spain with his friend Anthony Blunt and in Iceland with Auden. With his friend Dodds leaving for Oxford, MacNeice felt isolated in Birmingham and accepted a lectureship in Greek at Bedford College of the University of London.

MacNeice continued to try his hand at drama. At least one play from this time ("Blacklegs") remains unstaged and unpublished, but the Group Theatre, which had staged his *Agamemnon* translation, accepted another play, this time written with them in mind, *Out of the Picture* (produced and published in 1937). In this play, MacNeice's own interest may have been in the central character, a failed (or failing) artist, but whatever possibilities the story may have had are swallowed up in surrealistic farcical tragedy, political caricatures, and theatrical tricks. It belongs to roughly the same genre as Auden and Christopher Isherwood's *The Dog Beneath the Skin* (1935), but it was less successful than its model or MacNeice's *Agamemnon*.

MacNeice's most interesting work in the years dominated by the loss of his wife was his collaboration with Auden on *Letters from Iceland* (1937). One of the most entertaining travel books of this century, it is also one of the oddest. In the poem which closes the book, "Postscript to Iceland for W. H. Auden," MacNeice cites Auden as saying that "the North begins inside," and the book as a whole has more to say about the interior life of its authors and about the world they left behind them than it does about Iceland. There are, it is true, two prose chapters recounting their trip to Iceland and giving specific advice to would-be travelers there, but poetry bulks larger than prose in the volume, and its tone is set by five chapters devoted to a long "letter" in terza rima from Auden to Lord Byron. Besides the "Postscript to Iceland for W. H. Auden" MacNeice contributed a "letter" in heroic couplets (to his friends Graham and Anna Shepard) and an "Eclogue from Iceland," while collaborating with Auden on a "Last Will and Testament." The only one of these to rise above amusing occasional verse is the "Eclogue from Iceland," in which the main speakers are Craven (Auden), Ryan (MacNeice), and the ghost of a saga hero, with interruptions from a self-pitying Voice of Europe. The ghost advises the touring poets to go back to their native lands to fight the good fight, pat advice that seems especially ironic in light of Auden's later immigration to America and MacNeice's continued rejection of Ireland. The book attracted considerable critical attention and helped MacNeice's career, though it is Auden's "Letter to Byron" which has given it such durability as it possesses.

Offers from publishers led to two MacNeice books published in 1938, *I Crossed the Minch* and *Zoo*. In his autobiography MacNeice describes these as "prose books for which I had no vocation but which, I thought to myself, I could do as well as the next man. It flattered me that publishers should ask me to do something unsuitable." *I Crossed the Minch*, a journal of a trip to the Hebrides, is perhaps better than these remarks suggest. Lacking any knowledge of Gaelic and finding the islands distressingly modern, MacNeice contributes no new insights about the Hebrides, but his digressions in poetry and prose are often amusing. *Zoo* offers impressions of the London zoo with side trips to the Paris zoo and the city of Belfast; MacNeice shows no special sympathy with his subjects.

A more important prose work from 1938 is *Modern Poetry*. Several "case-book" chapters record MacNeice's own development as a poet. The book as a whole offers a defense of modern poetry, in particular the poetry of Auden, Spender, Day Lewis, and MacNeice himself. MacNeice wants to reduce the romantic distinction between the poet and the ordinary man. His poet is concerned with communication, though he is no propagandist but "a blend of the entertainer and the critic or informer." The poet looks, in fact, rather like MacNeice himself: "I would have a poet able-bodied, fond of talking, a reader of the newspapers, capable of pity and laughter, informed in economics, appreciative of women, involved in personal relationships, actively interested in politics, susceptible to physical impressions." Although taken by some at the time as a manifesto for the Auden group's poetry of social commitment, *Modern Poetry* treats political beliefs as just one sort of belief which may animate a poet, and it insists that all such beliefs must be disciplined by personal observation.

MacNeice's new volume of poetry in the same year, *The Earth Compels* (1938), is a slim one, reflecting both his personal troubles and the time he had devoted to prose and drama over the past few years. There has been little development in manner, and little was added to his reputation. Of the poems in this volume not previously published, "Carrickfergus" has some special biographical interest for its use of childhood memories, and it can be taken to signal MacNeice's growth toward a more balanced view of the Ireland he had left. The most popular MacNeice poem of this period, however, is not from this volume but from *I Crossed the Minch*: "Bagpipe Music" is a swinging, slangy poem which attempts to recreate the feeling of bagpipes and has proven a favorite with critics and readers. Under the jaunty rhythms, the subject of the poem is a Depression-induced despair: "It's no go the Herring Board, it's no go the Bible, / All we want is a packet of fags when our hands are idle." In this poem, the poet is certainly both "entertainer" and "critic or informer"; he is not a propagandist or prophet, for no solutions are endorsed, and many are rejected outright.

Autumn Journal (1939) is the closest thing to a "major" poem in the MacNeice oeuvre, though at the same time it is quite openly an "occasional" poem, a verse diary of the closing months of 1938. It is made up of twenty-four cantos composed of interwoven quatrains, rhyming on alternate lines—usually the second and fourth, sometimes the first and third. The lines vary in length from two to six feet, with the changes in rhythm controlled by an informal, colloquial tone and frequent use of enjambment. The poem begins at breakfast time in the suburbs, and other cantos follow the poet to London for his working days and nights. Events in the present stir old memories—of Ireland, rejected with hatred; of his own schooling, remembered with irony; of his wife, much missed, still loved. But the poet cannot immerse himself in his personal past and present. The voice of Hitler, speaking on the wireless, intrudes upon his life, and the eventual settlement at Munich fills him with shame. He visits Paris and Barcelona, where the Spanish speak to him of the necessity of choice and action. "The New Year comes with bombs," and we can only hope that it will prove possible to "pray for a possible land" better than our own.

The technical merits of *Autumn Journal* have been generally conceded. The poem retains the coherence of tone and rhythm through its many subjects and variations. The poem also convinces most readers of its essential honesty. It is not a confessional poem of intimate revelations, but the reader feels that the poet is doing his best to communicate what it is like to be Louis MacNeice in the fall of 1938, a man who is both "involved in personal relationships" and "a reader of newspapers." The tone in some places at first seems false—for example, "There ain't no universals in this man's town." Yet it is acceptable in a journal entry. To the extent that MacNeice was representative of a larger class of liberal individualists trapped in a polarized world which made their personal values seem less and less relevant, the poem earns the praise it has sometimes received as a historical document.

For some critics, however, the poem's strengths are also symptoms of its ultimate failure. Technical facility is never a substitute for substance, and the poem's honesty in mirroring MacNeice's bafflement in the face of history leaves the poem empty at the center, brought to a conclusion only by the conventions of the calendar. Such critics would argue that MacNeice fails to demonstrate the kind of belief or system he himself thought necessary for great poetry. The issue is a basic one, since the virtues and limitations of *Autumn Journal* are those of most of MacNeice's work.

In the spring of 1939, MacNeice visited America to give some lectures and fell in love with a young woman there. He returned to America the next spring to teach at Cornell. While there, he worked on an autobiography; left unfinished, it was edited and published after MacNeice's death by E. R. Dodds as *The Strings Are False* (1965). Many of his friends urged him to escape the war by staying in America, and the woman he loved would not return with him to England; nevertheless, MacNeice felt he had to go back. After some months of delay caused by a serious illness, he recrossed the Atlantic late in 1940. Barred from active service by bad eyesight, he joined the Features Department of the British Broadcasting Corporation in the spring of 1941.

MacNeice's next collection, *The Last Ditch* (1940), was published by the Cuala Press in Dublin. Despite the harsh things he had said of Ireland in *Autumn Journal*, MacNeice spent much of the fall of 1939 there, even applying unsuccessfully for a teaching position at Trinity College in Dublin. He wrote now of Dublin's fascination for him, though "This was never my town" and "she will not / Have me alive or dead" ("Dublin"). In a few lyrics he seems interested in exploring the possibilities of specifically Irish subject matter. *The Last Ditch* as a whole gives the impression that MacNeice was

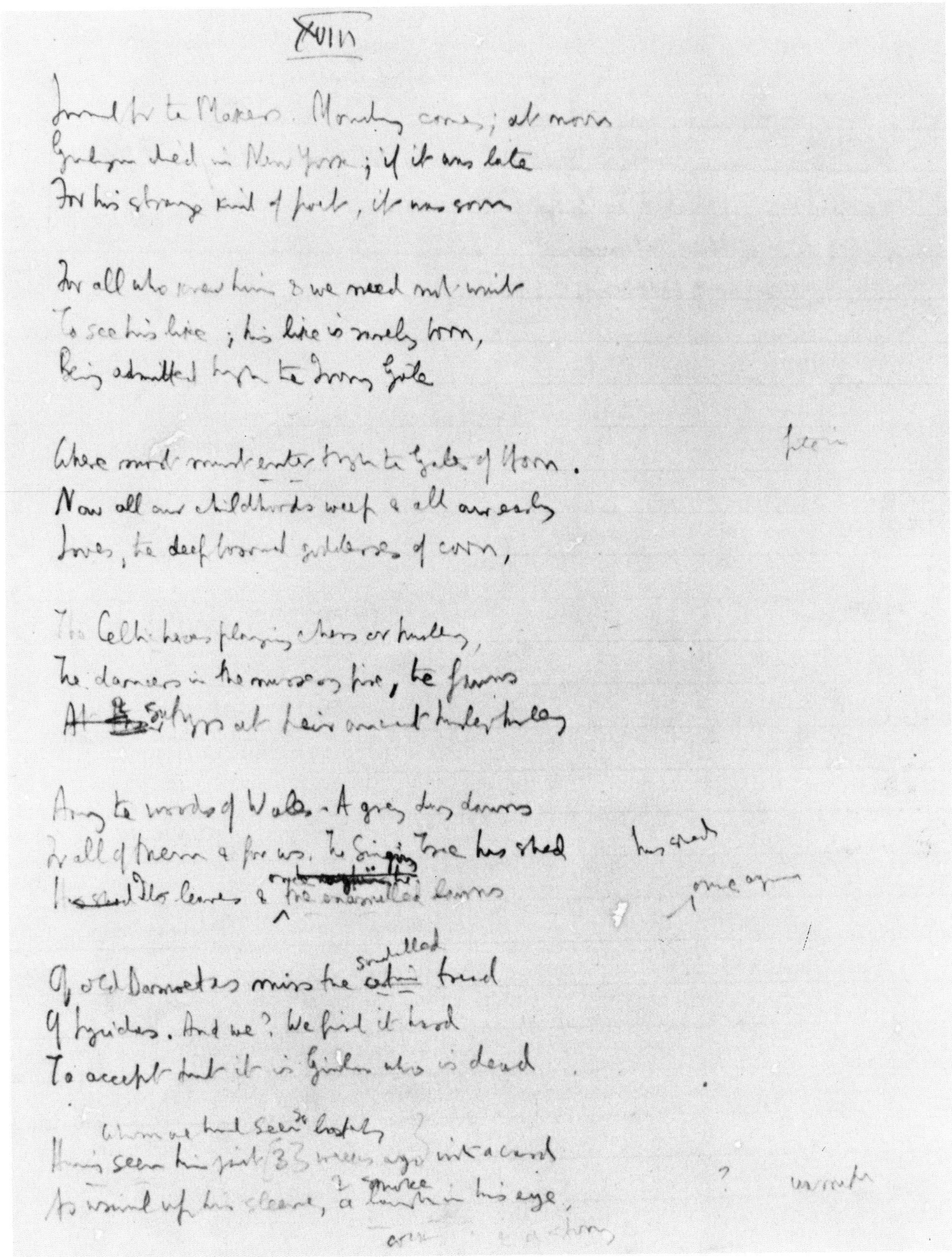

Page from an early draft of MacNeice's lament for Dylan Thomas, canto eighteen of Autumn Sequel *(Henry W. and Albert A. Berg Collection of English and American Literature, New York Public Library)*

looking for new directions after the impasse depicted in *Autumn Journal*. His old manner is represented in a poem of satirical observation, "The British Museum Reading Room." His American romance is presumably responsible for the inclusion of a number of love poems such as "Meeting Point." Risking—and sometimes falling into—sentimentality, the new love poems are distinguished by the relative absence of MacNeice's habitual, protective irony and of any trace of social consciousness. A series of five "Novelettes" present brief narratives of character; the most successful of these, "The Old Story," evidently derives from a meeting with his former wife and her new husband while on his American lecture tour. The love lyrics and character vignettes of this volume look forward to later work.

MacNeice's renewed interest in Ireland may also be seen in his *The Poetry of W. B. Yeats* (1941). A leading Yeats scholar, Richard Ellmann, wrote in 1967 that this book "is still as good an introduction to that poet as we have, with the added interest that it is also an introduction to MacNeice." That generous judgment may no longer be true, but MacNeice's book retains the special interest which attaches to books by one poet on another. MacNeice's intellectual problem in this work was to reconcile his admiration for Yeats's poetry with his reservations about Yeats's politics, spiritualism, and poetics. As a nonbeliever who valued beliefs, MacNeice had little trouble in accepting Yeats's strange system of beliefs as a basis for poetry. Yeats's aesthetic doctrines posed more of a problem, which MacNeice resolved partly by distinguishing between Yeats's pronouncements and his practice and partly by retreating from stands he himself had taken in *Modern Poetry*. Poetry, MacNeice now conceded, could be more than communication, and even mystic experiences have their place in it.

The 1930s were over, and *Plant and Phantom* (1941) marks the end of MacNeice's career as a bright young poet of the 1930s. The technique had matured and the poet grown, but in some ways the poet seems in much the same situation as the undergraduate of *Oxford Poetry, 1929* and *Blind Fireworks*. Like *The Last Ditch*, from which some poems are included, *Plant and Phantom* has a miscellaneous character, as though the poet had exhausted the possibilities of an old poetic identity without finding a new one. There are poems of Ireland and America, urban poems in MacNeice's old manner and new "Novelettes" to add to those from *The Last Ditch*. *Plant and Phantom* closes with one of MacNeice's best love lyrics, "Cradle Song for

Louis MacNeice at the BBC, 1942 (BBC Hulton)

Eleanor," rounding off this period in MacNeice's career with a poem which reminds one of the "Cradle Song" he had published in *Oxford Poetry*. The earlier lyric (for "Miriam") had been written for the woman who had married him and left him for America; the new poem was written for the woman he left behind to return to England and the war.

From 1941 until his death, Louis MacNeice was a man of the BBC. He remained a scriptwriter and producer with the Features Department until 1961 and worked with the department on a contract basis from then until his death. Although he traveled frequently after the war and eventually moved to the country, he remained a familiar figure in London pubs, approachable, but aloof with strangers. His interest in drama and his preference for poetry that communicates made him one of the leaders among those poets who, mostly for the BBC, brought to maturity the short-lived genre of radio drama in verse. MacNeice was a prolific scriptwriter, creating more than 150 scripts in his years of association with the BBC and serving as producer for many of them. A dozen of his radio plays have been published: *Christopher Columbus* (1944), *The Dark Tower and Other Radio Scripts* (1947), *The Mad*

Islands and The Administrator (1964), and *Persons from Porlock and Other Plays for Radio* (1969). Although critics generally regard radio drama as a minor genre—or ignore it completely—MacNeice's achievements within that genre deserve recognition.

The most widely read product of MacNeice's work with the BBC is his abridged translation of *Goethe's Faust, Parts I and II* (1951), which was produced first as a four-part BBC broadcast. MacNeice undertook this task with some initial reluctance, for his command of German was imperfect. His verse translation was prepared by E. L. Stahl and with the aid of frequent consultations with Stahl. The character of the abridgment was naturally affected by the demands and limitations of radio as a medium. From a purist's standpoint, no abridged translation can be considered satisfactory, but the superior qualities of its verse have made MacNeice's one of the most popular and well-regarded English versions of *Faust*.

The best of MacNeice's verse in the 1940s is in his radio dramas. The two new volumes of poetry he produced in this decade, *Springboard, Poems 1941-1944* (1944), and *Holes in the Sky, Poems 1944-1947* (1948), maintain the level of his earlier work but represent no advance upon it. MacNeice continues the series of character vignettes begun with *The Last Ditch*, but both his satirical portraits of contemporary types and his tributes to living and dead friends are among his weaker efforts. Religious and philosophical preoccupations seem somewhat more prominent, but MacNeice's ultimate skepticism makes most of these efforts seem too inconclusive to be satisfying. In the title poem of *Springboard* he finds an effective image for his own dilemma in the figure of a man poised high on his springboard above London, prepared to sacrifice himself but uncertain what the gain would be, crucified by his own unbelief. The most attractive poem of *Holes in the Sky* owes its inspiration to his second wife, the singer Hedli Anderson, whom he maried in April 1942, and to whom both *Springboard* and *Holes in the Sky* are dedicated. (They were separated in 1960.) "The Streets of Laredo" was written for his wife to sing to an arrangement of the traditional American cowboy song; the streets of Laredo become the bombed streets of London after the war, and the last two stanzas are whispered in the singer's ear by the Angel of Death. Despite such felicities, MacNeice's

Louis MacNeice and Michael Yates on the Iceland trip that inspired MacNeice and W. H. Auden's Letters from Iceland

reputation was declining in an age inclined to turn its back on the 1930s and its enthusiasms. Reviewing MacNeice's achievement in the light of his postwar volumes and of *Collected Poems, 1925-1948* (1949), many critics were inclined to dismiss MacNeice as a minor poet whose time was passed. MacNeice himself seemed to anticipate this judgment, including in *Holes in the Sky* an "Elegy for Minor Poets" which ends with "These debtors preclude our scorn—/ Did we not underwrite them when we were born?"

At the beginning of 1950 MacNeice, taking a leave of absence from the BBC, went to Athens, Greece, as the Director of the British Institute. When it was merged with the British Council the next fall, he stayed on as assistant representative through June 1951. While in Greece he wrote the ten long poems of *Ten Burnt Offerings* (1952), some of which were broadcast on the BBC. Each of the poems is in four movements; a great variety of stanza forms are employed. The poems are mannered and allusive meditations on religious and historical topics. The most successful is "Didymus," about the Apostle Thomas, whose doubts made him a congenial topic for MacNeice. Working as a cultural ambassador, MacNeice produced highly cultured poems which did little to still the growing suspicion that he was played out as a poet. In one of them, he himself remarks that "This middle stretch / Of life is bad for poets" ("Day of Renewal"). Few readers thought his new manner an improvement.

His two remaining volumes of the 1950s also suggest a poet grown weary. *Autumn Sequel: A Rhetorical Poem* (1954) reverts to the manner and matter of *Autumn Journal* but generally lacks either the historical or the poetic interest of the earlier poem. The short lyrics of *Visitations* (1957) combine the philosophical preoccupations of *Ten Burnt Offerings* with the colloquial manner more characteristic of MacNeice but with only partial success. These lyrics did, however, point the way toward more successful efforts in the same vein in his last two collections, *Solstices* (1961) and *The Burning Perch* (1963). Both of these volumes also contain a number of love lyrics, in a simpler style, which are among the best MacNeice ever wrote. In *The Burning Perch*, there are several poems in which the poet contemplates death, always the envisioned end of it all for the melancholy MacNeice but surely more real than ever for a man in his late fifties. His actual death was unexpected: despite a recent illness, he insisted on accompanying underground the sound engineers recording special effects for a radio play of his; he caught a severe chill and did not seek treatment until it had developed into pneumonia, which proved fatal.

Louis MacNeice

Besides the radio plays and autobiography already mentioned, there were several posthumous publications of works by MacNeice. *Astrology* (1964) is a prose potboiler surveying that subject. *One for the Grave* (1968) is a play reminiscent of *Out of the Picture* in style, with a television studio as an image of life and Death as the floor manager. The attractions of this style for MacNeice may be explained by the fondness for Spenser and more modern parablists revealed by his 1963 Clark Lectures at Cambridge, published as *Varieties of Parable* (1965).

The most important of these posthumous publications was *The Collected Poems of Louis MacNeice* (1966), edited by his longtime friend E. R. Dodds. Despite the more personal note sounded by a few love lyrics, MacNeice is an Apollonian, a Horatian poet. His individual lyrics rarely dazzle the reader with their boldness. His best remembered individual poems, such as "Bagpipe Music" and "The Streets of Laredo," impress themselves on the memory more through strong rhythms than through sharp images. MacNeice offers his readers irony rather than passionate commitment, understatement rather than hyperbole. His unobtrusive virtues of technical mastery and honesty are best appreciated when one surveys his work as a whole. The posthumous collected poems, following the renewed vigor of his last two volumes, improved MacNeice's standing, which had suffered from the relatively weak work of the 1940s and 1950s. There has been some continuing critical interest in his work, and though it seems unlikely that he will be upgraded to the status of a major poet, his reputation is certainly as high as that of any British poet of the 1930s other than Auden.

Plays:

The Agamemnon of Aeschylus, translated by MacNeice, London, Westminster Theatre, 4 November 1937;

Out of the Picture, London, Westminster Theatre, 2 December 1937;

Station Bell, Birmingham, Birmingham University, 1937;

Traitors in Our Way, Belfast, Lyric Theatre, March 1957;

One for the Grave, Dublin, Abbey Theatre, October 1966.

Radio Plays:

Christopher Columbus, BBC, 12 October 1942;

The Nosebag, BBC, 13 March 1944;

He Had a Date, BBC, 28 June 1944;

Sunbeams in His Hat, BBC, 16 July 1944;

The March Hare Resigns, BBC, 29 March 1945;

The Dark Tower, BBC, 21 January 1946;

Salute to All Fools, BBC, 1 April 1946;

Enter Caesar, BBC, 20 September 1946;

The Queen of Air and Darkness, BBC, 28 March 1949;

Faust, translated by MacNeice and E. L. Stahl, BBC, 30 October-21 November 1949;

Prisoner's Progress, BBC, 27 April 1954;

The Waves, adapted from Virginia Woolf's novel, BBC, 18 and 19 March 1955;

East of the Sun and West of the Moon, BBC, 25 July 1959;

They Met on Good Friday, BBC, 8 December 1959;

The Administrator, BBC, 10 March 1961;

The Mad Islands, BBC, 4 April 1962;

Persons from Porlock, BBC, 30 August 1963.

Other:

Oxford Poetry, 1929, edited by MacNeice and Stephen Spender (London: Oxford University Press, 1929);

The Agamemnon of Aeschylus, translated by MacNeice (London: Faber & Faber, 1936; New York: Harcourt, Brace, 1937);

"Experiences with Images," *Orpheus*, 2 (1949): 124-132;

Goethe's Faust, Parts I and II, translated by MacNeice (London: Faber & Faber, 1951; New York: Oxford University Press, 1952).

Bibliography:

Christopher Armitage and Neil Clark, *A Bibliography of the Works of Louis MacNeice* (London: Kaye & Ward, 1973).

References:

Terence Brown, *Louis MacNeice: Sceptical Vision* (New York: Barnes & Noble, 1975);

Barbara Coulton, *Louis MacNeice in the BBC* (London & Boston: Faber & Faber, 1980);

G. S. Fraser, "Evasive Honesty," in his *Vision and Rhetoric* (London: Faber & Faber, 1959), pp. 179-192;

William T. McKinnon, *Apollo's Blended Dream: A Study of the Poetry of Louis MacNeice* (London, New York & Toronto: Oxford University Press, 1971);

D. B. Moore, *The Poetry of Louis MacNeice* (Leicester: Leicester University Press, 1972);

John Press, *Louis MacNeice* (London: Longmans, Green, 1965);

Elton Edward Smith, *The Angry Young Men of the Thirties* (Carbondale: Southern Illinois University Press, 1975), pp. 69-92;

Smith, *Louis MacNeice* (New York: Twayne, 1970);

James G. Southworth, *Sowing the Spring* (Oxford: Blackwell, 1940), pp. 165-178;

Derek Stanford, *Stephen Spender, Louis MacNeice, Cecil Day Lewis* (Grand Rapids, Mich.: Eerdmans, 1969);

A. T. Tolley, *The Poetry of the Thirties* (London: Gollancz, 1975), pp. 175-191.

Papers:

The largest collection of MacNeice manuscripts and drafts is in the Humanities Research Center at the University of Texas, Austin. Additional manuscripts and materials are in the Berg Collection of the New York Public Library. A large number of radio scripts are in the archives of the British Broadcasting Corporation. Some other papers can be found at the Butler Library, Columbia University, and the Lockwood Memorial Library of the State University of New York at Buffalo.

Edwin Muir

James K. Robinson
University of Cincinnati

Edwin Muir (Mark Gerson)

BIRTH: The Folly, Parish of Deerness, Mainland, Orkney, 15 May 1887, to James and Elizabeth Cormack Muir.

MARRIAGE: 7 June 1919 to Wilhelmina (Willa) Anderson; child: Gavin.

AWARDS AND HONORS: Ph.D., Charles University, Prague, 1947; LL.D., University of Edinburgh, 1947; Docteur-ès-Lettres, University of Rennes, 1949; Foyle Prize, 1950; Heinemann Award, 1953; Fellow, Royal Society of Literature, 1953; Commander, Order of the British Empire, 1953; Frederick Niven Literary Award, 1953; Litt.D., University of Leeds, 1955; Russell Loines Award, 1957; Saltire Society Prize, 1957; Litt.D., Cambridge University, 1958.

DEATH: Swaffham Prior, Cambridgeshire, England, 3 January 1959.

SELECTED BOOKS: *We Moderns: Enigmas and Guesses*, as Edward Moore (London: Allen & Unwin, 1918; New York: Knopf, 1920);

Latitudes (London: Melrose, 1924; New York: Huebsch, 1924);

First Poems (London: Hogarth Press, 1925; New York: Huebsch, 1925);

Chorus of the Newly Dead (London: Hogarth Press, 1926);

Transition: Essays on Contemporary Literature (London: Hogarth Press, 1926; New York: Viking, 1926);

The Marionette (London: Hogarth Press, 1927; New York: Viking, 1927);

The Structure of the Novel (London: Hogarth Press, 1928; New York: Harcourt, Brace, 1929);

John Knox: Portrait of a Calvinist (London: Cape, 1929; New York: Viking, 1929);

The Three Brothers (London: Heinemann, 1931; New York: Doubleday, Doran, 1931);

Poor Tom (London: Dent, 1932);

Variations on a Time Theme (London: Dent, 1934);

Scottish Journey (London: Heinemann / Gollancz, 1935);

Scott and Scotland: The Predicament of the Scottish Writer (London: Routledge, 1936; New York: Speller, 1938);

Journeys and Places (London: Dent, 1937);

The Present Age, From 1914 (London: Cresset, 1939; New York: McBride, 1940);

The Story and the Fable: An Autobiography (London, Toronto, Bombay & Sydney: Harrap, 1940); revised and enlarged as *An Autobiography* (London: Hogarth Press, 1954; New York: Sloane, 1954);

The Narrow Place (London: Faber & Faber, 1943);

The Voyage and Other Poems (London: Faber & Faber, 1946);

Essays on Literature and Society (London: Hogarth Press, 1949; revised and enlarged, 1965; Cambridge: Harvard University Press, 1965);

The Labyrinth (London: Faber & Faber, 1949);
Collected Poems, 1921-1951 (London: Faber & Faber, 1951; New York: Grove, 1953);
One Foot in Eden (London: Faber & Faber, 1956; New York: Grove, 1956);
Collected Poems, 1921-1958, edited by Willa Muir and J. C. Hall (London: Faber & Faber, 1960; revised and enlarged, 1963; New York: Oxford University Press, 1965);
The Estate of Poetry (London: Hogarth Press, 1962; Cambridge: Harvard University Press, 1962);
Selected Poems (London: Faber & Faber, 1965);
Edwin Muir: Uncollected Scottish Criticism, edited by Andrew Noble (New York: Barnes & Noble, 1981).

Though the translations of Kafka he did with his wife, Willa Muir, have long given Edwin Muir a secure place in modern literature, his reputation as a modern British poet of the first rank came only late in his life. While Yeats, Pound, and Eliot, responding to French symbolism, established Anglo-American modernism as the dominant mode of poetry in English, Muir took another road. Starting with ballads and seminal events of his early childhood and nourishing his imagination on such German writers as Hölderlin, Rilke, and Kafka, Muir achieved a poetry that was visionary, generously moral, romantically lyrical, personal but not private.

Muir's earliest years were literally outlandish. He was born on a farm on Mainland, Orkney, due west of the southern tip of Norway. When he was two his family moved to the Orkney island of Wyre, two miles long and a mile wide, where for five years they lived at the Bu (an Old Norse word meaning "farmstead"), the largest of eight farms on the island. Though Muirs had come from Scotland in the sixteenth century, Muir once insisted that he was "not Scotch" but an Orkney man, a good Scandinavian whose "true country is Norway, or Denmark, or Iceland." Speech was a mixture of Norse and Scots and Irish Gaelic. The five years at the Bu remained for Muir among the happiest in his life. He loved the world of farm animals (especially horses), gentle, cooperative farmers, the long light of summers in a northern latitude. He assimilated century-old patterns of thought and feeling. He was frail and so was not sent to school. Perhaps the only disadvantages to this idyllic seed time were that it was so brief and that it included indoctrination in one of the harsher forms of Calvinism. The Muirs belong to the United Presbyterian Church, a conservative offshoot of the Church of Scotland which united Covenanters and Seceders. As Elgin W. Mellown has observed, "Though the daily lives of the Orkney farmers were patterned by timeless nature, their religious attitudes were dictated by strict Calvinism. They knew Hell and Salvation from it for the Elect as real entities, and they accepted without question the authority of the Bible, which they interpreted literally. They emphasized such Old Testament concepts as restrictions and punishments, rather than the New Testament ideas of an Incarnate Deity, and the need for love and mercy." The Bu may have been the nearest to Eden Muir knew in childhood, but the Calvinism he contracted there was a virus he spent the rest of his life battling. Since Calvinists regarded such profane literature as poetry a vanity, it is not surprising that there were few books, or that these included the Bible and Bunyan's *Pilgrim's Progress*. Muir's art long reflected his self-portrayal as Pilgrim. The bulk, though little of it the best, of the poetry Muir was later to write focused on journeys, voyages, pilgrimages not far removed from Bunyan's allegory. The redeeming poetry at the Bu was not in any book but in the ballads and songs, literally hundreds of them, which had been handed down for generations. For Muir, first and last, ballads contained some of the truest poetry; what Muir learned from the ballad tradition was a salubrious corrective to the moralistic, judgmental world of Bunyan.

In 1894 the family moved to a poorer farm on Wyre, Helzigartha (Old Norse: "Helye's farmstead"), and Edwin attended, spasmodically, the island's one-room school along with fifteen other children. It was during the Helye year that a schoolmate, Freddie Sinclair, whom earlier Muir had defeated in a fight over a knife, chased Muir home. Thirty years later the terror of that experience was purged in "Ballad of Hector in Hades." At the end of the year the Scottish landlord, Gen. Frederick Burroughs, drove them out, as he had driven them out of the Bu, by high rental demands. The next six years were spent on Mainland, first at the farm Garth, four miles south of Kirkwall, and then, the last year, in Kirkwall. Fortunes and health declined, but Edwin gained two advantages: he enjoyed several years at the excellent Kirkwall Burgh School and, while he was still at Garth, decided to be a writer. Since his parents objected to profane literature, he decided he would write a life of Christ.

It was nearly forty years before he got around to Christ. In the winter of 1901-1902 the family moved to Glasgow, and Edwin got his first harrowing view of hell. As Muir was to remark forty years later, when he was at last beginning to hit the poetic stride which he maintained the last twenty years of his life, "I was born before the Industrial Revolution, and am now about two hundred years old. But I have skipped about a hundred and fifty of them. I was really born in 1737, and till I was fourteen no time-accidents happened to me. Then in 1751 I set out from Orkney for Glasgow. When I arrived I found that it was not 1751, but 1901, and that a hundred and fifty years had been burned up in my two days' journey. But I myself was still in 1751, and remained there for a long time. All my life since I have been trying to overhaul that invisible leeway. No wonder I am obsessed with time." Though the Muirs settled in a flat in the respectable south Glasgow suburb of Crosshill, Edwin was not shielded from the human by-products of the Industrial Revolution. Having got a job as a clerk in the central business district, he found himself walking to work through some of the largest and most violent slums in Europe. To make matters much worse, Muir's father, mother, and two brothers died between October 1902 and February 1907. As Muir has recorded in his autobiography, "I was too young for so much death." So much death made an already insecure adolescence miserably guilt-ridden. As Muir recalled in a letter written to Sydney Schiff in 1924: "My life had been a continuous enemy of my inner development. At 14 I had had to begin work in a commercial office—hours 9 to 6; at 18 I was thrown upon the world to live on the 14/- a week that I earned at the cost of ill-health and psychological misery; and I am still a little surprised to this hour that all this time I read, learned to love music and, being a Scotsman, speculation, without knowing for years a single person to whom I could speak of those things."

About the only misery Muir was spared was military service in World War I; he failed the physical exam. Sparing him from the tedium and fatigue of Glasgow were summer holidays in Orkney. Sustaining him throughout these years was a strong creative drive which began to find release after an Orkney holiday he spent reading of Heine. Muir began to write verse and, in 1913, to have it published in the *New Age*. Ten poems, juvenilia in both senses of the word, appeared within the next sixteen months. The first stanza of the first published poem, "Salutation," is a fair sample of his work:

I read, ye poets of today
Your verses grim, your verses gay.
But little got I for my pains.
My soul is weary of your strains.

It is perhaps just as well he signed Edward Moore to these squibs. It is a sign of Muir's powers of self-criticism that he stopped having his effusions published. Not until a few weeks after his thirty-fifth birthday did he again have a poem published, and then, for the first time, he signed his own name.

Muir's first poetic period may properly be said to have taken its origin from three events in 1919; all of them took place in London. He married Willa Anderson, went to work for A. R. Orage as assistant editor of the *New Age*, and undertook a course in psychoanalysis. As Muir has quite accurately remarked, "My marriage was the most important event in my life." Born in the Shetlands but reared in Montrose, Willa Anderson had had a brilliant academic career, having won first-class honors in classics at St. Andrews University and then proceeding to a promising teaching career. Her linguistic skill was of intensely practical advantage over the next twenty years, when a considerable portion of their income was to come from translating from the German, especially Kafka. Her character and personality complemented Muir's beautifully: she was adventurous and gay, unencumbered by Calvinist inhibitions. Her self-confidence was a great support to her more diffident husband.

Orage not only gave Muir much needed employment, he recognized that the bridegroom, however blessed in his new marital state, was in bad shape from nearly eighteen years of Glasgow clerking. Therefore he persuaded Muir to accept the offer of a well-known Harley Street psychoanalyst, Maurice Nicoll, to analyze him "for the mere interest of the thing, and without asking for any payment." Muir had read a good deal about psychoanalysis, and Nicoll's generous offer was all the more attractive since he had studied under both Freud and Jung, preferring Jung. For a bit under two years, Muir was in analysis, at first with Nicoll, then with a colleague. Though for years he had not dreamed, now, with professional encouragement, he began to dream profusely and to record his dreams in notebooks. Though analysis had to be terminated prematurely when the Muirs left in August 1921 for Prague, the course was immensely valuable. Indeed, Muir may be the only important British poet fully to have taken advantage of analysis. The effects of treatment lasted a lifetime, though they did not surface until early 1922 when the Muirs were about to leave Prague for Dresden. Vague fears were gone; dreams continued; contact with unconscious life became practically continuous; the sense of timelessness with which Muir had been instilled in his Orkney childhood but which had been lost in his Glasgow youth and young manhood returned. "In dreams," Yeats wrote, "begin responsibilities." For Muir in dreams began liberation from guilt and shame, freedom to create.

Psychologically free to create, Muir found himself economically free to create. With assurance of $120 a month for two articles for the *Freeman* and somewhat less than that for weekly articles for the *New Age*, the Muirs gave up work in London and went to Prague, like Muir newly liberated. They were warmly received, and they at once set about to learn Czech. Muir spent weeks in "an orgy of looking," unlearning the Glasgow regimen of averting eyes from sights too violent or ugly to be assimilated. He sent the *Freeman* articles recording impressions of Prague, impressions that did not include a meeting with Kafka, which would have been possible, for the master of modern fiction was in the city in early 1922. As Willa Muir has written, "We were so busily involved in Czech doings . . . that we never knew about the German life going on in pockets here and there in Prague. We never got even a hint that Kafka or his friends had ever existed in the city. An invisible but unyielding barrier cut off German-speakers from Czech-speakers and it was only the Czech-speakers that we came to know." Yet surely familiarity with Prague must have been part of the attraction to begin translating Kafka just a few years later and to return to Prague not long after World War II ended in Europe.

Marriage, psychoanalysis, travel to Prague were a prelude to the year, from spring 1922 to spring 1923, in Dresden and nearby Hellerau. There, as Willa Muir observed, Edwin Muir became carefree as never before in his life. In his happiness he began to write poetry again, this time poetry to which he could with satisfaction sign his real name. The first two poems, published in the *New Age* on 8 June and 6 July 1922, were aptly entitled "Re-Birth" and "Ballad of Eternal Life."

The Muirs' Grand Tour was to last another year, with stays in northern Italy and in Austria—at Salzburg, at Vienna, and at Rosenau. At Rosenau, in the spring of 1924, came a very significant opportunity; the American publisher Huebsch invited them to translate three of Gerhart Hauptmann's verse plays. As Peter H. Butter has observed, "they naturally jumped at the offer, though they had no formal training in German, having picked it up by talking, reading and singing with friends in cafés. By chance they had found a means of making a steady living, one which was to take up an inordinate part of their time during the next fifteen years."

Edwin Muir in Glasgow, 1917

Translation was to provide employment (and drudgery) for years, but, before that drudgery had well begun, Muir was able to write the first significant poetry of his life. Largely relieved of rippling psychological conflicts, Muir could draw on vividly recalled childhood experiences and on ballads he had learned as a child. An important essay in Muir's *Latitudes*, published in 1924, was entitled "A Note on the Scottish Ballads." Here Muir was to proclaim a lifelong interest; in his Charles Eliot Norton lectures delivered at Harvard in 1955-1956 and published as *The Estate of Poetry* (1962), there are extended discussions of the nature, value, and significance of ballads. It was to be predicted that the second section of Muir's *First Poems*, hand-printed and published by Leonard and Virginia Woolf at the Hogarth Press in April 1925, should be headed "Ballads." "In recalling his early years," says Roger Knight, "and in studying the ballads he was reanimating a vital and long-suppressed part of his imaginative life. It was that rather than the pressure of contemporary poetic example that counted in his early poetic development." As Butter has noted, two of the ballads in *First Poems*, "Ballad of the Flood" and "Ballad of the Monk," are of interest for being written in Scots. The former begins,

> Last night I dreamed a ghastly dream,
> Before the dirl o' day.
> A twining worm cam out the wast,
> Its back was like the slae.

(*dirl*: break, turning; *wast*: west; *slae*: slow or blind worm)

The ballad engagingly incorporates rhythms and idioms known to Muir since childhood and taps the world of the unconscious made accessible in his psychoanalysis. Another ballad, "Ballad of Eternal Life," (not republished until 1960, when it appeared as "Ballad of the Soul" in *Collected Poems*) had its source in a waking dream Muir experienced in psychoanalysis. "A Ballad of the Nightingale" stems from Muir's Heine period in the 1910s. The most striking, "Ballad of Hector in Hades," goes back to Muir's childhood on Wyre, resuscitating the afternoon when he ran away, "in real terror," from Freddie Sinclair on the way home from school. This ballad has come in for praise from such discerning critics as R. P. Blackmur, Douglas Bush, Peter H. Butter, Daniel Hoffman, Elizabeth Huberman, and Christopher Wiseman. Writing the poem rid Muir of a terror felt for thirty years. The image of flight described by Hector came "quite spontaneously." Muir wrote out the poem, "almost complete, at one sitting." The poem cleared Muir's conscience: "I saw that my shame was a fantastically elongated shadow of a childish moment, imperfectly remembered; an untapped part of my mind supplied what my conscious recollection left out, and I could at last see the incident whole by seeing it as happening, on a great and tragic scale, to some one else." Of the process which brought about the creation of the poem, Muir goes on, "My feeling about the Achilles and Hector poem is not of a suppression suddenly removed, but rather of something which has worked itself out. Such events happen again and again in everyone's life; they may happen in dreams; they always happen unexpectedly. . . ." As important as was the poem's therapeutic value, it is its quality as an aesthetic entity that is more striking. In "Ballad of Hector in Hades" Muir has found an apt objective correlative, a universally accessible formula for his fear and shame. The mound above his father's house becomes the eternal battlefield of Troy. Event becomes a part of history as pattern emerges. As Kathleen Raine has so perceptively said, "The themes of major poetry are epic, and cosmic; Muir wrote no epic, yet an epic sense haunts his work."

Edwin Muir in Vienna, circa 1923

Less successful than "Ballad of Hector in Hades" were two other poems dating back to experiences on Wyre: "Childhood" and "Horses." "Childhood" anticipates Dylan Thomas's "Fern Hill" in its portrait of an Edenic, seemingly timeless time. "Horses" recalls Wordsworth's "Ode: Intimations of Immortality for Recollections of Early Childhood" with its evocation of a fading vision. Except for "Ballad of Hector" the best work in *First Poems* appears in renderings of scenes recently perceived: "Autumn near Prague," a 1921 landscape, and "October at Hellbrünn," inspired by an "orgy of looking" indulged in two years later near Salzburg. In these poems Muir revealed that at least he was overcoming a tendency not to look prompted by the ugliness of eighteen years in Glasgow. There were no signs yet of another recrudescence from childhood, carry-overs from readings of the Bible and of *Pilgrim's Progress*, a preoccupation with moral and spiritual dilemmas. But, as Knight has noted, he had first to rediscover life and therefore establish a foundation for that poetry. He had also to improve his technical skills.

The second phase of Muir's poetical career—roughly from 1925 to 1938—was the least impressive of the four (1919-1925, 1925-1938, 1938-1945, 1945-1959). Its fruits might have discouraged a less gifted and resilient man. One reason for the slump was that far too much time and energy went into work not as a creative artist but as a general man of letters: translator, book reviewer, essayist, publisher's reader, travel writer, biographer. There were, of course, advantages other than economic to these enterprises. Frequent reviewing and essay writing enabled Muir to give himself a literary education. Books on Scotland (*John Knox: Portrait of a Calvinist*, 1929; *Scottish Journey*, 1935; *Scott and Scotland*, 1936) provided a means for coming to terms with a country he had left with such relief in 1919. The book on Knox was the most important; it helped Muir purge himself of some long nourished grievances against the religious culture by which he had been traumatized. And there was a good deal of merit in Muir's charge that "what Knox really did was to rob Scotland of all the benefits of the Renaissance." Translation doubtless sensitized Muir to literary language. Most relevantly, it led him to Kafka. As Joyce Crick has pertinently observed, "There were from the start affinities between Muir and Kafka which make of the translating a deeply congruent part of Muir's own creative life. His formative experiences—the loss of religious transcendence, the failure of secular remedies, the closeness to dream and archetype, the tidy, weary office hours, the vision of horror—all have their equivalents in Kafka's world, including two peculiarly Scottish cradle gifts: the Calvinist conscience and a problematic relationship to a national culture and language. . . . The novels of the one and the poems of the other point beyond the immediate, . . . they provoke the reader into the effort towards interpretation." As early as July 1929 Muir declared in a letter to a friend his fascination with Kafka. That fascination grew so strong it became an influence. In the summer of 1929 Muir persuaded Secker to publish *The Castle*, and the Muirs began their careers as Kafka's first English translators. They produced *The Castle* (1930), *The Great Wall of China, and Other Pieces* (1933), *The Trial* (1937), and *America* (1938). For Edwin Muir translation provided contact with the master artist of the first half of the twentieth century.

Energies of Muir's second phase were not only diverted to critical tasks, they were also misapplied creatively. Though they may have helped Muir disencumber himself of the burden of his past, the three more or less autobiographical novels he wrote during this period (*The Marionette*, 1927; *The Three Brothers*, 1931; and *Poor Tom*, 1932) conclusively demonstrated that Muir was no novelist, that he lacked dramatic power, an ability to create a number of believable characters in action.

It was not until near the end of Muir's second poetic phase that the creative energy he applied to the writing of poetry began to produce rewards. The decade in England from 1925 to 1935, a nomadic time of residences in Bucks, Surrey, Sussex, and Hampstead, was especially discouraging. An ambitious long poem, *Chorus of the Newly Dead* (1926), which undertook to come to terms with the Glasgow years, was a nearly complete failure. When he came to collect his poems in 1951, no work from this volume was included. As Muir remarked, "The idea greatly moved me, but my imaginative excitement never managed to communicate itself, or at best now and then, to the poem; the old disability. . . , a simple lack of skill, still held me up. In any case the theme was far too great for my powers. . . ." Still struggling, Muir brought out, in 1934, a long poem, *Variations on a Time Theme*. Butter is among the kinder of critics when he notes in it "an advance on *First Poems* both in content and style," but he finds "greater complexity bought at the price of some obscurity," leading him to the conclusion that this book was "perhaps Muir's least attractive volume of poetry." Yet Muir's *Variations on a Time Theme* probably had to be written, however unsuccessfully, before he could address himself to man in time. *Journeys and Places* (1937) offered ample evidence that Muir had survived his dark poetic decade and was on his way toward much more impressive achievement. Of the "journey" poems "Tristram's Journey" is noteworthy, but the most brilliant is "Hölderlin's Journey," the first of Muir's poems accepted by T. S. Eliot for publication in the *Criterion* (it appeared in the January 1937 issue). Hölderlin had seized Muir's imagination as early as the autumn of 1922, when, at Hellerau, an "impoverished Junker, Ivo Von Lucken, succeeded in making me begin to understand that great poet." Muir had periodical articles on Hölderlin published in 1923, 1925, 1926, and 1935. "Hölderlin's Journey" succeeds, perhaps, because, like the best of Muir's ballad poems, "Ballad of Hector in Hades," it has its basis in an actual experience, that of Hölderlin's return to Frankfurt from Bordeaux in hope of reunion with his "Diotima." The poem begins,

> When Hölderlin started from Bordeaux
>   He was not mad but lost in mind,
> For time and space had fled away
>   With her he had to find.

Dominant motifs of Muir's second phase, time and space, are introduced with a characteristic puzzlement. Life was, in nearly all of Muir's poetry, dominated by the metaphor of the journey, the pilgrimage of human life, a pilgrimage in time under the

Edwin Muir with Francis George Scott, Scott's son, and Hugh MacDiarmid in Montrose, 1924

aspect of eternity. In "Hölderlin's Journey" Muir was choosing the better way, what might be called the ballad way, rather than the more abstract, Bunyanesque way of so much of the unsuccessful poetry of this period. Even the prosody suggests the ballad with the thumping rhythms, the quatrains with rhymed second and fourth verses and occasional proximate rhyme in the first and third verses, and the tetrameter varied with several fourth-verse trimeters. And like so many ballads, this poem ends, as Hoffman notes, "in a perfect epiphany of despair." There is profound pathos in the final description of Hölderlin, "Dragging in pain a broken mind / And giving thanks to God and men." The best "journey" poems are about believable journeys. The best "place" poems take their origins from subjects already accessible to readers in literary legend and therefore challenging Muir to work concretely within certain recognizable limits; thus the success of "Merlin" and "The Enchanted Knight," Muir's version of "La Belle Dame Sans Merci." The triumph in this vein is "Troy." One remembers that Muir was married to a woman who had taken a first-class degree in classics. If he did not read Greek, she did. And Troy, as we have seen from "Ballad of Hector in Hades," had long had personal associations for him. If the Gawain poet could elaborately trace Britain back to Troy, Muir felt the mound on Wyre *was* Troy. Further, he had a precedent in a Scottish poet he greatly admired, Robert Henryson, for treating an ending at Troy on a tragic note. "Troy" is a remarkable poem. Auden's "September 1, 1939" may evoke shivers of anxiety over the terrors to come, but Muir's "Troy," as John Holloway has said, "strikes today's reader as a vision of post-war Europe, of the chaos of the late 1940s." Troy, of all places, may be all places in Europe. In the poem's grimly ironic phrase, "proud history has such sackends." Though the young 1930s poets of the Left felt themselves political poets, Muir, who never called himself one, surely is. He presents the ruined city in the appropriate language, the language of nightmare.

Muir's third poetic period, from 1938 through 1945, coincided, not surprisingly, with preparations for war and war in Europe. Early in 1938 Muir was "more unhappy than he had been since 1919," Butter says, "and as in the earlier period he worked toward a cure by self-discovery and by returning to the sources of strength in the past. He began to collect material for an autobiography; or rather, perhaps, he began a process of self-discovery which then led to the idea of writing the autobiography." Work on the autobiography, finished in December 1939, must have had some connection with a turning point in Muir's life. As Muir wrote in his diary on 1 March 1939: "Last night, going to bed alone [Willa Muir was in hospital], I suddenly found myself . . . reciting the Lord's Prayer in a loud, emphatic voice—a thing I had not done for many years—with deep urgency and profound disturbed emotion." Muir came to believe that he was a Christian, though he did not turn to any church. He certainly was not tempted to return to any Calvinist position. As he wrote Herbert Read on 26 January 1940, linking Calvinism and communism, "where I disagree violently with them both is in their seeing a divine principle in wrath, like the Calvinist, and the only liberating human principle in wrath, like the Communist. I think both theories are extraordinarily alike here, alike, that is, in elevating the form of most human activity (which I suppose is struggle and anger) into the principle of human activity, and beyond that, into the principle of good, at least of advancement."

The autumn of 1940 was a dark time in Muir's life. Naturally, with the outbreak of war demands for translation from the German had ceased. The Communists, acting on their "liberating human principle of wrath," had occupied what Germany left of Poland, also the Baltic nations. The Germans took Denmark, Norway, Holland, Belgium, and France. Over 300,000 British and French troops were evacuated to Britain from beaches around Dunkirk. Butter reports that Muir found himself a clerk in the food office in Dundee, "stamping ration books and doing other such routine chores in the back office at £3 a week. After twenty-one years he was back again as a clerk, earning less than he had in 1919 and doing less responsible work." In six months Muir became ill and had to give up even this unsuitable, low-paying job. It was not until March 1942 that his fortunes changed for the better. He joined the British Council staff in Edinburgh with the responsibility of organizing evening programs for Polish, Czech, and French servicemen and refugees—and later, American servicemen. The Edinburgh years, which lasted until July 1945, when he was sent by the British Council to Prague, were Muir's happiest in Scotland. And, despite the demands of his work at the council, Muir wrote more poetry in the three years in Edinburgh than he had in the preceding seven years in St. Andrews. At last, approaching his fifty-eighth birthday, Muir had an appropriate, full-time position and some economic security. It is understandable that from this time on, until his retirement at the age of sixty-nine, with an end to constant economic distress, with positions in which his talents were used, and with honors beginning to come in, Muir's poetry came into its own.

A fitting prelude to *The Narrow Place* (1943) and *The Voyage and Other Poems* (1946), Muir's two volumes of poetry assembled during the war years, was *The Story and the Fable*, published in May 1940. This, the greatest of Muir's prose works, is also one of the century's finest autobiographies. In it Muir documents his deeply held conviction that man lives both a story, his individual life, and a fable, "an endlessly repeated performance of the life of man." Just as Yeats's *A Vision* (1925) offers a valuable theoretical base for much of the poetry, so *The Story and the Fable*, later extended to cover Muir's life up to the assumption of duties as warden at Newbattle Abbey College in 1950, gives the reader of Muir's poetry a rich sense of the life tree from which the finest fruit of that tree, the poetry, came. The poetry in *The Narrow Place* does not give the reader a clear clue to the spiritual development traced in *The Story and the Fable*. As Mellown has noted, "Muir is less concerned . . . with man's spiritual origins than with man's present, temporal life, a change in attitude that reflects his own personal circumstances after he was swept into a world of activity. . . ." There are a number of notable poems set in Scotland—"The Refugees," "The Wayside Station," "Scotland 1941," and "The Ring," which Elizabeth Huberman has called "a landmark on Muir's journey up from the depths." Huberman goes on to say that this virtuoso poem in terza rima treats "the disaster that wrecked Scotland, the spiritual, political, and economic division experienced in that country, . . . a paradigm of the division that has fragmented both contemporary man and his world." It is fitting that after these dark poems on Scotland comes "The Gate," which looks back to Muir's Orkney childhood. This powerful poem may be said to distill Muir's mature work. And there is what may be the earliest borrowing from Rilke in the isolated final line: "And then behind us the huge gate swung open."

Of *The Voyage*, consisting largely of poems written during the happy Edinburgh years, it may be enough to say that Muir here achieves a command, an ease, a peace of mind, only occasionally to be found in *Journeys and Places* and *The Narrow Place*. Among the most notable poems are "The Voyage," "In Love for Long," "The Fathers," "On Seeing

Two Lovers in the Street," and "A Birthday"—the last a striking rejoinder to Robert Frost's "To Earthward." The best lyric in *The Voyage* is "The Myth," which, as Roger Knight says, "draws a thread across from childhood to approaching old age and conjures forth a profound metaphysical unity." "Childhood," which appeared in *First Poems*, caught the feelings of a little boy, but "The Myth" follows that boy to an adult vision. The poem begins,

> My childhood all a myth
> Enacted on a distant isle;
> Time with his hourglass and his scythe
> Stood dreaming on the dial,

and ends,

> Consolidated flesh and bone
> And its designs grow halt and lame;
> Unshakeable arise alone
> The reverie and the name.
> And at each border of the land,
> Like monuments a deluge leaves,
> Guarding the invisible sheaves
> The risen watchers stand.

If Muir's childhood was a myth enacted on the distant isle of Wyre, one of the tiniest of the inhabited North Isles in the Orkneys, he came to full manhood in the center of Europe shortly after World War II ended in Europe. The fourth, last, and by far the most distinguished phase of his poetical career, from 1945 until his death in January 1959 began. Muir's posting to Prague as director of the British Council Institute was, after his marriage and psychoanalysis, the most important event in his life. Prague revisited after a lapse of nearly a quarter century and the violent punctuation of war proved an incalculable stimulus. Not only did Muir ably administer an important cultural center and conduct classes in English literature, at the institute and at Charles University, but, according to Butter, he wrote "most, probably all, of the poems in *The Labyrinth*." And *The Labyrinth* (1949), in the opinion of Muir himself and of such discerning critics as Butter, Jennings, Knight, and Mellown, is his best book of poems. Muir's energy and command came from clear sources: though he was by this time fifty-eight years old, for the first time in his life he was actually in charge of an important activity; he was back in a city where he had begun to emerge from the nightmare memories of Glasgow into an "orgy of looking" and where once more, as Muir notes in his autobiography, he "began to learn the visible world all over again." This time he had three years rather than six months to look. Happy in a soul-fulfilling position in a favorite city, Muir was further in touch with the master spirit of the age and the object of close scrutiny over a period of fifteen years, Franz Kafka.

It was while he was in Prague that Muir was able to resume, with Willa Muir, the Kafka translations which the war had interrupted. *Parables, in German and English*, mainly translated by the Muirs, appeared in 1947; *In the Penal Settlement: Tales and Short Pieces* was published in 1948. In the 1930s had appeared five introductory notes and essays on Kafka. In 1947 Muir's essay, in Czech, "Poznámka k Franzi Kafkovi" ("A Note on Franz Kafka") was published in *Franz Kafka a Praha*. This essay, which was reprinted in English in *Essays on Literature and Society* (1949), is, as Joyce Crick says, "the most coherent and elegant and all-of-a-piece of his Kafka articles." Michael Hamburger, in an *Encounter* article in 1960, was the first to call attention to the Prague essay. He may have been exaggerating the theoretical difference of this essay from predecessors in asserting that in the introductions Muir "had interpreted Kafka's fiction as allegory" and, in 1947, had "corrected this view and stressed the purely imaginative character of Kafka's works." Indeed, Muir does say in his essay, of *The Castle* and *The Trial*, "These stories are not allegories. The truths they bring out are surprising or startling, not conventional and expected, as the truths of allegories tend to be. They are more like serious fantasies. . . ." As Crick pertinently concludes, "but since he had never meant allegory in the narrow sense in the first place, this amounts to less of a change in his evaluation than does the redoubled importance he ascribes to the autonomy of Kafka's imagined world."

The impact of Kafka on Muir's poetry of his greatest period is so pervasive it is impossible to assess precisely. It may suffice to mention three poems in *The Labyrinth* which not only recall the terrors of war, not least of which were the death camps, but also draw upon the inventiveness of Kafka in depicting suffering, torture, oppression, and invisible evil. These are "The Helmet," "The Bridge of Dread," and "The Combat." "The Combat," which Muir considered one of his best poems, and is surely one of his best known, offers a Kafkaesque nightmare of defenselessness. Indeed, it is based on one of Muir's dreams when he was undergoing psychoanalysis. A further reminder of *The Trial* appears in "The Interrogation," an almost reportorial account of what happened to the Muirs as they left Czechoslovakia after their work was rendered impossible by the Communist takeover in February 1948.

An influence so powerful does not quickly exhaust itself, so it is not surprising that Kafka may be felt in the last collection published during Muir's lifetime, *One Foot in Eden* (1956), most transparently in "The Road," "The Heroes," and "To Franz Kafka," a poem which heads the second half of the collection. Though "To Franz Kafka" is not the best poem Muir has written, it is among his most encyclopedic; it clearly justifies Muir's long journey from Calvin to Kafka and as such, and because it has the admirable brevity of the sonnet, it may be quoted in full:

If we, the proximate damned, presumptive blest,
Were called one day to some high consultation
With the authentic ones, the worst and best
Picked from all time, how mean would be our station.
Oh we could never bear the standing shame,
Equivocal ignominy of non-election;
We who will hardly answer to our name,
And on the road direct ignore direction.
But you, dear Franz, sad champion of the drab
And half, would watch the tell-tale shames drift in
(As if they were troves of treasure) not aloof,
But with a famishing passion quick to grab
Meaning, and read on all the leaves of sin
Eternity's secret script, the saving proof.

Dust jacket for Muir's 1956 collection, the last book published during his lifetime

Muir came late, and resorted seldom, to the sonnet form. Sonnets first appear, four of them, in *The Voyage*; three are to be found in *The Labyrinth*; and seven in *One Foot in Eden*. The rhyme pattern—English in the octave, Italian in the sestet—"To Franz Kafka" shares only with "The Heroes," another sonnet first published in *One Foot in Eden*. The diction may appear at first characteristically abstract, but here it is abstract to specific purposes. In the octave such terms as "proximate damned, presumptive blest" echo Calvinist references to the Church Militant, while "authentic ones" suggest members of the Church Triumphant, the saved. "Equivocal ignominy of non-election" is a stern reminder of the terror flooding the life of sinful man; election is never assured until one enters heaven. The sestet puts an end to the cold abstractions of the octave and repudiates the position Muir had previously taken (In "Epitaph," 1946, he refers to a "flickering soul . . . half and half," and in "Scotland 1941," [1941] appears the line, "We, fanatics of the frustrate and the half"). Kafka corrects the absolutism of Calvin and Knox (and Muir). In his art there is not rejection but acceptance and welcome of "the drab / And half." As Mellown has succinctly remarked, "The poem declares the worth of the individual and praises the artist who can discern that worth." Further, "To Franz Kafka" establishes Muir's final philosophical and religious position. There are, as Muir was to say on the way to his final hospitalization, "no absolutes," and good and evil are to be perceived as inextricably, and desirably, bound together. From this sonnet such late poems as "One Foot in Eden" and "The Annunciation" follow quite naturally.

If Kafka the humane, imaginative artist is the subject of Muir's late sonnet, it is Kafka the depicter of trials who contributes to the success of several poems in *The Labyrinth*. The title poem of this volume, as Bush remarks, "only touches Theseus and the Minotaur" and is "an inner debate between nihilism and faith somewhat akin to Tennyson's *Two Voices*. The speaker could not live unless convinced that 'the endless maze' of life and time and self is illusion, that there are gods in an 'eternal dialogue' of peace. . . ." This poem, appropriately written late in 1946 in Kafka's native Czechoslovakia, is almost as labyrinthine as a Kafka novel; the opening statement runs for thirty-five lines, in its hesitations, punctuations, changes of course, it acts out Theseus's journey. But if the poem ostensibly begins in Greek myth, it expands to embrace Muir's personal experience and the chaotic state of central Europe after World War II. Muir's dreams and nightmares are matched by whole peoples'. Along the same lines, perhaps even more successful, or so at least think Butter, Knight, and Brian Keeble, is "The Transfiguration." His *great* poem, still in the Kafka vein, is "The Journey Back," all the more impressive, in Knight's view, because it was written when Muir was over sixty.

Events in Czechoslovakia became literally Kafkaesque in February 1948 with the Communist takeover. It became imprudent for Czechs to continue associations with the British Council. By July it was clear that Muir's work in Prague was over, so Edwin and Willa Muir left. At least three poems bear significantly on the political situation in Czechoslovakia. The title characters of "The Usurpers," most obviously Gestapo types, justify their "freedom." "The Good Town" asks the perhaps unanswerable question of how a town comes to lose its goodness and instead of ivy "From post to post across the prison door" gets a "fine new prison." "The Interrogation" has the numbing force of *The Trial*. The poem ends on a note of endless oppression: "And still the interrogation is going on."

Another native of Prague, Rilke, is also recalled in three of the Prague poems. Muir uses the isolated final line, as Harvey Gross has pointed out, to fix "the poem's emotional climax in significant isolation—a frequent mannerism of Rilke's." There are any number of such lines in Rilke's *The Life of the Virgin Mary*. In Muir appear such isolated lines in "The Good Town":

> 'Our peace betrayed us; we betrayed our peace.
> Look at it well. This was the good town once.'
>
> These thoughts we have, walking among our ruins.

in "The Usurpers":

> We have thought sometimes the rocks looked strangely on us,
> Heard dark runes murmuring in the autumn wind,
> Muttering and murmuring like old toothless women
> That prophesied against us in ancient tongues.
>
> These are imaginations. We are free.

Muir is not overdoing the device when he uses it yet once more in "The Animals," a poem written in Rome in 1949:

> All is new and near
> In the unchanging Here
> Of the fifth great day of God,
> That shall remain the same,
> Never shall pass away.
>
> On the sixth day we came.

Before his posting to Rome by the British Council in January 1949 Muir had to emerge from the severe trauma he suffered from the Communist takeover in Czechoslovakia and his premature departure from that country at the end of July 1948. As he wrote his friend Joseph Chiari from Cambridge on 8 September 1948: "For months now I have been suffering from both physical and nervous exhaustion, and to have them both put me in a curious blind dejection for days at a time—a thing I haven't suffered from since a bad time I had as a young man." A poem which captures the glazing of feeling wrought by the shock is "The Charm." The beginning lines, the end of the first stanza, and the last lines give a sense of the poem's thrust:

> There was a drug that Helen knew.
> Dropped in the wine-cup it could take
> All memory and all grief away,
> . . . .
> all the charities, unborn,
> Slept soundly in his burdened breast
> As he took his heavy rest,
> Careless, thoughtless and forlorn.
> . . . .
> But far within him something cried
> For the great tragedy to start,

The pang in lingering mercy fall,
And sorrow break upon his heart.

This eloquent description of deep depression also contains an emergent new perspective on the ordinary world. Muir no longer aspires to Eden alone. He embraces the world outside Eden, a world in which there are human feelings, human emotions, the tears of things. It is not surprising that, having come so far, Muir came through this breakdown in a few months of rest in Cambridge and was off, in January 1949, to Rome as director of the British Council Institute.

The years in Prague prompted Muir's finest poems of struggle; the eighteen months in Italy released a flood of poems of harmony, joy, peace, reconciliation: "Loss and Gain," "The Mediterranean Island," "The Annunciation," "The Animals," "The Days," "Adam's Dream," "The Succession," "The Late Wasp." "Loss and Gain," retitled "One Foot in Eden" to stand as title poem of the last volume Muir had published in his lifetime, makes explicit the direction indicated in "The Charm." Some key lines run:

still from Eden springs the root
As clean as on the starting day.
. . . .
But famished field and blackened tree
Bear flowers in Eden never known.
Blossoms of grief and charity
Bloom in these darkened fields alone.
What had Eden ever to say
Of hope and faith and pity and love
Until was buried all its day
And memory found its treasure trove?
Strange blessings never in Paradise
Fall from these beclouded skies.

Like Milton in *Paradise Lost* Muir embraces the paradox of the fortunate Fall, "A paradise within thee happier far." It was going to Rome that gave Muir the opportunity to come to terms, at last, a man in his early sixties, with difficulties of religious faith traceable all the way back to the "Edenic" childhood years in the Orkneys. Of the Roman experience Muir writes in his autobiography: "During the time when as a boy I attended the United Presbyterian Church in Orkney, I was aware of religion chiefly as the sacred Word, and the church itself,

Edwin Muir, Louise Bogan, and James Merrill at Mount Holyoke College, 1956

severe and decent, with its touching bareness and austerity, seemed to cut off religion from the rest of life and from all the week-day world, as if it were a quite specific thing shut within itself, almost jealously, by its white-washed walls, furnished with its bare brown varnished benches unlike any others in the whole world, and filled with the odour of ancient Bibles. . . . In figures such as these [two Orkney ministers] the Word became something more than a word in my childish mind; but nothing told me that Christ was born in the flesh and had lived on the earth.

"In Rome that image was to be seen everywhere, not only in churches, but on the walls of houses, at crossroads in the suburbs, in wayside shrines in the parks, and in private rooms. I remember stopping for a long time one day to look at a little plaque on the wall of a house in the Via degli Artisti, representing the Annunciation. An angel and a young girl, their bodies inclined towards each other, their knees bent as if they were overcome by love, 'tutto tremante,' gazed upon each other like Dante's pair; and that representation of a human love so intense that it could not reach farther seemed the perfect earthly symbol of the love that passes understanding. A religion that dared to show forth such a mystery for everyone to see would have shocked the congregations of the north, would have seemed a sort of blasphemy, perhaps even an indecency. But here it was publicly shown, as Christ showed himself on the earth.

"That these images should appear everywhere, reminding everyone of the Incarnation, seemed to me natural and right."

From this beautifully described experience came one of Muir's best religious poems, first entitled "From a Roman Bas Relief," and retitled "The Annunciation." Kathleen Raine's comment is apt: "His poem of the Annunciation is as profoundly spiritual, in its way, as Fra Angelico (whose painting he had in mind), yet it is not because he was a Christian but because he rediscovered the symbols from within that this is so. For him, the meeting of the Angel and the woman is essentially a poem about the eternal nature of love, not a poem describing an unique historical event. The theme is none the less holy for that; for Muir, like Plato, understood that lovers are winged—that is to say uplifted into a spiritual order, whose mystery is reflected in the earthly event." Yet Muir did not envision any forthcoming universal embracing of the idea and spirit of the Incarnation. In what Sir Herbert Read considers one of Muir's finest poems, "The Incarnate One," Muir less than five years later reminds the reader of northern resistance to the Incarnation, "Calvin's kirk crowning the barren brae." The poem ends:

> Yet I know well
> The bloodless world will battle for its own
> Invisibly in brain and nerve and cell.
> The generations tell
> Their personal tale: the One has far to go
> Past the mirages and the murdering snow.

The Roman assignment, which had offered such rich spiritual experiences, ended in just a year and a half. Council funds had been cut, and the Roman branch was closed. The Muirs returned to Scotland in July 1950. As Muir wrote a friend shortly before leaving Italy, he was "grateful to Rome for curing me. . . ." Cured, he assumed the post of warden of Newbattle Abbey College, Dalkeith, an adult education residential college a few miles south of Edinburgh. This post he held for five years, resigning it in 1955 to spend a year at Harvard as Charles Eliot Norton Professor, giving the brilliant lectures which constituted his last book, *The Estate of Poetry* (1962). At Newbattle Muir was again

Willa Muir, 1967

powerful, important, economically secure. The run of good poems which had begun in Prague in 1945 continued—indeed, continued right up to his death in January 1959. During the years at Newbattle, or on summer holidays in the Orkneys in 1951 and 1952, came such masterpieces as "Orpheus' Dream," "Telemachus Remembers," "The Incarnate One," "The Horses," "Milton," and "To Franz Kafka."

"Orpheus' Dream" justifies Holloway's description of Muir as "the outstanding British love poet since Yeats." This brilliant lyric was not tossed off. Butter informs us that "the MS of this poem in the National Library of Scotland enables us to see how much hard work went into its making. Four MS sheets, all but the last heavily revised, contain four separate drafts." And the work did not begin with Orpheus. Muir is a poet of returns. As far back as 1937, "Hölderlin's Journey," one of his first successful poems, appeared in the January *Criterion*. "The Return [of Odysseus]" appeared in *The Narrow Place* (1943) and "The Return [of the Greeks]" in *The Voyage* (1946). Muir was doubtless aware of Orpheus's solitary return from such earlier versions of the story as those in Plato's *Symposium*, in Vergil's fourth *Georgic*, in Ovid's *Metamorphoses*, book ten, and in Rilke's *Sonnets to Orpheus* (he reviewed J. B. Leishman's translation of this last for the *Scotsman* in 1936). Muir's version of the myth is a radical departure from its predecessors. It gives us an archetypal voyager, going his journey in dreams, as Muir's speakers so often do. The poet who had been psychoanalyzed never ceased to turn the key to self, which a recording and examination of dreams made possible. The poet of dreams could draw on his own experiences to offer a poetical realization of unity in love in the dreamt-of reunion of Orpheus and Eurydice:

> And she was there. The little boat
> Coasting the perilous isles of sleep,
> Zones of oblivion and despair,
> Stopped, for Eurydice was there.
> The foundering skiff could scarcely keep
> All that felicity afloat.
>
> As if we had left earth's frontier wood
> Long since and from this sea had won
> The lost original of the soul,
> The moment gave us pure and whole
> Each back to each, and swept us on
> Past every choice to boundless good.
>
> Forgiveness, truth, atonement, all
> Our love at once—till we could dare
> At last to turn our heads and see
> The poor ghost of Eurydice
> Still sitting in her silver chair,
> Alone in Hades' empty hall.

The manifest properties of dream are here: perilous isles, skiff floundering with "all that felicity afloat," a ghost in a silver chair in an empty hall. The persuasions of dream are here too: what in classical myth might have seemed illusion is now reality, ultimate reality, unity in love. The intensity of dream in a moment joins the lovers. Orpheus does not "forget" and turn his head; the lovers, forever one, can "dare" to turn their heads to see the "poor ghost of Eurydice / . . . / Alone in Hades' empty hall," empty because the real Eurydice has returned with Orpheus. Dream has triumphed, but its triumph is couched in terms which relate to Muir's lifelong struggle to free himself from the crippling Calvinism of his childhood. The moment brings, along with "all / Our love at once," "Forgiveness, truth, atonement." Love conquers all, even a sense of guilt. "Orpheus' Dream" is a quiet triumph of the late Muir in a personal prophetic vein.

Another triumphant reworking of Greek myth appears in "Telemachus Remembers," written about July 1952 in the Orkneys, a great improvement over a poem on the same subject, "The Return of Odysseus," of a decade before. In the first we are given a moving image of Penelope's orderly fidelity in her long weaving and unweaving. In the second, Telemachus, grown up, remembers and now understands not merely the pathos of her waiting but the "Pride and fidelity and love" that went into it. But much more important, we as readers see that Muir is presenting a different moral choice: Penelope might, many times, have created a masterpiece of art. In her unweaving, her temporizing, she has opted for another good, a precious marriage.

Odysseus will return from the archetypal Trojan War. Muir knew about war. He had seen, in the 1920s, the stifling effect of World War I on German and Austrian economies. He had seen what the Nazis had done to Czechoslovakia in World War II. He had witnessed the snuffing out of a proud, independent nation in the Communist putsch of 1948. This quiet, acute observer, at the center of events as no other British poet since 1920 had been, not surprisingly grasped the implications of nuclear fission by the United States in 1952 and by the Soviet Union in 1953. One of his most important early poems about childhood in the Orkneys was called "Horses," in which he portrays the huge farm animals with eyes that "Gleamed with a cruel apocalyptic light." In "The Horses" Muir returns to what appears to be another Orkney setting after an imagined nuclear war. The poem is grandly apocalyptic in its repudiation of the industrialism, technology, and materialism which generate modern war and in its espousal of a simple world of interdependent men and beasts. The poem, composed in an austere yet supple blank verse, concludes with an experience of Grace, the coming of strange horses and their foals:

> We did not dare go near them. Yet they waited,
> Stubborn and shy, as if they had been sent
> By an old command to find our whereabouts
> And that long-lost archaic companionship.
> In the first moment we had never a thought
> That they were creatures to be owned and used.
> Among them were some half-a-dozen colts
> Dropped in some wilderness of the broken world.
> Yet new as if they had come from their own Eden.
> Since then they have pulled our ploughs and borne our loads,
> But that free servitude still can pierce our hearts.
> Our life is changed; their coming our beginning.

In this climactic statement of Muir's abiding theme, the fabulous world of innocence intersecting the storied, tragic world of time, he has, as T. S. Eliot has remarked, concentrated his own experience and that of mid-twentieth century Europe into "that great, that terrifying poem of the 'atomic age.' "

Though Muir continued to write superior poetry right up to his death in January 1959, with no diminution of poetic power, he is most likely to be remembered for the poems in *The Labyrinth* (1949) and in *One Foot in Eden* (1956). Though his later work was championed by Eliot and has been illuminatingly praised by such acute critics as Blackmur, Butter, Hoffman, Huberman, and Knight, it is fair to say that not all able critics have joined the chorus of praise. Donald Davie puts well critics' reservations: "What dismays me . . . is a pervasive slackness—not in perception nor in seriousness . . . but simply in artistic ambition. . . . The medium is used scrupulously and well, to good and important ends; but it is *not wrought up to the highest pitch*. He does not say a thing once for all, then move on fast to another thing."

Accepting Davie's standards, one cannot rank Muir, say, with Hardy, Yeats, and Eliot. But he stands well in the company which follows. Despite discovering his talent very late, and arriving at competence perhaps later than any poet who has written in English, despite the handicaps of Calvinist upbringing and rudimentary formal education, nevertheless, by dint of a talent that could not be stilled, Edwin Muir achieved a secure place in the history of British poetry in the twentieth century.

Selected Translations (with Willa Muir):

Gerhart Hauptmann, *Poetic Dramas*, volume 8 of *The Dramatic Works* (London: Secker, 1925; New York: Huebsch, 1925);

Hauptmann, *The Island of the Great Mother* (London: Secker, 1925; New York: Viking, 1925);

Lion Feuchtwanger, *Jew Süss* (London: Secker, 1926); republished as *Power* (New York: Viking, 1928);

Feuchtwanger, *The Ugly Duchess* (London: Secker, 1927; New York: Viking, 1928);

Hauptmann, *Historic and Legendary Dramas*, volume 9 of *The Dramatic Works* (London: Secker, 1929; New York: Viking, 1929);

Franz Kafka, *The Castle* (London: Secker, 1930; New York: Knopf, 1930):

Hermann Broch, *The Sleepwalkers* (London: Secker, 1932; Boston: Little, Brown, 1932);

Kafka, *The Great Wall of China, and Other Pieces* (London: Secker, 1933);

Heinrich Mann, *Hill of Lies* (London: Jarrolds, 1934; New York: Dutton, 1935);

Broch, *The Unknown Quality* (London: Collins, 1935; New York: Viking, 1935);

Kafka, *The Trial* (London: Gollancz, 1937; New York: Knopf, 1937);

Kafka, *America* (London: Routledge, 1938; New York: New Directions, 1940);

Kafka, *Parables, in German and English*, translated by the Muirs and Clement Greenberg (New York: Schocken, 1947);

Kafka, *In the Penal Settlement: Tales and Short Pieces* (London: Secker, 1948; New York: Schocken, 1948).

Letters:

Selected Letters of Edwin Muir, edited by P. H. Butter (London: Hogarth, 1974).

Bibliographies:

Elgin W. Mellown, *Bibliography of the Writings of Edwin Muir* (University: University of Alabama Press, 1964);

Mellown, *Supplement to Bibliography of the Writings of Edwin Muir* (University: University of Alabama Press, 1970);

Peter C. Hoy and Mellown, *A Checklist of Writings About Edwin Muir* (Troy, N.Y.: Whitson Publishing Company, 1971).

Biographies:

Peter H. Butter, *Edwin Muir: Man and Poet* (Edinburgh: Oliver & Boyd, 1966);

Willa Muir, *Belonging: A Memoir* (London: Hogarth Press, 1968).

References:

R. P. Blackmur, "Edwin Muir: between the Tiger's Paws," in *Poets on Poetry*, edited by D. C. Allen (Baltimore: Johns Hopkins University Press, 1953), pp. 24-43;

Douglas Bush, *Pagan Myth and Christian Tradition in English Poetry* (Philadelphia: American Philosophical Society, 1968), pp. 92-98;

Peter H. Butter, *Edwin Muir* (Edinburgh: Oliver & Boyd, 1962; New York: Grove Press, 1962);

Joyce Crick, "Kafka and the Muirs," in *The World of Franz Kafka*, edited by J. P. Stern (New York: Holt, Rinehart & Winston, 1980), pp. 159-174;

Harvey Gross, *Sound and Form in Modern Poetry* (Ann Arbor: University of Michigan Press, 1964), pp. 68-72;

J. C. Hall, *Edwin Muir* (London: Longmans, Green, 1956);

Michael Hamburger, *Art as Second Nature: Occasional Pieces, 1950-74* (Cheadle Hulme, Cheshire: Carcanet New Press, 1975), pp. 86-106;

Allie Corbin Hixson, *Edwin Muir: A Critical Study* (New York: Vantage, 1977);

Daniel Hoffman, *Barbarous Knowledge: Myth in the Poetry of Yeats, Graves, and Muir* (New York: Oxford University Press, 1967), pp. 225-256;

John Holloway, *The Colours of Clarity: Essays on Contemporary Literature and Education* (London: Routledge & Kegan Paul, 1964), pp. 95-112;

Elizabeth Huberman, *The Poetry of Edwin Muir: The Field of Good and Evil* (New York: Oxford University Press, 1971);

Elizabeth Jennings, *Every Changing Shape* (London: Deutsch, 1961), pp. 148-162;

Brian Keeble, "Edwin Muir: Our Contemporary and Mentor," *Agenda*, 12, no. 4-13, no. 1 (Winter-Spring 1975): 79-87;

Roger Knight, *Edwin Muir: an introduction to his work* (London & New York: Longman, 1980);

Elgin W. Mellown, *Edwin Muir* (Boston: Twayne, 1979);

Ralph J. Mills, Jr., "Edwin Muir on Poetry," *Christian Scholar*, 45, no. 3 (1962): 238-248;

Willa Muir, *Living with Ballads* (New York: Oxford University Press, 1965);

Michael Phillips, *Edwin Muir: a master of modern poetry* (Indianapolis: Hackett, 1978);

Kathleen Raine, *Defending Ancient Springs* (London: Oxford University Press, 1967), pp. 1-16;

Herbert Read, *The Cult of Sincerity* (New York: Horizon Press, 1969), pp. 178-184;

James K. Robinson, "Terror Lumped and Split," *Southern Review*, new series 6 (Winter 1970): 216-228;

Christopher Wiseman, *Beyond the Labyrinth: A Study of Edwin Muir's Poetry* (Victoria: Sono Nis Press, 1978).

Papers:

Most of Muir's papers are in the National Library of Scotland, Edinburgh.

Alfred Noyes

(16 September 1880-23 June 1958)

Margaret B. McDowell
University of Iowa

SELECTED BOOKS: *The Loom of Years* (London: Richards, 1902);

The Flower of Old Japan (London: Richards, 1903);

Poems (Edinburgh & London: Blackwood, 1904);

The Forest of Wild Thyme (Edinburgh & London: Blackwood, 1905);

Poems (New York: Macmillan, 1906; London: Macmillan, 1906);

Drake: An English Epic (2 volumes, Edinburgh & London: Blackwood, 1906-1908; 1 volume, New York: Stokes, 1909);

The Flower of Old Japan and Other Poems (New York & London: Macmillan, 1907);

Forty Singing Seamen and Other Poems (Edinburgh & London: Blackwood, 1907; New York: Stokes, 1913);

The Golden Hynde and Other Poems (New York: Macmillan, 1908);

William Morris (London: Macmillan, 1908);

In Memory of Swinburne (Cleveland: Privately printed, 1909);

The Enchanted Island and Other Poems (Edinburgh & London: Blackwood, 1909; New York: Stokes, 1910);

Collected Poems (volumes 1-2, Edinburgh & London: Blackwood, 1910; New York: Stokes, 1913; volume 3, Edinburgh & London: Blackwood, 1920; New York: Stokes, 1920; revised and enlarged edition, 4 volumes, Edinburgh & London: Blackwood, 1927);

Sherwood, or Robin Hood and the Three Kings (New York: Stokes, 1911); revised as *Robin Hood* (Edinburgh & London: Blackwood, 1926);

The Carol of the Fir Tree (London: Burns & Oates, 1912);

Tales of the Mermaid Tavern (Edinburgh & London: Blackwood, 1913; New York: Stokes, 1913);

The Wine-Press; a Tale of War (Edinburgh & London: Blackwood, 1913; New York: Stokes, 1913);

Rada (New York: Stokes, 1914); revised and enlarged as *Rada, A Belgian Christmas Eve* (London: Methuen, 1915); republished as *A Belgian Christmas Eve* (New York: Stokes, 1915);

The Lord of Misrule and Other Poems (New York: Stokes, 1915);

A Salute from the Fleet and Other Poems (London: Methuen, 1915);

Mystery Ships, Trapping the U Boat (London: Hodder & Stoughton, 1916);

Open Boats (Edinburgh & London: Blackwood, 1917; New York: Stokes, 1917);

The New Morning, Poems (New York: Stokes, 1918);

Walking Shadows (London & New York: Cassell, 1918; New York: Stokes, 1918);

Beyond the Desert (New York: Stokes, 1920);

The Elfin Artist and Other Poems (Edinburgh & London: Blackwood, 1920; New York: Stokes, 1920);

The Watchers of the Sky, volume 1 of *The Torch-Bearers* (Edinburgh & London: Blackwood, 1922; New York: Stokes, 1922);

The Hidden Player (London: Hodder & Stoughton, 1924; New York: Stokes, 1924);

Some Aspects of Modern Poetry (London: Hodder &

Stoughton, 1924; New York, Stokes, 1924);
Songs of Shadow-of-a-Leaf and Other Poems (Edinburgh & London: Blackwood, 1924);
The Book of Earth, volume 2 of *The Torch-Bearers* (Edinburgh & London: Blackwood, 1925; New York: Stokes, 1925);
Dick Turpin's Ride and Other Poems (New York: Stokes, 1927);
New Essays and American Impressions (New York: Holt, 1927);
Ballads and Poems (Edinburgh & London: Blackwood, 1928);
The Opalescent Parrot (London: Sheed & Ward, 1929);
The Return of the Scare-Crow (London: Cassell, 1929); republished as *The Sun Cure* (New York: Cosmopolitan Book, 1929);
The Last Voyage, volume 3 of *The Torch-Bearers* (Edinburgh & London: Blackwood, 1930; New York: Stokes, 1930);
Tennyson (Edinburgh & London: Blackwood, 1932);
The Unknown God (London: Sheed & Ward, 1934; New York: Sheed & Ward, 1934);
Voltaire (London: Sheed & Ward, 1936; New York: Sheed & Ward, 1936);
Orchard's Bay (London: Sheed & Ward, 1939; New York: Sheed & Ward, 1939); republished as *The Incompleat Gardener* (London: Sheed & Ward, 1955);
The Last Man (London: Murray, 1940); republished as *No Other Man* (New York: Stokes, 1940);
Pageant of Letters (New York: Sheed & Ward, 1940);
If Judgment Comes (New York: Stokes, 1941);
Shadows on the Down and Other Poems (New York & Toronto: Stokes, 1941; London & New York: Hutchinson, 1945);
The Edge of the Abyss (New York: Dutton, 1942; London: Murray, 1944);
Poems of the New World (Philadelphia & New York: Lippincott, 1942);
The Secret of Pooduck Island (New York & Philadelphia: Stokes, 1943; London: Hutchinson, 1946);
Horace: A Portrait (New York: Sheed & Ward, 1947); republished as *Portrait of Horace* (London: Sheed & Ward, 1947);
Collected Poems (Philadelphia: Lippincott, 1947; London: Murray, 1950; enlarged edition, London: Murray, 1963; New York: McCutcheon, 1966);
Daddy Fell Into the Pond and Other Poems for Children (New York: Sheed & Ward, 1952);
Two Worlds for Memory (London & New York: Sheed & Ward, 1953; Philadelphia & New York: Lippincott, 1953);
The Devil Takes a Holiday (London: Murray, 1955);
A Letter to Lucian and Other Poems (London: Murray, 1956; Philadelphia: Lippincott, 1957);
The Accusing Ghost; or, Justice for Casement (London: Gollancz, 1957); republished as *The Accusing Ghost of Roger Casement* (New York: Citadel Press, 1957).

For his contemporaries the strong popular appeal of Alfred Noyes's poems lay in their lyrical and technical aspects—the heartiness of the songs, the heavy beat of the ballads, and the variety of metrical forms which he used with grace and apparent ease. The vitality of rhythm and rhyme in songs often marked by sonorous lines and memorable refrains made them especially popular for oral presentation. His appeal lay also in the optimistic view of the world which prevails in most of his work. He lent persuasive rhetoric in poetry and prose to support patriotism, heroism in war, and pursuit of international peace, and his poems reflect his faith in God, his belief in and appreciation of the harmony of nature, and his admiration for the explorers of the world of science. Noyes wrote poetry on less weighty subjects than these—for example, the satisfaction achieved through gardens and the escape to childhood, particularly through fantasies of fairyland, the songs of Robin Hood and his men, or those of good-natured sailors and pirates. Noyes was primarily a poet, but his works also include short stories, novels, plays, biographies, autobiography, and essays on literary subjects, religion, the philosophy and history of science, the waging of war, and the achieving of a lasting peace. Extremely prolific, he produced about sixty books in the course of his career.

In literature he praised the ancient and modern classics, paying homage to Chaucer, Shakespeare and the other Elizabethans, Milton, Pope, Samuel Johnson and his circle, Addison, James Thomson (1700-1748), Scott, Wordsworth, Shelley, Tennyson, Morris, Swinburne, Henley, and Stevenson. Although he never compared his work with Kipling's, many others have done so. Art for Noyes was humanistic in its implications, and in his critical essays he conceived of literary tradition as growing incrementally over the centuries, as an enlarging phenomenon to which all significant writers contributed. His essays are appreciative and enthusiastic rather than sharply discriminating. The ideas expressed in his trilogy on the history and philosophy of science, *The Torch-Bearers* (1922, 1925, 1930), parallel those that underlie his thoughts on literature. Individual researchers, inventors, and theorists contribute to the whole of scientific understanding by passing on the torch to the next generation, and their achievement helps enlarge the boundaries of human knowledge and understanding. In the case of both artists and scientists, their achievement is not only important in itself but also because it expands the frontiers of human culture.

In contrast to his positive responses to earlier writers, Noyes scorned the work of his most prominent contemporaries. In fiction he was hostile to works that attempted to register the nuances of inner experience through such innovative techniques as stream of consciousness. While he was capable of probing many levels of his own consciousness in the spiritual questioning that culminated in his alignment with Roman Catholicism and in his writing of *The Unknown God* (1934), he preferred a fiction that was conventional and realistic to one that was experimental. He regarded James Joyce's work as "filth," and he criticized what he perceived as Joyce's willful obscurity and vulgarity in *Ulysses*. Ironically, with the increased interest in science fantasy, his few experiments in fiction with necromancy, the occult, violence, and the subconscious have increased in popularity since 1975. Among his contemporaries in poetry, Noyes disapproved of innovative or unconventional writers. In the work of T. S. Eliot, he believed that excessive intellectual complexity detracted from clarity of expression and from the conveying of emotion. Noyes disliked the use of free verse, of esoteric allusions, of imagery private to the poetry, and of calculated ambiguity.

Noyes shared the interest of some of his contemporaries in Japanese art and culture, but he was national rather than international in his focus and interests. He believed it was most important for people of England and the United States to understand their common literary heritage, because civilization would survive only if these two countries developed an invincible bond of understanding and purpose. He thought he was almost alone in espousing this view during his early career, but he lived to see this idea become a more general conviction after two world wars.

Alfred Noyes appeared to move with remarkable assurance through his childhood, his youth, and then his career of fifty years. Born in Wolverhampton, Noyes was the eldest of the three sons of Amelia Adams Rawley Noyes and Alfred Noyes, a grocer who later became a teacher. In his autobiography Noyes remarks that his childhood, which seems to have been unclouded, provided him with no reason for "the slightest cry of self-pity." He, nevertheless, comments parenthetically that his mother remained an invalid after the birth of his younger brother and that her nervous illness precluded all normal relationships and activities for the rest of her life. His father, who had given up his chance to attend a university and become an Anglican clergyman so that his younger brother could have a university education instead, devoted all of his time to the care of the invalid and their children. He taught his son Latin and Greek, and gave him a Greek New Testament, which he encouraged him to follow as the English version was read in church services. Alfred Noyes grew up enjoying the mountainous Welsh sea coast and rambling over Welsh hills. In school in Aberystwyth, Wales, his only problem occurred when a teacher one day rapped him on the head because he had hidden a volume of Spenser's poetry behind the copy of Euclid that he was supposed to be studying. For him, Oxford, where he went in 1898, was an intense and positive experience, but he left without a degree. As a repository of the traditions that he loved, Oxford, he felt, kept the past alive in its cloisters, and "the great cultural traditions of Christendom" haunted the place. Although he helped organize a small group of students at Queen's College who were "keenly interested in literature and especially in poetry," and although he was writing poetry and having it published (his first collection, *The Loom of Years*, was published in 1902 when he was a twenty-one-year-old undergraduate), he also could say that for a time during those years rowing was the most important thing in life. In 1907 he married Garnett Daniels. Their marriage was childless. Prompt arrival of his royalty checks was a necessity, but Noyes recalled their nineteen years together as "without a cloud." Garnett Daniels was an American, and the couple lived about a third of the time in the United States—New Jersey, New York, and California. Garnett died in 1926, having kept her impending death a secret from her husband. That year Noyes became a Roman Catholic. The following year he married Mary Angela Mayne Weld-Blundell, the mother of an eleven-year-old daughter, Agnes, by her first husband, Richard Weld-Blundell, who had been a member of one of the oldest and most prominent Catholic families in England and who had died in action in World War I in 1916 a few months after their marriage. During the next decade Alfred and Mary Noyes had three children—Henry, Veronica, and Margaret. Noyes's literary work, especially his poetry, supported a comfortable upper-class mode of living for his family during a time when it was virtually impossible for a poet to depend solely on income from his work. Besides his residences in England and America, Noyes maintained a country place on the Isle of Wight.

Although Noyes now seems out of step with the major movements in British poetry between 1900 and 1950, his success as the most popular poet of his time did not—in the first two decades of his career at least—exclude him from enjoying the respect of several major writers whose careers had flourished before his own began. *The Loom of Years* received the compliments of George Meredith and William Butler Yeats. In 1907 the aging Swinburne entertained Noyes several times. Noyes, a devout Christian, could complacently brush aside the earlier flamboyant paganism of Swinburne and write that the "real Swinburne" impressed him "with the essential nobility of his mind and spirit." Edmund Gosse enhanced Noyes's reputation by including him in many gatherings. The two shared such enthusiasms as Browning, Swinburne, Christina Rossetti, and Coventry Patmore. It was at Gosse's home that Noyes met Prime Minister Herbert Asquith. In the early years of his career he also enjoyed the stimulus of writers such as A. A. Milne and G. K. Chesterton. During Noyes's first trip to the United States in 1907, Longfellow's daughters and Emerson's son entertained him, and he became a close friend of the family of Thomas Bailey Aldrich, a writer whom Noyes admired and who had just died. On a later visit, in 1919, he had afternoon tea with Theodore Roosevelt a few hours before Roosevelt's unexpected death.

So prolific was Noyes that by the time he was thirty, in 1910, he had produced his first biography, *William Morris* (1908), and had collected his poems in eight full-length books: *The Loom of Years* (1902), *The Flower of Old Japan* (1903), *Poems* (1904), *The Forest of Wild Thyme* (1905), *Drake: An English Epic* (1906-1908), *Forty Singing Seamen and Other Poems* (1907), *The Golden Hynde and Other Poems* (1908), and *The Enchanted Island and Other Poems* (1909). They were widely reviewed and several were published in both Britain and the United States.

Perhaps the most ambitious of Noyes's poetic works is *Drake: An English Epic*, a twelve-book, two-hundred-page epic in blank verse, primarily about the events surrounding the British defeat of the Spanish Armada. While the poem is too long, the scope and energy of the work are remarkable. Felicitously, for the purpose of a metrical variety he placed many songs in other meters throughout the epic. While the catalogues of historical data and events are perhaps overly extended, Noyes reveals some notable originality and force in the development of William Cecil, Lord Burghley, as a man of evil who frequently opposed Drake's ideas, and in the description of the tragedy of Thomas Doughty's execution by Drake, after he had been found guilty of plotting a mutiny during Drake's expedition to South America. Another intense episode occurs when Drake returns to Bess of Sydenham, the "queen of his heart," just before her father forces her to marry someone else. Noyes's epic is not the equal of Homer or Milton, but it is a work of ambition and sustained craft. When the first volume was published in 1906 and again when the second appeared in 1908, the London *Times Literary Supplement* devoted its main feature articles to *Drake*.

Also in 1908 Noyes produced his first book in prose, the critical biography *William Morris*, which reviewers and scholars, including Andrew Lang, mostly praised. A later critic, C. S. Lewis, concluded that Noyes had given the "true picture of the real Morris." In his prose works Noyes generally reveals his breadth of interests and his enthusiasms, rather than relying on meticulous scholarship or creative imagination. An anonymous reviewer in the *Saturday Review*, for example, questioned Noyes's rather uncritical admiration for all of Morris's work and the depth of his study of the poet, and he maintained that the studies of Morris already done by Mackail, Pater, Symons, and Yeats had presented him with greater subtlety, delicacy, and discrimination.

In Noyes's early career the commentators emphasized his energy and his enthusiasm. Occasionally a reviewer commented that Noyes had not yet attained that fusion of content and expression that betokens poetic maturity. Generally, however, critics suspended judgment while thousands of readers bought Noyes's books of poems, cherished them, and even memorized parts of them. In the first ten or fifteen years of his career those who qualified their praise did so equivocally; for example, a reviewer in a 1907 issue of the *Atlantic Monthly* commented, "There is a proficiency in the workmanship that, coupled with Mr. Noyes' humorous tenderness in approaching his theme, all but disarms criticism." A reviewer who suggested that *Drake* was a failure concluded by calling it the best poem since Tennyson. Not until World War I did Noyes's critics become more stringent in their judgments; many of them then pointed out the triteness, the false profundities, and the pedestrianism of vision and workmanship in some of the poems.

During the impressive first decade of Noyes's career, he wrote the two poems for which he became best known, "The Barrel Organ" (usually identified by its refrain, "Come down to Kew in lilac time") and "The Highwayman." Because "The Barrel Organ" varies in form from section to section and the transitions between sections are abrupt, the poem conveys an impression of loose construction. The work is, in fact, carefully organized and executed, with repetitions fitting into intricate patterns. The poet communicates a variety of moods in the serious songs of the organ, in the songs of knights marching to battle, and in the joyous refrains, as the poet insists that everyone leave work-a-day London and "Come down to Kew in lilac time."

Noyes reported that he wrote "The Highwayman" in two days when he was twenty-four, "the age when I was genuinely excited by that kind of romantic story." The night wind and moonlight add much to the effect as Noyes uses repeated phrases to secure an atmosphere of hypnosis. In view of his outspoken disapproval of the explicitly sexual or abnormal in the works of his contemporaries, it is somewhat surprising to encounter the sadistic violence in this poem: Police officers tie the highwayman's sweetheart to a bedpost so that she must watch the torture and death of her lover when he appears. They fit the muzzle of the shotgun beneath her breast. When she struggles with her bloodied hands to free herself from the ropes so that she may warn her highwayman lover, the gun goes off, and she is mutilated. There is also violence when the robber races back to secure revenge and finally lies in his blood on the highway. (Some other poems written early in Noyes's career suggest a derivation from Swinburne and Baudelaire. "Necromancy" and "Love's Ghost," for example, are both concerned with necrophilic sexual experience.)

In 1913 Noyes produced a long poem, *The Wine-Press; a Tale of War*, in which Johann, a woodcutter in the Balkans, leaves his wife and their baby to enlist, after being recruited by five men who carry "little disks of gold." It is not long before Johann and other recruits find themselves caught up in the frenzy of battle, and at one point Johann is so caught up in bayoneting swarms of attackers that he fails to realize that the slippery lumps over which he attempts to walk in the dark are the faces of the dead and wounded. The blood oozing from them is like wine from trampled grapes—hence, the title of the thirty-page poem.

Noyes's recognition in America was assured in 1913 when, at the age of thirty-three, he received from the hands of former President William Howard Taft an honorary doctor of letters from Yale University. (He later was awarded honorary doctorates from the University of Edinburgh in 1927, Syracuse University in 1943, and the University of California in 1944.) He was invited to give the Lowell Lectures at Harvard University in the spring of 1913 and chose as his subject for the lectures, "The Sea in English Poetry." In 1914 he was awarded a three-year appointment to the Murray Professorship of Literature at Princeton University. Noyes held this post until 1923, except for a term beginning in 1916 when he served the British government in the International News Service. The position at Princeton required two lectures a week for one semester each year. Among Noyes's students in one seminar were F. Scott Fitzgerald, Edmund Wilson, and John Peale Bishop. He established strong relationships during this time with guests of the university, including Sir Cecil Spring-Rice, British ambassador to Washington, and George Ellery Hale, a noted astronomer who later at Wilson Ob-

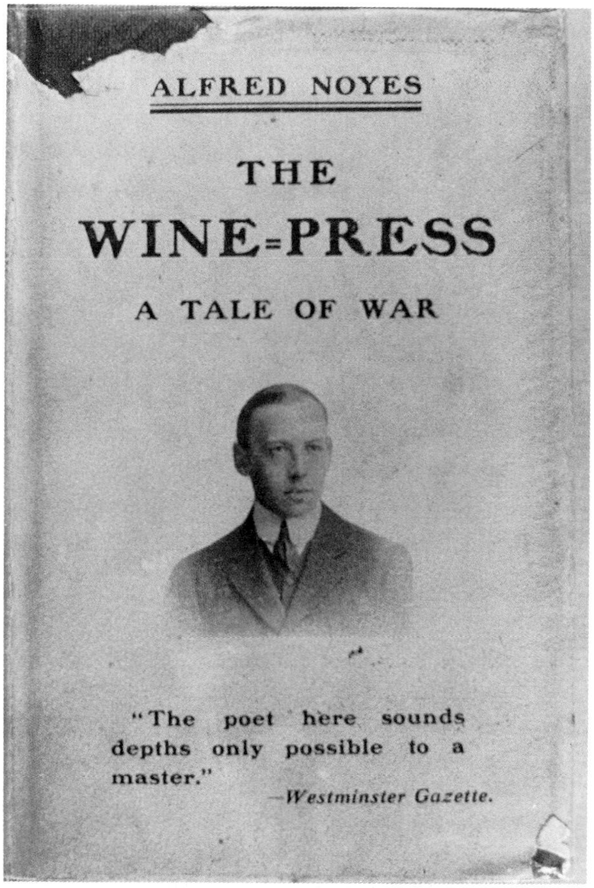

Dust jacket for Noyes's 1913 narrative poem, emphasizing war's dehumanization of the individual

servatory in California gave Noyes the idea for *The Torch-Bearers*.

On the eve of World War I Noyes produced two works which might be considered propaganda in verse. *Rada*, a one-act play published in 1914, was rewritten and enlarged for republication in 1915. Set in a Belgian village on Christmas Eve the play deals with Rada, the village physician's wife, who shoots her twelve-year-old daughter and herself as an alternative to their being raped by the invading Germans.

During World War I Noyes produced *Open Boats* (1917), about the trawlers that rescued from their open boats the survivors from ships sunk by German submarines, and *Mystery Ships, Trapping the U Boat* (1916). Noyes maintained throughout his career a strong interest in the sea and seafarers, reflecting his childhood love of hiding in his "mountain nook" overlooking the sea as he read or daydreamed. The appeal of his work on this theme extends to present-day readers, as the biographical sketch of Noyes in the *Oxford Companion to Ships and the Sea* (1976), edited by Peter Kemp, suggests. Related to the war also are the short stories in the collection *Walking Shadows* (1918).

World War I stimulated Noyes's interest in fiction, particularly fiction related to strange psychic experience or extrasensory powers. His earlier preoccupation with sensational subjects is apparent later in a far more sinister fusion of pain, cruelty, rape, and torture in *The Wine-Press* and *Rada*. More subtly in *Walking Shadows*, a half-dozen stories about submarine sailors, he blended documentary realism with supernatural endings. *The Hidden Player* (1924) is a collection of eleven short stories focusing on the mysterious and ineffable dimensions of religious experience. *The Last Man* (1940) is a fantasy novel describing the aftermath of super-weapon holocaust in which almost all human beings are destroyed. Although Noyes's popularity as a poet has waned, he has received favorable critical comment in recent books on fantasy and science fiction such as Mike Asley's *Horror and Fantasy Fiction* (1977) and Richard Reginald's *Science Fiction and Fantasy Literature* (1979).

The events of World War I also influenced some works of later years. Near the close of the war, he reported for the International News Service and the British government on the case of Roger Casement and his alleged commitment to separatist politics in Ireland. Casement was accused of going to Germany to recruit Irish soldiers being held as prisoners of war in Germany, who would be released upon agreement to take part in an Irish liberation offensive. He was convicted and sentenced to death for high treason in spring 1916. During the summer, many in America and England sought to block the execution of Casement, a retired employee of the British Foreign Service who had been knighted for his contributions to the Empire. Arthur Conan Doyle, for example, gathered long lists of names on petitions to stay the execution—including literary figures like Arnold Bennett, John Galsworthy, and G. K. Chesterton. In the meantime, however, typed pages purporting to be the personal diaries kept by Casement in 1903 and 1911 were widely circulated. The diaries, which mentioned homosexual encounters, proved highly prejudicial. Noyes wrote a denunciation of Casement's morality, which was not published until the execution took place. While Noyes took the word of government officials and believed the diaries to be authentic, it is now thought likely that they were forged.

Noyes received the Commander of the Order of the British Empire in 1918, in part for his reporting on the Casement case. He also received adverse publicity for it. In 1916 in Philadelphia he was denounced by Casement's sister, Nina, before a crowd of 2,000, when he rose to speak. In 1937, he was named derisively by William Butler Yeats in his poem "Roger Casement": "Come Alfred Noyes, come all the troop / That cried it far and wide / . . . / Come speak your bit in public / That some amends be made." Yeats later changed the beginning of the first line of the stanza to "Come Tom and Dick. . . ." Yeats, like other Irish patriots, saw Casement as a martyr. Such veneration and anger raised interest in the dramatization of Noyes's book *The Accusing Ghost; or, Justice for Casement* (1957). Noyes collaborated with Robert McHugh on the five-act dramatization, which was presented on the Dublin stage in 1958.

In 1917 Noyes visited the new telescope being installed at Mount Wilson, California, and was inspired to begin his ambitious, three-volume work, *The Torch-Bearers*, which celebrates the scientific, scholarly, theological, and philosophical growth of mankind. The three volumes—*The Watchers of the Sky* (1922), *The Book of Earth* (1925), and *The Last Voyage* (1930)—gained mixed reviews, but the scope of the undertaking brought Noyes considerable attention.

The last of the volumes of *The Torch-Bearers* reflects the intensity of Noyes's theological search for one's destiny after life on earth and his increased preoccupation with religion following the death of Garnett. He strenuously denied that his impending marriage to a Catholic had precipitated his entrance into the church in 1926. He stressed, rather, his lifelong spiritual aspirations, which were fostered in early childhood by his father. He also believed that he moved gradually toward Catholicism through the influence of eighteenth- and nineteenth-century free thinkers. In their thinking he thought he saw a common thread, expressed best by Voltaire—a classification of knowledge and reality into two parts, physically verifiable knowledge as contrasted with knowledge of experience that lies beyond empirical understanding. This concept freed him to accept Catholic interpretations of what lies beyond physical verification. Noyes's *Tennyson* (1932) reflects the belief that the agnostic's doubt can guide some to surer faith. *The Unknown God* (1934) and *Voltaire* (1936) emphasize a similar dual view of reality, and through a brief misunderstanding, *Voltaire* suffered from a "suspension of approval" by the Vatican when a careless reader assumed that, because he presented Voltaire's thought processes in a positive manner, Noyes's own ideas about theology were like Voltaire's.

Noyes's political views sometimes derived simplistically from his Catholic faith. He was a strong believer in the alliance of "English-speaking nations," by which he tended to mean England, Canada, and the United States. Peace and survival for the world lay in the close alliance of England and America and in the strong dedication of these countries to Christianity. The plea for British-American unity and for the revival of Christian religion in these nations underlies such wartime books as *If Judgment Comes* (1941) and *The Edge of the Abyss* (1942). Noyes's interest in religion had much to do with the optimism characteristic of his earlier poems and with the views on nature expressed in them. Like the romantics, he once said that all nature is a parable directing the individual to spiritual truth, but he also was convinced of this truth in Christian terms. This point of view is clear in *Orchard's Bay* (1939), which he later retitled *The Incompleat Gardener*. In this series of personal essays he reflects upon his garden on the Isle of Wight and intersperses forty new poems among the informal comments. Everywhere in his meditations he finds the peace of God, even though he is living in a country at war and directly beneath a major air corridor for fighter planes.

Noyes's teaching and lecturing in the United States from 1913 to 1923 and again during World War II resulted in several volumes of miscellaneous literary essays: *Some Aspects of Modern Poetry* (1924), *New Essays and American Impressions* (1927), *The Opalescent Parrot* (1929), *Pageant of Letters* (1940), and *Horace: A Portrait* (1947). The range of his reading and of his literary appreciation is evident in the contents of *The Opalescent Parrot*, which includes essays on Baudelaire, Longfellow, Carlyle, Poe, Milton, Bunyan, Meredith, Keats, Shakespeare, Bacon, and Whitman. Similarly, *Pageant of Letters* collects essays on Chaucer, Marlowe, Shakespeare, Bacon, Milton, Samuel Johnson, Thomson, Shelley, Landor, Dickens, Browning, Emerson, Whitman, Addison, Stevenson, Meredith, Swinburne, and Alice Meynell. Such essays provided the basis for lectures, which often accompanied his platform readings of poetry in more than 1,000 American communities.

In the early days of World War II Noyes remained in his home on the Isle of Wight and produced *Orchard's Bay*, the poems in *Shadows on the Down and Other Poems* (1941), and began work on *A Letter to Lucian and Other Poems* (1956), which was completed after the war. Because of the dangers in living on the Isle of Wight, he placed his children in Canadian boarding schools and, beginning in 1940, traveled and lectured in the United States. *Poems of the New World* (1942) is a sort of travelogue in poetry. In separate poems Noyes celebrates the particular places and people he and Mary Noyes visited in the United States and Canada. While Noyes lived until 1958, most of his poetry was written by 1942, when glaucoma claimed his eyesight. At this time he began collecting and revising the poems that were to appear in the single-volume edition, *Collected Poems* (1947). The 1963 edition of this collection added only nine poems, all from *A Letter to Lucian and Other Poems*, and was edited by his son, Henry Noyes.

On the Isle of Wight after the war, Noyes dictated his prose works: *Horace* (1947), his autobiography *Two Worlds for Memory* (1953), the satiric *The Devil Takes a Holiday* (1955), and *The Accusing Ghost; or, Justice for Casement* (1957). In addition, he wrote two children's books: *The Secret of Pooduck Island* (1943) about the family's hideaway in Maine, and *Daddy Fell Into the Pond and Other Poems for Children* (1952). The first of these won the Pro Parvulis Book Club's Downey Award in 1943.

In *Two Worlds for Memory* Noyes engagingly tells of his travels and his encounters with famous people on both sides of the Atlantic. He describes, for example, his private audience with Premier Benito Mussolini just before the war broke out in 1939. Each man pretended awkwardly to understand the language of the other. He also tells how he and the irreverent Hugh Walpole covered the 1939 funeral of Pope Pius XI for the International News

Alfred Noyes, 1914 (BBC Hulton)

Service and how, a few months later, he threw Walpole out of his house for trying to entice one of his children to read James Joyce's *Ulysses*.

Though he lacks the incisiveness, the concentration, and the radical originality of a major poet, Alfred Noyes will surely be remembered for the variety, vitality, and imaginative facility of his poetry. The best of his work makes him far more than a skillful versifier. His sense of the dramatic, his mastery of verbal melody and rhythmic movement, and his ability to recreate a scene with a single line make his contribution to British literature substantial. Poems such as "The Barrel Organ" and "The Highwayman" and many of his nature poems possess timeless appeal. One can agree with Osbert Sitwell's 1935 comment that Noyes spent too much time defending great writers against crimes they had never been accused of. One might also agree with Sitwell that " 'Come down to Kew in lilac time' should have been—and perhaps was—whistled by every errand boy in town" and that with as many books of verse as Noyes has to his credit, "it would not . . . be fair . . . to expect every poem to be a good one." But it is surprising how many good poems there are in his collections and how readable and enjoyable they still can be.

Other:

The Magic Casement: An Anthology of Fairy Poetry, edited, with an introduction, by Noyes (London: Chapman & Hall, 1908; New York: Dutton, 1909);

The Golden Book of Catholic Poetry, edited by Noyes (Philadelphia and New York: Lippincott, 1946).

Bibliography:

James E. Tobin, "Alfred Noyes: A Corrected Bibliography," *Catholic Library World*, 15 (March 1944): 181-184, 189.

References:
Patrick Braybrooke, *Some Victorian and Georgian Catholics* (London: Burns, Oates & Washbourne, 1936), pp. 171-202;
Edward Davison, *Some Modern Poets and Other Critical Essays* (New York: Harper, 1928), pp. 197-218;
Hoxie Neale Fairchild, *Gods of a Changing Poetry, 1880-1920*, volume 5 of *Religious Trends in English Poetry* (New York: Columbia University Press, 1961), pp. 195-221;
Walter Copeland Jerrold, *Alfred Noyes* (London: Shaylor, 1930);
Arthur St. John Adcock, *Gods of Modern Grub Street* (New York: Stokes, 1923);
Osbert Sitwell, *Penny Foolish* (London: Macmillan, 1935), pp. 334-338.

Wilfred Owen

Margaret B. McDowell
University of Iowa

BIRTH: Plas Wilmot, Oswestry, Shropshire, 18 March 1893, to Thomas and Susan Shaw Owen.

AWARD: Military Cross, 1918;

DEATH: Sambre and Olse Canal, north of Ors, France, 4 November 1918.

SELECTED BOOKS: *Poems*, edited by Siegfried Sassoon (London: Chatto & Windus, 1920; New York: Huebsch, 1921);
The Poems of Wilfred Owen, edited by Edmund Blunden (London: Chatto & Windus, 1931; New York: Viking, 1931);
Thirteen Poems (Northampton, Mass.: Gehenna Press, 1956);
The Collected Poems of Wilfred Owen, edited by C. Day Lewis (London: Chatto & Windus, 1963; New York: New Directions, 1964);
War Poems and Others, edited by Dominic Hibberd (London: Chatto & Windus, 1973);
Ten War Poems (Oxford: Taurus Press, 1974).

Wilfred Owen, 1916

Wilfred Owen, who wrote some of the best British poetry on World War I, composed nearly all of his poems in slightly over a year, from August 1917 to September 1918. In November 1918 he was killed in action at the age of twenty-five, one week before the Armistice. Only five poems were published in his lifetime—three in the *Nation* and two that appeared anonymously in the *Hydra*, a journal he edited in 1917 when he was a patient at Craiglockhart War Hospital in Edinburgh. Shortly after his death, seven more of his poems appeared in the 1919 volume of Edith Sitwell's annual anthology, *Wheels*, a volume dedicated to his memory, and in 1919 and 1920 seven other poems appeared in periodicals. Almost all of Owen's poems, therefore, appeared posthumously: *Poems* (1920), edited by Siegfried Sassoon with the assistance of Edith Sitwell, contains twenty-three poems; *The Poems of Wilfred Owen* (1931), edited by Edmund Blunden, adds nineteen poems to this number; and *The Collected Poems of Wilfred Owen* (1963), edited by C. Day Lewis, contains eighty poems, adding some juvenilia, minor poems, and fragments but omitting a few of the poems from Blunden's edition.

Wilfred Edward Salter Owen was born on 18 March 1893, in Oswestry, on the Welsh border of Shropshire, in the beautiful and spacious home of his maternal grandfather. Wilfred's father, Thomas, a former seaman, had returned from India to marry Susan Shaw; throughout the rest of his life Thomas felt constrained by his somewhat dull and low-paid position as a railway station master. Owen's mother felt that her marriage limited her intellectual, musical, and economic ambitions. Both parents seem to have been of Welsh descent, and Susan's family had been relatively affluent during her childhood but had lost ground economically. As the oldest of four children born in rapid succession, Wilfred developed a protective attitude toward the others and an especially close relationship with his mother. After he turned four, the family moved from the grandfather's home to a modest house in Birkenhead, where Owen attended Birkenhead Institute from 1900 to 1907. The family then moved to another modest house, in Shrewsbury, where Owen attended Shrewsbury Technical School and graduated in 1911 at the age of eighteen. Having attempted unsuccessfully to win a scholarship to attend London University, he tried to measure his aptitude for a religious vocation by becoming an unpaid lay assistant to the Reverend Herbert Wigan, a vicar of evangelical inclinations in the Church of England, at Dunsden, Oxfordshire. In return for the tutorial instruction he was to receive, but which did not significantly materialize, Owen agreed to assist with the care of the poor and sick in the parish and to decide within two years whether he should commit himself to further training as a clergyman. At Dunsden he achieved a fuller understanding of social and economic issues and developed his humanitarian propensities, but as a consequence of this heightened sensitivity, he became disillusioned with the inadequate response of the Church of England to the sufferings of the underprivileged and the dispossessed. In his spare time, he read widely and began to write poetry. In his initial verses he wrote on the conventional subjects of the time, but his work also manifested some stylistic qualities that even then tended to set him apart, especially his keen ear for sound and his instinct for the modulating of rhythm, talents related perhaps to the musical ability that he shared with both of his parents.

In 1913 he returned home, seriously ill with a respiratory infection that his living in a damp, unheated room at the vicarage had exacerbated. He talked of poetry, music, or graphic art as possible vocational choices, but his father urged him to seek employment that would result in a steady income. After eight months of convalescence at home, Owen taught for one year in Bordeaux at the Berlitz School of Languages, and he spent a second year in France with a Catholic family, tutoring their two boys. As a result of these experiences, he became a Francophile. Later these years undoubtedly heightened his sense of the degree to which the war disrupted the life of the French populace and caused widespread suffering among civilians as the Allies pursued the retreating Germans through French villages in the summer and fall of 1918.

In September 1915, nearly a year after England and Germany had gone to war, Owen returned to England, uncertain as to whether he should enlist. By October he had enlisted and was at first in the Artists' Rifles. In June 1916 he received a commission as lieutenant in the Manchester Regiment, and on 29 December 1916 he left for France with the Lancashire Fusiliers.

Judging by his first letters to his mother from France, one might have anticipated that Owen would write poetry in the idealistic vein of Rupert Brooke: "There is a fine heroic feeling about being in France. . . ." But by 6 January 1917 he wrote of the marching, "The awful state of the roads, and the enormous weight carried was too much for scores of men." Outfitted in hip-length rubber waders, on 8 January he had waded through two and a half miles of trenches with "a mean depth of two feet of water." By 9 January he was housed in a hut where only seventy yards away a howitzer fired every minute day and night. On 12 January occurred the march and attack of poison gas he later reported in "Dulce et Decorum Est." They marched three miles over a shelled road and three more along a flooded trench, where those who got stuck in the heavy mud had to leave their waders, as well as some clothing and equipment, and move ahead on bleeding and

Wilfred Owen at Dunsden Vicarage, early 1912

freezing feet. They were under machine-gun fire, shelled by heavy explosives throughout the cold march, and were almost unconscious from fatigue when the poison-gas attack occurred. Another incident that month, in which one of Owen's men was blown from a ladder in their trench and blinded, forms the basis of "The Sentry." In February Owen attended an infantry school at Amiens. On 19 March he was hospitalized for a brain concussion suffered six nights earlier, when he fell into a fifteen-foot-deep shell hole while searching in the dark for a soldier overcome by fatigue. Blunden dates the writing of Owen's sonnet "To A Friend (With an Identity Disc)" to these few days in the hospital. Throughout April the battalion suffered incredible physical privations caused by the record-breaking cold and snow and by the heavy shelling. For four days and nights Owen and his men remained in an open field in the snow, with no support forces arriving to relieve them and with no chance to change wet, frozen clothes or to sleep: "I kept alive on brandy, the fear of death, and the glorious prospect of the cathedral town just below us, glittering with the morning." Three weeks later on 25 April he continued to write his mother of the intense shelling: "For twelve days I did not wash my face, nor take off my boots, nor sleep a deep sleep. For twelve days we lay in holes where at any moment a shell might put us out." One wet night during this time he was blown into the air while he slept. For the next several days he hid in a hole too small for his body, with the body of a friend, now dead, huddled in a similar hole opposite him, and less than six feet away. In these letters to his mother he directed his bitterness not at the enemy but at the people back in England "who might relieve us and will not."

Having endured such experiences in January, March, and April, Owen was sent to a series of hospitals between 1 May and 26 June 1917 because of severe headaches. He thought them related to his brain concussion, but they were eventually diagnosed as symptoms of shell shock, and he was sent to Craiglockhart War Hospital in Edinburgh to become a patient of Dr. A. Brock, the associate of Dr. W. H. R. Rivers, the noted neurologist and psychologist to whom Siegfried Sassoon was assigned when he arrived six weeks later.

Owen's annus mirabilis as a poet apparently began in the summer of 1917, but he had, in fact, been preparing himself haphazardly but determinedly for a career as poet throughout the preceding five or six years. He had worshipped Keats and later Shelley during adolescence; during his two years at Dunsden he had read and written poetry in the isolated evenings at the vicarage; in Bordeaux, the elderly symbolist poet and pacifist writer Laurent Tailhade had encouraged him in his ambition to become a poet. Also in France in 1913 and 1914 he probably read and studied the works of novelist and poet Jules Romains, who was experimenting with pararhyme and assonance, although Romains's treatise on half-rhyme or *accords* (*Petit Traite de Versification*, written with G. Chenneviere) which describes several devices that Owen himself used, was not published until after Owen's death. While he was stationed in London in 1915 and 1916, he found stimulation in discussions with another older poet, Harold Monro, who ran the Poetry Bookshop, a meeting place for poets; and in 1916, he read Rupert Brooke, William Butler Yeats, and A. E. Housman. In the fall and winter of 1916, Owen, his cousin Leslie Gunston, and a friend of Gunston's engaged in an extended literary game in which the three decided upon a topic and then mailed to one another the verses they wrote on that topic. Owen was developing his skill in versification, his technique as a poet, and his appreciation for the poetry of others, especially that of his more important contemporaries, but until 1917 he was not expressing his own significant experiences and convictions except in letters to his mother and brother.

This preparation, the three bitter months of suffering, the warmth of the people of Edinburgh who "adopted" the patients, the insight of Dr. Brock, and the coincidental arrival of Siegfried Sassoon brought forth the poet and the creative outpouring of his single year of maturity.

Before Sassoon arrived at Craiglockhart in mid-August, Dr. Brock encouraged Owen to edit the hospital journal, the *Hydra*, which went through twelve issues before Owen left. Later in Owen's stay Brock also arranged for him to play in a community orchestra, to renew his interests in biology and archaeology, to participate in a debating society, to give lectures at Tynecastle School, and to do historical research at the Edinburgh Advocates Library.

It seems likely that this sensitive psychologist and enthusiastic friend assisted Owen in confronting the furthermost ramifications of his violent experiences in France so that he could write of the terrifying experiences in poems such as "Dulce et Decorum Est," "The Sentry," and "The Show." He may also have helped him confront his shyness; his apparently excessive involvement with his mother and his attempt, at the same time, to become more independent; his resentment of his father's disapproval of his ambition for a career as a poet; his ambivalence about Christianity and his disillusionment with Christian religion in the practices of the contemporary church; his expressed annoyance with all women except his mother and his attraction to other men; and his decision to return to his comrades in the trenches rather than to stay in England to protest the continuation of the war.

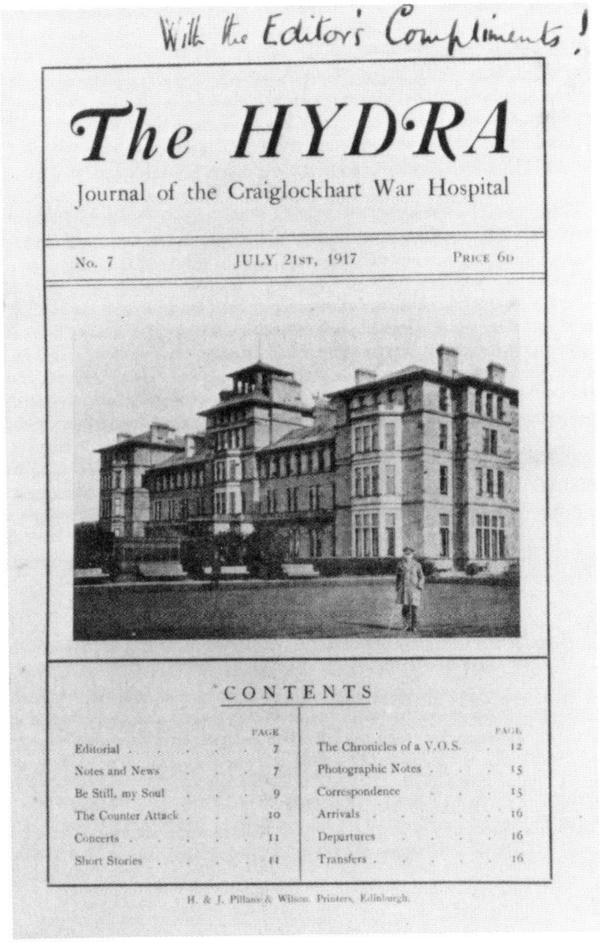
With the Editor's Compliments!

The HYDRA

Journal of the Craiglockhart War Hospital

No. 7 JULY 21st, 1917 PRICE 6d

CONTENTS

	PAGE		PAGE
Editorial	7	The Chronicles of a V.O.S.	12
Notes and News	7	Photographic Notes	15
Be Still, my Soul	9	Correspondence	15
The Counter Attack	10	Arrivals	16
Concerts	11	Departures	16
Short Stories	11	Transfers	16

H. & J. Pillans & Wilson, Printers, Edinburgh.

Front cover, inscribed by Owen, of an issue of the magazine he edited at Craiglockhart War Hospital

When Sassoon arrived, it took Owen two weeks to get the courage to knock on his door and identify himself as a poet. At that time Owen, like many others in the hospital, was speaking with a stammer. By autumn he was not only articulate with his new friends and lecturing in the community but was able to use his terrifying experiences in France, and his conflicts about returning, as the subject of poems expressing his own deepest feelings. He experienced an astonishing period of creative energy that lasted through several months, until he returned to France and the heavy fighting in the fall of 1918.

By the time they met, Owen and Sassoon shared the conviction that the war ought to be ended, since the total defeat of the Central Powers would entail additional destruction, casualties, and suffering of staggering magnitude. In 1917 and 1918 both found their creative stimulus in a compassionate identification with soldiers in combat and in the hospital. In spite of their strong desire to remain in England to protest the continuation of the war, both finally returned to their comrades in the trenches. Whatever the exact causes of Owen's sudden emergence as "true poet" in the summer of 1917, he himself thought that Sassoon had "fixed" him in place as poet. By the time Sassoon arrived, his first volume of poetry, *The Old Huntsman* (1917), which includes some war poems, had gained wide attention, and he was already preparing *Counter-Attack* (1918), which was to have an even stronger impact on the English public. In the weeks immediately before he was sent to Craiglockhart under military orders, Sassoon had been the center of public attention for risking the possibility of court martial by mailing a formal protest against the war to the War Department. Further publicity resulted when he dramatized his protest by throwing his Military Cross into the River Mersey and when a member of the House of Commons read the letter of protest before the hostile members of the House, an incident instigated by Bertrand Russell in order to further the pacifist cause. Sassoon came from a wealthy and famous family. He had been to Cambridge, he was seven years older than Owen, and he had many friends among the London literati. Both pride and humility in having acquired Sassoon as friend characterized Owen's report to his mother of his visits to Sassoon's room in September. He remarked that he had not yet told his new friend "that I am not worthy to light his pipe. I simply sit tight and tell him where I think he goes wrong."

If their views on the war and their motivations in writing about it were similar, significant differences appear when one compares their work. In the poems written after he went to France in 1916 Sassoon consistently used a direct style with regular and exact rhyme, pronounced rhythms, colloquial language, a strongly satiric mode; and he also tended to present men and women in a stereotypical manner. After meeting Sassoon, Owen wrote several poems in Sassoon's drily satirical mode, but he soon rejected Sassoon's terseness or epigrammatic concision. Consequently, Owen created soldier figures who often express a fuller humanity and emotional range than those in Sassoon's more cryptic poems. In his war poems, whether ideological, meditative, or lyrical, Owen achieved greater breadth than Sassoon did in his war poetry. Even in some of the works that Owen wrote before he left Craiglockhart in the fall of 1917, he revealed a technical versatility and a mastery of sound through complex patterns of assonance, alliteration, dissonance, consonance, and various other kinds of slant rhyme—an experimental method of composition which went beyond any innovative versification that Sassoon achieved during his long career.

Wilfred Owen and Laurent Taihade, September 1914

While Owen wrote to Sassoon of his gratitude for his help in attaining a new birth as poet, Sassoon did not believe he had influenced Owen as radically and as dramatically as Owen maintained. Sassoon regarded his "touch of guidance" and his encouragement as fortunately coming at the moment when Owen most needed them, and he later maintained in *Siegfried's Journey, 1916-1920* that his "only claimable influence was that I stimulated him towards writing with compassionate and challenging realism. . . . My encouragement was opportune, and can claim to have given him a lively incentive during his rapid advance to self-revelation." Sassoon also saw what Owen may never have recognized—that Sassoon's technique "was almost elementary compared with his [Owen's] innovating experiments." Sassoon thought it important, however, that he had given Owen a copy of Henri Barbusse's *Le Feu*, from which he planned to quote in his introduction to *Counter-Attack*, and he appreciated the benefits of their "eager discussion of contemporary poets and the technical dodges which we were ourselves devising." Perhaps Sassoon's statement in late 1945 summarizes best the reciprocal influence the two poets had exerted upon one another: "imperceptible effects are obtained by people mingling their minds at a favorable moment."

Sassoon helped Owen by arranging for him, upon his discharge from the hospital, to meet Robert Ross, a London editor who was Sassoon's friend and the former publishing agent of Oscar Wilde. Ross, in turn, introduced Owen—then and in May 1918—to other literary figures, such as Robert Graves, Edith and Osbert Sitwell, Arnold Bennett, Thomas Hardy, and Captain Charles Scott Moncrieff, who later translated Proust. Knowing these important writers made Owen feel part of a community of literary people—one of the initiated. Accordingly, on New Year's Eve 1917, Owen wrote exuberantly to his mother of his poetic ambitions: "I am started. The tugs have left me. I feel the great swelling of the open sea taking my galleon." At the same time, association with other writers made him feel a sense of urgency—a sense that he must make up for lost time in his development as a poet. In May 1918, on leave in London, he wrote his mother: I am old already for a poet, and so little is yet achieved." But he added with his wry humor, "celebrity is the last infirmity I desire."

By May 1918 Owen regarded his poems not only as individual expressions of intense experience but also as part of a book that would give the reader a wide perspective on World War I. In spring 1918 it appeared that William Heinemann (in spite of the paper shortage that his publishing company faced) would assign Robert Ross to read Owen's manuscript when he submitted it to them. In a table of contents compiled before the end of July 1918 Owen followed a loosely thematic arrangement. Next to each title he wrote a brief description of the poem, and he also prepared in rough draft a brief, but eloquent, preface, in which he expresses his belief in the cathartic function of poetry. For a man who had written sentimental or decorative verse before his war poems of 1917 and 1918, Owen's preface reveals an unexpected strength of commitment and purpose as a writer, a commitment understandable enough in view of the overwhelming effects of the war upon him. In this preface Owen said the poetry in his book would express "the pity of War," rather than the "glory, honour, might, majesty, dominion, or power," which war had acquired in the popular mind. He distinguished also between the pity he sought to awaken by his poems ("The Poetry is in the Pity") and that conventionally expressed by writers who felt less intensely opposed to war by this time than he did. As they wrote their historically oriented laments or elegies for those fallen in wars, they sought to comfort and inspire readers by placing the deaths and war itself in the context of sacrifice for a significant cause. But Owen's message for his generation, he said, must be one of warning rather than of consolation. In his last declaration he appears to have heeded Sassoon's advice to him that he begin to use an unmitigated realism in his description of events: "the true poet must be truthful."

Owen's identification of himself as a poet, affirmed by his new literary friends, must have been especially important in the last few months of his life. Even the officer with whom he led the remnant of the company to safety on a night in October 1918 and with whom he won the Military Cross for his action later wrote to Blunden that neither he nor the rest of the men ever dreamed that Owen wrote poems.

When Owen first returned to the battlefields of France on 1 September 1918, after several months of limited service in England, he seemed confident about his decision: "I shall be better able to cry my outcry, playing my part." Once overseas, however, he wrote to Sassoon chiding him for having urged him to return to France, for having alleged that further exposure to combat would provide him with experience that he could transmute into poetry: "That is my consolation for feeling a fool," he wrote on 22 September 1918. He was bitterly angry at Clemenceau for expecting the war to be continued and for disregarding casualties even among children in the villages as the Allied troops pursued the German forces. He did not live long enough for this indignation or the war experiences of September and October to become part of his poetry, although both are vividly expressed in his letters.

In October Owen wrote of his satisfaction at being nominated for the Military Cross because receiving the award would give him more credibility at home, especially in his efforts to bring the war to an end. Lieutenant J. Foulkes, who shared command with him the night in October 1918 that all other officers were killed, described to Edmund Blunden the details of Owen's acts of "conspicuous gallantry." His company had successfully attacked what was considered a "second Hindenburg Line" in territory that was "well-wired." Losses were so heavy that among the commissioned officers only Foulkes and Owen survived. Owen took command and led the men to a place where he held the line for several hours from a captured German pill box, the only cover available. The pill box was, however, a potential death trap upon which the enemy concentrated its fire. By morning the few who survived were at last relieved by the Lancashire Fusiliers. Foulkes told Blunden, "This is where I admired his work—in leading his remnant, in the middle of the night, back to safety. . . . I was content to follow him with the utmost confidence." Early in his army career Owen wrote to his brother Harold that he knew he could not change his inward self in order to become a self-assured soldier, but that he might still be able to change his appearance and behavior so that others would get the impression he was a "good soldier." Such determination and conscientiousness account for the trust in his leadership that Foulkes expressed. (Harold Owen in his biography of his brother gives a more heroic version of the acts of valor that night, but Foulkes's emphasis on Owen's efforts to get the remaining troops back to safety seems in keeping with Owen's own account and his attitude toward the war and toward his men.) Owen was again moving among his men and offering encouragement when he was killed the next month.

In the last weeks of his life Owen seems to have coped with the stress of the heavy casualties among his battalion by "insensibility," much like that of soldiers he forgives in his poem of the same title, but condemns among civilians: "Happy are men who yet before they are killed / Can let their veins run cold." These men have walked "on the alleys cobbled with their brothers." "Alive, he is not vital overmuch; / Dying, not mortal overmuch." Owen wrote to Sassoon, after reading *Counter-Attack*, that Sassoon's war poems frightened him more than the actual experience of holding a soldier shot through the head and having the man's blood soak hot against his shoulder for a half hour. Two weeks before his death he wrote both to his mother and to Sassoon that his nerves were "in perfect order." But in the letter to Sassoon he explained, "I cannot say I suffered anything, having let my brain grow dull. . . . I shall feel anger again as soon as I dare, but now I must not. I don't take the cigarette out of

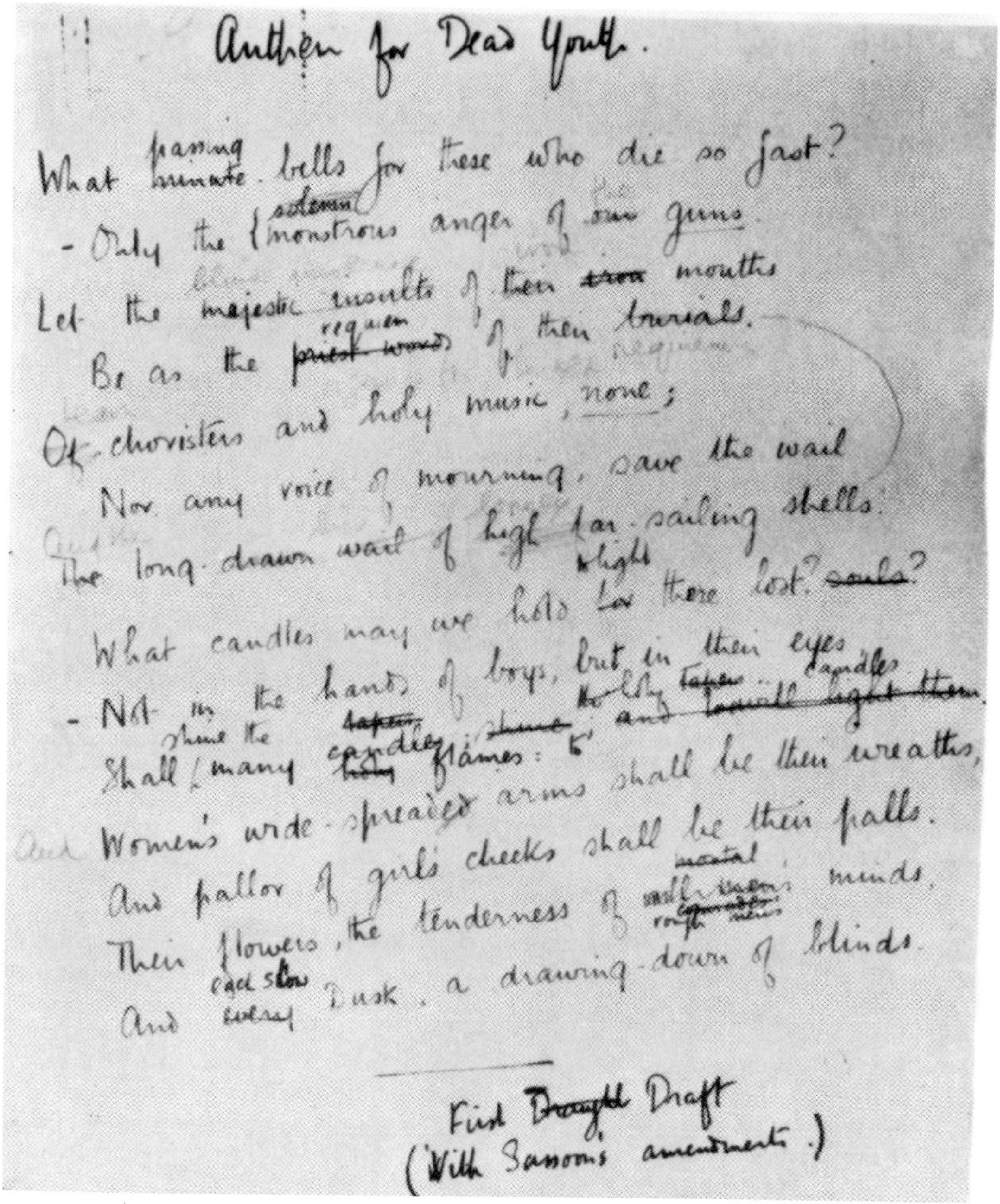
Anthem for Dead Youth.

What passing bells for these who die so fast?
- Only the monstrous anger of our guns.
Let the majestic insults of their iron mouths
Be as the requiem of their burials.
Of choristers and holy music, none;
Nor any voice of mourning, save the wail
The long-drawn wail of high far-sailing shells.
What candles may we hold for these lost? souls?
- Not in the hands of boys, but in their eyes
Shall many candles shine
Women's wide-spreaded arms shall be their wreaths,
And pallor of girls' cheeks shall be their palls.
Their flowers, the tenderness of mortal minds,
And every Dusk, a drawing-down of blinds.

First Draft
(With Sassoon's amendments.)

First draft for "Anthem for Doomed Youth," with revisions in pencil by Siegfried Sassoon (British Museum)

my mouth when I write Deceased over their letters. But one day I will write Deceased over many books."

After Wilfred Owen's death his mother attempted to present him as a more pious figure than he was. For his tombstone, she selected two lines from "The End"—"Shall life renew these bodies? Of a truth / All death will he annul, all tears assuage?"—but omitted the question mark at the close of the quotation. His grave thus memorializes a faith that he did not hold and ignores the doubt he expressed. In 1931 Blunden wrote Sassoon, with irritation, because Susan Owen had insisted that the collected edition of Owen's poems celebrate her son as a majestic and tall heroic figure: "Mrs. Owen has had her way, with a purple binding and a photograph Wh makes W look like a 6 foot Major who had been in East Africa or so for several years." (Owen was about a foot shorter than Sassoon.)

If, in October 1918, Owen coped with his anguishing experiences by imitating his mother's refusal to see reality, the difference is notable. He clearly recognized that he was temporarily refusing

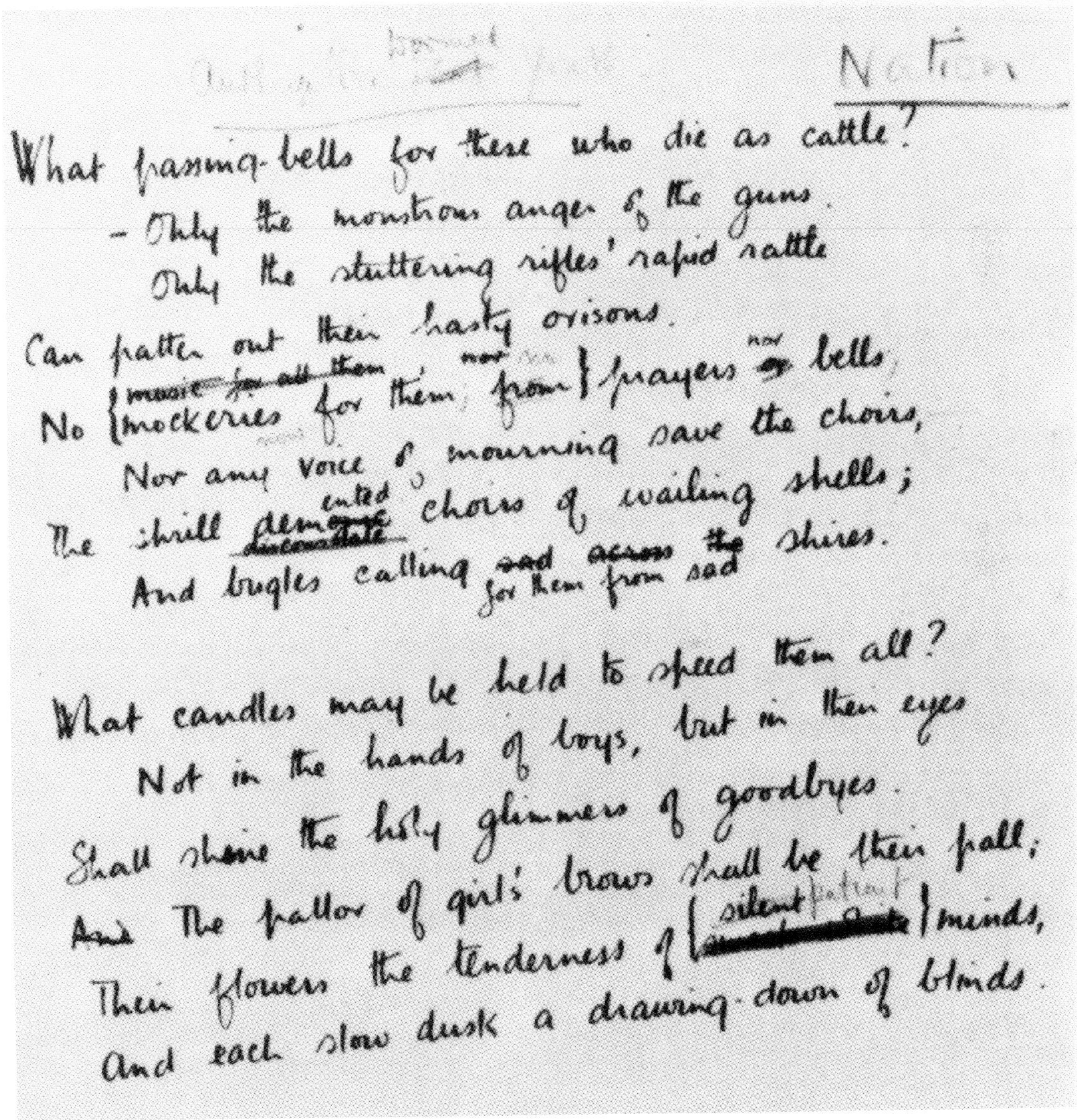
Nation

What passing-bells for these who die as cattle?
- Only the monstrous anger of the guns.
Only the stuttering rifles' rapid rattle
Can patter out their hasty orisons.
No {~~music for all them~~ mockeries for them; ~~from~~ nor} prayers ~~or~~ nor bells,
Nor any voice of mourning save the choirs,
The shrill ~~disconsolate~~ demented choirs of wailing shells;
And bugles calling ~~sad across the~~ for them from sad shires.

What candles may be held to speed them all?
Not in the hands of boys, but in their eyes
Shall shine the holy glimmers of goodbyes.
~~And~~ The pallor of girls' brows shall be their pall;
Their flowers the tenderness of {silent patient} minds,
And each slow dusk a drawing-down of blinds.

Final draft for "Anthem for Doomed Youth," with Sassoon's penciled revisions (British Museum)

to grieve—an act of carefully practiced discipline—but that in a quieter time he would recall those moments and create the "pity" in his poetry, as he had already done with the experience of January 1917 in "The Sentry" and "Dulce et Decorum Est." In "Insensibility" he condemns those who, away from the field of battle, refuse to share "the eternal reciprocity of tears."

Harold Owen succeeded in removing a reference to his brother as "an idealistic homosexual" from Robert Graves's *Goodbye to All That*, and specifically addressed in volume three of his biography the questions that had been raised about his brother's disinterest in women. Harold Owen insisted that his brother had been so dedicated to poetry that he had chosen, at least temporarily, the life of a celibate. He also explains, what was undoubtedly true, that Owen expressed himself impulsively and emotionally, that he was naive, and that he was given to hero worship of other men.

Owen's presentation of "boys" and "lads"—beautiful young men with golden hair, shining eyes, strong brown hands, white teeth—has homoerotic elements. One must recognize, however, such references had become stock literary devices in war poetry. The one poem which can clearly be called a love poem, "To A Friend (With an Identity Disc)," carefully avoids the use of either specifically masculine or feminine terms in addressing the friend. Eroticism in Owen's poems seems idealized, romantic, and platonic and is used frequently to contrast the ugly and horrible aspects of warfare. Of more consequence in considering Owen's sexual attitudes in relation to his poetry is the harshness in reference to wives, mothers, or sweethearts of the wounded or disabled soldiers. The fullness of his insight into "the pity of war" seems incomprehensibly limited in the presentation of women in "The Dead-Beat," "Disabled," "The Send-Off," and "S.I.W."

In several of his most effective war poems, Owen suggests that the experience of war for him was surrealistic, as when the infantrymen dream, hallucinate, begin freezing to death, continue to march after several nights without sleep, lose consciousness from loss of blood, or enter a hypnotic state from fear or excessive guilt. The resulting disconnected sensory perceptions and the speaker's confusion about his identity suggest that not only the speaker, but the whole humanity, has lost its moorings. The horror of war, then, becomes more universal, the tragedy more overwhelming, and the pity evoked more profound, because there is no rational explanation to account for the cataclysm.

In "Conscious" a wounded soldier, moving in and out of consciousness, cannot place in perspective the yellow flowers beside his hospital bed, nor can he recall blue sky. The soldiers in "Mental Cases" suffer hallucinations in which they observe everything through a haze of blood: "Sunlight becomes a blood-smear; dawn comes blood-black." In "Exposure," which displays Owen's mastery of assonance and alliteration, soldiers in merciless wind and snow find themselves overwhelmed by nature's hostility and unpredictability. They even lose hope that spring will arrive: "For God's invincible spring our love is made afraid." Anticipating the search that night for the bodies of fallen soldiers in no-man's-land, the speaker predicts that soon all of his comrades will be found as corpses with their eyes turned to ice. Ironically, as they begin freezing to death, their pain becomes numbness and then pleasurable warmth. As the snow gently fingers their cheeks, the freezing soldiers dream of summer: "so we drowse, sun-dozed / Littered with blossoms trickling where the blackbird fusses." Dreaming of warm hearths as "our ghosts drag home," they quietly "turn back to our dying." The speaker in "Asleep" envies the comfort of one who can sleep, even though the sleep is that of death: "He sleeps less tremulous, less cold / Than we who must awake, and waking, say Alas!" All these "dream poems" suggest that life is a nightmare in which the violence of war is an accepted norm. The cosmos seems either cruelly indifferent or else malignant, certainly incapable of being explained in any rational manner. A loving Christian God is nonexistent. The poem's surface incoherence suggests the utter irrationality of life. Even a retreat to the comfort of the unconscious state is vulnerable to sudden invasion from the hell of waking life.

One of Owen's most moving poems, "Dulce et Decorum Est," which had its origins in Owen's experiences of January 1917, describes explicitly the horror of the gas attack and the death of a wounded man who has been flung into a wagon. The horror intensifies, becoming a waking nightmare experienced by the exhausted viewer, who stares hypnotically at his comrade in the wagon ahead of him as he must continue to march.

The nightmare aspect reaches its apogee in "The Show." As the speaker gazes upon a desolate, war-ravaged landscape, it changes gradually to the magnified portion of a dead soldier's face, infested by thousands of caterpillars. The barbed wire of no-man's-land becomes the scraggly beard on the face; the shell holes become pockmarked skin. Only at the end does the poet's personal conflict become

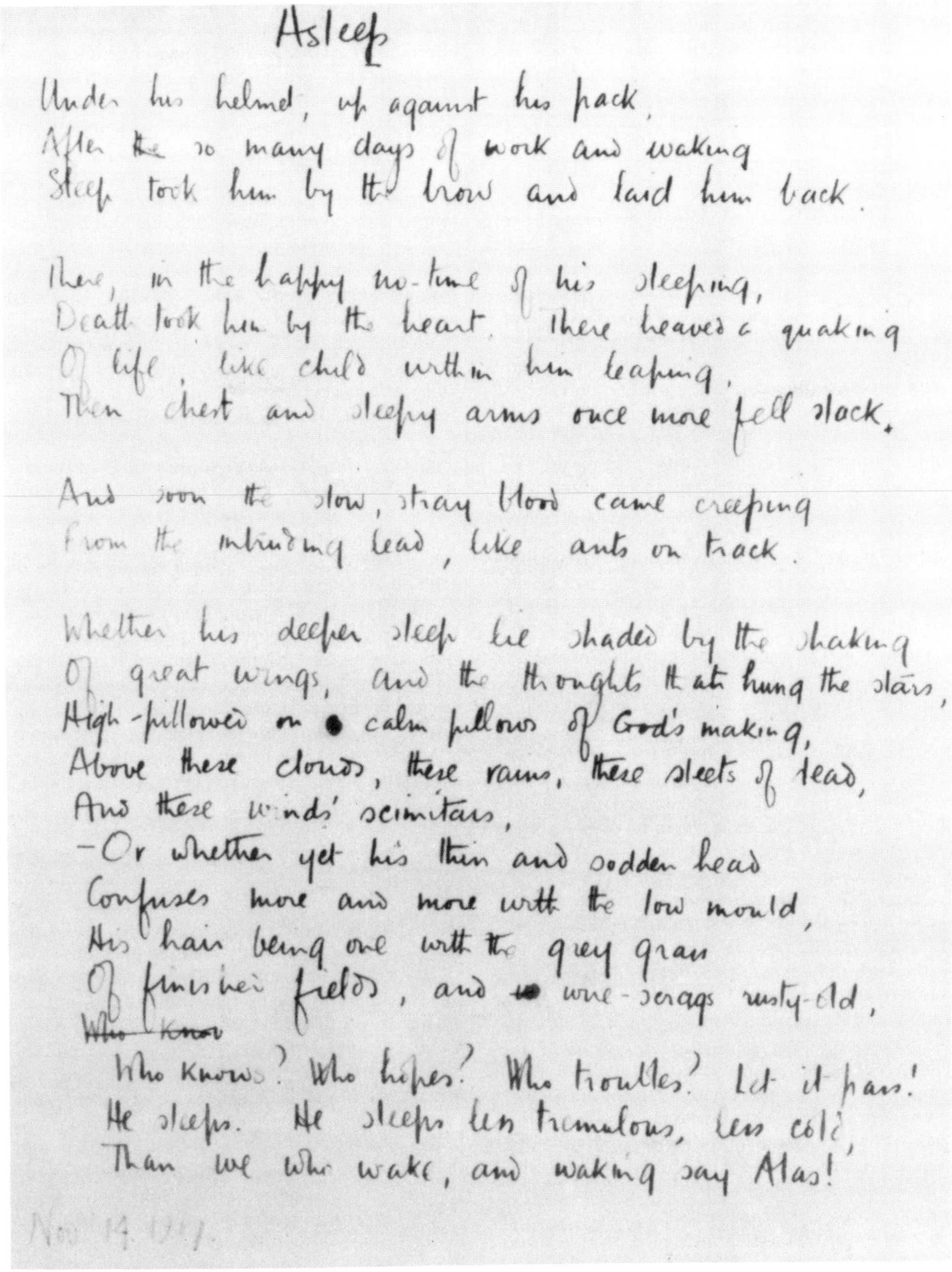

Asleep

Under his helmet, up against his pack,
After the so many days of work and waking
Sleep took him by the brow and laid him back.

There, in the happy no-time of his sleeping,
Death took him by the heart. There heaved a quaking
Of life, like child within him leaping,
Then chest and sleepy arms once more fell slack.

And soon the slow, stray blood came creeping
From the intruding lead, like ants on track.

Whether his deeper sleep lie shaded by the shaking
Of great wings, and the thoughts that hung the stars,
High-pillowed on calm pillows of God's making,
Above these clouds, these rains, these sleets of lead,
And these winds' scimitars,
—Or whether yet his thin and sodden head
Confuses more and more with the low mould,
His hair being one with the grey grass
Of finished fields, and wire-scraggs rusty-old,
~~Who Knows~~
Who knows? Who hopes? Who troubles? Let it pass!
He sleeps. He sleeps less tremulous, less cold,
Than we who wake, and waking say Alas!

Nov 14 1917.

Manuscript for "Asleep" (British Museum)

clear. Owen identifies himself as the severed head of a caterpillar and the many legs, still moving blindly, as the men of his command from whom he has been separated. The putrefying face, the sickening voraciousness of the caterpillars, and the utter desolation of the ruined landscape become symbolic of the lost hopes for humanity.

"Strange Meeting," another poem with a dreamlike frame, differs from those just described in its meditative tone and its less-concentrated use of figurative language. Two figures—the poet and the man he killed—gradually recognize each other and their similarity when they meet in the shadows of hell. In the background one becomes aware of multitudes of huddled sleepers, slightly moaning in their "encumbered" sleep—all men killed in "titanic wars." Because the second man speaks almost exclusively of death's thwarting of his purpose and ambition as a poet, he probably represents Owen's alter ego. Neither figure is differentiated by earthly association, and the "strange friend" may also represent an Everyman figure, suggesting the universality of the tragedy of war. The poem closes as the second speaker stops halfway through the last line to return to his eternal sleep. The abrupt halt drives home the point that killing a poet cuts off the promise of the one more line of poetry he might have written. The last line extends "the Pity of war" to a universal pity for all those who have been diminished through the ages by art which might have been created and was not.

Sassoon called "Strange Meeting" Owen's masterpiece, the finest elegy by a soldier who fought in World War I. T. S. Eliot, who praised it as "one of the most moving pieces of verse inspired by the war," recognized that its emotional power lies in Owen's "technical achievement of great originality." In "Strange Meeting," Owen sustains the dreamlike quality by a complex musical pattern, which unifies the poem and leads to an overwhelming sense of war's waste and a sense of pity that such conditions should continue to exist. John Middleton Murry in 1920 noted the extreme subtlety in Owen's use of couplets employing assonance and dissonance. Most readers, he said, assumed the poem was in blank verse but wondered why the sound of the words produced in them a cumulative sadness and inexorable uneasiness and why such effects lingered. Owen's use of slant-rhyme produces, in Murry's words, a "subterranean . . . forged unity, a welded, inexorable massiveness."

Although Owen does not use the dream frame in "Futility," this poem, like "Strange Meeting," is also a profound meditation on the horrifying significance of war. As in "Exposure," the elemental structure of the universe seems out of joint. Unlike the speaker in "Exposure," however, this one does not doubt that spring will come to warm the frozen battlefield, but he wonders why it should. Even the vital force of the universe—the sun's energy—no longer nurtures life.

One of the most perfectly structured of Owen's poems, "Anthem for Doomed Youth," convinced Sassoon in October 1917 that Owen was not only a "promising minor poet" but a poet with "classic and imaginative serenity" who possessed "impressive affinities with Keats." By using the fixed form of the sonnet, Owen gains compression and a close interweaving of symbols. In particular, he uses the break between octave and sestet to deepen the contrast between themes, while at the same time he minimizes that break with the use of sound patterns that continue throughout the poem and with the image of a bugle, which unifies three disparate groups of symbols. The structure depends, then, not only on the sonnet form but on a pattern of echoing sounds from the first line to the last, and upon Owen's careful organization of groups of symbols and of two contrasting themes—in the sestet the mockery of doomed youth, "dying like cattle," and in the octave the silent personal grief which is the acceptable response to immense tragedy. The symbols in the octave suggest cacophony; the visual images in the sestet suggest silence. The poem is unified throughout by a complex pattern of alliteration and assonance. Despite its complex structure, this sonnet achieves an effect of impressive simplicity.

Poems (1920), edited by Sassoon, established Owen as a war poet before public interest in the war had diminished in the 1920s. *The Poems of Wilfred Owen* (1931), edited by Blunden, aroused much more critical attention, especially that of W. H. Auden and the poets in his circle, Stephen Spender, C. Day Lewis, Christopher Isherwood, and Louis MacNeice. Blunden thought that Auden and his group were influenced primarily by three poets: Gerard Manley Hopkins, T. S. Eliot, and Wilfred Owen. The Auden group saw in Owen's poetry the incisiveness of political protest against injustice, but their interest in Owen was less in the content of his poems than in his artistry and technique. Though they were moved by the human experience described in Owen's best poems and understood clearly his revulsion toward war, they were appalled by the sheer waste of a great poet dying just as he had begun to realize fully his potential. Dylan Thomas, who, like Owen, possessed a brilliant metaphorical imagination, pride in Welsh ancestry, and an ability to dramatize in poetry his psychic experience, saw in Owen "a poet of all times, all places, and all wars. There is only one war, that of men against men."

C. Day Lewis, in the introduction to *The Collected Poems of Wilfred Owen* (1963), judiciously praised Owen's poems for "the originality and force of their language, the passionate nature of the indignation and pity they express, their blending of harsh realism with a sensuousness unatrophied by the horrors from which they flowered." Day Lewis's view that Owen's poems were "certainly the finest written by any English poet of the First War" is incontestable. With general agreement critics—J. Middleton Murry, Bonamy Dobree, Hoxie Fairchild, Ifor Evans, Kenneth Muir, and T. S. Eliot, for example—have written of his work for six decades. The best of Owen's 1917-1918 poems are great by any standard. Day Lewis's conclusion that they also are "probably the greatest poems about the war in our literature" may, if anything, be too tentative. His work will remain central in any discussion of war poetry or of poetry employing varied kinds of slant rhyme.

Periodical Publications:

"Song of Songs," anonymous, *Hydra: Journal of the Craiglockhart War Hospital*, no. 10 (1 September 1917);

"The Next War," anonymous, *Hydra: Journal of the Craiglockhart War Hospital*, no. 11 (29 September 1917).

Letters:

Collected Letters of Wilfred Owen, edited by John Bell and Harold Owen (London & New York: Oxford University Press, 1967).

Bibliography:

William White, "Wilfred Owen (1893-1918): A Bibliography," *Serif* (2 December 1965): 5-16.

Biography:

Harold Owen, *Journey From Obscurity: Wilfred Owen, 1893-1918*, 3 volumes (London & New York: Oxford University Press, 1963-1965).

References:

Sven Bäckman, *Tradition Transformed, Lund Studies in English*, no. 54 (Lund: Gleerup, 1979);

Bernard Bergonzi, *Heroes' Twilight* (London: Constable, 1965), pp. 121-135;

Paul Fussell, *The Great War in Modern Memory* (London & New York: Oxford University Press, 1975), pp. 285-299;

Robert Graves, *Goodbye to All That* (London: Cape, 1929; New York: Cape & Smith, 1930);

Dominic Hibberd, *Wilfred Owen* (London: Longman, 1975);

John Johnston, *English Poetry of the First World War* (Princeton: Princeton University Press, 1964), pp. 155-212;

Arthur Lane, *An Adequate Response* (Detroit: Wayne State University Press, 1972);

Jon Silkin, *Out of Battle: The Poetry of the Great War* (London: Oxford University Press, 1972), pp. 197-248;

Jon Stallworthy, *Wilfred Owen* (London: Chatto & Windus, 1974);

D. S. R. Welland, *Wilfred Owen: A Critical Study* (London: Chatto & Windus, 1960);

Gertrude White, *Wilfred Owen* (New York: Twayne, 1969).

Papers:

The major repository for manuscripts of Owen's poems is the British Museum. Owen's letters are at the University of Texas, Austin.

Ruth Pitter

(7 November 1897-   )

Francine Muffoletto Landreneau
Louisiana State University

SELECTED BOOKS: *First Poems* (London: Palmer, 1920);

First & Second Poems, 1912-1925 (London: Sheed & Ward, 1927; Garden City: Doubleday, Doran, 1930);

Persephone in Hades (Auch, Gers, France: Sauriac, 1931);

A Mad Lady's Garland (London: Cresset, 1934; New York: Macmillan, 1935);

A Trophy of Arms: Poems, 1926-1935 (London: Cresset, 1936; New York: Macmillan, 1936);

The Spirit Watches (London: Cresset, 1939; New York: Macmillan, 1940);

The Rude Potato (London: Cresset, 1941);

Poem (Southampton, U.K.: Shirley Press, 1943);

The Bridge: Poems, 1939-1944 (London: Cresset, 1945); republished as *The Bridge: Poems, 1939-1945* (New York: Macmillan, 1946);

On Cats (London: Cresset, 1947);

The Plain Facts, by a Plain but Amiable Cat (London: Joan Hassall, 1948);

Urania: Poems Selected from A Trophy of Arms, The Spirit Watches, and The Bridge (London: Cresset, 1950);

The Ermine: Poems, 1942-1952 (London: Cresset, 1953);

Still by Choice (London: Cresset, 1966);

Poems, 1926-1966 (London: Barrie & Rockliffe/ Cresset Press, 1968); republished as *Collected Poems* (New York: Macmillan, 1969);

End of Drought (London: Barrie & Jenkins/ Communica-Europa, 1975).

In 1955 Ruth Pitter became the first woman to receive the Queen's Gold Medal for Poetry. Queen Elizabeth broke precedent and presented the award in person. Though it is her most cherished, this award was not the first for Pitter. In 1937 *A Trophy of Arms* received the coveted Hawthornden Prize, and in 1954 Pitter was recipient of the William E. Heinemann Award for *The Ermine*. More recently, in 1979, Pitter was made a Commander of the British Empire. Not known widely but deeply appreciated by a few, Pitter is a poet of classical discipline writing in traditional forms but speaking in a modern voice and with mystical conviction. One only begins to identify her by saying that her work is religious though attached to no creed; that her love poems match Edna St. Vincent Millay's; that her nature lyrics compete with Robert Frost's; that her symbolic poems are equal to Stephen Crane's; that her lyrical integrity raises her above such British poets as Rudyard Kipling or Edith Sitwell. Though Pitter's verses do not now command the wide respect they deserve, her readers do not doubt their quality and wait for a revival of appreciation for classical form to establish her with a larger audience.

Pitter was born 7 November 1897, on the fringe of the East End countryside in Ilford, Essex, a suburb of London. Her father, George Pitter, and her mother, Louisa R. Murrell Pitter, whom Pitter describes as "of superior artisan class, intelligent, idealistic, country-lovers, poetic, altruistic," were assistant teachers in an East End elementary school. Hard workers, and poorly paid themselves, they understood well the problems of educating poorly nourished children in a system with high standards. Thus they imparted to their children a practical attitude of "the necessity for earning." This attitude was to influence Pitter's writing career. She wrote for *Twentieth Century Authors*, "From the very first I realized there was no money in poetry, and determined not to write for money. By commercial slavery and continual anxiety I have avoided patronage and the meal-ticket marriage, and am (as a writer) independent of politics, publishers, and jobbery. When I hear the observations of professional writers on these matters I thank Heaven for my dour foresight."

After Ruth was born her family moved to Goodmayes, another outlying suburb. Her recollections of these early years indicate her independent personality. At age five she attended the local school of about 1,000 students and was appalled by "That huge crowd of children, some of them pretty savage," but she recalls, "I was strong, and soon learnt to be belligerent because I was afraid."

It was at this early age that Ruth Pitter began to write poetry. Again, it was her parents' teaching that cultivated her inclinations. Poetry was not merely made available; it was taught: "They made us notice special beauties, and they made us learn poems by heart; but they paid us for this extra work, from a penny to sixpence a poem according to length." Her young mind was "wax to receive, marble to retain." She grew up reading Francis Turner Palgrave's influential anthology, *The Golden Treasury of the Best Songs and Lyrical Poems in the English Language*, Shakespeare's songs, Blake's *Songs of Innocence* (1789), and Wordsworth's Lucy poems. The elder Pitters' dedication to refining the minds of their children bore fruit. Though only Ruth continued to write poetry, her younger sister, Olive, became a successful novelist (Shirley Murrell), and her younger brother, Geoffrey, distinguished himself as a painter after retiring from architecture.

Another parental decision coincided with the children's study of lyrical poetry to become what Miss Pitter terms "the greatest single factor in early influences"—her "land of Canaan" and the center of her "joyful infancy." In a successful effort to forfend against raising bourgeois-minded children, the Pitters adopted rural life. In day-long tramps with her father, regardless of the time of year, Ruth came to know Hainault Forest, a portion of the royal hunting grounds of Epping since before the time of Elizabeth I. In time the Pitters managed to rent a primitive, decayed cottage cut off from road or water supply and "romantically situated" on Crabtree Hill in the Essex forest. The cottage appears in poem after poem and is the site of Pitter's "hermitage" in "Stormcock in Elder," her most frequently anthologized poem. Ruth recognized the value of her parents' sacrifice: "I am very grateful to my mother for squeezing out the rent, three and six pence a week, and for the drudgery both parents put in to make and keep it habitable as a holiday home."

Pitter's experiences in the Essex forest established her senses of the natural and of the mystic, which become inextricably fused in her work. The rigorous practicality which tempers this fusion and which invokes traditional form in her poetry was doubtlessly inherited from her parents, who were practical by reason rather than by convention, who worked diligently for an adequate living but found true sustenance in treasuries of lyrical poems and a romantically decayed cottage. The effect on Pitter is intimated in her very first line of poetry. Inherently sensitive to natural surroundings already (Arthur Wolseley Russell writes that her earliest, vivid memories of things are "her first bird's nest, her first red toadstool, and a bare green hill at sunset"), Pitter experienced her first poetic tears at the age of five, when an image of "a desolate and abandoned place" seen on one of the forest walks suddenly entered her mind as she sat on the back doorstep. She seized her stump of blue pencil and bit of torn paper to write in block letters those "painful capitals": "The old mill stands with broken shaft." The line could be considered an imagist poem in and of itself.

Pitter's poetry exhibits a fine intellect which is often powerful and incisive but not academic. Though Ruth's sister, Olive, earned the sought after annual allowance of £10 in the county scholarship examination, Ruth did not. Subsequently she was sent to an old City foundation, the Christian charity school that had at one time arranged domestic services for its girls. Coborn School at Bow, London, was trying for Ruth. Twelve years old now, she did not welcome the discipline and insistence on manners that had survived from the days of domestic training. But she writes, "The worst for me was the train journey, scrappy feeding (part poverty, part negligence) and the smelly factory surroundings." Despite these disadvantages, Coborn School provided Ruth with classes in art, cookery, French, mathematics, natural science, and Latin, where she gained an appreciation for Horace.

Still developing her craft and practicing with complicated and elaborate rhythms which she would later abandon for a style emphasizing lucidity over technique, Ruth was also resisting her father's compulsion to correct her work. His enthusiasm finally prompted him to send her verses to the *New Age* for publication. Its editor was a fellow socialist and schoolteacher, the politically influential Alfred Richard Orage, whom George Pitter had met when both were students at Culham College near Abingdon. With a genius for disseminating literature he published the writings of 700 different writers between 1907 and 1922, acquiring, without compensation, works by Hilaire Belloc, Arnold Bennett, G. K. Chesterton, Bernard Shaw, and H. G. Wells at the height of their fame and introducing to the British public for the first time such writers as Ezra Pound, Katherine Mansfield, Edwin Muir, T. E. Hulme, F. S. Flint, Herbert Read, and Dylan Thomas. He introduced Ruth Pitter to the public by publishing her poem "Field Glasses" in the 11 May 1911 issue. Ruth was thirteen. Her affiliation with the magazine was to last until it dissolved in 1921, and her first book (*First Poems*, 1920) included many of the poems which had been published in the *New Age*.

In the long run the attention Ruth received so early probably delayed her discovery of her own voice. By April of 1912 Orage had become as notorious a tutor as her father, to whom the editor mailed his critical comments: "We all like Ruth's new poems . . . . the prose rather less so. . . . Ruth is too much of a poet to make fanciful prose . . . by the way, would the young lady deign to change a single word in the *Song*? Verse 1 line 3 *amorous* kissed. The attribution of human emotions . . . to natural objects is fancy not imagination. Do ask Ruth if she will find the right word to take its place." Ruth did find the word, and the *New Age* published "Song" in its 23 May 1912 issue. *Amorous* had become *silently*.

Socially, Ruth became exposed to some of the literary "tigers." Well-liked by Orage and his mistress, the volatile Mrs. Beatrice Hastings, Ruth was frequently invited to visit. On one occasion she called upon Orage and found beads scattered over the floor. It was explained to her that Beatrice Hastings and Katherine Mansfield had "come to blows with their necklaces" (probably over Hastings's long poem "Echo," published in the *New Age*, January 1912, as an obvious attack on Mansfield's approach to writing).

Another social incident described by John Carswell in *Lives and Letters* (1978) is Ruth's visit in 1913 to Pease Pottage near Crawley, Sussex, where Orage and Hastings were currently taking their weekends. Here Ruth spent a "heavily chaperoned day," her progressive parents somewhat intolerant of open adultery. Ruth was shocked and shyly impressed "by Beatrice in her flowing oriental dress from Liberty's, and her preference for sitting on the floor, smoking, and making free use of the word 'damn.' " Hastings also "confided in the budding poet that she never wore drawers." Carswell comments, "As for Orage—no other man entered Ruth's mind for several years afterwards." Ruth was to remember years later having seen Hastings in London in 1925 "living in a shabby room in Charlotte Street subsisting on porridge turned up with jam and topped with condensed milk." When Orage in April 1932 began publication of his first number of the *New English Weekly* he thought to "pick up his early discoveries for further development." One of these was Ruth Pitter. During the time that she knew Orage he introduced her to the writings of Nietzsche, Freud, and Ernest Jones. She once noted that it took her years to get over her traumatic experience of Freud's case histories, even though she found her new knowledge of people and their motivations "salutary."

World War I broke out when Ruth was almost through her Intermediate Arts year. Without the knack for winning scholarships and without the funds to pay for her own schooling, the most practical course open to Pitter was work as a clerk in the War Office. Thus, her formal education came to an end.

Sometimes she regretted not having university experience, and she seems to have wondered in later years how this lack might show in her verses. A 31 October 1936 letter to her from Hilaire Belloc dismisses the suggested question: "As to the scholarship in your verses, you must remember that they give the *effect* of scholarship. What you tell me about the extent of your acquaintance with the classics I did not know—but most certainly you have the soul of them." This same letter included a grateful acceptance of some of Pitter's verse for publication in the *Weekly Review*, which Belloc was then editing for a short time.

At the War Office, Pitter acquired a temporary junior clerkship at twenty-five shillings a week and "stood it" for nearly two years. She detested the paperwork and got seventeen boils at one time ("partly from bad food, partly from contemplating officialdom"). The job became more bearable when she took over tea making for the fifty or so people there. By 1918 she was badly run down and feeling the urgency to be "some sort of artist, however humble."

Pitter regained her health while working for a couple named Jennings (an artist and an architect), who lived on the east coast of Suffolk, made furniture, and decorated the wares sold by the Walberswick Peasant Pottery Company. The Jennings couple furnished Ruth room and board and eventually some pay. Here she developed the hand skills which would eventually make her financially self-sufficient as well as quite well known for her wares, which were widely imitated. Her painted tea trays, signed R. P., sold for £ 1 or less and were shipped around the world. (Her friend Arthur Russell attributes much of this success to heredity, Pitter having one grandfather who was a master cabinetmaker and another who was a toolmaker.) At this time Pitter not only learned how to paint but how to use woodworking tools, and she found this work with her hands conducive to writing poetry.

The result of Pitter's writing at this time was her first book of poetry, *First Poems*, published in London by Cecil Palmer in 1920. As Hilaire Belloc stated a few years later, "The first volume appeared and fell dead." Pitter herself remarks of her long but glorious immaturity that her early poems were guilty "of almost every possible fault of adolescence." A brief notice in the *Times Literary Supplement* concurs with Pitter's idea that her early work concentrated too much on technical complexity: "In Miss Pitter's poems constructive ability reconciles us to the avoidance of an intellectual effort. She can remodel the secondary elements of life with such skill that we mistake many an affectation for reality."

In this first volume Pitter escapes sentimentality by maintaining an absolute distance between herself and her poems. Nonhuman or medieval subjects inhabit such poems as "The Elfin Heart" and "The Knightly Damoiseau." Archaic diction in such poems as "Fairy-gold" and a reliance on sound, color, and emotional wonder in "The Waters of Paradise" allow the poet to escape the complacency and cynicism of modern versifiers. Part of this escape was avoidance of her own voice. Pitter was still experimenting. Though all her critics have put by the term "pastiche" in favor of "eclectic variety," Pitter was weaving together, albeit smoothly, imitations of verses from Chaucer to Keats and Swinburne. The restrained voice which was slowly coming into its own through the cumulative heritage of lyricism was discerned by few.

Hilaire Belloc discerned it. Known for his refusal to write prefaces for new authors, he made an exception for Pitter. In a 6 August 1925 letter to her, he begged that she collect her poetry and promised to have it published with a preface by him, to send it out to the press, and to find a place of sale for it. *First & Second Poems, 1912-1925*, published in 1927, includes many of the poems from her first volume and eighty-nine additional ones. Belloc's preface insured reviews. He set the tone by praising Pitter as "an exceptional reappearance of the classical spirit" and its only "contemporary example." He offers her work: "Here is beauty and right order, singularly apparent in the midst of such a moral welter . . ."

Eda Lou Walton in the *Nation* called Pitter's "a seventeenth-century mind" of religious yearning. Gorham B. Munson in the *Commonweal* saw in her poems Elizabethan sentiment: "Fresh in feeling, spirited in composition, pastoral in quality, they shed on us the merry rays of the soul of a green England miraculously unsooted with factory smoke." Richard Church in the *Spectator* found a perfectly translated aesthetic expression of religious joy-sorrow whose fountain remained unseen: "All that we see is the trickle of water among the rocks, in the sand, through the grasses, and the consequent miracle of flowers and mosses." He discovered in her a spirit and mind which subdue personal desire and momentary moods "until they are willing to harmonize with a conviction and a faith that have tempered to permanence" and offer a criterion larger than the self.

In this volume Pitter moves beyond imitation. Committed to formal structure and using such forms as the sonnet, the rondeau, the ballade, and other fixed stanzaic patterns, she retains the noble splendor of feelings involved in the striving for perfection—classical form and noble feeling abandoned by many moderns. But the voice of *First Poems* has now grown through the past into a modern situation. The voice speaks with a newfound conviction in such poems as "Night," which opens "This is Finality who lives in the dark" and closes

> that's truth, I say,
> Which by no blackness can obscure be made.
> Small wonder, Lady, that fools fly from thee
> And all who wish the eternal seek that way!

The voice begins to deal with its own age. The modern age is addressed in "Confusion": "woe on this weary time" whose every good is "Bruised unto death, beggared and spat upon!"

From the beginning her critics have found such a sustained, cohesive crescendo of inner-ear music and nonparaphraseable thought moving through Pitter's poems that attempting to demonstrate her ability by excerpt or comparison remains inadequate. The line imbedded in her blank-verse poem "In Praise" speaks best to identify the tenor of the whole volume: "I am fidelity that still abideth."

Belloc was disappointed in his countrymen's lack of receptiveness to Pitter but noted that a restricted reading audience in America admired her work, first published there in 1930 by Doubleday.

After the war ended in November 1918 Pitter had moved to London with the Jenningses, and by 1926, she had been able to set up her own household above the Jennings' workshop. But by 1930 the job was not lucrative enough. She was offered "a ghost of a similar business" that year, and through the urgings of a fellow worker, with whom she pooled her savings, became partner and proprietor of the Deane and Forester Shop, Chelsea, London. Beginning with less that £600, Pitter and artist-friend Kathleen O'Hara (who was Ruth's senior by ten years) familiarized themselves with the business aspect of their trade, acquired a reliable traveling salesman, and worked at painting furniture and small objects from eight A. M. until midnight. After a six-month struggle they made a successful go of the business. Eventually they gave up their separate flats and moved in together above their workshop. They were to remain lifelong companions.

It was during the early struggle in this business that Pitter suffered the disaster which Arthur Russell sees as leading to "a fortunate result." Blindfolded for two months after being struck by the lid of an old acetate paint can that she was trying to open in hot weather, Pitter had a vision of a misselthrush in full song in February which she had studied close-up through the broken roof of the family cottage years earlier. This recollection is the basis of the frequently anthologized "Stormcock in Elder."

In the late 1920s Pitter was also contributing to the American magazine the *Dial*. Her most significant work of this period was the privately printed *Persephone in Hades*, a long poem in seven parts. One hundred copies were produced for private circulation in August 1931. William Rothenstein claims that Belloc financed the project. Certainly he approved it. Though he never mentions the poem by name in his 7 June 1930 letter to Pitter, his remarks about the poem that "excels in vision" can refer to no other work. Belloc comments on the insufficient presence of the caesura and then proceeds to remark on the generality of the poem which forbids particular point making and gives rise to the excellence of the metaphors, on the abundance of strong similes, on the effective double-syllable ending, and on the escape from monotony due to the passionate passages: "All put together it is the mind that is powerful behind the thing."

In *Persephone in Hades* Pitter's own mythmaking transforms the ancient legend by shifting its center of interest from Demeter to Persephone ("I sing the Daughter") and by focusing with intimate clarity upon the gradations of emotional experience in Persephone's descent "to the coast of being" and then to the ultimate beyond. In his letter Belloc speaks of this passage on the horror, presence, and experience of death as "not only the finest in the poem but the finest I know." He also mentions the swan simile in the passage preceding the descent and the jasper simile in the passage foreshadowing Persephone's subsequent ascent. Using the image of jasper, the poem speaks of "a glorious beam / Plunged into Hades. . . ," which "from Aidoneus' upward look evoked / A gleam of jasper, such as from the eyes / Of lions may dart when they behold the sun." Belloc begged Pitter to send him four or five copies of the poem when it was printed, and he mentioned it parenthetically in his preface to *A Mad Lady's Garland* when speaking of his admiration for Pitter's verse in the elegiac and tragic mode.

During the 1930s Pitter and Kate O'Hara's London gift shop was growing—the painted furniture replaced by the better-selling flower-painted trays. O'Hara took charge of the buying, the customers, and the employees who totaled twelve by 1938. Pitter did the painting and bookkeeping. Occasionally she got away from the city, and once, in the late spring of 1934, she spent a fortnight on the Donegal coast in Ireland as a guest of AE (George William Russell). Accompanied by her mother (who was as enthusiastic about the occult as AE was serious), Ruth was impressed with the supernatural air of the Irish landscape. Shortly after her visit AE wrote that he had had a vision of her "thought-body" roaming the ridge at Breaghy.

This same year the book that finally brought reviewers' attention was published. *A Mad Lady's Garland* collected the poems that Pitter had been having published in the *New English Weekly* under the heading "Pastiche." The poems in this collection are characterized by humor with the point of "a bodkin, not a dagger." Through the voice of a lamenting flea, a pious lady trout, an indignant cockroach addressing moderns; in the self-vindication of a coffin worm, in the Spenserian stanzas of a heretical caterpillar, in the complaint of an earwig who writes elegy but "would fain sing Epithalamion"; in lines that return to the cavalier lyric and Pope's heroic couplet; and in the skillful parody of *Piers Plowman*—what Poet Laureate John Masefield called "her judgments . . . merciful" and "her methods . . . merry," Pitter demonstrated her versatile talent with a wit that "broke no bones" and "made no enemies."

In his preface for this book Belloc attributed to Pitter "a perfect ear and exact epithet." In numerous lines alliteration, assonance, consonance, and rhyme flourish while remaining exempt from contrivance. In "The Kitten's Eclogue," Bogey Baby the black cat glories in the wantonness symbolized in her "sable hue":

> What sight more welcome than the night above?
> What hue more honoured in the courts of love?
> . . . .
> What music shall I have—what dying wails—
> The seldom female in a world of males!

The heroic earwig of another poem introduces himself grandly:

> Armed Earwig I, that erst in prideful plight
> Swanked in my mail and only swore by Mars;
> Unlucky warrior and wretched wight,

That am dashed down to darkness from the
stars!

Whereas Hardy in his *Satires of Circumstance* would seek to teach by eliciting the facile, superficial response that the embarrassed reader soon reprimands himself for making, Pitter prefers to elicit moral behavior by mocking the ridiculous. She accomplishes this end, ingeniously, by exposing and granting the ambiguity involved in any attitude one strikes. Thus, by the time he is cast out of bed by an awakened and horrified human beauty shrieking in "melodious thunders," the lovesick earwig's noble utterances provoke an empathetic response in spite of the ridiculous situation: "Most cruel, I continually say, / Who wouldst not crush but only cast away." Several editions of *A Mad Lady's Garland* were printed, and the 1935 American edition included an introduction by John Masefield.

The very next year *A Trophy of Arms: Poems 1926-1935* (1936) was published with a preface by James Stephens, who called Pitter a pure poet second to none but Yeats in current writing. This volume of serious verse won the prestigious Hawthornden Prize of 1937 for the best imaginative work by a British author published during the preceding twelve months.

Many readers first discoverd Pitter's work through *A Trophy of Arms*. Belloc wrote to her on 17 September 1936, "I heard a story about it [*A Trophy of Arms*] last night at dinner. . . . One of the younger generation, between 30 and 40, who apparently had not come across your work (which is understandable, considering the stuff they read and alone have the chance to see), came rushing in to a big restaurant, shouting that he had found a new poet who was worth all the others put together and waving your new book in his hand."

Julian Symons was the harshest critic. His brief review spent most of its time dissecting Stephens's rhetoric and brushed Pitter's verse aside as "dead words." Other reviewers were more enthusiastic and noted a "reticent strength," a "sensuous alertness," and an urgent directness in her contemplation of the soul, its destiny and esctasy, its dangers and peace.

In "Close, Mortal Eyes" the poet recognizes that only the "Eternal eyes" of the soul can understand joy. "Elegy to Mary" says that as a child the poet could "Mourn in the minor mode for a little matter," but as an adult she finds "Grace is fled from the tear." Adult mourners are "Ashamed and in secret, seated amid corruption." The diminishing hope of immortal joy participates in this grief, but once this grief is transcended, then is

All paradox seized and resolved, all evil
consumed,
All fear soared above, the depth and the
height reconciled,
The ultimate claimed, the great cry of unity
uttered.

Pitter realizes that recollected youth is the delirium of mortality. In "Reflection" faith in immortality is the only armor, the "proven mail." The faithful poet moves forward, not backward: "I cleave the chaos and prevail."

A Trophy of Arms was especially admired for the exquisite imagery, symbolism, and development of spiritual theme in such vividly concrete poems as "The Strawberry Plant" and "The Beautiful Negress." The strawberry plant, "flushed with wine, thought her last days her best." Her "one fruit achieved and ripe" is "an odorous vermilion ball / Tight with completion." The movement toward death is gay because in mortal life true bliss is like the plant in the rocky niche: "Perfection's self, and (rightly) out of reach." Consonant with this theme of advancing into death toward life is the imagery conjured up by the unhurrying, detached gait of the negress:

An unregretful elegiac song
Swelled in her wake; she gathered up my woe
Into epitome, and left it so;
Still dark, but made harmonious and strong.

And the poet asks

Did not the silent voice within the ear
Cry Fly with her to the soul's Africa,
Night, tragedy, the veiled, the end prefer?

Before the 1930s were over another collection of Pitter's verse was published. Taking its title from a phrase in the Persephone poem, *The Spirit Watches* was first published in 1939. This volume includes "The Downward-Pointing Muse" and "Burning the Bee-Tree," two poems selected by Thomas Moult to appear in his *The Best Poems of 1937*, and "The Stockdove," which appeared in *The Best Poems of 1938*. Pitter had also been represented in the 1934 and the 1936 selections of *The Best Poems* and was again represented in the 1940 and 1941 volumes.

The Spirit Watches was felt by some to be a falling off from the incisive penetration of *A Trophy of Arms*. The difference was a change in mood, not technique. Some recognized the value of the subtle change—a new calmness and sincerity of passion. Louis Untermeyer called it poise: "beneath the gently changing contours the shaping mind is firm and surprisingly edged." The natural and the mystical still combine, but in a grander, quieter space:

Silent as a falling leaf
To my heart there came a grief:
With a cold and pure despair,
Angerless, it settled there.

In "A Natural Sorrow" the poet speaks of acceptance:

I will not grudge to feel it so,
This dead leaf, this natural woe,
Neither will rage nor yet repine,
But let it lie there as a sign.

Grief is natural and to be accepted. *Natural* connotes "comfort," and the poet transforms grief into comfort through concrete, sensuous detail. The grief will lie as a sign,

Humble as the tattered nest
Which once felt the thrush's breast,
And harmless as the bustling wren
That trips about it now and then.

By 1940 Pitter was having poems published frequently on both sides of the Atlantic, with her work appearing in the *London Mercury*, *Life and Letters*, the *Dial*, the *Virginia Quarterly Review*, the *Poetry Review*, the *Commonweal*, *Literary Digest*, and *Wind and the Rain*. None of her books ever lost money, but they were never her sole means of support. The £50 to £70 annual income from poetry was mostly anthology fees. The year of *A Trophy of Arms* her income from these fees was £175. This poetry money was used to buy little luxuries, "a bottle of wine or . . . the theatre." Though Kate O'Hara scoffed at the sincerity of it, Pitter claimed that her own idea of material bliss is "a bed with an oyster satin eiderdown, and a bell that I can ping to summon a domestic who will fetch me another champagne cocktail." Elsewhere she has said, "My ultimate ambition is a cottage in some peaceful place, and enough strength left for gardening, my great love. I should not mind poverty in the country."

Pitter's fondness for gardening is evident in her book *The Rude Potato* (1941), illustrated by Roger Furse. The title poem of this slim volume pays tribute to the "freakish masterpiece" of a potato, whose life gives a joy "wild, bracing, and inconsequent." Other notable poems in the book are "The Morals of Pruning" and the dialectically rendered defense of "The Weed," from the mouth of a daughter weed. Of *The Rude Potato*, which was dear to her, Pitter writes: "America would not have it. It was rejected with horror as 'hamfisted, flat-footed, island British social satire.' " This book along with *A Mad Lady's Garland* and *On Cats* (1947) make up what Pitter terms her "grotesques or babouineries." She believes that mirth is both healthy and holy and claims to have written some unprintable lyrics. She sometimes contemplates the possibility of a comic work as austere and "unbearably" noble as *Oedipus Rex* and wonders if life's secret might not be "a final revelation potent to resolve time and matter and mutability into a supreme universal and divine laughter."

But in the early 1940s things were quite serious. The thriving gift-shop business ended with World War II. The employees were drafted, imported stock ran out, air raids interfered with work, and twice the glass roof of the workshop was blown in. Pitter and O'Hara then moved to the industrial south side of the river and took war jobs with the

Dust jacket for Pitter's 1941 book, one of her "grotesques or babouineries"

Morgan Crucible Company, Battersea, London.

In addition to this office job Pitter worked an evening a week in a machine shop turning carbon rods on a lathe for a shilling an hour. Despite rheumatism and dermatitis, she cherished the experience in the machine shop for the moral beauty she saw in the workers. Her often praised poem "The Cygnet" mourns one of these people, a young Irishwoman who was killed in a bombing. Ruth stayed on at the machine shop until after the war, sorting out the insurance cards of the 5,000 employees until September 1945.

Pitter was in her forties when she experienced a spiritual crisis. Relief came to her when she heard the religious broadcasts of C. S. Lewis. Believing that in middle age "one doesn't just fall into religion with adolescent emotion," she struggled hard to achieve intellectual satisfaction in religion as well. She leaned toward Roman Catholicism for a while but then decided that despite Henry VIII she had to be confirmed Anglican—in the traditional church of her country and in the religion in which she had been born and baptized, even though her parents had not been active churchgoers. The poem that records her deep religious struggle for decision, "On a Certain Philosophy," is reminiscent of Hopkins's religious poetry in stress, rhythm, and some word choice: "Out of the order, the calm, the mighty conclusions / Breathe as of balm, sing triumph, like adamant shine."

Pitter's war-years' poems were published in 1945 as *The Bridge, Poems 1939-1944*. This collection of serious verse moves back toward the metaphysical. "But for Lust," which had been published privately as *Poem* in an edition of 60 copies by John Arlott at the Southampton Shirley Press, is included in this volume. The title poem, "The Bridge," speaks of Pitter's move from the artist's section of Chelsea, where she made "peacock-jars," to the industrial section of London, where she worked for the crucible company that made "Simple as doom" vessels. Though the tragedy of war is felt throughout the volume, the pain is reconciled with the natural and the mystical—especially in such poems as "The Sparrow's Skull, memento mori, Written at the Fall of France."

On Cats was published in 1947. The verse is comic but also sympathetic of the real needs of real cats. Pitter once remarked that she found Eliot's "Old Possum's" cat verse "rather old-maidish." Though she respected Eliot as poet and critic and had thought about his work for twenty-five years, she finally decided that his innovations in English verse were "not I think to its advantage." They were acquainted with each other through the *New Age* people and occasionally attended the same Communion services at Chelsea Old Church early in the mornings. In 1968 she commented, "I am perfectly aware of his [Eliot's] stature as much superior to my own, but an English cat may look at an American king."

In 1950 *Urania* came out. This selection of poems was taken from *A Trophy of Arms*, *The Spirit Watches*, and *The Bridge*. The title page was a wood-engraving designed by Joan Hassall, who had designed the engraving for Pitter's 1948 Garland chapbook, *The Plain Facts, by a Plain but Amiable Cat*. This single poem later appeared in *End of Drought*.

Since January 1949 Pitter had been carrying on the giftware painting alone. O'Hara had retired from the business and was having success painting pictures. Heavy taxation after the war kept profits down. Pitter's ambition was to move with O'Hara from London to the country near Oxford, where they could see friends at the university and enjoy a milder climate. In 1952 Ruth and Kate bought The Hawthorns, a plain brick house in Long Crendon. Though she grieved over the lack of forest and vine, Pitter could now cultivate a year-round garden of flowers and vegetables.

In 1953 *The Ermine, Poems 1942-1952* was published and in 1954 this volume won the William E. Heinemann Award. The seriousness of the poems in this volume recall *A Trophy of Arms*—with a difference. In the earlier work the poems generally concentrate on nature or move, in a Wordsworthian way, from a contemplation of nature to a recollection of human experience juxtaposed with the natural imagery. For instance, the poem "Storm" opens, "I have seen daylight turn cadaverous, / And on the earth the fixed defeated look." Eventually this natural observation evokes the concept of storm within the mind. Calm follows nature's tempest and is observable. But the poet is unable to observe the calm of the mind, if there is one, and can only imagine and hope for it. The poems in *The Ermine* reverse the emphasis. The human element dominates and invokes a concept which eventually translates into a knowledge rather than a hope. "The Father Questioned" opens, "My mind alights like a bird in the dark tree." The sun, in this poem, is afflicted rather than afflicting: "The raw new sorrowful houses, the unmade road / Saddened the sun." In "Aged Man to Young Mother" the emphasis is on man's need for fellow man: "Now he is here, he needs a friend," and "Hold hard the lonely, bending hand / The hook that seeks a mooring." In "May 1947" the poet finds a dead daw:

There was a time this would have spoiled my
day;
But now I pick him up and go my way,
Walk in the spring with death as best I may.

The Ermine is Pitter's testament following her conversion to Anglo-Catholicism. The mystical vision of the poet has crystallized. She sees "The Transparent Earth" in "Five Dreams and a Vision":

Standing at midnight in the street
I saw the sun between my feet,
Shining up into my face
Through earth colourless as space;
Through an earth as clear as wine,
Colourless and crystalline.

This vision can be expressed in imagery that is hard, that reflects solid conviction. The mist has cleared. But the vision persists. Her earliest critics had faulted her for creating a world too fair—one in which no serious intellect could rest. In *The Ermine* Pitter anchors her vision where she has found her Christian answer on earth:

Solemn and lovely visions and holy dreams,
. . . .
Fade to the country that we never find:
For I am listening for that mortal tune,
The broken anthem of my fallen kind.

In the final passage of "Five Dreams and a Vision" the poet has faced "vincible" death. Now earthly reality is validated and can be embraced.

The next year, on 19 October 1955, Pitter was received by the Queen at Buckingham Palace to be awarded the Queen's Gold Medal for Poetry. She was fifty-seven. Poet Laureate John Masefield had made the recommendation to the committee, whose members were Neville Coghill, Walter de la Mare, Charles Morgan, Gilbert Murray, Vita Sackville-West, Sir Osbert Sitwell, and Masefield. The committee had been unanimous in its choice.

Shortly after 1955 Pitter began to appear on the BBC television Sunday afternoon live program "Brains Trusts," which had a viewing audience of three million. A question master would introduce questions written in by viewers and the guests would discuss answers for forty-five minutes. Pitter writes, "My great day was when I knew the *Chinese* word for something." In May 1960 Hilary Corke, one of the more caustic reviewers of the program, wrote that of the three guests on the most recent program "We should have just Miss Pitter and Lord David" since Pitter and Lord David Cecil shared "delicate sensibility," and "relaxed urbanity." This reviewer praised Pitter for presiding over "Ten thousand tutorials" and being "capable of holding an intellectual thread without dropping it."

During this time Pitter was also writing a regular weekly article on country experiences for the popular weekly magazine *Woman*, which had a readership of nine million. Its editor, Mary Grieve, wrote, "week after week Ruth revealed the small and the tender to an age hypnotised by the large, the noisy and the brash." And the audience of one of Ruth's BBC broadcasts, "Hunting the Unicorn," created such a demand for copies that it seemed to Pitter "as if it concerned their immortal souls' destiny."

In 1960 *Poetry Northwest* published a special Ruth Pitter issue, in which several essays about her appeared along with seven of her new poems, which later became part of the 1966 volume *Still by Choice*. The volume was dedicated to Arthur Russell. The simple language and concrete natural detail in these poems celebrate the mysteries of life with a growing optimism:

But see the living thing rejoice,
By freest love constrained:
Great-winged by nature, still by choice,
Supremely entertained.

In 1968 *Poems, 1926-1966* was published, and for the first time Pitter included some "old extravagances" of comic verse along with poems from the serious volumes: "They are as much a part of me as my ancestral fears and my immortal longings." Pitter states her literary credo in this volume: "I have tried to be faithful to delight, to beatitude. . . . I have not ignored the aches and pains; but neither have I wished to propagate them."

In 1969 Arthur Russell edited *Ruth Pitter: Homage to a Poet*, a collection of essays introduced by Lord David Cecil and concluded with a poem to Pitter by Russell. The essays are written by friends, critics, and fellow poets who "have homed on her signal." In 1974 Pitter became a Companion of Literature, and in 1975 was published her most recent book, *End of Drought*, which collects her new poems, four of which had appeared in the *Southern Review* in spring 1971. The poems in this volume exhibit the same controlled yet intense passion for the natural. The mystical has again refused to wear a misty mantle. From the nuptials of snakes in "So

Dust jacket for the American edition of Poems, 1926-1966, *in which Pitter writes, "I have tried to be faithful to delight, to beatitude. . . ."*

Good of Their Kind" to "The Brothers: A Dream" Pitter celebrates a life "Tragic yet loving: grievous and quite all right." In June 1979 Ruth Pitter was made a Commander of the British Empire. She writes, "I was so glad not to be a Dame, all petticoats. A Commander is much better. Some neighbours stood in formation and saluted!"

Ruth Pitter has completed her task with her volume *End of Drought* (1975). As "root-bound" in "this earthen Pot," the poet anticipates the time when she, as "A long-retarded Plant," may be given leave "to aspire and blow": "Where every past Despair and bygone Grief / I'll sublimate in each transcendent Leaf." These lines may well predict the future of her poetry:

> That all may say, "Why, here's a Flower indeed!"
> And crave a slip of me, or else a Seed.

References:

John Carswell, *Lives and Letters* (New York: New Directions, 1978);

Rudolph Gilbert, *Four Living Poets* (Santa Barbara, Calif.: Unicorn Press, 1944);

Poetry Northwest, special Pitter issue, 1 (Winter 1960);

Arthur Russell, ed., *Ruth Pitter: Homage to a Poet* (London: Rapp & Whiting, 1969);

E. I. Watkin, *Poets and Mystics* (London & New York: Sheed & Ward, 1953).

William Plomer

(10 December 1903-21 September 1973)

Robert K. Martin
Concordia University

SELECTED BOOKS: *Turbott Wolfe* (London: Leonard & Virginia Woolf, 1925; New York: Harcourt, Brace, 1926);

I Speak of Africa (London: Hogarth Press, 1927);

Notes for Poems (London: Hogarth Press, 1927);

The Family Tree (London: Leonard & Virginia Woolf, 1929);

Paper Houses (London: Leonard & Virginia Woolf, 1929; New York: Coward-McCann, 1929);

Sado (London: Leonard & Virginia Woolf, 1931); republished as *They Never Came Back* (New York: Coward-McCann, 1932);

The Case Is Altered (London: Leonard & Virginia Woolf, 1932; New York: Farrar & Rinehart, 1932);

The Fivefold Screen (London: Hogarth Press, 1932; New York: Coward-McCann, 1932);

Cecil Rhodes (London: Davies, 1933; New York: Appleton, 1933);

The Child of Queen Victoria, and Other Stories (London: Cape, 1933);

The Invaders (London: Cape, 1934);

Ali the Lion: Ali of Tebeleni, Pasha of Jannina, 1741-1822 (London: Cape, 1936);

Visiting the Caves (London: Cape, 1936);

Selected Poems (London: Hogarth Press, 1940);

Double Lives: An Autobiography (London: Cape, 1943; New York: Noonday, 1956);

The Dorking Thigh and Other Satires (London: Cape, 1945);

Four Countries (London: Cape, 1949);

Museum Pieces (London: Cape, 1952; New York: Noonday, 1954);

Gloriana: Opera in Three Acts, libretto by Plomer, music by Benjamin Britten (London: Boosey & Hawkes, 1953);

A Shot in the Park (London: Cape, 1955); republished as *Borderline Ballads* (New York: Noonday, 1955);

At Home: Memoirs (London: Cape, 1958; New York: Noonday, 1958);

Collected Poems (London: Cape, 1960; enlarged edition, London: Cape, 1973);

Curlew River: A Parable for Church Performance, based on *Sumidagawa*, by Juro Motomasa, libretto by Plomer, music by Britten (London: Faber & Faber, 1964);

The Burning Fiery Furnace: Second Parable for Church Performance, libretto by Plomer, music by Britten (London: Faber Music, 1966);

Taste and Remember (London: Cape, 1966);

The Prodigal Son: Third Parable for Church Performance, libretto by Plomer, music by Britten (London: Faber Music, 1968);

Celebrations (London: Cape, 1972);

The Butterfly Ball and The Grasshopper's Feast (Lon-

William Plomer

don: Cape, 1973; New York: Grossman, 1975);

Autobiography (London: Cape, 1975; New York: Taplinger, 1975).

William Plomer, poet, novelist, and librettist, earned lasting fame through his first book, a novel of South Africa, *Turbott Wolfe* (1925), begun when he was nineteen. This novel established Plomer's reputation as a discriminating writer of exceptional sensitivity and as an important social critic, angry at the injustices of South African life. Following publication of the novel, Plomer became friendly with two of South Africa's most important writers, Roy Campbell and Laurens van der Post. (Van der Post wrote a lengthy introduction to *Turbott Wolfe* when it was republished by the Hogarth Press in 1965.)

Born in Pietersburg, Transvaal, to Charles and Edythe Waite-Browne Plomer, William Charles Franklin Plomer spent his childhood in both South Africa and England. He was educated at Beechmont (near Seven Oaks, England), Rugby, and St. John's College in Johannesburg. Although he considered himself an English writer and not a South African ("I once had a cat that had kittens in an oven, but nobody mistook them for cakes."), the imagery drawn from his South African years remained an important part of his poetry, and his profound sense of injustice and his striving to overcome racial boundaries remained central aspects of his thought. The early South African poems are marked by a sharp contrast between the fates of black and white South Africans and an angry view of the "plundering city," Johannesburg, "this city where science is applied for profit."

While many of the poems make their points by direct statement and frontal attack, many others are cast in a satiric vein. Plomer's satiric verse would later become the principal means for his ironic view of a corrupt and distintegrating world. For example, "The Explorer," written circa 1927, depicts a "Romantic subject of the Great White Queen" who is untouched by his African experience:

> And now he dreams of oatmeal, Scotland and the Flag
> The nimble corncrake in his native heather,
> The handy corkscrew in his leather bag.

In all of the "serious" poems there is a sense of ominousness, of impending disaster: "And Silence waited where the snake lay coiled / And mocked at each mild, bright morning."

After a residence of seven years in South Af-

Young William Plomer with his father and his nurse, 1903

rica, Plomer sailed with van der Post for Japan in 1926 and remained there until 1929. A number of the poems written in Japan show the influence of Japanese poetry, in the increased use of visual imagery, in the use of understatement, and in the gradual reduction of didactic elements. Plomer must not, however, be linked with the Orientalists of the 1890s: as Earl Miner has said, he was one of the first Western poets to treat Japanese subject matter "without exoticism and without condescension." The stay in Japan helped Plomer to deal with the portrayal of emotion through the image, and his poems developed a valuable concision. A poem such as "Hotel Magnificent" shows that he had not completely abandoned the satiric mode, however. It also shows his assimilation of the new rhythms of the 1920s: the poem employs deliberate cacophony and exaggerated alliteration as means toward the creation of a hectic world of agitated sound.

Plomer returned to England in 1929 by way of Korea and Siberia. In England he met Anthony Butts, a painter who had previously written to him in Japan. Butts and Plomer became deeply attached to one another and remained intimate friends until Butts's death in 1941. Butts was convinced of the dislocation of western society and of the inevitable cataclysm which must ensue and encouraged Plomer in his belief that non-Western societies might offer an alternative to Western imperialism and materialism. In 1930 Butts and Plomer traveled together in Europe and spent some time in Greece, which had particular significance for Plomer and which was the occasion for some of his finest poems. In his autobiography Plomer expressed the wish that some child of his, had he had one, might spend a year in Italy and a year in Greece: "My hope would be that emotions would be awakened while knowledge was being extended, and that the influence of climate and culture would be heightened by feelings of tenderness as well as of excitement." "Three Pinks" is an exquisite love poem of this period, recalling an anonymous lover with "eyebrow-arches, wide, Byzantine, black, / White-wine coloured eyes in a rose-tan skin, / Antique young eyes!"

During the 1930s Plomer lived on the coast of England or in London and began the work as a publisher's reader which he continued until his death. The poems of this period are marked by an extraordinary depth of affection. "Visiting the Caves," the title poem of a volume published in 1936, is an extraordinary tribute to the power of a sustaining love:

> The lift, the gangway and the staircase lead to you,
> And you, my bed and pillow, give me rest;
> I visit the caves and am guided, and I know
> Those galleries are glittering within your breast;
> Whatever you receive I share
> And I carry you like a passport everywhere.

The poems of this period do not abandon their vision of a world that is often harsh and cruel, but they find in personal affection a hope for renewal.

At the same time Plomer began work on a series of ballads and other "light" narrative poems, for which he has gained a considerable reputation. These poems present a witty and sardonic view of modern life; they seem likely to have been an influence on similar work by W. H. Auden, including his "Miss Gee" (1937). John Betjeman praised Plomer as "a humourous and satiric poet," but many critics, such as John Fuller, have complained of his "heartlessness" and what Fuller called "the bland comedy of cruelty." The best explanation, and defense, of Plomer's work is provided by Howard Moss, who notes "the close linkage between the absurd and the terrible. Behind the middle- or upper-class facade, Mr. Plomer sees the true skull."

The wit of these poems is biting, because it is most often directed at the self-centered delusions of the English upper-middle classes as they ignore the signs of poverty and impending disaster that surround them. Plomer's portrait of "Mews Flat Mona" is a wonderful pen portrait of a bright young thing, a character who could just as well step out of a novel by Evelyn Waugh. Plomer had lost none of his sense of anger and engagement, but he had learned to channel it into caricature, through an accurate depiction of manners and mores.

The death of Anthony Butts was the occasion for one of the most moving of Plomer's poems, his elegy "In a Bombed House." The poem evokes the memory of Butts as one whose anger rose out of a sense of betrayal—the betrayal of a greater England by "a duller England where / Suburban civilization ruled at last." Although most of the poem is devoted to a presentation of Butts's character, above all his courage and his hatred of stupidity and meanness, the concluding stanza offers a warm and permanent tribute:

> As in a waste of seas the cruising shark
> Follows a raft, and never turns aside,
> Death followed him. But love was following too,
> Was with him when he died.

As the last lines of that poem suggest, Plomer had been reading Herman Melville, whose deep commitment to social justice, questioning of racial and political assumptions, and overwhelming affirmation of human brotherhood Plomer must have found sympathetic. In the following years Plomer edited editions of Melville's *Poems* (1943), *Billy Budd* (1946), and *White Jacket* (1952). (He had edited *Redburn* in 1937.) Much of his work during these years was editorial, including his work on Anthony Butts's book, *Curious Relations* (1945).

Through an invitation to lecture at Aldeburgh, Plomer became friendly with the composer Benjamin Britten, and it was Plomer who suggested *Billy Budd* as the subject of an opera. Plomer's friend E. M. Forster wrote the libretto. In later years Plomer was a frequent librettist for Britten: he wrote the libretto for *Gloriana* (1953), the opera performed for the coronation of Elizabeth II, and for three parables for church performance, *Curlew River* (1964), *The Burning Fiery Furnace* (1966), and *The Prodigal Son* (1968). All of them show the influence of Japanese Noh drama.

In 1956 Plomer returned to South Africa, for

the first time in thirty years, at the invitation of the University of Witwatersrand. His poems written during that visit are among his finest. Far more mature than the early South African poems, they have nonetheless lost none of the early sense of anger or doom. "Tugela River" presents Plomer's vision of the future uprising, embodied in the river itself:

> Cool, cool Tugela slid
> Haunted with unwritten myth,
> Swam like a noble savage, dark
> And muscular in shade, or clear
> In the sun an emerald angel swam.

The poem moves from the mythology of the river to the death of a Zulu youth Plomer had once seen and to his belief that that death, like all the others, will finally bring change:

> When patience breaks, the sinews act,
> Rage generates energy without end:
> Tugela River, in the time of drums
> And shouting of the war-dance flood

William Plomer

> Will break a trance, as revolutions do,
> Will promise order, and a future time
> Of honey, beer, and milk.

Plomer's last two volumes of adult poetry, *Taste and Remember* (1966) and *Celebrations* (1972), continue many of his earlier concerns and forms. There is an elegy for John Kennedy, in which his death seems to give rise to "the image or dream / Of attainable good," and a satirical portrait of "Mrs. Middleditch," which is a parody of the world of advertising:

> A Supermorning, madam,
> For Supermarketing!
> Our cut-price Superfoods
> Are best for each and all,
> Our Supergoods await you
> On every Supershelf,
> So take a Superbasket
> And help your Superself!

In the midst of this world, however, Mrs. Middleditch is seized by the vision of a starving child, and the poem turns abruptly from silliness to horror, the horror that Plomer has always seen at the heart of Western commercial society. A poem for Cavafy evokes the tender love of "A Casual Encounter." "A Victorian Album" finds the surprising image of a Muslim among the white faces, Osman, who is "great among grandparents, grand among great- / uncles and aunts, he who put friendship first." And "The Planes of Bedford Square" exquisitely evokes the lost world of Edwardian England, peopled by Ronald Firbank, Lady Ottoline Morrell, Bertrand Russell, and Nijinsky.

Some readers have found a falling-off in the later work, and others have criticized Plomer for abandoning his longstanding opposition to the social order. Although the last volumes do not have the sustained vigor of some of the earlier books, it does not seem fair to say that Plomer abandoned his convictions. He did accept Christianity, but a Christianity of Christ, "saboteur / of received ideas." Although he had been asked by E. M. Forster to write Forster's life, he eventually grew away from both Forster and their mutual friend J. R. Ackerley and did not write the planned biography. Part of the disagreement concerned openness about homosexuality: although a number of Plomer's poems and novels treat the subject, they all do so in a discreet manner. It seems certain, nonetheless, that his strong sense of racial injustice was heightened by a sense of sexual injustice, and that the love of non-Westerners was, for Plomer, as for Forster, a means of attempting to bridge the gap between nations and races by a personal force of affection and love. After finishing the children's verses for *The Butterfly Ball and The Grasshopper's Feast* (1973), Plomer died of a heart attack on 21 September 1973 at his home in Hassocks, Sussex.

Plomer's poetry has not reached a large public. Some readers have found it too reserved and the poet too cold. Plomer was a man who required solitude, and the forbidden nature of his own sexuality did sometimes oblige him to assume a certain evasive manner. Although he does not have the scope or the extraordinary technical skill of Auden, their poetry has many similarities. Plomer's apparently light verse deserves a much larger audience, and his travel poems are masterpieces of their sort. They use the confrontation with a strange landscape as the occasion for the exploration of self. His anger and his simultaneous belief in the future of South Africa, the land itself and its peoples, should make him one of the most distinguished poets to have arisen out of that tormented history. Plomer's is a humane voice speaking for a civilized society that has disappeared. His minor key has come to seem inadequate, not because of its own weakness, but because in an age of shouting, his tones of irony and hope can no longer be heard.

References:

"About William Plomer," *London Magazine*, new series 13 (December 1973/January 1974): 5-29;

J. R. Doyle, *William Plomer* (New York: Twayne, 1969);

Howard Moss, "Over the Border," review of *Borderline Ballads*, *Poetry*, 88 (1956): 396-398.

Papers:

Plomer's papers are at the University of Durham.

F. T. Prince

(13 September 1912-)

David Tacium
Concordia University

SELECTED BOOKS: *Poems* (London: Faber & Faber, 1938);

Poems (Norfolk, Conn.: New Directions, 1941);

Soldiers Bathing and Other Poems (London: Fortune Press, 1954);

The Italian Element in Milton's Verse (Oxford: Clarendon Press, 1954);

William Shakespeare: The Poems (London: Longmans, Green, 1963);

The Doors of Stone: Poems 1938-1962 (London: Hart-Davis, 1963);

Memoirs in Oxford (London: Fulcrum Press, 1970);

Drypoints of the Hasidim (London: Menard Press, 1975);

Afterword on Rupert Brooke (London: Menard Press, 1976);

Collected Poems (London: Menard & Anvil Presses, 1979; New York: Sheep Meadow Press, 1979);

The Yüan Chên Variations (New York: Sheep Meadow Press, 1981).

On reading *Soldiers Bathing*, E. M. Forster claimed it was one of the three most outstanding books to have appeared in England in 1954. In general, however, knowledge of the work of F. T. Prince has been confined to other poets, the best of whom have repeatedly called his lyrical talent as fine as that of the most accomplished of modern poets. Long intervals between publications—one of the conditions of his level of workmanship—have no doubt delayed his recognition by a wider audience.

Frank Templeton Prince was born at Kimberley in South Africa, into a provincial bourgeois setting. His parents, Henry and Margaret Hetherington Prince, a businessman and a teacher, were English. Extremely important to all he was and would become was his mother, even though they saw little of one another in later years. He later wrote in the long poem *Memoirs in Oxford* (1970):

> But I must thank my mother's mind,
> Her fiery rational sense of right
> And love of all things well-designed,
> Books, furniture, people—signed
> With logic, courage, wit and light.
>
> She gave us pictures and adventures,

Ballads and stories by the fire,
Echoes of Ruskin and Carlyle,
The notion that there could be 'style';
But most herself and her desire.

Prince was a withdrawn child whose sensibility to the African landscape foretold the keen detail which was to mark even his most meditative verse. He began to write at fifteen years of age, after an earlier interest in painting.

Nevertheless, it was decided he would become an architect. After little more than a year this intention was abandoned, and he left South Africa to study at Balliol College, Oxford, in 1931. He had made previous trips to Britain; now he had come to stay. He graduated in 1934 with a first-class honors degree in English. French he had learned in South Africa, having already plunged deeply into Rimbaud, Valéry, and Verlaine. (Verlaine has remained important for Prince's poetry, as poems such as "At Beaulieu" show.) At Oxford he continued to read French poets, including St-John Perse. A lifelong admiration for Henry James had fully taken root by this time—he has said that he would like to have written poetry that would have affinities with James's novels.

F. T. Prince

Meanwhile, he taught himself Italian by means of a bilingual edition of Dante and made vacation excursions to Italy. There he became enthusiastic for Renaissance art and architecture, as well as Renaissance poetry. Several years later, this enthusiasm ripened into the moving meditation on the vocation of the artist, "The Old Age of Michelangelo" (first collected in *The Doors of Stone*, 1963), one of his finest poems:

And my whole anxious life I see
As a combat with myself, that I do violence to
myself,
To bruise and beat and batter
And bring under
My own being,
Which is an infinite savage sea of love.

In 1934 he met T. S. Eliot, who saw him as a potential Faber poet. Late in 1935, Eliot published "An Epistle to a Patron" in the *Criterion*. Praise for the "opulent" language of this long poem, whose argument is similar to Valéry's in "Eupalinos ou l'architecte," has been widespread.

A year as a visiting fellow at the graduate College of Princeton University in 1935-1936 was not followed by further academic work. Returning to live in London in 1936, he worked at the Royal Institute of International Affairs (Chatham House) and continued to write. Meanwhile, he traveled to Dublin in late 1937 and was able to meet William Butler Yeats. Among the notes he took is Yeats's response (echoing a Upanishad) to the question of how to think clearly and go forward: "Think continually on those things which make you happy." Prince took this advice, and his verse at this time was strongly influenced by Yeats in other ways as well, in its speech rhythms and the verse paragraph which seems to take form from the logic of what is being said.

Prince has inevitably been lumped with other English poets of the 1930's, but this categorization is erroneous. He followed Auden and his friends by the space of a few years, and attitudes had already begun to change. Prince did not dally with Marxism, nor did he follow Auden's path into popular forms.

In 1940, Prince was commissioned into the Intelligence Corps of the British Army. He began in the Government Communications Centre at Bletchley Park. On 10 March 1943, before being sent on to Cairo, he married Elizabeth Bush, an Englishwoman whose parents had lived in India. Two children came from this marriage. Returning from Egypt in 1944, he spent his final six months in uniform as an interpreter in Italian P.O.W. camps in England.

Any estimate of Prince's poetry has to take account of his religious beliefs. He converted to Catholicism at the age of twenty-five, seeing Catholicism as a force for humanism, with its heritage of classical culture and social-moral-artistic inspiration, and preferring this response to the only other one in the air at the time, communism. Temperament and circumstance combined to force him to seek a way by which to live, to feel he had entered upon life. He was led to accept the kind of faith described by religious writers from Simone Weil back to Saint Augustine as valid for himself. Reading Kierkegaard in 1939 seemed to reinforce the logic of conversion, but rereading his work five years later stirred some resistance. His emphasis on the gap between faith and "aesthetic paganism" was no longer congenial.

During the period that covered the years of World War II, Prince's poetry took on a seriousness and intensity seldom found in modern poetry. His most anthologized poem, "Soldiers Bathing," succeeds on the basis of a direct religious reading of the "facts":

These dry themselves and dress.
Combing the hair, forget the fear and shame and nakedness.
Because to love is frightening
We prefer the freedom of our crimes. Yet, as I drink the dusky air,
I feel a strange delight that fills me full,
Strange gratitude, as if evil itself were beautiful,
And kiss the wound in thought, while in the west
I watch a streak of red that might have issued from Christ's breast.

The feeling here clusters around the sense of "tragic joy" which so much of the poetry conveys, exploring in various ways the single theme of life-in-death and death-in-life. The deeper sense of joy seems to come only after something like death has descended, though the two experiences are in themselves opposites, as in "Apollo and the Sibyl":

My mournful calcined life
Half-eaten by desires,
Brimming with light and sorrow,
Yet I do not repent me;
I remain in my pain that is
A golden distance endlessly.

Prince clung to Catholicism as the central spiritual heritage of the West, and later poems, such as "Drypoints of the Hasidim," continue to inquire into the nature of belief, with unspoken allusions to the Church. This poem of roughly 400 lines focuses on the Hasidic movement in its prime, presenting its essential unworldliness and inwardness (it was so remote and precarious that it was barely heard of in its day). For slightly different reasons, in *Memoirs in Oxford* Angela of Foligno, "an imperfect saint," takes on significance partly for having "escaped the canon":

and one sees
Why—there is sorrow and unease
In all she does or tries to do.

—Sorrow, unease or desperation:
But that is why she offers me
An emblem of the hope and strife
And death in life—the choice of life
In death—I'd have you see.

Much of Prince's postwar poetry was written as he was teaching at Southampton University, where he began as lecturer in the English department in 1946. These poems are written either in the first person or through the medium of a commentator (as in "Strafford"), but the first person is seldom if ever the poet himself; rather, he is a persona, often historical, who permits the "realisation" or "dramatisation" of a given theme, mood, or emotion. Prince has always been at odds with those who seek to give a reproduction of the poet's immediate experience and way of life. Choosing dramatic subjects, he has been able to convey multiple bearings and perspectives through them.

At Southampton, Prince established himself as a Milton scholar, with his book *The Italian Element in Milton's Verse* (1954). He also worked on Shakespeare's narrative poems and sonnets. From 1962 to 1965, he was dean of the Southampton faculty of arts; he spent 1968 to 1969 at Oxford as a visiting fellow of All Souls College; and in 1972 he was Clark Lecturer at Cambridge.

Since 1970, F. T. Prince has produced five poems, which are substantial both in length and in the matters they take in hand. He has always been a writer of *verse*; he is certainly among the finest of living poets writing in metrical forms. Two of these later poems reflect a willingness to explore a method new to him, the syllabic line. The second of these later poems, "A Last Attachment," is based on

Laurence Sterne's *Journal to Eliza* and demonstrates Prince's lifelong Stendhalian preoccupation to read *dans mes sensations*:

> Yet he says 'Our passions ebb and flow.
> The truth is thou hast but turn'd them all one way—
> they flow to thee.' And there, there is the lucidity
> That seeks an old delight, but new in sadness—

In 1975, Prince began to teach abroad, spending two summers at Dalhousie University in Halifax, three years at University of the West Indies in Jamaica, two at Brandeis University in Boston, and one at Washington University in St. Louis. The American poetry audience responded to his work with interest, owing in part to John Ashbery's long-standing admiration of him. He made many friends among American poets, not only those for whom the center of gravity is New York. Prince received an honorary doctorate of literature from Southampton in 1981 and another from New York University in 1982. He expects to continue teaching abroad, and for several years he and his wife have spent a part of each summer in a chalet in Minorca.

F. T. Prince's poetry has been called unfashionable, which may variously mean that it is not modern, that it does not conform to English or American trends and assumptions, or that it is too "other-worldly." But critics have also noticed that Prince deals consistently with recurring dilemmas—restlessness, solitude, love, growing old, the sufferings and joys of the imaginative life—in the spirit of a "composer" working with a recognizable theme as his subject. His poetry offers a faithful attention to "the thing itself" and a documentation of the inner life.

Other:

John Milton, *Samson Agonistes*, edited by Prince (Oxford: Oxford University Press, 1957);

"On the Last Two Books of *Paradise Lost*," in *Essays and Studies*, edited by Basil Willey (London: Murray, 1958), pp. 38-52;

"The Sonnet from Wyatt to Shakespeare," in *Elizabethan Poetry*, Stratford-upon-Avon Studies, no. 2 (New York: St. Martin's, 1960), pp. 11-29;

William Shakespeare, *The Poems*, edited by Prince (London: New Arden Editions, 1960);

Milton, *Paradise Lost, Books 1 and 2*, edited by Prince (Oxford: Oxford University Press, 1962);

"A Note on *Romeo and Juliet*, in *Shakespeare: The Writer and His Work*, edited by Bonamy Dobrée (London: Longmans, Green, 1964), pp. 329-333;

Milton, *Comus and Other Poems*, edited by Prince (Oxford: Oxford University Press, 1968);

"Milton and the Theatrical Sublime," in *Approaches to Paradise Lost*, edited by C. A. Patrides (London: Arnold, 1968), pp. 53-64.

Periodical Publications:

"The Influence of Tasso and Della Casa on Milton's Diction," *Review of English Studies*, 25 (January 1949): 232-236;

Rejoinder to "Verse and its Feet," by M. Whitely, *Review of English Studies*, new series, 9 (1958): 278-279;

"The Study of Form and the Renewal of Poetry," *Proceedings of the British Academy*, 50 (1964): 45-61;

"Modern Poetry in England," *Review of the University of Pietermaritzburg* (1967);

"Voice and Verse," *English*, 108 (Autumn 1971): 77-82;

"John Skelton," *Proceedings of the Accademmia dei Lincei* (1972).

Kathleen Raine

(14 June 1908-)

J'nan Morse Sellery
Harvey Mudd College

Kathleen Raine (photo by Germaine Kanova)

SELECTED BOOKS: *Stone and Flower Poems 1935-43* (London: Editions Poetry/Nicholson & Watson, 1943);

Living in Time (London: Editions Poetry/Nicholson & Watson, 1946);

The Pythoness, and Other Poems (London: Hamilton, 1949; New York: Farrar, Straus & Young, 1952);

William Blake (London: Longmans, Green, 1951; revised, 1958; revised again, 1965, revised again, 1969);

The Year One: Poems (London: Hamilton, 1952; New York: Farrar, Straus & Young, 1953);

Coleridge (London: Longmans, Green, 1953);

The Collected Poems of Kathleen Raine (London: Hamilton, 1956; New York: Random House, 1957);

Poetry in Relation to Traditional Wisdom (London: Guild of Pastoral Psychology, 1958);

Blake and England (Cambridge: Heffer, 1960; Folcroft, Pa.: Folcroft Library, 1973);

The Hollow Hill and Other Poems, 1960-1964 (London: Hamilton, 1965);

Defending Ancient Springs (London & New York: Oxford University Press, 1967);

The Written Word (London: Enitharmon Press, 1967);

Six Dreams and Other Poems (London: Enitharmon Press, 1968);

Blake and Tradition, 2 volumes (Princeton: Princeton University Press, 1968; London: Routledge & Kegan Paul, 1969); abridged as *Blake and Antiquity*, 1 volume (Princeton: Princeton University Press, 1977; London: Routledge, 1979);

A Question of Poetry (Crediton, U.K.: Gilbertson, 1969);

William Blake (London: Thames & Hudson, 1970; New York: Praeger, 1971);

The Lost Country (Dublin: Dolmen/London: Hamilton, 1971);

Yeats, The Tarot and the Golden Dawn, New Yeats Papers, volume 2 (Dublin: Dolmen, 1972);

Hopkins, Nature, and Human Nature (London: Hopkins Society, 1972);

Faces of Day and Night (London: Enitharmon Press, 1972);

Farewell Happy Fields: Memories of Childhood (London: Hamilton, 1973; New York: Braziller, 1977);

On a Deserted Shore: A Sequence of Poems (Dublin: Dolmen, 1973);

Death-in-Life and Life-in-Death: 'Cuchulain Comforted' and 'News for the Delphic Oracle,' New Yeats Papers, volume 8 (Dublin: Dolmen, 1974);

David Jones, Solitary Perfectionist (Ipswich: Golgonooza Press, 1974; enlarged, 1975);

The Land Unknown (London: Hamilton, 1975; New York: Braziller, 1975);

The Inner Journey of the Poet (Ipswich: Golgonooza

Press, 1976; enlarged edition, London: Allen & Unwin, 1982; New York: Braziller, 1982);

The Oval Portrait and Other Poems (London: Enitharmon / Hamilton, 1977);

The Lion's Mouth: Concluding Chapters of Autobiography (London: Hamilton, 1977; New York: Braziller, 1978);

David Jones and the Actually Loved and Known (Ipswich: Golgonooza Press, 1978);

Fifteen Short Poems (London: Enitharmon, 1978);

Blake and the New Age (London & Boston: Allen & Unwin, 1979);

From Blake to 'A Vision,' New Yeats Papers, volume 17 (Dublin: Dolmen, 1979);

Cecil Collins Painter of Paradise (Ipswich: Golgonooza Press, 1979);

The Oracle in the Heart, and Other Poems 1975-1978, (Dublin: Dolmen/London & Boston: Allen & Unwin, 1980);

'What Is Man?' (Ipswich: Golgonooza Press, 1980);

The Human Face of God: William Blake and the Book of Job (New York: Thames & Hudson, 1982).

Over more than forty years Kathleen Raine has written twelve volumes of poetry, three volumes of autobiography, several volumes of essays and criticism, numerous translations, and introductions to the work of other poets. The recipient of numerous awards and honors, she has remained, nevertheless, relatively unnoticed in the United States, and her work is often omitted from major anthologies of contemporary poetry. Since the 1930s British literary periodicals of the highest reputation have published her poetry, which reveals a mythological emphasis, a lyrical ease, and an intellectual framework that sets her squarely in a philosophical and poetic tradition extending from Plato through Plotinus, Milton, and Swedenborg, to Blake, Coleridge, Shelley, and Yeats. Raine sees herself as a defender of an earlier tradition of poetry that is "language of poetic symbol within Perennial Philosophy." She is attracted to mystical and visionary writers and at the same time eschews many of the prevailing attitudes of this century. Critics sometimes compare her to other twentieth-century poets such as Edwin Muir or Herbert Read. Indeed, her subject matter, perhaps following the Anglo-Scottish tradition and personal suggestions by Muir, relies heavily on external nature, archetypal ideas or Platonic forms, and personal dreams, in a word, upon man's precarious relationship to man in a violent or untrustworthy universe. For her, mythology and nature are viable modes for illustrating psychic development. The symbolic and somewhat hieratic language of Raine's poetry focuses on the psychic development of the self, with its need for spiritual and human relationships, as forming the core of woman's creativity. Raine's recent poetry is more sharply defined by woman's relationship to the feminine.

In general, three interlocking subjects shape Raine's canon: her perception of Blake's power as poet and as intellectual resource; her views of nature, mythology, and archetypal psychology; and her personal growth and pain as a woman. Blake's ideas obviously have influenced her views of innocence (Eden in her many mythic renderings), experience (loss of love and need for human relationships), and second innocence or transcendence (Platonic ideas). Raine's concern for nature, which began during her childhood, remains a dominant poetic expression. It rarely takes on symbolic significance; rather nature represents itself, and the poet's vision moves through and beyond the actual into a spiritual union. And her view of the "daimon" or poetry's creative voice, though influenced and sustained by her mother in Raine's early years, contains, more often, a Platonic ingredient or a psychological ambience reminiscent of Jung.

Kathleen Jessie Raine was born in Ilford, an East London suburb, to George and Jessie Wilkie Raine, and with the exception of the years of World War I when she was sent to live with "Aunt Peggy," her mother's spinster cousin who taught school at Bavington, Northumberland, and a similar period during World War II when she took her son and daughter to live in the Northumberland area, or when she was at Cambridge either as a student (1926-1929) or as a research fellow at Girton College (1955-1961), London has been her home.

Raine's three volumes of autobiography—*Farewell Happy Fields* (1973), *The Land Unknown* (1975), and *The Lion's Mouth* (1977)—and an earlier volume of autobiographical essays, *Faces of Day and Night* (1972), inform her poetic themes. The autobiographies depict Raine's growth from an adored, resentful child to a nurturer of the poetic gifts she received from her mother. *Farewell Happy Fields* covers, as the subtitle indicates, memories of childhood. As an only child, Raine heavily depended upon the nurture of her parents; her mother's roots were Scottish, and her father was English master at County High School in Ilford, and, Raine says, "in his work as a teacher and Housemaster, as a Wesleyan Methodist 'local preacher,' and as a worker for pacifism and the league of Nations Union, he found fulfilment, loved and respected by many who remember him to this day." Raine adds: "If from my mother's side I inherited however small a portion in the memories of Scotland embodied in song, speech, and heroic story my father stood for progress, education and the future." The split between the intellect of the father and the poetic feelings of the mother is always apparent in her writings. She was sent to Miss Hutchinson's School near West View, London, and after schooling in Bavington, to the Highlands School in Ilford. From Ilford she prepared for her entrance examinations to college. In particular she credits her father with helping her with Latin, and notes: "How often since, from the turmoil of emotion, I have sought and found sanctuary in the calm regions of the mind; and for this I have my father to thank." Yet she considers her mother's family her genuine people: "my father's people were never my people, in any living sense. Scotland is to this day a matriarchal country, and my mother's family naturally regarded me as my mother's daughter rather than my father's."

The Land Unknown shows the young woman's growth into adulthood, her willful or unconscious actions, and her consuming belief in dreams, nature, and the inspiration of poetry. At eighteen, Raine received a full scholarship to attend Girton College, the woman's college at Cambridge, as a student of natural sciences. She received an M.A. in botany and zoology in 1929. Raine's world view was dominated by her love of poetry. She admits, "I also chose science because our teacher of Botany at that time was one of those rare people whose subject was a passion." At Cambridge, poetry and science coalesced for her, bringing her mother's love of nature and poetry into conjunction with her father's rational thought.

At Girton, she recalls, she was impressed by Virginia Woolf's delivery of the lecture that was later to become *A Room of One's Own*. At that time, Raine was so focused on science and its values that she had not "read any of Virginia Woolf's novels. . . ; a few months before I had not even heard of her. Now . . . I learned for the first time . . . that the problems of 'a woman writer' were supposed to be different from the problems of a man who writes; that the problem is not one of writing but of living in such a way as to be able to write." From that experience, Raine decided that "to write well and write truly" was her only goal. Her poetry and autobiographies define and clarify the movement of her woman's perceptions, needs, and aspirations from childhood's innocence through puberty to maternal experience, and later to old age. Raine never has had the unearned income recommended by Woolf in *A Room of One's Own*, and for her to support herself and raise a family and to write poetry entailed a continuing uphill economic battle.

Raine married twice, first to Hugh Sykes Davies, after her third year at Cambridge, and, after their divorce, to Charles Madge. With her second husband, she had two children, James and Anna. In 1965 Raine remarked that she had recently attended the baptism of a grandson, and in her last volume of poetry she refers to a granddaughter. No other information is available about her children and grandchildren. Raine left Madge because she fell in love with a man whom she calls Alastair in her autobiography and to whom she dedicated her first volume of poetry. That relationship did not last, and since leaving Madge she has lived alone: "for marriage was, to me, a symbol of imprisonment. I knew in my heart that freedom is a state, a blessing, a task which I had yet again relinquished, sacrificed."

The Lion's Mouth records the writer's friendships with artists and her painful unrequited love, in the early 1950s, for Gavin Maxwell, to whom she dedicated her *Collected Poems* (1956). In this relationship, Raine came to realize that she was psychologically and emotionally possessed by love; yet she found that the experience of love also reveals valuable insights and visions. To share this experience with the world is what motivated her to have the final autobiographical volume published; but again the undercurrent in this volume is the inner vision begun and sustained by her mother. Both the autobiography and the poetry are centrally informed by Raine's drive to be a poet, goaded and nurtured by her mother's stated but unfulfilled dream.

Raine's attitudes concerning femininity, the world, and poetry derive from her mother's love of nature, myth and fantasy, and poetry. Her feelings toward her mother over the years oscillated between total adoration and complete rejection. Raine presents her identification with her mother and their common love of nature and poetry metaphorically in terms of the archetypal myth of Demeter-Persephone-Kore in which nature is fully identified with the two nature goddesses, Demeter and Persephone. In this myth the girl-child Kore, daughter of the corn goddess and archetypal mother Demeter, is abducted by Hades. After her loss of innocence, she becomes Persephone, the woman who is both queen of the underworld and goddess of nature's yearly renewal. Raine then integrates the Greek myth into the romantic tradition which relies on the fall from innocence in the Edenic myth. In this way she explains the female self's changing perceptions, creating a cluster of female correspondences. Her most recent voice, that of the "old" woman reverberates with sureness, vigor, and honesty in expressing its vivid perceptions of nature and time. However, disentangling Raine's feminine myth of self from mythic tradition is complex because the mother-daughter, nature-poetry patterns are so deeply embedded in her thoughts and feelings.

Raine's critical writings are related to her concerns as a poet. For her the major poetic tradition is that of the major romantic poets, spearheaded by Blake and carried on especially by Coleridge, Yeats, and Edwin Muir. Her view of poetry is also reinforced by the discoveries and theories of analytical psychology. In contemporary literary and psychological circles (particularly in Zurich, London, New York, San Francisco, and Los Angeles, and at the Eranos Conference in Ascona, Switzerland), Raine is known for her many studies of Blake and Yeats, for her sensitively written introductions to the works of contemporary British poets and painters, and for her lectures on culture, art, literature, and their impact on the individual and society. The culmination of her years of studying Blake's symbolism and mythology is the A. W. Mellon lectures of 1962, published as *Blake and Tradition* in two volumes, 1968.

Raine's defense of the romantics is a reaction to the structured intellectual tradition into which she was thrust at Cambridge. She chose to study science because she was fascinated with the subject of nature and because she felt that she needed no mentors to teach her how to be a poet. But the intellectual milieu, "a literature of the temporal . . . a literature compatible with Wittgenstein's and Russell's new logical positivism, Bloomsbury humanism, (represented in King's College by Maynard Keynes and G. Lowes Dickinson) and the materialist science of the Cavendish laboratory, . . . dominated all fields of Cambridge." In rejecting this milieu, Raine solidly reinforced her own view of poetry as resonating "the eternal, in and through the temporal."

In England in 1970 and in the United States in 1971 another volume on Blake appeared; and in 1979 *Blake and the New Age*, which contains lectures and essays written after 1969. These last were written for various occasions, and are "studies of Blake's thought as it has an immediate bearing in changes taking place at the present time." The main theme is that "mind, not matter," is "considered as the first principal of the universe in which we find ourselves but of which we can know so little. Of this reversal of premises the Romantic poets—especially Coleridge and Blake—were forerunners."

Raine's continuing interest in Blake is interwoven with her growing interest in Yeats. Raine affirms that both speak to the present generation, which fears existential ennui and catastrophic violence. Raine has connected these two great minds in "Yeats's Debt to William Blake," "Yeats, the Tarot and the Golden Dawn" (1972), "Death-in-Life and Life-in-Death: 'Cuchulain Comforted' and 'News for the Delphic Oracle' " (1974), and "Hades Wrapped in a Cloud" (1975). In 1979 Raine again portrayed both Yeats and Blake as falling within the central and primary tradition of British poetry in "From Blake to 'A Vision.' "

Raine had scores of poems published in periodicals before she was thirty, but she refrained from having a volume published, perhaps, on two accounts. One is that T. S. Eliot, rightly or wrongly, did not feel that her poetry was quite ready for publication in a book and dissuaded her. Another is that she was impressed by Virginia Woolf and followed her advice to young writers that they should not rush into print. When the first volume of poetry, *Stone and Flower*, including poems written between 1935 and 1943, appeared in 1943, it revealed a verse stripped bare; her scientific education had taught her to view nature with a microscope. The geometric lines of Barbara Hepworth's drawings which grace the volume are sustained in the structured verse forms. There is a feminine, though cold, beauty depicted in both these women's arts; and they are fully complementary in this volume. The poetry justifies the feeling of a deep and sober honesty about life.

These poems were written when the loss of human love, World War II, and her own personal commitment to Roman Catholicism were her chief concerns. Such poems as " 'See, see Christ's blood streams in the firmament,' " "Desire," and "Christmas Poem" corroborate these values. In "Prayer," the religious need is quietly raised to a higher plane, so that

> this humble joy of living
> May be the golden sowing of heaven's
> harvest,
> The texture of a song, the exaltation
> Of Christ most high, whose love is greatest.

These are not Raine's best poems, for they express desire for, rather than an assurance of, transcendent love. Pantheistic and mystic personifications intimate a lurking, but far from realized, presence.

For instance, in "Cattle Dream" and "Tiger Dream," Raine, by identifying with nature, finds her rare moments of happiness. Throughout these poems, Raine uses many images reminiscent of the major romantics: "starry sky," "jewelled eyes," and "angels feet." "Lyric," echoing Yeats, establishes the union of speaker and nature, while "The Seal-woman" recalls ballad or folk rhythms in a plaintive narrative tone evoking a bare disillusionment with life.

Overall, there is a strong, meditative, sober, and deep sincerity present in the poems. Despite her faith in nature and religion, there is also a strong awareness of death, and the focus on the present is often dark and empty. Consciousness of death tends to offer "the soul's unquenchable desire for God," yet the yearning rather than the possession of the mystical experience dominates.

Living in Time (1946) differs from *Stone and Flower* not in its major focus on nature but in its delineation of detail. Such poems as "Mourning in Spring 1943" appear to be spoken by a woman, and, while playing on the mythological, they recognize, as in "Sun in a Glass," that "Living in time is but to seem—/ Like green leaves on a tree we grow, / But each must fall and fade alone." Mutability in nature dramatizes woman's physiological changes. So, the speaker knows, as in "Sorrow," that human pain and sorrow "is true for everyone . . . / . . . / is deep and vast / . . . / the shape of man." Yet in "The Crystal Skull (II)" the speaker seeks love and finds it in the natural, metaphysical, and religious order of Roman Catholicism:

> Love was in the beginning—the desire
> That made a star,
> Made man.
> All that will remain
> Is desire
> Returning to God.

Love is intimately related to nature, as in "Winter Solstice": "and the sun, / That bridegroom, kind once, again, / Northward to me returning."

The title *Living in Time* is remarkably reminiscent of *Variations on a Time Theme*, a first volume of poetry by Raine's friend Edwin Muir, who suggested that she write from her dreams as he did from his. Time not only controls the speaker's epistemology, it also brings release: when practical worldly time fails, dream time dominates, as in "Pas Perdus": "Dreamer, our father, we are your children too, / Open your worlds within worlds." The dominant tone here, as in the first volume, is reflective. The speaker fears the power of engagement, thereby providing a distancing that shows a reluctance to experience action. This distancing requires a precise delineation of the observed but unwanted feelings. So a metaphysical spirituality, or a poetic expression which transcends the burdens of the collective present (these poems were written in 1941-1945) conveys considerable longing for resolution, as in "London Night":

> The sky above London
> Last night over my house shone with two kinds of being
> . . . .
> I saw Christ's imagined resurrection
> Arrayed behind the real September moonlight.

"Sparrows in March" unites man's yearning, symbolized in nature, and God's omnipotence: "They glint along invisible wires / . . . / So that not one of them tumbles down."

Raine's third volume, *The Pythoness, and Other Poems* (1949), establishes hesitantly but certainly the woman's voice which will show considerable development in her later work; that is, Raine moves toward a voice of her own by discarding the formal structure of Roman Catholicism and expressing the natural embodiments of water, sea, and sky endemic to her Northumberland childhood and to her fantasies of Scotland. At the same time the speaker is a prophetess who addresses her lover and poet, and the god Apollo, whom she serves as priestess. Where earlier poems tried different personae, here the emphasis is on the female voice in each of its passions and nuances. This voice has become steadily stronger and dominates the recent volumes.

The later poetry overcomes sentimentality so that the pain from lack of human love, though real, does not disintegrate into narcissistic self-pity. The early poems sometimes employ phrases or expressions that become in later work a basis for the presentation of human conflict and dynamic interchange often ending in death or dream. The first poems in *The Pythoness, and Other Poems* draw simply from the elementals: "Air," "Water," "Dust," "Fire," and "Storm." In "Storm" Raine uses a quasi-Blakean dialectic to identify God as "the four elements of storm / Raging in the shelterless landscape of the mind" and Shakespeare's Goneril as the "barred doors" of her heart. But all is not feeling in this thin volume. Such poems as "Optical Illusions" focus on the crystal sharp image of the mind as the harbinger and matrix of impulse:

> My house, my rooms, the landscape of my world
> Hang, like this honeycomb, upon a thought
> And breeding-cells still hatch within my brain
> Winged impulses.

Even as early as 1949, Raine began to explore dreams as ways of achieving temporary peace. In "Absolution" the speaker notes "Sometimes the heart is touched with mercy in a dream." "Mandala" integrates art, soul, and life as spiritual love, "as incarnation, seed of the tree." All new possibility turns about "I the infinity where all selves converge / Into the perennial circle of the sun."

Raine was coming increasingly under the influence of Jung's archetypal theories; however, Jung's universal patterns do not guarantee ease, as "Winter Fire" makes clear: "Essential fire is the unhindered spirit / . . . / Whose burning teaches love the way to die." In "Isis Wanderer," however, the speaker claims achievement: "I piece the divine fragments into the mandala / Whose center is the

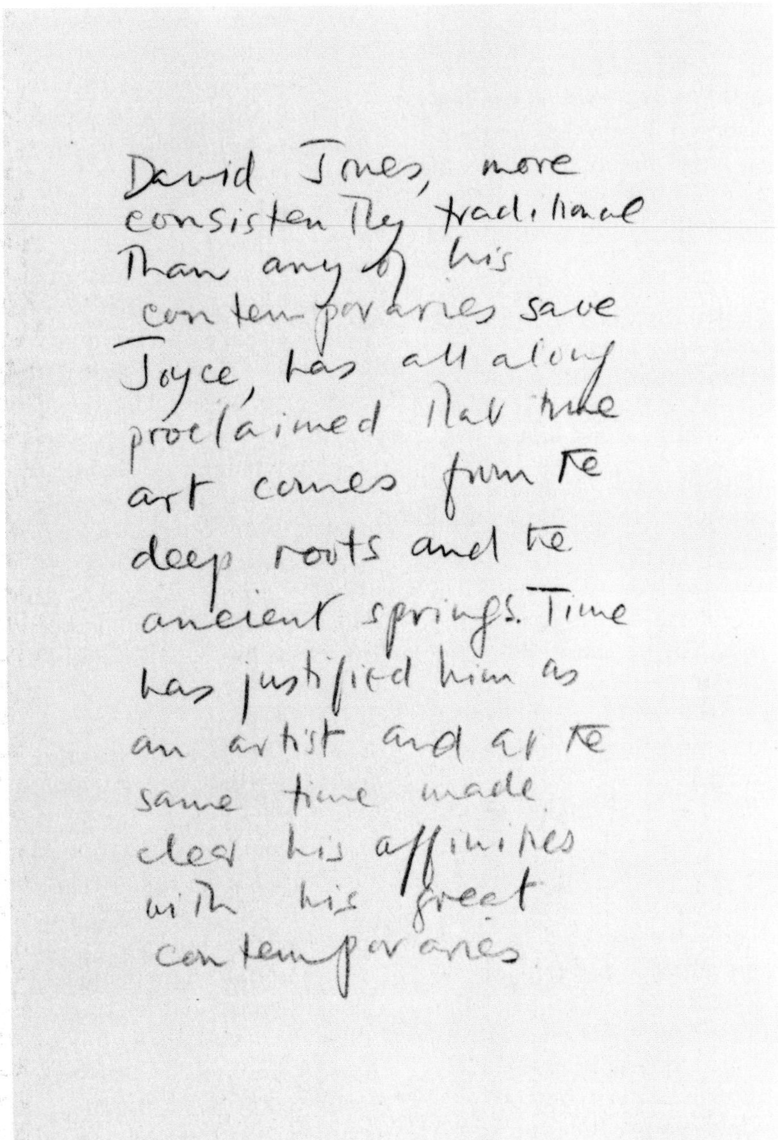
David Jones, more
consistently traditional
than any of his
contemporaries save
Joyce, has all along
proclaimed that true
art comes from the
deep roots and the
ancient springs. Time
has justified him as
an artist and at the
same time made
clear his affinities
with his great
contemporaries

Kathleen Raine's fair-copy manuscript that appeared as the frontispiece for David Jones, Solitary Perfectionist

lost creative power." Yet the completion seems willed. Only through her lover / brother Osiris can Isis feel creativity's surge. The lack, however, is powerfully apparent:

> Oh in the kitchen-midden of my dreams
> Turning over the potsherds of past days
> Shall I uncover his loved desecrated face?

A woman's abandonment dominates "The Transit of the Gods." Once extremely beautiful, "And I who have been virgin and Aphrodite," the speaker goes on to express the problems of being the "woman with an ageing body," waiting "for the last mummer, dread Persephone / To dance my dust at last into the tomb." The goddess-woman-speaker's awareness of the powerful control over all life represented by the pythoness ("I am that serpent-haunted cave / Whose navel breeds the fates of men,") can be juxtaposed against the virgin-woman-mother's defeat in the battle with time in "The Clue":

> For time undoes us, darkness defaces
> The figures of Penelope's night loom.
> Revolving stars wind up the tenuous treads of day-dream
> And the old spinner ravels skeins of death.

Beauty's demise and death dominate women's concerns from time immemorial. For Raine, there is no need, as there has been for other contemporary women poets, such as Sylvia Plath, Adrienne Rich, and Anne Sexton, to reconcile the two existential roles of woman and poet; for in Raine they have always been symbiotically unified. Like other poets of this century, Raine's personal life finds its way into her poetry, not in a confessional, but in a significantly distinctive, fashion.

As in *Living in Time*, lost love resides next to death. In the dream described in "Encounter" the beloved replies to the speaker, " 'This is death's house, where love must learn to die' / And time moved on again, and we were parted." In these poems Raine furthers her stanzaic development by virtue of variable line length, and she employs the voice of the woman who, with trepidation, controls her fate by recognizing and expressing the changes in her. Once again, the Edenic pattern controls both Raine's imaginative thoughts and poetic expression.

The poems found in *The Year One: Poems* (1952) were written during a three-year period, either on the Border or in Scotland, and reveal a loosening of line length, a freer and less concentrated style, and a reinforcing of the importance of nature imagery found in her early volumes. There is an emphasis on the felt correspondences between earthly and spiritual experience. Throughout this volume, her poetry invokes nature's forces as powerful realities often foreboding doom—the apocalyptic fire, the fecund water, the tempestuous air—all relating to the denuding of or joyous increase of creativity. Poetry for Raine is a mode of thought; she has committed herself to an "inspirational" vision of reality whose form is best elaborated through romantic poetic imagery. Poetry is a way of experiencing life: it is a "lyrical form, no less than a certain kind of imagery [that] is archetypal, and emerges when a certain level of consciousness is attained."

The Year One is the first of Raine's books to include the poetic-sequence form, which Raine employs in her later volumes *Six Dreams and Other Poems* (1968) and *On A Deserted Shore: A Sequence of Poems* (1973). The larger form permits her to develop various facets of an image without the constraints of a single situation or one highly charged symbol. It serves in *The Year One* to create an incantatory ritual or a rhythmic revelation. These early sequences show a variety that is exploratory and rich in promise. There is the "Northumbrian Sequence" containing six sections. The eight "Spell" poems struggle with an important concept for Raine, even though these short lines and repetitive incantations do not best convey love in its many guises. In addition, there are "Three Poems on Illusion," "Three Poems of Incarnations," and the death poems. The final poem on nature, time, love, and death utilizes refreshingly open lines, an unornamented style, and an almost conversational tone, which bespeak a fresh and energetic emergent voice. These poems directing experience into emotional inevitability show Raine's developing female voice.

From the beginning her poetry expresses a woman's sorrow, plight, loss, and defeat. She may be favorably compared with other Englishwomen poets such as Edith Sitwell and Anne Ridler. Raine writes about woman's passive waiting, her joyous sexual, emotional, or spiritual awakening, and the effort to develop a disciplined skill when the gender model, her mother, provides no worldly confidence or assertion. "The Marriage of Psyche," though carrying mythic baggage, never falls into a mere retelling of the tale but transforms the moment of awakening into love: "In sleep I was borne here / . . . / But into whose all-enfolding arms I sink in sleep. / He has married me with a ring, a ring of bright water." For Raine, personal love brings alive archetypal power: "Transcendent touch of love summons my world of being."

In this volume, the speaker appears to merge with the objects described so that nature reveals itself in porphyry, in obsidian darkness. This imagery is more than the symbolic language of nature, more than the words of a speaker identifying with cyclical natural patterns; it expresses a point of view about living reality. Nature lives, and man suffers or exists. The voice of the sparrow as speaker in "Northumbrian Sequence" is symbolically and femininely consistent with Raine's personal lifestyle—"I was never still, / I turned upon the axis of my joy, / I was the lonely dancer on the hill"—echoing the archetypal power that sustains her. Love in its human form, though longed for, is either painfully unrequited or destructive: "I weave upon the empty floor of space / The bridal dance, I dance the mysteries / That set the house of Pentheus ablaze." The speaker is caught by the mysterious Dionysian maenads; her frenzied dance leads to the destruction of the male heir. This is a matriarchal realm where men are subordinated, used, and discarded by the female. Also, socially it is a collective unconsciousness that must be brought to awareness by an individual. For Jung says that only through individual consciousness will collective consciousness be gained. The incomplete resolutions in the poem are expressed in the refrains alternating between the first and third, and second and fourth stanzas: "Into my dark I have drawn down his light" and "His radiance shines into my darkest place." Confusion resides in the insecurity of giver or given. In the first and third stanza, she controls; in the second and fourth, he does. But only in the dark is she the recipient of his power. This woman speaker has, as Yeats says of Leda in "Leda and the Swan," "put on his knowledge with his power," but until it is brought to light, or made conscious, it will be used against both men and women. Love is not shared in Raine's poetry nearly as much as it is imposed. She appears to believe, as Blake did, that one needs the extreme to know the mean. Her love poetry shows the dark extremes more than light and transcendence.

The symbolism in *The Year One*, in particular her temptation (she often consciously yearns for an Edenic posture) to view transcendence as imminently real and powerful, reflects a Blakean model. Representative of Raine's best poetry is the loose natural way that nature's cycle and human speech mesh, thereby exposing the roots of her later poetic success. The speaker in this volume is a forerunner of the new prevailing feminine voice, conceived out of a suffering woman's psychic space, haunted either by the loss of or longing for a sexual and spiritual relationship with man. Ultimately the poetry in *The Year One* is fraught with a varied yet genuine feeling for living as a woman in the twentieth century.

The *Collected Poems of Kathleen Raine* (1956) brings together poems Raine selected from her first four volumes of poetry, and its publication afforded critics the opportunity for retrospective assessment. They commented on her "rare and objective mind," her "clarity of insight" and "delicacy of feeling, and a purity of diction," and they found her to be "a meditative, intimate, feminine poet with a real gift." A less frequently noted, but more important characteristic of these poems is Raine's determination to speak in her own voice and to follow the demands of the creative spirit, be it represented by older poets such as Muir, love affairs, or mythic patterns of the goddess. Raine's recognition of self-primacy is all important.

With the publication of *The Hollow Hill and Other Poems* (1965), Raine's first collection of poems to appear for thirteen years and a choice of the Poetry Book Society, critics applauded her pure and chiseled images. The manner, attitudes, and poetic voice are rendered by a purity and fineness of poetic language that is only apparently restricted by a comparatively limited vocabulary and laconic tone. Certainly the visionary and hermetic element perceived in the early poetry continues in this volume, but the symbols gain emotional credence through her own experience and sensibility. The patterned sequence of "Ten Italian Poems," inspired by a visit, graphically reveals this interpenetration of the personal and the archetypal.

Other poetic sequences, "Bheinn Naomh" and "Eileann Chenaidh," in this volume of thirty-odd poems support and reinforce the visionary and hermetic succinctly carved in her earlier work. The book is prefaced by an epigraph from Plato's myth of the cave. Though Plato's and Blake's influences are clearly apparent, in "Night Thought" the conversation of ego and soul recalls W. B. Yeats's "A Dialogue of Self and Soul." The binding relationship of the speaker to the creative spirit asserts a past and future connection in "Eudaimon": "Bound and free, / I to you, you to me." The archetypal pattern of life before birth in "Night Sky" continues to involve the speaker in the realization that she is preformed. Yet though "Bound and bounded," she is joyous "To know the death I must."

The pattern present in "Thaumas" (and "Lachesis") makes clear her personal pain in love:

Kathleen Raine, circa 1951 (BBC Hulton, Picture Post*)*

and you and I,
My love, must suffer patiently what we are,
These parts of guilt and grief we play
Who must about our necks the millstone bear.

At the same time this personal note relies heavily on biblical or Buddhist symbols, or allusions to philosophical and religious writers: Blake, Coleridge, Milton, Dante, Yeats, Hopkins, and Plotinus.

The poems in *The Hollow Hill* begin the direct discussion of her relationship to her mother, a relationship which gives rise to powerful poetry. Explicit development of the mother / daughter relationship follows the earlier oblique exploration through the medium of myth, as in "The Marriage of Psyche." Raine is driven to live out her mother's goal, that is, to become the poet the mother could not become, but in many situations, she must have wondered whether she would really succeed. This drive to become the poet her mother wished her to be is evident also in the later volumes, culminating in *The Oval Portrait* (1977), and it is expressed in the three autobiographies. The poem "Kore in Hades" first sets this pattern: "Mother, daughter, daughter, mother, never / Is now: there is nothing, nothing for ever." In "Childhood Memory" the speaker says that her mother kept her in Edenic innocence:

Dear and familiar face
That beamed on childhood,
Shining on morning fields and flower smile
What emptiness veiled,
Chasms of inhuman darkness veiled.

The other major poetic theme begun in the 1960s and carried into greater prominence in later volumes is Raine's reliance upon dreams as important keys to personal direction. "The Hollow Hill," a six-part poem, is dedicated to Willa Muir, with whom Raine stayed at Swaffham Prior after she gave up her research fellowship at Girton in 1961. It is Edwin Muir's poetry, values, and sensitivity to the manifest permanence of life reflected in dreams that Raine relies on:

One night in a dream
The poet who had died a year ago
Led me up the ancient stair
Of an ancestral tower of stone.
Towards us out of the dark blew such sweet air
It was the warm breath of the spirit, I knew,
Fragrant with wild thyme that grew
In childhood's fields; he led me on,
Touched a thin partition, and was gone.
Beyond the fallen barrier
Bright over sweet meadows rose the sun.

In Raine's as well as in Muir's poetry the movement away from childhood and Eden leads to losing oneself in the labyrinthian complexities of confusion, despair, and disappointment. To find true being requires death and transcendence. As this death must be psychological rather than actual and as the world Raine knows continues to deliver the expected pain and disillusionment, she incorporates Jung's theories of dream interpretation with Blake's visionary convictions and Muir's reliance upon dreams in poetry. Through dream, the poet translates the sacred and eternal for her readers.

Six Dreams and Other Poems (1968) fully manifests the use of dreams in literature. The opening poem, "Written in 1967," establishes the transcendent qualities of dreams and the poet's reliance upon them. The meaning of natural and spiritual objects has been lost in the waking world and is only restored "inviolate in dream." "Dreams" contains six parts revealing an archetypal tale of consciousness. The traditional mythic story of the knight saving the sleeping maiden is inverted. Here it is the woman dreamer with "diamond blade" sheathed "in an old scabbard" before whom the "wounded knight / Stirred as with the first wave of an inflowing tide." Raine's poetic myth of woman's odyssey or search for meaning portrays the woman longing for the spiritual union before she has confronted the primordial power of the archetypal mother.

Knowledge of and longing for the past, together with the relationship of mother and daughter, reinforce the Eve image in "By the River Eden," a three-part poem which depicts the natural environment of Eden from the perspectives of a child and an old woman. The Adam and Eve myth, suggested by the title, plays only around the poem's periphery, for there are no males in this "unchanging scene." The environment of the poem is wholly a woman's world, limited to mother and daughter, and more important, the child is both the mother of the speaker and the speaker. The child marks "pebbles in the sand / . . . / As once I did, and was," while the mother "Was that same child" noticing "the red spots on the yellow mimulus / That nodded in the burn." What has been experienced by one is observed by the other and articulated by the speaker-child. Raine's growing awareness, both of her extended identification with her mother and of her longing for her own poetic voice uncontaminated by the personal or archetypal mother, appears even in maturity as nearly irreconcilable. The poet continues to wonder about the role her mother really played in her compulsion to devote her life not primarily to personal relationships but to poetry.

The Lost Country (1971) has two major sections. The first section of twenty-three poems includes "By the River Eden" and "Ninfa Revisited," both previously published. The second sequence of poems entitled "Dream" includes nine poems, three of which were formerly published in *Six Dreams*. Within the traditional pattern of nature's luminous reality, mythology's archetypal resonance, and dream's essence, Raine documents her many friendships in dedicatory poems. These relationships depend upon their common meeting grounds: love of art, literature, music, and philosophy. Her painful but consuming love for Gavin Maxwell picks up another of the volume's threads, while the return to Eden and her childhood, her need to face old age, and her consuming dreams provide other recurring themes.

Speaking from the far side of youth, her voice, never strident nor harsh, emphasizes woman's natural aging and concomitant changing definitions of living. For instance, "Childhood" centers on age's contentment with the present in its reflection on the past. The poem begins in the immediacy of childhood's innocent solipsism, "I see all, am all, all," and concludes powerfully with the speaker consciously, realistically, and firmly declaring: "Never, never, never will I go home to be a child." The speaker reluctantly realizes the past is dead and gone.

In the three-stanza lyric "Old Age" the speaker, after lamenting she has "seen and known, too much," moves from despair and frustration to complete acceptance of impermanence. Besides the loss of human beings known intimately, the speaker feels saddened that: "Some songs I had of mine, and words of secret power / In chaff of learning lost." The poem begins with the ego's eyes seeing too much and concludes with their vision as the record of a life.

Imagistically and aesthetically, nature dominates in Raine's poetry, symbolizing the growing and changing self. Looking backward and forward, the woman speaker in an untitled poem says: "I felt under my old breasts, this April day" and found a young girl, a Kore or the self, who was tired of the old "winter bark, this toil-worn body." The symbolic relationship of aging poet to young self, born in spring's April in the winter months of the poet's life, powerfully reinforces, obscures, and palliates the importance of the past doting or forlorn mother. The synthesis of the poetic persona of the old woman and the emerging self becomes the focus of the creative faculty of the artist. The aging poet sees that renewal in her own body, not only in the female experience but in the rejuvenated feminine soul. Now instead of giving birth to an infant, this old woman feels the rising breasts of another woman within. This experience is a spiritual birth occasioning both a warning and a promise. For a woman like Raine, the creative faculty is eternally feminine, as the inimitable poet shows: "Young or old / What was I but the story told / By an unageing one?"

On a Deserted Shore, a sequence of 130 poems, plus opening and closing poems, describes the speaker's longing for her departed lover. Raine's own longing for Gavin Maxwell is paramount. The poetry, however, transcends the personal. Nature, death, and dream dominate these anguished poems:

> We walked in the same dream:
> Do you, awake,

Dissolving clouds recall of hills once home
That sheltered us in sleep
Whose desolate ways I tread alone?

Raine's language continues to be philosophical, symbolic, mythological, and visionary, but it is uniquely channeled through the timeless voice of a woman—tender, plangent, mournful, and possessed by love. What emerges in the 1980s as the dominant poetic persona is a projection of the author's self as a continually changing consciousness, in the process of being fully and creatively in the world.

Raine's last five volumes of poetry, from *The Lost Country* through *The Oracle in the Heart* (1980), continue to clarify her relationship to her mother as a condition of her own poetry and her femininity. Central to Raine's responses and their interpretations are various mythic personae—Demeter, Kore, Persephone—through whom she vividly recalls and plumbs the mysteries and paradoxes of her beginnings as child, daughter, and poet. Raine celebrates not only herself as an old woman expressing her fantasy and dreams, but the lives of women of all ages and in particular her elderly mother about whose portrait "The Oval Portrait" was written. In the volume of that title, there are also nine other poems about the daughter's relationship to the mother, or her perception of the mother's life. For Raine, her mother's seventh decade was vitally important. So the poetry reveals the attitudes and feelings of two generations of seventy-year-old women: Jessie Wilkie Raine (1880-1973) and Kathleen Jessie Raine. The feminine voice's progression is from consistent anguished personal doubt and inner conflict to qualified lyrical ease, or from a preponderant early identification with myths to the vitally alive tone of ever-present security grounded in life's cycles.

Two other themes also dominate *The Oval Portrait*: the importance of travel and friends, and the possession of love lost through death. In old age, death surrounds or is the living reality. This fact is poignantly expressed in the short poem "What it is to be old. . . ." Though alive, the woman "dwells" in an almost physical sense on the idea of death as she reflects on her memories of youth and sees them as "dead" realities. The past is existentially dead, yet, in her memory, psychologically alive.

Raine followed *The Oval Portrait*, in which she began to consider her seventieth birthday, with a short, privately printed volume, *Fifteen Short Poems* (1978), in celebration of that event. There she reviews her life:

What have I to regret
Who, being old,
Have forgotten who I am?
I have known much in my time
But now behold
Procession of slow clouds across my sky.

The images of nature and the rhythm of the language point to the actual physical changes of the female and concomitantly to the woman's altering perceptions of life. Now recognizing the love her parents gave her, Raine says:

Dear ones in the house of the dead,
Can you forgive
An old woman who was your proud
Daughter, who now too late
Returns your love?

The past anxieties and rebellions appear to come to a sanguine acceptance of her life.

The most recent volume of poetry, *The Oracle in the Heart, and Other Poems 1975-1978*, dedicated "To my daughter Anna," brings the matriarchal poetic tradition full circle. The movement is from "Mother who made me," to daughter and finally to further daughters in their offspring: "And now my granddaughter is she / Who dreams undying dreams / And greets the high wind on the hills."

In "Spheres" the Platonic themes mingle with those of dream: "if one dreamer dreams all lives / . . . / . . . how vain / Our hopes and fears, since dreams are only dreams," to ask the usual question:

And what if the unsleeping one
Within our dreams with finger's touch
Should stir the strings of music.

Rounding out her career, this volume contains themes that reflect love held but lost, "Occasional Poems" to friends, and "Short Poems" similar in focus (on aging, loss, her mother) and controlled tone to poems in *On a Deserted Shore* and *Fifteen Short Poems*. In fact, some of the stanzas are gathered from earlier poems.

Again, the Paradisal myths of Eden recur in "Eve and the Angel," where she sees the loss of Eden as a person's self-chosen fate. And yet, despite her self-flagellation and despair, in "Fore-Mothers" Raine still relies on Eden: "And yet my dream tells still of Paradise." In the "Oracle of the Heart" she says:

Some other world, some other mode
Of being on the other side of dream

. . . .
. . . how bright a paradise
When the heart loves, or when the mind forgets
Memory's load, year by year laid on us,
And welcomes, as if for the first time and for ever, the glad day.

Raine's voice forcefully articulates the mythic and actual journey of the woman poet from childhood through adulthood into old age. In the twilight of the twentieth century, her most recent poetry provides a significant model: the voice of the old woman as a figure of the self.

Other:

Letters of Samuel Taylor Coleridge, edited by Raine (London: Grey Walls Press, 1950);

"English Poetry at Mid-Century," in *The Arts at Mid-Century*, edited by Robert Richman (New York: Horizon Press, 1954), pp. 214-220;

Selected Poems and Prose of Coleridge, edited by Raine (Harmondsworth, U.K.: Penguin, 1957);

Peter Russell, *Visions and Ruins*, foreword by Raine (Aylesford, Kent: Saint Albert's Press, 1964);

Selected Writings of Thomas Taylor the Platonist, edited, with introductions, by Raine and George Mills Harper (Princeton: Princeton University Press, 1969);

"Poetic Symbols as a Vehicle of Tradition: The Crisis of the Present in English Poetry," in *Tradition and Gegenwart, Eranos-Jahrbuch 37*, 1968 (Zurich: Rhein-Verlag, 1970);

Julian Trevelyan, *A Place, A State, A Suite of Drawings*, includes commentary by Raine (London: Enitharmon Press, 1974);

"Hades Wrapped in a Cloud," in *Yeats and the Occult*, edited by Harper (Toronto: Macmillan, 1975), pp. 80-107;

Rayne MacKinnon, *The Blasting of Billy P. and Other Poems*, foreword by Raine (London: Enitharmon Press, 1978);

Vernon Watkins, *The Ballad of the Outer Dark and Other Poems*, introduction by Raine (London: Enitharmon Press, 1979).

Translations:

Denis de Rougemont, *Talk of the Devil* (London: Eyre & Spottiswoode, 1945);

Paul Foulquié, *Existentialism* (London: Dobson, 1948);

Honoré de Balzac, *Cousin Bette* (London: Hamilton, 1948);

de Balzac, *The Lost Illusions* (London: Lehmann, 1951);

Calderon de la Barca, *Life's A Dream*, translated by Raine and R. M. Nadal (London: Hamilton, 1968; New York: Theatre Art Books, 1969).

Periodical Publications:

"Vernon Watkins: Poet of Tradition," *Texas Quarterly*, 7 (Summer 1964): 173-189;

"Traditional Symbolism in 'Kubla Khan,' " *Sewanee Review*, 72 (Autumn 1964): 626-642;

"The Poetic Symbol," *Southern Review*, new series 1 (April 1965): 243-258;

"The Use of the Beautiful," *Southern Review*, new series 2 (April 1966): 245-263;

"David Gascoyne and the Prophetic Role," *Sewanee Review*, 75 (Spring 1967): 193-229;

"An Essay on the Beautiful," *Southern Review*, 15 (Summer 1979): 524-544.

References:

Hazard Adams, "The Poetry of Kathleen Raine: Enchantress and Medium," *University of Texas Studies in English*, 37 (1958): 114-126;

H. Foltinek, "The Primitive Element in the Poetry of Kathleen Raine," *English Studies*, 42 (February 1961): 15-20;

Frederick Grubb, *A Vision of Reality: A Study of Liberalism in Twentieth Century Verse* (London: Chatto & Windus, 1965), pp. 105-116;

Ralph J. Mills, Jr., *Kathleen Raine: A Critical Essay* (Grand Rapids, Mich.: Eerdmans, 1967);

Derek Stanford, *The Freedom of Poetry: Studies in Contemporary Verse* (London: Falcon Press, 1947), pp. 200-223.

Papers:

The Humanities Research Center at the University of Texas, Austin, has drafts of poems, essays, and material on Blake. The library of the University of California, Irvine, has worksheets and notes for poems written during 1962-1969, as well as drafts and final versions of essays and hardbound volumes containing a holograph journal kept between 1952 and 1969. There are also collections of Raine's papers at the British Library, London; Lockwood Memorial Library, State University of New York at Buffalo; and the University of Victoria.

Herbert Read

(4 December 1893- 12 June 1968)

Ashley Brown
University of South Carolina

SELECTED BOOKS: *Songs of Chaos* (London: Elkin Mathews, 1915);

Eclogues: A Book of Poems (London: Beaumont, 1919);

Naked Warriors (London: Art and Letters, 1919);

Mutations of the Phoenix (Richmond: Leonard and Virginia Woolf, 1923);

In Retreat (London: Leonard and Virginia Woolf, 1925);

Reason and Romanticism (London: Faber & Gwyer, 1926; New York: Russell & Russell, 1963);

Collected Poems, 1913-25 (London: Faber & Gwyer, 1926);

English Stained Glass (London & New York: Putnam's, 1926);

English Prose Style (London: Bell, 1928; New York: Holt, 1928; revised edition, London: Bell, 1942; revised again, 1952);

Phases of English Poetry (London: Leonard and Virginia Woolf, 1928; New York: Harcourt, Brace, 1929; revised edition, London: Faber & Faber, 1950; Norfolk, Conn.: New Directions, 1950);

The Sense of Glory: Essays in Criticism (Cambridge: Cambridge University Press, 1929; Freeport, N. Y.: Books for Libraries Press, 1967);

Staffordshire Pottery Figures (London: Duckworth, 1929);

Ambush (London: Faber & Faber, 1930);

Julien Benda and the New Humanism (Seattle: University of Washington, 1930);

Wordsworth (London: Cape, 1930; New York: Cape & Smith, 1931);

The Place of Art in a University (Edinburgh & London: Oliver & Boyd, 1931);

The Meaning of Art (London: Faber & Faber, 1931); republished as *The Anatomy of Art* (New York: Dodd, Mead, 1932); revised and enlarged as *The Meaning of Art* (London: Faber & Faber, 1936; revised again, 1951);

Form in Modern Poetry (London: Sheed & Ward, 1932; revised edition, London: Vision, 1948);

The Innocent Eye (London: Faber & Faber, 1933);

Art Now: An Introduction to the Theory of Modern Painting and Sculpture (London: Faber & Faber, 1933; New York: Harcourt, Brace, 1937);

The End of a War (London: Faber & Faber, 1933);

Art and Industry: The Principles of Industrial Design (London: Faber & Faber, 1934; revised, 1944; revised again, 1953; New York: Horizon Press, 1954; revised again, London: Faber & Faber, 1956; revised again, 1966);

Essential Communism (London: Nott, 1935);

The Green Child: A Romance (London: Heinemann, 1935; New York: New Directions, 1948);

Poems, 1914-1934 (London: Faber & Faber, 1935; New York: Harcourt, Brace, 1935);

In Defense of Shelley and Other Essays (London: Heinemann, 1936);

Art and Society (London: Heinemann, 1937; New

Herbert Read (BBC Hulton)

York: Macmillan, 1937; revised edition, London: Faber & Faber, 1945; revised again, 1956; revised again, 1967);

Collected Essays in Literary Criticism (London: Faber & Faber, 1938); republished as *The Nature of Literature* (New York: Horizon Press, 1956);

Poetry and Anarchism (London: Faber & Faber, 1938);

Annals of Innocence and Experience (London: Faber & Faber, 1940; revised and enlarged, 1946); republished as *The Innocent Eye* (New York: Holt, 1947);

Thirty-Five Poems (London: Faber & Faber, 1940);

The Philosophy of Anarchism (London: Freedom Press, 1940);

To Hell with Culture (London: Kegan Paul, 1941);

Education Through Art (London: Faber & Faber, 1943; revised, 1958);

The Politics of the Unpolitical (London: Routledge, 1943);

A World Within a War: Poems (London: Faber & Faber, 1944; New York: Harcourt, Brace, 1945);

The Education of Free Men (London: Freedom Press, 1944);

A Coat of Many Colours: Occasional Essays (London: Routledge, 1945; revised, 1956; New York: Horizon Press, 1966);

Collected Poems (London: Faber & Faber, 1946; revised, 1953; Norfolk, Conn.: New Directions, 1953; revised again, London: Faber & Faber, 1966; New York: Horizon Press, 1966);

The Grass Roots of Art (New York: Wittenborn, 1947; London: Drummond, 1947; revised edition, London: Faber & Faber, 1955; New York: Wittenborn, 1947);

Culture and Education in World Order (New York: Museum of Modern Art, 1948);

Coleridge as Critic (London: Faber & Faber, 1949);

Education for Peace (New York: Scribners, 1949; London: Routledge & Kegan Paul, 1950);

Byron (London & New York: Longmans, Green, 1951);

Contemporary British Art (Harmondsworth: Penguin, 1951; revised, 1954; revised again, 1961);

The Philosophy of Modern Art: Collected Essays (London: Faber & Faber, 1952; New York: Horizon Press, 1953);

The True Voice of Feeling: Studies in English Romantic Poetry (London: Faber & Faber, 1953; New York: Pantheon, 1953);

Anarchy and Order: Essays in Politics (London: Faber & Faber, 1954);

Icon and Idea: The Function of Art in the Development of Human Consciousness (London: Faber & Faber, 1955; Cambridge: Harvard University Press, 1955);

Moon's Farm and Poems Mostly Elegiac (London: Faber & Faber, 1955; New York: Horizon Press, 1956);

The Art of Sculpture (London: Faber & Faber, 1956; New York: Pantheon, 1956);

The Tenth Muse: Essays in Criticism (London: Routledge & Kegan Paul, 1957; New York: Horizon Press, 1958);

A Concise History of Modern Painting (London: Thames & Hudson, 1959; New York: Praeger, 1959);

The Forms of Things Unknown: Essays towards an Aesthetic Philosophy (London: Faber & Faber, 1960; New York: Horizon Press, 1960);

Truth Is More Sacred, by Read and Edward Dahlberg (New York: Horizon Press, 1961; London: Routledge & Kegan Paul, 1961);

A Letter to a Young Painter (London: Thames & Hudson, 1962; New York: Horizon Press, 1962);

To Hell with Culture, and Other Essays in Art and Society (London: Routledge & Kegan Paul, 1963; New York: Schocken, 1963);

The Contrary Experience: Autobiographies (London: Faber & Faber, 1963; New York: Horizon Press, 1963);

Lord Byron at the Opera: A Play for Broadcasting (North Harrow: Ward, 1963);

Selected Writings: Poetry and Criticism(London: Faber & Faber, 1963);

A Concise History of Modern Sculpture (London: Thames & Hudson, 1964; New York: Praeger, 1964);

Henry Moore: A Study of His Life and Work (London: Thames & Hudson, 1965; New York: Praeger, 1966);

The Origins of Form in Art (London: Thames & Hudson, 1965; New York: Horizon Press, 1965);

The Redemption of the Robot: My Encounter with Education through Art (New York: Trident Press, 1966; London: Faber & Faber, 1970);

Art and Alienation: The Role of the Artist in Society (London: Thames & Hudson, 1967; New York: Horizon Press, 1967);

Poetry and Experience (London: Vision, 1967);

The Cult of Sincerity (London: Faber & Faber, 1968).

Herbert Read was one of the most distinguished men of letters in his generation, and it is not easy to disengage the poet from the literary critic, the critic of social ideas, the tireless expositor of modern art, or the author of several works of autobiography and fiction. Indeed some of his friends, including Graham Greene, would probably rate his account of his childhood, *The Innocent Eye* (1933), and his novel, *The Green Child* (1935), as prose poems and Read's outstanding "creative" achievements. But Read himself always thought of his verse as the center of his life's work. His poems, written over a period of half a century, run to about 250 pages in the latest collected edition—not a large body of poetry by some standards, but one sufficiently various and accomplished to merit attention.

Read was born on a farm near Kirbymoorside, Yorkshire, in 1893, the son of Herbert and Eliza (Strickland) Read. In later years he made a great deal out of his origins in northern England, and it was no accident that his heroes included Wordsworth and the sculptor Henry Moore. After World War II, when he was a famous international figure, he returned to Yorkshire to live; in fact his house at Stonegrave lies only a few miles from the modest farmhouse where he grew up. His idyllic boyhood is described in precise detail in his memoir *The Innocent Eye*. This book, however, takes him only to his tenth year, when his father died and the farm was sold. He spent a rather unhappy few years at school at Halifax, then went to Leeds, where he worked briefly as a bank clerk. His literary interests were already highly developed, and about 1911 he managed to enter the new University of Leeds. By the time World War I broke out he was writing poetry. Somehow, during his years of active service in the army (he was an infantry officer who was decorated several times), he managed to write his poems and develop rapidly from the apprentice work of his first book, *Songs of Chaos* (1915).

Although Read is not usually included with the poets of World War I, there is good reason to start a discussion of his work with this momentous event. He was not killed in action, as were Isaac Rosenberg and Wilfred Owen; nor did he make the war his main subject, as did Siegfried Sassoon. But he was profoundly affected by what he went through in those four years, and some of his poems registered his response to this experience long afterward. George Woodcock, in the best study of Read written to date, *Herbert Read: The Stream and the Source* (1972), says: "As a theme, war recurred constantly in his poetry; it helped to shape his political and social thought, and even his views on art which, as he came to believe, held the last resort of peace and sanity."

By 1915 Read was beginning to contribute poems to the *Egoist*, the small avant-garde magazine published in London and usually associated with the early work of Pound, Eliot, and Joyce. Read did not meet these men for several years, but he obviously knew about the imagist credo which Pound, especially, represented. For Read imagism was "a new poetic awareness," and in theory he never abandoned its main principles. Certainly the best of his early poems, a group of seven called "The Scene of War" in *Naked Warriors* (1919), are thoroughly imagist, but they are less "pure" than typical imagist poems by Pound or H. D. Such, for instance, is "The Happy Warrior":

> His wild heart beats with painful sobs
> his strain'd hands clench an ice-cold rifle
> his aching jaws grip a hot parch'd tongue
> his wide eyes search unconsciously.
>
> He cannot shriek.
>
> Bloody saliva
> dribbles down his shapeless jacket.
> I saw him stab
> and stab again
> a well-killed Boche.
>
> This is the happy warrior,
> this is he. . . .

As Paul Fussell remarks in *The Great War and Modern Memory* (1975), Read "brutally inverts Wordsworth's celebration of the honorable, well-conducted soldier." One might extend Fussell's observation and point out that Read *depends* on Wordsworth's poem "Character of the Happy Warrior." For one thing, Wordsworth's perfectly regular rhythmic structure (iambic pentameter) is carried over to Read's poem as a kind of ground plan, but by the third line the irregularity has increased. Then at the end Wordsworth's penultimate line is quoted intact, but it is broken into half-lines. Read does not always have such a conventional basis for his rhythm, and it was unlikely that at this time (early 1917) he was aware of one alternative, the controlled free verse that was being developed by Wallace Stevens and William Carlos Williams in the United States. But he was as intent as any of his contemporaries on "making it new." In a fairly late critical book, *The True Voice of Feeling* (1953), which traces the course of English poetry from Wordsworth and Coleridge to Pound and Eliot, he demonstrates the astonishing rhythmic flexibility that set in as early as "The Rime of the Ancient Mariner." Clearly he based his concept of metrical freedom on a long study of his predecessors.

After the war Read settled in London, where he soon secured a post as assistant curator of ceramics and stained glass at the Victoria and Albert Museum. Although he gradually moved into the field of art history and criticism, his literary career continued to occupy much of his time. By 1919 he was a friend of Pound, Wyndham Lewis, Eliot, and others; indeed his friendship with Eliot meant a great deal to both of them. In 1922 Eliot founded the *Criterion*, and for the next seventeen years, while this journal lasted, Read was an unofficial associate editor and the most frequent contributor after Eliot himself. Eliot, it would seem, deliberately established Read as the friendly opponent in an ongoing dialectic of critical ideas: Read represented the "romantic" view (largely descended from Coleridge), Eliot the "classical." But in some ways the two men thought alike. Read, for instance, shared Eliot's admiration for the English metaphysical poets, and in 1923 he stated in his first *Criterion* essay: "Milton perhaps did more to destroy the true tradition of metaphysical poetry than any other agent. . . . in his too forceful fashion he crushed the life out of an only too subtle advance of human consciousness." Where Read parted company with Eliot was on the issue of the romantic poets: for Read the metaphysical tradition in English poetry lasted till Wordsworth. Perhaps he thought of himself, even more than Eliot, as retrieving this tradition. At any rate, the next phase of his verse, which came in *Mutations of the Phoenix* (1923), is heavily indebted to his study of Donne and Chapman.

The title poem, in eight sections, works out some of the implications of Shakespeare's "The Phoenix and the Turtle":

All existence
    past, present and to be
        is in this sea fringe.
There is no other temporal scene.

The phoenix burns spiritually
    among the fierce stars
    and in the docile brain's recesses.
Its ultimate spark
you cannot trace.

This is the poem that fascinated William Butler Yeats, who said (in the introduction to the *Oxford Book of Modern Verse*, 1936), "Herbert Read discovers that the flux is in the mind. . . . The Phoenix is finite mind rising in a nest of light from the sea or infinite. . . ." But the poem is not an unqualified success. Again, as with the early war poems, it has trouble in finding its rhythmic structure or, for that matter, its form in the larger sense. Read had some very considerable poetic virtues, but he lacked the dramatic sense that lies back of Eliot's major poems such as "Gerontion" or even the Ariel poems, "Marina" and "Journey of the Magi." This is apparent in the most ambitious piece in *Mutations of the Phoenix*, "John Donne Declines a Benefice," a dramatic monologue which makes considerable demands on his talent:

Once I was Jack Donne, burned by the vast
Energies of an eager lust,
And leapt with zeal
Into the mirage of a limpid pool
Which my impinging body crackt
Into a crater, a sulphurous hole
Of faithless lechery.
I reattained the fresh atmospheres
By the perfection of a fair fantasy,
This heart's concern, a sun to shine
In the night of lust.

One might have supposed that this poem would have some of the dramatic energy of Donne, or even Browning, but the speech which is the poem is hardly located in any precise situation that the reader can grasp; it is probably closer to the eloquent speeches of Chapman.

Rather better is "The Analysis of Love," in thirteen sections; this poem gains something from being written in fairly conventional though varied quatrains; at times it attains a quiet dignity that is impressive:

Since you are finite you will never find
    The hidden source of the mind's
                                        emotion;
It is a pool, secret in dusk and dawn,
    Deep in the chartless forest life has
                                        grown.

By 1926, when Read's first *Collected Poems* came out, his admirers included Eliot, Yeats, and Allen Tate, who included him with a group of young poets (among them Laura Riding and Archibald MacLeish) who, Tate thought for a time, might be the basis for a new school of metaphysical poetry. But, all things considered, this "metaphysical" phase of Read's poetry disappointed expectations. George Woodcock is surely correct in saying that "The impression created by the long poems of *Mutations of the Phoenix* is that Read is trying to work out a metaphysical system in verse, rather than utilizing an existing system (as Dante did that of St. Thomas

Aquinas) as the armature on which to build a poetic vision."

Herbert Read's "big" poem is "The End of a War" (1933), published by Eliot in the *Criterion* and included by Yeats in the *Oxford Book of Modern Verse* (1936). This poem is his fullest response to the horrors of a war which had ended almost fifteen years earlier. By the time he wrote it, he had published two remarkable prose narratives, *In Retreat* (1925) and *Ambush* (1930), and he had frequently reviewed books on the subject in the *Criterion*. The poem is based on an actual incident: a German officer deceived a British battalion into a virtual slaughter on 10 November 1918, the day before the Armistice; a young French girl in the village was killed and dismembered; and a British officer survived to be haunted by the incident. These three characters speak, but not to each other: the officers have meditations which frame a dialogue between the body and the soul of the murdered girl. The poem touches on many issues, some of them philosophical: the violation of innocence, the worship of the State, the ecstasy of battle. The British officer wakes up to the end of the war on Armistice Day, and he accepts "God's purpose":

> Evil can only to the Reason stand
> in scheme or scope beyond the human mind.
> God seeks the perfect man, plann'd
> to love him as a friend: our savage fate
> a fire to burn our dross
> to temper us to finer stock
> man emerging in some inconceived span
> as something more than remnant of a dream.

"The End of a War" is deeply felt, and it continues to have its admirers (among them Graham Greene), but it somehow does not engage Read's most intense poetic powers; in some ways it is *willed* into being as a kind of modern triptych, which may have been inspired by his study of painting. It would seem that Read had virtually deserted his early imagist credo; but in fact he was just about to write some of his finest short poems.

The best selection of Read's poetry is found in *The Faber Book of Modern Verse*, edited by Michael Roberts in 1936. Although Roberts included "The Analysis of Love," he drew attention mainly to the short poems that Read began writing in the early 1930s, poems that have both the sharp observation of the imagist phase and a new firmness of rhythm. One of these is "A Northern Legion": another war poem, ostensibly about a Roman legion in northern Britain during the decline of imperial power, but

Sir Herbert Read, circa 1956 (BBC Hulton)

indirectly about what was happening in Europe during the early 1930s:

> Eleven days this legion forced the ruin'd fields, the
> burnt homesteads and empty garths, the broken arches
> of bridges: desolation moving like a shadow before them, a
> rain of ashes. Endless their anxiety
>
> marching into a northern darkness: approaching
> a narrow defile, the waters falling fearfully
> the clotting menace of shadows and all the multiple
> instruments of death in ambush against them.
>
> The last of the vanguard sounds his doleful note.
> The legion now is lost. None will follow.

As the 1930s moved on toward world disaster

again, Read was often involved with events at the public level: he served on committees, wrote political pamphlets in favor of his rather gentle anarchist program, signed protests. This was a situation that more than likely would have done violence to his poetry, or at any rate have dulled it in the interests of political propaganda. But in fact two of his finest poems were written about the Spanish civil war and Hiroshima.

These poems might be described as Blakean, as though they came out of some modern *Songs of Innocence and of Experience* (1794). (In 1940 Read called his autobiography *Annals of Innocence and Experience*.) These are the first and third stanzas of "A Song for the Spanish Anarchists":

> The golden lemon is not made
> but grows on a green tree:
> A strong man and his crystal eyes
> is a man born free.
>
> . . . .
>
> And men are men who till the land
> and women are women who weave:
> Fifty men own the lemon grove
> and no man is a slave.

George Woodcock, himself an anarchist, points out that this poem "does not express directly a single anarchist doctrine, but in that moving picture of bucolic liberty all we need to know about the anarchist communes in Spain and the faith by which they lived is in fact implied."

Even more remarkable is "1945," which might be called the first poem of the atomic age:

> They came running over the perilous sands
> Children with their golden eyes
> Crying: *Look! We have found samphire*
> Holding out their bone-ridden hands.
>
> . . . .
>
> The children came running toward me.
>
> But I saw only the waves behind them
> Cold, salt and disastrous
> Lift their black banners and break
> Endlessly, without resurrection.

Here the poet has found his form by *reference* to Blake's songs: Blake, probably the first poet anywhere to admit children into the foreground of his poems and to judge experience from the child's point of view. But this is a rather disillusioned poem of the mid-twentieth century, and the point of view is that of an adult.

It was World War II that provided the occasion for Read's finest poetry, and not only the short poems such as "1945" and "To a Conscript of 1940," which is a meditation that takes the author back to his own entrance into military life in 1915. The short poems of this period tend to group themselves around "A World Within a War," which might be considered the closest thing to a masterpiece by this writer. It was published almost simultaneously by Allen Tate in the *Sewanee Review* and by Eliot through Faber and Faber. This poem in five sections perhaps owes something to Yeats in its larger form: it moves from one section to another through contrasts of stanza and tone; the mode is essentially meditative rather than dramatic, and one feels that Read has found his voice here in a way that he never quite did in the longer poems of the 1920s. The poem is set at Broom House, near Beaconsfield, which the poet had designed and built. But most of the time during the 1930s he lived close to the center of his public activities in London. Now, during the war, this "secular and insecure retreat" becomes a momentary point of stability in his life. The poem exhibits considerable variety of tone, for instance in the Keatsean evocation of the setting:

> For years the city like a stream of lava
> Crept towards us: now the flow
> Is frozen in fear. To the sere earth
> The ancient ritual returns: the months
> Have their heraldic labours once again.
> A tractor chugs through frozen clods
> And gold buds bead the gorse
> In coppices where besom-heads are cut.

It gradually builds up to a climax which embodies Herbert Read's favorite phrase, "the sense of glory," which recurs so often in his prose, a phrase which for him symbolizes the great potentiality of human existence:

> The sense of glory stirs the heart
> Out of its stillness: a white light
> Is in the hills and the thin cry
> Of a hunter's horn. We shall act
> We shall build
> A crystal city in the age of peace
> Setting out from an island of calm
> A limpid source of love.

But this momentary vision (which Herbert Read as anarchist has worked for) gives way to the "ravening death" which threatens to descend even here, "In a house beneath a beechwood / In an acre of wild land." This long poem must be read in its entirety to make its effect, which is cumulative. It is, as Tate said in 1963, "not only a great war poem but a great poem on a great subject: the impact upon the contemplative mind of universal violence, whether the violence be natural or man-made." (Tate's own "Seasons of the Soul," composed during the early 1940s, has much in common with "A World Within a War.")

Read continued to write his poems in the midst of a life that grew increasingly devoted to public causes, especially art and education—he was eventually knighted by the British government—but his best creative period was over. On two occasions he tried to move into verse drama without much success. In retrospect he reminds one of Arnold more than any other English writer, with his sense of idealism and public duty, his special kind of humanism; and as poet he also resembles Arnold in his occasional successes which take place, as it were, within a prose setting. There is much that is admirable about his work in poetry as well as his criticism.

References:

Paul Fussell, *The Great War and Modern Memory* (New York & London: Oxford University Press, 1975);

Robin Skelton, ed., *Herbert Read: A Memorial Symposium* (London: Methuen, 1970);

Henry Treece, ed., *Herbert Read: An Introduction to his Work by Various Hands* (London: Faber & Faber, 1944);

George Woodcock, *Herbert Read: The Stream and the Source* (London: Faber & Faber, 1972).

Papers:

An important collection of Read's papers is held by the University of Victoria, British Columbia.

Edgell Rickword

(22 October 1898-15 March 1982)

Alan Young

SELECTED BOOKS: *Behind the Eyes* (London: Sidgwick & Jackson, 1921);

Rimbaud: The Boy and the Poet (London: Heinemann, 1924; New York: Knopf, 1924);

Invocations to Angels and The Happy New Year (London: Wishart, 1928);

Love One Another: Seven Tales (London: Mandrake Press, 1929);

Twittingpan, and some others (London: Wishart, 1931);

War and Culture: The Decline of Culture Under Capitalism (London: Peace Library, 1936);

Collected Poems of Edgell Rickword (London: Bodley Head, 1947);

Fifty Poems: A Selection of Edgell Rickword (London: Enitharmon Press, 1970);

Gillray and Cruikshank, by Rickword and Michael Katanka (Aylesbury: Shire Publications, 1973);

Edgell Rickword: Essays and Opinions 1921-31, edited by Alan Young (Cheadle: Carcanet, 1974);

Behind the Eyes: Poems and Translations (Manchester: Carcanet, 1976);

Edgell Rickword: Literature and Society: essays 1931-1978, edited by Young (Manchester: Carcanet, 1978).

The reputation of Edgell Rickword as poet has been overshadowed to some extent by his better-known achievements as critic and editor. It has been limited too, no doubt, by the relative shortness of his poetry-writing career. His first collection appeared in 1921. Ten years later he had all but abandoned poetry. Only a small number of Rickword's verse satires and even fewer of his lyric poems have been published during the past fifty years. And yet Rickword the poet—as much as Rickword the brilliant literary and social critic or Rickword the outstanding editor—has been one of the models of creative intelligence in British culture since the end of World War I.

John Edgell Rickword was born in Colchester, Essex, England, where his father, George Rickword, was the town's first borough librarian. He attended the Royal Grammar School in Colchester and from there went directly into the army in autumn 1916. After a short period of service in Ireland he saw front-line action in France as a subaltern in the Royal Berkshire Regiment. He was wounded twice—losing the sight of one eye—and he won the Military Cross for distinguished service. Rickword's time in France helped to speed and to modify the development of his literary resources which, until then, had been largely imitative of such late-romantic writers as Tennyson and Swinburne. He taught himself French by reading French novels, but it was a young English poet who had the greatest influence on his early work. As he explained in an interview broadcast by the BBC's Radio 3 in 1977, it was above all the war poetry of Siegfried Sassoon which first showed him how the language of ordinary speech might be used in order to communicate terrifying battle experiences: "As I was going off leave back to France [in 1918] I picked up Sassoon's *Counter-Attack* which was devastating because he was the first poet I knew of who dealt with war in the vocabulary of war. And of course his satires were tremendous. This gave me a start towards writing more colloquially, and not in a second-hand literary fashion."

After the armistice Rickword was invalided out of the army. The following year he went up to Pembroke College, Oxford, to read French literature, but he left the university after only four terms there. He was disenchanted by Oxford's archaic literary studies, and, like so many other young men of his generation, he had been made prematurely wise and painfully disillusioned by war. Aged twenty-two and married, he started to earn a living as a free-lance literary reviewer for newspapers and for such well-known periodicals as the *New Statesman* and the *Times Literary Supplement*.

His first collection of verse, *Behind the Eyes* (1921), contains some war poems which exhibit the same colloquial directness and harsh irony as are to be found in Sassoon's war verse. Additionally these poems, including the much-anthologized "Trench Poets," "Winter Warfare," and "The Soldier addresses his Body," possess darker energies and a daring wit which were part of Rickword's already distinctive style (though, at this stage, he was still echoing his chosen masters, the English metaphysical poets and, at times, the French symbolists).

Love poems in this first volume range in mood and style from simply expressed tenderness for and sensual delight in the loved one to a fretful weariness with love viewed, in an archaic fin de siècle manner, as remote abstraction. Some of the love lyrics share the mysteriously dreamlike and disturbing moods of Rickword's few Rimbaudian short

Edgell Rickword in his study, Halstead, Essex, 1978

stories. None of the poems, however, has quite the bitterness and sudden violence of the lyric tales which were collected in 1929 under the title *Love One Another*.

The plainest and yet, perhaps, most moving language in *Behind the Eyes* is to be found in Rickword's compassionate laments for lost love or, more generally, for the human condition which entails inevitable loss. These simple elegies, especially "Regret for the Depopulation of Rural Districts" and "Regret for the Passing of the Entire Scheme of Things," exhibit within their helpless pessimism a degree of positive universal sympathy characteristic of the central recurring theme in all Rickword's writing—namely, the common natural bond which all human beings share. This profound sense of fellowship with ordinary people separates Rickword from most of the modernist writers who were his better-known contemporaries.

The early maturation of Rickword's critical faculties is remarkable enough; the range and balanced sureness of his critical perceptions are astonishing. His book *Rimbaud: The Boy and the Poet* appeared in 1924. This pioneering psychological study, which was described by Enid Starkie in the "Rimbaud Number" of *Adam* (1954) as the best book on Rimbaud to have appeared in any country by the mid-1920s, contained some fine translations by Rickword of the French poet's work. The book reached the provocative conclusion—one, some may think, prophetic in relation to Rickword's own subsequent career—that Rimbaud's abandonment of poetry was merely an early stage in a journey to greater imaginative maturity, which was to be reached at last when he became man-of-action and explorer in Abyssinia.

When Rickword's *Essays and Opinions 1921-31* came out in 1974, Clive James, reviewing the book for the *New Statesman*, wrote: "Rickword's mind and sensibility were of a piece—a brilliant unity reflected in his aesthetic, which did not admit of any easy division between style and substance." It is true also that the poets selected by Rickword for special analysis—Donne, Swift, Eliot, Baudelaire, Corbière, Laforgue, and Rimbaud—were those whose qualities of mind and sensibility as well as technical adventurousness and control were closest to his own creative aesthetic. His poetic manifesto for the mid-1920s included a total rejection of the prevailing sentimental romanticism in English poetry with its built-in emotional and linguistic taboos. As antidote, his essay "The Re-Creation of Poetry" (1925) prescribed the reintroduction of "negative emotions" into English poetry. Such emotions are to be

Lieutenant Edgell Rickword, circa 1917

found, for instance, in the nonromantic yet full individual satires of Swift, and they could provide the "means for a whole series of responses in parts of the mind which have been lying fallow for nearly two hundred years." In the same essay he made the comment, typical of his humanistic version of modernity, that "to himself the poet should be in the first place a man, not an author."

In 1925, with Douglas Garman and Bertram Higgins, Rickword launched a new literary periodical, the *Calendar of Modern Letters*; "The Re-Creation of Poetry" was, in fact, one of its earliest editorial pronouncements. Set up partly as a rival to Eliot's neoclassical the *Criterion*, the *Calendar* was certainly one of the finest literary reviews to be published in England, or perhaps anywhere, during this century. The balance which was achieved between superb creative work and lively, intelligent criticism is probably unique. Contributors included D. H. Lawrence, E. M. Forster, Edwin Muir, Robert Graves, John Crowe Ransom, Hart Crane, Allen Tate, as well as many writers in translation. The criticism included Rickword's notoriously trenchant "scrutiny" of the popular dramatist Sir James Barrie, as well as many more counterblasts against effete contemporary poets. The "Scrutinies," which were critical analyses of both underrated and overrated contemporary artists, led to the publication of two collections edited by Rickword—*Scrutinies* (1928) and *Scrutinies, Volume II* (1931). F. R. Leavis included a selection from the *Calendar*'s critical pages in *Towards Standards of Criticism* (1933), and he adopted "Scrutiny" as the title of his own influential critical review.

Many of the poems of Rickword's next collection, *Invocations to Angels and The Happy New Year* (1928), had first appeared in the *Calendar*, and they exhibit the tough intellectual qualities of that periodical. Metaphysical wit, sharp irony, sternly controlled verse forms, and the plainest diction are to be found in most of the lyric verses in *Invocations to Angels*. Many of the poems are far from simple to understand, however. There was obviously in Rickword's personality throughout the 1920s an increasingly anguished struggle to come to terms with personal tragedies and with a growing world-weary disillusionment and near-total despair.

The poet's delight in the world-illuminating magic of language is found only rarely, though most memorably, in "Terminology"—the first poem in the 1928 volume. A few love poems carry echoes of the innocent and gentle pleasures expressed in *Behind the Eyes*, but suffering and pain gradually overwhelm the private realms of lovers as insidiously as they do the social world around the lovers. "Absences" is a beautiful and profoundly moving three-part lament for a loved one—the poet's wife—but it is a rare exception to the prevailing universal bleakness of vision. In spite of the overall formal control, in many poems Rickword's images pulsate suddenly from the intimate and suburban to the cosmic and cosmopolitan, from finer human aspirations to our animal, and often beastly, origins. Rickword traces much of the angry unpleasantness of his second book of poems to his awareness that the social situation was worsening all the time and that "nothing could be obtained really without suffering somewhere else."

This developing sense of widespread social injustice created such bewildered antagonisms within the poet that some of his most energetic verses express anger against and mocking hatred for everything human, including himself. "Rim-

Edgell Rickword in 1961 with a bronze head made of him during the 1920s

baud in Africa" and "Theme for *The Pseudo-Faustus*" are just two of several poems in which deeply felt self-loathing and nihilistic disdain for the whole world are vividly combined.

The modern city, its whores and punks as well as the coarseness of the lives of all its other inhabitants, is savagely castigated in other poems. *The Happy New Year*—a wry verse drama, complete with presenter, chorus, and troupes of dancing girls—develops the theme of London's spiritual decadence in ways which call to mind both Eliot's postwar verse satires and, more interestingly, the political theater of Auden and Isherwood of the 1930s. By 1928, indeed, it was clear that Rickword's lyric impulse was deserting him almost completely and that he was moving already in the direction of political satire. Several critics have suggested that Rickword's poetry and criticism both failed at the time when he became associated with Marxism. Rickword denies this connection and gives a less sinister explanation: "One had given up dreaming, I suppose. I think dreaming is a very important factor in getting the imagery of poetry, the atmosphere. One tends to become so logical over twenty-five or twenty-six. One has to be logical to get along. You can, of course, live in very simple circumstances in a hut, and good luck! But that didn't suit me temperamentally. I like company and booze and so on."

Rickword's third and final book of verse, *Twittingpan, and some others*, appeared in 1931. The style is now entirely satirical, and the volume contains some memorable barbed attacks on establishment figures (including T.S. Eliot and certain well-known journalists) and on prevailing modes in the arts. The best-known poem in the collection is "The Encounter," which introduces the character Twittingpan, a purveyor of all the latest fashions in contemporary avant-garde art. The humor here is as keen and observant as ever, but the general tone of the book is far less intense than that of *Invocations to Angels*. Even the satirical vein in Rickword's verse was to give out eventually, but not before he had written one of the most effective and vigorous verse satires of the 1930s.

Rickword joined the Communist party in the early 1930s, and he became editor of *Left Review* at the beginning of 1936. His poem "To the Wife of any Non-Interventionist Statesman" appeared in *Left Review* in 1938; it is arguably the most successful political poem of the period, and it has been translated into many languages. In it Rickword prophesied, with nightmarish accuracy, how British cities would in time suffer the same fate as Spain's Guernica, which had been bombed by Fascist planes. The guilt lay with those British politicians whose upper-class upbringing gave them arrogant contempt for the masses and made them, with cowardly opportunism, attempt to appease the Fascist bullies and butchers instead of joining the common struggle against them.

During the war years and after Rickword wrote some superb social and literary criticism, including studies of the war poets of World War I, John Milton, and English radical thinkers of the early nineteenth century. Toward the end of the war he was invited to become editor of *Our Time*, a literary review which tried to create bridges, without condescension, between the arts and common people. During this period he wrote very little poetry of distinction, though he turned again to the writing of verse in later years; each of his collections published during the past thirty years included one or two new lyrics which reveal all the former lyrical tenderness and formal control undiminished. He had taken an active role in revising earlier poetry and prose, too, though without modifying any of his social or political opinion as they were expressed in his work at the time of first publication.

It is probably a pointless exercise to speculate about consequences for the development of British poetry had Rickword continued to write political poems after 1930. One critic who knew Rickword well from the late 1920s, Jack Lindsay, has argued: "If Edgell with his strong Baudelairian sense of the city had continued to compose and develop we should not have been left defenceless against the takeover by the Audens and Spenders in the thirties." Certainly in Rickword English poetry might have had a radically minded poet with actual roots in earlier literary modernism, but, as Rickword himself pointed out, his giving up of poetry when he did was not an act of volition, like Rimbaud's. Instead, he admitted candidly, it was a sort of artistic failure. But Rickword's actual contribution to the development of English poetry is undervalued even now, in spite of the fact that several selections from and collections of his poems have appeared at regular intervals since the end of World War II. Rickword's eyesight failed completely in his last years, though he was working on his memoirs up to the time of his death.

Rickword's work stands foursquare in English tradition, but it is in that tradition revolutionized by the same shaping forces of modernism which transformed Eliot's poetry. Rickword, with an intelligence and sensibility fully responsive to both French poetry and to English, opened up new paths for English poetry during the decade after World

War I. New generations of poets and readers are beginning to see that this modest, self-effacing poet and critic had much to teach. To be valued above all is his lesson that "to himself the poet should be in the first place a man, not an author." He certainly followed his own advice. As David Holbrook wrote (about Rickword's most caustic poetry of the late 1920s): "It strikes home, because underlying it is the tragic acceptance of man's situation, and the governed urbanity, civilisation and joy of a sensitive, responsible poet."

Other:

Scrutinies by Various Writers, collected by Rickword (London: Wishart, 1928);

François Porché, *Charles Baudelaire*, translated by Rickword and Douglas Mavin Garman as John Mavin (London: Wishart, 1928);

Aristophanes, *Women in Parliament (Ecclesiazusae)*, translated by Jack Lindsay, foreword by Rickword (London: Fanfrolico Press, 1929);

Scrutinies, Volume II by various writers, collected by Rickword (London: Wishart, 1931);

Marcel Coulon, *Poet under Saturn: The Tragedy of Verlaine*, translated, with an introduction, by Rickword (London: Toulmin, 1932);

A Handbook of Freedom: a record of English democracy through twelve centuries, edited by Rickword and Lindsay (London: Lawrence & Wishart, 1939; New York: International Publishers, 1939);

Christopher Caudwell (Christopher St. John Sprigg), *Further Studies in a Dying Culture*, edited, with a preface, by Rickword (London: Bodley Head, 1949);

Radical Squibs and Loyal Ripostes: Satirical Pamphlets of the Regency Period, 1819-1821, selected and annotated by Rickword (Bath: Adams & Dart, 1971);

Ronald Firbank, *La Princesse aux soleils; AND Harmonie . . .* , translated into French by Rickword (London: Enitharmon Press, 1974).

Interviews:

Ian Hamilton, "A Conversation with Edgell Rickword," *Review* (London), 11-12 (July 1964): 17-20;

Alan Young and Michael Schmidt, "A Conversation with Edgell Rickword," *Poetry Nation* (November 1973): 73-89;

John Lucas, "An Interview with Edgell Rickword," *Renaissance and Modern Studies*, 20 (1976): 5-13.

Bibliography:

Alan Munton and Alan Young, "Edgell Rickword," in *Seven Writers of the English Left: A Bibliography of Literature and Politics, 1916-1980* (New York: Garland, 1981), pp. 25-81.

References:

David Holbrook, "The Poetic Mind of Edgell Rickword," *Essays in Criticism*, 12 (July 1962): 273-291;

Jack Lindsay, *Fanfrolico and After* (London: Bodley Head, 1962);

Alan Munton, ed., "Edgell Rickword at Eighty: A Celebration," *Poetry Nation Review*, 9: supplement, i-xxxii.

W. R. Rodgers

(1 August 1909-1 February 1969)

John Wilson Foster
University of British Columbia

BOOKS: *Awake! and Other Poems* (London: Secker & Warburg, 1941); republished as *Awake! and Other Wartime Poems* (New York: Harcourt, Brace, 1942);

The Ulstermen and their Country (London & New York: Longmans, Green, 1947);

Europa and the Bull and Other Poems (London: Secker & Warburg, 1952; New York: Farrar, Straus & Young, 1952);

Ireland in Colour (London: Batsford, 1957; New York: Studio Publications, 1957);

Essex Roundabout (Colchester: Benham, 1963);

Collected Poems (London & New York: Oxford University Press, 1971);

Irish Literary Portraits: W. B. Yeats, James Joyce, George Moore, George Bernard Shaw, Oliver St. John Gogarty, F. R. Higgins, AE (London: British Broadcasting Corporation, 1972; New York: Taplinger, 1973).

W. R. Rodgers was one of only two Irish poets of his generation who enjoyed a substantial British and American reputation, the other being Louis MacNeice, a fellow Ulsterman. In the 1940s and 1950s Rodgers worked for the British Broadcasting Corporation in London and was a friend of MacNeice and also of Dylan Thomas, whose poetry Rodgers's occasionally resembles. Rodgers has suffered a sharper decline in reputation than his two friends, but, because of a few remarkable poems and a historical importance as a post-1930s romantic, he continues, and rightly, to find representation in anthologies of twentieth-century British and Irish verse.

The son of Robert Rodgers, who worked for an insurance company, and Jane McCarey Rodgers, William Robert Rodgers was born in Belfast into an Ulster Presbyterian (or Scots-Irish) family and had the puritan upbringing then widespread in the North of Ireland. His parents were, as the Ulster phrase has it, "good living," and they barred Shakespeare, full-length mirrors, and alcohol from their home. "Sunday dinner was cooked on Saturday," he recalled, "and the Sunday boots were polished the night before, and profane books and music were put away till Monday, and nothing, absolutely nothing, was allowed to disturb 'the Day of Dreadful Rest' as we restless children called it." In his poetry and later career, one can find ample evidence of Rodgers's reaction, early and late, against this upbringing, but there is evidence too, certainly in the early career, of its lasting influence and even benefit.

In 1931 Rodgers graduated from Queen's University, Belfast, with an honors B.A. in English literature, and after some hesitation he entered the neighboring Presbyterian theological college. He was ordained a minister in January 1935. Although he was interested in poetry during his years in college, Rodgers did not write his first poem until he was twenty-eight. "I was schooled," he explained, "in a backwater of literature out of sight of the running stream of contemporary verse. Some rumours of course I heard, but I was singularly ignorant of its extent and character. It was in the late 'thirties that I came to contemporary poetry, and I no longer stood dumb in the tied shops of speech or felt stifled in the stale air of convention." It was reading Auden, Spender, and MacNeice that triggered the release of verse: "I was particularly taken by Auden's work. I thought, well, if Auden can write in this very irregular way and rhythm, I'll have a go at it myself, so then I started."

Awake! and Other Poems, his first volume, contained the poems Rodgers wrote between 1938 and 1940. The book was sent to press in 1940, but the first printing was destroyed by enemy action. The book appeared the following year to enthusiastic acclaim, and the poet was heralded by some as a new Auden. The spendthrift and joyous use of language was, and is, the immediate and arresting quality of Rodgers's verse. "Always the arriving winds of words / Pour like Atlantic gales over these ears," one poem begins, and the reader, like the poet, is an astonished host to lines both buoyed and weighted by alliterations, assonances, puns, and breakneck rhythms and charged with exclamatory and imperative urgency. This new poet believed that for the poet words lead to ideas (whereas for the prose writer the process was reversed), a belief he later ascribed to Yeats, whose early line "Words alone are certain good" might be the motto of Rodgers's entire output. The power of words emanates in the beginning from their spoken effect: "I feel strongly that poetry should be read aloud. So often nowadays words are treated like children that should be seen and not heard. But I think poetry should be heard. As Yeats once said to a friend, he said, 'If you are writing poetry, write it as if you're shouting to a man on the other side of the street and he has to hear you.' "

The poems in *Awake! and Other Poems* are self-consciously Irish in spirit and carry, not always gracefully, the burden of Irish tradition, of Joyce, Yeats, and others. "The faculty of standing words or ideas on their heads—by means of pun, epigram, bull, or what-have-you—is," he later claimed, "a singularly Irish one. . . . To the English ear, which likes understatement, it is all rather excessive and therefore not quite in good taste. But to the Irish mind which likes gesture, bravado, gallivanting, and rhetoric, it is an acceptable tradition." It was indeed lapses in taste for which the English poet and critic Stephen Spender took Rodgers to task amid his general praise.

The dangerous qualities of relentless verve and dash Rodgers shares with his contemporaries George Barker and Dylan Thomas, and this suggests that they are not "singularly Irish." The theory of reality that lay, largely inchoate, behind Rodgers's use of language was one that developed in reaction to the dogmatic assurances of the 1930s, in contrast to which were the attractive linguistic experiments of Hopkins:

> I'd rather have the fickle run of things
> Like rivers any day. Stone is static,
> Is pat. Water alone is love, all else
> Is law and fixity.

We might hear Hopkins's "Pied Beauty" echoed in these lines from "The Fountain in the Public Square"; the Jesuit poet was early seen by critics as an influence on Rodgers. It has since been claimed that Rodgers was already a poet before he read Hopkins, but it is difficult to credit this assertion when we happen upon these lines from "Ireland":

> And Donard
> Where, high over all hanging,
> the strong hawk
> Held in his eyes whole kingdoms,
> sources, seas

Kenneth Rexroth suggested that Rodgers's long vowels and nasal music were "counter Hopkins," a poet whose "baroque irritability" expressed itself instead in staccato vowels and plosives. Rexroth suggested, not entirely convincingly, Andrew Marvell as a more helpful comparison.

Rodgers saw his native island as the supremely fickle and dappled country, and in "Ireland," one of his best-loved poems, he identifies himself and his poetry with it:

> O these lakes and all gills that live in them,
> These acres and all legs that walk on them,
> These tall winds and all wings that
> cling to them,
> Are part and parcel of me, bit and bundle,
> Thumb and thimble.

Yet life in Ulster has always been at one crucial level twofold, Protestant and Catholic, and Rodgers grew up vividly aware of this duality: "Gay goes up and grim comes down. The Puritan pepper and salt, if it

Dust jacket for Rodgers's posthumously published collection

looked like granite tasted like drama. It had two sides to it. Everything in Belfast had two sides." Later he ascribed this duality to the entire island, and he considered that all the subjects of his celebrated radio profiles displayed a "bi-partisan Irish background." One guise of this two-sidedness is the conflict in Ireland between the rebel and authority. "Directions to a Rebel" is a disturbing poem that goes against the grain of Rodgers's philosophy in advocating, apparently without irony, a fanatical and stonelike refusal to compromise or succumb to the fickle demands of others. It is as though the poem were a reply to the last stanza of Yeats's "Easter 1916" in which we are told that "Too long a sacrifice / Can make a stone of the heart." It has been reported that Brendan Behan told Rodgers that an Irishman in Parkhurst Gaol was sure the poem had been written for the IRA and had pinned it to the prison wall.

Since he so closely identified Ireland and poetry, it is not surprising that Rodgers considered poetry itself to originate in a violent duality: "I think all poetry is written out of conflict, out of a clash between two opposites, that that is where articulation comes from." That he has a somewhat crude version of Yeats's antinomies in mind is made clear when he adds, "As Yeats said, 'Out of the quarrel with ourselves we make poetry.' " Duality pervades all aspects of Rodgers's poetry. He delights in the kind of tandem phrases that open "Ireland" ("Thumb and thimble," "foils and fenders"). Two words will violently coalesce—"grotesticled," "tiptoadying," "eiderdowntrodden"—an unfortunate device (Joyce notwithstanding) to which Barker was also prey. Metaphors tend to be explicit and symmetrical: "scathing winds of hate," "bull's eye of truth."

In lines that Spender might have been thinking of when he said that Rodgers sometimes departed from good taste, Rodgers wrote in "Summer Holidays,"

> Note, now, how in us
> Each thing resists and buoys its opposite,
> Goodness is foreskinned and frisked by Evil

(At his worst, personified abstractions stalk through Rodgers's pages as obtrusively as through eighteenth-century satire; there is in Rodgers a vulgar allegorical urge that may have had its literary origin in the didacticism of 1930s verse. On such occasions one feels that the intellectual and creative processes have been short-circuited.) The troubling duality of marriage is captured more tastefully and successfully in "Paired Lives," a brief and almost metaphysical poem in which, like swing doors, husband and wife present "one smooth front / Of summed resistance" to outsiders, while each door in reality

> Is hung on its own hinge
> Of fear and hope, and in
> Its own reticence rests.

According to Rodgers, the wish to see life in terms of opposites can on occasions be counterproductive and premature, as when in "To the Preacher" the minister neatly separates good from evil, only to have "Bother" (fickleness) step in. This poem hints at a degree of discomfiture Rodgers felt as a minister, though by all accounts he was held in high esteem by his spiritual charges. For a dozen years, 1935-1946, he was minister at Cloveneden Presbyterian Church, Loughgall, County Armagh. The area has a rich and chromatic landscape that clearly inspired the poet. It was during his ministry, in 1936, that he married Marie Waddell, a doctor, who bore him two daughters. Outwardly happy, Rodgers in fact gradually tired somewhat of Loughgall's pastoral calm and of the burdens of his calling. The obtrusively apocalyptic theme and tone of many of the poems in *Awake! and Other Poems* associate him with Thomas and Barker and even with J. F. Hendry, Henry Treece, and Nicholas Moore, the poets of the apocalyptic anthologies (*The New Apocalypse*, 1939; *The White Horseman*, 1941), but more specifically they register a response to the opening salvoes of World War II (the volume's American title was *Awake! and Other Wartime Poems*), which from Loughgall could almost sound inviting. Many of the pieces are explicitly war poems, written by a noncombatant innocent of bloodshed, whose knowledge is filtered through newspapers and newsreels. The war is an unavoidable if distant fact that can spoil an otherwise ebullient day ("Stormy Day"), but, as "Escape" suggests, it can also attract the poet who feels isolated in a rural pocket of existence:

> You will be more free
> At the thoughtless centre of slaughter than
> you would be
> Standing chained to the telephone-end while
> the world cracks.

The apocalyptic voice in *Awake! and Other Poems* assumes various tones—rebuking, admonitory, euphoric, evangelical. They seem attempts on

Rodgers's part to resolve the growing oppositions in his life, to which marital unrest was now adding itself. The resolutions are in many poems premature, but that is understandable in a writer new to the exigencies of verse. Spender's reaction to *Awake! and Other Poems* seems, despite the passage of time, the just one: "With more economy he would be a wholly delightful, if somewhat spasmodic poet. With more thought the development of his poems would be strong and sweeping. As it is, his lines tend to arrest the attention, and then fail to develop beyond what is vivid and striking."

Before he left Loughgall for good, Rodgers made a visit to Dublin in 1941, during which he was initiated into that city's literary life. It was a trip fated to make him even more dissatisfied with his life in Armagh—"the lashings and leavings and lovings of good talk about writers and writing that was my first visit to Dublin." He met Austin Clarke, Geoffrey Taylor, Frank O'Connor, John Betjeman (on a wartime posting), and Sean O'Sullivan. There was a more melancholy visit to Oxford in 1943. The Rodgerses took to quarreling violently and often drunkenly, and Marie Rodgers became prey to bouts of anxiety and hysteria. She underwent analysis in Oxford, and the diagnosis was schizophrenia, a malady from which Rodgers, poet of dualities, seems himself not entirely free; he too visited a psychoanalyst and took to recording his troubling dreams.

Back in Ireland, Rodgers was approached in 1944 by Louis MacNeice, who was recruiting writers for the BBC's new Third Programme, and he offered Rodgers a job in London. Those were exciting times in British radio, for the BBC extended to writers the kind of lucrative sanctuary American colleges later extended, and the Third Programme was an uncompromising venture in highbrow culture. "Sound radio was expanding," Rodgers later wrote, "experiment was in the air, and with the inception of the BBC 'Third' Programme a sort of Indian summer of the imagination evolved." Yet Rodgers hesitated before accepting MacNeice's offer and resigning his ministry in 1946, breaking not only with the Church and with Loughgall and with Ireland, but also with Marie Rodgers, who was to study psychoanalysis in Edinburgh, and the children, who were to stay in Ulster.

His job as scriptwriter and producer for the BBC enabled Rodgers to live the life of a poet alongside MacNeice, Thomas, and others. In return, his love of poetry enriched his professional work, and he produced verse programs, including "Easter in Europe" and "Europe in Festival." "The Return Room," broadcast in 1955 (again in 1966 and 1969), has been called one of the most successful evocations of childhood in Belfast. As a producer and scriptwriter, Rodgers is chiefly remembered, however, for his series of broadcast profiles of the major twentieth-century Irish writers, a series that began in 1947 and ended in 1965. *Irish Literary Portraits*, an enormously entertaining transcript of these profiles, was published posthumously in 1972. The broadcasts are of interest in several respects. Rodgers interviewed those who had known his subjects (such as Yeats, George Moore, and Joyce), then edited the recordings, generally removing off-the-cuff responses, into collages that sometimes created the illusion of two informants (recorded perhaps miles and months apart) conversing in the same room. This method of radio portraiture was later in BBC circles called the "Rodgers technique." What the informants alleged or revealed about the great Irish writers has frequently been of intrinsic interest to literary critics as well as to delighters in literary gossip.

The broadcasts seem very much an extension of Rodgers's creative philosophy. They show Rodgers's enduring concern for the spoken word, a concern that nourished his great admiration for Ireland's traditional storytellers such as Peig Sayers to whose *An Old Woman's Reflections* he contributed an introduction in 1962. They even permitted Rodgers to imply his own (unscriptural) version of truth as a fickle, contrary thing: "In the end I was as well-informed about the contributors as I was about the subjects I discussed with them. I could tell fairly well how trustworthy or untrustworthy each one was on a particular point. As a Presbyterian clergyman I had learned to listen to a husband's and a wife's talk, each contradictory in every respect, yet each compulsively true and equally convincing. Everybody's story, I decided, was true, the only thing wrong was 'relationship'—the only thing that mattered. These radio 'portraits' are really studies in relationship, and a 'lie' therefore could be as informative as the 'truth,' and the myth as substantial as the reality. I knew very well before I finished how far any man's statement was trustworthy or factual, but truth is not the whole of life, or facts the whole of truth, and these people were, like myself, as honest as the day is long, and no more."

Rodgers's second volume of poems, *Europa and the Bull*, was published in 1952. It was a more ambitious if less brash performance than the first. There is a good deal of sensuality in the verse, and on occasions a worldly and confident treatment of sexuality. "The Net," for example, is cleverly poised in the manner of the Caroline poets between metaphysical conceit and innocent relish. A less abashed paganism (Rodgers's reaction against a Calvinist rearing, perhaps) pervades the ambitious narrative poems "Europa and the Bull" and "Pan and Syrinx," as well as "Apollo and Daphne." All three poems celebrate lives paired in sexual pursuit. Sexual flight is another provocative clash of desiring opposites and is a variation on the theme of hunting, a sport in which Rodgers became interested while living in Armagh. (In "Beagles," from *Awake! and Other Poems*, he identified himself with the quarry.) Each of these poems is a tour de force, partly because Rodgers's language was peculiarly suited to plotting what in "Pan and Syrinx" is called "The subterfuge of flesh." They are weaker in meditation than in celebration and narrative and tend to support Kathleen Raine's observation on Rodgers's style when she read the volume: "it is never dull, never flat—except when he has something to say of a philosophic nature, when he drops into bathos—but this seldom happens."

When he turned from classical to Christian episodes, Rodgers was barely orthodox and barely more contemplative. "Lent" is a powerful poem in which Mary Magdalene, "that easy woman," goes back to her old ways after two days of lenten self-denial and in doing so makes possible the rebirth of the dead Christ, who has been planted in her womb. Reborn, he returns to her the raiments and scents of her true and sensual self. Other poems, too, reinterpret New Testament episodes, for example "The Journey of the Magi," which plots another pursuit in a similar but more voluble, less successful fashion than Eliot's poem of the same title. In general, despite his penchant for parable and allegory, Rodgers in these Christian poems replaces the scriptural simplicity of his chosen episodes with a greater and untidier humanity. "This was a rough death," he begins a poem in "Resurrection: An Easter Sequence," "there was nothing tidy about it."

Rodgers was a laureate of dishevelment, and he loved this quality in Ireland's history and places. One of the most charming poems in *Europa and the Bull* has in its first line a perfectly employed Ulster dialect word:

> There is a through-otherness about Armagh
> Of tower and steeple,
> Up on the hill are the arguing graves
> of the kings,
> And below are the people.

In the poet's imagination, however, the through-other history of Celt and Dane, Norman and Saxon resolves itself into the union of his love for the city:

> There is a through-otherness about Armagh
> Delightful to me,
> Up on the hill are the graves of the
> garrulous kings
> Who can at last agree.

In the same way, scattered memories of dappled Ireland race "Round the mind's bowl, till at last all drop, / Lumped and leaden again, to one full stop" ("Ireland"). It is the poet who creates, in love and in the finitude of his poem, order in disorder.

The simple philosophic goal of Rodgers's life appears to have been at-one-ment, but it had to be reached through the illusion of chaos and the creative union of opposites. Life is, or ought to be, a kind of perpetual trinity in which "The idiosyncratic I" constantly confronts the through-otherness of the world, their union producing the son, Christ, love, truth, poetry, a union that heals "The split that was in man since time began."

In London Rodgers was happy with his semibohemian life, though pained by the guilt he felt in leaving his children. Marie Rodgers qualified as a psychoanalyst, but her mental health deteriorated; she attempted suicide, and then died suddenly in 1953. By that time Rodgers was living with Marianne Helweg; they had fallen in love with each other when he had first come to London, and she was the wife of Laurence Gilliam, Head of Features at the BBC, at whose home Rodgers stayed for a time. They married in 1953 and went to Essex, then Suffolk, to live. There was a daughter by the marriage, born in 1956. The influence of the love affair can perhaps be seen in the feelings of desire and guilt that pervade *Europa and the Bull*. In London Rodgers's life and art were at an altogether higher pitch than in Loughgall, and the public acknowledgment of this in career terms was his election in 1951 to the Irish Academy of Letters to fill the vacancy created by the death of Shaw.

Perhaps in Rodgers's case there was a price to pay for his delayed but later spasmodic happiness. Although Rodgers was productive of scripts, reviews, and essays, his only biographer, Darcy O'Brien, is aware of a mere six poems that Rodgers wrote between 1952 and his death in 1969: one poem every three years. In an interview published in 1966 Rodgers recalled, without intentional self-irony it seems, an incident: "I remember once having a drink in a pub in London; Louis MacNeice was there and Dylan Thomas and a few other poets and

Louis said to one of the poets, he says, 'Are you writing anything at the moment?' A kind of flush came over the other man's face and he says, 'Oh, Louis, I'm far too happy to write poetry.' "

However, one of his last poems was both eloquent and prophetic. "Home Thoughts From Abroad" is a backhanded greeting to the Reverend Ian Paisley, the political firebrand who played a prominent role in the troubles of Northern Ireland and who was, when the poem was written, achieving his notoriety. "I think of that brave man Paisley," Rodgers writes, using a two-edged Ulster adjective,

> eyeless
> In Gaza, with a daisy-chain of millstones
> Round his neck . . . .
> . . . .
> . . . I like his people and I like his guts
> But I dislike his gods who always end
> In gun-play.

For Rodgers, Paisley is the last of the Irish giants who, after their passing, live in shrunken form in the memories of the people. A pity, this diminution, but necessary, especially nowadays, and in the light, or darkness, of Paisley's "borborygmic roars / Of rhetoric." The poem is a eulogy that would prefer to be an obituary.

Rodgers repeatedly professed in his poetry a hatred of humbug and hubbub, and in "Words" (the second of his two poems of that title) he spoke of "the empty shop-fronts of abstraction," "the vendors of puffs," and "the tricks and tags of every demagogue." A certain measure of irony has to be registered here, for Rodgers's loud insistence on the orality of words, his repeated anticipation of apocalypse, and his rhetorical use of language all have their preacherly and demagogic aspect. Perhaps in his disgust with that side of Paisley and of the other preachers he assailed in his work we can see a degree of self-discomfort. And perhaps it was an attempt to deflect attention away from the rhetoric of his poetry that caused Rodgers to complain—for complaint it seems to be—that "when one first starts to write, and when one's first published, it is rather a grievance and a great disappointment to find that all critics write about the technique and the craft of your writing, but they never mention the ideas which you are trying."

In 1966 Rodgers became writer-in-residence at Pitzer College in Claremont, California. He was at first content, but then began to bridle at the bureaucratic demands of the American college system. He liked California, however, and wished to stay for the full three years of his visa, and when he was let go by Pitzer he secured a part-time post at California State Polytechnic College. He was taken ill in November 1968 and because he had no medical insurance was taken to the Los Angeles County General Hospital, where he died on 1 February 1969, surrounded by the poor and oppressed whom he befriended during his last days. His ashes were flown to Belfast and were taken to Cloveneden churchyard for burial.

Rodgers's eulogy for his dead friend Louis MacNeice, "A Last Word," has the punning eloquence we associate with MacNeice himself and with such an Ulster inheritor of MacNeice's gift as Derek Mahon. Yet Rodgers, though he was until the late 1960s one of the few Ulster poets of Irish or British stature, has had few imitators in Ulster or Ireland. It is partly because of literary fashion (after his romantic verse came the reaction of the Movement), partly because "his great virtue," as Rexroth claimed, "is that he speaks for himself." In the first poem of his first volume, he saw poetry and life as a "through-train of words," and he wondered "To what happy or calamitous terminus / I am bound, what anonymity or what renown." From his modest output of poems at least a dozen will live in the anthologies, and literary fashion may later rescue others from neglect. Stephen Spender, stressing the poet's individuality, has the last word: "Mr. Rodgers is an uneven poet, sometimes vivid and visual, sometimes vulgar. Everyone though should read him, because he is a poetic phenomenon."

References:

Terence Brown, *Northern Voices: Poets from Ulster* (Dublin: Gill & Macmillan, 1975), pp. 114-127;

Darcy O'Brien, *W. R. Rodgers: 1909-1969* (Lewisburg, Pa.: Bucknell University Press, 1970);

Peter Orr, ed., *The Poet Speaks: Interviews with Contemporary Poets* (London: Routledge & Kegan Paul, 1966), pp. 207-212;

Kenneth Rexroth, Commentary on Rodgers in *The New British Poets: An Anthology*, edited by Rexroth (Norfolk, Conn.: New Directions, 1949), p. xxi.

Isaac Rosenberg

(25 November 1890-1 April 1918)

Thomas F. Staley
University of Tulsa

BOOKS: *Night and Day* (London: Privately printed, 1912);
Youth (London: Privately printed, 1915);
Moses: A Play (London: Privately printed, 1916);
Poems, edited by Gordon Bottomley (London: Heinemann, 1922);
The Collected Works of Isaac Rosenberg, edited by Bottomley and Denys Harding (London: Chatto & Windus, 1937);
Collected Poems, edited by Bottomley and Harding (London: Chatto & Windus, 1949; New York: Schocken, 1949);
The Collected Works of Isaac Rosenberg: Poetry, Prose, Letters, Paintings, and Drawings, edited by Ian Parsons (London: Chatto & Windus, 1979; New York: Oxford University Press, 1979).

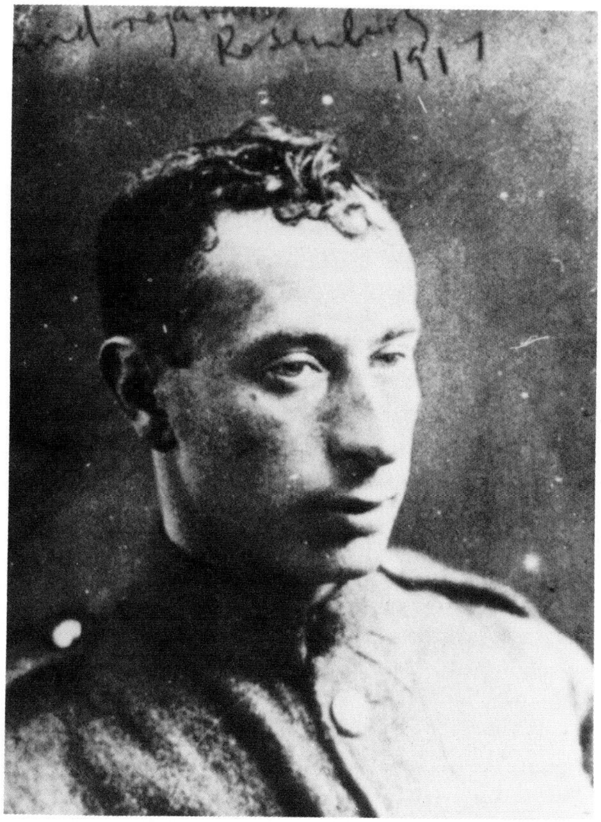

Isaac Rosenberg (London Borough of Tower Hamlets Amenities Committee)

Isaac Rosenberg was killed in battle on 1 April 1918 while on patrol out of the trenches south of Arras on the Somme. His body, however, was never found. Three days before, he had written to Edward Marsh and enclosed the last poem he was ever to write. By the time it arrived Rosenberg was dead. In this last poem, "Through These Pale Cold Days," he expressed not only the familiar themes of the "trench poets," sterility and deadness, but a longing for peace and tranquillity, the deeper concerns that preoccupied his later poetry. The themes and subjects of Rosenberg's mature work clearly identify him as a war poet, and he has been compared to Wilfred Owen, Rupert Brooke, Charles Sorley, and Julien Grenfell, but outside of their common experience of World War I, Rosenberg's life was as separate and distant from theirs as the English social and class system could make it.

Rosenberg was born in Bristol on 25 November 1890, to Dovber Rosenberg (who in England changed his first name to Barnett) and Hacha Davidov Rosenberg (also called Hannah or Chasa). Isaac's father, a Lithuanian, had emigrated from Russia and the family had only shortly arrived. The family moved to London's Jewish ghetto, where so many Jewish families had settled to avoid persecution in Eastern Europe. Barnett Rosenberg opened his own butcher shop, but it was subsequently confiscated by the authorities, and for most of the rest of his life he worked as an itinerant peddler. The poverty of the Rosenberg family was constant, and young Rosenberg's solace was a close and religious family and his talent and opportunity for education. By 1907 he was attending evening classes at Birkbeck College and had begun seriously the first part of his artistic career. He won the Mason prize in 1908 for nude studies and would go on to win other student awards. But his painting was done in the evenings, for during the day he spent long hours as an apprentice to an engraver.

Rosenberg's promising talent as a painter was recognized by a few people, who sponsored him at the Slade School, the important center for developments in English painting. The year of his entering at the Slade, 1911, was an important one for English art. Postimpressionism had only recently intruded into the insular art world of London, and the effects of Roger Fry's exhibition in 1910 had disturbing implications at the Slade. Rosenberg commuted from Whitechapel each day during his first year and as an outsider was probably less disturbed by these developments than most. His strongest affinity was for William Blake, whom he considered the finest artist England ever had. He admired Blake most of all for the "inspired quality" of his work, but he respected him almost as much for his "noble idea of form." There was, however, in Rosenberg's own early work a marked Pre-Raphaelite influence and little originality in anything he did during this early period at the Slade.

By 1912 Rosenberg had moved into a studio on Hampstead Road and that spring wrote to Laurence Binyon, Keeper of Prints and Drawings at the British Museum. He had sent Binyon some pages of verse and asked him for his criticism. Binyon was an established poet and thought well enough of Rosenberg's work to invite him for a visit. Mark Gertler, Rosenberg's fellow student at the Slade, has recalled how Rosenberg became increasingly interested in poetry during his first year. He also sent poems to the *English Review* and received encouragement from the editor, Austin Harrison. At his own expense he published in 1912 a twenty-four-page pamphlet, *Night and Day*. The poems in this thin volume are much like his early paintings in that they lacked originality, a distinctive voice. The influence of Shelley and Keats, especially Keats's "Endymion," is clear, and even the imagery is suffused with Keatsian diction. But the subject matter seems to probe beyond this influence to go backward in search of a more comprehensive vision of the world.

Rosenberg continued to study at the Slade. In 1913 he competed for the Prix de Rome, and his works were exhibited at the Imperial Institute Galleries in South Kensington. More important, however, in March of that year he met Edward Marsh, having been introduced to him by Mark Gertler. Marsh, the editor of *Georgian Poetry*, was a central figure in the art and literary world of London; Marsh was to become the most important literary personage in Rosenberg's short career. He purchased Rosenberg's paintings, encouraged him to write, and introduced him to many of the most important painters and writers in London, among them the imagist T. E. Hulme, Henri Gaudier-Brzeska, and Ezra Pound. Rosenberg came into contact with imagism at this time, and although he ultimately rejected it as a form inappropriate for his art, its purposes and techniques were felt. Imagism was not, however, solid and sinewy enough for Rosenberg's particular vision.

As Rosenberg's fledgling work in art and poetry was only beginning to attract some attention, his health began to break. He had spent part of the summer of 1913 on the Isle of Wight with David Bomberg, but by the winter of 1913-1914 his cough worsened, and by June he had sailed to Cape Town, South Africa, to stay with his sister, Minnie, and try to recover his health. He returned to England in March of 1915, seven months after the war with Germany had begun. The intellectual and cultural energy and excitement of the prewar years had dissipated. Rosenberg was without prospects and finally enlisted in the army in October 1915 to join the Bantam Battalion of 12 Suffolk Regiment, 40th Division. Upon his return to England earlier that year Rosenberg had, again at his own expense, published another pamphlet. He obtained the money by selling three paintings to Edward Marsh. The pamphlet was titled *Youth* and contained those poems of the two previous years that he wished to preserve.

Youth is an interesting collection both in its theme and arrangement. Rosenberg by this time had grown increasingly wary of the romantics and had grasped some of the aims of the imagists. Poetry, Rosenberg had come to feel, must attach

Self-portrait by Rosenberg, 1912 (Estate of Isaac Rosenberg, Imperial War Museum)

itself to "the earthly and the definite," beginning with "external notice" and moving to "human notice." The design of *Youth* begins with idealism and with the longing for experience mingled with fear. But by "Midsummer Frost" the imagery struggles with Rosenberg's confusion or uncertainty of the next direction, as experience intrudes on youthful idealism. Another poem in this section, "Wedded," symbolizes, as its title suggests, the loss of innocence and the strangeness of intimacy with another. And the last three poems, which form "The Cynic's Lamp," reveal the poet rejecting physical experience for a higher spiritual realm. Physical love is not lost in these last poems, and, in fact, as in Donne, it is celebrated, but also, in affinity with the later Donne, the poet seeks actively for God. The imagery in these poems is more complex and sustained than the imagists', and Rosenberg seeks out a kind of symbolic ordering for the rites of passage from youth to experience. In spite of some seeming confusion of purpose and a random willingness to expand some themes and leave others undeveloped, these poems reveal Rosenberg's clear if unsteady growth as a poet, albeit one who is still searching for his deeper subject matter.

Frail, very small, and in poor health, Rosenberg was probably one of the least likely candidates to enter the service. His enlistment did, however, provide some income for his impoverished family. And despite his contact with such prewar luminaries as Pound, Binyon, Gordon Bottomley, and that great patron of the arts, Edward Marsh, there was little to commend him as either painter or poet. His initial career in the army went as expected; he was surrounded by Jew-baiters, constantly forgot or lost his equipment, and was regarded as a "harmless freak." But in these unlikely circumstances of the last few years of his life, he became a poet of importance.

One crucial aspect of Rosenberg's life that cannot be ignored is his Jewishness. He early abandoned the immigrant Yiddish culture of his youth, but never the larger Jewish themes which he drew directly from biblical sources. His verse play *Moses*, a work that bridges his military experience, probes deeply the most sublime visions of Judaism. His Moses is able to summon the energies within himself for rebirth through his great personal desire. It is this central and pervasive Jewish element that brought an enormous prophetic urgency to his war poetry and gave it a character removed from the work of the other war poets. The patriotism of Brooke is countered by the individual will; the fatalism of Owen is countered by a redemptive vision seen through the power and longing of the Old Testament and the sensibility and personal vision of the modern isolato.

Rosenberg, in many ways the least prepared for war of all the trench poets, was in other ways the best prepared. He came to France, for example, without any illusions. Although he had yet to see the bloody, gory world that would envelop him, he knew he was not playing in a holy and glorious rite but rather he was entering a "land of ruin and woe." The following stanza in "From France" juxtaposes what in his imagination he might have expected from France with what the war had wrought there:

> The spirit dreams of café lights,
> And golden faces and soft tones,
> And hears men groan to broken men,
> 'This is not life in France.'

Self-portrait by Rosenberg (Estate of Isaac Rosenberg, Imperial War Museum)

As the war went on and Rosenberg's experience grew, his poetry held not only the deep pity and tender feeling of Wilfred Owen, but, as Maurice Bewley maintained, passed "beyond it into something new. He is aware that the suffering of war is too great to be comforted, and he cannot mistake pity for succor; in his poetry, suffering achieves something like classical composure." Heroic moral strength and stoicism characterize these later poems of Rosenberg's such as "Dead Man's Dump." This poem is deeply concerned with suffering, and yet the pain and agony never burden the classic poise, the detachment, clarity, and composure of the inquiring itself.

Nor do we find in Rosenberg's poems the bitterness which became characteristic of the later poems of the war. His most famous poem, for example, "Break of Day in the Trenches," although suffused with a subtle and penetrating irony, is, in the end, a deeply human statement about man's consciousness, its durability and its expressive feeling.

Before he went to war Rosenberg was beginning to reveal in his poetry the deep affinity he had with his Jewish roots in the Old Testament and the traditions of the Jewish people. The tragedy of war gave these affinities full expression in his later poems, and as war became the universe of his poetry, the power of his Jewish roots and the classical themes became the source of his moral vision as well as his poetic achievement.

References:

Marius Bewley, *Masks & Mirrors* (London: Chatto & Windus, 1970);

Joseph Cohen, *Journey to the Trenches* (London: Robson, 1975);

Isaac Rosenberg 1890-1918, A Poet Painter of The First World War (London: National Book League, 1975);

Jean Liddiard, *Isaac Rosenberg: The Half Used Life* (London: Gollancz, 1975);

Jean Moorcroft Wilson, *Isaac Rosenberg* (London: Cecil Woolf, 1975).

Siegfried Sassoon

Margaret B. McDowell
University of Iowa

BIRTH: Kent, England, 8 September 1886, to Alfred Ezra and Theresa Georgina Thornycroft Sassoon.

EDUCATION: Clare College, Cambridge University, 1905-1907.

MARRIAGE: 18 December 1933 to Hester Gatty; child: George.

AWARDS AND HONORS: Military Cross, 1916; bar for Military Cross, 1918; Hawthornden Prize for *Memoirs of a Fox-Hunting Man*, 1929; James Tait Black Memorial Prize for *Memoirs of a Fox-Hunting Man*, 1929; D.Litt., Liverpool University, 1931; Commander, Order of the British Empire, 1951; Honorary Fellow, Clare College, Cambridge University, 1953; Queen's Gold Medal for Poetry, 1957; D.Litt., Oxford University, 1965.

DEATH: Heytesbury House, near Warmister, Wiltshire, 3 September 1967.

SELECTED BOOKS: *Poems*, anonymous (London: Privately printed, 1906);

Orpheus in Diloeryium, anonymous (London: Privately printed, 1908);

Sonnets and Verses, anonymous (London: Privately printed, 1909);

Sonnets, anonymous (London: Privately printed, 1909);

Twelve Sonnets (London: Privately printed, 1911);

Poems (London: Privately printed, 1911);

Melodies, anonymous (London: Privately printed, 1912);

Hyacinth: An Idyll (London: Privately printed, 1912);

An Ode for Music (London: Privately printed, 1912);

The Daffodil Murderer, as Saul Kain (London: Privately printed, 1913);

Amyntas (London: Privately printed, 1913);

Discoveries (London: Privately printed, 1915);

Morning-Glory, anonymous (London: Privately printed, 1916);
The Redeemer (Cambridge: Heffer, 1916);
To Any Dead Officer (Cambridge: Severs, 1917);
The Old Huntsman and Other Poems (London: Heinemann, 1917; New York: Dutton, 1918);
Counter-Attack and Other Poems (London: Heinemann, 1918; New York: Dutton, 1918);
Picture Show (Cambridge: Privately printed, 1919); enlarged as *Picture-Show* (New York: Dutton, 1920);
The War Poems of Siegfried Sassoon (London: Heinemann, 1919);
Recreations (London: Privately printed, 1923);
Lingual Exercises for Advanced Vocabularians (Cambridge: Privately printed, 1925);
Selected Poems (London: Heinemann, 1925);
Satirical Poems (London: Heinemann, 1926; New York: Viking, 1926; enlarged edition, London: Heinemann, 1933);
Nativity (London: Faber & Gwyer, 1927; New York: Rudge, 1927);
The Heart's Journey (New York: Crosby Gaige/London: Heinemann, 1927);
To My Mother (London: Faber & Gwyer, 1928);
Memoirs of a Fox-Hunting Man, anonymous (London: Faber & Gwyer, 1928); as Sassoon (New York: Coward-McCann, 1929);
A Suppressed Poem (N.p.: Unknown Press, 1929);
Memoirs of an Infantry Officer, anonymous (London: Faber & Faber, 1930); as Sassoon (New York: Coward-McCann, 1930);
In Sicily (London: Faber & Faber, 1930);
Poems, as Pinchbeck Lyre (London: Duckworth, 1931);
To the Red Rose (London: Faber & Faber, 1931);
Prehistoric Burials (New York: Knopf, 1932);
The Road to Ruin (London: Faber & Faber, 1933);
Vigils (Bristol: Douglas Cleverdon, 1934; enlarged edition, London: Heinemann, 1935; New York: Viking, 1936);
Sherston's Progress (London: Faber & Faber, 1936; Garden City: Doubleday, Doran, 1936);
The Complete Memoirs of George Sherston (London: Faber & Faber, 1937); republished as *The Memoirs of George Sherston* (New York: Doubleday, Doran, 1937);
The Old Century and Seven More Years (London: Faber & Faber, 1938; New York: Viking, 1939);
On Poetry: Arthur Skemp Memorial Lecture (Bristol: University of Bristol, 1939);
Rhymed Ruminations (London: Chiswick Press, 1939; enlarged edition, London: Faber & Faber, 1940; New York: Viking, 1941);

Siegfried Sassoon, 1915 (BBC Hulton, photo by G. C. Beresford)

Poems Newly Selected, 1916-1935 (London: Faber & Faber, 1940);
The Flower Show Match and Other Pieces (London: Faber & Faber, 1941);
The Weald of Youth (London: Faber & Faber, 1942; New York: Viking, 1942);
Siegfried's Journey, 1916-1920 (London: Faber & Faber, 1945; New York: Viking, 1946);
Collected Poems (London: Faber & Faber, 1947; New York: Viking, 1949);
Meredith (London: Constable, 1948; New York: Viking, 1948);
Common Chords (Stanford Dingley: Mill House Press, 1950);
Emblems of Experience (Cambridge: Rampant Lion Press, 1951);
Faith Unfaithful (Worcester: Stanbrook Abbey, 1954?);
Renewals (Worcester: Stanbrook Abbey, 1954);
The Tasking (Cambridge: Cambridge University Press, 1954);

An Adjustment, as S. S. (Royston: Golden Head Press, 1955);
Sequences (London: Faber & Faber, 1956; New York: Viking, 1957);
Poems (Marlborough: Privately printed, 1958);
Lenten Illuminations and Sight Sufficient (Cambridge: Privately printed, 1958);
The Path to Peace: Selected Poems (Worcester: Stanbrook Abbey Press, 1960);
Arbor Vitae and Unfoldment (Worcester: Stanbrook Abbey Press, 1960);
Awaitment (Worcester: Stanbrook Abbey Press, 1960);
A Prayer at Pentecost (Worcester: Stanbrook Abbey Press, 1960);
Collected Poems, 1908-1956 (London: Faber & Faber, 1961);
Something About Myself (Worcester: Stanbrook Abbey Press, 1966);
An Octave: 8 September 1966 (London: Arts Council of Britain, 1966);
Siegfried Sassoon Diaries: 1915-1918, edited by Rupert Hart-Davis (London: Faber & Faber, 1981).

Siegfried Sassoon's poetry was published over a period of more than sixty years, almost to the moment of his death in 1967, a few days before his eighty-first birthday. In the history of British poetry, he will be remembered primarily for some one hundred poems—many satirical and almost all short—in which he protested the continuation of World War I through 1917 and 1918. Many of his war poems reflect with absolute authenticity the sufferings of the soldiers in the French trenches, in hospitals, or in their homeland after many of them returned disabled or traumatized. The poetry Sassoon wrote in the last half of his life drew less attention than his war poems and is, on the whole, far less arresting and original. For the most part, these later poems are meditative, reflecting his search for identity, and are important for their psychological revelations. His lyrics became increasingly religious in nature, a trend that reached its culmination in his last ten years, when he celebrated in his poems the spiritual peace and security that he had eventually found in Roman Catholicism in 1957.

Sassoon also wrote six memorable autobiographical books. In three of these—*Memoirs of a Fox-Hunting Man* (1928), *Memoirs of an Infantry Officer* (1930), and *Sherston's Progress* (1936)—he presented his life in a partially fictionalized form through the "journeys" of a character named George Sherston. (The trilogy appeared in one volume in 1937 as *The Complete Memoirs of George Sherston.*) *Memoirs of a Fox-Hunting Man* sold extremely well in both England and the United States and secured an audience for the two later volumes. It introduced Sassoon as an excellent writer in prose and won for him two distinguished awards: The Hawthornden Prize and the James Tait Black Memorial Prize. In a second autobiographical trilogy—*The Old Century and Seven More Years* (1938), *The Weald of Youth* (1942), and *Siegfried's Journey, 1916-1920* (1945)—Sassoon presented his life to 1920 without a fictional facade.

Siegfried Lorraine Sassoon grew up in Kent, loving the weald and the outdoor sports of the country gentry—fox hunting, golf, and cricket. His parents separated in 1901, and his father, Alfred Ezra Sassoon, died of tuberculosis when Siegfried was not quite nine. Because he had had little contact with his father, Siegfried Sassoon wrote in *The Weald of Youth* that he had not understood how long he should feel grief, after his father's funeral in London, which he was too upset to attend with his younger brother, Hamo, and older brother, Michael. Brought up by his mother, Theresa Georgina Thornycroft Sassoon, in the Church of England, Sassoon expressed surprise later in life at how deeply his Spanish-Jewish heritage affected him and at how greatly the psychological inheritance from his father's people had conditioned his responses, his values, and his attitudes: "I sometimes surmise that my eastern ancestry is stronger in me than the Thornycrofts'. The daemon in me is Jewish. Do you believe in racial memories? Some of my hypnogogic visions have seemed like it, and many of them were oriental architecture."

Alfred Ezra Sassoon, Siegfried's father, was the first Sassoon to marry a Gentile. Alfred's mother opposed the marriage, said all the Jewish funeral prayers for him, and uttered a curse upon his unborn children. Never relenting, she cut off his allowance and never permitted her grandchildren to visit her at Ashley Park, near Walton-on-the-Thames, an estate which included a large fifteenth-century hall, a cricket field, and a golf course. Sometimes called "the Rothschilds of the East," the millionaire Sassoon families had typically resided in India and in the Near East since the time of the Spanish Inquisition. In the mid-nineteenth century Siegfried's paternal grandfather and several of his uncles moved to Europe and were important in the arts as well as commerce and banking. In England some of the Sassoons exercised power in Parliament, and one entertained the Shah of Persia during his much-publicized visit to London in the

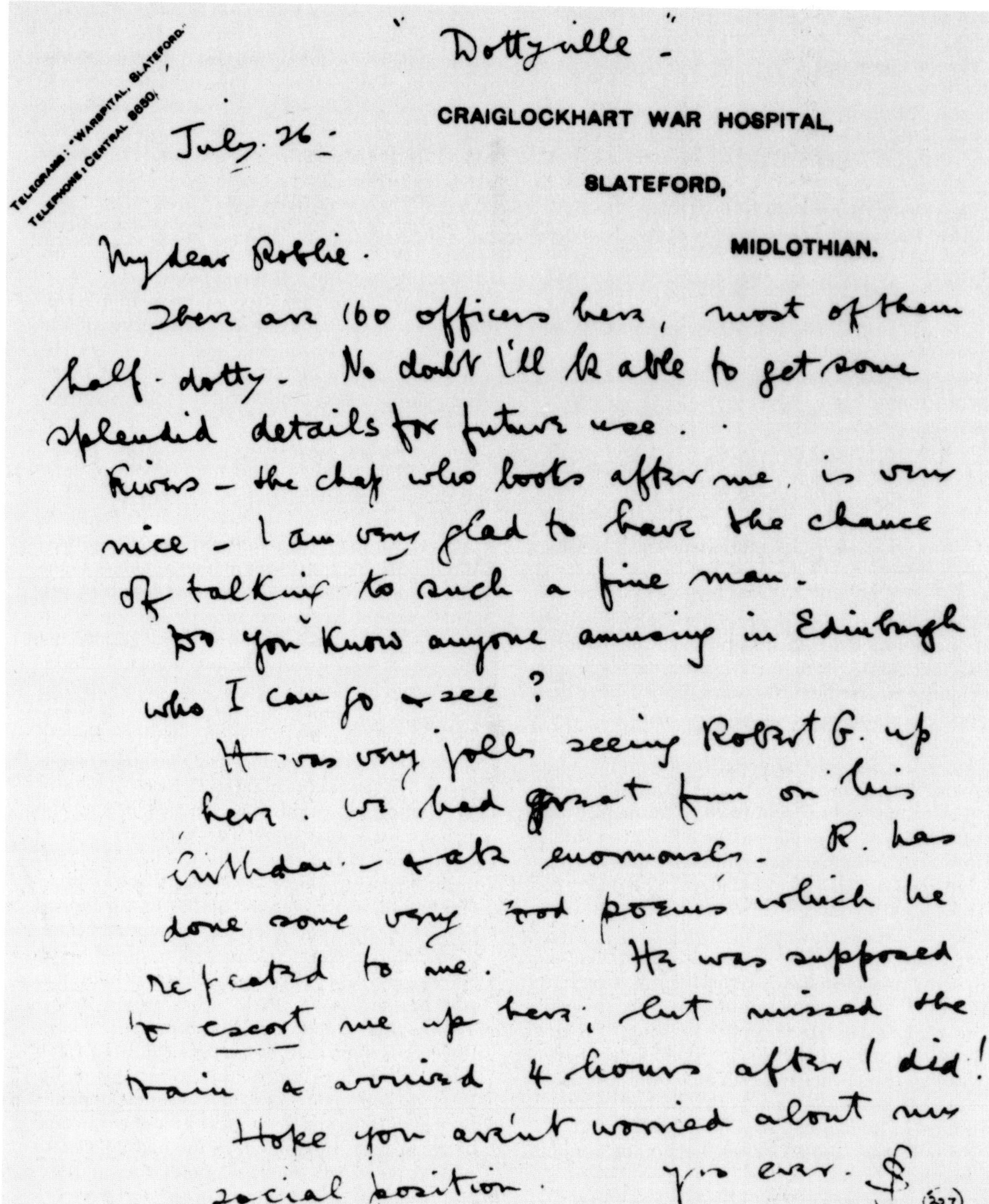

"Dottyville" -

TELEGRAMS: "WARSPITAL, SLATEFORD."
TELEPHONE: CENTRAL 8850.

CRAIGLOCKHART WAR HOSPITAL,
SLATEFORD,
MIDLOTHIAN.

July 26 -

My dear Robbie.

There are 160 officers here, most of them half-dotty. No doubt I'll be able to get some splendid details for future use.

Rivers - the chap who looks after me, is very nice - I am very glad to have the chance of talking to such a fine man.

Do you know anyone amusing in Edinburgh who I can go & see?

It was very jolly seeing Robert G. up here. We had great fun on his birthday - & ate enormously. R. has done some very good poems which he repeated to me. He was supposed to escort me up here, but missed the train & arrived 4 hours after I did!

Hope you aren't worried about my social position.

Yrs ever. S.S.

(327)

Letter from Sassoon to Robert Ross, 26 July 1917. "Robert G." is Robert Graves (Imperial War Museum).

1890s. Alfred Sassoon's sister, Rachel Beer, owned and edited two London newspapers, the *Observer* and the *Sunday Times*, from the early 1890s to 1904, and she wrote extensively for them. Against her mother's protests, she remained in close contact with Alfred's family and left an inheritance for Siegfried and his surviving brother, Michael, at her death in 1927.

Sassoon in *The Old Century and Seven More Years* suggested he had been endowed, in the Old Testament sense, with the gift of prophecy through his Jewish blood, and that this gift had found its most powerful expression in his crying out for social justice and compassion in his war poetry. Nevertheless, he identified more strongly with his mother than with his father. If he inherited from his father a contemplative spirit, an urge to speak as a minor prophet through his poetry, he, nevertheless, gained from the Thornycrofts the "common-sense" and the creative perspective that had allowed him to develop as an artist: "how I bless the Thornycroft sanity. . . . Introspective though I have been, I could stand aside and look at myself—and laugh." His mother chose his name because of her love of Wagner's *Der Ring des Nibelungen*, and he himself always liked the name for its heroic associations. In a letter to Dame Felicitas Corrigan in 1965, he remarked upon his mother's having given him for his third birthday a copy of Coleridge's *Lectures on Shakespeare*. Theresa's family, like the Sassoons, was wealthy, but its wealth derived from land. Her immediate family included notable sculptors: her grandfather John Francis; her father, Thomas; her mother, and her brother Hamo. Another brother, John, was an architect for the British navy. Theresa's mother painted many portraits of the royal family, and Theresa and her two sisters were minor painters and sculptors. Siegfried's education included private tutoring until he was fourteen, the study of law at Marlborough College from ages sixteen to nineteen, and the study of history—while he was also writing poetry—at Clare College, Cambridge. When he decided to return to Kent without taking a degree, he continued his writing and began to publish his poems privately. His mother introduced him to her friend Sir Edmund Gosse, who in turn introduced him to such literary figures as Edward Marsh and Rupert Brooke. Gosse encouraged Sassoon to spend much time in London. Marsh used some of Sassoon's early poems in his anthology, *Georgian Poetry, 1916-1917*. Sassoon later developed some doubts about Georgian poetry, which he described as "crocus-crowded lyrics."

In Sassoon's early poetry his ideas and his technique are conventional and sometimes reveal the influence of the Pre-Raphaelites or the Rhymers' Club poets, whom he had read as an adolescent and as a university student. Such poets as Algernon Charles Swinburne, Dante Gabriel Rossetti, Lionel Johnson, Ernest Dowson, Thomas Hardy, and George Meredith served as his models. Not all of his early poems have survived, but many appeared in pamphlets that he published privately between 1906 and 1916. Of those early efforts selected for inclusion in his collected poems, several bear titles that are pagan in orientation: "Goblin Revel," "Dryads," and "Arcady Unheeding." The poems are replete with romantic references to "hooded witches," "dulcimers," "mournful pennons," "the gloom of the glade," and gentle shepherds, and they include lines such as "The ghostly Sultan from his glimmering halls," "Dawn glimmers in the soul-forsaken face," and "Lord of Winged Sunrise and dim Arcady." As an older man, Sassoon attributed his frequent references to dawn in his early lyrics to the influence of George Meredith, and he thought his choice of archaic diction (words such as *noisome*, *darkling*, *marish*, *weir*, *jollity*) had derived from a desire to imitate Dante Gabriel Rossetti and other poets who had used medieval associations for romantic effects.

But these early poems also differ from the fin de siècle works that he read as a student. For example, his poems of fantasy have a more positive tone, a more direct style, and a more energetic pace than Dowson's fantasies, with their longing for death or for a return to lost innocence. In contrast to the older poets that Sassoon admired, he rarely wrote about love and sex. While in more than half of the early lyrics nature is a principal source of his imagery, his preoccupation with nature derives not only from attempts to follow pastoral conventions but also from a deeply felt love of outdoor life and an intimate knowledge of Kentish wildlife. Sassoon's depiction of nature even in the early poems reveals a freshness and a firsthand authenticity often absent in the poetry of the fin de siècle poets and the Georgian movement. This emphasis on nature continued throughout his lifetime. Even in his seventies a deep feeling for nature gave vitality to his poems of religion and the supernatural.

Much of his privately printed early verse was pallid and stilted, making his achievement as a war poet a few years later startling and unexpected. His revisions of early works, however, imply an ability to criticize his poetry and revise it in the direction of the simple and the specific. For example, in an essay, "Siegfried Sassoon's Poetry," his friend Edmund Blunden compares two versions of "Before Day," one from 1911 and the other from 1916. The line "In passional summer dawn I call for thee" Sassoon revised to the more forceful "In the still summer dawns that waken me." Yet, in moving away from conventional artifice in diction to a more direct language and syntax, he was still far from the forceful colloquial utterances in his best war poems.

Sassoon was the earliest of the World War I poets to enlist in the British service, although not the first to see action in France. On 1 August 1914 at the age of twenty-seven, he passed his examination for enlistment; England declared war on 4 August; and Sassoon found himself in uniform on 5 August. He left for France in November 1915 with the First Battalion of the Royal Welch Fusiliers.

Some of the eight poems included by Marsh in *Georgian Poetry: 1916-1917* and some printed in *The Old Huntsman and Other Poems* (1917) adumbrate the growth that was to occur between Sassoon's earliest poetry and the poetry that he produced during and after the Somme offensive in 1916. "Haunted," a two-page, blank-verse poem, is conventionally romantic in its descriptions and in the image of a pale and solitary forest wanderer, who is doomed by an evil spell. But a few lines also hint at Sassoon's developing realism. For example, he describes a sunset that has "Died in a smear of blood," and he depicts the pale victim's unequal encounter with Fate in terms as specific as those in the war poems: "the sweat of horror on his face," "his throat was choking. / Barbed brambles gripped and clawed him round his legs."

"The Kiss," written in 1916 (another poem in Marsh's anthology and in *The Old Huntsman*), depicts the violence of the war dramatically, but, unlike the war poems, written after he had seen action in the trenches, "The Kiss" seems to celebrate militarism. In this poem the soldier hopes that, as his heel holds his enemy, he will feel him "quail" as the bayonet penetrates. According to Sassoon, he wrote this poem after hearing a Colonel Campbell address his class in military training on "The Spirit of the Bayonet." It was written in the weeks when, according to Robert Graves, Sassoon was vacillating between being a "happy warrior" and a pacifist. Later Sassoon maintained that he had designed this poem as a satirical parody, but this assertion is of doubtful validity because he had similarly celebrated war as a cathartic experience in several other early poems.

Other poems written before his departure for France (or shortly after his arrival) present war as a positive agent that develops strength and character. In the chauvinistic "Absolution," composed in summer 1915, Sassoon writes, "war has made us wise / And, fighting for our freedom, we are free." Referring to the army as "the happy legion," he implies that soldiers may be glad to give up their lives in a great cause. The poet adopts the view that war occupies only a moment in history: "Time's but a golden wind that shakes the grass." This sense of war's brevity minimizes its agony, as does the comparison of that agony with the glory that comes from self-sacrifice. In "Absolution" Sassoon questions neither the necessity of the war nor the motives that led to it. This poem, influenced by poetry of Rupert Brooke, was written shortly after Brooke died.

In "The Redeemer," written in his first weeks in the trenches, Sassoon uses vivid details characteristic of his later war poems ("We lugged our clay-sucked boots"), and the soldier is depicted realistically as a "simple duffer," who loves "Good days of work and sport and homely song." The sardonic tone of Sassoon's later war poems is not yet fully developed. The speaker, seeing the duffer loaded down with planks across his shoulders in a midwinter rain, too readily envisions him as Christ. Unearned religious sentiment dominates the poem until it ends suddenly in a blunt declaration of nationalism, an assertion that the soldier will be "not uncontent to die / That Lancaster on Lune may stand sure."

Several conventional lyrics which emphasize nature (such as "Morning Glory," "Daybreak in a Garden," "Tree and Sky," "Storm and Sunlight," and "Wind in the Beechwood") appear in *The Old Huntsman and Other Poems*, and a number of the early war poems in the volume similarly treat nature in an artificial manner. "France" praises the "vivid green / Where sun and quivering foliage meet; / And in each soldier's heart serene." He comments that "they are fortunate, who fight / For gleaming landscapes." In another mood he complains in "To Victory," a poem written just after his arrival in France, of the colorlessness of the gray November landscape. In "The Dragon and the Undying" he identifies the bursting flares as dragons. The soldiers lying in the trenches relate to the landscape and the night sky as if meeting a significant destiny, in harmony with the cosmos. In "unshrouded night" the faces are "fair," and the dying men "hail the burning heavens." They have had "ageless dreams" and "wander in the dusk with chanting streams." "Before the Battle" is replete with similar language and conventional imagery. Such poetry—much like the popular war verse of Robert

Nichols—contrasts strikingly with even the better war poems that appear in this early book.

"To My Brother" (Autumn 1915) holds special personal significance because in it Sassoon—still in training in England—addresses his younger brother, Hamo, who was killed in action on the Gallipoli Peninsula in August 1915 and buried at sea. This graceful work is not an elegy or lament but an expression of the author's anxiety that fear may overwhelm him and of his longing for his brother's companionship in the ordeal he faces on the battlefield: "Look on these eyes lest I should think of shame." Unfortunately, Sassoon allows the speaker's uncertainty to be too easily resolved in the last two lines, in which the heroism of the dead is hailed impersonally as an omen of victory: "But in the gloom I see your laurell'd head / And through your victory I shall win the light."

A second loss was to come a few months later with the death of Sassoon's "dream friend," Lt. David Thomas, whom Sassoon calls Dick Tiltwood in the Sherston trilogy. Thomas is lamented in "The Last Meeting," written in May 1916 at Flixecourt, during Sassoon's brief respite from front-line action. In these calm surroundings after months of devastating warfare, Sassoon also wrote the excellent poem "Stand-To: Good Friday Morning," which he later identified as the single poem which pointed toward the satirical style that was to prove so successful in many of his poems in the next three years.

Besides the war poems and the pastoral poems in *The Old Huntsman*, the long title poem is of particular interest. Marked by colloquial diction and conversational rhythms, this poem is a blank-verse monologue in which an old huntsman recalls scenes and people from his past. He wonders about the religious convictions of "the old Duke" and of the clergy he has known, but he himself feels remote from heaven and hell—and finally also remote from a world "that's full of wars." The huntsman's series of descriptive pictures reveal a grasp of realistic detail, and the huntsman's speech is an improvement over Sassoon's only other long poem in colloquial blank verse, *The Daffodil Murderer* (1913), a parody on John Masefield.

Of even greater interest, however, are the new war poems, written after Sassoon was sent to the front. These poems present trench warfare graphically, stress the ordinariness and the humanity of the soldiers, and usually employ colloquial diction and conversational rhythms. While "The Old Huntsman" is relaxed and humorous, the majority of the war poems in this volume lament human suffering and express rage at the futile deaths of the young men.

Sassoon's combat career from 1916 to 1918 was marked by several long leaves and hospitalizations for injuries and illnesses. For example, he was hospitalized for a gastric illness, so that he missed the worst fighting of the Somme offensive, in which British casualties were heaviest, from July to October 1916. He also found himself in 1916 and again in 1917 in close contact in England with influential pacifists: art critic Robert Ross; Lady Ottoline Morrell and her husband, an influential pacifist member of Parliament; Bertrand Russell, who had already lost his professorship because of his antiwar statements at Cambridge; and John Middleton Murry, literary critic and friend of antiwar authors such as D. H. Lawrence. Sassoon, in part through the urging of these friends, made a formal declaration of protest against the war in July 1917. He had already received the Military Cross for bringing in under heavy fire a wounded lance-corporal who had fallen near the German lines; and he had been recommended for the Victoria Cross after he captured alone some German trenches in the Hindenburg Line. When he sent his letter of protest to the war department, he threw the ribbon of his Military Cross into the River Mersey. In the protest, Sassoon said: "I believe that the War is being deliberately prolonged by those who have the power to end it. . . . I believe that this War, on which I entered as a war of defence and liberation, has now become a war of aggression and conquest. I believe that the purpose for which I and my fellow soldiers entered upon this war should have been so clearly stated as to have made it impossible to change them, and that, had this been done, the objects which actuated us would now be attainable by negotiation. . . . I can no longer be a party to prolong these sufferings for ends which I believe to be evil and unjust. I am not protesting against the conduct of the war, but against the political errors and insincerities for which the fighting men are being sacrificed." Sassoon's declaration was read in the House of Commons at the instigation of Bertrand Russell, and he was in danger of court-martial. Robert Graves, a fellow poet, interceded at his hearing, pleading his view that Sassoon was suffering shell shock. As a result, in July 1917 Sassoon entered Craiglockhart War Hospital in Edinburgh, where Wilfred Owen was already receiving treatment. Sassoon and Owen became friends. (After Owen was killed during the week of the Armistice, Sassoon collected and edited Owen's poems—almost all previously unpublished—for publication in 1920.) By summer 1917

The Old Huntsman had been widely read, and Sassoon was writing and compiling the poems that were to appear in *Counter-Attack*.

While *The Old Huntsman and Other Poems* includes a variety of poems, the next volume, *Counter-Attack and Other Poems* (1918), does not. All thirty-nine poems are harshly realistic laments or satires. The typical satirical poem is short and marked by rhythms of conversation, strong and regular rhyme, considerable slang, and often a singsong, lilting verse at variance with the tragic subject. Sassoon's satires are marked by bitter irony, and they specifically attack patriotic and complacent civilians, politicians unconcerned with peacemaking, military strategists in high positions, clergymen who preach an apparently merciless God and who identify warlikeness with godliness, and all the popular media, especially the kind of journalism which emphasized military goals of absolute conquest and minimized the extent of British casualties.

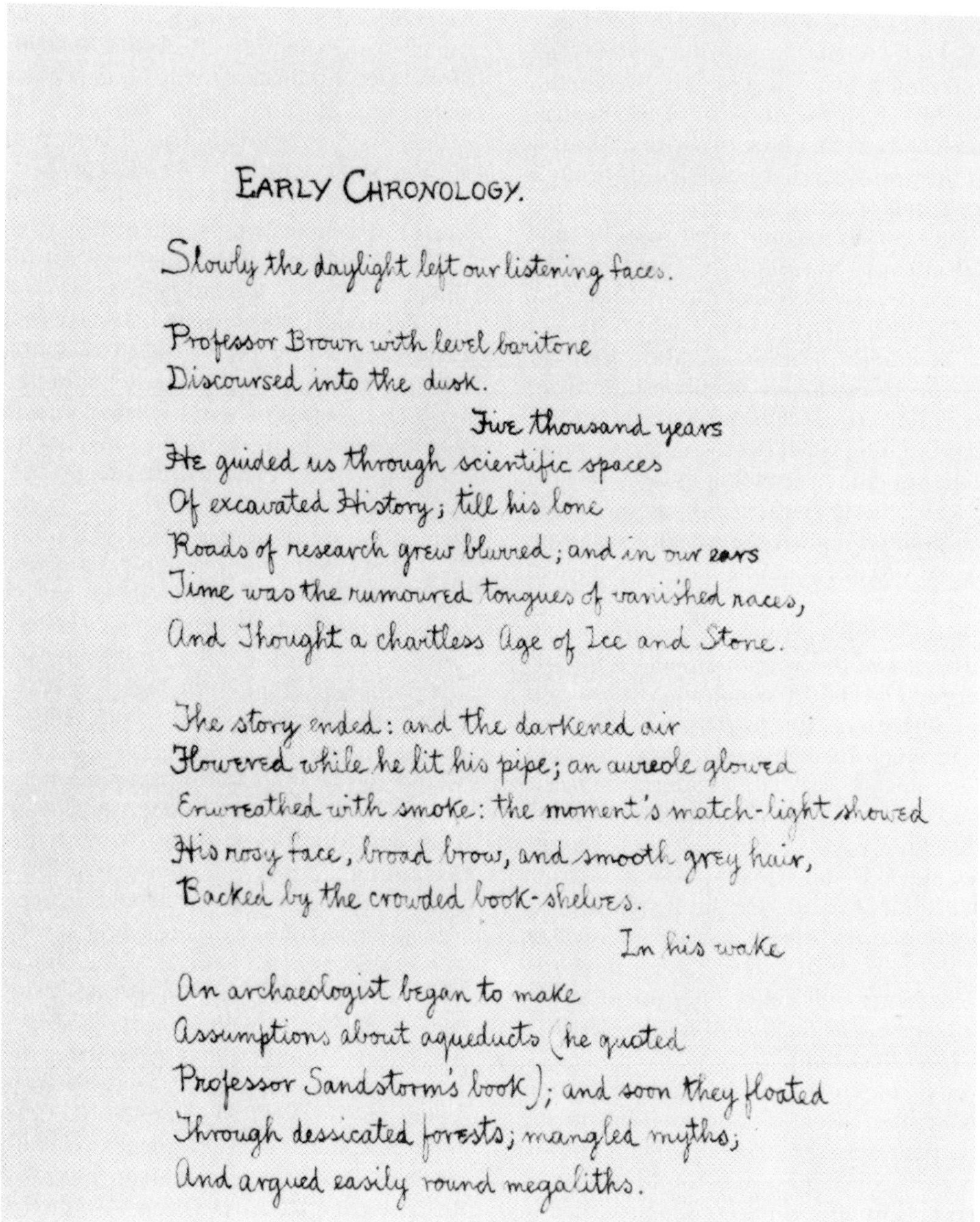

EARLY CHRONOLOGY.

Slowly the daylight left our listening faces.

Professor Brown with level baritone
Discoursed into the dusk.
Five thousand years
He guided us through scientific spaces
Of excavated History; till his lone
Roads of research grew blurred; and in our ears
Time was the rumoured tongues of vanished races,
And Thought a chartless Age of Ice and Stone.

The story ended: and the darkened air
Flowered while he lit his pipe; an aureole glowed
Enwreathed with smoke: the moment's match-light showed
His rosy face, broad brow, and smooth grey hair,
Backed by the crowded book-shelves.
In his wake
An archaeologist began to make
Assumptions about aqueducts (he quoted
Professor Sandstorm's book); and soon they floated
Through dessicated forests; mangled myths;
And argued easily round megaliths.

Manuscript for one of the poems added to the 1920 edition of Picture-Show *(Geoffrey Keynes,* A Bibliography of Siegfried Sassoon*)*

The horror of the battlefield and the trenches emerges as Sassoon relentlessly builds detail upon detail (rats, fragments of dead bodies, stench of rotting flesh, winter rain, mud that slows each step, sounds of guns, and sounds of ominous silence before shelling).

At the close of the war when Sassoon selected sixty-four poems for *The War Poems of Siegfried Sassoon* (1919), he included eighteen from *The Old Huntsman* (1917), nearly all of the poems in *Counter-Attack* (1918), and nine from the privately published volume *Picture Show* (1919). The war poems he excluded were primarily those in *The Old Huntsman* that were written prior to his combat experience—poems such as "Absolution," "The Redeemer," and "Victory"—that romanticized warfare. Most of the poems included in *The War Poems* were written in 1917 and 1918. Some reflect his own hospital experience; many were undoubtedly written in the hospital or rest home during the long leaves that Sassoon had in England and Scotland during the last year and a half of his army service. Although these periods of relief from combat service permitted him to see his experiences in perspective, he was still far from tranquil when he wrote about them. He admitted to Robert Graves that when he was back in England, he had at times visions of horror in which he saw the bodies of the dead on the city pavements. During his long leave at Craiglockhart in the summer and fall of 1917, Sassoon was torn between his wish to return to the front in order to share the sufferings of his comrades and his wish to stay in England in order to continue his protest against continuing the war to absolute victory. Poems reflecting his hospital experience include "Sick Leave," "Banishment," "Repression of War Experience," "Autumn," and "Survivors."

Public response to *Counter-Attack* was more vocal and violent than the response to *The Old Huntsman* had been in the previous year. The satirical poems in the earlier volume followed the genial, long title poem, and harsh poems were interspersed among more conventional lyrics primarily in praise of nature. Even the gray and black book cover of *The Old Huntsman* contrasted with the cover of *Counter-Attack*, an orange cover overlaid with red, as if to call attention to the violent experiences described inside. *Counter-Attack* featured an introduction by Robert Nichols, whose war poetry, though inferior in its sentimentality and its lack of artistry, enjoyed great popularity in 1915-1917. (Sassoon's *The Old Huntsman* sold even more copies in 1917 than did Nichols's *Ardours and Endurances*.) In the introduction to *Counter-Attack*, Nichols acknowledged that war destroys more often than it develops nobility in men. He suggests, however, that Sassoon's anger may weaken his poems aesthetically. Both the British and American editions of *Counter-Attack* began with an excerpt from Fitzwater Wray's translation of Henri Barbusse's *Le Feu*, a book that Sassoon had read at Craiglockhart. The passage from *Le Feu* maintains that war destroys its participants morally as well as physically: war, in short, "outrages common sense, debases noble ideas, and dictates all kind of crime." It enlarges "every evil instinct."

The satirical poems here are all short. In most of them Sassoon employs epigrammatic statements, often climactically in the last line or two. There is also a tautness in the diction and structure evident in many of the poems. The typical figure is a simple, honorable, and patient soldier who is incapable of sophisticated argument against war. The soldiers are "poor duffers" who accept their unheroic lot. The poetry is not marked by an unusual degree of richness, and there is not much subtlety or ambiguity present. If the soldier protagonist is capable of intense feeling, the poetry is seldom complicated enough to require reflection and analysis on the reader's part.

Some readers became angry with Sassoon's blatant lack of patriotism in poems such as "Lamentations" and "How to Die." Some others became angry with Sassoon's apparent blasphemy and disrespect for the Christian religion in poems such as "The Investiture," "To Any Dead Officer," "Stand To: Good Friday Morning," "The Choral Union," and "They." In "Stand To: Good Friday Morning," for example, a soldier mocks the benevolence and compassion universally attributed to Christ, and in his hope for a sick leave shouts, "O Jesus, send me a wound today, / And I'll believe in your bread and wine." Similarly glad for a wound that has allowed him to go home, the veteran in "The One-Legged Man" breathes a prayer in the last line, "Thank God they had to amputate!"

Even the responses of Wilfred Owen, John Middleton Murry, and Virginia Woolf to *Counter-Attack* were not wholeheartedly enthusiastic, although their points of view on the war were similar to Sassoon's. Like Nichols, they questioned whether Sassoon's technique of shocking the reader is aesthetically valid and whether he might not be writing propaganda rather than poetry. Not long before he was killed in action, Wilfred Owen wrote Sassoon in October 1918 that he had been made more fearful by reading the *Counter-Attack* poems than he had been when he had held a young soldier wounded in the head for half an hour and felt the soldier's blood soak through to his own shoulder. He wrote, "My senses are charred." For Owen, Sassoon's poetry failed to place the intense and horrible moment into a more general context of human association. Rather, Sassoon's poetry tended to hypnotize the reader so that he saw the horrible moment only in isolation. The reader is confronted with a violent "spot in time" which, intense in itself, leads to no discernible resolution or reasoned conclusion. In his preoccupation with the irrationality of war, Sassoon deliberately angered the reader and left him with a cryptic epigram that could give him little comfort. Owen at least must have appreciated Sassoon's revulsion against war, even though Sassoon was apparently unable to attain Owen's measured response to it.

John Middleton Murry wrote in his review of *Counter-Attack* that he found a city of pain in each poem, but he did not find a finished artistry. After reading Sassoon's poems, Murry could only conclude that there was no meaning at all left to human experience. Sassoon, said Murry, tends to numb his readers, to terrify them, and to deaden their sensibilities, all responses fatal to full aesthetic experience. For Murry, Sassoon failed to universalize his experience, because he concentrated so fanatically on one part of it. A truly great poet, Murry contended, must be able to get beyond even an annihilating experience to see it in its unusual implications; Sassoon gave us only the shocking intensity of the annihilating moment in many of his poems. Murry cited two lines from "Prelude: The Troops" to illustrate the element of balance he could not find in most of the poems: "To the land where all / Is ruin and nothing blossoms but the sky." These lines, because of the reference to the blossoming sky, present "a full octave of emotional experience . . . from serenity to desolation," a range of emotion lacking in most of Sassoon's grim new poems. Murry thought, moreover, that Sassoon had become too greatly dependent upon a single mode of expression in these poems, "the irony epigram."

Virginia Woolf's views on *Counter-Attack* are similar to Murry's. She suggested in the *Times Literary Supplement* that Sassoon had deserted art in his compulsion to express the intolerable. "Beauty and art have something too universal about them to meet our particular case," she commented as she criticized the narrow range of the individual poems. Like Murry, Woolf felt that rage by itself could never lead to the aesthetic effect that requires its presentation against a background of harmony—or some hope, however dim, of an orderly universe with which the horrible moment contrasts. Some sense of harmonious resolution must be present for a genuine artistic expression of emotional experience. Yet, in spite of Sassoon's inability to reach a largeness of vision in his war poetry, Woolf sees in his "contempt for palliative or subterfuge . . . the raw stuff of poetry." She says, in effect, that without his unusual and violent experience Sassoon would not have written at all.

Actually, at times in his war poems Sassoon shows the range of imaginative power that Murry and Woolf deny him. In these instances he can relate the violence about which he writes to a larger humanistic context, and his irony depends upon his suggestion that what would be the normally expected in peacetime cannot be relied upon to happen in wartime when human values must at times yield to struggle for survival. In two poems, "The Rear-Guard, Hindenburg Line, April, 1917" (sometimes published under the title "The Deceiver") and "The Dug-Out, St. Venant, July, 1918," Sassoon relates incidents in which a soldier mistakes a comrade's death for sleep in one case and mistakes a comrade's sleep for death in the other. The protagonist's terror in "The Rear-Guard" when he discovers the man is dead strikes suddenly. In "The Dug-Out," the narrator's recognition that the boy is only asleep calms his fears—but only for the moment. Any sleeping man can remind him of the many dead men he has seen. The incident punctuates his chronic fear, a fear which is appropriate in the trenches and the only possible emotion, perhaps, that can be experienced in the uncertainty of existence there. (Sassoon also describes this incident in *Sherston's Progress*.) In "The Rear-Guard" the soldier's actions and speech are presented by a detached narrator. In "The Dug-Out" the point of view is first person as the protagonist muses but never speaks aloud to the sleeping boy. In "The Rear-Guard" the poet implies that sleep constitutes the normal state and death is a shocking aberration. Conversely, in "The Dug-Out" the poet's awareness that death is the norm in the trenches has made sleep an abnormal state. Sassoon masterfully communicates that in wartime the normal expectations of one's previous experience are unlikely to be realized and that the unexpected converse of these expectations becomes the usual pattern for men who live under abnormal and distorted circumstances.

In spite of Murry's implication that a balanced view is unusual for Sassoon, Sassoon frequently uses natural backgrounds of beauty—sky, sunset, or dawn—to intensify his sense of desolation in the

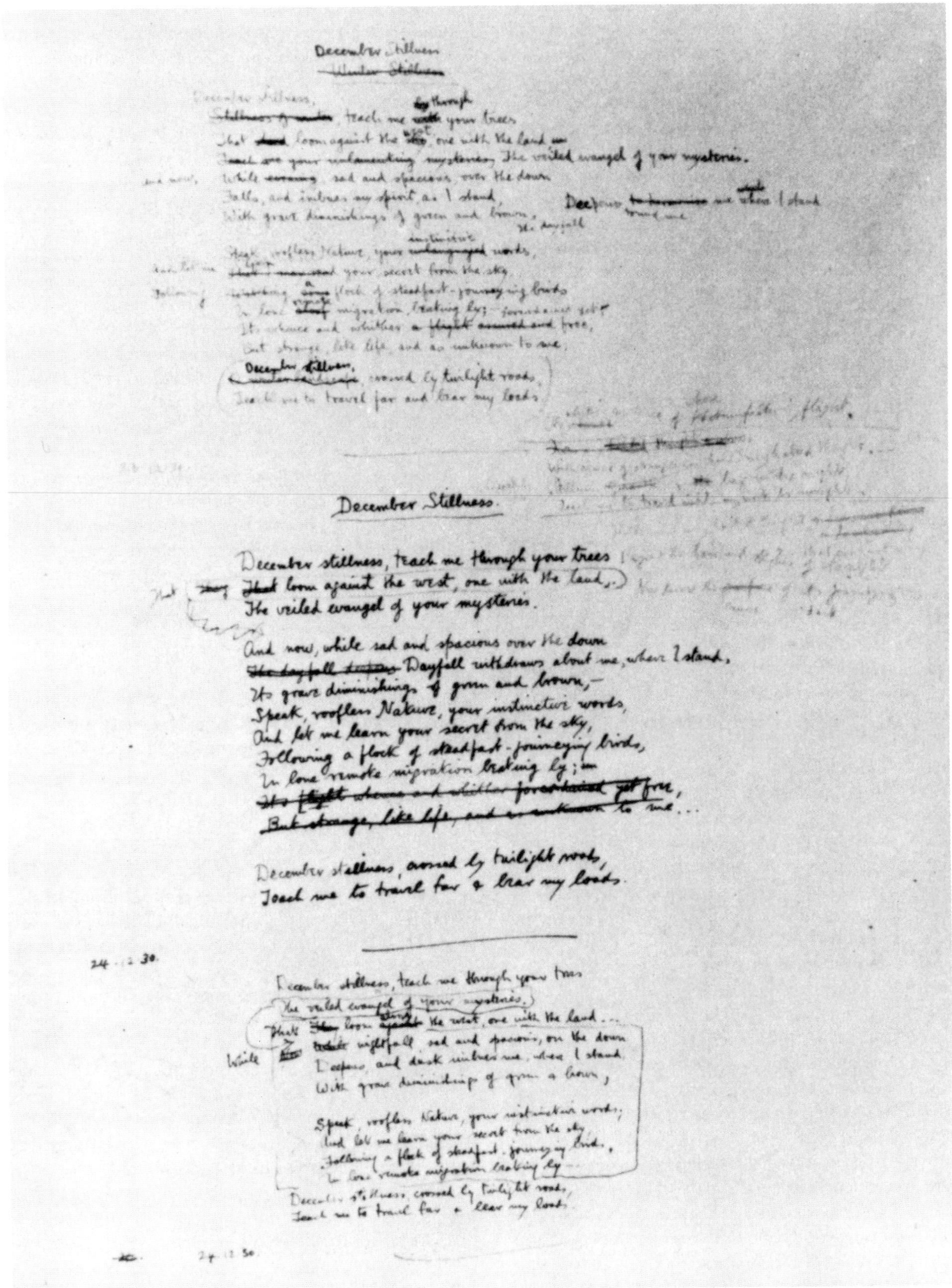
December Stillness

December stillness, teach me through your trees
That loom against the west, one with the land,
The veiled evangel of your mysteries.

And now, while sad and spacious over the down
Dayfall withdraws about me, where I stand,
Its grave diminishings of green and brown,—
Speak, roofless Nature, your instinctive words,
And let me learn your secret from the sky,
Following a flock of steadfast-journeying birds,
In lone remote migration beating by;
~~Its flight whence and whither foreordained yet free,~~
~~But strange, like life, and as unknown to me~~...

December stillness, crossed by twilight roads,
Teach me to travel far & bear my loads.

24.12.30.

December stillness, teach me through your trees
The veiled evangel of your mysteries,
That loom against the west, one with the land...
While nightfall sad and spacious, on the down
Deepens, and dusk withdraws me, where I stand,
With grave diminishings of green & brown,

Speak, roofless Nature, your instinctive words;
And let me learn your secret from the sky,
Following a flock of steadfast-journeying birds,
In lone remote migration beating by—
December stillness, crossed by twilight roads,
Teach me to travel far & bear my loads.

24.12.30.

Page from Sassoon's 1932-1933 poetry notebook (Sotheby Parke Bernet, sale 4934, 15 October 1982)

trenches. Always he describes the desolation of no-man's-land for what it is. Sassoon's poems avoid the artifice in some sentimental and popular war poems. No nightingale or lark is needed to heighten the effect of Sassoon's battlefields with their blighted trees and twisted wire, as in this description from "Counter-Attack":

> The place was rotten with dead; green clumsy legs
> High-booted, sprawled and grovelled along the saps
> And trunks, face downward in the sucking mud,
> Wallowed like trodden sand-bags loosely filled;
> And naked sodden buttocks, mats of hair,
> Bulged, clotted heads slept in the plastering slime,
> And then the rain began—the jolly old rain!

The depth and intensity of Sassoon's rendition of experience in itself provide a degree of universality in his poems which his critics often felt was not there.

Though Sassoon's satirical war poems possess strengths that his early critics tended to ignore, these works also reveal some weaknesses. In "Base Details" and "The General" Sassoon satirizes too easily the high-ranking military officers. His complacent generals and his irresponsible majors are so stereotypical that they become scapegoats without much human substance. More effective, but equally biased, are poems which regard women as insensitive civilians. In "The Hero" a soldier visits his comrade's mother and tries to keep secret his knowledge that her son was not courageous under fire. She continues to idealize the boy and refuses to recognize that he might have been a fearful and suffering individual before he died. In "Their Frailty" Sassoon presents women as complacent about the deaths of thousands of men mowed down by German machine guns, as long as the men in their own families are safe. In "Glory of Women" Sassoon inveighs against women who demand that soldiers be heroes and who do not realize that even British soldiers may flee from combat when fear grips them: "When hell's last horror breaks them, and they run, / Trampling the terrible corpses." In the last three lines of the poem Sassoon shifts abruptly to German grandmothers who knit socks for their men—men whose faces have already been ground into the mud by the retreating British. These complacent women, like the British women, cannot view their soldiers as suffering human beings. Sassoon's characteristic distrust of women, revealed in all his verse, finds its strongest expression in these poems.

In Sassoon's best war poems he achieved new dimensions in literary art through his use of techniques already established in fiction but not common in poetry—short, trenchant statements; colloquial language punctuated with oaths; the accumulation of graphic detail; the use of cryptic language; and the presentation of shocking incidents accompanied by little authorial comment. If his prewar poems had been overly conventional and dulled by artifice, his war poems either succeeded or failed because of their unconventionality and unpredictability. In his poems written after the war he seldom sought to shock, he used satire far less frequently, and he seldom employed the colloquial and epigrammatic technique that had marked his wartime verse. He did not lapse into the conventionality of his prewar romantic poems, but his work was more traditional and the emotional appeal was muted. His diction, though consistently simple, was not colloquial. His maturity as poet appeared in the order and grace of the verse rather than in its originality of thought or image. He aptly described his own style in the decades after the war as his "cello voice."

In July 1918 Sassoon was accidentally shot in the head by a member of his own company, and he was discharged prior to the Armistice. He seems to have lost his subject for a time. He briefly but vigorously supported the campaign of Philip Snowden in the general election following Armistice because Snowden had attempted to shorten the war and had supported postwar assistance for widows and for unemployed former soldiers. Since Snowden was involved in the Labour movement, Sassoon's "Tory-minded," fox-hunting companions taunted him for becoming a "budding Bolshevik."

If his occasional poems, often requested in the 1920s and 1930s, addressed social problems, the prophetic fervor and the intensity that had characterized the poems from 1915 to 1919 had largely vanished. In his war poems he had attained considerable universality, attacking war itself rather than the German forces or even World War I itself. Nevertheless, after the Armistice was signed, his rage against war and its madness, which had given the war poems their intensity, was inadequate to the resolution of the complex social and political problems emanating from the war and to the treatment of contemporary issues generally.

Sassoon spent nearly all of 1920 in the United States, speaking and reading his poetry to large audiences. In collecting new war poems in *Picture*

Show (1919) and collecting previously published war poems for republication in *The War Poems of Siegfried Sassoon* (1919), he saw the need to exhort readers not to forget the horror of one war, lest another war might someday occur. Such purpose also prompted his writing of the poems in *The Road to Ruin* (1933). In the satiric "An Unveiling" he has an orator call for the building of a "bomb-proof roofed Metropolis" in London, dedicated to "for What-they-died-for's sake," and the orator praises the courage of victims of poison gas. Sassoon did not protest England's entry into World War II and regarded that war as necessary to exorcize the evil of Hitler's regime. In his old age, he still regarded his protest declaration and his poems of World War I as a significant dramatization of the horror of war, although he had begun to doubt their permanent impact.

Sassoon returned to his practice of having single poems or small pamphlet editions of a few poems privately printed, particularly in the 1920s and again following World War II. The poems in these small publications were periodically collected in larger, commercially published volumes. In his old age, he said that *The Heart's Journey* (1927) was the last of his books of poetry to receive any favorable or full acknowledgment. Actually, in the twenty-five years following World War I, Sassoon wrote relatively little poetry and concentrated upon his seven major prose works: *Meredith* (1948) and the two autobiographical trilogies. Perhaps the best of his war poems is a lyric which heralds the Armistice, "Everyone Sang" (*Picture Show*, 1919). "Everyone suddenly burst out singing" as if imprisoned birds have been released and can be seen "Winging wildly across the white / Orchards and dark-green fields; on— on— on—and out of sight." In 1965, two years before his death, Sassoon was startled to see this poem printed on the back page of the *Times* as a memorial to Winston Churchill, who as a member of Parliament had fifty years before heard his protest against war. The lyric, with its childlike simplicity and joyous spirit, typifies much in Sassoon's maturity and old age.

Siegfried Sassoon, 1961 (photo by Maurice Wiggin for the Sunday Times*)*

In each decade Sassoon produced a few fine poems, which are not widely known. In "Alone" (1924) he shows his ability to enliven an abstract lament with the sharp specificity of the ordinary. As he speaks of the strange person that one becomes when alone, he contrasts that desolate state with the everyday, ritualistic, common acts of community. In "Revisitation" (*Vigils*, 1934) he speaks to his psychiatrist, Dr. W. H. R. Rivers, who returns as a ghost to his "heart room"; they continue to talk as they had done in summer 1917 at Craiglockhart. Sassoon portrays Rivers as a man who is both a good scientist and a "fathering friend." In him Sassoon sees "human sainthood," and he recognizes that the spiritual healing which Rivers had begun in him has been truly augmented by memory in the passing years. The poem's dignity precludes sentimentality.

During the late 1930s Sassoon wrote several brief poems on his son's birth and early years. In the best of these, "Meeting and Parting," Sassoon looks with love at his newborn son and then thinks of the grown-up man looking down at him at the time of his death. (Sassoon in his last years commented on the pleasure he had in talking with his son, who had recognized in his father his "second self." George Sassoon was present at his father's death.)

In the 1950s and 1960s Sassoon wrote meditative and philosophical poetry, focusing often on religious issues. He was preoccupied with such issues as the essential mystery of God as other and God as immanent in the spirit of the individual. The poems lack concentration and intensity and seldom achieve profundity. Very short—often only four lines long—they articulate momentary insights into what constitutes for Sassoon an ultimate reality, or they represent momentary affirmations of belief, or they are prayerlike and spontaneous celebrations of a unity recognized between God and himself. Often the poems of this period focus on a single image, like the opening of one flower. Biblical juxtapositions recur with the oxymoronic overtones that sometimes occur in the scriptures: losing oneself in order to find the self, becoming blind in order to see, dying in order to live. Familiar truths and paradoxes are presented with a sense of rediscovery or surprise.

In 1953 Sassoon remarked that he had remained under the spell of Swinburne, not only in his prewar poems but in all of his poetry after the war—that he had the rhythms of Swinburne in his mind and that their effect continued to hypnotize him. He related Swinburne's overpowering "auditory" influence to his own "cello voice" in a poetry characterized by the use of melancholy, nostalgic, and somewhat monotonous rhythms. Actually, in his best poems Sassoon may still have found Thomas Hardy to be a more dominant influence than Swinburne. During the war Sassoon had dedicated his first commercially produced collection, *The Old Huntsman and Other Poems*, to Hardy, and he had referred to his having read Hardy's novels in a dugout and not wanting to be killed before finishing the Hardy novel that he was then reading. In one of the later poems that reflects Hardy's ability to create graceful, if rugged, poems and to limn a sharp portrait, Sassoon created a memorable picture of the aged Hardy. The sonnet "At Max Gate" (1950) recalls a visit to Hardy in 1924. Hardy sits beside the fire, petting his dog, and appears as a man of hope and contentment. In the ironic and surprising last line—typical of Hardy but in its subtlety less typical of Sassoon's final lines—the poet expresses his recognition in 1950 that someone else "had taken Mr. Hardy's place."

In 1953 Sassoon sought to describe in his diary his various types of poetry: (1) his declamatory poems with their "loud-speaker" style; (2) his "strongly-drawn cartoons," which had given him wartime success as a satirist but had not satisfied him; (3) his poems characterized by an "indirect" style, which he felt that he had not yet perfected but which he longed to perfect; and (4) his "soliloquies," which dominate his late work. He observed that his poems were not visually evocative, and that he had much difficulty in trying to make them so, although while writing them he had always thought in terms of visual images. He also expressed distaste for the "loud ones" with their closing "fortissimo line," which had brought him fame thirty-five years earlier. He now saw himself as a poet whose work could not be appropriately evaluated aesthetically because of stereotypical opinions about it. He had been typed as a war poet who had written dramatic and strident poems. Sassoon felt that the poet should communicate directly with the common reader, and he believed that his audience had diminished as critics turned readers toward the predominant mode of the period, an intense, concentrated, elliptical, and intellectualized kind of poetry. To Sassoon, T. S. Eliot seemed "too professorial," and he commented that he could make neither head nor tail of *The Waste Land*. But he amiably conceded a few years before his death that Eliot had become an important touchstone by which his contemporaries were to be measured: "Anyhow, he was there to put us all in our place." Sassoon thought that even his friend Dame Edith Sitwell had been encouraged to turn away from his work as "old-fashioned," and he also felt that it was difficult for devotional religious poetry to be evaluated on its aesthetic merits.

Sassoon chose to live a relatively solitary existence in the last two decades of his life, but he was never a recluse. In 1933, at the age of forty-seven, he had married Hester Gatty and became a father three years later. The couple apparently lived together about ten years and then separated, but they remained good friends. During the years of World War II, Heytesbury House was largely taken over for refugees—some of whom Sassoon complained were unclean and ill-behaved. He complained also of the cold in the large house during those years, but the years of his son's childhood were happy ones for him. In the 1950s and 1960s his letters and diary entries comment on the extended visits of his son and his wife. Though he was practicing a disciplined preparation for death and eternity through meditation and prayer and writing, he had considerable contact with neighbors, particularly the nuns from Stanbrook Abbey. He greatly missed old friends such as Thomas Hardy, Max Beerbohm, Robert Ross, T. E. Lawrence, Edith Sitwell, E. M. Forster, and Walter de la Mare. (One of his last public speeches was the dedication of the memorial for de la Mare at St. Paul's Cathedral in December 1961.) But some old friends remained. He wrote that the high point of his eightieth birthday, 8 September 1966, was his having received a letter from John Masefield, the poet he had parodied in *The Daffodil Murderer* (1913), and he also rejoiced that year that his old friend of fifty years, Edmund Blunden, had received double the votes "of his

American adversary, Robert Lowell" for the Oxford Professorship of Poetry: "So, for once, an exceptionally modest man is given his due."

For his eightieth birthday, the Arts Council of Britain honored him with the publication of eight short poems, *An Octave*. In honor of this birthday the Stanbrook Abbey Press presented him with a calligraphic edition of *Something About Myself*, a story about cats that Sassoon had written at age eleven and illustrated for his mother. The dedication described Sassoon as "poet, warrior, and fox-hunting man, who even to serene old age has kept the heart of a child." As the dedication indicates, Sassoon had lived the active life of one concerned about and enjoying society, and he had lived the passive, contemplative life. The paradox is that as a poet he had actualized his career as a soldier so much more memorably than his life as a religious seeker. On 3 September 1967, he died in the company of his son quietly at home, an occasion toward which he had looked with joyful anticipation.

Other:

Wilfred Owen, *Poems*, edited, with an introduction, by Sassoon (London: Chatto & Windus, 1920; New York: Huebsch, 1921).

Letters:

Letters to a Critic by Siegfried Sassoon, edited by Michael Thorpe (Nettlestead: Kent Editions, 1976).

Bibliography:

Sir Geoffrey Keynes, *A Bibliography of Siegfried Sassoon* (London: Hart-Davis, 1962).

Biography:

Dame Felicitas Corrigan, *Siegfried Sassoon: Poet's Pilgrimage* (London: Gollancz, 1973).

References:

Bernard Bergonzi, *Heroes' Twilight* (London: Constable, 1965);

Paul Fussell, *The Great War and Modern Memory* (London & New York: Oxford University Press, 1975);

Robert Graves: *Goodbye to All That* (London: Cape, 1929; New York: Cape & Smith, 1930);

John H. Johnston, *English Poetry of the First World War* (Princeton: Princeton University Press, 1964);

Arthur E. Lane, *An Adequate Response* (Detroit: Wayne State University Press, 1972);

John Lehmann, *The English Poets of the First World War* (New York: Thames & Hudson, 1982);

John Silkin, *Out of Battle: The Poetry of the Great War* (London: Oxford University Press, 1972);

Michael Thorpe, *Siegfried Sassoon, A Critical Study* (London: Oxford University Press, 1967).

Papers:

The McFarlin Library at the University of Tulsa and the Edmund Blunden Collection at the University of Iowa have collections of Sassoon's papers.

Edith Sitwell

(7 September 1887-11 December 1964)

Robert K. Martin
Concordia University

SELECTED BOOKS: *The Mother and Other Poems* (Oxford: Blackwell, 1915);

Twentieth-Century Harlequinade and Other Poems, by Edith Sitwell and Osbert Sitwell (Oxford: Blackwell, 1916);

Clowns' Houses (Oxford: Blackwell, 1918);

The Wooden Pegasus (Oxford: Blackwell, 1920);

Façade (Kensington: Favil Press, 1922);

Bucolic Comedies (London: Duckworth, 1923);

The Sleeping Beauty (London: Duckworth, 1924; New York: Knopf, 1924);

Troy Park (London: Duckworth, 1925; New York: Knopf, 1925);

Poor Young People, by Edith Sitwell, Osbert Sitwell, and Sacheverell Sitwell (London: Fleuron, 1925);

Poetry and Criticism (London: Hogarth Press, 1925; New York: Holt, 1926);

Edith Sitwell (BBC Hulton, photo by Elliot & Fry Ltd.)

Elegy on Dead Fashion (London: Duckworth, 1926);
Rustic Elegies (London: Duckworth, 1927; New York: Knopf, 1927);
Gold Coast Customs (London: Duckworth, 1929; Boston & New York: Houghton Mifflin, 1929);
Alexander Pope (London: Faber & Faber, 1930; New York: Cosmopolitan Book Company,. 1930);
Collected Poems (London: Duckworth/Boston: Houghton Mifflin, 1930);
Bath (London: Faber & Faber, 1932; New York: Harrison Smith, 1932);
The English Eccentrics (London: Faber & Faber, 1933; Boston & New York: Houghton Mifflin, 1933; revised and enlarged edition, New York: Vanguard, 1957; London: Dobson, 1958);
Five Variations on a Theme (London: Duckworth, 1933);
Aspects of Modern Poetry (London: Duckworth, 1934);
Victoria of England (London: Faber & Faber, 1936; Boston: Houghton Mifflin, 1936);
Selected Poems (London: Duckworth, 1936; Boston: Houghton Mifflin, 1937);
I Live Under a Black Sun (London: Gollancz, 1937; Garden City: Doubleday, Doran, 1938);
Poems New and Old (London: Faber & Faber, 1940);
Street Songs (London: Macmillan, 1942);
English Women (London: Collins, 1942);
A Poet's Notebook (London: Macmillan, 1943);
Green Song & Other Poems (London: Macmillan, 1944; New York: View Editions, 1946);
The Song of the Cold (London: Macmillan, 1945);
Fanfare for Elizabeth (New York: Macmillan, 1946; London: Macmillan, 1946);
The Shadow of Cain (London: Lehmann, 1947);
A Notebook on William Shakespeare (London: Macmillan, 1948; Boston: Beacon Press, 1961);
The Canticle of the Rose: Selected Poems 1920-1947 (London: Macmillan, 1949); republished as *The Canticle of the Rose: Poems 1917-49* (New York: Vanguard, 1949);
Poor Men's Music (London: Fore Publications, 1950; Denver: Swallow, 1950);
Façade and Other Poems, 1920-1935 (London: Duckworth, 1950);
A Poet's Notebook (Boston: Little, Brown, 1950)—contains most of *A Poet's Notebook* (1943) and *A Notebook on William Shakespeare* (1948);
Selected Poems (Harmondsworth: Penguin, 1952);
Gardeners and Astronomers (London: Macmillan, 1953; abridged edition, New York: Vanguard, 1953);
Collected Poems (New York: Vanguard, 1954; enlarged edition, London: Macmillan, 1957);
The Outcasts (London: Macmillan, 1962); enlarged as *Music and Ceremonies* (New York: Vanguard, 1963);
The Queens of the Hive (London: Macmillan, 1962; Boston & Toronto: Little, Brown, 1962);
Taken Care Of (London: Hutchinson, 1965; New York: Atheneum, 1965);
Selected Poems of Edith Sitwell, edited by John Lehmann (London, Melbourne, & Toronto: Macmillan, 1965).

Of all the modern poets who came of age during the second decade of the twentieth century, Edith Sitwell remains the least understood and least appreciated. The reasons for this apparent neglect are several: sex prejudice, reluctance to admit a woman to Parnassus; class prejudice, reluctance to accept as a serious poet the granddaughter of the Earl of Londesborough; a belief in poetry as a private art, which made Edith Sitwell's public notoriety, as well as her performances of her poetry, suspect; and the mistaken idea, derived from a misreading of the early poems, that Sitwell was a poet without ideas. Edith Sitwell was born into an aristocratic country family. She was the daughter of Sir George Sitwell and his wife, Lady Ida Denison, daughter of Lord and Lady Londesborough. Her childhood was spent at her parents' home, Renishaw Hall in Derbyshire, and at her grandparents' home in Scarborough. The first child of an odd and unhappy marriage, Edith Sitwell had two younger brothers, Osbert, born in 1892, and Sacheverell, born in 1897. Renishaw gave Edith Sitwell a strong sense of family and history, and it was to play a large part in her poetic world. She was educated at home and began writing poetry when she was about twenty, but the major change in her life came when she moved to London in 1914 to share a flat with Helen Rootham, her former governess.

Although Sitwell had already produced a book of poems, *The Mother and Other Poems* (1915), she first came to public notice as the editor of *Wheels*, an anthology of contemporary verse published in six volumes, or "cycles," from 1916 to 1921. These anthologies were designed to provide an alternative to poetry of the Georgians. Against the Georgians' rural, nostalgic values, the group that Edith and her brothers Osbert and Sacheverell gathered about them were developing the bright, hard satiric style that came to be their trademark. The most significant contribution of *Wheels* to the history of modern poetry was the publication of seven poems by Wilfred Owen in the fourth cycle (1919). Like her brother Osbert, Edith Sitwell began her poetic career as an opponent of the monstrosity of war and of the foolish self-satisfaction of Edwardian England. Later she would continue this concern and become the most distinguished poet of World War II, with her poems "Still Falls the Rain," based on the air raids on England at the beginning of the war, and "Three Poems of the Atomic Age," based on the bombing of Hiroshima.

The Sitwells gave their first reading in December 1917 at an evening arranged by Lady Sybil Colefax, where they were joined by T. S. Eliot. Readings became important means for the establishment of Edith Sitwell's reputation, and much of her early poetry owes its character to the presumption that it would be read aloud. For it was Edith Sitwell more than anyone else who realized the importance of sound and texture in modern poetry and who introduced a poetry designed to take full advantage of the flexible rhythms of the spoken voice. Her interest in spoken poetry reached its fullest expression in the sequence of poems entitled *Façade*, first published in 1922.

The idea of declaiming poetry set to music was not invented by Sitwell, although her performances of *Façade* gave it its most distinguished form. Among the important precedents for the form were Arnold Schoenberg's *Pierrot Lunaire* (1912) and Erik Satie's *Parade* (1917). Sitwell's interest in modern art was considerable, and *Façade* should be considered an integral part of the international movement that embraced poetry, painting, and dance. Half of the poems that eventually found a place in *Façade* were composed earlier, while the others were written for music by William Walton. The poems were recited through a Sengerphone, a large megaphone with a mouthpiece. Since the Sengerphone and the speaker were concealed behind a curtain, the spoken voice achieved simultaneous clarity and impersonality. Sitwell considered the poems abstract: patterns in sound or virtuoso exercises. She saw them as explorations of the qualities of rhythm, in which meaning was secondary. There are obvious connections between this view of the poetry and the development of various schools of abstraction in painting. By allying herself with this forthright modernism, Sitwell was emphasizing her break with the Georgians. She was also exploring the possible application of the means of one medium to another. While this practice had already become frequent in the poetry of the French symbolists and their successors, nothing quite like it had been seen in English verse.

The poems were not sung but read, thereby emphasizing the inherently rhythmic quality of spoken verse. Sitwell explored the possibilities of rhyme, alliteration, assonance, and what she termed "colour." Her imagery was also startling, heightened by condensation. Sitwell linked her condensed imagery to Swedenborg's theory of correspondences, which is given its most permanent poetic form in Baudelaire's poem of that name. The poems in *Façade* create striking synesthetic effects, as in these lines from "Waltz":

> Her hair seemed gold trees on the
> honey-cell sand
> When the thickest gold spangles, on deep
> water seen,
> Were like twanging guitar and cold
> mandoline.

Many of the poems have titles linking them to popular dances ("Fox Trot," "Polka," "Mazurka"—this last poem not set to music by Walton), and the musical settings often enhance their parodic character. "I do like to be beside the Seaside" is set to a music-hall melody that underscores the poem's satire of romance and seduction. The comic feminine rhymes and lilting anapests contribute to the poem's jaunty effect:

For the lady and her friend from Le Touquet
In the very shady trees upon the sand
Were plucking a white satin bouquet
Of foam, while the sand's brassy band
Blared in the wind.

The poems of *Façade* seem very much a part of the post-World War I decade. As Sitwell claimed, they show an extraordinary mastery of sound and rhythm, but they also reflect the sense of disillusionment and accelerated movement that characterized those years of social transformation. Drawing on Russian ballet as well as fairy tale and romance, Sitwell created a poetic world that vigorously asserted its modernity. The targets are many, ranging from the upper-middle class of "En Famille" to the lingering Calvinism of "Scotch Rhapsody" or Lord Tennyson and his poetic imitators in "When Sir Beelzebub." The early poems and their public performances in 1923, 1926, and 1928 established Edith Sitwell as a leader in the movement of the Young Turks. It was she who consolidated the forces of revolution in modern poetry and brought them to public notice, and by so doing she confirmed the death of Victorianism.

Although published the year after *Façade*, the poems of *Bucolic Comedies* (1923) were for the most part written earlier. Nonetheless there are a number of similarities to the poems of *Façade*, despite Sitwell's statement that there are no technical experiments in *Bucolic Comedies*. The fairy-tale rhyming couplets of "Aubade" recall (or anticipate) some of the rhythms of *Façade*, and there is already considerable use of feminine rhymes (or partial rhymes) for comic effect: pollard/dullard, noodle/flopdoodle, affection/direction, Palestrina/leaner. The overall tone of the volume is far more serious and elegiac. Several of the poems introduce autobiographical elements, which became increasingly important in her work. The poems are based on memory of an enchanted world, but they also recognize the living death of that world which Edith Sitwell associated with her childhood at Renishaw Hall and at Scarborough, the seat of the Londesboroughs. In "Winter," Osbert Sitwell is present as Dagobert, and Edith Sitwell is five-year old Anne in the frozen and strangely blighted world of the "Countess of L—." The final lines of the poem capture the sterility of her family's world and give an important indication of her development of the central images of gold and fire as symbols of creative energy:

Can this be Eternity?—snow peach-cold,
Sleeping and rising and growing old,

While she lies embalmed in the fire's
gold sheen,
Like a cross wasp in a ripe nectarine,

And the golden seed of the fire droops dead
And ripens not in the heart or head!

In "The Man with the Green Patch," Sitwell's critique of her parents' world takes more specific form: although they provide access to a timeless and fairy-tale world, they are each blind in one eye and unable or unwilling to see

The real world, terrible and old,
Where seraphs in the mart are sold
And fires from Bedlam's madness flare
Like blue palm-trees in desert air;
The prisons where the maimed men pined
Because their mothers bore them blind.

Despite this strong indictment of the spiritual blindness of her family's class, Sitwell's attitude toward her past was always ambivalent, for her upbringing had also permitted her access to a timeless world of pure music:

For there my youth passed like a sleep,
Yet in my heart, still murmuring deep,
The small green airs from Eternity,
Murmuring softly, never die.

Troy Park (1925) is the major collection of poems dealing with her family and her relationship to the past. In "Colonel Fantock," probably the most successful of the poems in this volume, Osbert, Sacheverell, and Edith Sitwell are present as "Dagobert, and Peregrine and I," and Colonel Fantock is a real person, a retired military man who had served as tutor to the Sitwells. Although parts of the poem are devoted to reminiscence, much of the poem is a meditation upon death. Colonel Fantock is seen as the comic character he apparently was, but he is also remembered for his magical qualities, his ability to transform reality into legend:

Edith and Osbert Sitwell (BBC Hulton)

> For us he wandered over each old lie,
> Changing the flowering hawthorn,
> full of bees,
> Into the silver helm of Hercules,
> For us defended Troy from the top stair
> Outside the nursery.

The mood is turned into grief, though, as Sitwell recounts the day that Colonel Fantock overhears a remark about his advancing age. On that day the magic is broken, and awareness of death has gained the "first citadel."

"The Little Ghost Who Died for Love" is narrated by Deborah Churchill (1678-1708), who was hanged for shielding her lover in a duel. Sitwell drew upon historical material to evoke a romantic world that is doomed to destruction, and although the poem is cast as an elegy for the dead woman, it is also a prophetic poem, warning of the impending death of a society that has so punished love. The poem shifts from mourning lines of great simplicity to evocation of spring and rebirth in bright lines of exuberant imagery, as if to state its truth that good and evil, beauty and ugliness, are contained one within the other. In her final words, Deborah proclaims her victory: "for it is not I / But this old world, is sick and soon must die!"

During the 1920s, the period of her greatest creative activity, Sitwell lived in a flat in Bayswater, London, with Helen Rootham, her former governess, although she spent the summers at Renishaw Hall. She participated with her brothers in the literary life of the capital and entertained on her own. Their friends included T. S. Eliot and Aldous Huxley, although there was a break with Huxley in 1922, following the publication of a story by him which included a very unkind portrait of Osbert. Edith Sitwell was an admirer of Eliot's work, but she was also concerned by the fact that *The Waste Land* (1922) got far better reviews and far more critical attention than her books. Although an acquaintance of Virginia Woolf's, she was never more than on the fringes of Bloomsbury, which she thought of as somewhat too "closely serried" for her rather independent tastes; nonetheless there were affinities between the Sitwells and Bloomsbury, including their reaction against the Edwardian establishment and their strong opposition to war.

Throughout the 1920s Sitwell's poems displayed a mixture of elegiac memory with the sense of a world lost through the recognition of evil. Her long poem *The Sleeping Beauty* (1924) evokes the enchanted fairy-tale world "of ghostly flowers, all poignant with spring rain. / Smelling of youth that will not come again." But this world is clearly departed, and the poet recognizes her need to go beyond these memories, to be reborn out of the timeless world of the dream and into reality: "And now the brutish forests close around / The beauty sleeping in enchanted ground." The culmination of this development toward a position as a poet of social commentary occurred with the publication of the long poem *Gold Coast Customs* (1929). Although many of the poem's forms are obviously reminiscent of her earlier work (the elaborate use of both end rhymes and internal rhymes, as well as strong rhythmic patterns), the purpose to which these forms is put is much more resolutely critical. Sitwell had begun her move from the satiric and parodic to the revolutionary and visionary.

Gold Coast Customs interweaves the funeral customs of the Ashantee nation and contemporary society life of London. Sitwell's contemporary figure, Lady Bamburgher, is a symbol of the moral and social corruption that lies beneath the surface of fashionable life. The poem's strong beat and clear voice give a striking portrayal of an historical pattern of decay and betrayal. It concludes, however, with a vision of transformation and salvation:

> Yet the time will come
> To the heart's dark slum
> When the rich man's gold and the rich man's wheat
> Will grow in the street, that the starved may eat,—
> And the sea of the rich will give up its dead—
> And the last blood and fire from my side will be shed.
> For the fires of God go marching on.

As Jack Lindsay, a Marxist critic, has noted in his important introduction to *Façade and Other Poems, 1920-1935* (1950), *Gold Coast Customs* represented "the deepest—almost the only—political poetry" of the age in England, but Sitwell was never to be recognized as a political poet, perhaps because of her public reputation as a performer and aesthete, perhaps because of her social position. It is even more likely that admiration for Sitwell's political poetry was withheld because her sense of injustice and impending revolution was almost always accompanied, as in this poem, with religious imagery of rebirth at a time when religious faith in poetry had become unpopular. What was only a suggestion in *Gold Coast Customs* would later become the keynote of her poetry.

Technically, *Gold Coast Customs* is a major accomplishment. It illustrates the almost complete abandonment of straightforward narrative line. Instead the poem is structured around a series of contrasts, its effects cumulative rather than progressive. Geoffrey Singleton has linked Sitwell's practice to the film techniques of Sergei Eisenstein, showing her mastery of montage to accomplish rapid transitions back and forth among the levels (or tiers, as she called them) of the poem. Sitwell calls upon her reader to follow the action on various planes simultaneously by cutting from one to the other and hence by suggesting the interrelationships among the various periods or levels of civilization. The poem has also been said to have a polyphonic structure, bringing together several separate, although related, voice lines.

If the decade of the 1920s represented a period of great poetic advance and considerable public acclaim, the following decade was one of relative silence and personal loss. Sitwell devoted a large part of her energies to caring for Helen Rootham, who was seriously ill and would never recover. What writing Sitwell did was primarily in prose, which does, however, shed considerable light on her interests as a poet. In 1930 she produced a biography, *Alexander Pope*, in which she indicated her sympathy for this lonely man with a misshapen body and with whom she identified herself repeatedly. That identification was not only personal, but, more important, poetic: she identified Pope as an important part of the English poetic tradition from which she sprang; the failure to appreciate Pope adequately thus indicated her own fate at the hands of the critics. She praised Pope above all for his "rhetoric and formalism" and his refusal to give in to the hopeful formulas of his day. He was also praised for his ability to join intellect and personal expression; as Sitwell put it, "a poem begins in the poet's head, and then grows in his blood." Her other major work of prose during these years was her novel, *I Live under a Black Sun* (1937), based on the life of Jonathan Swift. Her structure is radical: a montage which shifts from the Middle Ages to World War I, moving Swift adroitly through time and place. Swift's acid satires and bleak vision of human folly were a perfect expression of her own state of mind. Her despair at the madness of war broadened into a recognition of mankind's self-destructive nature and was sustained by her own sense of personal loss.

Sitwell lived mostly in Paris with Helen Rootham from 1932 until Rootham's death in 1938, and in Paris she made the acquaintance of the great love of her life, the surrealist painter Pavel Tchelitchew, through Gertrude Stein. Since Tchelitchew was homosexual, the love remained unfulfilled, and Sitwell often felt betrayed by him. Nonetheless she remained a constant friend and

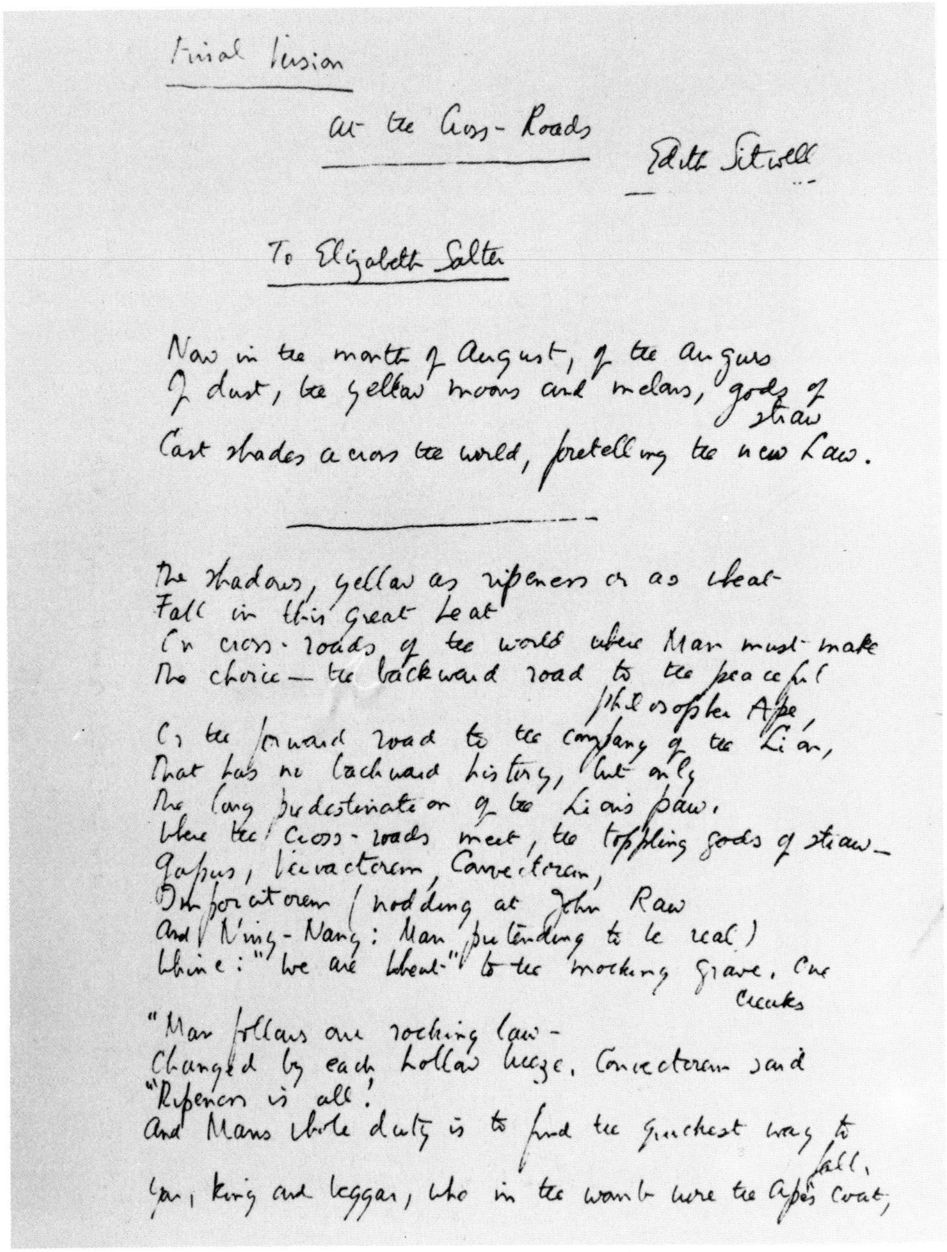
Final Version

At the Cross-Roads

Edith Sitwell

To Elizabeth Salter

Now in the month of August, of the augurs
Of dust, the yellow moons and melons, gods of straw
Cast shades across the world, foretelling the new Law.

The shadows, yellow as ripeness or as wheat
Fall in this great heat
On cross-roads of the world where Man must make
The choice — the backward road to the peaceful philosopher Ape,
Or the forward road to the company of the Lion,
That has no backward history, but only
The long predestination of the Lion's paw.
Where the Cross-roads meet, the toppling gods of straw —
Gogus, Wiseacreum, Conventicum,
Dunforatorem (nodding at John Raw
And Ning-Nang: Man pretending to be real)
Whine: "We are wheat" to the mocking grave. One creaks
"Man follows one rocking law —
Changed by each hollow breeze. Conventicum said
"Ripeness is all!
And Man's whole duty is to find the quickest way to fall,
Yes, king and beggar, who in the womb wore the Ape's coat,

Page from the manuscript for "At the Crossroads" (Elizabeth Salter, Edith Sitwell*)*

supporter over many years and attempted to find buyers for Tchelitchew's paintings. Since Osbert Sitwell was also homosexual, it is certain that Edith Sitwell often moved in a homosexual milieu; most of her biographers believe, however, that she preferred to ignore this fact. The one poem which Sitwell wrote during the 1930s, "Romance," is a moving testimony to the power of the love which she felt for Tchelitchew. The poem is written largely in heroic couplets; Sitwell draws upon all her poetic resources to subtly work within the iambic-pentameter line to create a subtly rich harmony of sound and rhythm. The imagery is lush and erotic:

> Green were the pomp and pleasure
> of the shade
> Wherein they dwelt; like country
> temples green
> The huge leaves bear a dark-mosaic's sheen
> Like gold on forest temples richly laid.
>
> In that smooth darkness, the gourds
> dark as caves
> Hold thick gold honey for their
> fountain waves,
> Figs, dark and wrinkled as Silenus, hold
> Rubies and garnets, and the melons cold
> Waves dancing . . .

The poem also recognizes the dominion of time and loss and finds strength out of suffering; although recognizing that winter must fall and that "I must wake alone / With a void coffin of sad flesh and bone," nonetheless the poet finds consolation in memory's "strange perfume."

Sitwell's other prose works during this period include a biography of Queen Victoria (1936), a book about Bath (1932), and *The English Eccentrics* (1933), a celebration of the kind of deliberate and outrageous nonconformity that she was making her own hallmark. For Sitwell, who had always suffered from a sense that she was an inadequate woman because she was not beautiful enough, learned to make of her unusual appearance an element of theatrical beauty, which is reflected in a number of the portraits of her. Cecil Beaton turned her into a gauzy romantic creature, Tchelitchew into a brooding Renaissance Madonna. Her own clothing was chosen to reflect timelessness; heavy brocade dresses, turbans, and enormous jewels gave her a

Edith, Sacheverell, and Osbert Sitwell (photo by Baron)

dignity and a kind of impersonality that were necessary to complete her rebellion against the Edwardian upper class.

The outbreak of World War II confirmed Sitwell's sense of cultural despair and gave renewed impetus to her search for emblems of healing and renewal. "Still Falls the Rain" (in *Street Songs*, 1942) is significantly subtitled "Night and Dawn," a reference not only to the actual times of the poem but to the hope for spiritual rebirth out of agony. The form of the poem is loose; although the rhythms are largely iambic, the lines are varied in length from two to seven feet. The title phrase, with its extraordinary power and sonority, is repeated seven times. It is rhymed, significantly, with "human brain," "pain," and "lain," and it acts as the organizing principle for a series of repetitions based on parallelism underscoring human failing and sin. The sixth stanza offers a dramatic reversal, with a recognition of the Crucifixion and its offering of redemption, and the final stanza concludes with its line ironically echoing the dominant chord, "Still do I love, still shed my innocent light, my Blood, for thee." Although the poem is described as a work about the air raids, it uses that rain of destruction as a representative of man's self-destruction, what Sitwell calls "the self-murdered heart, the wounds of the sad uncomprehending dark." Out of the agony of a nation, Sitwell turned to faith as the means for human recovery.

Other poems in *Street Songs* are equally powerful; the volume has been widely hailed as Sitwell's finest. Several, brilliantly blending Sitwell's personal feelings with cultural myth, are poems of age (Sitwell was in her fifties) and of hope, poems indicating that Sitwell has passed through her crises of the 1930s just as she believed mankind might pass through the crises of the war. Central to these poems is the symbolism of wheat, most often associated with gold. For Sitwell took as her principal persona in these poems a harvest goddess, offering birth from within herself. While a poem such as "Invocation" shows some relationship to Eliot's *The Waste Land* in its turn to myths of renewal and in its images of sterility ("the Lost Men / Who ask the city stones if they are bread / And the stones of the city weep"), it lacks the deep pessimism of Eliot's poem. "Invocation" sees in the goddess the hope that was lacking in the civilization of darkness that surrounded her. The poems in *Street Songs* gain power by their dramatic-monologue form, in which Sitwell speaks through the voice of the goddess. "Eurydice" is perhaps the finest of the series, melding personal love with the evocative power of myth. Although Eurydice has been touched by the freezing hand of Death, she finds recuperation within herself: "I cast the grandeur of Death away / And homeward came to the small things of Love, the building of the hearth, the kneading of daily bread." Led away from death by her lover (Orpheus or Adonis), she comes out of the tomb and into the light: "I turned to greet you— / And when I touched your mouth, it was the Sun."

Edith Sitwell's great power as a love poet has been inadequately recognized. It is hard to think of another poet of the twentieth century, except perhaps her disciple Dylan Thomas, who has so powerfully written of the ecstasy of personal love and its power to transform. Sitwell's "Mary Stuart to James Boswell (Casket Letter No. II)" is an example of her love poetry at its finest. She is able to transform herself into the historic person and make her come alive. There is no better way of capturing the excess, and the grandeur, of love than these concluding lines in which Mary is transported by the vision of her love:

> But how should Pity stand between
> you and me!
> The Devil sunder us from our mates,
> and God
> Knit us together
> Until nor man nor devil could tell
> lover from lover
> In our heaven of damnation! Could these
> sunder our clay,
> Or the seas of our blood? As well might they
> part the fires
> That would burn to the bottom of
> Hell . . . . But there is no Hell—
> We have kissed it away.

Sitwell had little sympathy for female poets—she singled out only Sappho, Christina Rossetti, and Emily Dickinson for partial exoneration from her general scorn of incompetence and flabbiness—but her own work depended upon a deep sense of affinity for women, such as Mary Stuart, destroyed for faith and love. And "Mary Stuart to James Boswell" does show a certain likeness to Dickinson's "I cannot live with you" despite obvious differences of poetic technique.

The end of the war brought the horror of the atom-bomb explosions in Japan and prompted *The Shadow of Cain* (1947), Sitwell's memorable poem of destruction and regeneration. Still echoing Eliot, Sitwell wrote of the alienation between men which had given rise to universal sterility. The poem is set in "that Spring when there were no flowers" and joins imagery of metal and darkness to convey the evil of man's murderous impulse: "And now the Earth lies flat beneath the shade of an iron wing." The gold which had been the alchemical symbol of perfection and the natural color of the wheat has been transformed into human greed, as men seek their own power and wealth and abandon their concern for their brothers. But in the midst of this horror, in the rain of destruction, there is also the potential for renewed fertility, as in the blood of Christ; there is new life for man. In the midst of destruction is renewed hope: "He walks upon the Seas of Blood, He comes in the terrible Rain."

In 1948 Edith and Osbert Sitwell undertook a lecture tour of the United States which lasted almost six months. It was highly successful and contributed greatly to her reputation in America. She made a new recording of *Façade*, and she was the guest of honor at a party given by the Gotham Book Mart, to which Marianne Moore, Randall Jarrell, Elizabeth Bishop, Gore Vidal, Tennessee Williams, and W. H. Auden, among others, came. The success of this tour led to a second one in 1950, which included a visit to Hollywood, where she read from *Macbeth*. Her interest in Shakespeare had grown considerably over the past few years, and several of the plays, including particularly *King Lear*, had a marked influence on her work. Her interest in the Elizabethan period included a fascination with Elizabeth I, which gave rise to her book *Fanfare for Elizabeth* (1946) and the ill-fated plans for a Hollywood film based on it, to be directed by George Cukor.

Largely unrecognized or scorned during her earlier years, Edith Sitwell was heaped with honors in her last years. In 1951 she received an honorary D. Litt. from Oxford (of which she was very proud, at the same time that she never forgave her father for a conventional girl's upbringing that had prevented her from obtaining a proper education and knowledge of Greek and Latin). Three years later, in 1954, she was made a Dame Commander of the Order of the British Empire by the Queen. Her seventieth birthday was celebrated by a luncheon given by the *Sunday Times* and her seventy-fifth by a concert at the Royal Festival Hall, which included Benjamin Britten's setting of "Still Falls the Rain" as well as a performance of *Façade*. During these years she also worked hard on behalf of young artists whom she had admired. She had always helped younger writers, beginning with the discovery and editing of Wilfred Owen and including the support given Dylan Thomas, and her new enthusiasms included Robert Lowell, Allen Ginsberg, and James Purdy.

Edith Sitwell, 1956 (BBC Hulton, photo by Baron)

In the meantime Sitwell's religious beliefs had intensified, and she decided to be accepted into the Roman Catholic Church in 1955. She received instruction from Father Martin D'Arcy and was baptized at the Farm Street church in London. Evelyn Waugh and Roy Campbell were her godfathers. The church provided consolation for her during her last years of loneliness and ill health. She received the last rites of the church before her death in London on 11 December 1964.

Critical appraisal of her work has been mixed. Babette Deutsch praises the "luxurious beauty" of her poems but argues that sometimes they are hurt by an excess of richness, "an extravagance of imagery that sometimes almost overwhelms the poem." David Daiches, who sees her sources in the art and poetry of the seventeenth and eighteenth centuries, as well as in French symbolism, comments, "The deliberate confusion of the senses . . . , the highly personal rococo images, the painted artificiality, the playfulness alternating with a half-suppressed grimness, the dream quality hovering between farce and nightmare, the marshalling of bright and brittle phrases with deliberate disregard of their relation to each other, the carefully fantastic situations, the tom-tom rhythms, the preference for geometric rather than natural form, the clowning, the anarchy, the individuality—all these features of Edith Sitwell's poetry suggest a culture that has lost its roots and its normal function and as a result is being used as a quarry from which to dig up coloured counters that are tossed into the air with the skill of an expert conjuror yet in a mood of suppressed hysteria." Other poets have praised her extraordinary technical skills; Marianne Moore called her "a virtuoso of rhythm and accent" and "an expert of the condensed phrase."

Sitwell's reputation has always suffered from the exceptional success of *Façade*, which was often treated as if it were the only work she had ever written. Inadequate attention has been paid to her development as a social poet, as a religious poet, and as a visionary. Her career traces the development of English poetry from the immediate post-World War I period of brightness and jazzy rhythms through the political involvements of the 1930s and the return to spiritual values after World War II. Her technique evolved, and, although she always remained a poet committed to the exploration of sound, she came to use sound patterns as an element in the construction of deep philosophic poems that reflect on her time and on man's condition. Edith Sitwell needs to be remembered not only as the bright young parodist of *Façade*, but as the angry chronicler of social injustice, as a poet who has found forms adequate to the atomic age and its horrors, and as a foremost poet of love. Her work displays enormous range of subject and of form. With her contemporary Eliot she remains one of the most important voices of twentieth-century English poetry.

Other:

Wheels, edited by Sitwell (Oxford: Blackwell, 1916);

Wheels, Second Cycle, edited by Sitwell (Oxford: Blackwell, 1917);

Wheels, Third Cycle, edited by Sitwell (Oxford: Blackwell, 1919);

Wheels, Fourth Cycle, edited by Sitwell (Oxford: Blackwell, 1919);

Wheels, Fifth Cycle, edited by Sitwell (London: Parsons, 1920);

Wheels, Sixth Cycle, edited by Sitwell (London: Daniel, 1921);

The Pleasures of Poetry, First Series: Milton and the Augustan Age, edited by Sitwell (London: Duckworth, 1930; New York: Norton, 1934);

The Pleasures of Poetry, Second Series: The Romantic Revival, edited by Sitwell (London: Duckworth, 1931; New York: Norton, 1934);

The Pleasures of Poetry, Third Series: The Victorian Age, edited by Sitwell (London: Duckworth, 1932; New York: Norton, 1934);

The American Genius, edited by Sitwell (London: Lehmann, 1951).

Bibliography:

Richard Fifoot, *A Bibliography of Edith, Osbert, and Sacheverell Sitwell*, revised edition (Hamden, Conn.: Archon, 1971).

Biographies:

John Lehmann, *A Nest of Tigers: The Sitwells in Their Times* (London: Macmillan, 1968);

John Pearson, *Façades: Edith, Osbert and Sacheverell Sitwell* (London: Macmillan, 1978); republished as *The Sitwell's: A Family Biography* (New York: Harcourt, Brace, 1979);

Victoria Glendinning, *Edith Sitwell: A Unicorn Among Lions* (London: Weidenfeld & Nicolson, 1981).

References:

C. M. Bowra, *Edith Sitwell* (Monaco: Lyrebird, 1947);

James Brophy, *Edith Sitwell: The Symbolist Order* (Carbondale: Southern Illinois University Press, 1968);

David Daiches, *Poetry and the Modern World* (Chicago: University of Chicago Press, 1940), pp. 85-89;

Babette Deutsch, *Poetry in Our Times* (New York: Columbia University Press, 1956), pp. 220-228;

G. S. Fraser, *The Modern Writer and His World* (London: André Deutsch, 1964), pp. 283-286;

Horace Gregory, "The 'Vita-Nuova' of Baroque Art in the Recent Poetry of Edith Sitwell," *Poetry*, 66 (June 1945): 148-156;

John Lehmann, Introduction to *Selected Poems of Edith Sitwell* (London: Macmillan, 1965);

Jack Lindsay, Introduction to *Façade and Other Poems, 1920-1935* (London: Duckworth, 1950);

Ralph J. Mills, *Edith Sitwell* (Grand Rapids, Mich.: Eerdmans, 1966);

Marianne Moore, "Edith Sitwell, Virtuoso" in her *A Marianne Moore Reader* (New York: Viking, 1965), pp. 210-215;

Vivian de Sola Pinto, *Crisis in English Poetry: 1880-1940* (London: Hutchinson, 1967), pp. 190-193, 205-208;

John Press, *A Map of Modern English Verse* (London: Oxford University Press, 1969), pp. 157-159;
Geoffrey Singleton, *Edith Sitwell: The Hymn to Life* (London: Fortune Press, 1960);
José Garcia Villa, ed., *A Celebration for Edith Sitwell* (New York: New Directions, 1948; republished, Freeport, N.Y.: Books for Libraries Press, 1972).

Papers:
Edith Sitwell's manuscripts are in the Humanities Research Center at the University of Texas, Austin.

Stevie Smith
(20 September 1902-7 March 1971)

Linda Rahm Hallett

BOOKS: *Novel on Yellow Paper* (London: Cape, 1936; New York: Morris, 1937);
A Good Time Was Had By All (London & Toronto: Cape, 1937);
Over the Frontier (London: Cape, 1938);
Tender Only to One (London: Cape, 1938);
Mother, What Is Man? (London & Toronto: Cape, 1942);
The Holiday (London: Chapman & Hall, 1949);
Harold's Leap (London: Chapman & Hall, 1950);
Not Waving but Drowning (London: Deutsch, 1957);
Some Are More Human than Others: Sketchbook (London: Gaberbocchus, 1958);
Selected Poems (London: Longmans, Green, 1962; Norfolk, Conn.: New Directions, 1964);
The Frog Prince and Other Poems (London: Longmans, Green, 1966);
The Best Beast (New York: Knopf, 1969);
Scorpion and Other Poems (London: Longman, 1972);
The Collected Poems of Stevie Smith (London: Allen Lane, 1975; New York: Oxford University Press, 1976);
Me Again: Uncollected Writings of Stevie Smith, edited by Jack Barbera and William McBrien (London: Virago, 1981; New York: Farrar, Straus & Giroux, 1982).

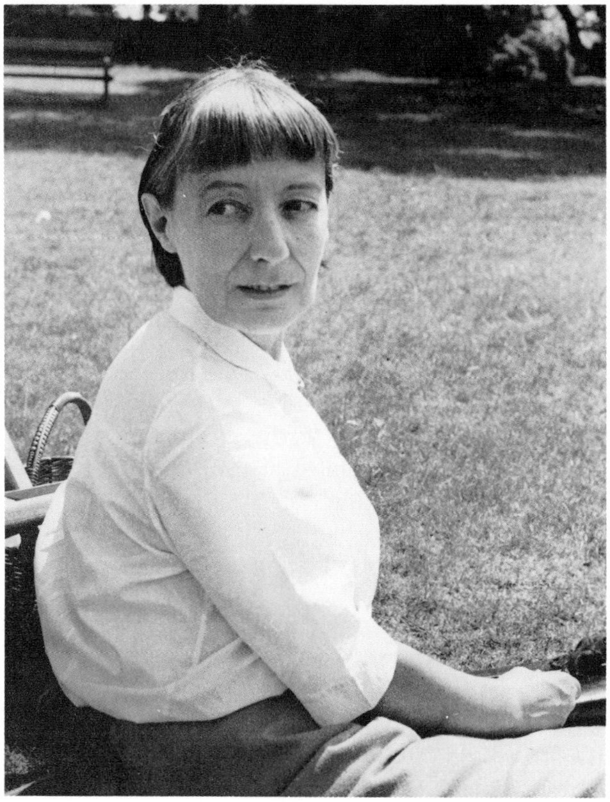

Stevie Smith, 1954 (BBC Hulton)

Stevie Smith's work, like her life, does not readily yield the interesting patterns of change and development favored by literary biographers. She lived in the same house from the age of three until her death in 1971 and held the same job, with the London publishing firm of George Newnes, for some thirty years. She had many friends, but no significant literary relationships. She read little contemporary poetry, and, of her own work, she said to Peter Orr in 1961, "I don't think my poems have changed very much since I started writing." The *Times Literary Supplement* mentioned her first collection of poetry under the category "Humor," and the sometimes disconcerting mixture of wit and seriousness noted by that early reviewer continued to characterize her later volumes, making her at once one of the most consistent and most elusive of poets. Like the swimmer's gesture in her best-known poem, Smith's seemingly light verse in fact signals not waving but drowning. Without identifying itself with any particular school of modern poetics, her voice is nevertheless very much that of what she once called the "age of unrest" through which she lived.

Florence Margaret Smith was born in Hull, Yorkshire, in 1902. The nickname, Stevie, which she adopted as her nom de plume, came later, when a friend with whom she was riding jokingly compared her to a jockey named Steve Donoghue. Her mother having made what she dryly termed "an unsuitable marriage," Smith seldom saw her father, who left his family and joined the North Sea Patrol soon after the birth of his second daughter. Allusion to this fact was to occur repeatedly in Smith's writing, both directly, as in *Novel on Yellow Paper* (1936) and in poems such as "Papa Love Baby" and "Infant," and indirectly, in her frequent portrayals of lost or abandoned children.

Despite what was effectively a desertion by one parent and her own frequent illnesses, including tuberculosis at the age of five, Smith's childhood was not an insecure one. In 1906 her mother moved with her sister and two small children to the North London suburb of Palmers Green, which was to be Smith's home for the rest of her life. In the late, "absolutely autobiographical" poem, "A House of Mercy," she describes the underlying strength and courage of that "house of female habitation"; in particular, the poem is one of her many tributes to "The noble aunt"—the "Lion of Hull" of the novels—who cared for the two, by then teen-aged, children after their mother's early death and who remained the single most important person in Stevie Smith's life.

After attending high school and the North London Collegiate School for Girls, Smith obtained a secretarial position with George Newnes, magazine publishers, eventually becoming private secretary to Sir Nevill Pearson and Sir Frank Newnes. She began writing poetry seriously in her twenties, and some of her early work appeared in *Granta* magazine. However, when she approached a publisher with her first collection of poems in 1935, she was advised to write a novel instead. She took the advice, but not without having a private joke at publishers in general, producing a "foot-off-the-ground novel," typed during office hours at Newnes on the yellow paper used for carbon copies and punctuated with specimens of her rejected poetry.

In *Novel on Yellow Paper*, as in her two subsequent novels, Smith draws heavily on her own life in creating the narrator—called Pompey Casmilus in the first two novels and Celia in the third—through whose eyes she explores the consciousness, and conscience, of World War II England. Like Smith, Pompey/Celia is a poet, holding down a rather boring London job and living with her maiden aunt in a middle-class suburb. Unmarried but passionately, if often critically, attached to her aunt and various friends and lovers, Smith's speaker develops her narrative chiefly through the interplay between the private turmoil of personal relationships and the public turmoil and dislocation of the years surrounding and including the war.

Perhaps even more than most fiction by poets, Smith's prose overlaps with her verse, both in themes and in approach to language and structure. "Over-Dew," a short story which she incorporated into her third novel, *The Holiday* (1949), was discovered to scan so perfectly that she later had it published as a poem, without any alteration except for the establishing of line and stanza divisions. Rather than plot or character study, Smith's novels emphasize discussion and reflection and the verbal ingenuity of the narrative voice. By including poems in all three of the novels, Smith contributes to the idea that they are, in a sense, extensions of the poetry; she also clarifies the effect of her historical context—or perhaps, more accurately, the questions raised by her historical context—on her writing.

Smith later expressed dissatisfaction with *Novel on Yellow Paper*, calling it overly mannered, but the book brought her important early recognition, and Jonathan Cape, who had published it in 1936, quickly followed with her first book of poems, *A Good Time Was Had By All*, in 1937, as well as her second novel, *Over the Frontier* and a second volume of poetry, *Tender Only to One*, in 1938. *A Good Time Was Had By All* established Smith's custom of embellishing her books with her own sketches, line drawings of people and animals which tend to comment on, rather than merely illustrate, the poems themselves. The volume also shows that Smith had already developed the stylistic features which were to mark her poetry throughout her career—the economy of expression, the verbal eclecticism which mixes archaic forms with modern colloquialisms and phrases in foreign languages, the presence of Gothic and fairy-tale devices, the building of poems around brief narratives or character sketches, and, perhaps most distinctive, the use of prosody reminiscent of humorous or popular verse to convey profoundly serious themes.

The opening poem, "The Hound of Ulster,"

finds Smith making use of two characteristic devices—the child as central figure and a light, almost nursery-rhyme meter—to probe the mysterious, rather sinister reality which lurks behind appealing or innocent appearances. Like many of her poems, it suggests, but does not impose, an allegorical reading. Smith takes both voices in the poem, that of the inquiring child and that of the "courteous stranger" who first tempts and then warns the child, and it is not unusual in her work for a single poem or several poems taken together to produce the effect of dialogue. No advocate of the strictly "pure" lyric, Smith did not hesitate to make use of prosaic statements, opinions, and judgments in her poetry, but her ability to adopt a variety of voices and points of view means that apparently straightforward pronouncements are constantly being reassessed, questioned, transformed by irony.

Smith subtitled *Novel on Yellow Paper, Work it out for Yourself*, and her poetry, too, tends to confront the reader with the problem of interpretation as a thematic, rather than simply a critical, issue. A later poem, "Not Waving but Drowning," is an example of how even the most urgent meaning can be misunderstood. Before her reformation, the orphan in "The Orphan Reformed" cries out in despair for parents; afterward, "when she cries, Father, Mother, it is only to please," and the people, no longer distressed, "say she is a mild tease." However, we have only the speaker's assurance that "now she is right" and that the orphan's words now bear an entirely different significance. Frequently, Smith also uses prosody or drawings to indicate other possible ways of interpreting the meaning of a poem's words. "Death Bereaves our Common Mother Nature Grieves for my Dead Brother," a poem about a dead lamb which seems just verging on the bathetic, suddenly acquires further perspectives with the final couplet rhyme of "mutton / button" and with the accompanying sketch, which portrays a mournful human figure and a lamblike creature lying on its back with four legs sticking up stiffly into the air.

Stevie Smith (photo by John Goldblatt for the Daily Telegraph*)*

Another important poem in Smith's first volume, "The River Deben" (republished in *Over the Frontier*), introduces one of her favorite images, water, and a recurrent theme, the fascination of death. There is perhaps some overstatement in Smith's remark to Kay Dick in 1970 that "nearly every poem's about suicide, more or less," but it is true that she frequently treats the attraction of death, and her feeling for life is enhanced by the idea—repeated throughout her writing, perhaps most affectingly in her final poem, "Come, Death (II)"—that death is "the only god / Who comes as a servant when he is called, you know."

What deepens and complicates this preoccupation with death in her poetry is Smith's ongoing concern with questions of religion. Brought up an Anglican, Smith rejected orthodox Christianity and yet could also call herself (again, to Kay Dick) "a backslider as a non-believer." Her position as both believer and nonbeliever is articulated in the poem "God the Eater," which begins,

> There is a god in whom I do not believe
> Yet to this god my love stretches,
> This god whom I do not believe in is
> My whole life, my life and I am his.

Smith went on, in her interview with Dick, to say that "being alive is like being in enemy territory," and many a Smith speaker, like Scorpion in the late poem of the same name, "wishes to be

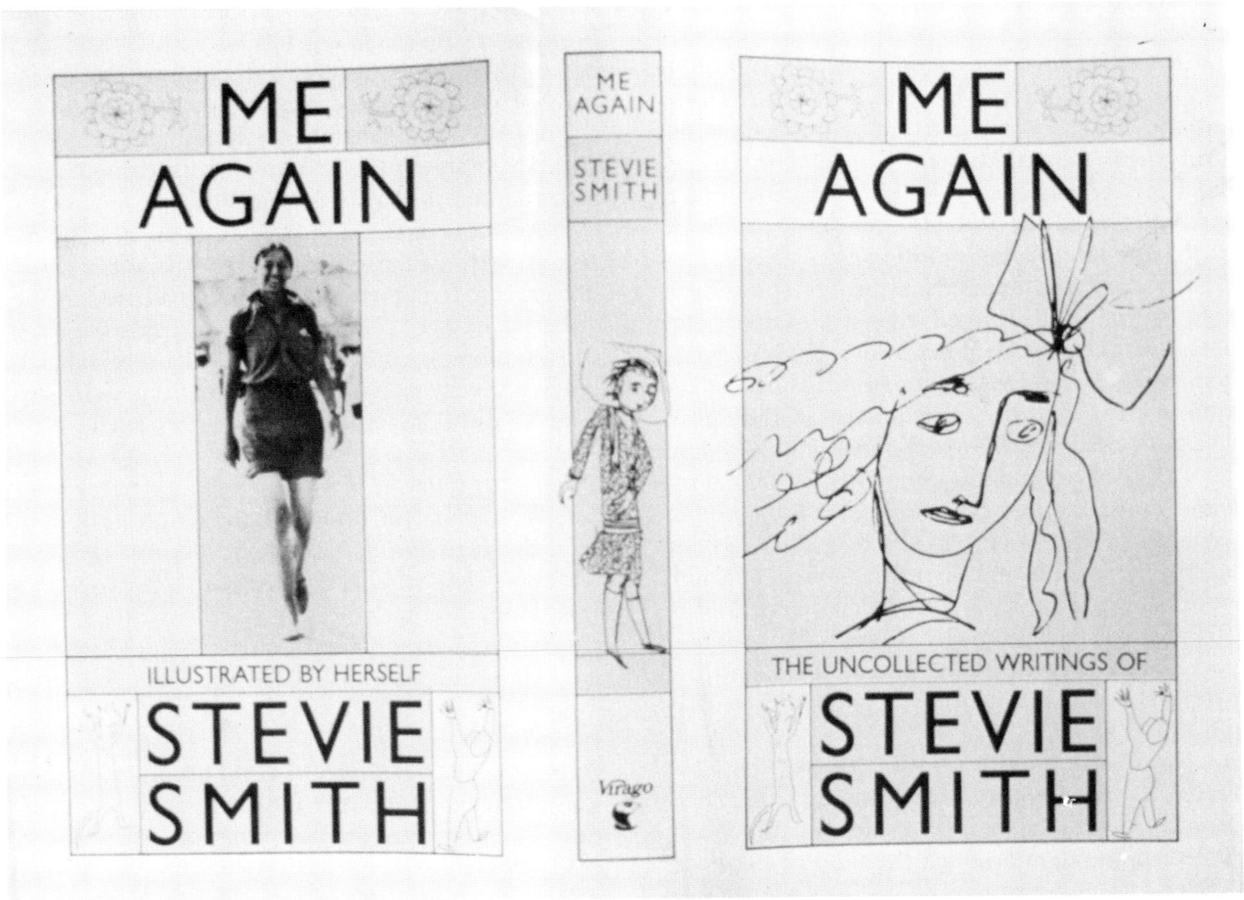

Dust jacket for the 1981 volume of Smith's previously uncollected work

gone." The frog prince of another poem expresses the dilemma of his dual nature, "fairly happy / In a frog's doom" and yet perpetually thinking of the "heavenly" disenchantment which he both fears and desires. In "Thoughts about the Person from Porlock," Smith transforms Coleridge's unwelcome visitor into an image of longed-for release, "To bring my thoughts to an end." Again and again, in her prose as well as in her poetry, Smith comes back to this theme of thought, of human consciousness—the individual's struggles with what is both "my glory and my bitter bane" ("Egocentric") and the modern age's struggle with the problem of how "To be good without enchantment" ("How do you see?").

If the consciousness she describes is modern, however, her inspiration often came from works of the past—history, theology, the fairy tales of the Brothers Grimm. Poetic influences, in the strict sense of the term, are difficult to trace in Smith's work, but there are certainly affinities with Blake and the seventeenth-century devotional poets, as well as occasional echoes of nineteenth-century writers she enjoyed reading, such as Tennyson and Browning. Aware of the tendency for contemporaries to exercise a perhaps unconscious influence upon one another's work, she told Peter Orr that she read few contemporary poets, because "one will get the lines crossed and begin writing their poems and they will begin writing one's own."

That very independence and uniqueness of style attracted considerable attention to Smith's early books, but after the rapid succession of publications in the late 1930's, she had some difficulty placing poems. *Mother, What Is Man?* (1942) was her only collection to appear in the 1940's, and her final novel, *The Holiday*, which was written during the war, did not find a publisher until 1949. Through all these years, Smith maintained a carefully controlled, seemingly uneventful private life. She admitted that, like Pompey Casmilus in *Novel on Yellow Paper*, she had once seriously considered marriage, but decided against it. Certainly, Pompey seems to speak for her creator in preferring "the rhythm of friendship," the freedom to come and go, which she realized was "antipathetic to marriage." Friendships were always important to Smith; however, although she thoroughly enjoyed her busy social life in London, she refused to move from the unfashionable, inconveniently located house in Palmers Green, which was presided over by her aunt and which clearly provided the stability and sense of escape which were also necessary to her.

In 1953, prompted by ill health, she retired from Newnes and devoted herself to writing and caring for her aunt until her aunt's death in 1968. Simultaneously, her reputation once again began to build, with several books of poetry, including an American edition of *Selected Poems*, published in 1964. Official recognition came with the Cholmondeley Award for Poetry in 1966 and the Queen's Gold Medal for Poetry in 1969. Following her death, of a brain tumor, in 1971, interest in Smith continued to grow; the *Collected Poems* appeared in 1975, all three of her novels became available in new editions after years of being out of print, and her life even became the subject of a popular stage play and film.

Critical attention, except for reviews, has tended to come more slowly, although the *Times Literary Supplement*'s review of her posthumously published book *Scorpion and Other Poems*, in 1972, indicated an important area for discussion when it called her, at her best, "one of the most musical poets of her generation." Smith herself once referred to her poems as "sound vehicles" and always laid great emphasis on oral reading, experimenting with singing or chanting her poems in public recitations, and sometimes setting poems to well-known tunes, much as Hopkins supplied his own stress marks to serve as guides to readers. Smith's way of interpreting the relationship between sound and meaning in poetry is one of the most original features of a style notable for its originality and possibly the one on which her fame will most securely rest.

Inevitably, a highly individualistic poetic style is vulnerable to shifts in critical taste and to the charges of eccentricity, a charge which Smith risked, and in a sense even flirted with, throughout her career. However, the integrity with which she adhered to her own style earned Stevie Smith a considerable amount of respect, and, more than ten years after her death, her reputation with both readers and fellow poets is deservedly high.

Other:

Cats in Colour, introduction by Smith (London: Batsford, 1959; New York: Viking, 1960);

The Poet's Garden, edited by Smith (New York: Viking, 1970);

The Batsford Book of Children's Verse, edited by Smith (London: Batsford, 1970).

Interviews:

Peter Orr, ed., *The Poet Speaks* (London: Routledge & Kegan Paul, 1966), pp. 225-231;

Kay Dick, *Ivy and Stevie* (London: Duckworth, 1971).

References:

Calvin Bedient, *Eight Contemporary Poets* (London: Oxford University Press, 1974), pp. 139-158;

Mark Storey, "Why Stevie Smith Matters," *Critical Quarterly*, 21, no. 2 (1979): 41-55;

"The Voice of Genteel Decay," *Times Literary Supplement*, 14 July 1972, p. 820.

Stephen Spender

Doris L. Eder
University of New Haven

BIRTH: London, 28 February 1909, to Edward Harold and Violet Hilda Schuster Spender.

EDUCATION: University College, Oxford, 1928-1930.

MARRIAGES: 1936 to Agnes Marie Pearn, divorced. April 1941 to Natasha Litvin; children: Matthew Francis and Elizabeth.

AWARDS AND HONORS: Honorary member American Academy and Institute of Arts and Letters; honorary member Phi Beta Kappa, Harvard University; Commander of the British Empire, 1962; fellow, Institute of Advanced Studies, Wesleyan University, 1967.

SELECTED BOOKS: *Nine Experiments: Being Poems Written at the Age of Eighteen*, as S. H. S. (Hampstead: Privately printed, 1928);
Twenty Poems (Oxford: Blackwell, 1930);
Poems (London: Faber & Faber, 1933; revised and enlarged, 1934; New York: Random House, 1934);
Vienna (London: Faber & Faber, 1934);
The Destructive Element: A Study of Modern Writers and Beliefs (London: Cape, 1935; Boston & New York: Houghton Mifflin, 1936);
The Burning Cactus (London: Faber & Faber, 1936; New York: Random House, 1936);
Forward from Liberalism (London: Gollancz, 1937; New York: Random House, 1937);
Trial of a Judge (London: Faber & Faber, 1938);
The Still Centre (London: Faber & Faber, 1939);
Selected Poems (London: Faber & Faber, 1940; New York: Random House, 1940);
The Backward Son (London: Hogarth Press, 1940);
Ruins and Visions (London: Faber & Faber, 1942; New York: Random House, 1942);
Life and the Poet (London: Secker & Warburg, 1942);
Citizens in War–And After (London, Toronto, Bombay & Sydney: Harrap, 1945);
European Witness (London: Hamilton, 1946; New York: Reynal & Hitchcock, 1946);
Poetry Since 1939 (London, New York & Toronto: Longmans, Green, 1946);
Poems of Dedication (London: Faber & Faber, 1947; New York: Random House, 1947);
The Edge of Being (London: Faber & Faber, 1949; New York: Random House, 1949);
World Within World (London: Hamilton, 1951; New York: Harcourt, Brace, 1951);
Shelley (London, New York & Toronto: Longmans, Green, 1952);
Learning Laughter (London: Weidenfeld & Nicolson, 1952; New York: Harcourt, Brace, 1953);
The Creative Element: A Study of Vision, Despair and Orthodoxy (London: Hamilton, 1953);
Collected Poems, 1928-1953 (London: Faber & Faber, 1955; New York: Random House, 1955);
The Making of a Poem (London: Hamilton, 1955; New York: Norton, 1962);
Engaged in Writing and The Fool and the Princess

Stephen Spender, 1932 (photo by Humphrey Spender)

(London: Hamilton, 1958; New York: Farrar, Straus & Cudahy, 1958);

The Imagination in the Modern World (Washington, D.C.: Library of Congress, 1962);

The Struggle of the Modern (London: Hamish Hamilton, 1963; Berkeley & Los Angeles: University of California Press, 1963);

Chaos and Control in Poetry (Washington, D. C.: Library of Congress, 1966);

The Year of the Young Rebels (London: Weidenfeld & Nicolson, 1969; New York: Random House, 1969);

The Generous Days (Boston: Godine, 1969; enlarged edition, London: Faber & Faber, 1971);

Love-Hate Relations: A Study of Anglo-American Sensibilities (London: Hamilton, 1974; New York: Random House, 1974);

Eliot (London: Fontana, 1975); republished as *T. S. Eliot* (New York: Viking, 1975);

The Thirties and After: Poetry, Politics, People, 1933-1970 (New York: Random House, 1978; London: Macmillan, 1978);

Henry Moore: Sculptures in Landscape (London: Studio Vista, 1979; New York: Potter, 1979).

Stephen Spender is one of a group of poets—the Auden or Oxford Generation—which also includes Louis MacNeice and C. Day Lewis. They began having their poetry published in the early 1930s, a decade whose ever-worsening crises—depression and massive unemployment, the rise of Fascism, and the approach of World War II—increasingly turned their poetry toward political themes. A lyricist of considerable gifts, though overshadowed by the major talent of his mentor, W. H. Auden, Spender forced his poems of the 1930s into a political mold. At the end of that decade, he returned to a more personal poetic mode. He is remembered chiefly for poems he wrote in his twenties. From the 1950s through the 1970s Spender almost abandoned poetry for literary criticism and political journalism. As a critic, Spender, despite a broad comparative knowledge of the arts and plentiful ideas, is basically an unanalytical, unsystematic thinker. His prose is clumsy and repetitive and has the quality of thinking out loud. As V. S. Pritchett observes, Spender's "insights are better than his arguments and he is best when he proceeds, as we would expect a poet to do, by vision." Stephen Spender is a visionary with an acute sense of his world and times, who has dedicated himself to the difficult integration of self with society.

Stephen Harold Spender is a younger son of the liberal political journalist, Harold Spender. His mother, Hilda Spender, was an invalid, and both parents died while he was still an adolescent. Like most members of the 1930s generation, who grew up *entre deux guerres* and whose lives were lived in parentheses of crises "bracketed by war," Spender was acutely aware of the gulf separating generation from generation and English life before World War I from English life after that war. World War I, he said, "knocked the ballroom-floor from under middle-class English life." The Spender family was of mixed German, Jewish, and English origin. Stephen did not discover his Jewish ancestry until he was sixteen, when the discovery made a profound impact: "I began to realize that I had more in common with the sensitive, rather soft, inquisitive, interior Jewish boys than with the aloof, hard, external English. There was a vulnerability, a tendency to self-hatred and self-pity, an underlying perpetual mourning amounting at times to spiritual defeatism, about my own nature which, even to myself, in my English surroundings, seemed foreign. . . . my feeling for the English was at times almost like being in love with an alien race." Spender's autobiography, *World Within World* (1951), indicates he has felt himself an outsider much of his life and that he possesses an innate sympathy for outsiders and underdogs. He is also an ardent idealist. From his father he appears to have inherited not only an interest in politics and a craving for recognition but a strong Platonic strain, despite his rebellion against these traits. Spender views himself as having been brought up in a "puritan-decadent" tradition, against which he revolted in his teens. In his youth "the abstract conception of Work and Duties was constantly being thrust on me, so that I saw beyond tasks themselves to pure qualities of moral and intellectual existence, quite emptied of things," he says. Although he deplored his father's habit of turning everything into rhetorical abstraction, Spender is often guilty of the same defect in his criticism, and his poetry sometimes evinces a disembodied Platonism, also "quite emptied of things." Comparing himself with Auden, he observes that Auden could quote reams of poetry by heart while he prefers not to recall the actual words because "I wanted to remember not the words and the lines, but a line beyond the lines"—the essence of a poem, as it were. Spender, having been anatomized by Auden and Isherwood at Oxford, shrewdly diagnoses himself: "My problem was that of the idealist. . . . [who] expects too much of himself and others. He is like an artist who cannot relate inspiration to form because the shift from vision to the discipline of form" is almost certain to diminish or dim vision.

Spender denies that the 1930s poets formed a group or movement, though he affirms Auden's preeminence, saying "a group of emergent artists existed in his mind, like a cabinet in the mind of a party leader." Thus, Auden introduced Isherwood to Spender as "the Novelist." Spender says "MacSpaunday" (MacNeice, Spender, Auden, and Day Lewis) "never met as a group, never referred to ourselves as a movement; curiously, the original three [Auden, Day Lewis, and Spender] didn't meet each other collectively until September 1949 in Venice." At Oxford in the late 1920s Spender felt isolated. He found Oxford divided into hearties and aesthetes, fell in love with one of the hearties ("Marston," who inspired a number of fine early lyrics), and did not really blossom on his own account until 1930, after Auden left. Spender thinks the atmosphere of Oxford in his day so strange it would take a Dostoevski to describe it adequately. It was so cloistered that he came to identify the town surrounding the colleges as the real world. The profound awareness of the subject/object dichotomy that informs Spender's thought and work was sharpened by his university education.

In the summer of 1930, before his senior year, Spender left Oxford without a degree and followed Isherwood to Germany. The attractions of Germany for young Englishmen during the *Weimardaemmerung* were social, homosexual, and literary. Sexual liberation, literary and political ferment, and social unrest were rife and the 1920s cult of hedonism at its height. Both Spender and Isherwood have described sojourns in those modern Sodoms, Hamburg and Berlin, with unforgettable vividness. *World Within World* evokes the extraordinary mixture of "nihilism, sophistication and primitive vitality" that was the *Zeitgeist* of Germany in the late 1920s and early 1930s: "all this German youth . . . born into war, starved in the blockade, stripped in the inflation—and . . . now, with no money and no beliefs and an extraordinary anonymous beauty, sprang like a breed of dragon's teeth waiting for its leader, into the centre of Europe." Nude sun worshippers crowded the beaches, while storm troopers trained in nearby forests.

Spender's first important volume, *Poems*, appeared in 1933, the year in which Hitler assumed the chancellorship of the Third Reich. Like so many young English intellectuals, Spender watched the

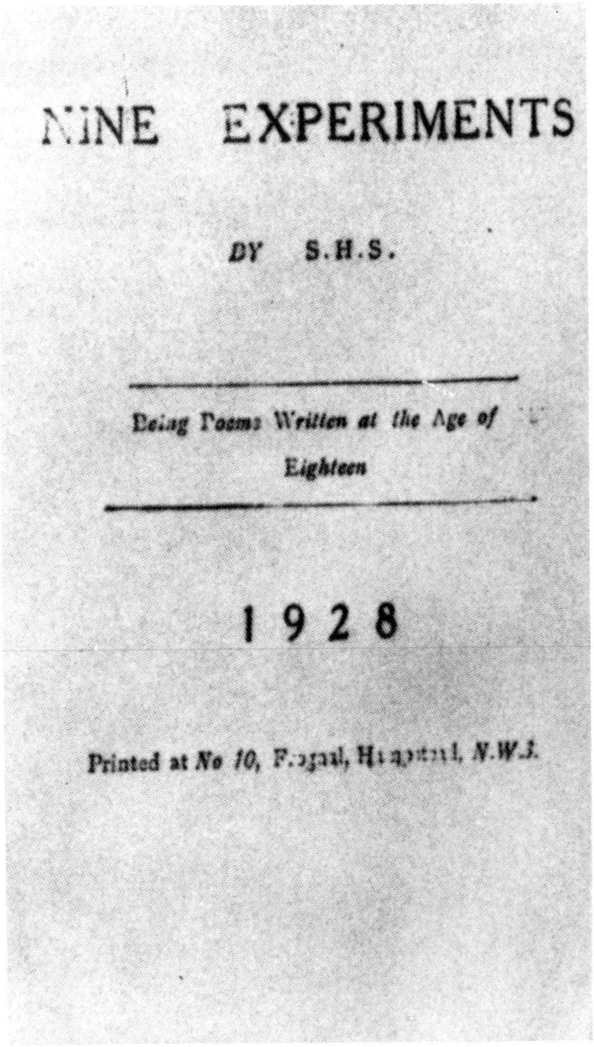
NINE EXPERIMENTS

BY S.H.S.

Being Poems Written at the Age of Eighteen

1928

Printed at No 10, Frognal, Hampstead, N.W.3.

Title page for Spender's first book, which he printed on a small handpress

rise of fascism, appalled. With Auden and Isherwood, he had a ringside seat in Berlin and Vienna. Spender's career exemplifies the split between personal and political life felt by his generation. A world lurching from crisis to crisis under the threat of Fascist domination made luxuries of poetry and the private life. Spender and his colleagues felt obliged to write public, "committed," political, even polemical, verse. But they distrusted such literature even as they wrote it. Says Spender: "We were divided between our literary vocation and an urge to save the world from Fascism. We were the Divided Generation of Hamlets who found the world out of joint and failed to set it right." Like many of his generation, Spender briefly embraced communism—he had a party card but never attended a meeting—and went to Spain to promote anti-Fascist propaganda during the Spanish civil war. (The chairman of the British Communist party urged Spender to go to Spain and, preferably, to get killed, so as to give the Loyalist cause a Byron.) Katharine Hoskins in *Today the Struggle: Literature & Politics in England During the Spanish Civil War* (1969) remarks that Spender's "first and only act as a Communist was to write an article in the *Daily Worker* announcing his having joined but simultaneously attacking Party policy on all points at which he 'disagreed with it.' " Spender describes his experience of communism and the Spanish civil war in his contribution to Richard Crossman's *The God That Failed* (1949). Hoskins sketches Spender's political evolution: "He had come from a wealthy Liberal family with strong traditions of social responsibility, and he had trod the well-worn path from liberalism to socialism and then, because of the apparent failure of social democracy and the growing menace of fascism, to communism." Spender has said that embracing communism in the 1930s was less a matter of belief than of conscience: for a while it appeared the only viable alternative to fascism.

At the age of twenty-seven, Spender married Agnes (Inez) Pearn, an Oxford student, a scholar of Spanish, and a member of the Spanish Aid Committee. They had known each other only briefly when Spender, on impulse, proposed. He was on the rebound after the end of an affair with another woman in Austria and also after the end of a long drawn-out, complex, and painful relationship with his secretary T. A. R. Hyndman, who figures in his autobiography as "Jimmy Younger." In *World Within World* Spender is candid about being bisexual, as he is about everything else. He says he sought out men for intellectual and artistic comradeship, for relationships in which total identification was the aim, and women for a more sensual, mystical kind of union. In his own words, he became aware of an acute, irremediable "ambivalence in my attitude towards men and women. Love for a friend expressed a need for self-identification. Love for a woman, the need for a relationship with someone different, indeed opposite, to myself." Looking back from the perspective of mid-life, Spender declares in his autobiography that he finds his relationships with women to have been more satisfying and lasting than those with men. However, in a recent interview with John Gruen (in *Vogue*), Spender reiterates the fear expressed in *World Within World* that intimacy with the opposite sex might rob him of his own identity. Spender also matter-of-factly observes that his mother was mad and expresses a fear of being controlled by women. The sharp dualism he discerns in male/female relations is likely traceable to his early childhood and was probably exacerbated by English methods of rearing and educating the sexes separately, since it appears symptomatic of many Englishmen of Spender's class and age. Spender's first marriage was childless and disintegrated in 1939, on the eve of war, at which time he underwent a period of suffering and self-doubt so intense that he feared he might never write again. The poems of this period reflect his inner turmoil. For therapy at this time Spender once again took up painting and underwent psychoanalysis.

In 1939 Spender and Cyril Connolly became coeditors of the magazine *Horizon*. In 1941 he married Natasha Litvin, a pianist, who bore him a son and a daughter. During the war Spender continued to live in London and served in the Auxiliary Fire Service, about which he writes engagingly in *World Within World*. This experience also inspired some vivid war poems. To the poets of the 1930s, who had watched the events of that "low dishonest decade" building to their cataclysmic climax, World War II had a profound and terrible significance. For Spender it signaled above all the end of individualism and of human control over destructive technology: "From now on, the fate of individuals was more and more controlled by a public fate which itself seemed beyond control. For control implies not merely putting a machinery into motion, but also being able to make it stop: modern war is a machine easy to make start, but it can only be stopped at the moment when it has destroyed or been destroyed by another war machine. Control means being able to relate a programme of action to the results of the action. . . . All this was only leading to . . . plans for making atomic and hydrogen bombs to defend East against West or West against East in a meaningless struggle between potential ashes to gain a world of ashes."

Since World War II Spender has had little poetry published but has produced an increasing number of prose works, including literary criticism, social and intellectual history, political and travel literature, translations, and reviews. In 1947 he made his first visit to the United States to see his old friends Auden and Isherwood. Spender and Auden frequently spent half the year in England, half abroad in an antithetical environment. In later life, they regularly crossed the Atlantic for their six-month sojourn in this country. During the 1950s and 1960s Spender divided his time about equally between England and the United States. During those years he held visiting professorships and lectureships at a number of prestigious American and English universities, including the University of Cincinnati (1953), the University of California at Berkeley (1959), Northwestern University (1963), Cambridge University (1965-1966), the University of Connecticut (1968-1970), and University College, London (1969). He was consultant in poetry in English at the Library of Congress in 1965-1966, and from 1953 to 1967 he coedited *Encounter* magazine with Irving Kristol and Melvin Lasky. He had for some years been looking for a literary vehicle, transatlantic in scope, to publish the foremost literary talents of the contemporary world. Spender describes in *The Year of the Young Rebels* (1969) how neither he nor Frank Kermode (who succeeded him as *Encounter*'s British editor when he became corresponding American editor) realized until late that the journal had received funds from the C. I. A. When Spender and Kermode discovered this fact, they resigned. From 1970 to 1975 Spender occupied the Chair of English Literature at University College in London, retiring in 1975. He continues to be a literary-political spokesman and cultural ambassador for the transatlantic community, and in 1981 he was a visiting professor at the University of South Carolina.

The autobiographical impulse is obvious in Spender's poetry. He has said that all his work, whether verse or prose, constitutes fragments of an autobiography and that his poems "all attempt to record . . . truthfully . . . experience which, within reality, seemed to be poetry." The obsessive themes of the poetry are also those of his critical prose: how to connect outer and inner reality, the active and contemplative, the political and personal; how, in Wallace Stevens's words, to bring a "world quite round" in an age of unbelief. Spender's poetry has been a search for a valid, sustaining faith. He has not attained such a faith, remaining a skeptic conducting continuous forays from the inner into the outer world, seeking to transform external fact or reality into internal truth. Spender's poetry shows a lifelong, strenuous effort to objectify the subjective or to subjectivize the object. He has been strongly influenced by the romantic poets in general and by Shelley in particular; indeed, he has been labeled the Shelley of the twentieth century, as well as the Rupert Brooke of the Depression. The former sobriquet is juster. Spender resembles Shelley in the nature of his lyrical gift, which is ethereal (F. R. Leavis calls it "glamorous-ineffable-vague"); in combining poetic with political interests; in his youthful idealism, now tempered; and in his somewhat feminine sensibility. Other influences have been Rainer Maria Rilke, T. S. Eliot, William Butler Yeats, D. H. Lawrence, and his contemporaries Auden and Isherwood.

Spender printed his first volume of poetry, *Nine Experiments: Being Poems Written at the Age of Eighteen* (1928), on his own handpress, on which he also printed Auden's *Poems* (1928). Spender later did not think well of this virgin enterprise and destroyed many copies. *Twenty Poems*, which appeared in 1930, comprises poems written between 1928 and 1930. Fourteen of these reappear in the volume that gained Spender recognition as a poet of the Auden Generation—*Poems*, published by Faber and Faber in 1933, with a revised, enlarged edition published the following year by Faber and Faber in England and by Random House in the United States. (The first edition of *Poems* contained thirty-three poems; the second, forty.) With this volume, at the age of twenty-four, Spender emerged as a mature poet. His particular poetic characteristics are already in evidence. Horace Gregory said in the *Nation* that Spender showed promise of becoming the best lyric poet of his generation, a promise he cannot be said to have fulfilled, for Spender has always been overshadowed, like the other members of the Oxford Group, by the intellectual brilliance and technical virtuosity of Auden. In *Poems* Spender's spontaneous lyric gift is constrained by a profoundly felt obligation to engage the ugliest, most recalcitrant features of the contemporary environment: the urban-industrial landscape, machinery and mechanization, unemployment, and fascism. (At the age of nineteen Spender had proclaimed, "Come let us praise the gasworks. . . .") "The Express" and "The Pylons," both included in *Poems*, have for decades been seen as exemplifying the tenacious grasp of the Auden group on the contemporary scene, its celebration of "the quick perspective of the future." In such poems Spender managed to fulfill his declared aim of enveloping the brute phenomena of his day in the poetic spirit. "The Express" is rhythmic and more concrete than many of his poems, which sometimes dissipate in an impressionistic haze. There are poems, however, in which the poet unflinchingly confronts the miseries of his time, finding them beyond poetry's power to console, vindicate, or transcend. Thus, in "In Railway Halls, on Pavements Near the Traffic," the poet, watching long lines of the unemployed, says:

> No, I shall wave no tracery of pen-ornament
> To make them birds upon my singing-tree:

Time merely drives these lives which do not live
As tides push rotten stuff along the shore.
. . . .
Paint here no draped despairs, no saddening clouds
Where the soul rests, proclaims eternity.
But let the wrong cry out, as raw as wounds
This time forgets and never heals, far less transcends.

Spender's poems are plainspoken without their meaning necessarily being plain. He likes truncated, sonnetlike but free-verse forms; as he developed, he used less rhyme or meter. The sound of his poems is distinctive. He is fully aware of the importance of sound, but he uses few seductive aural techniques, such as alliteration, assonance, full or near rhyme, or regular rhythms. The image is obviously of primary importance to this poet, but his images are often quite surreal, not easily visualized. The poetry, though painterly, often lacks concreteness. Some poems suffer from a Platonic blurring of the edges, similar to Shelley's; from first to last they are full of images of Shelleyan light, effulgence. Lyric and prosaic impulses are frequently at odds in his poetry. Spender's instinct for direct, lyric utterance is often betrayed by his predilection for the rhetorical, didactic, or homilectic, a weakness he attributes to the fatal attraction platform speaking has for him. As a *Times Literary Supplement* reviewer said of *Collected Poems, 1928-1953* (1955), "The typical quality of his style, arising from this paradoxical combination of a desire to 'let himself go' and a fear of 'letting himself go' is a stumbling eloquence or a sweeping gesture suddenly arrested." The justly praised "Not Palaces, an Era's Crown" (in *Poems*) illustrates most of these traits. Apparently a strong-willed, forward-looking call for human equality, it is nevertheless full of latent nostalgia for an abjured, abandoned past evoked in "family pride," "beauty's filtered dusts," "gardens," and "singing feasts." The justly famous invocation—

Eye, gazelle, delicate wanderer,
Drinker of horizon's fluid line;
Ear that suspends on a chord
The spirit drinking timelessness—

exemplifies Spender's use of surrealistic images, here synesthetic and memorable, though difficult to visualize. (Spender is an amateur painter, as well informed about painting as poetry; he is also knowledgeable about music.) Though he loves nature and greatly admires the ability of a writer like Lawrence to depict the outer world, Spender's own sensitive eye is inclined to be internal, a dilated pupil looking inward quite as much as it gazes on the outward scene. Thus, A. K. Weatherhead in *Stephen Spender and the Thirties* (1975) is right to say that Spender has written "no poetry that was not mediated through an analytic cerebration."

Vienna (1934) was written in 1934 while Spender was living half the year in Austria (as Auden did for many years). It is a long poem about the Dollfuss regime's brutal suppression of the February 1934 socialist insurrection in Austria and the heroic death of Kaloman Wallisch, the socialist mayor of Bruck-an-der-Mur, who was executed by the Dollfuss regime. Interwoven with political events is the poet's personal life, enmeshed in guilt over his bisexuality. A four-part poem that shows the influence of the Eliot of "Gerontion" and of Auden, *Vienna* is full of clogged images, obscure and dated allusions, and prosy passages. Spender later repudiated it because it failed in its grand objective of fusing inner and outer worlds. In *World Within World* Spender says of this nightmarish time, when he was observing at firsthand the brutalities of fascism, "in spite of everything, I did not plunge myself wholly in public affairs. Therefore a poetry which rejected private experience would have been untrue to me. Moreover, I dimly saw that the conflict between personal life and public causes must be carried forward into public life itself. . . . For our individualistic civilization to be reborn within the order of a new world, people must be complex as individuals, simple as social forces." Spender's ambivalent admiration for men of action, compact figures of will and single unified identity, is always offset by his realization of the painful (and peculiarly modern) necessity of being passive, will-less, and multivalent, a realization expressed in his elliptical, Audenesque, early poem, "An 'I' can never be great man." In *Vienna* he cannot make his inner world cohere, let alone connect his life to the turbulent outer world.

Vienna looks forward to Spender's only excursion into drama, *Trial of a Judge* (1938), a verse tragedy in five acts written for Rupert Doone's Group Theatre, which premiered the play on 18 March 1938. Its protagonist is a liberal judge who, under a Fascist regime, convicts the brutal anti-Semitic murderers of an unarmed man and is then compelled (by new antigun legislation) also to convict a group of Communists who, in a scuffle with the Fascists, have accidentally wounded a policeman. *Trial of a Judge* enacts in strong verse the judge's struggle of conscience as he is finally brought to condemn both Fascists and Communists, the former for violating all principles of law and justice, the latter for travestying justice by creating and trying to enforce their own laws. The play is too monologuic to be dramatic, but it is highly charged poetry. Louis MacNeice observed, "The intended moral of the play was that liberalism today was weak and wrong, communism was strong and right. But this moral was sabotaged by [Spender's] unconscious integrity." MacNeice describes how, at a meeting of comrades at the Group Theatre to discuss the play, an old man approached the youthful poet-playwright to say that he was sure he must be mistaken, but the play seemed to be advocating "Abstract Justice, a thing we know is non-existent." MacNeice records in *The Strings Are False: an Unfinished Autobiography* (1966) how Spender "deliberately towered into blasphemy. Abstract Justice, he said, of course he meant it; and what was more it existed." In *World Within World* Spender reveals his intense moralism. "My mind appeared to be a vehicle for a thought which existed independently of my own reasoning. This was that at some stage of our eternal and personal existence, we become aware of our significance in other lives, measured in terms of happiness and unhappiness, good and evil. . . . It was unbearable to me to think that people could do great good or great evil, without ever being completely aware, even for a moment . . . of what they had become as a result of what they had done."

Stephen Spender in his Auxiliary Fire Service Uniform (The British Council)

Spender has made several forays into fiction. Five short stories published under the title *The Burning Cactus* in 1936 are close in quality to his poetry, haunted, haunting, sometimes vivid, and reminiscent of Lawrence in their intense, suppressed emotionality and of Isherwood in their subject matter. The protagonists are hypersensitive, epicene, isolated, alienated, even solipsistic; interest is displaced from social to psychic contact and conflict. After World War II, Spender wrote two satirical sketches of postwar European life, *Engaged in Writing and The Fool and the Princess* (1958). His only full-length novel, *The Backward Son* (1940), is a thinly disguised autobiographical account of English boarding school life, which he hated.

The Still Centre (1939) is a key volume in Spender's poetic oeuvre because, although it contains many political poems, including some fine Spanish civil war poems, in the course of the book Spender turns from public and political verse back to the private and personal. He reiterates the need for the poet "to relate [his] small truth to the . . . wider truth outside his experience," but he also remarks, "Poetry does not state truth, it states the conditions within which something felt is true." That is, poetry is not, like science, concerned with discovering facts, but with conveying the "felt truth" of reality. *The Still Centre* includes some longer poems, such as "Exiles from Their Land" and "The Uncreating Chaos" which, by the time they appeared in Spender's *Collected Poems* (1955), had been revised and abridged.

The poems growing out of Spender's experience in the Spanish civil war in 1937 show his powers of empathy and humanity and the influence of Wilfred Owen's poetry of World War I, as well as of Auden. Spender thought Owen the best of the World War I poets. Less involved and steeped in suffering than Owen's, Spender's poems are sympathetic without being sentimental, always focused on the individual pressed into inhuman activity, dwarfed in the huge, insensate violence of war. Their bittersweet ironic spirit is reminiscent of Stephen Crane's "War is Kind." In "Two Armies" extraordinary effects are achieved through sudden, Auden-like shifts in perspective, from close up to far removed. The two armies, furiously pitted against each other by day, are seen by night as

Stephen Spender, circa 1951 (BBC Hulton)

sharing a common suffering:

> Clean silence drops at night, when a little walk
> Divides the sleeping armies, each
> Huddled in linen woven by remote hands.
> When the machines are stilled, a common suffering
> Whitens the air with breath and makes both one
> As though these enemies slept in each other's arms.

"*Ultima Ratio Regum*" explores the ultimate pity and waste of war. Somewhat facile opening lines—"The guns spell money's ultimate reason / In letters of lead on the Spring hillside"—lead to a brief lyric meditation on a dead boy lying under the olive trees, "a better target for a kiss" than a bullet. Again, the vast machinery and *materiel* of modern warfare are contrasted with the frail individual life, now extinguished. With wringing irony, the poet asks: "Was so much expenditure justified / On the death of one so young, and so silly / Lying under the olive trees. . . ?"

A recurrent theme in the political and personal poems of *The Still Centre* is the search for "unity of being or an image of the integrated self," as A. K. Weatherhead observes in *Stephen Spender and the Thirties* (1975). The most remarkable poem in this regard is "Darkness and Light," which Spender also uses as an epigraph to his autobiography. A loose sestina in form, its imagery of light and darkness exemplifies the two poles between which Spender's universe is suspended. "To break out of the chaos of my darkness / Into a lucid day, is all my will," the poem begins. But, equally, "to avoid that lucid day / And to preserve my darkness, is all my will." This poem is Spender's most concentrated and masterful exposition of his conflict between subject and object, inner and outer, activity and passivity, center that is nowhere and circumference that is everywhere. The whole drive of the poem is to reconcile these opposites that have so bedeviled the poet's life: they are reconciled within the poem, but not in life. Weatherhead sees the "still centre" of Spender's title as "that residue of self . . . which, washed over by all tides of public occurrences, is finally untouched and lives independent of any conditioning whatsoever." Thus, this manichaeistic conflict is also one between freedom and determinism.

Ruins and Visions (1942) is a revision of *The Still Centre*, with some new poems added. Spender's next volume, *Poems of Dedication*, which did not appear until five years later, in 1947, contains "Elegy for Margaret," a long poem in six parts written on the death of a beloved sister-in-law, the wife of Humphrey Spender. Despite some moving passages, this poem is flawed, falling far short of its aim. Reviewing this volume for the *New York Herald Tribune*, Babette Deutsch observed that Spender's "technical ability has not kept pace with the increase in scope and depth of his themes."

The Edge of Being (1949) is a slim volume, balanced between the longing for concrete existence and for abstract nonbeing, as Weatherhead observes. It contains some interesting new poems, such as "Rejoice in the Abyss," one of Spender's World War II poems, which, though not as directly apprehended as those written in the Spanish civil war, is impressive nonetheless. During World War II, Spender, serving in the Auxiliary Fire Service, experienced the fire and destruction of the London Blitz. "Rejoice in the Abyss" is Blakean, striving for that strange fusion of cockney concreteness with gnomic abstractness Blake achieves in "London." The poem's theme is that espoused in Spender's critical works, *The Destructive Element* (1935) and *The Creative Element* (1953): the Conradian "In the Destructive Element Immerse . . .":

hollow is the skull, the vacuum
In the gold ball under St. Paul's cross.
Unless you will accept the emptiness
Within the bells of fox-gloves and cathedrals,
Each life must feed upon the deaths of others.

An almost surreal technique (roof slates jabbering, houses kneeling, the sky foaming with a Milky Way of saints ascending) is wedded to a long-cherished theme, but theme and technique are not fused at all points. The end, in particular, seems willed and didactic. This volume also contains a brief, deeply moving lyric on the subject of the Holocaust, "Memento."

Spender's *Selected Poems* appeared in the inauspicious year of 1940. Of the forty-six poems in the *Selected Poems*, only a handful do not appear in *Collected Poems, 1928-1953*, published a decade and a half later in 1955. This later volume, published by Faber and Faber in England and by Random House in the United States, comprises 111 poems, only a few of which had not appeared in previous volumes. Most date from the 1930s, many from the original *Poems*. Louis Untermeyer has rightly characterized Spender's *Collected Poems* as "doggedly comprehensive." In his introduction, Spender describes the conscientious, painstaking method by which he put the volume together: "To collect and select these

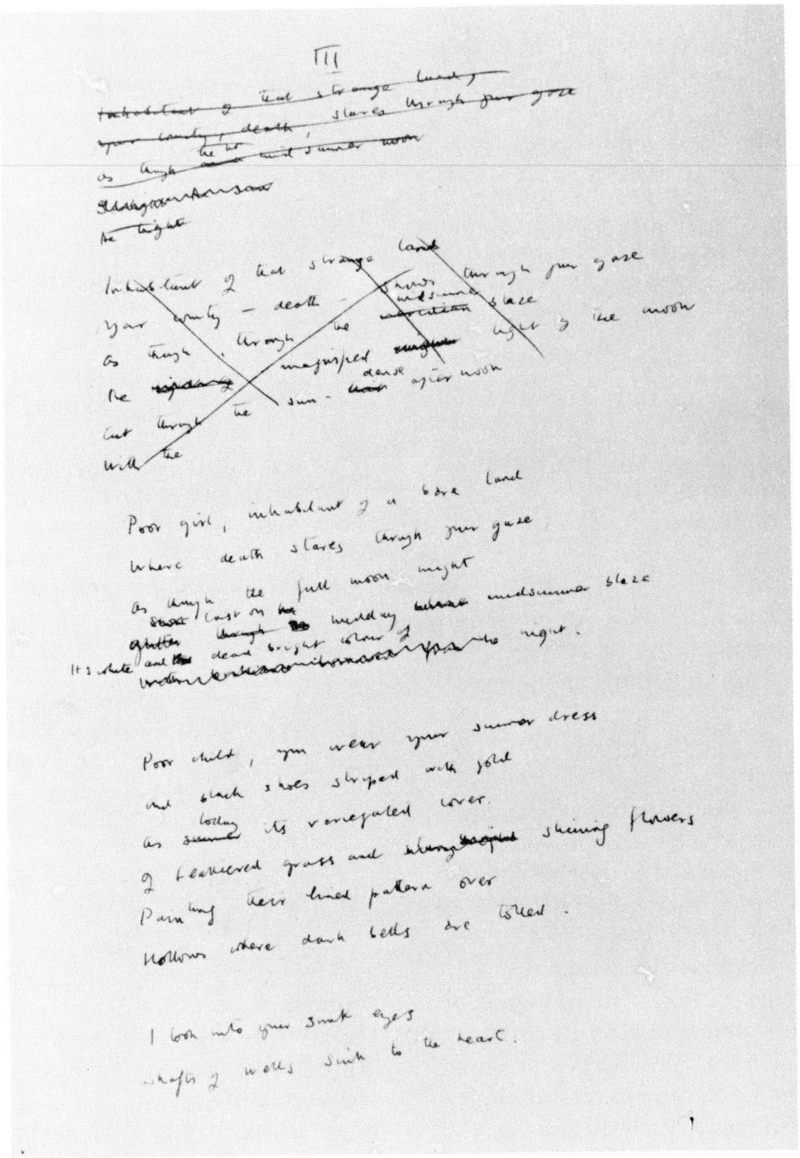
Poor girl, inhabitant of a bare land
Where death stares through your gaze,
As though the full moon might … midsummer blaze

Poor child, you wear your summer dress
and black shoes striped with gold
as … its variegated cover.
of feathered grass and … shining flowers
Painting their lined pattern over
Hollows where dark bells are tolled.

I look into your sunk eyes
shafts of wells sink to the heart.

Page from Spender's notebook in which he made revisions for Collected Poems,1928-1953
(Humanities Research Center, University of Texas at Austin)

poems, I copied them out into a large note-book, then typed them out and tried to consider how each poem would best take its place in a single volume. In this way, I have spent several months reconsidering and even re-experiencing poems I have written over the past twenty-five years. . . . my aim has been to retrieve as many past mistakes, and to make as many improvements, as possible, without 'cheating'. . . . Poetry is a game played with the reader according to rules, but it is also a truth game in which the truth is outside the rules." So Spender's revisions are technical, not thematic. He included poems of the 1930s that embarrassed him in the 1950s by their youthful ardor or awkwardness. His revisions are mostly for clarity or specificity, sometimes for metaphorical elaboration. Spender is no perfectionist like Yeats, Eliot, or Pound and rarely wrestles sufficiently to arrive at *le mot juste*. He says so of his prose, but the same is true of his poetry. In the "Elegy for Margaret," to cite only one example, he amended

> Since, darling, there is never a night
> But the restored prime of your youth
> With all its flags does not float
> Upon my sleep like a boat.

to

> Since, Margaret, there is never a night
> But the beflagged pride of your youth
> In all its joy, does not float
> Upon my sleep, as on a boat.

The sought-for improvement is spoiled by the single preposition *as*, which undoes a fine image, for Margaret's youthful image *is* the vessel riding the flood of the poet's sleep; it is not, as it were, a passenger on a vessel.

Reading through Spender's *Collected Poems*, one is struck by a dozen or so poems that stand out as finely crafted, memorable, the poet's best. Most of these are early poems, written while he was still in his twenties and first published in *Poems* of 1933. Preeminent among them, flawlessly lyrical, is "I Think Continually of Those Who Were Truly Great." Here Spender allows his innate romanticism free rein: the poem is full of the nostalgia of Wordsworth's "Ode: Intimations of Immortality from Recollections of Early Childhood," extolling the glory and the dream still "appareled in celestial light." Spender's characteristically luminous and Shelleyan imagery of light is beautifully integrated from first to last strophe. The rhythm is harmonious and hypnotic, and each word is chosen with extreme care. Streaming images of light, fire, spirit, voices, streams, mountains, winds, grasses, sun, and air flow into one another with an extraordinary élan to celebrate the devotees of life. The final two lines—"Born of the sun they traveled a short while towards the sun, / And left the vivid air signed with their honor"—poignantly convey Spender's simultaneous sense of man's frailty and his grandeur, for he sets the spirit in its ephemeral perdurability against the immense background of time-space. The poem is one of the purest evocations of spirit imaginable, so that it seems severe of Weatherhead to complain of its impalpability and self-reflexiveness, or of its "delivering only the vaguest kind of intelligence."

The overriding theme of Spender's poems is the union of self with world. Bent as he is in fusing subject and object, on merging existence and being, there remains a thin integument separating the poet from the external world. In poems about art, as in war poems, Spender is aware of the transparent curtain dividing art from life, life from death. "The Living Values," like Auden's "*Musée des Beaux Arts*," concerns the relationships between art and life and life and death, as they are and as they are portrayed by the Old Masters. The curtain separating these realms of being is astonishingly thin; pierced in a moment, it leads to a looking-glass world:

> Alas for the sad standards
> In the eyes of the new-dead young
> Sprawled in the mud of battle.
> Stare back, stare back, with dust over glazed
> Eyes, their gaze at partridges,
> Their dreams of nudes, and their collected
> Hearts wound up with love, like little watch springs.
> To ram them outside Time, violence
> Of wills that ride this cresting day
> Struck them with lead so swift
> They look at us through its glass trajectory
> And we, living, look back at them through glass,
> Their bodies now sunk inch-deep in gold frames.

Similarly, in "An Elementary School Classroom in a Slum," the poet sees the life of slum children as too removed from that depicted in schoolbooks, maps, travel posters of alpine valleys, a bust of Shakespeare, for any of these windows opening upon other worlds really to free them from their cramped, impoverished lives in the catacombs of modern industrial cities. Art is perpetrating a fraud on life. Unless, the poet proclaims in a final,

Blakean stanza, these windows magically burst open to liberate these prisoned minds and lives:

Unless, governor, teacher, inspector, visitor,
This map becomes their window and these windows
That shut upon their lives like catacombs,
Break O break open till they break the town
And show the children to green fields, and make their world
Run azure on gold sands, and let their tongues
Run naked into books, the white and green leaves open
History theirs whose language is the sun.

It seems unfair of Robert Graves to damn with faint praise what he calls Spender's "poor-little-rich-boy poems," full of pity for the poor. Though Spender's sympathy may be liberal and bookish, his entire work and life express a passion for social justice.

Spender has also written poems about the stealthy depredations of time, the gradual ruin of the flesh that is poignantly contrasted with the longing for perfection of the unquenchable spirit. His apprehension of time's power is profound, cosmic: "Time's ambition is all space, and hangs its flags / In night that never reaches us, years to which this world is dead." In poem number 12 in *Collected Poems*, about youth's great expectations, he writes:

What I had not foreseen
Was the gradual day
Weakening the will
Leaking the brightness away . . .
. . . .
Expecting always
Some brightness to hold in trust,
Some final innocence
Exempt from dust,
That, hanging solid,

Louis MacNeice, Ted Hughes, T. S. Eliot, W. H. Auden, and Stephen Spender, 1960

Would dangle through all,
Like the created poem,
Or faceted crystal.

If he has written few poems that achieve such crystalline perfection, Spender's is a true lyric gift, his voice one of deep and humane feeling.

Spender's most recent volume of verse, *The Generous Days*, shows a new leanness; his free verse is becoming tauter, compressing more meaning into smaller compass. The American edition of *The Generous Days*, published by Godine in 1969, contains only ten poems, the English edition brought out by Faber & Faber in 1971, forty-seven. One is a sonnet to Auden on his sixtieth birthday. It is interesting to compare the late styles of these two poets, for, while Auden grew more colloquial, leisurely, and diffuse, Spender has become more disciplined, spare, laconic. Of late his free verse is more lean and effective. The most effective poems are those in which Spender so shapes inspiration within form as to attain the union of flesh and spirit, the two becoming one.

Because criticism has become an increasingly important part of his work and because his critical roles have had some effect on his own poetry, a brief discussion of it is appropriate here. Spender's first important critical work was *The Destructive Element*, published in England in 1935, in the United States the following year. He has described how "the idea for a book on James gradually resolved itself . . . in my mind into that of a book about modern writers and beliefs, or unbeliefs; which turned again into a picture of writers grouped round the 'destructive element,' wondering whether or not to immerse themselves." Spender's version of the Conradian allusion, his definition of the destructive element is a world devoid of belief or shared values. He defines James's quintessential qualities as "his morality, his pity, his humanity, his feminine genius and feminine courage, his gift of profound understanding." He writes of James that his "morality is fogged and confused by the fact that a very great deal of his work is about nothing except that he is a New Englander who has spent his life trying to reconcile a Puritan New England code of morals with his idea of the European tradition."

Spender follows chapters on James with briefer assessments of W. B. Yeats, T. S. Eliot, and D. H. Lawrence. He complains that, compared with Eliot's, Yeats's poetry is deficient in magic. (Spender dislikes Yeats's supernaturalism, which he finds bogus, and Eliot's orthodoxy, which he finds constraining.) He finds the poetry and criticism of Eliot remarkable for their power of internalizing the external world. Like Eliot, Spender is obsessed by the modern dissociation of sensibility, by the sundering of inner from outer reality. He views Eliot, Rilke, Proust, and Woolf as subjective artists with an extraordinary capacity for absorbing the outer into the inner self and transforming it, but he prefers D. H. Lawrence's respect, indeed reverence, for the external and tries to emulate the balance Lawrence strikes between inner and outer. Lawrence has profoundly influenced Spender. The outsider in Spender recognizes the outsider in Lawrence. He praises Lawrence for recognizing that "each person is outside everyone else and outside nature. It is on the basis of this separation of polarities that there is meeting. . . . Out of a fusion of opposites, a spark is struck." Spender also understands and explains well Lawrence's belief in the collective unconscious, for Spender has since childhood had a profound sense of the finitude and frailty of microcosmic human personality, at the same time that he senses the expansiveness and durability of the macrocosmic consciousness contained within it.

The Creative Element (an adaptation of the Elliston lectures at the University of Cincinnati in 1953) is a companion volume or sequel to *The Destructive Element*. Whereas the first work was subtitled *A Study of Modern Writers and Beliefs*, the second has the subtitle *A Study of Vision, Despair and Orthodoxy*. Spender defines the creative element as "the individual vision of the writer who realizes in his work the decline of modern values while isolating his own individual values from the context of society. . . . The main impulse of the whole great 'modern movement' has been the individual vision," and therefore the emphasis in this book is on the great moderns as visionaries with the center still the subjective consciousness of the artist, the circumference the circumambient external world.

The Creative Element is also concerned with the central problem of belief. Spender disagrees with Arnold that poetry can take the place of religion in the modern world, yet proposes a role for poetry that is close to this. He sees poetry's task as "to restore the lost connection between man-made objects and inner life," to translate the life of the soul into the language of the modern city and, through the rediscovery or reinvention of traditional symbols and the forging of new ones, to create provisional faiths. Among his visionaries, Spender includes Rimbaud, Rilke, Eliot, Forster, Lawrence, and Yeats.

Like *The Destructive Element*, *The Struggle of the Modern* (1963) is clearly a product of the temporal

Stephen Spender, 28 November 1968 (BBC Hulton, photo by J. Jackson)

context in which it was written. (This book comprises lectures given at the University of California at Berkeley in 1959 and at the Library of Congress in 1962.) Spender looks back at the modern from the perspective of the contemporary literary scene, finding the split between art and life (like that between the individual and society), ever widening, *Dichtung* and *Wahrheit* drawing further apart. He views as endemic to the modern movement the endeavor to heal this split, to see life as a whole. This endeavor necessitates, in Spender's view, confronting the present with the past. This technique of juxtaposing present and past is strikingly present in Eliot, Yeats, Joyce, Woolf, Lawrence, and others. He diagnoses nostalgia as the dominant emotion of modern art, because past has been amputated from present. Exploring and retrieving the past is the only way, as Eliot wrote of Joyce's mythic method in *Ulysses*, of "controlling, of ordering, of giving a shape and significance to the immense panorama of futility and anarchy, which is contemporary history." Paradoxically, the vision of the whole the modernists aspire to is achieved only through assembling fragments—"These fragments I have shored against my ruins," as Eliot wrote at the end of *The Waste Land*.

Further Spender observes that modernism was a movement in which all the arts cross-fertilized one another—poets, prose writers, painters, and musicians learned from one another. He traces the influence of painting on poetry and of poetry on prose, notably through impressionism and imagism, showing how concentration on modes of perceiving became itself an object of perception and how emphasis on the image gave the technique of stream-of-consciousness in Proust and Woolf and Joyce its living power.

The Making of a Poem was published in 1955, between the publication of *The Creative Element* and *The Struggle of the Modern*. Since it assembles reviews and occasional pieces, it is a more loosely organized, desultory collection of critical pieces than the other books and makes a less unified impression. Spender discusses Auden, Dylan Thomas, A. E. Housman, and Georgianism, among other topics. The best essay is "Goethe and the English Mind," in which Spender compares Goethe with Shakespeare and the Goethean conception of *Dichtung* with the English conception of poetry. This essay, like the title essay, "The Making of a Poem," reveals a great deal about Spender and his own poems. He argues that English poetry springs from inhibition, guilt, and puritan repression. It is less an expression of public than of private life and conscience. It denies the dichotomy of form and content that Goethe could equably contemplate and exploit.

"The Making of a Poem" emphasizes poetry's dependence upon memory, establishing an equivalence of imagination and memory by remarking we can imagine nothing we have not experienced in some way. He describes his own memory as self-centered, which is why his art is essentially autobiographical. He also confesses, "My mind is not clear, my will is weak, I suffer from excess of ideas and a weak sense of form," judgments the serious student of his poetry will corroborate.

Love-Hate Relations: A Study of Anglo-American Sensibilities, published in 1974, is a recasting of the Clark Lectures Spender delivered at Cambridge in 1965. It is concerned with Anglo-American literary relations during the past hundred years, with the West-East immigration of Pound, Eliot, and other American writers to Europe and with the reverse East-West migration of Spender's friends and contemporaries—Auden, Isherwood, Huxley, and Lawrence. The subject is a fascinating one, about which Spender is well informed, but his study is vitiated by a diminished capacity for intellectual analysis.

The acme of Spender's achievement in prose is his autobiography, *World Within World*, by any standard, a fine example of its genre, completed when the writer was in his early forties. The book corroborates and vindicates Spender's claim that all his art is essentially autobiographical: "what I write are fragments of autobiography: sometimes . . . poems, sometimes stories, and the longer passages may take the form of novels." The title is one of Spender's master metaphors or key symbols: that of microcosm with macrocosm, center within circumference, the individual contained within society and the universe. The personality revealed in the autobiography is intense, honest, generous, but also neurotic, ambivalent, and masochistic. Spender's candor is incandescent. At the age of twenty he noted in a journal, "I have no character or will power outside my work." He consistently judges himself objectively and dispassionately, even when such judgment shows him in an unfavorable light.

Spender's most important works, *The Destructive Element* and *The Struggle of the Modern*, contain some insights original at the time of publication, but on the whole Spender's criticism is repetitious and prolix, full of overgeneralizations and projective judgments. At its best, however, both Spender's poetry and his prose fuse the concrete and the abstract vividly, unifying flesh and the spirit, inner and outer existence.

Other:

Richard Crossman, ed., *The God That Failed: Six Studies in Communism*, includes a chapter by Spender (New York: Harper, 1949);

The Writer's Dilemma: Essays First Published in the Times Literary Supplement Under the Heading "Limits of Control," introduction by Spender (London, New York & Toronto: Oxford University Press, 1961);

The Concise Encyclopedia of English and American Poets and Poetry, edited by Spender and Donald Hall (New York: Hawthorn Books, 1963);

Encounters: An Anthology from the First Ten Years of Encounter Magazine, edited by Spender, Irving Kristol, and Melvin J. Lasky (New York: Basic Books, 1963);

D. H. Lawrence, edited by Spender (New York, Evanston, San Francisco & London: Harper & Row, 1973);

W. H. Auden: A Tribute, edited by Spender (London: Weidenfeld & Nicolson, 1974; New York: Macmillan, 1975).

Translations:

Rainer Maria Rilke, *Duino Elegies*, translated by Spender and J. B. Leishman (London: Hogarth Press, 1939; New York: Norton, 1939);

Georg Büchner, *Danton's Death*, translated by Spender and Goronwy Rees (London: Faber & Faber, 1939);

Federico García Lorca, *Poems*, translated by Spender and J. L. Gili (London: Dolphin, 1939);

García Lorca, *Selected Poems*, translated by Spender and Gili (London: Hogarth Press, 1943);

Paul Eluard, *Le Dur Désir de Durer*, translated by Spender and Frances Cornford (Philadelphia: Grey Falcon Press, 1950);

Rilke, *The Life of the Virgin Mary*, translated, with an introduction, by Spender (London: Vision Press, 1951);

Frank Wedekind, *Five Tragedies of Sex*, translated by Spender and Frances Fawcett (New York: Theatre Arts Books, 1952);

Schiller's Mary Stuart, freely translated and adapted by Spender (London: Faber & Faber, 1959).

Letters:

Letters to Christopher: Stephen Spender's Letters to Christopher Isherwood, 1920-1939, With "The Line of the Branch"–Two Thirties Journals, edited by Lee Bartlett (Santa Barbara: Black Sparrow, 1980).

Bibliography:

H. B. Kulkarni, *Stephen Spender; Works and Criticism: An Annotated Bibliography* (New York & London: Garland, 1976).

References:

J. J. Connors, *Poets & Politics: A Study of the Careers of C. Day Lewis, Stephen Spender & W. H. Auden in the 1930's* (New Haven: Yale University Press, 1967);

George S. Fraser, *Vision & Rhetoric* (London: Faber & Faber, 1959; New York: Barnes & Noble, 1960);

Katharine B. Hoskins, *Today the Struggle: Literature & Politics in England During the Spanish Civil War* (Austin & London: University of Texas Press, 1969);

Christopher Isherwood, *Christopher & His Kind, 1929-1939* (New York: Farrar, Straus & Giroux, 1976; London: Eyre Methuen, 1977);

Isherwood, *Lions & Shadows: An Education in the Twenties* (London: Hogarth Press, 1938; Nor-

folk, Conn.: New Directions, 1947);
H. B. Kulkarni, *Stephen Spender: Poet in Crisis* (Glasgow: Blackie, 1970);
D. E. S. Maxwell, *Poets of the Thirties* (London: Routledge & Kegan Paul, 1969; New York: Barnes & Noble, 1969);
Howard Nemerov, *Poetry & Fiction* (New Brunswick, N. J.: Rutgers University Press, 1963);
John Press, *A Map of Modern English Verse* (London & New York: Oxford University Press, 1969);
Francis Scarfe, *Auden & After: The Liberation of Poetry, 1930-1941* (London: Routledge, 1942);
Hugh Thomas, *The Spanish Civil War* (London: Eyre & Spottiswoode, 1961; New York: Harper & Row, 1961);
A. K. Weatherhead, *Stephen Spender and the Thirties* (Lewisburg, Pa.: Bucknell University Press / London: Associated University Presses, 1975).

Papers:
The principal repository of unpublished Spender papers is the Library of Northwestern University, Evanston, Illinois, which has a collection of 450 catalogued manuscripts and 131 letters, including considerable correspondence with T. S. Eliot. The Bancroft Library of the University of California at Berkeley has a collection of uncatalogued manuscripts, as well as notebooks containing drafts of poems, personal journals, and correspondence with Eliot, Pound, Forster, Huxley, Edith Sitwell, and others. Other libraries having Spender papers are the University of Notre Dame and the Humanities Research Center of the University of Texas, Austin.

Dylan Thomas

David E. Middleton
Nicholls State University

See also the Thomas entry in *DLB 13, British Dramatists Since World War II*.

BIRTH: Swansea, Wales, 27 October 1914, to D. J. and Florence Hannah Williams Thomas.

MARRIAGE: 11 July 1937 to Caitlin Macnamara; children: Llewelyn, Aeron, Colm.

AWARDS AND HONORS: "Poets' Corner" Prize of the *Sunday Referee*, 1934; Blumenthal Poetry Prize, 1938; Levinson Poetry Prize, 1945; grant from The Authors' Society Travelling Scholarship Fund, 1947; Foyle's Poetry Prize for *Collected Poems: 1934-1952*, 1952.

DEATH: New York, New York, 9 November 1953.

SELECTED BOOKS: *18 Poems* (London: *Sunday Referee* / Parton Bookshop, 1934);
Twenty-Five Poems (London: Dent, 1936);
The Map of Love (London: Dent, 1939);
The World I Breathe (Norfolk, Conn.: New Directions, 1939);
Portrait of the Artist as a Young Dog (London: Dent, 1940; Norfolk, Conn.: New Directions, 1940);
New Poems (Norfolk, Conn.: New Directions, 1943);
Deaths and Entrances (London: Dent, 1946);
Selected Writings of Dylan Thomas (New York: New Directions, 1946);
In Country Sleep and Other Poems (New York: New Directions, 1952);
Collected Poems: 1934-1952 (London: Dent, 1952); republished as *The Collected Poems of Dylan Thomas* (New York: New Directions, 1953);
The Doctor and the Devils, adapted from Donald Taylor's story (London: Dent, 1953; New York: New Directions, 1953);
Under Milk Wood (London: Dent, 1954; New York: New Directions, 1954);
Quite Early One Morning (London: Dent, 1954; enlarged edition, New York: New Directions, 1954);
A Prospect of the Sea and Other Stories and Prose Writings, edited by Daniel Jones (London: Dent, 1955);
Adventures in the Skin Trade and Other Stories (New York: New Directions, 1955); republished as *Adventures in the Skin Trade* (London: Putnam's, 1955);

Dylan Thomas, circa 1946 (BBC Hulton)

A Child's Christmas in Wales (Norfolk, Conn.: New Directions, 1955);

The Beach of Falesá, based on Robert Louis Stevenson's story (New York: Stein & Day, 1963; London: Cape, 1964);

Twenty Years A-Growing, adapted from Maurice O'Sullivan's story (London: Dent, 1964);

Rebecca's Daughters (London: Triton, 1965; Boston: Little, Brown, 1965);

Me and My Bike (New York: McGraw-Hill, 1965; London: Triton, 1965);

The Doctor and the Devils and Other Scripts (New York: New Directions, 1966);

The Notebooks of Dylan Thomas, edited by Ralph Maud (New York: New Directions, 1967); republished as *Poet in the Making* (London: Dent, 1968);

Dylan Thomas: Early Prose Writings (London: Dent, 1971; New York: New Directions, 1971);

The Poems of Dylan Thomas, edited by Jones (London: Dent, 1971; New York: New Directions, 1971);

Dylan Thomas: Selected Poems, edited by Walford Davies (London: Dent, 1974);

The Death of the King's Canary, by Thomas and John Davenport (London: Hutchinson, 1976).

Dylan Thomas's life, work, and stature among twentieth-century poets are all matters of controversy and speculation. An essentially shy and modest man when sober, Thomas called himself the "captain of the second eleven" on the team of modern poets, an uneasy, pivotal ranking between the clearly major and the clearly minor poets. Others, too, such as John Crowe Ransom, have found difficulty in formulating a final opinion of Thomas: is he really only the best of the minor poets—those who achieve distinction within inherited modes and procedures—or is he the weak man, if that, among the major poets—those who absorb the tradition of ideas and forms which they then in some way radically change?

Until recently, Thomas's spectacular public life and personality, essentially distinct from the serious craftsman within, obscured the critical view of the body of work which the poet left behind. The burning ground of Thomas's four reading tours in America (1950-1953)—the endless drunkenness, the exhibitionist behavior, the masterful and deeply moving public readings, the early death from alcoholism at thirty-nine in New York—these events and more make Thomas's biography, like Byron's or Rimbaud's, an interesting story in itself. Yet as Thomas's closest childhood friend, Dr. Daniel Jones, said, Thomas's artistic sensibility was at war with his outer life. In Thomas's words, there was a traditional romantic conflict between the "interior world" of childhood fantasy, dream, poetic imagination and the "exterior, wrong world" of objective, adult reality, what Thomas fearfully called "the world-of-the-others."

Not only Thomas's life but even his poetry is dominated by the problem of the relation of inner and outer, of self and world. In a letter of 1933, written during the single greatest year of Thomas's poetic activity, the eighteen-year-old poet speculated about this troubling matter of "worlds": "Perhaps the greatest works of art are those that reconcile, perfectly, inner and outer." This problem remains the underlying theme of Thomas's poetry in its three major phases: (1) the early juvenilia, the poems in the notebooks, and the post-notebook poems of 1934-1936; (2) the middle-phase poetry of the late 1930s to mid-1940s; and (3) the final poetry of the postwar years (1946-1953). Less centrally, the immediate themes of the poetry in the three periods evolve from an early obsession with a visionary, often demonic fusion of the processes of the body, especially intercourse and gestation, with the processes of nature and the cosmos, through a more directly personal encounter with the "exterior" challenges of marriage, fatherhood, and war, to a final period of imaginative recollection and dramatic evocation of a lost Wordsworthian childhood and a loving vision of nature and death as holy, sacramental, and good.

Dylan Marlais Thomas was born at home, No. 5 Cwmdonkin Drive, in the middle-class Uplands district of Swansea, Wales, on 27 October 1914. His father, D. J. Thomas, was a schoolmaster in English at the Swansea Grammar School, while his mother, Florence Williams Thomas, was a housewife who had previously given birth to a daughter, Nancy, nearly nine years older than Dylan. A bitter, disappointed man who thought his schoolmaster's job beneath his abilities, Thomas's father was rather cold, somewhat given to drink in his youth, an atheist who paradoxically cursed God for changes in the weather, yet a brilliant reader of Shakespeare to his class and to the preschool Dylan, and the owner of a surprisingly up-to-date library of modern and nineteenth-century poets which his son absorbed. Dylan feared, respected, and deeply loved this rather terrifying father, and in some sense his life was an attempt to realize his father's frustrated dream of being a great poet. His mother, on the other hand, was a simple woman, loving and overly protective. She spoiled Dylan as a child and adolescent and even at the end of his life found no fault in his public behavior and drinking habits. Thomas's lifelong desire to remain in some way a child and to be free of adult responsibility probably results from his mother's overindulgence and from his own rebellion against his stricter, more demanding father.

Swansea and the Gower peninsula, No. 5 Cwmdonkin Drive, Cwmdonkin Park, Fernhill—these are the places which meant the most to Thomas in childhood and adolescence, from his earliest years until he moved to London for his first long stay in 1934. In Thomas's time, Swansea had around 100,000 residents. Built on hills curving around a bay (hills through which the River Tawe flows), Swansea was a middle-class, Anglicized seaport town, adjacent to the beautifully wild, heath-covered Gower peninsula. From his room at No. 5 Cwmdonkin Drive, the young poet could see the bay and also, across the street, Cwmdonkin Park, where he played as a child and which figures in poems such as "The Hunchback in the Park" as an Edenic place, visionary nature as seen by the poet as child. Fernhill was the farm near Llangain, owned by his uncle Jack Jones, husband of his mother's oldest sister, Annie, the subject of Thomas's poem "After the Funeral: in memory of Ann Jones." Here, Dylan spent many vacations as a child, as recounted in his most famous poem, "Fern Hill." Like Cwmdonkin Park, Fernhill (as it is normally spelled) became, in Thomas's later life, the focus of nostalgic yearnings for the lost world of the romantic child.

Schooling proved to be no real threat to such childhood happiness as Thomas grew into adolescence. In 1925, he entered the Swansea Grammar School, where he stayed on until 1931. Under headmaster Trevor Owen, the school was run in a relaxed, liberal atmosphere, one in which the studious boys were encouraged and the lazy ones, like Dylan, left pretty much alone.

As Thomas later said, his real education came from the freedom to read anything in his father's library, and more. He absorbed a bewildering array of works and authors: "Sir Thomas Browne, Robert W. Service, de Quincey, Henry Newbolt, Blake, Baroness Orczy, Marlowe, *Chums*, the Imagists, the Bible, the *Magnet*, Poe, Grimm, Keats, Lawrence, Austin Dobson and Dostoievski, Anon and Shakespeare." The Bible and Shakespeare were particularly important sources of Thomas's imagery, rhythms, and poetic syntax. Keats was for Thomas a conscious model and measuring rod to whom he frequently compared himself. Of Blake, Thomas once said that "I am in the path of Blake, but so far behind him that only the wings of his heels are in sight."

During his stay at the grammar school, Thomas edited, almost single-handedly, the *Swansea Grammar School Magazine*. Here he published his juvenilia—comic and wittily imitative poems that do not reveal Thomas's private struggle to achieve a serious, profoundly original voice. That struggle was occurring, in utmost privacy, in the notebooks (1930-1934), of which four survive. These notebooks chart Thomas's gradual development of the famous early style. That a young boy, sixteen to nineteen years old, in a Welsh sea town should create such original poetry at first seems amazing, but a precocious essay called "Modern Poetry" (1929) shows Thomas to be aware of many modern poets: Hardy, Bridges, Hopkins, the Sitwells, Yeats, the World War I poets, Lawrence, Pound.

Another important influence on the young poet was his friendship with Dan Jones, later Dr. Daniel Jones, musical composer and editor of *The Poems of Dylan Thomas* (1971). Dan's house was called Warmley, and there Thomas found many books on modern poetry. The two young artists composed poems together, and they created, like the Brontë children, a vast fantasy world of poets, musicians, and others whose works were "broadcast" through jerry-rigged loudspeakers over the Warmley Broadcasting System. The word games and poetic exercises were part of Thomas's deliberate but essentially private development from school wit to serious young poet in the notebooks. When Thomas left school for good in July 1931, he entered into the most productive three-year period of his life. From mid-1931 until he moved to London in late 1934, Thomas lived an intense poetic life, as recorded in the notebooks.

In the Swansea of the depression year of 1931, Thomas was lucky to land a job, probably with D. J. Thomas's help, as copyreader and then reporter for the *South Wales Evening Post*. Thomas held this job for nearly a year and a half, leaving at Christmas 1932 by mutual agreement. From all accounts, he was a terrible news reporter: he got facts wrong, and he failed to show up to cover events, preferring instead the pool hall or coffee at the local artistic hangout, the Kardomah Café. Thomas's most significant journalism from this period is a series of articles for the *Herald of Wales* (weekend complement to the *Post*) on "The Poets of Swansea." The most intriguing of these critical essays is the one on Llewelyn Prichard, a fiery nineteenth-century figure whose personality and fate forecast in eerie fashion Thomas's own: "No one can deny that the most attractive figures in literature are always those around whom a world of lies and legends have been woven, those half mythical artists whose real characters become cloaked for ever under a veil of the bizarre. They become known not as creatures of flesh and blood, living day by day as prosaically as the rest of us, but as men stepping on clouds, snaring a world of beauty from the trees and sky, half wild, half human." Thomas also wrote about his reporter days in his poignant BBC reminiscence of prewar Swansea, "Return Journey," in which an old reporter and two young reporters discuss the long gone young Thomas. The narrator, too, recalls Thomas the young poet and reporter: "He'd be about seventeen or eighteen . . . and above medium height. Above medium height for Wales, I mean, he's five foot six and a half. Thick blubber lips; snub nose; curly mouse-brown hair; one front tooth broken after playing a game called Cats and Dogs, in the Mermaid, Mumbles; speaks rather fancy; truculent; plausible; a bit of a shower-off; plus-fours and no breakfast, you know; used to have poems printed in the *Herald of Wales* . . . a bombastic adolescent provincial Bohemian with a thick-knotted artist's tie made out of his sister's scarf, she never knew where it had gone, and a cricket-shirt dyed bottle-green; a gabbing, ambitious, mock-tough, pretentious young man; and mole-y, too."

As a self-affectedly bohemian poseur, Thomas began acquiring his reputation as a great drinker, the "conscious Woodbine" cigarette dangling from his lips. He began to develop a public persona as jokester and storyteller which became his trademark later on in the London years. Thomas's first visit to London seems to have occurred in August 1933. Only one poem, "And Death Shall Have No Dominion," had appeared in a London publication before this first trip, and that was in A. R. Orage's *New English Weekly* (May 1933). Contacts made in August 1933 and on later trips led to the publication of a number of early poems in the *Adelphi*, the *Listener*, *New Verse*, and T. S. Eliot's *Criterion*. Although Eliot subsequently declined Thomas's poems for Faber and Faber, he wrote to Thomas's biographer Constantine FitzGibbon that "I certainly regarded him always as a poet of considerable importance." In 1933, however, it was the unlikely figure of Victor Neuburg, a strange poet who was once under the influence of the occultist Aleister

Crowley, who discovered and widely promoted Thomas's work. Neuburg edited the "Poets' Corner" in Mark Goulden's newspaper, the *Sunday Referee*. Between 1933 and 1935, Neuburg published seven poems by Thomas in the "Poets' Corner." In March 1934 Thomas followed Pamela Hansford Johnson in receiving the second "Poets' Corner" Prize: the publication of a first book of poems. David Archer, owner of the Parton Bookshop, shared printing costs with the *Referee*, and *18 Poems* by Dylan Thomas was published on 18 December 1934. Earlier, in 1933, the first recipient of the *Referee* prize, Pamela Hansford Johnson, had written Thomas a letter in admiration of the poem "That Sanity Be Kept" (*Sunday Referee*, 3 September 1933). From this letter developed Thomas's most extensive correspondence on the ideas embodied in his early poetry. Although in love with Thomas, Johnson sensed that his irregular life and especially his drinking would not do, and the relationship was eventually broken off.

In his letters to Johnson, Thomas clearly stated his defiantly romantic view of poetry: "There is no necessity for the artist to do anything. There is no necessity. He is a law unto himself, and his greatness or smallness rises or falls by that. He has only one limitation, and that is the widest of all: the limitation of form. Poetry finds its own form; form should never be superimposed; the structure should rise out of the words and the expression of them. I do not want to express only what other people have felt; I want to rip something away and show what they have never seen." In another letter, Thomas described his characteristic method in the early poems of linking cosmic and bodily processes: "All thoughts and actions emanate from the body. Therefore the description of a thought or action—however abstruse it may be—can be beaten home by bringing it onto a physical level. Every idea, intuitive or intellectual, can be imaged and translated in terms of the body, its flesh, skin, blood, sinews, veins, glands, organs, cells, or senses. Through my small, bone-bound island I have learnt all I know, experienced all, and sensed all. All I write is inseparable from the island. As much as possible, therefore, I employ the scenery of the island to describe the scenery of my thoughts, the earthquake of the body to describe the earthquake of the heart." For Thomas, the poet is the great healer and unifier, for whom words are living things and living things are words. To Johnson, too, he said what he would often repeat, that poets either work *toward* words or *out of* words. He himself worked *out of* words, trying to release from words, like a shaman, their magical powers that would unite all opposites of human experience. Such a procedure often led to obscurity, as Thomas confessed to Johnson in May 1934, when he wrote to her of himself as "a freak *user* of words, not a poet."

In October 1934 on the eve of his departure for London, Thomas discussed his poetic goals more affirmatively in answers to a *New Verse* questionnaire. There he defined poetry as "the rhythmic, inevitably narrative, movement from an overclothed blindness to a naked vision. . . . My poetry is, or should be, useful to me for one reason: it is the record of my individual struggle from darkness towards some measure of light." He also accepted Freud and revolution. Shortly after his arrival in London, Thomas wrote to Swansea friend Charles Fisher about "my theory of poetry." Slightly altering his quotation from Blake, Thomas pronounced: "I like things that are difficult to write and difficult to understand; I like 'redeeming the contraries' with secretive images; I like contradicting my images, saying two things at once in one word, four in two and one in six. . . . Poetry . . . should be as orgiastic and organic as copulation, dividing and unifying, personal but not private, propagating the individual in the mass and the mass in the individual." This statement is matched by his famous response to Henry Treece about his imagistic method of composition. A poem of his begins, he said, with a "host of images," one image breeding another, often its opposite, a "dialectical method" that begins with the "central seed" and proceeds through a series of "creations, recreations, destructions, contradictions" to reach "that momentary peace which is a poem."

The years 1935-1936 brought to a close the first phase of Dylan Thomas's life and art. In these years, he reworked most of the best of the remaining notebook poems and wrote new long poems that led up to the ten sonnets of the "Altarwise by Owl-light" sequence. This time period also found Thomas plunging into London's art world and bohemian quarters, establishing a reputation as poet, pub crawler, character, storyteller, and "damned soul," in the nineteenth-century French tradition, the demonically destructive angel-child whom many acquaintances wished to mother and protect.

Thomas lived first at 5 Redcliffe Street, near Earl's Court in South Kensington. He shared rooms with Swansea artist friends Fred Janes, Mervyn Levy, and William Scott. Soon, however, he was living in one place and then another, as girls or friends came and went, making do with beer and

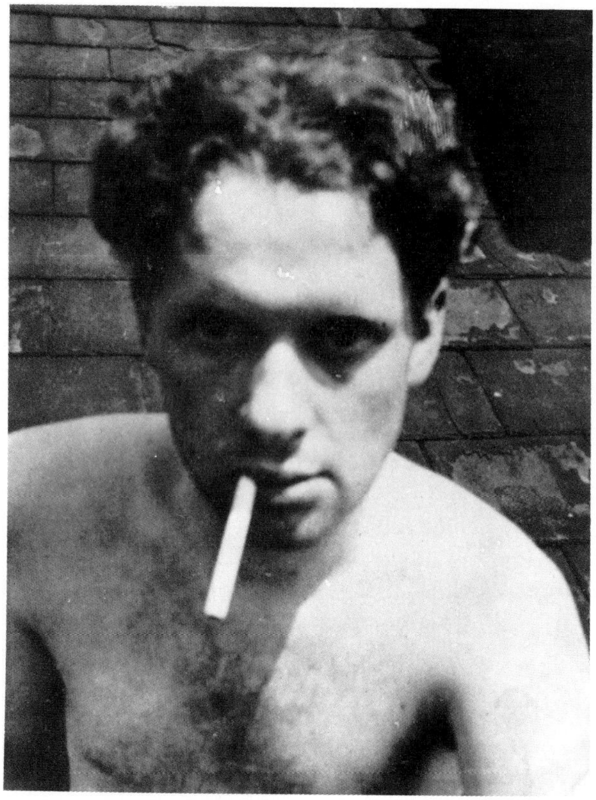

Dylan Thomas in Kensington, 1935

cake or an apple for breakfast, no pajamas, and only a mattress on the floor at Janes's flat, when he was there at all. His squalid domestic and hygienic habits earned him the nicknames "Ditch" and "The Ugly Suckling," among others. Relishing the image of the poet-in-the-gutter, Thomas loved to be sung to sleep by Levy with a song whose line "For I am waiting and watching, an outlaw defiant" the poet loved best.

In public, Thomas lived up to this image of the artist as "an outlaw defiant" in his often outrageous, sometimes hilarious, at other times disgusting behavior. He made up strange fantasies about "Night Custard," or a universe in which all things are made from oil (an "oily verse"), about the delectability of a sandwich of dried eyes. Most of Thomas's pub stories and jokes are lost, and the fragments still recalled by listeners usually pale without Thomas's presence, delivering voice, and the beer; nevertheless, countless reports seem to confirm that before getting too drunk for wit, Dylan Thomas was one of the great conversationalists of his day. In June 1936 he fit right in at the famous international Surrealist Exhibition at the Burlington Galleries, London, where he carried around a cup of boiled string, asking "weak or strong?" At a poetry recitation there, he read—a postcard. Apparently, too, he caught a social disease from a girl at this time and went home to Wales to recuperate. In fact, from 1934 on, Thomas established a lifelong pattern of travel between London and some rural retreat, usually in Wales. London meant drink, possibly employment by the BBC, and no work on poems. Wales and elsewhere meant work on poems, somewhat less to drink, but no employment, eventual boredom, and the inevitable return to London for dissipation.

Thomas's second book, *Twenty-Five Poems*, was published in 1936 by J. M. Dent, second only to Faber and Faber as a poetry press, through the offices of Lascelles Abercrombie, who knew an editor at Dent, Richard Church, who accepted *Twenty-Five Poems* in spite of his fear that the poems were too obscure and fashionably surrealistic. Although Thomas denied the charge and Dent published the volume, his poetry was becoming more and more obscure and continued to be so until World War II. In a letter to Vernon Watkins, Thomas admitted his fears: "now, I'm almost afraid of all the once-necessary artifices and obscurities, and can't, for the life or the death of me, get any real liberation, any diffusion or dilution or anything, into the churning bulk of the words." Thomas's own fears were echoed in the mixed reviews of *Twenty-Five Poems*, although sales were high, with four printings of over 3,000 copies by October 1944.

Thomas first met Caitlin Macnamara in the Wheatsheaf, a London pub, in 1936, accompanied by Augustus John, the painter, with whom she was intimate. Blue-eyed, yellow-haired, once called a true poet's girl, a corn goddess, Caitlin Macnamara was a fair-skinned Irish beauty, strong-willed, violently emotional and argumentative at times, a truer bohemian than the essentially middle-class Thomas, a good writer, and a superb free-style dancer who had a brief career in Paris and London before becoming Thomas's wife.

Thomas fell in love with Caitlin at first sight. They had an affair at the Eiffel Tower Hotel on John's tab but were afterward separated when Thomas went to Cornwall. In July 1936 Thomas met her again at Richard Hughes's house in Laugharne where she and John were staying. A fight ensued between Thomas and the much older John, with John knocking Thomas down and driving off with Caitlin. However, by 11 July 1937, Thomas and Caitlin were married, in Cornwall, and the first phase of Thomas's short life came to an end.

The critical reception of Dylan Thomas's poetry may be divided into three phases. First, there was a generally polemical reception of the various volumes of poetry from *18 Poems* (1934) through *Collected Poems* (1952). This critical debate occurred mainly in the review columns and editorial pages of the important English and Welsh newspapers and poetry journals of the day. Second, with the exception of Henry Treece's *Dylan Thomas* (1949), the 1950s and 1960s saw the appearance of the first book-length critical studies of Thomas's poems. Most of these studies were general surveys of Thomas's work emphasizing the immediate problem of explicating difficult texts for the general reader. Third, in the middle 1960s and the 1970s, academic studies shifted to an interest in placing Thomas in one of several contexts such as Jungian psychology, Gnosticism, Christianity, Nietzchean Dionysianism, or the Welsh bardic tradition. Each of the studies in this third phase sought to give unity to Thomas's poetry by defining his poetic development in terms of one of these contexts.

Thomas's first book, *18 Poems*, appeared in a poetic decade usually characterized as one in which the poet's political responsibility and awareness were paramount in influencing the kind of poetry he wrote. Yet the poets of the 1930s are not as homogeneous a group as might first be thought. In his 1952 *Spectator* review of Thomas's *Collected Poems: 1934-1952*, Stephen Spender looked back on Thomas as having purposefully rebelled against the conscious intellectualism, wit, and political emphasis of "Macspaunday" (his name for MacNeice, himself, Auden, and Day Lewis, often called the Auden Generation). The romantic personalism of the poetry of Edith Sitwell and the blossoming of the British variety of surrealism in the 1930s gave that decade a more complex character than is sometimes acknowledged. Certainly the reviewers of the period saw Thomas in a romantic context. The subjective, expressionistic nature of his poetry was emphasized as well as its struggle to articulate a new mode of consciousness. Some critics condemned him for being a surrealist or for not being more politically aware. By the end of the decade, however, Thomas himself was adopted as the patron saint of a group of British poets known as the Apocalypse, whose most important members, Henry Treece and J. F. Hendry, were advocates of a new romantic poetry, surrealistic and antimechanistic in style.

Although Dylan Thomas said that he preferred "what I think about verse to be *in* the verse," he left numerous letters, essays, broadcasts, and lecture notes that contain important statements of his views on the nature of poetry. Like the letters to Pamela Hansford Johnson, Thomas's other prose statements are a rich source of evidence in support of the proposition that the problem of *self* and *world*, of subject-object relations, as inherited from the romantic tradition, is a central concern of Thomas as a poet. Thomas often expresses this theme in terms of the romantic myth, that is, the romantic displacement of the Creation, Fall, and Redemption phases of the Christian version of history into a secular, psychological context. In the romantic scheme Creation is the sense of unity of being, present most clearly in childhood, a sense of oneness with nature and a unity among the faculties of the mind. The Fall is the decline of the child into adulthood and attendant self-consciousness, a sense of isolation, estrangement, division. Redemption, then, becomes the self-generated effort of the romantic to achieve reintegration by exercising the poetic imagination in such a way as to release a healing love into the world. Keeping the theme of self and world as embodied in the romantic myth in mind as the key to Thomas's poetry, one may list a number of important secondary traits that emanate from that central concern. These include the importance of the imagination as an image-making power; the epiphanic moment; poetry as the expression of intense emotion; the poet as the hero of his own poems, an exile from society; the organic nature of the image and the poetic process; the desire of the poet to remove the ontological barrier between word and thing; the inner quest for psychic unity; the problem of self-consciousness; the child as a figure of unity of being; the displacement of religious values into psychological and poetic terms; the importance of the relation of man and nature; and the poetic significance of the power of love.

The most authoritative comments on the question of Thomas's periods of poetic development are two made by Thomas himself. In a conversation in a New York bar with the critic William York Tindall, Thomas agreed with Tindall's division of the poetry into three phases: (1) a "womb-tomb" period that included the poems in *18 Poems* and *Twenty-Five Poems*, (2) a troubled middle period about marriage and war in *The Map of Love* and *Deaths and Entrances*, and (3) a final "period of humanity" or acceptance of the tragedy of the human condition in some of the later poems in *Deaths and Entrances* and in the poems of *In Country Sleep*. However much overlapping there might be between the volumes that make up these periods, there seems to be little doubt among critics that Thomas brought to fruition two major strains of poetry. The first strain is that of the early poems, originating mostly from the notebooks, written in a packed stanza of intense, obscure imagery, making use of assonantal and consonantal rhyme, and concerned with the development of an assertive romantic self, a development that culminates in the spiritual and poetic autobiography, "Altarwise by Owl-light," the quest-romance that closes *Twenty-Five Poems* and which Thomas himself came to see as the ultimate development of the tendencies in his first major period of creativity.

The second strain of major achievement begins with poems in *Deaths and Entrances*—"Poem in October," "A Winter's Tale," and the volume's final poem, "Fern Hill"—and ends with three finished sections of the projected poem "In Country Heaven" ("In Country Sleep," "Over Sir John's Hill," and "In the White Giant's Thigh"), the final birthday poem entitled "Poem on his Birthday," and the "Author's Prologue" to *Collected Poems*. This second period of major poetry is one in which the romantic self finds its true place in the role of priestly interpreter of nature and purveyor of the forces of imaginative perception and of love that redeem humanity from isolating self-consciousness and destructive rationality by revealing nature as a place of holiness.

In between these early poems of the assertive romantic self and the later poems of regenerative landscapes falls what some call a separate period, often designated as Thomas's "dark," "troubled," or "transitional" phase. The poems in this middle period are the "marriage" poems and the "war" poems in *The Map of Love* and in *Deaths and Entrances*. What the marriage and the war poems have in common is that both represent serious incursions of what Thomas called the "exterior" world of the "others" into the "interior" world of the youthful Swansea poet. The central question posed by the problem of marriage and of armed conflict was whether the romantic self's claim that it could govern its relation to the outer world was valid. In seeking a way out of this dilemma, Thomas discovered the romantic self's true task in the fostering of love and in the praise of the spiritualized landscape in face of the threats to humanity and the natural world posed by the atomic bomb. This final task of the self, then, becomes the subject of the later poems.

One difficulty with any examination of Thomas's poems is what may be called the problem of chronology. Because he wrote so slowly, Thomas reworked poems from the notebooks for inclusion in his second and third volumes, *Twenty-Five Poems* and *The Map of Love*. Most of the poems in his first volume, *18 Poems*, came from the last notebook, begun in August 1933. Thus, many of Thomas's poems written before those in *18 Poems* were first published in book form in the two volumes that followed *18 Poems*. The only valid way to see Thomas's poetic development clearly in the early period is to examine the poems as they appear in the four extant notebooks first, and then, if necessary, to examine radical revisions of notebook poems when these revisions result in the virtual creation of a new poem.

Although written concurrently with some unimportant schoolboy verses, the private notebook poems represent a more intensely serious effort at poetic composition. Headed "Mainly Free Verse Poems," the poems in the 1930 notebook show the obvious influence of certain poets and poetic schools, including Yeats, Pound, the imagists, and Keats. The first group contains poems that deal with the tendency of the self to transform or to absorb the world, usually by way of the process of poetic creation. In poem eleven, for instance, the poet takes two growing plants—a cornstalk and a blue flower—and speculates on how his imagination must operate to "free" the corn and flower from the restrictions of rational perception, of the laws of growth and decay in the fallen world. A second group of poems examines the relation of the self and world in terms of the self's desire for or fear of absorption into the external world. Poem twenty-seven is spoken by a bird, a favorite image of Thomas's, in this case to be identified with the poet in the act of poetic creation. Poem eighteen seems heavily indebted to Keats's "Ode to a Nightingale." The poet experiences a romantic moment of the loss of self-consciousness: "So I sink myself in the moment, / I let the fiery stream run." He becomes a garden in which the bird sits and sings, bringing such intense joy that the poet is "all but cut by the scent's arc" as in Keats's poem.

The idea of a perfect woman who wavers between the status of nature and art is the subject of poem thirty-three. The poet addresses a real woman who has been transformed into an ideal by the poet's imagination. Thus he says,"I bought you for a thought," and calls his mind "your panopticon," or distorting mirror that makes the woman over to suit his desires.

Other poems compare the poet to the natural world. Sometimes Thomas sees nature as a place of vitalistic, primitive energy, where human self-consciousness does not disturb the harmony. For instance, poem eight, a Lawrentian beast poem, expresses a desire to be like the lion who is "balanced," has a "clean" mind without superfluous vanity, and who is a "vital, dominant creature," unlike the "unbalanced," "frail" poet. More often, nature is seen as an object for imaginative redemption or as a desirable object for union with the isolated self. As an object for redemption, nature in its fallen form is released by imagination in the poem on the endlessly growing cornstalk and blue flowers (poem eleven) or the similarly unlimited expansion of sacramental trees (poem twelve).

Several of these poems on nature link the virtues of the natural world with the poet's quest for a love that would bring release from self-consciousness. In the 1930 notebook, love appears as pure sensuality or mundane human love, as the poet's anima or its dark reverse, the femme fatale, or as an agent of redemption. Three poems—poems twenty-one, thirty-nine, and forty-two—contain the figure of the female dancer who unites art and nature, spirit and body, pattern and embodiment in one. Poem thirteen apparently invites an Egyptian goddess ("Oh, eagle-mouthed") into the poet's inner world while poem twenty invites an angel, a seraph, to enter a cavernous Jordan of the imagination. Poems ten and thirty-eight take opposite attitudes toward the union of the poet's lover or anima with natural powers, the former seeing the lover-anima as drawing strength from nature and the latter bemoaning Artemis's degradation from myth into the material world.

All of the themes of the 1930 notebook continue in the 1930-1932 notebook which immediately followed. Somewhere in the middle of this notebook emerges Thomas's most characteristic early style, one containing a dense, packed line, heavily rhythmical, a catalogue of arcane images which often seek to become polysemous metaphors for three simultaneously presented creative processes: nature, sex, and poetry. Besides this emergence of a more sophisticated style, what distinguishes the 1930-1932 notebook from its predecessor is the poet's increasing awareness of the necessity and yet supreme difficulty of exercising the imagination in poetic composition in order to govern the external world on terms congenial to the self. A growing sense of deathliness in nature as well as a sense of the multiple faces of love—sexuality, necrophilia, the ideal woman or anima—and the experience of the relative failure of these forms in redeeming the self from isolation are also major themes of the second extant notebook.

Poem two ("To-day, this hour I breathe") addresses the problem of the artist whose imagination, operating according to the same organic laws that govern nature, encounters recalcitrant objects that violate its own laws. In an epiphanic moment, the poet and nature are linked by the romantic metaphor of the correspondent breeze by which internal symbol and external object are made one: "To-day, this hour I breathe / In symbols, be they so light, of tongue and air."

A poem whose subjects are nature, imagination, and love is poem eighty, the 1932 version of "The Hunchback in the Park." Though alone in nature, "a solitary mister," the hunchback is not isolated from nature; rather nature lends support to the hunchback, "propped between trees and water." From the degraded perspective of modern urban dwellers, the hunchback is a madman, "going daft," while his physical deformity brings on the cruel laughter of children. They call him only "mister" as if to deny him identity, yet with some irony it is they who tease him and run into the oblivion beyond the park, the limit of the hunchback's perception: "Past lake and rockery / On out of sight." At night, when the park is emptied of all

Dylan and Caitlin Thomas at Sea View, Laugharne, circa 1938 (photo by Nora Summers)

but the Yeatsian "three veteran swans," the hunchback assumes his true identity as romantic poet by creating in the mind a figure of ideal feminine beauty, which he then transposes from the inner self to the outer landscape. He makes

> A figure without fault
> And sees it on the gravel paths
> Or walking on the water.

The feminine ideal brings unity of being and may be a nature spirit, for she is "frozen all the winter" and appears only in the summer. That the hunchback is a poet exercising imagination we know directly: "It is a poem and it is a woman figure." She calls to him from the water of the lake, and, while he responded angrily to the taunting children, he now smiles at the woman who has left his imagination to live in the park.

A similar poem in Thomas's emerging early style is poem twenty-one ("High on a Hill"), which attempts to create a polysemous metaphor for the self's relation to nature, sex, and poetic creation. The poet seems to be riding a hill like a bucking bronco, yet this hill is surprisingly female—"straddle her wrinkled knees"—just as the adder, snake, and shell-bursting bird are creatures of nature but also representative of the penis. The poetic dimension of the imagery is made explicit in the exclamation "Christ, let me write from the heart," which makes the "carnal stem" not only flower stalk and penis but also the poet's phallic fountain pen which deflowers the virgin paper, a frequent metaphor in Thomas's letters. As he writes from the "heart," the "blood's ebb" is of the detumescent penis and the receding moment of poetic inspiration.

The 1930-1932 notebook also marks the emergence of Thomas's brooding over the endless cycles of creation and decay in the universe, an imprisoning cycle from which he seeks escape by trying to invoke the power of poetic creation to reverse or end the cycle. Poem twenty-five is an obscure meditation on two impulses toward poetic creation—death and love—both of which relieve the poet of his burden of self-consciousness. Even as the poet writes, death's promise comes nearer in the passing of time: "I have a friend in death, / Daywise, the grave's inertia."

Ralph Maud designates the February 1933 notebook and the surviving poems from the lost 1932-1933 notebook as the beginning of Thomas's famous "inlooking" poems, phantasmagoric evocations of "process" in the body and in the natural world to which the body is linked. Actually, Thomas's romantic concern with self and world and the links between the two (sex, death, imagination) begins with his earliest poetry. The real changes in successive notebooks or published volumes are Thomas's increasing mastery of poetic technique and the periodic risings and fallings off of his faith in the ability of imagination to heal the gap between subject and object.

One of the most despairing in this group of poems on poetry and nature is "Especially When the November Wind," a 1932-1933 version of the well-known "Especially When the October Wind," from which it radically differs. One month further into the cold than its later version, the 1932-1933 poem has as its theme the paradox that the more intensely the poet writes in order to find a way to link himself to the outer world the more self-conscious he becomes of his isolation, an isolation seemingly made worse by the very self-consciousness of the act of poetic creation itself. An evil version of the romantic metaphor of the correspondent breeze, the "November wind / With frosty fingers, punishes my hair" as the poet's fingers respond to the creative breezes of inspiration. The poet seems to face two unpleasant choices: to expend his animal youth in a nature that is killing him even as he enjoys the release from the burdens of human thought or else to compose an aesthetic poetry that cannot create unity of being for the fully human poet in a fully natural world. Thus, the "raw / Spirits of words" and "arid syllables" oppress brain and heart. Being caught in the "chain of words" and "shut in a tower of words," the poet envies animals, children, or unself-conscious men, who in their primitive "language" or in silence find the unity with nature that escapes the poet.

A nearly complete version of "Ears in the Turrets Hear" dramatizes the isolation of the poet from the outer world. The poet is both an island and a tower (imagination) to which ships and their sailors come to make threatening noises. A masterpiece of sound and rhythm in an essentially trimeter line with appropriate trochaic and anapestic substitutions, the poem imagines intrusive sounds being made outside the tower door by surrealistically disordered pieces of the human anatomy (both his own and the intruders'):

> Ears in the turrets hear
> Hands grumble on the door,
> Eyes in the gables see
> The fingers at the locks.

The tower is surrounded by "a thin sea of flesh / And a bone coast" beyond which lies the unreal outer world: "The land lies out of sound / And the hills out of mind." But fiery winds and anchoring ships entice the poet either to death or to salvation in the outer world:

Shall I run to the ships,
With the wind in my hair
Or stay to the day I die,
And welcome no sailor?
Hands, hold you poison or grapes?

Is the poet lured on by a correspondent breeze in sea and hair? He certainly comes to know that his isolation from the world is no final solution.

As equally self-divided as Thomas's attitudes toward nature in the February 1933 notebook are his attitudes therein toward love. Poem eighteen ("Make Me a Mask") calls for a mask to repel the outer world where the poet perceives "Others betraying the inner love" that motivates him. The degradation of love is sometimes associated with Eliotic cityscapes, as in the typescript poem thirty-three, where we are sardonically told of "a girl whose single bed held two / To make ends meet" or in poem twenty-four, whose hero-quester sees in the dark nighttime city women's faces "with serpents' mouths and scalecophidian voids." Other corruptions of love include religious prudery, in poem fifty-three, and onanism, in poem forty-three.

That the August 1933 notebook marks Thomas's substantial arrival as an important poet seems undeniable. From the forty-odd poems in this notebook, Thomas chose thirteen of the poems for *18 Poems* as well as five poems for *Twenty-Five Poems*. Poems in the August notebook mark the emergence of the endless "process" of birth and death as an obsessive theme. Even more important, however, the many poems that address the central romantic problem of the relation of self and world begin to fall clearly into the three phases of the romantic myth—Creation, Fall, Redemption. Undoubtedly, the awareness of "process," the natural cycle of birth and death, led Thomas first to identify himself with the cycles but second to hope for some final end to these cycles in a vision of unfallen nature, some final religious apocalypse, or the poet's own exercising of imagination in the world.

Several poems key on the creation phase of the myth. A unified sensibility may be associated with a sacramental nature, the experience of one's own birth, an awakening apprehension of the unity between the evolving individual consciousness and the evolving outer world, or else a feeling of identity between God's creating Word and the poet's creating words.

With a natural bias toward the inner world, Thomas could write poems that attempt to describe simultaneously inner and outer processes, the goal of the polysemous metaphor. Two famous examples of this process are the August 1933 notebook versions of "Light Breaks Where No Sun Shines" (poem thirty) and "In the Beginning" (poem forty). The first of these begins mysteriously:

Light breaks where no sun shines;
Where no sea runs, the waters of the heart
Push in their tides;
And, broken ghosts with glowworms in their heads,
The things of light
File through the flesh where no flesh decks the bones.

These opening lines may be read as an evocation of the dawn of consciousness, the physical act of conception, and the first creation of the cosmos.

The action of "In the Beginning" is obviously a creation, primarily, one assumes, of the universe; but it is also clear that Thomas is attempting to identify the poet's words and creative imagination with the creation of the cosmos and of the child, these two creations being the objects of simultaneous presentation in the five stanzas of the poem. Thus, in stanza one:

In the beginning was the three-pointed star,
One smile of light across the empty face;
One bough of bone across the rooting air,
The substance spread that marrowed the first sun;
And, burning ciphers on the round of space,
Heaven and hell mixed as they spun.

Several important poems in the August 1933 notebook emphasize the fall of man. This fall is not the result of moral transgression but the inevitable consequence of birth, the agonies of self-consciousness and isolation being overcome in the twin extremes of prenatal existence and death or else in a moment when nature's unfallen form is revealed to the poet.

Poem seven ("Before I Knocked") differs from the version in *18 Poems* only by the presence of two stanzas later cut and two words later changed. The central issue of the poem is the identification of the speaking "I" who has been called a sperm cell, an

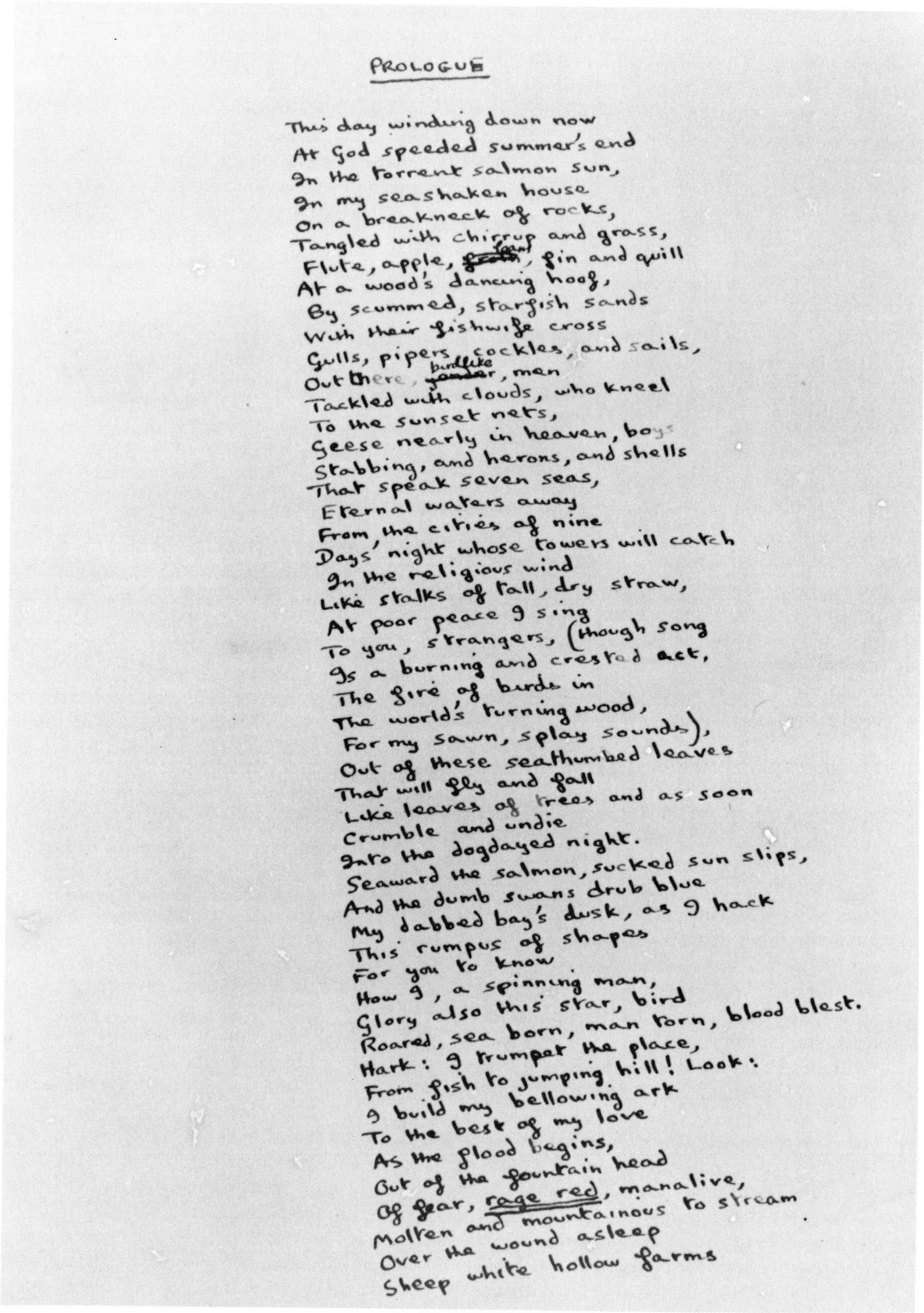

PROLOGUE

This day winding down now
At God speeded summer's end
In the torrent salmon sun,
In my seashaken house
On a breakneck of rocks,
Tangled with chirrup and grass,
Flute, apple, ~~froth~~ foam, fin and quill
At a wood's dancing hoof,
By scummed, starfish sands
With their fishwife cross
Gulls, pipers, cockles, and sails,
Out there, ~~yonder~~ birdlike, men
Tackled with clouds, who kneel
To the sunset nets,
Geese nearly in heaven, boys
Stabbing, and herons, and shells
That speak seven seas,
Eternal waters away
From the cities of nine
Days' night whose towers will catch
In the religious wind
Like stalks of tall, dry straw,
At poor peace I sing
To you, strangers, (though song
Is a burning and crested act,
The fire of birds in
The world's turning wood,
For my sawn, splay sounds),
Out of these seathumbed leaves
That will fly and fall
Like leaves of trees and as soon
Crumble and undie
Into the dogdayed night.
Seaward the salmon, sucked sun slips,
And the dumb swans drub blue
My dabbed bay's dusk, as I hack
This rumpus of shapes
For you to know
How I, a spinning man,
Glory also this star, bird
Roared, sea born, man torn, blood blest.
Hark: I trumpet the place,
From fish to jumping hill! Look:
I build my bellowing ark
To the best of my love
As the flood begins,
Out of the fountain head
Of fear, rage red, manalive,
Molten and mountainous to stream
Over the wound asleep
Sheep white hollow farms

Page from a late draft for Thomas's "Author's Prologue" to Collected Poems: 1934-1952 *(Houghton Library, Harvard University)*

unreleased female egg, the unborn Christ, the unborn poet, or the spirit of the child entering its body at conception:

> Before I knocked and flesh let enter,
> With liquid hands tapped on the womb,
> I who was shapeless as the water
> That shaped the Jordan near my home,
> Was brother to Mnetha's daughter
> And sister to the fathering worm.

The images describe the conception, gestation, birth, brief life, and crucifixion-death of a speaker who is essentially a composite of the poet and Christ. The true subject of the images that evoke pictures of these actions is the psychological experience of a fall from unity into division, and, in this poem, not redemption but death. The biblical pattern of creation-fall-redemption is thus internalized in two senses: the images describe the inner processes of gestation and this imaged process of an action of the body figures forth the psychic experience of a fall into self-consciousness.

A final group of poems in the August 1933 notebook dealing with the relation of self and world includes the famous "process" poems: poem twenty-three ("The Force That Through the Green Fuse Drives the Flower") and poem thirty-five ("A Process in the Weather of the Heart"). Many readers have noted that "The Force That Through the Green Fuse Drives the Flower" has as an important theme the idea that the process of growth and decay that exists in the external world also exists in the inner world of the poet's body. Each of the first three five-line stanzas presents one and a half lines devoted to the process of inner and outer growth, one and half lines devoted to the process of inner and outer decay, and two refrainlike lines that are the poet's commentary on the first three lines:

> The hand that whirls the water in the pool
> Stirs the quicksand; that ropes the blowing wind
> Hauls my shroud sail.
> And I am dumb to tell the hanging man
> How of my clay is made the hangman's lime.

The final two lines of each stanza hold the key to the most crucial theme of the poem. For instance, in stanza one: "And I am dumb to tell the crooked rose / My youth is bent with the same wintry fever." Far from rejoicing in his unity with nature, the poet is all too aware that this oneness is a oneness of death; furthermore, as a poet, he is unable in this poem to use his poet's language as a means of establishing a deeper communion with nature (the rose), his own body (the veins), or another human being (the hanging man). In other words, this poem is really about the limits of poetic language, the poet's feeling of self-consciousness that estranges him intellectually from the world.

One of the most striking features of the August 1933 notebook in comparison to the February 1933 notebook is the revival of the idea of love as a healing power. A good example of this theme is in poem forty-one ("If I was Tickled by the Rub of Love"). Although it is probably just chance that this poem ends the fourth of the extraordinary notebooks that document a young poet's emergence as a significant talent, "If I was Tickled by the Rub of Love" is distinguished by being the only one of several autobiographical notebook poems that combines the form of the spiritual autobiography of the poet-as-poet with the theme of love as a redemptive agent.

In the poem, the proposition "If I was tickled by the rub of love" is counterbalanced in stanzas one through four by a description of the poet's progress through his own love autobiography: (1) conception by his parents, (2) gestation and birth, (3) childhood and adolescence, and (4) manhood and old age. In each stanza, the poet is saying that if love could be shown to be a restorative power he would not fear any of its attendant drawbacks or downright evils.

Throughout the four notebooks, Thomas's line of development has been consistent with the statements in his letters that the reconciliation of inner and outer worlds by the imaginative identification of microcosmic man and macrocosmic universe to form something like Blake's Universal Man is his ultimate goal. But Thomas-the-Christ, whose "wordy wounds" are a romantic displacement of Christ's sacrificial blood into a secular variety of redemptive love, never averted his face from the realities of death, time, narcissism, evil, and the limitations of love itself. Still, it is the "rub of love" that must fuse man with the cosmos. Thomas's great attempt to embody that action is the sonnet sequence "Altarwise by Owl-light," written in 1935-1936.

"Altarwise by Owl-light" is in the romantic tradition of the internalized quest romance and the spiritual autobiography of the poet-as-poet. In sonnet ten, the last, Thomas takes upon himself a part of the role and power of Christ and achieves a reintegration of all opposites in the image of Eden rising up from the drowned waters, the romantic variation on directional movement toward redemption, from the Christian idea of heaven as "up there" to the romantic concept of an inner heaven of psychic unity and undivided, visionary perception "down there" in the deeper regions of the human mind and in nature.

In sonnet one the birth of the poet and the death of Christ are presented simultaneously by polysemous metaphors. Christ, having risen from the tomb, visits the poet in the poet's cradle just as the Magi visited Christ; Christ addresses the infant poet and reveals His nature to him. In romantic terms, the poet is describing his sense of estrangement from the world and the arising from the subconscious ("that night of time") of his own Blakean Christhood that promises inner and outer unity. Having received this vision of his own greater poetic self, the poet describes in sonnets two through ten the long quest to realize in himself that Christhood which he only sees in a vision in sonnet one.

Undoubtedly, sonnet two may be said to be a continuation of the autobiography of the poet which began in the first sonnet's description of the poet's conception and birth. The poet's early infancy is discussed and his future "fall" into self-division and estrangement from nature is outlined; and, as in sonnet one, the figure of Christ weaves in and out of the narrative, now fusing and now separating from that of the poet, but always providing the final model of achieved power over opposites and over fallen nature that the growing poet wishes to take for his own.

Sonnet three seeks out the origins of the "fall" into division and thereby defines the role of the Christ-poet composite in overcoming that division. Adam's fall from paradise necessitated Christ's sacrificial entrance into history and/or the poet's childhood unity with nature gave way to a sense of deathliness in nature and dark sexual process; as a result, in both cases, Christ and the poet as incarnate powers engaged in battle with the forces of decay, and, by the theory of progression through opposites, were able to link natural regeneration (spring) to the more permanent springs of Christian salvation and/or the romantic apocalypse of imagination.

The primary concern of sonnet four is the growth of the poet into a later phase of childhood where his incessant questioning indicates a precocious facility for language that will later blossom into mature poetry. Having become increasingly aware of his tool of imagination, the creative word, and love, the young poet turns, in the zany and obscure sonnet five, to a scrutiny of his inherited answer to all questions: orthodox Christianity.

In sonnet five the young poet rejects orthodoxy and embarks on a quest through the uncharted waters of world and mind. Institutionalized Christianity has become a self-serving body which perverts Christ's true nature and cheats its members with false dogma; thus the poet has left the church to search for his own version of Adam's paradise, but what he has found initially was that he was cast forth on a phantasmagoric quest in a weird, natural-supernatural landscape, an exile in the sea of his own experience with no inherited cosmology to order his perceptions. This sonnet's final line seems a conjuration of the romantic poet's creative faculty, the anima, counterbalanced by the opposing figure of the fatal sirens, the voyaging poet's double-natured source of his own power as he goes forth to forge his own relation to the world and to his own mental faculties.

Still churning about in the fantastic seas of sonnet five, the young poet comes to see in sonnet six the integrated processes of poetic and sexual creation as the avenues by which his own self-redeeming Christhood may be obtained. Beginning in the womb or his sea-cliff room at No. 5 Cwmdonkin Drive, the poet begins the process of poetic creation and the breaking down of the barrier between word and thing; by doing so, the poet discovers that the power of love is released into the world, thus purifying his own perceptions and rendering harmless to him all embodiments of the male and female principles which are integrated in poetry and love; finally, the young poet begins to write his early poems—the poems of the notebooks—which are predominantly poems about the fall into self-division but which also develop the concurrent theme, fully realized in "Altarwise by Owl-light" itself, of the poet as his own Christ.

The Christlike nature of the poet's self-sacrificing, expressionist act having been established, Thomas proceeds in sonnet seven to examine the young poet's first attempts to write poems that unite language and nature as sacrament. In sonnet eight the poet achieves his own Christhood. Christian myth and romantic poetics are fused in this climactic sonnet of the sequence. A lucid, simultaneous presentation of Christ's crucifixion on Golgotha and the poet's "self-immolation in the agonies of the imagination," sonnet eight describes the ultimate romantic epiphany, in which the poet's imagination unites itself with a redeemed external world to which it is linked by a love that, for once, transcends the cycles of sex.

In sonnet nine desert burial is a symbol of the tribulations of the poet's poem of redemption: pub-

Dylan Thomas in London, circa 1939 (photo by Bill Brandt)

lishers, critics, and the ravages of time. Abruptly switching from Christian to Egyptian myth, Thomas explores the ill fate of the orthodox "version" of Christ and the fate of his own poems in the hands of critics. Finally, in sonnet ten the poet comes to an understanding of the nature of his poetry, his quest, and his final fate. The poet commands his own usurpation of the role of the orthodox Christ and prophesies a final restoration of nature and the self to their Edenic states by the reconciliation of all opposites: let the poet who has displaced Christian myth into a secular, poetic context thus unite the creative word to nature, which that word redeems by using and shaping any myth to suit its own purposes. Let Simon Peter, first Pope and founder of the orthodox church, lean out from heaven to ask Christ or Aphrodite what phallic poet this is who has caused Eden to rise out of the waters of nature and of mind; whatever its own nature, may that garden with its two trees rise up forever on Judgment Day, its central tree (phallus, cross, world tree) a whole made up of various opposites: good and evil, male and female, fruition and decay, the self (phallus) and the world (the world tree), and others.

With all its awkwardnesses, obscurities, and even grotesqueries, "Altarwise by Owl-light," written by a poet of twenty-one, is a heroic attempt to create a powerful romantic self whose imaginative powers might bring about the realization of the redemption phase of the romantic myth. A history of the young poet's inner world as well as a history of the poetic self's relation to the external world which it hopes to redeem, "Altarwise by Owl-light" marks the final fruition of the early poetry.

The second phase of Thomas's life and art extends from 1937, the year of his marriage, to 1945, the year of the conclusion of World War II and of the composition of "Fern Hill." This poem marks the end of Thomas's successful transition from his early obscure, subjective, "cosmic" style to his later clear, objective, odelike style with its prelapsarian vision of a sacramental landscape, perceived and experienced by the child, celebrated by the death-conscious adult poet. Marriage, fatherhood, and war—the three resistantly objective, outer experiences which form the poet's biography in these years—were also stimuli to the development, in this transitional middle phase, of the later, clearer style.

The Thomases spent part of the summer of 1937 in Swansea, then moved on to Caitlin Thomas's mother's house in Hampshire for the winter and spring of 1937-1938. Dylan's sole new poem of 1937 was "I Make This in a Warring Absence," a marriage poem whose subject—a spat—is inappropriately embodied in the clotted imagery of the early style. In the spring of 1938, Thomas's radical revision of "After the Funeral" from the notebooks marks the first real movement toward clarity, the poem emerging as a more sympathetic elegy for his aunt. Thomas's third volume, a mix of sixteen poems and seven short stories, *The Map of Love*, appeared in 1939, and in 1940 appeared his book of objectively realistic stories of his childhood and adolescence in Swansea, *Portrait of the Artist as a Young Dog*.

Thomas's marriage satisfied him deeply, but it also created problems that would aggravate his personal flaws and lead him down the road to America and death. In the 1938-1940 period, the Thomases moved back and forth between his parents and her mother, London, and Laugharne, where they lived in houses called Eros and Sea View. Caitlin Thomas was pregnant in 1938 and gave birth to the couple's first child, a son, Llewelyn, on 30 January 1939. Turned down for a grant from the Royal Literary Fund, Thomas obtained a little money from doing book reviews, from writing begging letters to friends, and from the Blumenthal Poetry Prize, which brought him $100. He tried to start his own literary fund, "Thomas Flotation Limited," but with no luck. On 18 October 1938 he did his second stint for BBC Radio, appearing on the program "The Modern Muse" with Auden, Spender, Day Lewis, and MacNeice.

One source of income that failed was a projected collection of early stories to be called "The Burning Baby." Both Dent and Europa Press in Paris backed out, for they feared that obscenity charges might arise. In addition, *The Map of Love* and *Portrait of the Artist as a Young Dog* did not sell too well, probably because of the change of mood caused by the outbreak of war in Europe in 1939. However, Thomas's earlier negotiations with his first American publisher, James Laughlin of New Directions, climaxed with the publication of selections from his work in *The World I Breathe* (December 1939). There also survive from this period a few episodes from his unfinished novel about a young provincial poet's initiation into London, *Adventures in the Skin Trade* (1955), and a comic novel written in collaboration, first with Charles Fisher and later with John Davenport, *The Death of the King's Canary* (1976), a wild detective story whose suspects are caricatures of famous poets and other writers of the day.

Thomas's reaction to the war was complex. Superficially, his only concern was to avoid conscription, to which end he tried sponsoring a writers' antiwar petition and considered declaring himself a conscientious objector on religious grounds. Thomas's letters on this matter are unseemly and narrowly selfish at best. In any case, he need not have worried, for he failed his medical exam, though the reason he did so remains unclear—possibly asthma or weak lungs.

Thomas's deeper response to the war is contained in his moving elegies "Ceremony After A Fire-Raid" and "A Refusal to Mourn the Death, by Fire, of a Child in London." Here, the holiness and the horror of human suffering in war are captured in what may well be the two greatest poems in English written about World War II. The successive experiences of marriage, fatherhood, and war also led to the emergence, in the poems of 1941-1945, of an intense nostalgia for the world of the romantic child, the world of vision in which pantheistic nature is sacred and all things appear in imagination's eye. Thomas's desire to recapture the lost world of the visionary child of romantic tradition was made more intense as the war continued from 1940 to 1945.

Thomas's life during the war years centered around the necessity of avoiding the London bombing yet the need for traveling to London to work with Ivan Moffatt and Donald Taylor for Strand Films, Taylor's company, now involved in making war documentaries for the Ministry of Information. Here Thomas earned £8-10 weekly for the duration of the war. Still, Thomas was always short of money and ill-advisedly sold the rights to *18 Poems* for £15. In a more complicated move, he sold his notebooks to the Lockwood Memorial Library in Buffalo, New York, in the spring of 1941. At the time, he spoke of having to "burn your boats" and of his lifelong sense of competition with Keats. Keats died at twenty-six, and Thomas was twenty-six when he sold the notebooks. The young bohemian poet was dead, and Thomas resolved not to keep going back to the notebooks for more poems. After a dry period as poet (1941-1943), Thomas emerged at the war's end as the poet of "Poem in October" and "Fern Hill," writing of lost childhoods in odes of great clarity and wide feeling.

The movements of the Thomases during the war years are complex. Spending Christmas of 1939 with Caitlin Thomas's mother, the Thomases moved on, in the summer of 1940, to Marshfield, the country home of the gregarious poet and critic John Davenport. A man of means, Davenport decided to entertain friends lavishly that summer as the war entered its darkest phase. Davenport and Thomas worked on their comic detective novel, *The Death of the King's Canary*, and caroused, while Caitlin Thomas played Mozart on the gramophone and danced. In late 1940 and throughout 1941, the Thomases wandered from one place to another, looking for safety for Caitlin and Llewelyn Thomas: Bishopston, Talsarn in Cardiganshire, and Laugharne Castle. In 1942 they returned to London, where they lived in two bare studios: first, Sir Alan Herbert's in Hammersmith, and later, No. 3, Wentworth Studios, off the Manresa Road in Chelsea. Caitlin Thomas was pregnant again and gave birth to a daughter, Aeron, in March of 1943.

Caitlin Thomas disapproved of Thomas's work on Taylor's films, and, near the end of the war, of his work for the BBC as broadcaster of various prose reminiscences of his Swansea youth. These activities, along with the increasing dominance of the clowning, drunken, "public" Thomas over the introspective, "private" Thomas who wrote the poems, disturbed her greatly. After leaving No. 5 Cwmdonkin Drive, Thomas always did his best work in Wales in rural isolation. In 1944 and 1945, in fact, he enjoyed a second flowering as a poet in just such surroundings, producing poems such as "A Winter's Tale," "A Refusal to Mourn the Death, by Fire, of a Child in London," and "Fern Hill." The widening split between Thomas's roaring London life and persona and his poetic life in Wales became critical by the end of the war, so that the pattern of London partying followed by recuperation and work in Wales was "writ large" as America, especially New York, displaced London in this deadly scheme.

Of Thomas's wartime and postwar filmscripts and broadcasts, little need be said. Most of the scripts were hackwork, written as part of Thomas's job. *These Are the Men* (written in 1942) is the Leni Reifenstahl film of a 1934 Nuremberg Rally, *Triumph of the Will*, with Thomas's dissenting commentary added. *Our Country* surveys wartime Britain, while *Is Your Ernie Really Necessary?* was detected by the Ministry of Information as parody and suppressed. Thomas also wrote scripts for feature films. These include *The Doctor and the Devils* (written in 1944), based on Burke and Hare, the famous Scottish body snatchers, and *Twenty Years A-Growing* (also written in 1944), an incomplete but interesting dramatization of the idyllic childhood on the Blasket Islands of Maurice O'Sullivan. After the war, in 1948, Thomas also wrote a script version of the Robert Louis Stevenson tale *The Beach of Falesá*.

More relevant to Thomas's postwar poetry of childhood in nature are the prose reminiscences, written during the last decade of Thomas's life. These are collected in the volume *Quite Early One Morning* (1954). The first of these recollections, "Reminiscences of Childhood" (1943), is a camera's-eye view of the poet's Swansea childhood, Cwmdonkin Park being his "world within the world"—its hunchback, celebrated in "The Hunchback in the Park," the centerpiece of the broadcast—and ending with Thomas the child flying in fancy over the town now lost in time: "The memories of childhood have no order and no end." The talk "Quite Early One Morning" is a humorous account of a Welsh seaport (New Quay) waking up—a study for his play for voices concerning a whole day in such a town, *Under Milk Wood* (1954). "Memories of Christmas" and the famous "A Child's Christmas in Wales"—the latter a rival still today to Dickens's classic *A Christmas Carol*—also appeared as broadcasts. "A Child's Christmas in Wales" is a masterful and fantastically detailed recollection of Christmas—its weather, sights, sounds, its food, presents, and its melancholy close—as perceived by the happy child Thomas apparently was. Matching these evocations of Thomas's childhood is the later broadcast "Return Journey" (1947). Here Thomas returns to Swansea, whose town center was gutted by German air raids during the war, in search of his old haunts as adolescent poet and reporter. The narrator inquires after the young Thomas, but the boy, like the pubs and stores and friends he knew, is lost. The narrator's quest comes to an end in Cwmdonkin Park where the old park keeper answers the question of young Thomas's fate: "Dead . . . Dead . . . Dead . . . Dead . . . Dead . . . Dead."

In addition to these filmscripts and broadcasts about his early life, Thomas often read his own and others' poetry for BBC Radio and took part in dramatic readings. A few BBC talks on poets and poetry also survive as well as prose introductions to his own poetry readings in America. Like the early surrealist short stories, the more realistic, autobiographical stories of *Portrait of the Artist as a Young Dog*, the unfinished London novel, *Adventures in the Skin Trade*, the coauthored parody with Davenport, and a few other fugitive pieces in prose, the scripts and talks of the 1940s and the 1950s were essentially done for money or diversion from the poetry, and their importance extends little beyond whatever light they shed on the poetry.

The "Altarwise by Owl-light" sequence represented what Thomas recognized as a carrying of "certain features to their logical conclusion," a task that "had . . . to be done" even though the result be "mad parody." If the earlier phase clearly ends with this sequence's positing of an almost omnipotent Christlike poetic self whose imagination is capable of releasing love into the world, the remainder of Thomas's poetry may be viewed as a second phase (1936-1953) or as two phases, a transitional "middle" phase that consists of the poems on marriage and war (1936-1945) and a final phase, emerging only slightly later than the middle phase (1946-1953) but becoming increasingly dominant in its depiction of the particular sacramental landscapes of childhood. The dominant feature of these later poems is the transformation of the assertive, apocalypse-fostering romantic self as Christ whose testament is "Altarwise by Owl-light," into a less domineering self, a self as priest, functionary, agent, medium of the divine power in nature whose interpreter the poet is. This shift implies that Thomas came more and more to realize the resistant otherness of the external world, too easily absorbed into the self in many of the earlier poems by the cosmic analogy, and that subsequently he relinquished his claims to contain all necessary power to transform the outer world. Relying on visionary memory to evoke the spiritualized landscapes of his childhood, Thomas came to find in a vision of sac-

The Boat House, Laugharne, Thomas's home from 1949 until his death (BBC Hulton)

ramental love infusing the landscape the final answer to the problem of the recalcitrant *other* that baffled him in most of the marriage poems and that posed an almost insurmountable threat in the war poems. The poet's final task was, through imaginative action, to release that power of love into the world.

A number of poems on the poetic process from this period register Thomas's struggle to realize the substantial otherness of the external world while at the same time fostering a relationship between self and world based on love. One of these, "Once It was the Colour of Saying," deals with the poet's fears that his early, florid style (a synesthetic "*colour* of *saying*"—italics added) was only a way of drowning external reality, not of achieving any valid relationship with it. Now viewing his earlier verse as a sort of aesthetic indulgence, he calls for a chastening of style that gives the outer world its due as a separate entity. Lines 1-6 describe the earlier verse that "soaked my table" or created a "capsized field" (that is a field that is both overturned and the size of a cap—a field that fits the poet's head) or "seaslides of saying." These colorful words enlivened the outer world, yet now he fears that his imaginative coloring of the external world was an illusion that he must "undo" so that "the charmingly drowned" innundated by the magical charm of the imagination may "arise" in their separateness to live and die as themselves. In a basic change, Thomas is announcing that his future poems of love will seek not to transform the outer world radically to the heart's desire but rather to honor the integrity and otherness of the object even as he still hopes that a single spirit of love may unite the two.

One of Thomas's most beautiful lyrics, "In My Craft or Sullen Art," affirms that his poetic audience is common humanity. As Thomas says, he writes his poems not for the proud and the great

> But for the lovers, their arms
> Round the griefs of the ages,
> Who pay no praise or wages
> Nor heed my craft or art.

These lines also exhibit Thomas's newly won clarity of expression, so often absent in the earlier poems.

Unlike the poems on poetics—most of which are successful definitions of Thomas's own views on the relation of imagination, nature, and love—ten poems, spread over a decade, that deal with Thomas's own fiery marriage to Caitlin and his subsequent fatherhood have been almost universally condemned. Tindall calls these poems "coagulated" while Kidder sees in them evidence of "reintegrated disintegration," a patchwork of fragments, a "whipped mixture of oil and water" remaining in "unstable union." Trying to discover cosmic implications in a lovers' quarrel or ecstatic union or reunion, Thomas somehow failed in the majority of these poems.

A representative example of the marriage poems is "Into Her Lying Down Head," the immediate occasion for which seems to have been a marriage argument resulting from the poet's sexual jealousy and fears. The specific complaint of the poet is that in sleep Caitlin Thomas dreams of imaginary male lovers who exclude the poet from the crucial consummation of physical love. Egocentrically conceived, this poem seems to argue that the poet's particular needs in his inspiring mate dominate her own needs for an ideal mental lover, a lover that Thomas applauded as a good thing for the poet in poems such as "The Hunchback in the Park" and "Love in the Asylum." Apparently, Thomas is saying that unity of being within himself, between the lovers, and between the lovers and nature depends upon a union of the imagined and the real. Thus, section one may be paraphrased as follows: through orifices of maidenhead, eye, and ear, a woman's imaginary lovers enter her body; the erotic power of nature and the unconscious rise mightily to take her, her conjured images of that power ranging from kings and queens to famous lovers of those betrayed in love or attractive persons passed on the street or stair; behind all these images a single young "blade" scythes the hayfield of her thighs; all England seems her love, the giant Albion, who brought her the new sleep of lost innocence and pregnancy. In section two the poet, meditating on the consequences of the woman's betrayal of him in her dreams, finds that their sacramental love has been turned into a satanic sacrament instead. Then, elaborating largely on how betrayal of human love leads directly to similar betrayals in nature, the poet takes us through analogies between the human lovers and two sand grains, a she bird, grass blade, and stone, lamenting at the end his exclusion from the woman's dream because only his union with her could reverse the similar process of betrayal in nature.

The poem ends with the poet's final lament over his absence from the ceremony of sacramental love. He is "torn up" and mourning in the "sole night" where she is also "alone and still" though unconscious of her betrayal or the poet's loss. What she sought to do with "the incestuous secret brother," her dream lover, is what only lovemaking with her human lover could accomplish: "to perpetuate the stars" (have children). The imaginary lovers, by separating two human lovers, myriad natural lovers (bird, stone), and the divine from the material in all, deserve their final name—"the severers"—who "bury their dead" of imaginary, infertile sperm in the woman's sleep. In an earlier version, the poem's final lines equally clearly associate human love and reproduction, divinity in woman, and the sustaining of an external nature informed by goodness:

> Will his lovely hands let run the daughters
> and sons of the blood?
> Will he rest his pulse in the built breast of
> impossible great god?
> Over the world uncoupling the moon rises up
> to no good.

Symbol of love, nature, and imagination, the moon, by her betrayal, turns evil, and nature itself is torn apart like the human lovers—"the world uncoupling."

If the first threat to Thomas's early poetry's obsessive theme of the imaginative identification of poet and cosmos was his experience of marriage and fatherhood, the second, and in many ways more powerful threat, was his experience of the Blitz in wartime London. The war was a "pressure of reality" that had to be balanced by a "pressure of imagination," but as tragic subject it had to be handled with the greatest delicacy yet also without flinching before the human suffering of the "others" who had died. Of the handful of poems written on the war, Thomas composed at least two extremely fine poems—"A Refusal to Mourn the Death, by Fire, of a Child in London" and "Ceremony After a Fire-Raid"—that, unlike many war poems, have completely survived their original occasions and contexts.

"A Refusal to Mourn the Death, by Fire, of a Child in London" explains its occasion in its title. Written in four stanzas rhyming *abcabc* with lines 2 and 5 of each stanza being short lines of five syllables, and with the first thirteen lines of the poem forming a single, syntactically grandiloquent sentence, the poem achieves an oracular, stately tone that is appropriate to its grave, weird, and awesome subject: an elegy without mourning for a young girl killed in an air raid in wartime London.

Thomas quite consciously and deliberately embeds within his elegiac statements about the child, himself, and the child's future existence as a part of nature such language that makes the psychic and the physical life of all creation and of the single human being correspond to significant stages in the Christian myth: creation (stanza one), Old Testament Judaism (stanza two), New Testament Christianity (stanza three), and, in a significant historical addition, romantic pantheism (stanza four), which is also a return to the Genesis and creation of stanza one.

In a famous series of compound adjectives modifying the noun *darkness*, with the hyphens left out for ambiguity, Thomas, in stanza one, magnificently recapitulates the arising of natural creation out of the void and begins to tell us the only conditions (the impending end of all things in an apocalypse of dark stillness) under which he would mourn the child's death:

> Never until the mankind making
> Bird beast and flower
> Fathering and all humbling darkness
> Tells with silence the last light breaking

And the still hour
Is come of the sea tumbling in harness.

If stanza one reveals the single human life and the history of nature as parallel to Christian creation, stanza two takes us into the Old Testament for sacramental images of the self's final fusion with nature:

And I must enter again the round
Zion of the water bead
And the synagogue of the ear of corn.

Moving farther along in the Christian myth as analogue, Thomas, in stanza three, describes the girl's death as a merely physical crucifixion ("the mankind of her going"). He refuses to utter the "grave truth" of the Anglican burial service nor will he "blaspheme" down his own "stations of the breath" by speaking of the self-evident youthfulness of the child. Having developed his feelings about the child and pantheism by displacing Genesis, Judaism, and Christianity into romantic personalism, Thomas completes the cycle in stanza four by touching briefly on Genesis again before moving, without any further analogy to the Christian myth, into direct statements about the union of self and nature according to romantic doctrine. Although she is "London's daughter," the child is not associated with a single image from the modern cityscape. Instead, she escapes the city, the war, and adulthood's estranging self-consciousness to join "the first dead," Adam and Eve, as well as the Londoners first killed in the air raids:

Deep with the first dead lies London's daughter,
Robed in the long friends,
The grains beyond age, the dark veins of her mother,
Secret by the unmourning water
Of the riding Thames.
After the first death, there is no other.

The stateliness of the "riding Thames" brings to mind Spenser's "Sweet Thames, run softly till I end my song" in *Prothalamion*, a not inappropriate association to make, for Thomas's unmourning pseudoelegy celebrates the child's marriage to nature and nature's ongoing fertile power of renewal.

"Poem in October" and "Fern Hill" in *Deaths and Entrances*, two odelike poems whose subjects are the poet's imaginative recollection of his childhood in nature, forecast the dominant pastoral concerns of his final volume of new poems, *In Country Sleep*. "Poem in October" is listed by Watkins as among those poems that Thomas wrote in 1944-1945 after the horror of living through wartime London "compelled his imagination forward . . . to the beautiful poems evoking childhood." What is significant about "Poem in October" is that it is Thomas's first acknowledged "place poem," a poem set in a particularized landscape. "Poem in October" is set both in the seaside village of Laugharne and on Sir John's Hill, whose green-wooded shouldering cliffs protrude into the neighboring estuary on which Thomas's seaside house was situated.

Beginning in the town (stanzas one and two), the poet climbs Sir John's Hill (stanzas three and four), and there he undergoes a transformation, as he regains his childhood sense of wonder in nature (stanzas five through seven). Identifying the occasion as his thirtieth birthday, Thomas sets the poem in a definite time (1944) as well as in a definite place, thus making "Poem in October" a striking example of a greater romantic lyric. Beginning with a description of the landscape in the present by the poet

Dylan Thomas in Laugharne graveyard a few months after his father's death in December 1952 (photo by John Deakin for Condé Nast Publications)

as an adult (stanzas one through five), he then vividly recalls the same landscape as he saw it so differently as a child (stanzas five and six and stanza seven, lines 1-4), and he ends by returning to his adult self in the present landscape (stanza seven, lines 5-10) where his exclamation of hope for the future represents the rejuvenating power of visionary memory.

Leaving Laugharne on his thirtieth birthday, the poet climbs Sir John's Hill among all the sights and sounds of nature. Then, in a long evocative description, the adult regains his childhood's spontaneous apprehension of nature as ordered, benevolent, divine. Moving from adult "fancy" to childhood "imagination," Thomas quite clearly indicates the differences in intensity of perception. The merely "blithe country" perceived by the adult is left behind to *turn* down "the other air" and "the blue altered sky" of imaginative perception. Not merely a marvel, now it is a "wonder of summer" with its apples, pears, currants, and the poet is possessed by familiar sights seen by the imagination:

> And I saw in the turning so clearly a child's
> Forgotten mornings when he walked with his
> mother
> Through the parables
> Of sun light
> And the legends of the green chapels.

In a spot of time or moment of epiphany, the adult poet perceives nature once more as fully divine, its own decipherable language. The poet now possesses completely his own childhood, called "the twice told fields of infancy" because once lived and a second time recollected, and, in one of Thomas's simplest and most moving lines, the poet says of his recovered childhood self: "his tears burned my cheek and his heart moved in mine."

A greater romantic lyric concludes with an anticipation of the future. Thus, in the short third section of Thomas's poem (stanza seven, lines 5-10), the poet ends the long vision of childhood simply and briefly:

> O may my heart's truth
> Still be sung
> On this high hill in a year's turning.

Though the "town below lay leaved in October blood" of reddened, fallen leaves, the poet "stood there then in the summer noon" of hilltop and childhood, knowing he must again descend to the town. It was on this high hill of the joyful romantic child and his heightened consciousness that Thomas wished to stay. "Poem in October," however, stands almost alone in its nearly unadulterated joy and affirmation—possibly the reason it reflects more than any other of his poems the exact form of the greater romantic lyric.

"Fern Hill," the final poem in *Deaths and Entrances*, represents a peak in Thomas's development, just as "Altarwise by Owl-light" was the culmination of the tendencies in the earlier poems. "Fern Hill" superimposes the adult's less visionary view of nature on top of the child's by various devices from irony and ambiguity to direct statement, progressive clusters of images, and several parallel syntactical structures that contain these images. "Fern Hill" is an example of the romantic concern with the growth of a poet's mind, for we see the "fall" of the child's spontaneous perception of visionary nature, the growing into adolescence with its sexual awakening, and adulthood with its consciousness of estrangement, death, and time. Against this dismal flow, however, emerges implicitly a faith in imagination and memory, the faculties of mind that are able to recover, embody, and thus evoke forever the lost childhood vision.

Composed in lines strictly syllabic and with assonantal rhyme, stanza one is the first of three which describe the cycle of a single day at Fernhill from night to day to night. Following the pattern of creation in Genesis, these three stanzas present all the child's days at Fernhill as a single, holy day, enclosed by a night that only completes the day and is unthreatening. Narrated by the poet as an adult, the poem contains from the very first line a contrast of the Wordsworthian "two consciousnesses" (child and adult) and the twin landscapes they perceive; but though present, the adult's view lurks more often only in certain disturbing ambiguities than in direct statement. In stanza two, the child's joy in nature builds to a climax:

> Time let me play and be
> Golden in the mercy of his means,
> And green and golden I was huntsman and
> herdsman, the calves
> Sang to my horn, the foxes on the hills barked
> clear and cold,
> And the sabbath rang slowly
> In the pebbles of the holy streams.

In stanzas three and four, the child sleeps and wakes in utmost security, although hints about death, sad wisdom, and nascent adolescent sexuality foreshadow the inevitable end of the child's world.

Stanza four ends with a vision of creation that is stunning in effect:

So it must have been after the birth of the
simple light
In the first, spinning place, the spellbound
horses walking warm
Out of the whinnying green stable
On to the fields of praise.

The last two stanzas are more completely dominated by the adult poet's understanding of the child's lost world. The poem ends with a full recognition both of the true joy of the child's world and the ineluctable fact of its loss:

Nothing I cared, in the lamb white days, that
time would take me
Up to the swallow thronged loft by the
shadow of my hand,
In the moon that is always rising,
Nor that riding to sleep
I should hear him fly with the high fields
And wake to the farm forever fled from the
childless land.
Oh as I was young and easy in the mercy
of his means,
Time held me green and dying
Though I sang in my chains like the sea.

Thus, in "Fern Hill," as in "Poem in October," Thomas imaginatively reenters his own childhood consciousness, savoring it, knowing it, and finally recapturing it, but not out of a corrupting nostalgia; for the adult consciousness is also fully developed as a dramatic counterweight to the lost childhood vision.

The last years of Thomas's life (1946-1953) may be divided into two periods: the immediate postwar struggle to find a job and money in England (1946-1949) and the period of the famous reading tours in America (1950-1953).

In 1946-1949 Thomas spent most of his time looking for steady employment in films and at the BBC and for publishers from whom he sought and sometimes received advances on books that he often did not deliver. Both his actual drinking and his reputation for drinking meant that a permanent job with the BBC was out of the question, although he made frequent broadcasts over radio until the end of his life. In 1948, he signed a contract with Gainsborough Films to produce three scripts during the year, which he did, but his scriptwriting career ended there, and only one of the films was produced.

As early as 1945, Thomas was writing to Oscar Williams about a possible job at Harvard or *Time* magazine, should he decide to emigrate. James Laughlin, his American publisher, was also approached, in 1946, about Thomas's moving to the United States. These inquiries were fruitless, however, and the Thomases were soon moving again from place to place, with no money. In 1945, Thomas left New Quay for London and spent Christmas of 1945 with A. J. P. Taylor and his wife Margaret in Oxford. Margaret Taylor let the Thomases stay in a summerhouse on the grounds for some months, until The Authors' Society granted Thomas £150 from its Travelling Scholarship Fund for an Italian holiday. The Thomases spent time in Rapallo, Florence, and Elba during their vacation, which lasted from April to August 1947. The heat, the language barrier, and the intelligentsia they met in Florence (near which the Thomases had rented a villa) all exasperated Thomas, who drank a great deal of wine and completed his poem "In Country Sleep," a section of his long unfinished "In Country Heaven."

Thomas was now more and more in demand for public appearances. He did a number of readings in London, often performing brilliantly, if he was not too drunk. His failure to show up for an address to the Swansea chapter of the British Medical Association in 1949 was atypical. When it came to public readings, Thomas was unusually reliable. In March of 1949, he even attended a conference in Prague, celebrating the beginning of the Czechoslovak Writers' Union. Politically naive, Thomas did little there besides party and make a vague speech about the international brotherhood of writers.

In May of 1949, the Thomases moved to another house bought for them by Margaret Taylor. This was the now well-known Boat House, in Laugharne, a picturesque seaside village in Wales whose inhabitants are lovingly caricatured in *Under Milk Wood*. Set up on stilts high on a cliff overlooking an estuary into which three small rivers flow, with Sir John's Hill to one side, and surrounded by the gulls and herons that inhabit the poems written during his time there, the Boat House, with its nearby shed (Thomas's workroom), is as romantic in appearance as it must have been uncomfortable to live in. Except for the inevitable, lethal sprees in London and, later, in America, Thomas lived in Laugharne for most of the rest of his life. The Boat House is now a shrine for tourists.

The Thomas which some of these tourists seek is not Thomas, the poet, but Thomas-the-Poet, the roaring public image of the Romantic Bard which

Thomas had cultivated since adolescence. The final exaggerated, grotesque, and deadly version of this persona found the ideal stage for its bloody fifth act when Thomas received an invitation that May from John Malcolm Brinnin, a young American poet and newly appointed director of the YM-YWHA Poetry Center in New York. Thomas asked Brinnin to arrange readings, both in New York and at universities all across America, and suggested January or February 1950 as a convenient time for him to come. From May 1949 until February 1950, Thomas was able to work on poetry again, and on 21 February 1950 he arrived at Idlewild Airport in New York, where Brinnin was waiting for him.

Thomas's first tour of America (21 February-1 June 1950) set the pattern for the next three. Beginning with a series of parties and readings in or near New York, Thomas moved on to read at numerous universities. Thomas recorded his poetry for the Lamont Library at Harvard and for the Library of Congress. Most of the stories about Thomas's wild behavior are collected in Brinnin's book, *Dylan Thomas in America* (1955). In retrospect, many of the incidents seem merely boorish or boyish, but in the America of the early 1950s, Thomas managed briefly to maintain a reputation as the Dionysian minstrel.

Most of the Thomas stories concern his drinking, awkward sexual advances, petty thievery (especially of shirts), witty remarks, and yet his admittedly miraculous ability to recover from dishevelment to perform stunning readings of his own and others' poetry. He was, he said—in parody of Eliot's self-designation as classicist, royalist, and Anglican—a drunkard, a Welshman, and a lover of women. He had come to America "to continue my lifelong search for naked women in wet mackintoshes." During one party, he lifted Katherine Anne Porter (age fifty-nine) up to the ceiling; at another, an explicit four-letter-word descriptive of the sexual theme of his "Ballad of the Long-Legged Bait" silenced conversation. Women babied him, and some slept with him. Academics, whom Thomas as a dropout always feared, did not know how to put him at ease. One party with Yale professors was especially uncomfortable.

From the point of view of money, the tour should have been a success—but it was not. Thomas spent most of what he earned on the spot. Brinnin, in fact, secretly placed $800 in a handbag (a gift for Caitlin Thomas) to insure that the poet's wife saw at least that much of Thomas's earnings. Thomas saw Robert Lowell in Iowa City, and in New York City he was introduced to Theodore Roethke, the one American poet he especially wanted to meet. In California, he fell in love with San Francisco and spent an evening with a childhood idol, Charlie Chaplin. Back in New York, Thomas survived a series of farewell parties, began a liaison with a woman whom Paul Ferris and Constantine FitzGibbon call "Sarah," and sailed home on the Queen Elizabeth on June 1.

The next eighteen months of Thomas's life were spent in England, with one exception. That was a brief trip to Persia in January 1951 to do a documentary film for the Anglo-Iranian Oil Company. Prior to the trip, in the previous September, Caitlin Thomas had caught her husband renewing his affair with Sarah, who was in England. Thomas's marriage was severely strained in 1950-1951, and Caitlin Thomas was forever suspicious thereafter. Throughout the spring and summer of 1951, Thomas strove to repair his marriage and enjoyed his last brief flowering as a lyric poet. He wrote "Lament," "Do Not Go Gentle Into That Good Night," "Poem on His Birthday," and worked on *Under Milk Wood* and the verse prologue to his forthcoming *Collected Poems: 1934-1952*, "Author's Prologue."

Thomas's second American tour (20 January-16 May 1952) was much like the first, except that this time Caitlin Thomas went along, so even more money was spent, and a number of partygoers were treated to the Thomases' publicly enacted spats. New Directions published his *In Country Sleep*, the six poems written since *Deaths and Entrances*, in February, and the young founders of Caedmon Records persuaded Thomas to record his poetry for their label, an event that would eventually produce a great deal of money, though Thomas would not live to see it. As at the end of the first tour, Thomas again left America with little profit and totally exhausted.

Back in Laugharne, Thomas spent the summer of 1952 working on *Under Milk Wood*. "Author's Prologue" was completed, and on 10 November 1952, Thomas's *Collected Poems: 1934-1952* appeared. The collection was prefaced by an author's note in which Thomas said that his poems were written "for the love of man and in praise of God." In the 102-line "Author's Prologue," Thomas addresses the readers, the "strangers," in the guise of a modern Noah who would save the creatures of the natural world in his ark of art from the molten flood of nuclear holocaust. Looking over this body of early and recent work, most critics granted Thomas the status of major poet. Philip Toynbee called Thomas "the greatest living poet" writing in En-

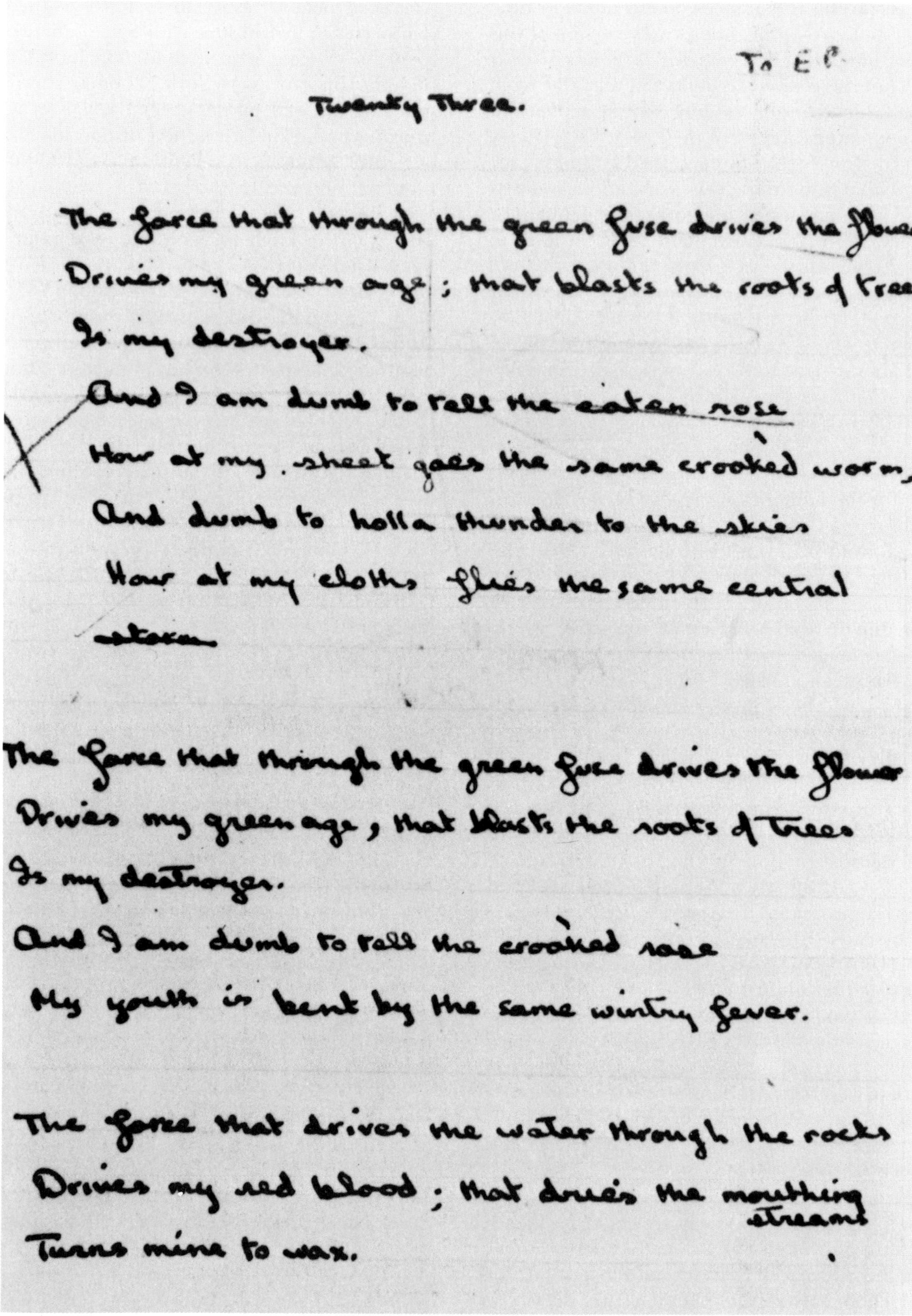
To E P.

Twenty Three.

The force that through the green fuse drives the flower
Drives my green age; that blasts the roots of trees
Is my destroyer.
And I am dumb to tell the eaten rose
How at my sheet goes the same crooked worm,
And dumb to holla thunder to the skies
How at my cloths flies the same central
storm

The force that through the green fuse drives the flower
Drives my green age, that blasts the roots of trees
Is my destroyer.
And I am dumb to tell the crooked rose
My youth is bent by the same wintry fever.

The force that drives the water through the rocks
Drives my red blood; that dries the mouthing streams
Turns mine to wax.

Page from the manuscript for "The force that through the green fuse drives the flower" (Lockwood Memorial Library, State University of New York at Buffalo)

glish. Many were charmed by the pastoral poems such as "Poem in October," "A Winter's Tale," "In Country Sleep," and the instant favorite, "Fern Hill." Thomas received £250 for winning the Foyle's Poetry Prize for *Collected Poems*.

Thomas's third tour of America was somewhat shorter than the first two, lasting from 21 April to 3 June 1953. This tour saw the premiere of Thomas's play for voices, *Under Milk Wood*, on which Thomas had been meditating and working since the late 1930s. Earlier entitled "The Town That Was Mad" and "Llareggub: A Piece for Radio Perhaps," *Under Milk Wood* borrows the daylong structure of Joyce's *Ulysses* (1922) as Thomas takes the listener through a typical day in the lives of a host of inhabitants of a small Welsh sea town. The geography of the village, from Milk Wood to Coronation Street and down to Cockle Row and the sea, is reminiscent of that of New Quay, but the flavor of the work, the caricatured citizens with their Dickensian eccentricities, reflects Thomas's years in Laugharne.

Under Milk Wood celebrates the town, what the First Voice calls "this place of love," and the play becomes a comic variant of the happy pastoral world of the late poems. Love in all its forms and guises flourishes in the forgiving presence of Captain Cat. As the play begins and ends at night, the brief day of love and sun that the inhabitants enjoy seems more poignant than the superficially playful tone of the piece might suggest. When Captain Cat, for instance, converses with the image of his long-dead Rosie, she fades away at last with the lines:

> Remember her.
> She is forgetting.
> The earth which filled her mouth
> Is vanishing from her.
> Remember me.
> I have forgotten you.
> I am going into the darkness of the darkness forever.
> I have forgotten that I was ever born.

Like much great comedy, *Under Milk Wood* holds within itself a tragic sense of the brevity and the preciousness of human love and life.

Under Milk Wood had its premiere at the Fogg Museum, Harvard, on 3 May 1953, in an unfinished state, with Thomas reading all the parts. On 14 May the first full-cast reading occurred at the YM-YWHA Poetry Center in New York with Thomas reading the parts of First Voice, Reverend Eli Jenkins, and the Second and Fifth Drowned. This production, as well as the second one done two weeks later, was a great success with the audience. During this time also, Thomas eagerly agreed to write the libretto for a proposed opera with Stravinsky. The subject was intriguing and reflected Thomas's deepest feelings about language and innocence: after a nuclear holocaust, a new Adam would recreate for his Eve a new language in which there would be no abstractions. The words would blow from a new Tree of Knowledge, each of whose leaves would be imprinted with one letter of the alphabet. It would be a world of physical perception only—people, things, and words referring to things. (Thomas was about to fly to meet Stravinsky in California to begin work on this opera when he died.) On 3 June, Coronation Day, when he flew back to London, he seemed on the verge of becoming as successful as a writer of more dramatic, public works—like the radio play and the proposed opera—as he had been as a successful lyric poet for the last twenty years.

Between June and October 1953 Thomas was in Britain. He covered the International Eisteddfod in Wales that July, worked on "Elegy," for his father, and, over Caitlin Thomas's strong objections, resolved to go back to America that year. Alcoholism and the chronic inability to take charge of his life so as to solve the problem of money and regular employment made another trip to America seem the only escape from an impossible situation.

Thomas's fourth and final American tour began on 19 October 1953 and ended with his death on 9 November at St. Vincent's Hospital in New York City. On 24 and 25 October Thomas read First Voice in the third and fourth productions of *Under Milk Wood* at the YM-YWHA. He participated in a "Poetry and the Film" discussion, organized by Cinema 16, on 28 October. A New York doctor, Milton Feltenstein, who had treated him on his third visit, was called in to give Thomas an injection of ACTH to relieve the effects of incessant drinking. Thomas must have known the end was near. To one person he said: "I've seen the gates of hell tonight," and to his intimate friend Liz Reitell he said he wished to die and "to go into the garden of Eden." Waking up during the night of 3 November Thomas left his room at the Chelsea Hotel and returned in an hour or so, saying "I've had eighteen straight whiskeys. I think that's the record." The next night, 4 November, he fell into unconsciousness and was rushed to St. Vincent's. He lingered in an irreversible coma, caused by a lifetime of alcoholic poisoning, but probably aggravated by Feltenstein's ill-advised injections (possibly of morphine) earlier in the day on 4 November. Caitlin Thomas arrived before he died, went into hysterics and was temporarily straitjacketed and placed in a Long Island clinic. After his death on 9 November, Thomas was buried in the churchyard in Laugharne, where a simple white cross marks his grave. He was thirty-nine.

Between 1946 and his death in 1953 Thomas composed only nine poems, two of which are fragments, in addition to several BBC broadcasts on childhood and the play *Under Milk Wood*. Six of the nine poems appeared in the volume *In Country Sleep* (1952): "In Country Sleep," "Over Sir John's Hill," "In the White Giant's Thigh," "Poem on His Birthday," "Lament," and "Do Not Go Gentle Into That Good Night." In addition to these poems, Thomas wrote "Author's Prologue," the long verse preface to *Collected Poems*. "Elegy," left unfinished at the poet's death, was, after "Do Not Go Gentle Into That Good Night," Thomas's second poem on his father's death. "In Country Heaven," the framing poem of the ambitious unfinished sequence by the same name, exists in several drafts.

In the final poems, the poet still appears as an intermediary figure—father, Aesop, lapidary, local historian, Noah, sea voyager—but one who is less an active agent than a more deeply satisfied, happily resigned observer, spectator, describer, witness, perceiver of a spiritualized landscape whose mysteries now seem more fathomable. The great evils of both the early and the middle poems, time and death, are finally worked into the poet's vision of nature as holy; in fact, all of the last nine poems deal with death in some fashion. Finally, Thomas tried to create poems in which what he understood as "God" and "man," "heaven" and "earth," becomes clear. In trying to come to terms with death and God, the natural and the supernatural, Thomas begins but does not complete a reintroduction of the "cosmic" perspective of the earlier poems as a background to poems that still continue to be set in a localized landscape.

The most ambitious of these poems of his last years is the unfinished "In Country Heaven." In a long prose synopsis of the epic action of this poem and in an extant fragment of a framing poem "In Country Heaven," Thomas tells us that the earth has destroyed itself in an atomic war. Learning of the death of earth, God weeps, and his pastoral retainers, "heavenly hedgerow-men," recall what they can of their lives on earth. The three poem sections that Thomas completed for the overall poem are "In Country Sleep," "Over Sir John's Hill," and "In the White Giant's Thigh."

Like its predecessors, "Poem in October" and "Fern Hill," "In Country Sleep" deals with the problem of the perception of nature by the child and by the adult. Unlike the earlier poems, however, "In Country Sleep" greatly lessens, in fact, almost entirely abolishes, the sense of a great divide between child and adult in the perception of nature as holy. Although the poet, speaking the poem to his sleeping infant daughter, identifies a mysterious figure called the "thief" who will visit the child, this thief, a development of the similar figure of "Time" in "Fern Hill," robs the child of its visionary perception of nature only in order to perpetuate a higher unity and greater good after adulthood's separation from continuous vision: that greater good is the assumption of the grown-up child into Country Heaven, where it shall enjoy an eternal, deepened apprehension of nature as vision. Significantly, it is the father in the poem who describes, in a long chain of epiphanies, the revelation of Country Heaven *within* the landscape. Unlike "Poem in October" and "Fern Hill," in which the perception of holy nature was carefully ascribed to the child, here that distinction is pointedly omitted. In fact, the child remains asleep throughout the entire poem, and the poet, who addresses her directly in section one, moves to the more objective third-person perspective in section two, in order to show that these epiphanies are his as well as hers. Only the father's adult knowledge that the thief must come and his less intense response to nature separate him from his daughter.

Unlike "In Country Sleep" with its sweeping landscape, the second of the three poem sections, "Over Sir John's Hill," is almost a case history or outdoor laboratory experiment seeking answers to two questions: how can particular acts of killing in nature be justified and how can the poet possibly write poems about visionary landscapes that keep collapsing into scenes of death?

"Over Sir John's Hill" is written in a complicated stanza of twelve lines of various lengths, carefully patterned with syllabics and end rhymes that may be full or assonantal and with a free use of sprung rhythm. The general action of the poem's five stanzas is as follows: above Sir John's Hill, a hawk waits to kill sparrows and other small birds, while, below, a heron and the poet observe. While the sparrows answer the hawk's call for their deaths, the poet praises both hawk and sparrows for the parts they play in the natural, holy cycle. Described as a saint or priest, the heron seems as conscious as the poet of the mystery of death, and his mournful singing is transcribed by the lapidary-poet onto a stone by the shore. God is asked to have mercy on the sparrows and to save their souls.

Observing the slaughter, the poet is a priest reading from the psalter, nature's priest who interprets her actions, as well as being an Aesop, whose animal tales ended with moral statements drawn from the action of the tale. Also, in creating his own poems, the poet makes the poem a critique of nature: nature is a book the poet reads, and his poem is his analysis of that book. By recreating the landscape in his poem, entwining within that recreation his own sympathies and thematic interpretation of the outer landscape, the poet is completing the process of understanding nature by linking outer landscape to inner, subjective response in a single imaginative act.

The birds that engaged in child's play were innocent and are now guilty, that were living are now dead, that received justice are now candidates for mercy. These opposites are significant to an understanding of the poet's call on God to "have mercy" on the birds "For their souls' song." God exists not independently but as an immanence in nature ("God in his whirlwind silence save"). There is even a hint that the birds are a part of God, his voice, like the hymning heron and the fabling poet, without all of whom God cannot speak or sing. The final completed poem section of "In Country Heaven" is "In the White Giant's Thigh." Like the paternal and Aesopian roles of the previous two poems, the poet's role here as what Walford Davies calls "the sad historian of a Welsh pastoral community" is one that places him at some distance from the landscape but in a position of teacher, interpreter, chronicler, and commemorator of the events, past and present, that make up the landscape's history. Walking on a hillside, the poet dreams of women, long dead, who once met, and made love to, their lovers there. Though the women and their lovers are now turned to dust, the poet longs to know their undying love: "Teach me the love that is evergreen." The poem becomes a great celebration of the physical joys of love in a rustic setting.

Another moving poem on love and death is the villanelle Thomas addressed to his dying father, "Do Not Go Gentle Into That Good Night." The point of the poem is contained in its double refrain: "Do not go gentle into that good night. / Rage, rage against the dying of the light." Thomas examines different ways to meet death—that of wise men, good men, wild men, and grave men (such as philosophers, moralists, hedonists, everyman)—and finds all ways of meeting death inadequate. The only solution is to live each moment of life with a burning intensity, yet also recognizing inevitable death as "good," a part of the scheme of things. "Do Not Go Gentle Into That Good Night," in its powerful simplicity and genuine sympathy for the dying father, is one of the best villanelles in English. Equally moving is an elegy to his father, the unfinished poem in terza rima, "Elegy," found among Thomas's papers after his death.

Two final poems that draw on the landscape of Laugharne to assert the poet's faith in life and sacramental nature are "Poem on His Birthday" and "Author's Prologue." In the birthday poem, Thomas affirms ambiguously his faith in "fabulous, dear God" and in "Heaven that never was / Nor will be ever" yet which nonetheless is "always true." Like the seaside world of fish and fowl, the poet rejoices in life and resolves to praise life even as he approaches his own end:

That the closer I move
To death, one man through his sundered hulks,
The louder the sun blooms
And the tusked, ramshackling sea exults;
And every wave of the way
And gale I tackle, the whole world then,
With more triumphant faith
That ever was since the world was said,
Spins its morning of praise.

Thomas's last finished poem, and one of his best, is "Author's Prologue" to *Collected Poems: 1934-1952*. Set in the Laugharne estuary, with the poet at work

John Malcolm Brinnin and Dylan Thomas

in his cliffside hut, the poem divides into two parts. The first half is in four sections: an opening description of the seaside below Thomas's workshop window in Laugharne; a contrasting description of the great cities of the world that the poet imagines will be gutted by nuclear firestorms; a meditation on the nature of poetic creation in light of these two descriptions; and finally, a description of a terrible molten flood that is flowing westward from London toward Wales, where the poet as Noah is building his ark-poems against the coming flood. Nature is holy, but the poet is deeply disturbed. Nuclear war threatens to annihilate the world, which it is his task to praise. Building his ark-poems out of love, the poet symbolically serves the members of creation by releasing a saving love into the world of the Cold War. The second half of the poem, in fact, is a long call to the animals to come into the poet's wordy ark and ride out the molten flood in safety. At the end of the poem, in Shelleyan fashion, love transforms hatred and destruction:

> We will ride out alone, and then,
> Under the stars of Wales,
> Cry, Multitudes of arks! Across
> The water lidded lands,
> Manned with their loves they'll move,
> Like wooden islands, hill to hill,
> Huloo, my proud dove with a flute!
> Ahoy, old, sea-legged fox,
> Tom tit and Dai mouse!
> My ark sings in the sun
> At God speeded summer's end
> And the flood flowers now.

The sun shines over the ark into the stilled flood water, transforming the rage and fear of humanity into flowers. The fire and water images that first signaled natural order and then man-made deathliness now again coalesce fruitfully and peacefully in the poem's consummate flowering flood. The sailing arks are flowers on the flood because they are also seeds of windblown puffballs. The flowering flood, too, is all of the poems in *Collected Poems*. Poetry, nature, and love—the flood is inseminated by the beams of the sun and "flowers" into a new creation of life on earth. Finally, the rainbow, symbol of divine covenant with an earlier Noah, is also the flower of the flood.

A complete integration of Thomas's romantic concerns, "Author's Prologue" presents a landscape in whose events we can see the projection of Thomas's complete inner poetic life: the endless struggle of the self to find its place in the landscape without being annihilated by absorption into it; the linkage of inner poetic process and events in the external, natural world; the linkage of word and thing both in nature and man as not ontologically dissimilar; the fostering of love by imaginative action as the poet's way of deeply communing with all that is outside the self; the poet's assumption of the role of Christlike saviour, first of himself, and, in his latest poems, of the natural world threatened by the dark products of scientific rationalism and the antinatural "cities of nine / Days' night"; and even that most difficult of romantic concerns, the integration of poetic creation with revolutionary political action.

During the last years of his life and just after his death, Dylan Thomas may well have been the most popular major poet since Byron. Unlike Byron, whose life and poetry enhanced and illuminated one another, Thomas lived a life at odds with his deepest poetic instincts. Thomas wrote his best poems in Wales and about Wales—about his childhood and experience of nature there as a child. He worked best in comfortable, utterly middle-class surroundings, whether in his room at No. 5 Cwmdonkin Drive or in one of the many places in rural Wales and England that Caitlin made into a home for him. In London or in New York, little truly creative work was done, and Thomas's public image and attendant drunkenness eventually created an unbridgeable split in his nature. Like Rimbaud, Verlaine, Hart Crane, and others, Thomas became ultimately self-destructive.

Dylan Thomas the legend now seems sadly dated, and the hour of his public fame has passed as other suicidally Dionysian figures in art and the entertainment world fill his place, but Thomas the man remains fascinating, pitiable, yet tragically heroic as well, for in spite of the dark side of his nature, he did produce a substantial body of poems, modern in technique and romantic in theme, the best of which seem able to stand the test of time and the shifts in poetic fashion which it brings. Criticism of Thomas's poetry has, of course, been severe. It has been called narrow in emotional and intellectual range, hopelessly obscure in the earlier years, narcissistic, nostalgic, lacking in nuance and subtlety, and incurably adolescent in sensibility. Yet T. S. Eliot, W. H. Auden, Stephen Spender, Edith Sitwell, Kathleen Raine, and many other poets have praised Thomas's best work.

If, as Yvor Winters once said, a great poet is a poet who has written at least one great poem, then Thomas may well be just inside the circle of major poets in the twentieth century. Certainly on the basis of such poems as "Altarwise by Owl-light,"

"The Hunchback in the Park," "A Refusal to Mourn the Death, by Fire, of a Child in London," "Ceremony After A Fire-Raid," "A Winter's Tale," "Poem in October," "Fern Hill," and "Do Not Go Gentle Into That Good Night" Thomas is, at the very least, one of the greatest lyricists in the ongoing romantic tradition.

Screenplay:

Me and My Bike, Gainsborough, 1948.

Periodical Publications:

"On Poetry: A Discussion," *Encounter*, 3 (November 1954): 23-26;

"Dylan Thomas On Reading His Poetry," *Mademoiselle*, 43 (July 1956): 34-37;

"Dylan Thomas on Edgar Lee Masters," *Harper's Bazaar*, 96 (June 1963): 68-69, 115;

"Poetry and the Film: A Symposium," *Film Culture*, 29 (Summer 1963): 55-63.

Letters:

Letters to Vernon Watkins, edited by Vernon Watkins (London: Dent & Faber, 1957; New York: New Directions, 1957);

"Love Letters From a Poet to his Wife," *McCall's*, 93 (February 1966): 78, 173;

Selected Letters of Dylan Thomas, edited by Constantine FitzGibbon (London: Dent, 1966; New York: New Directions, 1967);

Twelve More Letters (Stoke Ferry, Norfolk, U.K.: Turret Books, 1969).

Bibliographies:

J. Alexander Rolph, *Dylan Thomas: A Bibliography* (London: Dent, 1956; New York: New Directions, 1956);

Ralph Maud, *Dylan Thomas in Print: A Bibliographical History* (Pittsburgh: University of Pittsburgh Press, 1970).

Biographies:

John Malcolm Brinnin, *Dylan Thomas in America* (Boston: Atlantic/Little, Brown, 1955);

Caitlin Thomas, *Leftover Life to Kill* (London: Putnam's, 1957; Boston: Atlantic/Little, Brown, 1957);

Bill Read, *The Days of Dylan Thomas* (London: Weidenfeld & Nicolson, 1964; New York: McGraw-Hill, 1964);

Constantine FitzGibbon, *The Life of Dylan Thomas* (London: Dent, 1965; Boston: Atlantic/Little, Brown, 1965);

Nicolette Devas, *Two Flamboyant Fathers* (London: Collins, 1966);

Andrew Sinclair, *Dylan Thomas: No Man More Magical* (New York: Holt, Rinehart & Winston, 1975);

Paul Ferris, *Dylan Thomas* (London: Hodder & Stoughton, 1977; New York: Dial Press, 1977);

Daniel Jones, *My Friend Dylan Thomas* (London: Dent, 1977).

References:

John Ackerman, *Dylan Thomas: His Life and Work* (London: Oxford University Press, 1964);

Sam Adams, ed., *Poetry Wales: A Dylan Thomas Number*, 9 (Autumn 1973);

John Bayley, *The Romantic Survival* (London: Constable, 1957);

John Malcolm Brinnin, ed., *A Casebook on Dylan Thomas* (New York: Crowell, 1960);

Robert K. Burdette, *The Saga of Prayer: The Poetry of Dylan Thomas* (The Hague: Mouton, 1972);

C. B. Cox, ed., *Dylan Thomas: A Collection of Critical Essays* (Englewood Cliffs, N.J.: Prentice-Hall, 1966);

Aneirin Talfan Davies, *Dylan: Druid of the Broken Body* (London: Dent, 1964);

Walford Davies, *Dylan Thomas* (Cardiff: University of Wales Press, 1972);

Davies, *Dylan Thomas* (Portsmouth, U.K.: Open University Press, 1976);

Davies, Introduction and notes in *Dylan Thomas: Selected Poems* (London: Dent, 1974);

Davies, ed., *Dylan Thomas: New Critical Essays* (London: Dent, 1972);

Clark Emery, *The World of Dylan Thomas* (Coral Gables: University of Miami Press, 1962; London: Dent, 1971);

J. M. and M. G. Farringdon, *A Concordance and Word Lists to the Poems of Dylan Thomas* (Swansea: Ariel House, 1980);

G. S. Fraser, *Dylan Thomas* (London: Longmans, Green, 1957; revised, 1972);

David Holbrook, *Dylan Thomas: The Code of Night* (London: Athlone Press, 1972);

Holbrook, *Llareggub Revisited: Dylan Thomas and the State of Modern Poetry* (London: Bowes & Bowes, 1962);

T. H. Jones, *Dylan Thomas* (Edinburgh: Oliver & Boyd, 1963);

R. B. Kershner, *Dylan Thomas: The Poet and His Critics* (Chicago: American Library Association, 1976);

Rushworth Kidder, *Dylan Thomas: The Country of the*

Spirit (Princeton: Princeton University Press, 1973);
H. H. Kleinman, *The Religious Sonnets of Dylan Thomas* (Berkeley & Los Angeles: University of California Press, 1963);
Jacob Korg, *Dylan Thomas* (New York: Twayne, 1965);
Gary Lane, *A Concordance to the Poems of Dylan Thomas* (Metuchen, N.J.: Scarecrow Press, 1976);
Min Lewis, *Laugharne and Dylan Thomas* (London: Dobson, 1967);
Ralph Maud, *Entrances to Dylan Thomas' Poetry* (Pittsburgh: University of Pittsburgh Press, 1963);
J. Hillis Miller, *Poets of Reality* (Cambridge: Harvard University Press, 1966);
William Moynihan, *The Craft and Art of Dylan Thomas* (Ithaca, N.Y.: Cornell University Press, 1966);
Louise Murdy, *Sound and Sense in Dylan Thomas's Poetry* (The Hague: Mouton, 1966);
H. R. Neuville, *The Major Poems of Dylan Thomas* (New York: Monarch, 1965);
Elder Olson, *The Poetry of Dylan Thomas* (Chicago: University of Chicago Press, 1954);
Annis Pratt, *Dylan Thomas's Early Prose: A Study in Creative Mythology* (Pittsburgh: University of Pittsburgh Press, 1970);
A. M. Reddington, *Dylan Thomas: A Journey from Darkness to Light* (New York: Paulist Press, 1968);
Don Sinnock, *The Dylan Thomas Landscape* (Swansea: Celtic Educational Services, 1975);
Derek Stanford, *Dylan Thomas: A Literary Study* (London: Spearman, 1954; revised, 1964);
E. W. Tedlock, ed., *Dylan Thomas: The Legend and the Poet* (London: Heinemann, 1960);
William York Tindall, *A Reader's Guide to Dylan Thomas* (New York: Farrar, Straus, 1962);
Henry Treece, *Dylan Thomas* (London: Drummond, 1949; revised edition, London: Benn, 1956);
Robert C. Williams, *A Concordance to the Collected Poems of Dylan Thomas* (Lincoln: University of Nebraska Press, 1967).

Papers:
Thomas's notebooks are located in the Lockwood Memorial Library of the State University of New York at Buffalo. The Humanities Research Center of the University of Texas, Austin, has a large miscellaneous collection. Other material exists in the BBC Archives, the British Library at the British Museum, at M.I.T., and at Harvard.

Vernon Watkins
(27 June 1906-8 October 1967)

Michael J. Collins
Georgetown University

SELECTED BOOKS: *Ballad of the Mari Lwyd and Other Poems* (London: Faber & Faber, 1941);
The Lamp and the Veil (London: Faber & Faber, 1945);
The Lady with the Unicorn (London: Faber & Faber, 1948);
Selected Poems (Norfolk, Conn.: New Directions, 1948);
The Death Bell (London: Faber & Faber, 1954; Norfolk, Conn.: New Directions, 1954);
Cypress and Acacia (London: Faber & Faber, 1959; Norfolk, Conn.: New Directions, 1960);
Affinities (London: Faber & Faber, 1962; Norfolk, Conn.: New Directions, 1963);
Selected Poems: 1930-1960 (London: Faber & Faber, 1967; New York: New Directions, 1967);
Fidelities (London: Faber & Faber, 1968; New York: New Directions, 1969);
Uncollected Poems, edited by Kathleen Raine (London: Enitharmon Press, 1969);
The Influences (Hayes, Middlesex: Bran's Head Press, 1976);
I That Was Born in Wales: A New Selection from the Poems of Vernon Watkins, edited by Gwen Watkins and Ruth Pryor (Cardiff: University of Wales Press, 1976);
Elegy for the Latest Dead (Edinburgh: Tragara Press, 1977);
Unity of the Stream: A New Selection of Poems (Llandysul, Dyfed: Gomer Press/Cardiff: Academi

Gymreig, 1978; Redding Ridge, Conn.: Black Swan, 1981);

The Ballad of the Outer Dark and Other Poems, edited by Pryor (London: Enitharmon Press, 1979);

The Breaking of the Waves (Ipswich: Golgonooza, 1979);

Yeats & Owen: Two Essays (Frome, U.K.: Hunting Raven, 1981).

On a wet day in November 1963 a crowd gathered in Cwmdonkin Park, Swansea, to take part in the dedication of a stone (carved by the sculptor Ronald Cour) to the memory of Dylan Thomas, who had died ten years before. Vernon Watkins was there to pay tribute to his friend and fellow poet by reading Thomas's "The Hunchback in the Park" and one of his own poems (of 138 lines) on Thomas, "A True Picture Restored." As he started to read, the weather grew worse, and the crowd began opening umbrellas and bundling up against a steady rain. But Vernon Watkins continued to read, "gravely and beautifully," as Elizabeth M. Jones describes it, cutting not a line in deference to the rain, affirming, as he did throughout his life, his unqualified commitment to his art and to his friends. "We all stood still and quiet," Jones recalls, "in affectionate recognition of an integrity which informed everything he wrote and did."

Vernon Watkins at work in the St. Helens branch of Lloyd's Bank, Swansea, circa 1951 (BBC Hulton)

Vernon Phillips Watkins was born on 27 June 1906, in the town of Maesteg (in Glamorgan, South Wales), the second of three children and the only son of William and Sarah Phillips Watkins. Although both his parents spoke Welsh, like many other parents of their generation, they did not pass the language on to their children. William Watkins, who had entered Lloyd's Bank at the age of seventeen, was manager of the branch in Maesteg, the youngest manager in the firm when his son was born. The family moved to Bridgend in 1908, to Llanelly in 1912, and to Swansea in 1913, as William Watkins's career in Lloyd's moved rapidly forward. (Vernon Watkins, who never sought promotion lest it interfere with poetry, would later joke about his own career in the bank by pointing out that while his father had been the youngest manager in Lloyd's, he would be the oldest cashier.) The family settled in Gower shortly after the move to Swansea, and except for school, his service in the Royal Air Force, and his visits to the University of Washington in Seattle, Vernon Watkins lived there for the rest of his life. "There's a special light about it," his wife would say later, "that makes Vernon's affirmations possible. He could never be so positive anywhere else."

Welsh poet Roland Mathias describes Vernon Watkins as a "bookish, sensitive, and rather withdrawn boy, whose nature and upbringing did not allow the appearance of overt precocity." Watkins showed interest in poetry at the age of five (his early favorites were Keats and Shelley), and he was writing poems himself at eight. At ten, he began to collect the works of the great English poets by giving them as Christmas and birthday gifts to his parents and sisters. "These books," he wrote later, "seemed to me at that time the most precious gifts one could give. Words in cadenced form, whether in rhyme or not, seemed to have an unrivalled power over the imagination."

After a year in Swansea Grammar School, his parents sent him, at age eleven, to Tyttenhanger Lodge, a highly regarded preparatory school in Seaford, Sussex, where he "counted every night," as he put it, "the lines of the Arthurian epic I was writing." He completed his preparatory studies in 1920 and entered Repton, a public school even farther from home in Derbyshire, perhaps, as his mother suggests, "to guard against too narrow an outlook on life."

At Repton, he stopped writing poetry for

eighteen months until, as he said later, "a lecture on Shelley by one of the masters brought back the irresistible impulse, and I wrote poems again . . . fairly continuously." While he no doubt improved his already excellent game of tennis, which he would play enthusiastically for the rest of his life, he was not, at least until the last eighteen months, very happy in the brutal world of a public school. Once in the sixth form, however, he could write to a friend, Eric Falk, "This place is wonderful; . . . so, also, is everybody and everything in it. . . . I used to criticize people so much, and now, with a few loathsome exceptions, everybody is being glorious." Although he had been raised in a Congregational family, he was confirmed in the Church of England at Repton. His strength there was in languages, and in his last term he won the Lancelot Saye Prizes and the Schreiber Prize for French and German as well as the Howe Verse Prize for a poem called "The Japanese Disaster." In June 1924 he left Repton with a romantic memory of happiness that would remain with him throughout his life. Thirty-three years later, on the occasion of its quadricentennial, he honored the school he had loved with a sequence of four intensely personal poems called "Revisited Waters."

In October 1924 Watkins entered Magdalene College, Cambridge, as a pensioner (that is, a student without a scholarship). He read modern languages (French and German) and was reasonably successful in the Intercollegiate Examination at the end of the year. But in June 1924, without discussing the matter with his parents, he decided suddenly to withdraw for good from the college, perhaps, as the poet Kathleen Raine suggests, in response to the " 'scientific' school of literary criticism" at Cambridge and its "denial of the imagination." In any case, his withdrawal was dramatic and irrevocable. When he told the master of the college, A. C. Benson, he would not remain at Cambridge and, as Roland Mathias puts it, have poetry "criticized out of him," Benson replied that if he intended to become a poet, he would curse the day he had been born. Saying he had already cursed it many times, he slammed the master's door as he left. But when he returned home and asked his father, who had with great difficulty paid his expenses at Cambridge, to support him in a year of travel in Italy, William Watkins refused, and in the fall of 1925, indifferent to other possibilities, wanting only to be a poet, Vernon Watkins, at the age of nineteen, joined Lloyd's Bank at Butetown, Cardiff, as a junior clerk.

The great crisis of Vernon Watkins's life was yet to take place. He worked regularly at the bank during the next two years, and while he still wrote poetry, he was continually unhappy. His life, as Mathias suggests, was schizophrenic: torn between the world of the bank and the world of the imagination, he was deeply depressed by his sense of the terrible gulf between ideal and real, between vision and fact. "At the age of twenty-one," Watkins said later, "the poems and letters of Keats, and the poetry of Shelley, Milton, and Blake so governed me that the everyday world scarcely existed for me except as a touchstone for protest and indignation." The inevitable breakdown came on a weekend in the fall of 1927.

As Watkins would later describe it, it began on a Saturday evening in Cardiff soon after he had returned to his lodgings. Extremely tense, he began rushing violently about his room, shouting to himself that he had conquered time and could control his own destiny and that of others. Coincidentally, he heard a loud crash outside and discovered the driver of a motorcycle dead and his bloodied passenger coming toward his window. He knew at once, he said later, that he had willed the accident, and he immediately passed out. The next morning, however, he took a train to Repton, where three years earlier he had been, he felt, ideally happy. He visited some students, attended chapel, and then later in the day burst into the study of the headmaster, Dr. Geoffrey Fisher, shouting it was Fisher who destroyed youth and at the same time attempting, without success, to assault him. He was soon restrained and finally brought, in a state of mental collapse, to a nursing home in Derby.

He remained there for several months, often under physical restraint, keeping the other patients awake at night with his recitals of Blake. During this period he had a profound visionary or religious experience that would henceforth determine what he called the "metaphysical" character of his poetry. His wife, Gwen Watkins, describes the experience as "comparable with that of St. Paul on the road to Damascus—not, indeed, that he was converted to Christianity, since he could never remember the time when he was not a Christian; but his eyes were opened to the nature of Time and Eternity." The experience was salutary as well, for he came to believe, as poet Leslie Norris puts it, "that time does not exist" and that the real world is no more than "a flawed copy" of another "perfect world." Watkins himself called it "a complete revolution of sensibility. I repudiated the verse I had written and knew that I could never again write a poem which could be dominated by time." "To create art and neglect the Greater Eternity," he would say later, "is to work in confusion."

When he returned home, his father (with considerable difficulty) managed to get him another position in Lloyd's, this time in the St. Helens branch in Swansea, where he would work faithfully for the rest of his life. (He said in a lecture in 1966 that his one distinguishing feature was that he had "worked longer in a bank than any other poet.") He destroyed all the poetry he had written earlier and began the long struggle to articulate his vision. The poems did not come easily. "It took," he said, "several years for my style to catch up with this experience, so powerful were the verbal legacies left me by the poets I had admired for so long. I now saw them in a new light, but I could not translate my transfigured vision of the world into language." Thus, in the mental breakdown he suffered at the age of twenty-one and in the experience that followed it, Watkins discovered not only his way of living with the world but the vision of reality he would struggle for the rest of his life to express in his poetry.

With his assignment to the bank in Swansea, Watkins's daily life took on the pattern it would retain, with only two interruptions, until his retirement in 1966. Each morning he went by bus to his job at the bank; each evening, after dinner, he wrote and revised his poems, putting them through an average of 50 drafts and at times through 500. Although he loved to tell hilarious stories of his incompetence as a cashier (setting banknotes aflame, chasing customers through the streets of Swansea to retrieve overpayments), he was, in fact, quite able, and he would occasionally entertain his coworkers by adding up five columns of figures simultaneously. "A poet can do any work in the world and not lose by it," he said, "provided that he is a poet first." He refused advancement in the bank, and since his work as a cashier made few demands upon him, he was free to dedicate himself to poetry. The job, indeed, seems to have been perfect for him: with the daily reconciliation and closing out of books, he closed out as well the world of Lloyd's bank and turned his attention fully to his craft.

Vernon Watkins and Dylan Thomas, circa 1936

Gwen Watkins has written that her husband's "two great experiences" in the years between 1928 and 1941 "were his discovery of the late poems of Yeats and his friendship with Dylan Thomas. Yeats remained a lasting influence on his poetic style, perhaps the only one." In reading Yeats, she added later, he came to recognize "that music could be made out of bare and ordinary language. . . . Until his style caught up with his feelings the real poet couldn't begin to develop, and this was what Yeats did for him."

His interest in Yeats began with the poems in *The Tower*, which was published in 1928. Here was a poet who had changed directions, as he was struggling to do, in the course of his career and who, like himself, sought to express in poetry his own vision of "the Greater Eternity." Critic Desiree Hirst has traced in great detail their affinities in theme, form, and language, and they are, as she shows, considerable, although the notion of the timeless, of "the Greater Eternity," often took a Christian form in Watkins, as it never did in Yeats.

In the summer of 1938 (only six months before Yeats's death) Watkins and a young friend, Francis Dufau-Labeyrie, traveled to Ireland to visit Yeats. They met one afternoon at Riversdale, Yeats's home in Dublin. The two poets talked about literature, politics, Ireland and Wales, Vernon Watkins's work at the bank, the Abbey Theatre. Shortly before they left, Watkins snapped a picture of Yeats in his garden and told him that "for ten years I have been greatly influenced by your work, more than by anyone else." On the train that evening from Dublin to Galway, as Francis Dufau-Labeyrie sat in silence across from him, Watkins completed the first draft of his long poem "Yeats in Dublin," which finally appeared in 1945 in *The Lamp and the Veil*. Years later, in his lectures on modern poetry at University College, Swansea, Watkins called Yeats "the greatest lyric poet of our age," who "had shown me something which the others had not been able to show: that is, how a lyric poet should grow old."

On their journey home from Ireland, Watkins and his friend stopped at Laugharne to visit Dylan Thomas, whom Watkins had met in 1935, a few months after the publication of Thomas's first book, *18 Poems* (1934). "We became close friends almost immediately," Watkins wrote later, "from an affinity which I think we both recognized at once." In fact, it seems to have been an attraction of opposites, of order and chaos, and all they finally seem to have shared was a commitment to poetry, although as Watkins recognized, "our approach to it and our way of working presented a complete contrast. Dylan worked upon a symmetrical abstract with tactile delicacy; out of a lump of texture or nest of phrases he created music, testing everything by physical feeling, working from the concrete image outwards. I worked from music and cadence towards the density of physical shape." He recognized as well their temperamental differences. In an address to the Poetry Society of Great Britain on 17 May 1966 he said, "Dylan was always glad that I worked in a bank, but I could never see him in the same position. He might have been Master of the Mint, and then there would have been more money all round. At least, for a time."

The two poets spent a great deal of time together, reading and commenting on their own poetry and that of others as well. "We were both religious poets," said Watkins, "and neither of us had any aptitude for political reform." They met every Wednesday with several friends (Tom Warner the composer, Alfred Jones the painter, and John Prichard the writer, among others) at the Kardomah Café in Swansea during Watkins's lunch hour. Thomas convinced his friend to submit his poetry for publication: he had, Gwen Watkins says, "up to this time . . . set himself against publishing any of his poems." After Watkins gave two of his poems to Thomas to be published in the first issue of *Wales*, a magazine of Anglo-Welsh prose and poetry, one of them, "Griefs of the Sea," appeared with a line left out and two others changed. Watkins's response was characteristic: he forgave Thomas and spent the next few days in a bookshop in Swansea surreptitiously correcting by hand every copy of *Wales* he could find. In spite of the experience, he continued to have his poems published.

The story of "Griefs of the Sea" seems to make clear the relationship of the two men. One is always disappointed at Thomas's failures and amazed at Watkins's loyalty. None of the letters Watkins wrote to Thomas, for example, has survived; Watkins preserved those he received from Thomas and had them published after his friend's death. When Watkins was married, the best man, Dylan Thomas, failed to show up, lost, he claimed later, in London. But Watkins seems always to have forgiven his friend, and his writings about him never suggest any bitterness or sense of betrayal. "Innocence," he said in an obituary for Thomas, "is always a paradox." He wrote nineteen poems about Thomas, named one of his sons for him, lent him money, and continually acknowledged a great debt to his friend. "It's an article of faith," he once told Mathias. "I have to believe the best of people." He remained loyal to his friend throughout his life, and as Gwen Watkins tells us, Thomas's "death in November 1953 was a grief from which Vernon never recovered."

In 1941, two months before he left for more than four years of service in the Royal Air Force, Faber and Faber, the firm that would publish seven volumes of his poetry, brought out his first collection, *Ballad of the Mari Lwyd and Other Poems*. The book was favorably reviewed (on 25 October 1941) in the *Times Literary Supplement*. The reviewer wrote that the poems "show the originality of Mr. Watkins's imagination, and his rhythm is as potent as his imagery. He translates the actual . . . into an essentially poetic reality. And he is equally passionate when he sings."

The title poem, 600 lines long, concerns the ancient Welsh new year's custom of the Mari Lwyd or Gray Mare. The model of a gray horse's head was carried from house to house on New Year's Eve, and the carriers tried to gain entry by defeating the inhabitants in a rhyming contest. The ballad is dramatic (it was staged by the Swansea Little Theatre in January 1948), a play of voices among the carriers, whom Watkins made the dead; the living, who dwell within the house; and others who are more or less detached from the confrontation. Writing soon after Watkins's death, Glyn Jones recalled his first reading of the *Ballad of the Mari Lwyd*. "The title poem," he said, "was to me a revelation, an unexpected masterpiece, easily the finest thing of Vernon's I had then seen. In the same volume were splendid poems like 'The Collier,' 'Sycamore,' and 'Griefs of the Sea' . . . , but . . . 'Ballad of the Mari Lwyd' was for me the outstanding work of the book and today . . . it still seems to me unsurpassed by anything he wrote later." Of the others Jones mentions, "Sycamore" is perhaps the most important, for the poem, which sees the tree as an image of the eternal, goes to the heart of Watkins's vision:

> Who sleeps? The young streams feed
> My boughs. The blind keys spin.
> Hark, he is dead indeed.
> Never shall fall again
> My natural winged seed,
> On this small-statured man.

With the outbreak of World War II Watkins joined the Home Guard. (He watched the fire-bombing of Swansea from his post on the cliffs of Gower.) In 1941 he was called up and joined the Royal Air Force as a policeman. (He thought he would make a better policeman than a cook, the only other job available.) While he enjoyed the physical training and proved an excellent marksman, he was not, to say the least, entirely successful in the Air Force police. The stories about Watkins the policeman rival those of Watkins the cashier: marching in a parade without a rifle, hosing a rank of airmen during a fire drill, failing to lower the flag during a ceremony, reading poetry at a train station where he had been posted to pick up drunks. In 1943 he transferred to the Intelligence Service, which he found more congenial. (He said of the Air Force police, "I don't suppose I'll ever meet a bigger bunch of crooks.")

In the Intelligence Service he was promoted to sergeant and stationed at Bradwell, near Oxford. (Poet Philip Larkin tells of his first meeting Watkins when he came to Oxford in uniform to read and discuss the poetry of Yeats.) He visited Dylan Thomas frequently in London during the war, and he met Gwendoline Mary Davies, also a member of the Intelligence Service, whom he married in London at the Church of St. Bartholomew the Great in the City on 2 October 1944. (They would have five children: Rhiannon Mary born in 1945; Gareth Vernon, 1947; William Tristan David, 1951; Dylan Valentine, 1954; and Conrad Meredith, 1958.) In January 1946 he was released from the Royal Air Force and returned with his wife and infant daughter to Gower, where he settled finally in Pennard and resumed his position in the bank.

In 1945, two months before his release from the Royal Air Force, his second collection, *The Lamp and the Veil*, had been published. The book contains only three poems: "Yeats in Dublin," which he had begun on the train to Galway after his meeting with Yeats in 1938, "Sea-Music for My Sister Travelling," written for Dorothy Watkins as she sailed on a troop ship to India, and "The Broken Sea," a poem "For my Godchild, Danielle Dufau-Labeyrie, born in Paris, May, 1940," part of which is about Dylan Thomas. It is an unusual collection for Watkins, for the poems are all longer than one would now expect of him. Although Thomas thought "Yeats in Dublin" too literal a report of the meeting (Watkins quotes Yeats verbatim in the poem), the reviewer in the *Times Literary Supplement* of 29 December 1945 found it written "with admirable control and exactness," and Glyn Jones lists it among Watkins's best. "Sea-Music for My Sister Travelling" is, in the words of Mathias, "essentially cadence-work amongst sea-words":

> In peaceful day, who knows how near
> you now,
> Black, the begetters clash like thunderclouds;
> Light in the rainbow from the prow
> Hides the ascending death where spirits,
> torn, begin
> To put on light, and shed their
> parted shrouds.
> O, the sea turns, and now your eyes look in.

The Lady with the Unicorn, his third volume of poems, was published in 1948. It is an important book, the "first collection," as Mathias says, "of unquestionable stature." The title poem, for Leslie Norris, is "not only . . . his most explicit statement of the power of art over time," but it also affirms "that human love, which inspired the making of the tapestries he describes and celebrates, is akin to divine love, sacred in its own right and a powerful force in the destruction of the idea of time." The poem that opens the collection, "Music of Colours—White Blossom," is one of the best Watkins ever wrote and one of his most important. It was suggested, he said, "in winter by a fall of snow on the sea cliff where I live. I walked out on the cliff and found that the foam of the sea, which had been brilliantly white the previous day, now looked grey":

> The spray looked white until this snowfall.
> Now the foam is grey, the wave is dull.
> Call nothing white again, we were deceived.
> The flood of Noah dies, the rainbow is lived.

Yet from the deluge of illusions an unknown color is saved. The things of nature, the finite things of the world are never purely white, never perfect, and yet white, pure white, does exist:

> If there is white, or has been white, it must
> have been

When His eyes looked down and made the leper clean.
White will not be, apart, though trees try
Spirals of blossom, their green conspiracy.
She who touched His garment saw no white tree.

The eternal, the timeless, the unchanging, the perfect is never seen in nature, but the poet knows and affirms its existence. As the reviewer for the *Times Literary Supplement* wrote, "this poetry . . . conveys through sensuous images the meaning of a spiritual experience that has, in fact, for the poet transformed the sensuous world."

In 1951 Watkins's American publisher, New Directions, brought out *The North Sea*, his translations of poems by the German poet Heinrich Heine. With his gift for languages, it is not surprising that, as the posthumous collection of 1977, *Selected Verse Translations*, reveals, the translation of poetry engaged Watkins throughout his life. He worked not only in German but in ancient Greek, Italian, French, Spanish, and (with prose translations of the poems of Jozsef Attila) even Hungarian, although German and French were most frequent. His choices were diverse and wide-ranging: as critic Ian Hilton puts it, "he translated the things he liked and he liked many different kinds of poetry."

In discussing the process of translation in an essay for the first issue of *Contemporary Literature in Translation*, Watkins distinguished between the scholar's translation and the poet's: "The first consideration of a scholar's translation is that it should be accurate; the first consideration of a poet's, that it be alive. . . . His object is to create, not a paraphrase, but an equivalent poem." Watkins, of course, translated as a poet, and his "strong point," as Hilton points out, was "the relaying of the rhythm and the musicality of a poem. . . . His ability to capture the internal rhymes, and movement sound in vowels in Heine's verse, for example, has rightly been praised." Watkins's translations are an important part of his work not only in themselves but in what they suggest about the way he wrote his own poems, about the influences of other poets on them, and about his affinities (to use one of his own words) with the poets whose work he translated.

His next collection, *The Death Bell*, appeared in 1954 and was the first choice of the newly formed Poetry Book Society. The book is divided into two parts—poems and ballads—and it continues, particularly in the first part, the themes of *The Lady with the Unicorn*. "Music of Colours: The Blossom Scattered" recalls the earlier "Music of Colours—White Blossom" and affirms that in the "flashes" of the "world's colours" some at least can glimpse the timeless, the perfect:

The marguerite's petal is white, is wet with rain,
Is white, then loses white, and then is white again
Not from time's course, but from the living spring,
Miraculous whiteness, a petal, a wing,
Like light, like lightning, soft thunder, white as jet,
Ageing on ageless breaths. The ages are not yet.

With "Taliesin in Gower"—the first poem he published on the sixth-century Welsh poet who proclaimed (in an ancient Welsh tale of the Mabinogion) that he lives out of time, through all of history—Watkins introduced a figure he would use repeatedly to express not only his affirmation of the eternal but his belief in the poet's occult, visionary knowledge. The review of *The Death Bell* in the *Times Literary Supplement* of 14 May 1954, while recognizing the difficulty of the poetry, was particularly laudatory. "The central experience of these poems is a sustained wonder at the glories of the created world, told in twin and merging moods of rhapsodic acceptance and grave meditation. The themes that Mr. Watkins chooses to dwell on are relatively few; but they are the great ones, and it is a measure of the intensity of his gift that, in trying to give them fresh expression, he seems to be straining at times at the very limits of the communicable."

Beginning in 1951, when he was elected a fellow of the Royal Society of Literature, Watkins received several prestigious awards for his poetry: the Quarterly Review of Literature Prize in 1952, the Levinson Prize from *Poetry* (Chicago) in 1953, the Guinness Prize for "The Tributary Seasons" in 1957, and two traveling scholarships from the Society of Authors in 1952 and 1956.

In 1959 *Cypress and Acacia* was published. In the judgment of the reviewer in the *Times Literary Supplement* of 11 December 1959, the collection "represents a steady development of gifts his admirers already knew about rather than a radically new departure." Taliesin appears again in an important poem, "Taliesin and the Spring of Vision." Here the ageless poet momentarily sees through time to eternity, to "the kingdom of love." But the vision is only momentary, and the poem ends with his prayer for finite, human wisdom:

"I have encountered the irreducible diamond
In the rock, Yet now it is over. Omniscience is not for man.
Christen me, therefore, that my acts in the dark may be just,
And adapt my partial vision to the limitations of time."

In the concluding stanza of "Great Nights Returning," the last poem in the volume, the poet affirms again, now in the dead of winter, the defeat of time:

Now the soul knows the fire that first composed it
Sinks not with time but is renewed hereafter.
Death cannot steal the light which love has kindled
Nor the years change it.

By 1959, as the reviewer in the *Times* suggested, after the publication of Philip Larkin's *The Less Deceived* (1955) and the production of John Osborne's *Look Back in Anger* (1956), Vernon Watkins's beliefs about the nature of the world and the writing of poetry, always at odds with those of his contemporaries, seemed utterly anachronistic. But as *Cypress and Acacia* makes clear, he remained, as he had throughout his life, true to what he believed, and the review in the *Times* pays tribute not just to his artistry but to his integrity: "He is a poet who has created his own immediately recognizable world; and who, in an age in love with ambiguity and hedging, can declare with obvious dignity, 'Truth is simple.' "

Affinities, the last collection of verse published in his lifetime, appeared in 1962. The familiar theme of time and eternity recurs, most clearly perhaps in two more poems on Taliesin and the last poem in the "Music of Colours" sequence, "Music of Colours: Dragonfoil and the Furnace of Colours." But *Affinities* also calls attention to another of Watkins's beliefs, one that helps explain his unqualified commitment to his craft. Many of the poems are about particular poets with whom he felt some affinity, and together the poems celebrate the peculiar wisdom and distinct mission of all poets. While such poems had appeared earlier, particularly in *Cypress and Acacia*, they predominate in *Affinities* and include, among others, poems on Eliot, Thomas, Holderlin, and Heine. As always, Watkins affirmed the profound importance of the poet's unique vision and the craft that makes it known. As he wrote in "The Demands of the Poet," "Art is the principle of all creation, / And there the desert is, where art is not."

In the spring of 1964, Watkins took a leave of absence from Lloyd's to become Visiting Professor of Poetry at the University of Washington in Seattle. He stayed from March to June and lectured on Yeats and Hopkins. Two years later, after forty years of service, he finally retired from Lloyd's, and in the same year, in recognition of his life's work in poetry, he was awarded an honorary Doctor of Literature from University College, Swansea. Soon afterward, he received a Gulbenkian Scholarship that provided, for two years, a position in the department of English at University College, Swansea, and another offer (this time for a full year) as a visiting professor at Washington. He spent a year (1966-1967) at Swansea and then in the fall of 1967 left for Seattle with his wife and three youngest children. On Sunday, 8 October 1967, soon after their arrival in Seattle, he collapsed during a game of tennis and died at the age of sixty-one. (He had learned some two years earlier that he had a serious heart condition, but he did not alter his way of life.) Two collections of poems were brought out soon afterward: *Fidelities*, which he had prepared for publication before his death, was published by Faber and Faber in 1968, and *Uncollected Poems*, selected and edited from manuscripts by Kathleen Raine, was published by Enitharmon Press in 1969. The notice of his death in the *Times* revealed that he had been one of the five or six poets under consideration for the Poet Laureate of England.

Since his death, Vernon Watkins has come to be recognized as one of the best poets of his generation, highly praised, if not widely read. He was a contemporary of W. H. Auden, Stephen Spender, and C. Day Lewis, but he was not, in any way, a political writer: "I am," he said, "entirely concerned with metaphysical truth." While he was born and lived almost all his life in Wales, he has little in common with the Anglo-Welsh writers of his time, and despite the poems on Taliesin, the Mari Lwyd, and Gower, "it is," as Glyn Jones says, "vain to look in his work for the influence of Welsh-language poetry, ancient or modern." Watkins went his own way as a poet, and if he never matched the achievement of Yeats, Eliot, or David Jones, he has been called by Kathleen Raine "the greatest lyric poet of my generation."

The way he went, of course, was not a popular one. While he is, in the words of Roland Mathias, "one of the very few twentieth century representatives of the great metaphysical tradition in English poetry," the century has had little sympathy for the meanings of that tradition, particularly in the Christian form it sometimes takes in Watkins's poetry. And the poems themselves are difficult, first because the vision that inspires them is profound and ineffable and then because their range of symbol and allusion, growing out of the poet's wide familarity with classical and modern literature, makes great demands on the reader.

Watkins was, above all perhaps, an able, meticulous, dedicated artist. His poetry is formal and carefully structured, and in the judgment of Roland Mathias, "as a craftsman of line and rhythm he belongs to an order rarely, if ever, seen in English poetry since the day of the now equally disregarded Tennyson." His commitment to poetry was unqualified, and it yielded poems that will forever reward careful and sensitive reading. As Alan Brownjohn put it in his review of *Fidelities* in the *New Statesman*, Watkins "was, by any standards, a major talent" who achieved "a splendid late perfection of his style."

If Vernon Watkins was a greatly gifted poet, he was also a rare human being—modest, generous, and loving. His letters from David Jones, the essays written after his death by those who knew him, his friendship with Dylan Thomas all attest to the goodness of the man and his loyalty and love for everyone he knew. In the brief biographical sketch she wrote of her husband shortly after his death, Gwen Watkins seems to find, in a single sentence, the perfect epitaph for the poet and the man: "he believed that lyric poetry should be exalted, and that it existed as an affirmation of love."

Recording:

Vernon Watkins Reads From His Own Works (Carillon Records, YP317, 1961).

Other:

Heinrich Heine, *The North Sea*, translated by Watkins (New York: New Directions, 1951);

Dylan Thomas: Letters to Vernon Watkins, edited, with an introduction, by Watkins (London: Dent / Faber & Faber, 1957);

"The Translation of Poetry," *Contemporary Literature in Translation*, 1 (1968): 39-41;

Selected Verse Translations (London: Enitharmon Press, 1977).

References:

Roland Mathias, "Grief and the Circus Horse: A Study of the Mythic and Christian Themes in the Early Poetry of Vernon Watkins," in *Triskel One: Essays on Welsh and Anglo-Welsh Literature*, edited by Sam Adams and Gwilym Rees Hughes (Swansea & Llandybie: Davies, 1971), pp. 96-138;

Mathias, *Vernon Watkins* (Cardiff: University of Wales Press, 1974);

Leslie Norris, "Seeing Eternity: Vernon Watkins and the Poet's Task," in *Triskel Two: Essays on Welsh and Anglo-Welsh Literature*, edited by Adams and Hughes (Llandybie: Davies, 1973), pp. 88-110;

Norris, ed., *Vernon Watkins 1906-1967* (London: Faber & Faber, 1970);

Poetry Wales, special Vernon Watkins issue, 12 (Summer 1977);

Dora Polk, *Vernon Watkins and the Spring of Vision* (Swansea: Davies, 1977);

Ruth Pryor, ed., *David Jones: Letters to Vernon Watkins* (Cardiff: University of Wales Press, 1976);

Kathleen Raine, "Vernon Watkins and the Bardic Tradition," in her *Defending Ancient Springs* (London: Oxford University Press, 1967), pp. 17-34.

Contributors

Allan E. Austin .... *University of Guelph*
Ashley Brown .... *University of South Carolina*
Kenneth Buthlay .... *University of Glasgow*
Robert H. Canary .... *University of Wisconsin, Parkside*
Catherine Cantalupo .... *Rutgers University*
John Clarke .... *University College, London*
Michael J. Collins .... *Georgetown University*
Terry Comito .... *George Mason University*
Diane D'Amico .... *Western Illinois University*
Terence Diggory .... *Skidmore College*
Carol M. Dole .... *Cornell University*
Doris L. Eder .... *University of New Haven*
John Finlay .... *Enterprise, Alabama*
Mary FitzGerald .... *University of New Orleans*
John Wilson Foster .... *University of British Columbia*
Philip Gardner .... *Memorial University of Newfoundland*
Jo Marie Gulledge .... *Louisiana State University*
Linda Rahm Hallett .... *Hassocks, England*
Richard Johnson .... *Mount Holyoke College*
Patrick J. Keane .... *LeMoyne College*
Francine Muffoletto Landreneau .... *Louisiana State University*
Barbara E. Lesch .... *Sonoma State University*
Robert K. Martin .... *Concordia University*
Margaret B. McDowell .... *University of Iowa*
Peter MCMillan .... *University of South Carolina*
David E. Middleton .... *Nicholls State University*
D. S. J. Parsons .... *University of Saskatchewan*
James K. Robinson .... *University of Cincinnati*
J'nan Morse Sellery .... *Harvey Mudd College*
Vincent B. Sherry, Jr. .... *Villanova University*
Thomas F. Staley .... *University of Tulsa*
Andrew Swarbrick .... *Birmingham, England*
David Tacium .... *Concordia University*
A. T. Tolley .... *Carleton University*
Alan Young .... *Cheshire, England*

Cumulative Index

Dictionary of Literary Biography, Volumes 1-20
Dictionary of Literary Biography Yearbook, 1980, 1981, 1982
Dictionary of Literary Biography Documentary Series, Volumes 1-3

Cumulative Index

DLB before number: *Dictionary of Literary Biography*, Volumes 1-20
Y before number: *Dictionary of Literary Biography Yearbook*, 1980, 1981, 1982
DS before number: *Dictionary of Literary Biography Documentary Series*, Volumes 1-3

A

Abbott, Jacob 1803-1879 .... DLB1
Abercrombie, Lascelles 1881-1938 .... DLB19
Adamic, Louis 1898-1951 .... DLB9
Adams, Henry 1838-1918 .... DLB12
Adams, James Truslow 1878-1949 .... DLB17
Ade, George 1866-1944 .... DLB11
Adeler, Max (see Clark, Charles Heber)
AE 1869-1935 .... DLB19
Agassiz, Jean Louis Rodolphe 1807-1873 .... DLB1
Agee, James 1909-1955 .... DLB2
Aiken, Conrad 1889-1973 .... DLB9
Albee, Edward 1928- DLB7
Alcott, Amos Bronson 1799-1888 .... DLB1
Alcott, Louisa May 1832-1888 .... DLB1
Alcott, William Andrus 1798-1859 .... DLB1
Aldington, Richard 1892-1962 .... DLB20
Aldiss, Brian W. 1925- DLB14
Algren, Nelson 1909-1981 .... DLB9; Y81,82
Alldritt, Keith 1935- DLB14
Allen, Hervey 1889-1949 .... DLB9
Josiah Allen's Wife (see Holly, Marietta)
Allott, Kenneth 1912-1973 .... DLB20
Allston, Washington 1779-1843 .... DLB1
Alvarez, A. 1929- DLB14
Amis, Kingsley 1922- DLB15
Amis, Martin 1949- DLB14
Ammons, A. R. 1926- DLB5
Anderson, Margaret 1886-1973 .... DLB4
Anderson, Maxwell 1888-1959 .... DLB7
Anderson, Poul 1926- DLB8
Anderson, Robert 1917- DLB7
Anderson, Sherwood 1876-1941 .... DLB4, 9; DS1
Andrews, Charles M. 1863-1943 .... DLB17
Anthony, Piers 1934- DLB8
Archer, William 1856-1924 .... DLB10
Arden, John 1930- DLB13
Arensberg, Ann 1937- Y82
Arnow, Harriette Simpson 1908- DLB6
Arp, Bill (see Smith, Charles Henry)
Arthur, Timothy Shay 1809-1885 .... DLB3
Asch, Nathan 1902-1964 .... DLB4
Ashbery, John 1927- DLB5; Y81
Ashton, Winifred (see Dane, Clemence)
Asimov, Isaac 1920- DLB8
Atherton, Gertrude 1857-1948 .... DLB9
Auchincloss, Louis 1917- DLB2; Y80
Auden, W. H. 1907-1973 .... DLB10, 20
Austin, Mary 1868-1934 .... DLB9
Ayckbourn, Alan 1939- DLB13

B

Bacon, Delia 1811-1859 .... DLB1
Bagnold, Enid 1889-1981 .... DLB13
Bailey, Paul 1937- DLB14
Bailyn, Bernard 1922- DLB17

C

D

E

G

H

I

J

K

L

M

N

O

S

T

U

V

W

Y

Z